Hear the **Gospel of the Lord**, or rather hear the Lord Himself saying of Himself: "This," says He, "is life eternal, that they may know Thee, the only true God, and Jesus Christ whom Thou hast sent." You heard above that the Word of God was sent to heal mankind: here you are told that He who was sent is Jesus Christ.

John Cassian, *The Incarnation* 4.5

When this man, beloved brethren, came to us with such condescension of the Lord, illustrious by the testimony and wonder of the very man who had persecuted him, what else behoved to be done except that he should be placed on the pulpit, that is, on the tribunal of the Church; that, resting on the loftiness of a higher station, and conspicuous to the whole people for the brightness of his honour, he should read the precepts and **Gospel of the Lord**, which he so bravely and faithfully follows? Let the voice that has confessed the Lord daily be heard in those things which the Lord spoke. Let it be seen whether there is any further degree to which he can be advanced in the Church. There is nothing in which a confessor can do more good to the brethren than that, while the reading of the Gospel is heard from his lips, everyone who hears should imitate the faith of the reader.

Cyprian, *Epistle* 33.4

The Gospel of the Lord

How the Early Church
Wrote the Story of Jesus

Michael F. Bird

WILLIAM B. EERDMANS PUBLISHING COMPANY
GRAND RAPIDS, MICHIGAN / CAMBRIDGE, U.K.

Published 2014 by

Wm. B. Eerdmans Publishing Co.

2140 Oak Industrial Drive N.E., Grand Rapids, Michigan 49505 /

P.O. Box 163, Cambridge CB3 9PU U.K.

Printed in the United States of America

20 19 18 17 16 15 14   7 6 5 4 3 2 1

Library of Congress Cataloging-in-Publication Data

Bird, Michael F.

The gospel of the Lord: how the early church wrote the story of Jesus / Michael F. Bird.

pages   cm

Includes bibliographical references and indexes.

ISBN 978-0-8028-6776-6 (pbk.: alk. paper)

1. Jesus Christ — Historicity   2. Jesus Christ —Biography —Sources

3. Bible. Gospels — Authorship.   I. Title.

BT303.2.B57   2014

226′.066 — dc23

2014002599

www.eerdmans.com

Contents

Preface

I am convinced that we are about to see a resurgence in scholarly interest in the Gospels. The "Third Quest" for the historical Jesus appears to be in a bit of a lull with some folks reconsidering the whole historical Jesus enterprise, others questioning the very idea of finding authentic traditions in the Gospels, and then again others shifting their interests into adjacent domains of the theological and narrative texture of the Gospels. I lament that unless new energy is injected into the field, then the Quest looks destined to enter a period of suspended animation. In Pauline studies the "New Perspective on Paul" seems to have essentially prevailed, albeit in a chastened form, achieving a kind of equilibrium that offers nuanced views of Judaism, more social realism in Paul, and yet maintains and even magnifies the primary concerns of traditional readings of Paul about grace, faith, and divine initiative in salvation. Unless the equilibrium is disturbed by some mad monk from Wittenberg or a holy man from the east, we need not expect much to change here any time soon.

If my reading of the scholarly scene is correct, then "Gospels" is very probably the next big thing in biblical studies. And why not? There is so much to do. The deployment of social memory and performance criticism constitute new ways of attempting to conceive of the formation of the oral tradition underlying the Gospels. The genre of the Gospels is always up for a good debate. Although the two-source theory of the priority of Mark and "Q" has dominated the scholarly consensus with respect to the literary relationships between the Gospels, there are still defenders of alternative theories like the Griesbach hypothesis (Matthean priority) and the Farrer-Goulder-Goodacre scheme (where Luke used Matthew). And when will some brave soul be bold enough to argue at length that Matthew used Luke?

We can only wait and see! In addition, the use of the Old Testament by the Evangelists remains fertile ground for toiling exegetes. The question of why the early church chose four Gospels instead of just one is likewise an immense theological, literary, and social matter to ponder. There are outstanding text-critical questions like the ending of Mark's Gospel and the witness of the apostolic fathers to the text of the Gospels. Then we might ask if there is a single gospel theology that can be constructed from the four canonical Gospels as well. Alas, the fields are white for scholarly harvest. Good evidence for a spike in Gospels research is that not long after I submitted the manuscript of this book to Eerdmans a number of very excellent volumes came out that I sadly did not have time to interact with including Francis Watson, *Gospel Writing*, Vernon Robbins, *Who Do People Say I Am*, Eric Eve, *Behind the Gospels*, Richard Horsley, *The Prophet Jesus and the Renewal of Israel*, James Dunn, *The Oral Gospel Tradition*, and Rafael Rodriguez, *Oral Tradition and the New Testament*, a smorgasbord of Gospel studies!

My own background has been largely in Jesus and Gospel studies. I cut my scholarly teeth writing a thesis on the historical Jesus and the development of the Gentile mission. I followed that up with a study on whether the historical Jesus thought of himself as a messianic claimant.[1] However, because of my Reformed theological pedigree, I have frequently found myself conscripted into debates about Paul, justification, and the New Perspective on Paul. In fact, nearly every speaking engagement I have had has had something to do with Pauline studies. Do not get me wrong. I love the Apostle Paul. I immensely enjoy reading, preaching, and teaching from his letters. Even so, it is nice every now and then to leave Paul and go back to Jesus. For Paul may rock, but Jesus surely reigns! So I enjoy a return to Gospel studies whenever I can. After spending a winter in the trenches of Pauline warfare, I have come to long for the dramatic panache of St. Mark, the ambitious socio-theological project of St. Matthew, the mixture of joy and prophetic drive in St. Luke, and the spiritual depth of St. John. So here again I return to Jesus and the Gospels as much for my own benefit as for that of readers.

I do not pretend for a moment that this study will solve every contentious subject on the Gospels. I am concerned primarily with the questions of how the Gospels came to be, what kinds of literature they are, and how they relate to Christian discourse about God. I want to explore how the Gospels

---

1. Michael F. Bird, *Jesus and the Origins of the Gentile Mission* (LNTS 331; London: Clark, 2006); idem, *Are You the One Who Is to Come? The Historical Jesus and the Messianic Question* (Grand Rapids: Baker, 2009).

were shaped by the Christian movement and how they also came to shape that movement themselves. Now along the way many other questions come up and I deal with them where I can, often in excursuses, but primarily this volume is focused on the origins and development of the books we call "Gospels" in the context of the early church.

Several of the chapters in this book have appeared in an earlier form. Chapter 2 ("The Purpose and Preservation of the Jesus Tradition") originally appeared in *Bulletin for Biblical Research* 15.2 (2005): 161-85. Chapter 3 ("The Formation of the Jesus Tradition") originally appeared in *Westminster Theological Journal* 67.1 (2005): 113-34. The excursus in chapter 3 ("The Failure of Form Criticism") is largely indebted to an article published in *European Journal of Theology* 15.1 (2006): 5-13. All these chapters have been heavily revised for this book in light of recent research. I remain grateful to the editors of those journals (Richard Hess, Vern S. Poythress, and Pieter Lalleman) for permission to reuse that material here.

I am grateful to many people for helping bring this book to fruition. Stephen Morton, librarian at Brisbane School of Theology, helped secure many of the volumes I needed for the researching of this project. Conversations with several of my students such as Ovi Buciu were fruitful as well. A number of friends also read chapters of this book in draft form including Markus Bockmuehl, Richard Burridge, Kirrily Drew, Benjamin Sutton, Joel Willitts, Rick Brannan, Paul Foster, Robert Gundry, Michael Holmes, and Christopher Skinner. Thanks also to Michael Thomson of Eerdmans for getting behind this book and for his support and encouragement along the way. As ever, my family has to be thanked for allowing me to be distracted with the joys and strains of my writing ministry, especially during a period of illness related to an acute sleep disorder. The best times I have had reading the Gospels are when I am reading them to my children Alexis, Alyssa, Markus, and Theodore. Together we have spent much time thinking about the "Way" of Jesus Christ.

Finally, I dedicate this volume to Rt. Rev. Prof. N. T. Wright. Back in 1999 on a trip to Atlanta, just after my first year of seminary, I entered a book shop and for the first time I saw a copy of *Jesus and the Victory of God*. It had a nice glossy cover and I was intrigued since I had read several reviews of the book that had left me very curious about the author's unique take on the life of Jesus of Nazareth. When I returned to Australia one of the first things I did was to go to the library and check out a copy of *Jesus and the Victory of God*. Thereafter, I remember coming across page 14, which said: "For many conservative theologians it would have been sufficient if Jesus had been born of a virgin (at any time in human history, and perhaps from any race), lived a sinless life, died a sacrificial death, and risen again three days later." Reading those words felt like being slapped in the face with a very soggy fish. That was exactly how I read the Gospels. They beheld Jesus, the Lord of Glory, the propitiatory sacrifice of Paul's theology, but they were just the *hors d'oeuvres* to Paul's meaty theology of atonement and justification. I knew why Jesus died, but I had nothing in my theological repertoire to justify why he lived. On this point, I confess that Wright did for me what David Hume did for Immanuel Kant: he interrupted my "dogmatic slumber." Or as I tell my students, this was the point that I left the Matrix. Wright's many publications on the Gospels have inspired me and also enabled a generation of Christians to discover Jesus for the first time.[2] In fact, the Catholic Archbishop of Brisbane, the Rt. Rev. John Bathersby, said very much the same thing when he introduced Wright during his visit to the diocese in 2006. Those in diverse Christian traditions have benefited from Wright's ability to teach about the mission of Jesus as it relates to the mission of the church. I was thus greatly honored to be the respondent to Wright's paper at the Institute for Biblical Research meeting in Atlanta in 2010 on the subject of the cross and the kingdom of God. Like many younger scholars of my generation, I remain grateful for Wright's industrious scholarly work and commitment to Christian ministry. I pray that Wright will be granted many more years of productive labor to challenge the churches to continually return to the Gospels of Jesus since the story of Jesus is the story we are all called to live by.

---

2. N. T. Wright, *Who Was Jesus?* (London: SPCK, 1993); idem, *Jesus and the Victory of God* (COQG 2; London: SPCK, 1996); idem, *The Challenge of Jesus* (London: SPCK, 1999); idem, *Simply Jesus: A New Vision of Who He Was, What He Did, and Why He Matters* (New York: HarperOne, 2011); idem, *How God Became King: The Forgotten Story of the Gospels* (New York: HarperOne, 2012).

Abbreviations

AB	Anchor Bible
ABD	D. N. Freedman, ed., *Anchor Bible Dictionary* (New York: Double-day, 1992)
ABRL	Anchor Bible Reference Library
Adv. Haer.	Irenaeus, *Adversus Haereses*
Adv. Marc.	Tertullian, *Adversus Marcionem*
ANRW	*Aufstieg und Niederang der römischen Welt*
Ant.	Josephus, *Antiquities of the Jews*
1 Apol.	Justin, *First Apology*
2 Apol.	Justin, *Second Apology*
b.	Babylonian Talmud
BBR	Bulletin for Biblical Research
BDAG	W. Bauer, F. W. Danker, W. F. Arndt, and F. W. Gingrich, *A Greek-English Lexicon of the New Testament and Other Early Christian Literature* (3rd ed.; Chicago: University of Chicago Press, 1999)
BETL	Bibliotheca Ephemeridum Theologicarum Lovaniensium
Bib	*Biblica*
BJRL	*Bulletin of the John Rylands Library*
b. Shab.	Babylonian Talmud, tractate *Shabbat*
BSL	Biblical Studies Library
BTB	*Biblical Theology Bulletin*
BZNW	Beihefte zur Zeitschrift für die Neutestamentliche Wissenschaft
CBNTS	Coniectanea biblica Neotestamentica Studia
CBR	*Currents in Biblical Research*
CITM	Christianity in the Making
1 Clem.	*1 Clement*
2 Clem.	*2 Clement*
COQG	Christian Origins and the Question of God

CRBS	*Currents in Research: Biblical Studies*
De vir.	Jerome, *De Viris Illustribis*
Dial Tryph.	Justin, *Dialogue with Trypho*
Diatr.	Epictetus, *Diatribes*
Did.	*Didache*
DJG	J. B. Green and S. McKnight, eds., *Dictionary of Jesus and the Gospels* (Downers Grove: InterVarsity, 1992)
DNTB	C. A. Evans and S. E. Porter, eds., *Dictionary of New Testament Background* (Downers Grove: InterVarsity, 2000)
DPL	G. F. Hawthorne and R. P. Martin, eds., *Dictionary of Paul and His Letters* (Downers Grove: InterVarsity, 1993)
ECC	Eerdmans Critical Commentary
ed.	Editor or edition
EDNT	H. Balz and G. Schneider, eds., *Exegetical Dictionary of the New Testament* (Grand Rapids: Eerdmans, 1990-93)
EJTh	*European Journal of Theology*
Ep.	*Epistle(s)*
Ep. Diogn.	*Epistle to Diognetus*
Eph.	Ignatius, *Ephesians*
Epigr.	Martial, *Epigrams*
EQ	*Evangelical Quarterly*
esp.	especially
ETS	Erfurter theologische Schriftten
ExpT	*Expository Times*
FB	Forschung zur Bibel
FRLANT	Forschungen zur Religion und Literatur des Alten und Neuen Testaments
FS	Festschift
GELS	T. Muraoka, *A Greek-English Lexicon of the Septuagint* (Louvain: Peeters, 2009)
HeyJ	*Heythrop Journal*
Hist. Conscr.	Lucian, *Quomodo historia conscribenda sit*
Hist. Eccl.	Eusebius, *Historia Ecclesiastica*
HSHJ	T. Holmén and S. E. Porter, eds., *Handbook for the Study of the Historical Jesus* (Leiden: Brill, 2007)
HTK	Herders theologischer Kommentar
HTR	*Harvard Theological Review*
HTS	*Hervormde Teologiese Studies*
Inst.	Quintilian, *Institutio Oratio*
Inter	*Interpretation*
JBL	*Journal of Biblical Literature*
JECS	*Journal of Early Christian Studies*

Abbreviations

JETS	*Journal of the Evangelical Theological Society*
JGRChJ	*Journal of Graeco-Roman Christianity and Judaism*
JR	*Journal of Religion*
JSHJ	*Journal for the Study of the Historical Jesus*
JSNT	*Journal for the Study of the New Testament*
JSNTSup	Journal for the Study of the New Testament Supplement
JTS	*Journal of Theological Studies*
L&N	J. P. Louw and E. A. Nida, *Greek-English Lexicon of the New Testament Based on Semantic Domains* (2nd ed.; New York: United Bible Societies, 1989)
LAE	A. Deissmann, *Light from the Ancient East: The New Testament Illustrated by Recently Discovered Texts of the Graeco-Roman World* (New York: Doran, 1927)
LNTS	Library of New Testament Studies
LSJ	H. G. Liddell, G. R. Scott, and J. S. Jones, *A Greek-English Lexicon* (9th ed., with revised supplement; Oxford: Oxford University Press, 1996)
LXX	Septuagint
m.	Mishnah
Magn.	Ignatius, *Magnesians*
Mart. Pol.	*Martyrdom of Polycarp*
ms(s).	manuscript(s)
MT	Masoretic Text
NA[28]	B. Aland, K. Aland, et al., eds., *Nestle-Aland Novum Testamentum Graece* (28th ed.; Stuttgart: Deutsche Bibelgesellschaft, 2012)
NDIEC	G. H. Horsley and S. Llewelyn, *New Documents Illustrating Early Christianity* (Grand Rapids: Eerdmans, 1981-)
NeoT	*Neotestamentica*
NHC	Nag Hammadi Codices
NICNT	New International Commentary on the New Testament
NIDNTT	C. Brown, ed., *New International Dictionary of New Testament Theology* (Grand Rapids: Zondervan, 1975-85)
NIGTC	New International Greek Testament Commentary
NovT	*Novum Testamentum*
NovTSup	Novum Testamentum Supplement
NRSV	New Revised Standard Version
NSBT	New Studies in Biblical Theology
NTR	New Testament Readings
NTS	*New Testament Studies*
NTTS	New Testament Tools and Studies
Od.	Homer, *Odyssey*

OGIS	W. Dittenberger, ed., *Orientis Graeci Inscriptiones Selectae* (Leipzig: Hirzel, 1903-5)
Phild.	Ignatius, *Philadelphians*
Pomp.	Plutarch, *Pompey*
Pss. Sol.	*Psalms of Solomon*
RB	*Revue Biblique*
RGG	K. Galling, ed., *Religion in Geschichte und Gegenwart* (3rd ed.; Tübingen: Mohr, 1957-65)
ResQ	*Restoration Quarterly*
Rom.	Ignatius, *Romans*
SBJT	*Southern Baptist Journal of Theology*
Smyrn.	Ignatius, *Smyrnaeans*
SNTSMS	Society of New Testament Studies Monograph Series
SNTU	Studien zum Neuen Testament und seiner Umwelt
STI	Studies in Theological Interpretation
STR	*Sewanee Theological Review*
Strom.	Clement of Alexandria, *Stromata*
TANZ	Texte und Arbeiten zum neutestamentlichen Zeitalter
TDNT	G. Kittel and G. Friedrich, eds., *Theological Dictionary of the New Testament* (Grand Rapids: Eerdmans, 1964-76)
TNTC	Tyndale New Testament Commentary
Trall.	Ignatius, *Trallians*
TrinJ	*Trinity Journal*
TSAJ	Texte und Studien zum antiken Judentum
TT	*Theology Today*
TynBul	Tyndale Bulletin
TZ	*Theologische Zeitschrift*
UBS[4]	B. Aland, J. Karavidopoulos, C. M. Martini, B. M. Metzger, B. M. Newman, and K. Aland, eds., *The Greek New Testamament* (4th ed.; New York: United Bible Societies, 2010)
VC	*Vigiliae Christianae*
War	Josephus, *Jewish War*
WBC	Word Biblical Commentary
WTJ	*Westminster Theological Journal*
WUNT	Wissenschaftliche Untersuchungen Zum Neuen Testament
ZNW	*Zeitschrift für die neutestamentliche Wissenschaft*
ZWB	Zürcher Werkkomentare zur Bibel

CHAPTER 1

Introduction: From Jesus to Gospels

In his "Prologue to the New Testament," the English Reformer William Tyndale movingly wrote:

> Euagelio (that we cal gospel) is a greke worde,
> and signyfyth good, mery, glad and joyfull tydings,
> that maketh a mannes hert glad,
> and maketh him synge, duance and leepe for ioye.[1]

Tyndale's remarks convey the thought that the Gospels are actually good news and a cause for merriment and joy. They narrate a glad message about Jesus, his life and passion, and communicate that men and women can have a share in the kingdom of God. No wonder then that the Gospels have been among the centerpieces of Christian devotion, theology, and spirituality. Citations from the Gospels fill the pages of patristic, medieval, Reformed, and even modern theologians. Literature such as John Milton's *Paradise Regained* and musicals like *Godspell* and *Jesus Christ Superstar* are shaped by the Gospels.

Reverence for the Gospels as Scripture, that is, celebrating the sacred story that brings readers into contact with the person of Jesus, has a long pedigree. Justin Martyr (d. 160 CE) mentions in passing an early Christian worship service where the Gospels were read as the source for scriptural exhortation: "And on the day called Sunday, all who live in cities or in the country gather together to one place, and the memoirs of the apostles or

---

1. Cited from Richard I. Deibert, *Mark* (*Inter*; Louisville: Westminster John Knox, 1999), 6.

the writings of the prophets are read, as long as time permits; then, when the reader has ceased, the president verbally instructs, and exhorts to the imitation of these good things."[2] In the homiletical additions to the *Epistle of Diognetus,* the author declares that "The fear of the law is sung, the grace of the prophets is made manifest, and the faith of the gospels is established," clearly putting the Gospels on a par with the law and prophets.[3] Some later manuscripts extend the titles of the Gospels to the "Holy Gospel" according to each Evangelist, further underscoring their sacred texture.[4]

In the ancient church, the four Gospels, often bound together in a single codex, remained the proverbial bestseller among believers. According to leading text critic David Parker:

> The Four Gospels, the Tetraevangelium, is *the* book of Christianity — not four books, but one codex. Such manuscripts comprise more than a half of all continuous-text Greek copies of New Testament writing. In every ancient language of Christianity, copies of the Gospels predominate among what survives. And in case this preoccupation is seen as an ancient phenomenon, be it noted that the Gospels in these ancient languages are traditionally far better served with editions and results of research than is any other part of the New Testament. Moreover, more editions of the Gospel manuscripts have been published, in facsimile or in some other form.[5]

How this codex with four Gospels, four life-stories of Jesus, seemingly repetitive, and allegedly contradictory in places, came to be the most cherished section of the Christian Bible is a fascinating subject.

Sometime around 27-28 CE, Jesus of Nazareth began preaching the "gospel of the kingdom of God" in the environs of Judea and Galilee.[6] Then in ca. 180 CE, a mere hundred and fifty years later, an Asian bishop in France named Irenaeus offered a robust defense as to why there can be no more and no less than four Gospels with reference to the magnificence and mesmerizing nature of the number four.[7] In this move from Jesus to Irenaeus two

---

2. Justin Martyr, *1 Apol.* 67.3.

3. *Ep. Diogn.* 11.6.

4. Mss. 209, 579.

5. David Parker, *An Introduction to New Testament Manuscripts and Their Texts* (Cambridge: Cambridge University Press, 2008), 311 (italics original).

6. Mark 1:14.

7. Irenaeus, *Adv. Haer.* 3.11.8-9.

important things have happened: (1) Jesus is not only the proclaimer of the gospel, but now also the proclaimed in the Gospel, and (2) the oral message of the "gospel" has morphed into a literary genre known as "Gospel." There has been a monumental shift in the gospel-language of the early church whereby the "gospel" — often accompanied by a genitive modifier as the gospel *of God,* the gospel *of Christ,* or the gospel *of the Lord* — now means the message of salvation given in the fourfold Gospel of the biblical canon.

There are so many questions about the Gospels that need to be answered. Why would anyone write a "Jesus book" like these,[8] how did they compile and compose them, and why were these four Jesus books and not others accepted as canonical by the ancient church? Such questions should be of interest not only to historians of the early church but to all thoughtful readers of the Gospels. One can better appreciate the Gospels when one knows something of what they are, how they were written, why they were written, and how they were read by their first generations of readers. The Evangelists evidently wrote a story about Jesus, but to understand that story it helps if we can go behind the scenes, look at the story behind the story, and understand something of why these Gospels emerged in the shape they are in. A task of this order requires good detective work to uncover the blueprints from which the Gospels were made. As such, I think there are four big questions that need to be addressed in any account of the origins of the Gospels.

First, we have to look at the "big bang" behind the Jesus tradition. The "Jesus tradition" is the body of oral tradition transmitted in the early church which rehearsed the words of Jesus and stories about Jesus. This tradition coexisted with and even coalesced with the kergymatic message of Jesus' saving death and resurrection.[9] Yet for what purpose were Jesus' words recalled in the early church, and what was the point of preserving them? The Jesus tradition had a particular content focused on Jesus' teaching, ministry, and death, and it held a particular currency among followers of Jesus. The question is "why?" Why make an effort to pass on Jesus' sayings to others,

---

8. On the Gospels as "Jesus books," see Larry W. Hurtado, *Lord Jesus Christ: Devotion to Jesus in Earliest Christianity* (Grand Rapids: Eerdmans, 2003), 269.

9. On definitions, oral tradition refers to transmission of a tradition in the oral medium, while oral history is concerned with the historical data within oral tradition. Also, while *didachē* and kerygma were in some ways separate species of Christian discourse, nonetheless, the lines between them were flexible and fuzzy as both drew from each other. Acts 15:25 provides a clear example where "teaching" and "preaching the gospel" are both regarded as elements of the same "Word of the Lord."

why tell stories about Jesus, and what has that to do with anything that was happening in the early church? I think it possible to have a fresh look at why the church attributed such authority to Jesus' words and to then explore the role that the Jesus tradition had in shaping the early churches.

Second, how was the Jesus tradition transmitted? Some like to imagine that the transmission of the Jesus tradition was much like a game of "telephone" or "Chinese whispers." On such an analogy, an initial message like "Send reinforcements: we are going to advance" is funneled down a chain of persons and gets so distorted in transmission that it ends up as something garbled like "Send three and sixpence: we are going to a dance."[10] Was the transmission of Jesus' words really that messy, or was the church more careful in its attempt to transmit the Jesus tradition to others? Are the Evangelists merely reading their own beliefs into the life of Jesus, or are they providing accounts of Jesus' life that are in some way accurate? If accurate, how accurate, and what kind of accuracy: Wall Street Journal accurate or Fox News accurate?

Third, there is a constellation of critical questions pertaining to the sources, literary genus, and purposes of the Gospels. Specifically, what were the sources behind the Gospels, what genre are the Gospels, and why would anyone even write a Gospel? While these are three different questions I believe that they are all umbilically linked. Critical matters related to Gospel sources cannot be properly solved until we get a grip on the genre of the Gospels, and the genre question is closely connected to the purposes for the Gospels. Dense and dreary as these historical-critical questions often are, they remain crucial for getting a grip on what the Evangelists were doing and what they were trying to achieve. The nitty-gritty questions of sources, genre, and purpose bring us close to the heart of the Gospels and what kind of goals they were written to achieve!

10. Bart Ehrman (*Jesus, Interrupted: Revealing the Hidden Contradictions in the Bible [And Why We Don't Know About Them]* [New York: HarperOne, 2009], 146-47) uses the children's "telephone game" as an analogy to explain how contradictions emerged in the Jesus tradition. Anthony Le Donne (*Historical Jesus: What Can We Know and How Can We Know It?* [Grand Rapids: Eerdmans, 2011], 70) objects to this analogy: "It must be said that this [game] is *not* a controlled exercise in orality. It is an exercise in variation without stability. The vast majority of human civilizations operated with largely illiterate cultures. Are we to imagine that all these civilizations were the equivalent of giggling children? That the golden ages of Egypt, Rome, Britain, the Maya, etcetera had no confidence in the stability of social communication? No. Oral cultures have been capable of tremendous competence. The human mind can remember vast amounts of information with great accuracy when it remains active and fluid. The oral culture in which Jesus was reared trained their brightest children to remember entire libraries of story, law, poetry, song, etcetera."

Fourth, anyone with a shred of canonical sense is bound to ask at some point: Why do we have four Gospels? Why not just one? And if more than one, then why not several, or a dozen? The theological rationale behind our fourfold Gospel canon is worth exploring, especially in light of the various alternatives to a fourfold Gospel that were readily available to the early church. An answer to this question will, I hope, give us a greater appreciation for the value of the four-ness of our canonical Gospels.

That is the task which lies ahead: mapping out how the Gospels emerged and why they took on the shape and character that they did. Hopefully a study of this order will prove illuminating for both our understanding of the Gospels as historical artifacts and also be equally informative in learning about the people who wrote them and collected them as Scripture. Reading and studying the Gospels should inevitably draw one closer toward the Lord about whom they are written, and inspire those who live under the mantle of his lordship with an ever increasing appreciation for the authors and communities who risked all so that this story could be told to others.

EXCURSUS
FROM ORAL GOSPEL TO WRITTEN GOSPEL

1. The Meaning of "Gospel" in the Ancient World

A Gospel is a distinctive literary entity in the ancient world. As we consider the origins of this literary form, an obvious starting point is the background and Christian usage of the word "gospel." The Gospels were composed to put the oral message of Jesus into written form, so we must consider the link between the oral "gospel" and the written "Gospels."[11]

To begin with, our English word "gospel" comes from the old English word "godspel," which means something akin to "good tale." In an English language perspective, the New Testament Gospels are the good news about Jesus. The English is a translation of the Latin *evangelium* and the Greek εὐαγγέλιον (the verbal form in Greek is εὐαγγελίζομαι). The lexical root of these words signifies notions of glad tidings and joyous news that is declared to others.[12] For a more precise understand-

---

11. Cf. Tom Thatcher, "The Gospel Genre: What Are We After?" *ResQ* 36 (1994): 137.

12. GELS, 297; BDAG, 402-3; L&N, 412-13; *NIDNTT* 2.107-15; *EDNT* 2.69-74; *TDNT* 2.707-37; *NDIEC* 3:10-15. See studies by Adolf von Harnack, "Gospel: History of the Conception in the Earliest Church," in *The Constitution and Law of the Church in the First Two Centuries* (London: William & Norgate, 1910), 275-331; Julius Schniewind, *Euangelion: Ursprung und erste Gestalt des Begriffs Evangelium, Untersuchung* (Gütersloh: Bertelsmann, 1927); Peter

ing of the terms it is profitable to explore the Greco-Roman and Jewish usage of the noun "gospel" and the verb "to announce the gospel."

In the Greco-Roman world, the noun εὐαγγέλιον was primarily associated with positive news in general and news of military victory in particular, while the verb εὐαγγελίζομαι described the specific act of declaring the good news. In some cases εὐαγγέλιον was associated with the gift that one received for bringing the good news.[13] On other occasions it is linked with the sacrifice offered as a thanksgiving for the good news.[14] John Dickson observes the link among these associations about glad tidings:

> Εὐαγγελίζομαι denotes the activity of the εὐαγγέλος, the messenger of ancient Greece who was sent from the field of battle by ship, by horse, or as a swift runner, to proclaim to the awaiting city the victory — εὐτυχής is commonly associated with the announcement — of the army or the death or capture of an enemy or some other significant announcement. The noun εὐαγγέλιον, an adjective used as a substantive, derives from εὐαγγέλος and means simply "that which is proper to the εὐαγγέλος," thus allowing the two-fold usage of antiquity, "reward/offering for tidings" and the "tidings" themselves.[15]

Importantly, when the good news is associated with news of military victory, it is sometimes invested with religious connotations like divine favor and a gift of providence. Plutarch is a rich source of information about the "gospel" of Greco-Roman military news. Plutarch records how the Spartans would give a reward of meat to "the man who brought good news of victory (εὐαγγέλιον ἐκ φιδιτίου)."[16] The Roman General Quintus Sertorius claimed to have had a magical doe that gave him dreams about military tactics:

Stuhlmacher, "The Pauline Gospel," in *The Gospel and the Gospels*, ed. P. Stuhlmacher (Grand Rapids: Eerdmans, 1991), 149-72; Graham Stanton, *Jesus and Gospel* (Cambridge: Cambridge University Press, 2004), 9-62; William Horbury, "'Gospel' in Herodian Judea," in *The Written Gospel*, ed. M. Bockmuehl and D. A. Hagner (Cambridge: Cambridge University Press, 2005), 7-30; John Dickson, "Gospel as News: εὐαγγελ- from Aristophanes to the Apostle Paul," *NTS* 51 (2005): 212-30; Steve Mason, *Josephus, Judea, and Christian Origins: Methods and Categories* (Peabody: Hendrickson, 2009), 283-302; Petr Pokorný, *From the Gospel to the Gospels: History, Theology and Impact of the Biblical Term "Euangelion"* (BZNW 195; Berlin: de Gruyter, 2013); James D. G. Dunn, "The Gospel and the Gospels," *EQ* 85 (2013): 291-308; David E. Aune, "The Meaning of Εὐαγγέλιον in the *Inscriptiones* of the Canonical Gospels," in *Jesus, Gospel Traditions and Paul in the Context of Jewish and Greco-Roman Antiquity: Collected Essays II* (WUNT 303; Tübingen: Mohr, 2013), 3-24.

13. Cf. Homer, *Od.* 14.152; 2 Sam 4:10; 18:22 (LXX); Plutarch, *Demetrius* 17.5.

14. Aeschines, *Against Ctesiphon* 160; Isocrates, *Areopagiticus* 10; Xenophon, *Hellenica* 1.6.37; 4.3.14; Josephus, *Jewish War* 4.618.

15. Dickson, "Gospel as News," 212-13.

16. Plutarch, *Moralia* 347D.

Whenever he had secret intelligence that the enemy had made an incursion into the territory which he commanded, or were trying to bring a city to revolt from him, he would pretend that the doe had conversed with him in his dreams, bidding him to hold his forces in readiness. Again, when he got news of some victory won by his generals, he would hide the messenger, and bring forth the doe wearing garlands for the receipt of good news (εὐαγγελίοις), exhorting his men to be of good cheer and to sacrifice to the gods, assured that they were to learn of some good fortune.[17]

While the Roman general Pompey and his army were en route to Petra, he was met with the "good news" of the death of his adversary, King Mithridates of Pontus: "For when he came within a short distance of Petra . . . news-bearers rode up from Pontus bringing good news (εὐαγγέλια)."[18] Plutarch also describes a situation where allies of Pompey had, presumptuously it turned out, declared Pompey's victory over Julius Caesar as "a number of people sailed for Lesbos, wishing to announce to Cornelia the good news (εὐαγγελιζόμενοι) that the war was over."[19] Elsewhere we find much the same. In a surviving private letter, an author refers to "a slave coming to bring the good news of victory and success (εὐαγγελίζοντι τὰ τῆς νείκης)" from the early second century.[20]

Jewish authors of the first century similarly wrote about the good news of imperial power. Philo, in his *Embassy to Gaius,* described how the news of Gaius Caligula's accession to the throne was received in Jerusalem, noting that it was "from our city that rumor to carry the good news (εὐαγγελιουμένη) sped to others."[21] Josephus refers to the report about Vespasian's accession to the imperial throne, narrating how "every city celebrated the good news (εὐαγγέλια) and offered sacrifices on his behalf."[22] Then later, Josephus adds, "On reaching Alexandria Vespasian was greeted by the good news (εὐαγγέλια) from Rome and embassies of congratulation from every quarter of the world now his own . . . the whole empire being now secured and the Roman state saved beyond expectation."[23] The accession of Vespasian to imperial power was not just political headlines. His accession was reported and celebrated as the socio-political salvation of the Roman Empire from the disastrous year of 68-69 CE that had seen three emperors (Galba, Otho, and Vitellius) all quickly rise and fall in the wake of Nero's suicide. It was also a religious event, which implied that Vespasian was supported by the gods and served now as a priestly mediator for the Roman people.

17. Plutarch, *Sertorius* 11.4.
18. Plutarch, *Pompeius* 41.3.
19. Plutarch, *Pompeius* 66.3.
20. *P.Giss.* 27, cited in *NDIEC* 3:12.
21. Philo, *Ad Gaium* 231.
22. Josephus, *Jewish War* 4.618.
23. Josephus, *Jewish War* 4.656-57.

The imperial cult had its own "gospel" for celebrating the benefaction of the emperor. The Priene inscription, containing the official Calendar Decree of the Asian League (9 BCE), was written at the suggestion of the proconsul Paulus Fabius Maximus, and it mandated that the birthday of Emperor Augustus (September 23) would mark the beginning of the Asian new year. The proconsul sent out letters with accompanying documents to several Asian cities recommending the decision, guaranteeing the widespread dissemination of the decree among the populace. The decree celebrated the birth of Caesar as a renewal of the natural order and his life as a means of beneficence and benefaction to all the peoples of Asia.

> It seemed good to the Greeks of Asia, in the opinion of the high priest Apollonius of Menophilus Azanitus: "Since Providence, which has ordered all things and is deeply interested in our life, has set in most perfect order by giving us Augustus, whom she filled with virtue that he might benefit humankind, sending him as a savior, both for us and for our descendants, that he might end war and arrange all things, and since he, Caesar, by his appearance (excelled even our anticipations), surpassing all previous benefactors, and not even leaving to posterity any hope of surpassing what he has done, and since the birthday of the god Augustus was the beginning of the good tidings for the world that came by reason of him (ἦρξεν δὲ τῶι κόσμωι τῶν δι᾽ αὐτὸν εὐαγγελίων ἡ γενέθλιος τοῦ θεοῦ)," which Asia resolved in Smyrna.[24]

Other ancient archaeological evidence points in the same direction. In one inscription it is said that the day when a son of Augustus takes on the toga (i.e., comes of age into manhood) is "good news for the city" (εὐαγγελίσθη ἡ πόλις).[25] An Egyptian papyrus from the early third century describes the author's joy at hearing "the good news concerning the proclaiming of Caesar [i.e., Gaius Julius Verus Maximus Augustus]," which the author thinks should be celebrated with a procession for the gods.[26] And an inscription at Amphiaraia on the Oropos from around 1 CE mentions the "good news of Rome's victory" (εὐαγγέλια τῆς Ῥωμαίων νίκης).

Again and again we find that "gospel" is associated primarily with news of military victory and with the benefits associated with the emperor's birth, coming of age, or accession. There are occasions where "good news" simply means a favorable report, but the technical usage of the language applies to settings that have social, religious, and political connotations. If a war has been won, then the gods have given victory and sacrifices must be made. If Caesar is reigning, it means peace and prosperity to all, and the gods are working through him to provide benefaction to the world. This is the Greco-Roman gospel into which Jesus first announced "the

24. *OGIS* 458.
25. *NDIEC* 3:12.
26. Deissmann, *LAE* 367; *NDIEC* 3:12.

gospel of the kingdom" and Mark and Paul declared "the gospel of Jesus the Messiah." Of course, we cannot jump from Plutarch to Paul without first looking at the Jewish background to εὐαγγέλιον as well.

In the Old Testament the noun בְּשֹׂרָה refers to the reward for good news or to the good news itself, with the verbal cognate בָּשַׂר meaning "announce good news" and the participle מְבַשֵּׂר used substantively for the "messenger of good news." In the Septuagint, these Hebrew words are translated with the verb εὐαγγελίζω for declaring good news, the participle εὐαγγελιζόμενος to designate the one announcing the good news, the neuter plural noun εὐαγγέλια for the reward for bringing the good news, and the feminine singular noun εὐαγγελία for the good news itself. The semantic frame for these words pertains to the news of victory, the announcer of victory, and the reward for bringing good news of victory.

In 2 Samuel is the story of an Amalekite who presumed that if he announced good news to David about the death of Saul (מְבַשֵּׂר/εὐαγγελιζόμενος) he would be rewarded (בְּשֹׂרָה/εὐαγγέλια), but the reward for his news was death (2 Sam/2 Kgdms 4:10, referring back to 2 Sam/2 Kgdms 1:1-16). Similarly, after the death of Absalom, Ahimaaz wanted to run to David and "carry tidings (בָּשַׂר/εὐαγγελιῶ) to the king that the Lord had delivered him from the power of his enemies." Yet Joab tells him not to bother, he sent a Cushite instead because Ahimaaz will "have no reward for the tidings (בְּשֹׂרָה/εὐαγγελία)" given the grievous state David will be in when he hears the news (2 Sam/2 Kgdms 18:19-20). Even though the death of Absalom is reported as good news that Yahweh has given victory to David (בְּשֹׂרָה /εὐαγγελία), David still weeps bitterly for Absalom (2 Sam 18:21-33).

Earlier in 1 Samuel, after the Philistines killed Saul and his sons, they scavenged the battlefield, took Saul's body, and we are told: "They cut off his head, stripped off his armor, and sent messengers throughout the land of the Philistines to carry the good news (בָּשַׂר/εὐαγγελίζοντες) to the houses of their idols and to the people" (1 Sam/1 Kgdms 31:9; cf. 1 Chron 10:9-10). They also deposited Saul's relics in the temple of their god. His death was good news and so was declared to the Philistine gods and people. Strategically, the Israelite king's death meant that the military threat had been defeated. Theologically, the Philistine gods seemed to have defeated Yahweh. So the report of military victory leads to a religious claim: the gods of the Philistines have triumphed over the Israelite deity.[27]

While Adonijah, the son of David, was sumptuously feasting and presuming his ascension to the Judean throne, David's confidant Jonathan brought Adonijah "good news" (בָּשַׂר/εὐαγγελίσαι) that David had formally anointed Solomon as his successor to the throne (1 Kgs/3 Kgdms 1:42). The good news of Solomon's kingship was in fact bad news for Adonijah, who then fled to grasp the horns of the altar in the temple to claim sanctuary (1 Kgs 1:42-50).

27. Walter Brueggemann, *First and Second Samuel* (*Inter*; Louisville: John Knox, 1990), 208-9.

The Psalms also contribute to this picture of the good news of the victory and reign of Israel's God. Psalm 68 (67 LXX) is prayerful praise to the God who casts away his enemies like smoke and melts them like wax. Israel's God provides for and defends the people, so that Israel's story is a long and glorious recital of the victories of Yahweh. In fact, in vv. 11-12 (12-13), the Lord speaks the word that determines the result of the battle. In the Greek text we read how "the Lord will give a word to those who bring good news (המבשׂר/τοῖς εὐαγγελιζομένοις) to a large host of people" about the defeat of kings, and then women rejoice as their city is filled with the spoils of battle. Importantly in the psalm, God proves his kingship by delivering Israel from foreign threats, and he himself directs, or perhaps even reveals the news of his victory to the people. Psalm 96 (95 LXX), one of the enthronement psalms, celebrates the kingship and reign of Yahweh over the nations. Israel's worship takes on a kerygmatic character, as the worshippers are to "Sing to the LORD, bless his name; preach good news (בשׂר/εὐαγγελίζεσθε) of his salvation from day to day. Declare his glory among the nations, his marvelous works among all the peoples" (vv. 2-3). The psalm includes a denunciation of idol worship and an invitation to the families of the earth to worship Yahweh in his temple. They should because Yahweh is king and is coming to judge the world in righteousness (vv. 10-13). The Psalmist here is like an international messenger, telling the nations the news of Yahweh's victory and their imminent defeat, and they are invited to become his vassals and to worship him.

It is in Isaiah, however, that we see the most concrete example of Israel's "gospel," where the news of God's coming reign and his deliverance of the exiles are set forth as part of a prophetic picture of hope for the ruined nation.[28] According to Isaiah 40–66, in the aftermath of judgment, Israel's fortunes are to be restored, and a herald is commissioned to tell the cities of Judah the momentous news of their imminent salvation: "Go up to a high mountain, you who herald good news (מבשׂרת/ ὁ εὐαγγελιζόμενος) to Zion; lift up your voice with strength, you who bring good news (מבשׂרת/ὁ εὐαγγελιζόμενος) to Jerusalem, lift it up, do not fear; say to the cities of Judah, 'See your God!' See, the Lord GOD comes with strength, and his arm rules for him; see, his reward is with him, and his recompense is before him" (Isa 40:9-10).[29] The major theme here is the coming new exodus, with God beginning again with Israel in the wilderness, and leading the captives into the promised land like a shepherd leading his flock. The long awaited end to the exile finds its embryonic beginning in the prophetic announcement that God is coming with kingly power. Later, the same theme emerges again, where Zion is awoken from the slumbers of captivity with the jubilant news from the Lord: "I am here, like springtime upon the mountains, like the feet of one bringing good news (מבשׂר/εὐαγγελιζομένου) reporting peace, like one

---

28. Cf. precedents in the eighth-century prophets Joel 2:32 and Nah 1:15 about news of God's victory and deliverance for the people.

29. In the MT, Zion/Jerusalem is the deliverer of good news, while in the LXX, Zion/Jerusalem is the recipient of the good news.

bringing good news (מבשׂר/εὐαγγελιζομένου) of good things, because I will make your salvation heard, telling Zion, 'Your God shall reign'" (52:6-7). The good news is that God is king, that his purposes will prevail over the nations, and that he has planned redemption for the exiles. Also, Israel's restoration will be of such grandeur that peoples from the surrounding nations will converge on Jerusalem with gifts of gold and frankincense, and there "proclaim good news (בשׂר/εὐαγγελιοῦνται) of the salvation of the LORD" (60:6). A special figure enlisted to herald this message is the "Servant," who is commissioned with these words: "The Spirit of the Lord GOD is upon me, because he has anointed me; he has sent me to bring good news (בשׂר/εὐαγγελίσασθαι) to the poor, to heal the brokenhearted, to proclaim liberation to the captives, recovery of sight to the blind, to summon the welcomed to the year of the LORD and the day of reckoning, to comfort all who mourn, a garment of glory instead of a spirit of tiredness" (61:1-3). All in all, in Isaiah 40–66, we detect the "glad tidings" of Israel's salvation (60:6), the restoration of the nation (61:1-6), God coming in strength (40:9), and a message simply and suitably summarized as "your God reigns" (52:7).[30] Thus, Isaiah's "gospel," if we may speak of one, pertains to God's intention to demonstrate his faithfulness to the nation by redeeming them from exile, returning them to the land, and restoring their socio-political fortunes in a new creation.

The Isaianic "glad tidings," with its canvas of national deliverance, appears to have significantly impacted several later pieces of Jewish literature. The *Psalms of Solomon,* probably deriving from the Herodian period, include a psalm in which Solomon looks ahead to the end of Israel's dispersion among the nations. In this psalm, God literally changes the landscape so that the dispersed tribes can return to Jerusalem, where God's glory has taken up residence once more. "Blow the trumpet in Zion with a trumpeting signal to summon the holy ones; proclaim in Jerusalem the voice of one who brings good news (εὐαγγελιζομένου); for the God of Israel has shown mercy in his visitation to them."[31] This psalm is part of a sequence in which Israel has fallen under divine judgment and been taken into a foreign land (*Pss. Sol.* 9), leading to an appeal to the God who is righteous, yet avails in mercy (*Pss. Sol.* 10), who will show mercy by releasing Israel from exile, and this is the good news that Zion must hear (*Pss. Sol.* 11).

In the Qumran scrolls, the "glad tidings" from Isaiah are integrated with wider scriptural hopes that are believed to affect the future of the sectarian community. In the Melchizedek scroll (11Q13), the scribe envisages a coming messenger, one anointed with the Spirit, who brings a message about a "divine being" and declares that Melchizedek will deliver the sect from the power of Belial. More precisely, rehearsing the words of Isa 52:7, this messenger is the one who declares good news to

---

30. Cf. Jonathan T. Pennington, *Reading the Gospels Wisely: A Narrative and Theological Introduction* (Grand Rapids: Baker, 2012), 14-17.

31. *Pss. Sol.* 11.1.

Zion about God's reign. He is identified as the anointed one from Dan 9:26 who is cut off from the people (i.e., he dies), and his chief tasks are to declare God's favor and to comfort all who mourn, which is straight out of Isa 61:2. What really stands out is that the good news of Isa 52:7 is given the interpretation that "Zion" (equated with the congregation of the sons of righteousness) hears that a "divine being" (identified as the heavenly Melchizedek), will rescue them from the power of Belial.[32] Looking elsewhere in the scrolls, in the Messianic Apocalypse (4Q521), the Messiah is the one through whom the Lord shall heal the wounded, revive the dead, and "send good news to the poor" (ענוים יבשר) — terms all taken from Isaiah and associated with the signs of the day of restoration, here applied to the renewal of the faithful and their sharing in God's eternal kingdom.[33]

Bringing this together, in the *Psalms of Solomon*, Isaiah's good news is for the end of Israel's exile and a new beginning to God's mercy, while in the Qumran scrolls the Isaianic herald of good news is either a proclaimer of the heavenly Melchizedek or the Messiah who performs the signs which indicate that the day of national restoration is coming. In any case, this preaching of good news is not just a generic announcement about "salvation," but constitutes a declaration about God's faithfulness to Israel and his victory over the pagan powers. The good news, Isaiah's glad tidings, is composed of assertions about God's kingship, mercy, and the sociopolitical deliverance it will entail for Israel.

Despite the paucity of the εὐαγγέλ- root in the Septuagint, it seems likely that "gospel" language was extant in Judea through Hebrew בשׂרה and Aramaic בסורת as they can be found in several ancient Jewish sources. Several scholars have drawn attention to Aramaic vocabulary pertaining to "good news" for family and national life in pre-Mishnaic Aramaic, the targumim, and the Qumran writings, and how they were often connected to divine kingship. Thus, the biblically derived vocabulary of the "good news," including the noun and verb cognates, was extant in Judea in Greek and Aramaic forms, influenced by both biblical tradition and eastern ruler cults.[34]

I infer, against all three major NT lexicons, that it is most definitely not the case that New Testament usage of εὐαγγέλιον and εὐαγγελίζομαι is derived simply from the Roman imperial cult.[35] I think there might be some parodying of the lan-

---

32. 11Q13 2.15-25.

33. 4Q521 2.1-14; compare with Matt 11:5/Luke 7:22.

34. As cogently argued by Horbury, "'Gospel' in Herodian Judaea," 9-20; see also J. W. Bowman, "The Term *Gospel* and Its Cognates in the Palestinian Syriac," in *New Testament Essays*, ed. A. J. B. Higgins (FS T. W. Manson; Manchester: Manchester University Press, 1959), 54-57, and Peter Stuhlmacher, *Das paulinische Evangelium* (Göttingen: Vandenhoeck & Ruprecht, 1968), 129-35. Influence by "classical and biblical traditions" is conceived by Murray J. Smith, "The Gospels in Early Christian Literature," in *The Content and Setting of the Gospel Tradition*, ed. M. Harding and A. Nobbs (Grand Rapids: Eerdmans, 2010), 182.

35. Cf. *TDNT* 2.725; *NIDNTT* 2.109; *EDNT* 2.71. Horbury ("'Gospel' in Herodian Judaea," 11, 15) argues for a "convergence" of influence from the imperial cult and biblical and

guage of the imperial cult, even an implicit critique of its propaganda, but the roots for the New Testament "gospel" lay elsewhere. Rather, it is the prophetic vision of Isaiah, with the "glad tidings" of Yahweh's reign, the end of the exile, and Israel's restoration, drawn from the Aramaic vocabulary of Herodian Judea, that forms the immediate background of "gospel" on the lips of Jesus, in the preaching of the early church, and on the pages of the Gospels.[36] So much so that Isaiah is appropriately called the "fifth Gospel" of the church.[37]

2. From Jesus' "Gospel of the Kingdom" to Mark's "Beginning of the Gospel of Jesus the Messiah"

An often overlooked factor in the development of the Gospels is the proclamation of the "gospel" by Jesus of Nazareth.[38] Now a common line in scholarship has been that Jesus did not preach a gospel and that all the places in the Gospels where "gospel" is on the lips of Jesus or where Jesus "preaches the gospel" are to be understood as

---

later Jewish documents on the Christian gospel. On the Christian Gospels and the imperial cult, see Stanton, *Jesus and Gospel*, 25-35, 59, and Craig A. Evans, "Mark's Incipit and the Priene Calendar: From Jewish Gospel to Greco-Roman Gospel," *JGRChJ* 1 (2000): 67-81.

36. Contra Helmut Koester (*Ancient Christian Gospels: Their History and Development* [London: SCM, 1992], 3), who argues that "There is no evidence that the earliest Christian use of εὐαγγέλιον and εὐαγγελίζεσθαι in its formative stages is in any way influenced by these prophetic passages from the Old Testament." But we are left wondering why Isaiah's "gospel" would have any less influence on the first Christians than on the Qumranites or the *Psalms of Solomon*. Isaiah's "gospel" seem to have definitely shaped Mark, Paul, and Luke in the very least. In fact, they did not invent the Isaiah-Jesus connection and were probably amplifying a tradition that they had already received. See, e.g., Rikki E. Watts, *Isaiah's New Exodus in Mark* (BSL; Grand Rapids: Baker, 1997); J. Ross Wagner, *Heralds of the Good News: Isaiah and Paul in Concert in the Letter to the Romans* (Leiden: Brill, 2003); Peter Mallen, *The Reading and Transformation of Isaiah in Luke-Acts* (LNTS 367; London: T&T Clark, 2008) ; Pokorný, *From the Gospel to the Gospels*, 41-44.

37. Cf. John F. A. Sawyer, *The Fifth Gospel: Isaiah in the History of Christianity* (Cambridge: Cambridge University Press, 1996).

38. Pokorný (*From the Gospel to the Gospels*, 53) surveys Marcan and Q traditions and concludes: "Jesus considered his proclamation of the kingdom of God to be identical with the prophetic proclamation of good news [from Isaiah 61]. The fact that the two earliest documents including traditions about Jesus (Q and Mark) indicate the use of the term *euangelion* in his lifetime, may speak in favour of a traditional consciousness according to which Jesus proclaimed the 'good news' which, in this case, is identical with his teaching about the kingdom of God." In contrast, Klyne Snodgrass ("The Gospel of Jesus," in *The Written Gospel*, ed. M. Bockmuehl and D. A. Hagner [Cambridge: Cambridge University Press, 2005], 31-45) treats "gospel" as a descriptor for Jesus' message, but is unsure if Jesus used any Aramaic equivalent for "gospel."

anachronistic Christianizations of the Galilean rabbi from Nazareth.[39] Yet I think that such a scholarly view, dominant and durable as it has been, is about as sure-footed as a mountain goat on a very steep iceberg!

First, we have a good *prima facie* claim to historical authenticity for Jesus proclaiming a gospel because Jesus himself is not the focal point in his "gospel." He preaches the kingdom of God. He does not preach the good news of his own death and resurrection with justification by faith or the forgiveness of sins as its chief benefit. This is good evidence that we are not reading a later Christianized write-up of his message. Now obviously kingdom and cross do go together and form a crucial thread in the tapestry of how the divine victory will be won, but Jesus did not preach a gospel ripped directly from Paul's letter to the Romans.[40] Instead, his message was God's reign and God's plan to renew Israel, packed densely with echoes of scriptural hopes and warnings of judgment and setting forth the response that Israel needs to make in this day of decision.

Second, if we situate the historical Jesus in the context of Jewish restorationist eschatology, as I and others have previously argued, then it makes perfect sense for Jesus to proclaim glad tidings of God's coming kingship.[41] In Aramaic, something like the בסורה אמלכות ("good news of the kingdom") would prick the ears of hearers with an exciting announcement of God's kingship and deliverance.[42] Jesus announced that Israel stood on the precipice between God's victory and God's judgment, and how they responded to him would determine their standing before

39. Cf., e.g., *EDNT* 2.70-71.

40. On which, see N. T. Wright, *How Did God Become King?* (London: SPCK, 2011), 175-249.

41. Cf. Ben F. Meyer, *The Aims of Jesus* (London: SCM, 1979); E. P. Sanders, *Jesus and Judaism* (Philadelphia: Fortress 1985); N. T. Wright, *Jesus and the Victory of God* (COQG 2; London: SPCK, 1996); Scot McKnight, *A New Vision for Israel* (Grand Rapids: Eerdmans, 1999); Brant Pitre, *Jesus, the Tribulation, and the End of the Exile: Restoration Eschatology and the Origin of the Atonement* (Grand Rapids: Baker, 2005); Michael F. Bird, *Jesus and the Origins of the Gentile Mission* (LNTS 331; London: T&T Clark, 2006), esp. 26-45.

42. While some argue that Jesus used the Aramaic verb rather than the noun, given the prevalence of the verb in the Hebrew and Greek forms of Isaiah (e.g., Stanton, *Jesus and Gospel*, 18-20), I remain agnostic since we just do not know for sure. But I would not rule out Jesus' use of the noun because: (1) εὐαγγέλιον can be retroverted from the Greek of the Gospels into "preachable" Aramaic easily enough, (2) "believe in the gospel" (Mark 1:15) might even rest on a Semitic idiom (so Stuhlmacher, "Gospel and the Gospels," 20-21), and (3) there is a good chance that reference to a "gospel" or "gospelizing" was part of early Christian Palestinian tradition from the dawn of the early church (see Matt 24:14/Mark 13:10; Matt 26:13/Mark 14:9; Acts 15:7; Rom 1:1; Rev 14:6-7). Mark's exclusive use of the noun does not mean that he is dependent on Pauline influence, as if Paul was the only one who announced a "gospel" (contra Willi Marxsen, *Mark the Evangelist: Studies on Redaction History of the Gospel* [Nashville: Abingdon, 1969], 125). Mark might simply be following a mixture of Pauline influence and earlier tradition for the use of the noun *euangelion* in the story of Jesus.

the God of the covenant in a future reordering of power. Jesus took up the Isaianic script about the good news of God's coming reign and declared that this reign was now becoming a reality in and through his work as the messianic herald of salvation (Mark 1:14-15; Matt 4:23; 9:35; Luke 4:18-21, 43; 8:1; 9:6; Luke 7:22/Matt 11:5). For Jesus, the deeds that he does — healings, exorcisms, preaching to the poor — are all signs that God is becoming king and that Israel's hopes for restoration are really, visibly, and tangibly happening. In other words, victory is on the horizon. The constellation of hopes associated with Israel's restoration, of which Isaiah contributed much to, included items like the advent of a messianic king, a new exodus, the return of the dispersed tribes to Israel, the pilgrimage of the Gentiles to Jerusalem, the defeat of national enemies, the rebuilding of the temple, Yahweh's visitation to Zion, and a return to covenant righteousness, and all of these can be coordinated with the program and preaching of Jesus of Nazareth. This was his gospel, his declaration.[43]

Third, a knee-jerk response to the claim just made might be to rattle off the dictum that Jesus proclaimed the kingdom, but the church preached Jesus! So even if Jesus did proclaim a gospel of sorts, it was clearly different from the post-Easter gospel of the early church. A genuine concern is lodged here since Easter did introduce a transformation of sorts between Jesus' pre-Easter gospel and the post-Easter gospel of the early church, but the contrast does not have to be posed quite so starkly. For a start, though Jesus did not preach expressly about himself, there was always an implicit self-reference in Jesus' preaching of the kingdom. Jesus asserted to his critics, "But if it is by the finger/Spirit of God that I cast out the demons, then the kingdom of God has come to you" (Luke 11:20/Matt 12:28). So it is *his work* of mediating God's Spirit and *his words* activating prophetic hopes that usher in God's kingdom. What is more, we have to also ask what role Jesus thought he would personally play in this coming kingdom. The impression we get from our sources, especially from Jesus' final week in Jerusalem, is that he saw himself as the messianic king, God's vice-regent, ruling over a restored Israel (see esp. Matt 19:28/Luke 22:30).[44] In addition, the passion predictions, prophetic intimations of his suffering, and many of his parables all suggest that he considered his death to be instrumental for the victory of the kingdom.[45]

Not only that, but within the early church, the ascription of an atoning function to Jesus' death and belief in his resurrection and exaltation did not lead to an abandonment of his kingdom message. On the contrary, the early church seemed to

43. Cf. E. P. Sanders, *Judaism: Practice and Belief, 63 BCE–66 CE* (London: SCM, 1992), 279-303; N. T. Wright, *The New Testament and the People of God* (COQG 1; London: SPCK, 1992), 145-338; James D. G. Dunn, *Jesus Remembered* (CITM 1; Grand Rapids: Eerdmans, 2003), 393-96.

44. Cf. Michael F. Bird, *Are You the One Who Is to Come? The Historical Jesus and the Messianic Question* (Grand Rapids: Baker, 2009), 104-7.

45. Cf. Michael F. Bird, "Passion Predictions," in *Encyclopedia of the Historical Jesus,* ed. C. A. Evans (New York: Routledge, 2008), 442-46.

have understood themselves quite consciously as a "kingdom" movement of sorts, for whom the cross became a central symbol for what the kingdom stood for. Paul's few scattered reference to "kingdom" suggests that it was a virtual abbreviation for the work that he was doing (Rom 14:17; 1 Cor 4:20; Col 1:13; 4:11), something still to be entered into or inherited in the future (1 Cor 6:9-10; 15:24, 50; Gal 5:21; 1 Thess 2:12; 2 Thess 1:5), and something that was also christologically constituted so that he could regard Jesus the Messiah and God's kingdom as items intertwined together (see Acts 28:31; Col 1:12-14; Eph 5:5; 2 Tim 4:1).[46] Luke's précis of apostolic preaching gives the deliberate impression that the good news was closely connected to Jesus' announcement of the kingdom, since the church retained the hope for Israel's restoration as part of the overall divine purpose, even while it focused on Jesus' death and resurrection (Acts 3:19-21; 8:12; 14:22; 19:8; 20:25; 28:23, 31). While all four Gospels, in varying ways, associate Jesus with the kingdom, they all climax with descriptions of the kingship of the crucified as the chief emblem of the kingdom's advent. Hence, the gospel preached by Jesus remains the crucial presupposition for the church's gospel about Jesus.

For those reasons, I am skeptical of those who try to drive a wedge between the message of the Gospels and the gospel of Paul. For example, Howard Clark Kee argues that Paul's gospel emphasizes Jesus' death and resurrection, while the Gospels focus on Jesus' role as conveyer of the purpose of God for his covenant people. Kee writes: "What we are confronted with, therefore, is not merely a difference between 'gospel' as a message in Paul and as a narrative account in Mark, but a different understanding of the meaning of Jesus for faith."[47] This is, once more, a false dichotomy, as both corpora know of Jesus as God's redemptive agent sent to Israel and the saving message of his death and resurrection. All the Gospels culminate in Jesus' death and resurrection as the climax of the saving news about Jesus, while Paul emphasizes in places Jesus as the Servant and Savior of Israel (e.g., Gal 4:4-5; Rom 1:16; 15:8; cf. Acts 13:23-24; 28:20).

A further plank of proof for continuity between Jesus and the church on the gospel is that Jesus very probably prepared others to continue the proclamation of his message.[48] During his prophetic career, Jesus sent out disciples on itinerant missions to imitate his deeds and to replicate his message (Mark 6:6b-13, 30; Matt 10:1-42; Luke 9:1-6, 10; 10:1-20). This "gospel" of the "kingdom" (Matt 10:7; Luke 9:6; 10:9) undertaken by his disciples was regarded by Jesus as part of God's victory over Satan effecting the rescue of God's people (Luke 10:18). According to the Olivet discourse,

46. Cf. Simon Gathercole, "The Gospel of Paul and the Kingdom of God," in *God's Power to Save*, ed. C. Green (Nottingham: InterVarsity, 2006), 138-54; Brian Vickers, "The Kingdom of God in Paul's Gospel," *SBJT* 12 (2008): 52-67.

47. Howard Clark Kee, *The Beginnings of Christianity: An Introduction to the New Testament* (New York: T&T Clark/Continuum, 2005), 65, 80.

48. Cf. *1 Clem.* 42.1: "The apostles received the gospel for us from the Lord Jesus Christ," a theme that proved to be important to later authors like Irenaeus who believed that the church's gospel was itself given and authorized by Jesus.

Jesus believed that, before the destruction of Jerusalem, the "gospel" must first be preached to all nations, then the elect will be saved and the Son of Man vindicated (Mark 13:10; Matt 24:14).[49] In the story of the anonymous woman who anointed Jesus at Bethany (Mark 14:3-9; Matt 26:6-13) Jesus promises that "wherever the gospel is preached throughout the world, what she has done will also be told, in memory of her" (Mark 14:9; Matt 26:13). Jesus intimated a future and further preaching of the "gospel," one connected with his approaching death in Jerusalem, indebted to his own kingdom message, which would be taken by his followers beyond Israel.[50]

What we have seen above is good proof that the post-Easter gospel of the early church has antecedent connections with the pre-Easter gospel of the historical Jesus. Jesus takes up the Isaianic script for restoration, with himself cast as the "servant" and the "anointed one," who heralds the "gospel" that God's reign is coming. As a demonstration of that fact he performs a ministry of healings and miracles, connected closely as well with his implicit messianic claims and climaxing in his death. Afterward, the early church, as witnesses to his resurrection and recipients of the Spirit, believed that it was entirely appropriate to engage in devotion to Jesus as Lord and to declare the gospel of God's kingdom with due emphasis on the king who inaugurated it. The good news of God's victory in Isaiah turns out to be God's victory in the life, death, and resurrection of Jesus the Messiah. Thereafter the story of Jesus' messianic work for God's kingdom becomes determinative for the content of the church's gospel. That is why the "gospel of God" and the "gospel of the kingdom," when their contents are unpacked, are tantamount to the "gospel of Jesus the Messiah." That is why the apostolic preaching in Acts can narrate the gospel beginning with a synopsis of Jesus' life and then expounding the saving significance of his resurrection and exaltation (see Acts 10:34-43; 13:15-41). That is why Mark's "beginning of the Gospel of Jesus the Messiah" must refer to Jesus preaching the "gospel of God" (Mark 1:1, 14-15). Later, for Ignatius of Antioch, the gospel is Jesus' "cross and death and the faith that comes through him,"[51] but in its extended form it encompasses Jesus' birth, baptism, and Davidic lineage: "For our God, Jesus the Christ, was conceived by Mary according to God's plan, both from the seed of David and of the Holy Spirit. He was born and was baptized in order that by his suffering he might cleanse the water."[52] It would appear that the early church's gospel, where

49. On the authenticity and meaning of this passage, see Bird, *Jesus and the Origins of the Gentile Mission*, 138-42, and Pitre, *Jesus, the Tribulation*, 253-92.

50. Cf. further Bird, *Jesus and the Origins of the Gentile Mission*, 162-68.

51. Ignatius, *Phild.* 8.2.

52. Ignatius, *Eph.* 18.2. Koester (*Ancient Christian Gospels*, 7-8) regards the additional topics as a supplement to the core focus on Jesus' death and resurrection, originating in an incipient anti-docetist controversy. While it is undoubtedly true that much of Ignatius's framing of the gospel has an eye to the docetist controversy (esp. *Trall.* 9.1-2), the presence of similar topics in Rom 1:3-4; Gal 4:4-5; and 2 Tim 2:8 shows that references to Jesus' birth and Davidic origin are not necessarily motivated by docetist controversies.

Jesus is God's chief actor to bring forth the kingdom, represented the hub of their worldview, story-telling, community practice, political rhetoric, and future hopes.

The transition from Jesus' own preaching vocabulary and Jewish Christian usage of בשׂרה and בסורת into the Greek εὐαγγέλιον was probably facilitated by Greek-speaking Jewish Christians in the Jerusalem church, for the "glad tidings" concerning Jesus the Messiah.[53] A message in the early church known as the "gospel" appears to be have been shared widely (see Gal 2:7; 1 Thess 2:4; 1 Cor 15:3-5, 11; Rom 1:3-4; 1 Pet 4:17; Heb 4:6; Rev 14:6; 2 Tim 2:8).[54] The message was influenced also by Christian exegesis of Isaiah 40–66, like Paul's usage of Isa 52:7 in Rom 10:15-18, the Lucan Peter's echo of the same text about God preaching peace through Jesus the Messiah in Acts 10:36; and Mark's incipit (Mark 1:1-2), which links the gospel to Isaiah's exodus motif to the extent that "the 'gospel of Jesus Christ is that gospel about which Isaiah wrote."[55]

But what about Paul we might ask next? Does he resonate with the notion of the gospel as a divine victory, and does the career of Jesus hold a place in Paul's gospel? I believe that we can answer "yes" on both counts.

First, Paul's gospel was resolutely focused on Jesus' identity as the Messiah and Lord (Rom 1:3-4) and the saving message of his death and resurrection (see Gal 3:1; 1 Cor 1:18–2:2; 15:3-8; 2 Cor 5:15; 1 Thess 4:14, etc.).[56] Hence Paul's traditional summary that "the Messiah died for our sins in accordance with the Scriptures, and that he was buried, and that he was raised on the third day in accordance with the Scriptures" (1 Cor 15:3-4). God's action in Jesus, executed according to Scripture, brought forgiveness, reconciliation, redemption, and justification, to name a few benefits that accrue to believers. The death and resurrection of Jesus were paramount in Paul's articulation of how God's purposes for the salvation of his people were effected through the Lord Jesus.

Second, Paul's gospel, perhaps cued by local expressions of the imperial cult, placed a particular accent on Jesus' victory. Romans is arguably Paul's exposition of

53. Cf. Stanton, *Jesus and Gospel*, 23-24 ; Pokorný, *From the Gospel to the Gospels*, 45. Koester seems unsure *(Ancient Christian Gospels)*, writing in one place that εὐαγγέλιον and εὐαγγελίζεσθαι derived from the early Hellenistic church prior to Paul (4 n. 3), but then later contending that the technical use of the terms became established in the Pauline communities (9). Similar is Dunn, "Gospel and the Gospels," 292, who thinks it was Paul who introduced the noun into Christian vocabulary.

54. Contra Mason *(Josephus, Judea,* 282-302) who regards τό εὐαγγέλιον as a Pauline neologism for "The Announcement." However, knowledge of τό εὐαγγέλιον as a message seems to have been accepted outside of the Pauline circle as evidenced by Paul's discussion with Peter, James, and John in Jerusalem (Gal 2:2, 7). It is also attested in 1 Pet 1:12; 4:6, 17; and Rev 14:6, and usage in those places is distinctively non-Pauline.

55. Watts, *Isaiah's New Exodus*, 56.

56. Cf. Michael F. Bird, *A Bird's-Eye View of Paul: The Man, His Mission, and His Message* (Nottingham: InterVarsity, 2008), 74-81.

his gospel, and its first theological summit is Paul's claim that believers are "more than conquerors" through the love of Christ (Rom 8:37). Then, at the end of Romans, in a theological postscript, the Apostle adds, "The God of peace will shortly crush Satan under your feet" (16:20). First Corinthians 15 begins with some traditional material about the gospel and features an explication of the nature of the resurrection body, yet the climax of the discourse is Paul's closing exhortation, "thanks be to God, who gives us the victory through our Lord Jesus Christ" (1 Cor 15:57). Let us not forget that Paul was put to death, not because of some interiorized spirituality but because he was traveling around the eastern Mediterranean declaring the kingship and victory of the Lord Jesus on the turf claimed by Caesar (see Acts 17:7).

Third, the career of Jesus must have figured prominently in Paul's christological discourse at some point.[57] The mere fact that Paul narrates the crucifixion of Jesus as Israel's Messiah seems to presuppose something of Jesus' biographical story and the historical mission of the Messiah, subjects that Paul must have expounded at some point in either his proclamation or instruction. One gets the impression that Paul may have even acted out, as in a one-man drama, the passion story of Jesus since he says that "It was before your eyes that Jesus Christ was publicly exhibited as crucified" (Gal 3:1). Paul received and passed on the tradition about Jesus' last meal with his disciples (1 Cor 11:23-26). He had met with Peter, a source of the Jesus tradition (Gal 1:18; 2:7-8; 1 Cor 9:5). Members of the Jerusalem church such as Barnabas and Mark traveled with Paul for a time (Acts 13:1–15:39; 1 Cor 9:6; Gal 2:1-14; Col 4:10). Concrete connections between Paul's parenesis and the Jesus tradition can also be found across the epistles (e.g., 1 Thess 4:15; 1 Cor 7:10).

Coming now to the Gospels, particularly the Synoptics, it seems that among their chief aims is to narrate the gospel of God's kingdom through the story of Jesus' career, crucifixion, and resurrection. Telling the gospel in a continuous narrative was hardly innovative since the gospel always included a recital of Jesus' career climaxing in his death and resurrection, as evidenced by the evangelistic sermons in Acts. The Gospels, therefore, reflect the kergymatic declarations of the early church about the saving message of Jesus precisely because they weld together Jesus' career and crucifixion in its eschatological coordinates. So Mark cannot be credited with expanding the meaning of the gospel to include Jesus' career in addition to the cross and resurrection, for the two were always connected together.[58]

Mark's "beginning of the gospel" is, then, entirely appropriate to describe a book about Jesus' preaching of the "kingdom of God" and the "gospel of God" (Mark

---

57. Cf. further Bird, *Bird's-Eye View of Paul*, 52-55; Graham Stanton, *Jesus of Nazareth in New Testament Preaching* (Cambridge: Cambridge University Press, 1974), 86-116; Martin Hengel, *The Four Gospels and the One Gospel of Jesus: An Investigation of the Collection and Origin of the Canonical Gospels* (Harrisburg: Trinity, 2000), 86; Dunn, "Gospel and the Gospels," 295-97.

58. Robert H. Gundry, *Mark: A Commentary on His Apology for the Cross* (Grand Rapids: Eerdmans, 1993), 1050; Hengel, *Four Gospels*, 92-94; Stanton, *Jesus and Gospel*, 53; *pace* Marxsen, *Mark the Evangelist*, 117-50.

1:1, 14-15). Mark does not distinguish terminologically between the gospel of Jesus and the post-Easter gospel about Jesus, for he assumes that the church's proclamation of the gospel springs forth from the word of Jesus (see esp. Mark 13:10; 14:9).[59]

However, there are tangible differences between an oral message and a written book, and this is not insignificant. The Gospels are not constrained by the limitations of oral performance, but are carefully devised literary constructs. The Gospels reflect not only ancient orality, but also ancient book culture. The oral gospel is to a written Gospel what a writer's notebook is to a finished novel.[60] The Gospels are not simply narrations of sermons, as they are heavily augmented to deal with didactic, apologetic, and communal needs. The Gospels reflect the literary crystallization of the Jesus tradition, supplement Christian preaching about Jesus with didactic content, and exemplify early Christian interpretation of the Old Testament. All this is located in a theologically loaded narrative designed to promote the message of Jesus among communities both local and geographically adjacent. At some point the orally taught gospel, with its scant outline of Jesus' ministry and resolute focus on Jesus' passion, was supplemented with sayings and anecdotes from his life, padded out to add a thickness to the church's presentation of Jesus. What Mark did was to standardize this process somewhat by combining preaching and teaching about Jesus into a single written account. By doing so, he birthed the literary genre we call "Gospel." Viewed this way, the movement from oral gospel to written Gospel was, as Aune notes, "gradual and inevitable"[61] since it became necessary to conserve the core elements of the gospel while simultaneously augmenting it with additional Jesus traditions. Accordingly, the Gospels are biographical expansions of the preached gospel, developed into a known literary form, for a wide array of purposes including evangelistic, didactic, and formative.

I have thus far argued that the Gospels constitute a strong continuity with the oral gospel, different only by virtue of development of the content by augmentation from the Jesus tradition, overlaid with interpretation of the Old Testament, and placed in the literary form of a biography. The Gospels signify the victory of God in the mission, passion, and resurrection of Jesus. They announce this victory in a biographical narrative. Mark's achievement was not to combine the Jesus tradition with the kerygma, for the Jesus story was always part of the kerygma; rather, his achievement was to put the gospel of Jesus into a biographical medium to which it was already well suited. The fact that this was seized upon by others and emulated shows that a biographical Jesus book met a deep and universal need among Christian groups.

---

59. *EDNT* 2.73. According to Pokorný (*From the Gospel to the Gospels*, 196-97): "The story of Jesus is the necessary beginning (pre-history) of the Easter gospel, which appears at the very end of the Gospel in Mark 16:6-7 as a proclamation. This means that the gospel of Jesus (Mark 1:14-15) also belongs to the Easter gospel as its 'beginning.'"

60. David Aune, *The New Testament in Its Literary Environment* (Philadelphia: Westminster, 1987), 24.

61. Aune, *New Testament in Its Literary Environment*, 24.

CHAPTER 2

The Purpose and Preservation of the Jesus Tradition

A study of how the oral traditions about Jesus circulating in the early Christian movement came to be incorporated into the Gospels is a necessary prolegomenon to Jesus research. Conclusions drawn about the nature of the oral tradition underlying the Gospels largely impacts what one thinks about the Gospels as historical witnesses to Jesus.

One immediate issue is scholarly *suspicion* directed toward the historical integrity of the traditions embedded in the Gospels. Doubts about the reliability of the Gospel accounts are generated by a host of factors, including the twenty- to seventy-year gap between Jesus' life and the composition of the Gospels, a perception that the oral tradition was fluid and vulnerable to unsupervised alteration, the theological creativity of the Evangelists in refashioning the tradition to suit themselves, as well as postmodern misgivings about attempts to uncover history itself. For such reasons, Harm Hollander states that "the Christian gospels do not give us a historically reliable account of his [Jesus'] life."[1] Such an understanding of the formation of the Gospels may effectively derail historical Jesus study before it has begun,[2] in which case one would have to concede to Martin Kähler's claim that historical Jesus research constitutes a "blind alley."[3]

---

1. Harm W. Hollander, "The Words of Jesus: From Oral Traditions to Written Record in Paul and Q," *NovT* 42 (2000): 341.

2. On skepticism toward the Synoptic Gospels in particular, see discussion in Gerd Theissen and Annette Merz, *The Historical Jesus: A Comprehensive Guide*, trans. John Bowden (Minneapolis: Fortress, 1998), 90-121; E. Earle Ellis, "The Synoptic Gospels and History," in *Authenticating the Activities of Jesus*, ed. Bruce D. Chilton and Craig A. Evans (NTTS 28; Leiden: Brill, 1999), 51-53; Grant R. Osborne, "History and Theology in the Synoptic Gospels," *TrinJ* 24 (2003): 5-22.

3. Martin Kähler, *The So-Called Historical Jesus and the Historic Biblical Christ*, trans. and

Another obstruction is the *plurality of proposals* for describing the formation of the Jesus tradition. The models are diverse, ranging from those that espouse strong control of the tradition to those that advocate a liquid tradition created out of the life-setting of the early church. The impact of this multiplicity is pointed out by David du Toit, who attributes the diversity in Jesus research to a lack of consensus regarding the formation of the Jesus tradition.

> Current reconstructions of the historical Jesus are either based on an-tiquated form-critical principles or they are constructed without being at all set within the framework of a theory about the processes and the modalities of transmission in early Christianity. The extreme diversity in current Jesus research could therefore be an indication of the urgent need to develop a comprehensive theory of the process of transmission of tradition in early Christianity, which could serve as an alternative to form criticism and provide new analytical tools for the quest for the historical origins of Christianity.[4]

It is in the context of scholarly skepticism and a plurality of perspectives that it is worthwhile to explore anew this old problem about the nature of the Jesus tradition. Martin Dibelius identified long ago the task at hand when he suggested that what is required is a theory explaining both the *motive* for the spreading of the reminiscences of Jesus and the *laws* concerning how they were kept.[5] In fresher terms we might say that we are pursuing the *purpose* and *preservation* of the Jesus tradition. Why did Jesus' followers attempt to keep his teachings alive, tell stories about him, and narrate the story of his death and resurrection? In addition, did they transmit these stories and traditions in a way that faithfully communicated what actually happened?

---

ed. Carl E. Braaten (Philadelphia: Fortress, 1988 [1896]), 46. See a similar view more recently in Scot McKnight, "The Jesus We'll Never Know," *Christianity Today* 54.4 (2010): 22.

4. David S. du Toit, "Redefining Jesus: Current Trends in Jesus Research," in *Jesus, Mark and Q: The Teaching of Jesus and Its Earliest Records*, ed. M. Labahn and A. Schmidt (JSNTSup 214; Sheffield: Sheffield Academic, 2001), 123-24.

5. Martin Dibelius, *From Tradition to Gospel*, trans. Bertram Lee Woolf (Cambridge: Clarke, 1971 [1919]), 11. Cf. C. K. Barrett, *Jesus and the Gospel Tradition* (London: SPCK, 1967), 7: "Why then was historical tradition about the earthly life of Jesus of Nazareth preserved, and how did it come to be preserved in the form we have it?"; Graham Stanton, *Jesus of Nazareth in New Testament Preaching* (SNTSMS 27; Cambridge: Cambridge University Press, 1974), 172: "Why did the early church retain the traditions about Jesus? How did the evangelists use the traditions on which they drew?"

Therefore, it will be the aim of this chapter to make a case as to how the Jesus tradition might have been preserved and why it was important for the early church that it be preserved.

I. The Purpose of the Jesus Tradition

If we can identify the purpose that the Jesus tradition had in the early church, then we have arrived close to a satisfactory explanation for its enduring existence. Several such reasons can be postulated.

The Historical Jesus as Properly Basic to Faith

A central purpose of the Jesus tradition was to provide content to the faith of the early church. The kerygmatic formula "Jesus died and rose" is one of the most basic and well attested beliefs of the early Christians (1 Thess 4:14; 1 Cor 15:3-8; 2 Cor 5:15; Rom 4:25). Yet this creedal formula presupposes or at least raises the further question of the identity of the one who is proclaimed as the crucified and risen Lord. Jesus' passion and his exaltation to the Father's right hand cannot be separated from his earthly vocation since the prophetic career, messianic task, and redemptive death of Jesus are all intertwined in the New Testament. Samuel Byrskog writes, "the kerygma, the story of the present Lord, remains, after all, intrinsically linked with the Jesus of the past."[6] In which case, it is presumptuous to assert that the early church had an entirely kerygmatic faith focused exclusively on the death and resurrection of Jesus, entirely divorced from any interest in his earthly life.[7] Without the narration of the Jesus tradition, the kerygma of

---

6. Samuel Byrskog, *Story as History — History as Story: The Gospel Tradition in the Context of Ancient Oral History* (WUNT 123; Tübingen: Mohr, 2000), 6. Cf. Vincent Taylor, *The Formation of the Gospel Tradition* (London: Macmillan, 1949), 173-74, for a balanced assessment of interest in both Jesus' life and his passion.

7. Hence the words of Rudolf Bultmann, *History of the Synoptic Tradition,* trans. J. Marsh (2nd ed.; New York: Harper & Row, 1963 [1921]), 372: "There is no historical-biographical interest in the Gospels, and that is why they have nothing to say about Jesus' human personality, his appearance and character, his origin, education, and development." Vincent Taylor, *The Formation of the Gospel Tradition* (London: Macmillan, 1935), 143-44, supposes that prior to the Gospels "a Christianity had existed which was destitute of the biographical interest" which is why "no one thought of recording the life of Christ for the first decades of the church."

Jesus' redemptive death would have been incomprehensible to the church from the beginning.[8]

Ernst Käsemann, in a direct and deliberate critique of his mentor Rudolf Bultmann, argued that the early church never lost interest in the life of Jesus as being properly basic to its faith.[9] This makes sense since the canonical Gospels, written as they are from the vantage point of faith in the risen Jesus, still include the ministry of Jesus as an important component of their christological portrait, not just as a preamble to the passion narrative. The Gospels certainly culminate in the death and resurrection of Jesus, but nonetheless they still spend the vast amount of their limited manuscript space in detailing the mission and message of Jesus in the context of Herodian Galilee and Roman Judea. In many ways it is the ministry of Jesus that provides the all-important context in which the significance of Jesus' death and resurrection makes sense. If the Gospels were exclusively stories of encounters with the risen Christ, then one might reasonably infer an ahistorical interest in Jesus' life (as is arguably the case in a Gnostic resurrection dialogue like *Pistis Sophia*). However, that is not what one finds. The death of Jesus made no sense apart from his life, his teaching, and his deliberate effort to follow a prophetic script for his work.

The faith in Jesus that the Evangelists attempt to evoke or affirm is one that seemingly includes both the proclamation of the crucified and risen Jesus as well as teaching about the span of his public ministry. The "gospel of Jesus Christ," as the saving message of the crucified and risen Lord, must also include the "Gospel of Jesus Christ" as the story of Jesus' mission to restore Israel.[10] If one grants the broadly evangelistic nature of the Gospels

8. Martin Hengel, "Eye-Witness Memory and the Writing of the Gospels," in *The Written Gospel*, ed. M. Bockmuehl and D. A. Hagner (Cambridge: Cambridge University Press, 2005), 75-76. See also Eugene E. Lemcio, *The Past of Jesus in the Gospels* (SNTSMS 68; Cambridge: Cambridge University Press, 1991), 2: "Kergymatic expressions of 'faith' found outside of the gospels were *not* projected back onto the narrative" (italics original). Rafael Rodriguez, *Structuring Early Christian Memory: Jesus in Tradition, Performance, and Text* (LNTS 407; London: Clark, 2010), 5: "Jesus' followers spoke of *Jesus,* and they did so knowing that the events of his life belonged to the past" (italics original).

9. Ernst Käsemann, "The Problem of the Historical Jesus," in *Essays on New Testament Themes,* trans. W. J. Montague (London: SCM, 1964), 15-47. Cf. Dieter Lührmann, "Jesus: History and Remembrance," in *Jesus Christ and Human Freedom,* ed. E. Schillebeeckx and B. van Iersel (New York: Herder & Herder, 1974), 46: "[I]f the kerygma was in fact an historical given of this kind, and its substance was Jesus of Nazareth, an historical individual, surely one then must ask what support that kerygma had in that individual and his activity."

10. For instance, the opening of Mark's Gospel commences in 1:1 with "The Gospel

and the recounting of Jesus' prophetic career in the missionary speeches of Acts, then one can discover a setting for remembering Jesus in the proclamation of Jesus by the early church.[11] The declaration of the gospel entailed a narration of Jesus' life, ministry, death, and resurrection, all in the context of Israel's sacred traditions. When it comes to the genesis of the Jesus tradition, Dibelius was basically right: "In the beginning was the sermon."[12]

One obvious purpose, then, for the Jesus tradition, when remembered and retold, when transmitted and taught, when passed on and proclaimed, was to provide content to faith, to recite the story of the one called "Savior." Who Jesus is and yet will be could never be explained apart from who Jesus was. Furthermore, the question "Who is this Jesus?" did not begin in eighteenth-century Germany. The question of who Jesus is and who he thought he was commenced in his own lifetime. Such questions were broached by followers, supplicants for healing, critics, opponents, and later by early converts to Christianity, expounded upon by early teachers, and later epitomized by the Evangelists. Richard Bauckham puts it well: "Thus, at the deepest level, it was for profoundly theological reasons — their understanding of God and salvation — that the early Christians were concerned with faithful memory of the really past story of Jesus. The present in which they lived in relationship with the risen and exalted Christ was the effect of this past history, presupposing its pastness and not at all dissolving it."[13]

---

of Jesus Christ" and in 1:15 it introduces Jesus as proclaiming "the gospel of God." If 1:1-15 is taken as a complete introductory unit where "gospel" functions as an *inclusio,* then Mark has introduced the objective Gospel about Jesus with the subjective gospel proclaimed by Jesus in his prologue. See further Edward Schillebeeckx, *Jesus: An Experiment in Christology,* trans. Hubert Hoskins (London: Collins, 1979), 108; John Painter, *Mark's Gospel: Worlds in Conflict* (NTR; London: Routledge, 1997), 35; Harald Riesenfeld, *The Gospel Tradition* (Oxford: Blackwell, 1970), 29.

11. On this point, see the older studies by C. H. Dodd, *The Apostolic Preaching and Its Developments* (London: Hodder & Stoughton, 1936), 21-22, 28-29, 56; Stanton, *Jesus of Nazareth in New Testament Preaching,* 172-85 (esp. 176-77). Of course, this does not mean that preaching was the *only* setting in which the deeds and words of Jesus were remembered. The transmission process had a definite purpose and setting, but it probably included a mixture of loci related to proclamation, exhortation, internal and external debate, and pure curiosity in Jesus' life. Though Martin Dibelius, *From Tradition to Gospel* (New York: Scribner, 1965), 15, sees the life of Jesus as not contained in evangelistic preaching but instead belonging to a later catechetical phase.

12. Martin Dibelius, *Die Formgeschichte des Evangelium* (Berlin: Evangelische Verlag, 1969), 242.

13. Richard Bauckham, *Jesus and the Eyewitnesses* (Grand Rapids: Eerdmans, 2006), 277-78. See also C. H. Dodd, *Historical Tradition in the Fourth Gospel* (Cambridge: Cambridge

The Practical Value of Jesus' Teachings

It is quite likely the early Christians were very interested in the words and actions of Jesus if only for their practical significance. That Jesus was perceived as an oracular prophet, teacher, rabbi, and sage is the overall impression one gets from the Gospels. The veneration of Jesus as a teacher and the "echoes" one finds of the Jesus tradition in early Christian literature testifies further to the impact that Jesus had as a didactic authority.

The impact that Jesus had as a teacher can be easily compared to that of other revered Jewish teachers. The wisdom of ben Sirach, the strictures of the Teacher of Righteousness, and the instruction of pharisaic figures like Hillel and Shammai were preserved by their closest followers precisely because their teachings were thought to be authoritative. Jesus' teaching was similarly imbibed and retained by his followers because his words carried a particular didactic weight and even an air of divine authority. In the Gospels, Jesus is addressed as "teacher," "master," and "rabbi." He evidently attached a particular importance to his own instruction in light of his eschatological conception of God's coming reign and the coming Son of Man.

The Gospels "recount," by which I mean both retrieve and re-create, the words and deeds of Jesus because they addressed the needs and situation of the later church. Samuel Byrskog argues that Matthew in particular accents the role of Jesus as teacher. Matthew identified an inherent value in Jesus' instruction located in the context of his life and ministry; Matthew amplified the image of Jesus as teacher in order to underscore the importance of following his commands. Hence the emphasis on "hearing" and "doing" so prevalent in Matthew's Gospel. Byrskog surmises that the transmitters of the Jesus tradition in Matthean circles lived out the Jesus tradition in practical obedience comprising adherence to his teaching and imitation of his example. He writes: "Within a setting where transmission is a specific act motivated by a special interest in the teaching as integrated within the past history of Jesus, the aim to preserve and protect the Jesus tradition remained essential."[14]

In the Pauline corpus, Jesus material occurs in one of two forms, either

---

University Press, 1963), 7: "The [Jesus] tradition served (among other purposes) to guard and hand on what was remembered and believed concerning that which Jesus had done, said and suffered — in other words, the raw material of gospel composition."

14. Samuel Byrskog, *Jesus the Only Teacher: Didactic Authority and Transmission in Ancient Israel, Ancient Judaism and the Matthean Community* (CBNTS 24; Stockholm: Almquist & Wiksell, 1994), 397.

in direct *citation* of Jesus' words or in passages that *echo* Jesus' teaching.[15] Notably, these citations and echoes of the Jesus tradition occur more frequently in parenetic sections that discuss practical matters (1 Corinthians 7–15; Romans 12–15; Colossians 3; 1 Thessalonians 5). To give a few examples, in 1 Cor 7:10-11 Paul presents Jesus' prohibition on divorce (Mark 10:9-12; Matt 5:31-32; 19:3-9; Luke 16:18). The command to allow those who preach the gospel to make a living out of the gospel in 1 Cor 9:14 alludes to words of Jesus in the Lucan missionary discourse (Luke 10:7). The eucharistic tradition contained in 1 Cor 11:23-25 recalls the words of Jesus at the Last Supper (Mark 14:22-25; Matt 26:25-29; Luke 22:14-23). The "word of the Lord" denotes the instruction of Jesus about the eschatological denouement as part of Paul's response to the Thessalonian crisis (1 Thess 4:15).[16]

Elsewhere Paul's employment of the Jesus tradition is best described as re-presentation rather than as quotation. He often alludes to Jesus' teachings

---

15. For a list of such sayings, see Seyoon Kim, "Jesus, Sayings of," in *DPL*, ed. G. F. Hawthorne, R. P. Martin, and D. G. Reid (Downers Grove: InterVarsity, 1993), 481. See studies by Birger Gerhardsson, *Memory and Manuscript: Oral Tradition and Written Transmission in Rabbinic Judaism and Early Christianity* (2nd ed.; Grand Rapids: Eerdmans, 1998), 262-335; Dale C. Allison, "The Pauline Epistles and the Synoptic Gospels: The Pattern of the Parallels," *NTS* 28 (1982): 1-32; Michael Thompson, *Clothed with Christ: The Example and Teaching of Jesus in Romans 12.1–15.13* (JSNTSup 59; Sheffield: JSOT, 1991); Peter Stuhlmacher, "Jesustradition im Römerbrief," *Theologische Beiträge* 14 (1983): 240-50; P. Richardson and P. Gooch, "Logia of Jesus in 1 Corinthians," in *Gospel Perspectives 5: The Jesus Tradition Outside the Gospels*, ed. David Wenham (Sheffield: JSOT, 1985), 39-62; E. Earle Ellis, "Traditions in 1 Corinthians," *NTS* 32 (1986): 481-502; F. F. Bruce, *Paul: Apostle of the Heart Set Free* (Grand Rapids: Eerdmans, 1980), 100-112; David Wenham, "Paul's Use of the Jesus Tradition: Three Samples," in *Gospel Perspectives 5*, 7-37; idem, *Paul: Follower of Jesus or Founder of Christianity?* (Grand Rapids: Eerdmans, 1995); Ben Witherington, *Paul's Narrative Thought World: The Tapestry of Tragedy and Triumph* (Louisville: Westminster John Knox, 1994), 151-54; Rainer Riesner, "Paulus and die Jesus-Überlieferung," in *Evangelium — Schriftauslegung — Kirche*, ed. J. Ådna, S. Hafemann, and O. Hofius (FS P. Stuhlmacher; Göttingen: Vandenhoeck & Ruprecht, 1997), 346-65; James D. G. Dunn, "Jesus Tradition in Paul," in *Studying the Historical Jesus: Evaluations of the State of Current Research*, ed. Bruce Chilton and Craig A. Evans (NTTS 19; Leiden: Brill, 1994), 155-78; idem, *The Theology of Paul the Apostle* (Grand Rapids: Eerdmans, 1998), 189-95; Craig L. Blomberg, *Making Sense of the New Testament: Three Crucial Questions* (Grand Rapids: Baker, 2004), 73-88; Detlef Häusser, *Christusbekenntnis und Jesusüberlieferung bei Paulus* (WUNT 2.210; Tübingen: Mohr, 2006); Todd D. Still, ed., *Jesus and Paul Reconnected: Fresh Pathways into an Old Debate* (Grand Rapids: Eerdmans, 2007); David E. Aune, "Jesus Tradition and the Pauline Letters," in *Jesus in Memory: Traditions in Oral and Scribal Perspectives*, ed. W. H. Kelber and S. Byrkog (Waco: Baylor University Press, 2009), 63-86.

16. Cf. discussion in Michael W. Pahl, *Discerning the "Word of the Lord": The "Word of the Lord" in 1 Thessalonians 4:15* (LNTS 389; London: Clark, 2009).

by drawing on a few key words, following Jesuanic themes, and then putting things into his own words in light of the situation that he is speaking to.[17] His remark in Rom 14:14 that he is persuaded "in/by the Lord Jesus" (ἐν κυρίῳ Ἰησοῦ) that no foods are unclean, which corresponds to Mark 7:15, is a good example of re-presentation. Similar too are Paul's references to the love command in Rom 13:8-10 and Gal 5:14, which apparently draw on Jesus' particular use of Lev. 19:18 (Matt 22:34-40/Mark 12:28-34; Matt 5:43-46; Matt 19:19/Luke 10:27). The references to praying to God the Father as "Abba" that Paul makes (Rom 8:15; Gal 4:6) appear to be umbilically connected to the same style of prayer that Jesus modeled before his disciples (Mark 14:36; Luke 11:2). In fact, what Paul calls the "law of Christ" (1 Cor 9:21; Gal 6:2) may well represent a body of dominical tradition pertaining to the example of Jesus and the words of Jesus that is ethically normative for followers of Jesus.

The "Q" document, assuming for now that it existed, is equally illuminating in its use of the Jesus tradition. I remain highly skeptical of all attempts to state the tradition history of Q in terms of sapiential and eschatological editions and reconstructions from a hypothetical Q "community."[18] I suspect the most that we can say that is that "Q" was a document belonging to a network of Christians, probably in Galilee-Syria, who possessed a collection of sayings of Jesus written in Greek.[19] Much of Q's content reflects Jesus' ministry toward Israel and his warnings of national catastrophe shaped with stern ethical admonitions.[20] I am drawn toward the proposal that Q does not represent a form of kerygma-less Christianity with no concern for Jesus' death and resurrection, but instead constitutes general instruction for believers who already know the basic outlines of Jesus' life, death, and exaltation.[21] In such a document what one largely finds, though not exclusively,

17. Kim, "Jesus, Sayings of," 482.

18. Cf. Dennis Ingolfsland, "Kloppenborg's Stratification of Q and Its Significance for Historical Jesus Studies," *JETS* 46 (2003): 217-32; N. T. Wright, *The New Testament and the People of God* (COQG 1; London: SPCK, 1992), 435-43; James D. G. Dunn, *Jesus Remembered* (CITM 1; Grand Rapids: Eerdmans, 2003), 147-60; Christopher M. Tuckett, *Q and the History of Early Christianity: Studies on Q* (Edinburgh: Clark, 1996), 69-75, 82; idem, "Q and the Historical Jesus," in *Der historische Jesus. Tendenzen und Perspektiven der gegenwärtigen Forschung*, ed. J. Schröter and R. Brucker (BZNW 114; Berlin: de Gruyter, 2002), 213-41; Dale C. Allison, *The Jesus Tradition in Q* (Harrisburg: Trinity, 1997), 3-8.

19. For a minimalist list of the contents of Q, see Frans Neirynck, "The Reconstruction of Q and IQP and CritEd Parallels," in *The Sayings Source Q and the Historical Jesus*, ed. A. Lindemann (Leuven: Leuven University Press, 2001), 58.

20. Cf. David Catchpole, *Studies in Q* (Edinburgh: Clark, 1992).

21. T. W. Manson, *The Sayings of Jesus* (Oxford: Oxford University Press, 1937), 16.

is material that focuses on exhortation. To give a few brief examples, we find love for enemies (Matt 5:38-48/Luke 6:27-36), teaching about discipleship (Matt 8:18-22/Luke 9:57-62), encouragement to faithfulness (Matt 24:42-51/ Luke 12:35-48), and the like. The Q document, in whatever form it might have existed, was probably an early handbook on discipleship that drew its content mostly from circulating dominical tradition.

The epistle of James is likewise permeated with echoes of and allusions to the Jesus tradition. It probably represents a sermonic digest of Christian parenesis written to rural churches of Judea sometime in the mid-50s CE and is heavily indebted to Jewish wisdom traditions and also to the Jesus tradition. It is perhaps best characterized as a form of Jesuanic wisdom catechesis that draws from and is inspired by the Jesus tradition. Scot McKnight calls it a "wiki version" of the sayings of Jesus.[22] Although James is christologically "lite," with a paucity of references to Jesus (see Jas 1:1; 2:1), it is quite literally inundated with parallels to Jesus' teachings in the Synoptic Gospels, especially Matthew.[23] Once more, the parallels are largely ethical in nature: joy amid trials (Jas 1:2 with Matt 5:10-12/Luke 6:22-23), perfection (Jas 1:4 with Matt 5:48; 19:21), suspending anger (Jas 1:20 with Matt 5:22), the importance of being doers (Jas 1:22-25 with Matt 7:24-27/Luke 6:47-49), fulfilling the law (Jas 2:10 with Matt 5:19), showing mercy (Jas 2:13 with Matt 5:7), the call to peace (Jas 3:18 with Matt 5:9), humility and reward (Jas 4:10 with Matt 5:5), not judging (Jas 4:10 with Matt 7:1-5/Luke 6:37-38, 41-42), hostile reaction to rich oppressors (Jas 5:2-6 with Matt 6:24-34/Luke 16:13; 12:22-31), the patience of the prophets (Jas 5:10 with Matt 5:12/Luke 6:23), and prohibition of oaths (Jas 5:12 with Matt 5:33-37).[24] Scholars have debated whether James had access to Matthew, Q^Matt, Q, or to a free floating collection of logia.[25] The

---

22. Scot McKnight, *The Letter of James* (NICNT; Grand Rapids: Eerdmans, 2011), 27.

23. Cf. list of Matthew-James parallels in Ralph P. Martin, *James* (WBC; Waco: Word, 1988), lxxiv-lxxvi.

24. McKnight, *Letter of James*, 25-26.

25. Massey H. Shepherd "The Epistle of James and the Gospel of Matthew," *JBL* 75 (1956): 40-51; Peter H. Davids, "James and Jesus," in *Gospel Perspectives 5*, ed. D. Wenham, 63-84; Patrick Hartin, *James and the "Q" Sayings of Jesus* (JSNTSup 47; Sheffield: JSOT, 1991); idem, "James and the Jesus Tradition: Some Theological Reflections and Implications," in *Catholic Epistles and Apostolic Tradition*, ed. K.-W. Niebuhr and R. W. Wall (Waco: Baylor University Press, 2009), 55-70; Richard Bauckham, *James: Wisdom of James, Disciple of Jesus the Sage* (London: Routledge, 1999), 74-107; Todd C. Penner, "The Epistle of James in Current Research," *CRBS* 7 (1999): 287-88; Wesley H. Wachob, *The Voice of Jesus in the Social Rhetoric of James* (Cambridge: Cambridge University Press, 2000); Luke Timothy Johnson and Wesley H. Wachob, "The Sayings of Jesus in the Letter of James," in *Authenticating the Words of Jesus,*

parallels with Synoptic material are interesting: some are closer than others, but there seems nothing to show for sure that James knew canonical or pre-canonical Matthew.[26] In fact, the general allusions to common themes and loose verbal connections make it more likely that James was drawing from a common pool of oral traditions rather than from a fixed literary source akin to Matthew. It would seem, then, that James has familiarity with the Jesus tradition rather than knowledge of the Gospels themselves, as Martin Dibelius observed long ago.[27] The Jesus tradition, more emulated than recited in the letter, constitutes an important source of encouragement and exhortation for Christ-believers.

Taking together a survey of Paul's letters, Q, and James, all suggest that the Jesus tradition which survived the attrition of time was that which was continually relevant to the primitive church in terms of community praxis. In fact, the more radical and subversive Jesus' teachings were in terms of going against the grain of the Greco-Roman ethos, the more likely they were to be embedded in communal practice as visible affirmations of Christian identity.[28]

---

ed. Chilton and Evans, 431-50; John S. Kloppenborg, "The Reception of the Jesus Tradition in James," in *The Catholic Epistles and the Tradition*, ed. J. Schlosser (BETL 176; Leuven: Peeters, 2004), 91-139; idem, "The Emulation of the Jesus Tradition in the Letter of James," in *Reading James with New Eyes: Methodological Reassessments of the Letter of James*, ed. R. L. Webb and J. S. Kloppenborg (LNTS 342; London: Clark, 2007), 121-50; idem, "The Reception of the Jesus Tradition in James," in *Catholic Epistles and Apostolic Tradition*, ed. Niebuhr and Wall, 71-100; Alicia J. Batten, *What Are They Saying about the Letter of James?* (New York: Paulist, 2009), 72-83.

26. For instance, a comparison of Jas 5:12 and Matt 5:34-37 indicates a mixture of similarity and dissimilarity that makes a direct literary relationship unlikely. Indeed, the Jacobean version has good claim to being earlier and showing signs of an eyewitness account according to Byrskog, *Story as History*, 171-75.

27. Martin Dibelius, *James: A Commentary on the Epistle of James* (trans. M. A. Williams; Hermeneia; Philadelphia: Fortress, 1976), 28-29.

28. One cannot escape the genuine possibility that many of the sayings attributed to Jesus or the parallels between the Gospels and epistles are elements of anonymous Christian parenesis (see Hollander, "Words of Jesus," 346, 349). However, I would be prepared to argue that given: (1) the veneration of Jesus as a teacher in early Christianity (indeed "the only teacher" according to Matt 23:8; Ignatius, *Eph.* 15.1; *Magn.* 9.1) and (2) the multiple attestation of several sayings in non-Gospel sources (e.g., Paul on divorce, 1 Cor 7:9-11), the burden of proof lies on those who would demonstrate that sayings of Jesus in the Synoptic tradition arose from anonymous Christian parenesis. Demonstrating that this actually occurred, rather than merely assuming that it took place, is genuinely problematic for advocates such as Hollander.

Intra-Jewish Polemic and Christian Self-Definition

A plausible purpose for retelling the Jesus tradition was because it comprised the foundation of the early church's self-understanding. The Jesus tradition would have been crucial for the earliest disciples with respect to their identity formation and *raison d'être*. Such a tradition would be needed to explain why the group existed and how it was to subsist. As Bailey notes, "Those who accepted the new rabbi as the expected Messiah would record and transmit data concerning him as the source of their new identity."[29] The first believers saw themselves within a meta-narrative of which they were key characters: the *ekklēsia*, the "elect," the "Nazarenes," the "Israel of God," the rebuilt temple, and they were constituted as such strictly by virtue of their relationship with Jesus the Messiah. It was inevitable that they would look back to Jesus — his life, death, and resurrection — as the epicenter of their own story. The retelling of the story of Jesus and the beginning of church potentially kept alive their vision and hope and justified their existence under adverse conditions. For a Jewish sect whose relationship to mainstream Judaism, both in Palestine and in the Diaspora, was becoming increasingly strained and who found itself simultaneously at odds with the politics and pantheon of Greco-Roman society, the Jesus tradition enabled Christian communities to interpret the significance of its own adverse situation by remembering the past of Jesus.[30] In other words, the Gospels "seek to remember in order to make Christian identity in the present possible."[31]

The struggle of the early church to remain within the web of common Judaism amid controversial approaches to the Torah, temple, and Gentiles by its members probably precipitated conflict between Christ-believers and Jews. A dominant approach in New Testament scholarship has been to regard the controversy stories in the Gospels as reflecting the situation of the church in the post-70 CE and post-Yavneh era. However, Paul describes his own conflict with Jewish communities related to his messianic faith (Rom 15:31; 2 Cor 11:23-25; 1 Thess 2:15-16). Paul by his own admission had persecuted the church in an earlier phase of his life when he was a zealous Pharisee (Gal 1:23;

---

29. Kenneth E. Bailey, "Informal Controlled Oral Tradition and the Synoptic Gospels," *Themelios* 20 (1995): 10; idem, "Middle Eastern Oral Tradition and the Synoptic Gospels," *ExpT* 106 (1995): 367.

30. Bauckham (*Jesus and the Eyewitnesses*, 277) complains that the early church was less interested in self-identity than with salvation, though of course as he admits, the two are closely related.

31. Theissen and Merz, *Historical Jesus*, 104.

Phil 3:6; Acts 9:1-4). The martyrdoms of Stephen, James the son of Zebedee, and James the Just indicate further tensions between Christ-believers and the Judean leadership (Acts 7:54-60; 12:1-2; Josephus, *Ant.* 20.200-201). Indeed, the "criterion of execution,"[32] that is, formulating an explanation of why Jesus was crucified, necessitates some kind of conflict between Jesus and his Jewish contemporaries.[33] Therefore, the early church did not have to project its contemporary controversies back onto Jesus in order to justify its stance, but instead remembered similar conflicts that Jesus had with certain Jewish groups culminating in his death.[34] Similarly, the sectarians at Qumran could interpret their own *present* situation in view of the *previous* conflict between the Teacher of Righteousness and the Wicked Priest, but they did not invent the story of the conflict. According to Hengel and Deines:

32. On this criterion, see John P. Meier, *A Marginal Jew: Rethinking the Historical Jesus: The Roots of the Problem and the Person* (ABRL; New York: Doubleday, 1991), 177.

33. N. T. Wright, *Jesus and the Victory of God* (COQG 2; London: SPCK, 1996), 371-83; cf. Meier, *A Marginal Jew*; Craig A. Evans, *Jesus and His Contemporaries: Comparative Studies* (Leiden: Brill, 1995).

34. Some scholars advocate that there were no Pharisees in Galilee for Jesus to confront, implying that the Gospel authors have projected their own post-70 CE debates with Pharisaic Judaism onto Jesus: see E. P. Sanders, *Jesus and Judaism* (London: SCM, 1985), 270-93; idem, *The Historical Figure of Jesus* (London: Penguin, 1993), 205-37; Paula Fredriksen, *Jesus of Nazareth, King of the Jews* (New York: Vintage, 1999), 10-11. However, (1) Richard A. Horsley, *Galilee: History, Politics, People* (Valley Forge: Trinity, 1995), 70, 150-52, concedes that the Pharisees and scribes have a literary function as the agents of Jerusalem authorities in the plot of the Gospels and are also used as the foil for controversy in the pronouncement stories. Still, he writes that "they would have no credibility in either function unless they did, historically, on occasion at least, appear outside of their focus of operations in Jerusalem" (150). (2) The fact that upon the outbreak of hostilities in 66 CE the Jerusalem authorities sent a Pharisaic delegation to take control of the region renders the portrait of the Pharisees as delegates of the Jerusalem authorities to Galilee entirely plausible (Josephus, *Life* 191-93, 197). (3) Archaeological discoveries of white stone vessels, bone ossuaries, and ritual baths throughout Galilee are telltale signs of the adoption of a distinctly Pharisaic halakah in some quarters of the Galilee: see J. F. Strange, "Galilee," in *DNTB*, ed. C. A. Evans and S. E. Porter (Downers Grove: InterVarsity, 2000), 396; Jonathan L. Reed, *Archaeology and the Galilean Jesus* (Harrisburg: Trinity, 2000), 49-51, 125-31. (4) Maurice Casey has argued for the authenticity of two Sabbath controversy stories in Mark 2:23–3:6 on the basis of underlying Aramaic sources in *Aramaic Sources of Mark's Gospel* (SNTSMS 102; Cambridge: Cambridge University Press, 1998), 138-92, 257: "The Sitz im Leben of these disputes is in the life of Jesus. Jesus lived in first-century Judaism, where the question of how to observe the Law was a permanent focus of Jewish life. . . . These disputes have no Sitz im Leben in the early church, which was concerned about whether Christians, especially Gentile Christians, should observe the Law at all. These detailed disputes do not speak to that major issue" (192). (5) For a balanced critique of Sanders's view, see Wright, *Jesus and the Victory of God*, 376-83.

We would argue, however, that the evangelists have not made up Jesus' controversies with the scribes and Pharisees. Nor can they simply be laid at the door of the later Church (one would then have to ask: which one?). The earliest community of disciples in Jerusalem and Galilee may *also* have experienced such conflicts. Yet the Church did not simply freely invent "ideal scenes" in the Gospels, but rather formed them on the basis of concrete *memory.*[35]

These memories could be updated or contextualized to fit the situation of the author and audience but still retain an historical element (I think here principally of the warnings in the Fourth Gospel about being "dis-synagogued" [John 9:22; 12:42; 16:2] and references to "their synagogue" in the Synoptics [Mark 1:23; 1:39; Matt 4:23; 9:35; 10:17; 12:9; 13:54; Luke 4:15]). The circulation of such stories from the Jesus tradition would have the effect of justifying their continued resistance against efforts to reintegrate them into the matrix of Jewish social relationships centered within the synagogue in Greco-Roman cities. It would also validate their contentious beliefs and reinforce group boundaries. James Sanders writes:

> In fact, it is highly possible, in the realm of canonical criticism, that one reason the teachings of Jesus were so popular in the period after his death, and especially following the fall of Jerusalem in A.D. 69, is that reviewed in light of the needs of the struggling Christian community of that time, Jesus' prophetic strictures against his fellow Jews looked like the comfort and support they thought they needed for their own views of themselves as the New Israel.[36]

Several factors led the first Christians to remember and retell the conflicts that Jesus had with fellow Judeans leading up to his death, even if they updated and recontextualized those stories to fit their own immediate situations — situations like the struggle to define the church in the face of opposition, the task of securing the integrity of its message in debate with contempo-

---

35. Martin Hengel and Roland Deines, "E. P. Sander's 'Common Judaism,' Jesus, and the Pharisees," *JTS* 46 (1995): 11. Wright (*Jesus and the Victory of God*, 136): "The community's vital interest in affirming its identity by means of telling Jesus-stories, so long regarded within some critical circles as a good reason for reducing the stories to terms of the community, is in fact nothing of the kind."

36. James A. Sanders, "The Ethic of Election in Luke's Great Banquet Parable," in *Essays in Old Testament Ethics*, ed. J. L. Crenshaw and J. T. Willis (New York: Ktav, 1974), 253.

raries, and retaining a distinctive ethos against those who tended toward a broader trend of Hellenization. The conflict stories in the Gospels, therefore, cannot be wholly attributed to the inventiveness of the later church.

Jesus as Movement Founder

One of the sociological categories useful for describing Jesus is that of a "movement founder." Jesus called *Christ* was the primary cause for the existence and development of a movement called *Christians*. Jesus of *Nazareth* stood at the head of a sectarian group called *Nazarenes*. There is no denying that Jesus and the impact he had on his closest followers constituted the driving force in the emergence of the early church. So much so that James Dunn comments:

> Here, after all, were small house groups who designated themselves by reference to Jesus the Christ, or Christ Jesus. Sociology teaches us that such groups would almost certainly require founding traditions to explain to themselves as well as to others why they had formed distinct social groupings, why they were "Christians." It is unlikely that a bare kerygmatic formula like 1 Cor 15:1-8 would provide sufficient material for self-identification. . . . And stories of such diverse figures as Jeremiah and Diogenes were preserved by their disciples as part of the legitimation of their own commitment.[37]

In the first century there were various renewal movements within Israel. The Pharisees arguably attempted to manufacture the conditions for eschatological restoration through obedience to the Torah and strict adherence to ceremonial purity laws. The Jesus movement could be seen in a similar light where Jesus and his followers sought to implement a prophetic program for Israel's eschatological restoration. Gerd Theissen declares, "Earliest Christianity began as a renewal movement within Judaism brought into being through Jesus."[38] It is this setting in motion of a movement, however diverse it became, that represents the most visible impact left by the histor-

37. James D. G. Dunn, "Can the Third Quest Hope to Succeed?" in *Authenticating the Activities of Jesus,* ed. Chilton and Evans, 37; idem, *Jesus Remembered,* 175.
38. Gerd Theissen, *Sociology of Early Palestinian Christianity,* trans. John Bowden (Philadelphia: Fortress, 1978), 1.

ical Jesus. One is not thereby entertaining the far-flung notion that Jesus himself was a Christian and founded Christianity in the modern sense of the term. Steven Bryan states, "It may be anachronistic to think of Jesus as the 'founder of Christianity,' but Christianity must in some sense be seen as part of his effective history."[39] The existence and shape of the early Christian movement is a historical phenomenon perhaps best explained with recourse to a dynamic figure who had a momentous impact on his closest followers, who themselves made a significant impression upon the religious landscape of the Greco-Roman world.[40]

If so, the title of C. H. Dodd's little book, *The Founder of Christianity*, is not at all misleading even if it must be qualified. It is precisely because Jesus was a "movement founder" that the first disciples made concerted efforts to keep his teachings alive in the primitive Christian communities, whether by itinerants and villagers in Palestine or by Hellenistic Jewish Christians in Mediterranean cities. In a comparative sense, the followers of Luther, Calvin, and Wesley, founders of Christian denominations, had their teachings or "complete works" preserved by followers committed to their doctrines.

More analogous to the Jesus movement, the Teacher of Righteousness at Qumran as founder or refounder of the community arguably had his teachings recorded in literary form, including his unique interpretation of prophetic literature and laws pertaining to the celebration of festivals, and perhaps he even authorized a specific calendar. The Teacher was fondly remembered: God "raised up for them a teacher of righteousness to guide them in the way of his heart. He taught to later generations what God did to the generation deserving wrath, a company of traitors."[41] When due caution is given to the integrity of traditions concerning Hillel and Shammai

39. Steven M. Bryan, *Jesus and Israel's Traditions of Judgement and Restoration* (SNTS 117; Cambridge: Cambridge University Press, 2002), 9. Cf. C. H. Dodd, *Founder of Christianity* (New York: Macmillan, 1970), 90: Jesus' aim was "to constitute a community worthy of the name of a people of God"; Morton Smith, *Jesus the Magician* (New York: Harper & Row, 1978), 5: "Whatever else Jesus may or may not have done, he unquestionably started the process that became Christianity"; James D. G. Dunn, *The Living Word* (Philadelphia: Fortress, 1987), 27: "We need not become involved in complex christological questions in order to recognize Jesus as the founder of a new religious movement." Wright, *Jesus and the Victory of God*, 76, identifies Jesus specifically as a "movement catalyst."

40. Paul W. Barnett, *Jesus and the Logic of History* (NSBT 3; Leicester: Apollos, 1997), 35; idem, *Jesus and the Rise of Early Christianity: A History of New Testament Times* (Downers Grove: InterVarsity, 1999), 17; Hengel, "Eye-Witness Memory," 74-75.

41. CD 1.11-12.

in rabbinic literature, it still appears that their authentic teachings defined not only their respective houses of Pharisaism but also laid the bedrock for rabbinic Judaism. In each case — Jesus, Teacher of Righteousness, Hillel, or Shammai — one observes the deliberate conservation and perpetuation of a religious leader's message and biography because the leader has had a principal role in the formation of the community, a community that has inherited and consciously maintained the vision and teaching of that leader.

II. The Preservation of the Jesus Tradition

It is one thing to establish that the early church had a rationale for remembering Jesus but quite another issue as to whether they were equipped with the means to preserve that memory effectively. Several factors imply that they did.

Interest in Jesus

Earlier we saw that one purpose of the Jesus tradition was to provide content to the early church's faith in Jesus. It naturally follows that interest in Jesus then would have also constituted a reason for preserving and transmitting traditions about him.[42] As T. W. Manson put it: "It is at least conceivable that one of the chief motives for preserving the stories at all, and for selecting those that were embodied in the Gospels, was just plain admiration and love for their hero. It is conceivable that he was at least as interesting, *for his own sake,* to people in the first century as he is to historians in the twentieth."[43] This point we explore now.

The problem is that some scholars contest whether the early church was really interested in a "historical Jesus" when the Jesus of the church's proclamation was their first point of contact with Jesus. Long ago much was made of 2 Cor 5:16, where Paul refuses to know "Christ according to the flesh," which was taken as evidence of the Apostle's deliberate disinter-

---

42. Indeed, only material that is interesting and relevant to audiences would likely survive the attrition of time; see Ernst L. Abel, "The Psychology of Memory and Rumor Transmission and Their Bearing on Theories of Oral Transmission in Early Christianity," *JR* 51 (1971): 280.

43. T. W. Manson, "The Quest of the Historical Jesus — Continued," in *Studies in the Gospels and Epistles* (Manchester: Manchester University Press, 1962), 6.

est in the historical figure of Jesus.[44] On the contrary, Paul states that he formerly viewed Christ from a worldly perspective, but now comprehends Christ from the vantage of one who is "in Christ." Paul may be referring to his former knowledge of Christ, which operated with a false notion of messiahship, or else acknowledging his prior hostility toward the Jesus movement.[45] On either account there is no deprecating of interest in the historical Jesus.

Moreover, the hypothesis that the early church was not interested in the historical Jesus works best if one assumes that the early church, or at least constituent elements of it, were either second-century Gnostics or twentieth-century Existentialists. The Gnostics preferred the voice of the risen Jesus to the earthly Jesus. But the Gnosticism which is required for this theory to work lies beyond the horizon of the first century and emerges more fully in the second century. Scholars who take the line that the primitive Christian communities evolved out of the kerygma and had only the faintest interest in the life of Jesus, in my mind, retroject their own apparent disinterest in the historical Jesus onto the early church.[46] The ugly ditch of G. E. Lessing, whereby the accidental truths of history cannot prove to be the basis for theological truths, was traversed by many twentieth-century interpreters who retreated into the sphere of a Hegelian existentialism so that the proclaimed Word provided a veridical experience of the real Jesus as opposed to the Jesus of mere historical cause and effect. However, the early church appears to have maintained a steadfast conviction that history was the theater of God's activity: the kerygma was not anchored in the mere fact of Jesus' existence coupled with the need for an existentially laden faith.

44. Cf. Albert Schweitzer, *The Quest of the Historical Jesus,* trans. W. Montgomery (London: Black, 1945), 399; Rudolf Bultmann, "The Significance of the Historical Jesus for the Theology of Paul," in *Faith and Understanding* (London: SCM, 1969), 241-44; H. J. Schoeps, *Paul: The Theology of the Apostle in the Light of Jewish Religious History* (London: Lutterworth, 1961), 55-58, 72.

45. Cf. F. F. Bruce, "Paul and the Historical Jesus," *BJRL* 56 (1974): 321-23; W. G. Kümmel, *The Theology of the New Testament,* trans. John E. Steely (London: SCM, 1976), 166; N. T. Wright, "The Paul of History and the Apostle of Faith," *TynBul* 29 (1978): 72-73; Victor Paul Furnish, *II Corinthians* (AB; New York: Doubleday, 1984), 312-13; Witherington, *Paul's Narrative Thought World,* 153-54; Dunn, *Theology of Paul the Apostle,* 184-85; Thomas R. Schreiner, *Paul: Apostle of God's Glory in Christ* (Downers Grove: InterVarsity, 2001), 76-77.

46. In all fairness, one must keep in mind that this door swings both ways and that it is possible that other scholars project their own *interest* in the historical Jesus onto the early church, which did not know of the post-Enlightenment tendency of the criticizing the present by appeal to the past.

Instead, the proclamation of Jesus as the exalted Lord included with it the tacit assumption of his prior historical ministry to Israel. This is hinted at in early hymns and creeds, arguably discernible in Paul's echoes of the Jesus tradition, evident in Luke-Acts, which includes stories of both the pre-Easter Jesus and sermons proclaiming him as the exalted Lord, and confirmed by the symbol and praxis of the early church, where, for instance, the memorial of the Lord's Supper looked back to Jesus' ministry in Jerusalem, his betrayal, and his death and forward to his glorious return.

The Gospels themselves make a clear delineation between the historical ministry of Jesus and his post-Easter presence with his disciples. Becker notes, "When the gospels define the time of Jesus as Christianity's normative primeval time, they demonstrate their interest in the historical Jesus and show that they are not simply wanting to write a commentary on the post-Easter confession of faith."[47] It would also be quite surprising if a movement whose participants focused intently on one named "Jesus the Christ," who constructed creeds around his life and death, who initiated others into their midst through baptism in his name, who as "Christians" took on themselves the very name of that same individual would at the same time be uninterested in his life.[48] Thus, interest in the historical back-then-ness of the person of Jesus was not obliterated by faith in him as the crucified and risen Lord and not worn away by charismatic enthusiasm for the voice of the risen Lord, but inherent within the very praxis of the early Christian movement and epitomized in the Gospels.

47. Jürgen Becker, *Jesus of Nazareth*, trans. James E. Crouch (New York: de Gruyter, 1998), 6. Cf. Hengel, "Eye-Witness Memory," 70: "[T]he Synoptic Gospels consciously intend to narrate *a temporally removed event of the past, i.e., Jesus' unique history, which, of course, has fundamental significance for the present time of the evangelists* and the communities addressed through them" (italics original). Theissen and Merz, *Historical Jesus*, 103-4: "All the Gospels contain 'historicizing elements' which serve as distancing signals and through which past and present are distinguished (cf. Mark 2.20). . . . Thus we may not play off the interest in preaching, which is present in the Gospels as a matter of course, against their intention to remember. The Gospels are biographical narratives with distancing signals and offers of identification." Lemcio, *Past of Jesus in the Gospels*, 108: "The hardest available evidence from the gospels has confirmed the thesis that the Evangelists produced narratives about Jesus of Nazareth that were free of blatant attempts to infuse and overlay his story with their own later and developed estimates of his teaching, miracles, passion, and person." See also Barnett, *Jesus and the Logic of History*, 154-57.

48. Dunn, *Theology of the Apostle Paul*, 185; idem, *Living Word*, 34: "In short, the idea that the first Christians were *not* interested in the pre-Easter Jesus is little short of ludicrous" (italics original). See too Birger Gerhardsson, "The Path of the Gospel Tradition," in *The Gospel and the Gospels*, ed. Peter Stuhlmacher (Grand Rapids: Eerdmans, 1991), 77.

If there was a distinct absence of interest in the pre-Easter Jesus, then it raises the question of why the first Christians retrojected their hopes, debates, conflicts, and beliefs onto a historical figure whom they were purportedly not interested in, but still did so in order to authenticate certain teachings and practices. Moreover, why would they place these new teachings into a pre-Easter narrative? One would be more inclined to think that the voice of the risen Christ speaking through a contemporary prophet would be what such a group needed to hear in order to validate new teachings.

But if they were interested in the historical figure of Jesus, it seems unlikely that they would have allowed creation of sizeable amounts of material *ex nihilo* or the casting of existing traditions into trajectories which they knew to be contrary to the original shape. If they were *not* interested in the details of Jesus' life, then what rationale would they have for retrojecting material onto a historical Jesus within a historical setting? If I am right, then one of the standard party lines of Gospel scholarship concerning formation of the Jesus tradition appears to rest on a contradictory premise, namely, that the church was not interested in a historical Jesus, but interested enough to project their later debates into his life. Yet examination of the various strata of traditions about Jesus yields a continual ebb of interest in the contours of Jesus' pre-Easter ministry.

The members of the Jesus movement in both Palestine and the Hellenistic cities of the Mediterranean, pre- and post-70, testify to an awareness of traditions about Jesus. As Charlesworth writes, "The sheer existence of the Gospels — which include the celebration of the life and teachings of the pre-Easter Jesus — proves that from the earliest decades of the movement associated with Jesus there must have been some historical interest in Jesus of Nazareth."[49] Porter comments similarly, "The quest for the historical Jesus, in fact, clearly began soon after Jesus' death and is reflected in the writings of the early church."[50] Going further, interest in Jesus' person may have begun

49. James H. Charlesworth, *Jesus within Judaism: New Light from Exciting Archaeological Discoveries* (London: SPCK, 1989), 13. Cf. Henry Wansbrough, "Introduction," in *Jesus and the Oral Gospel Tradition*, ed. Wansbrough (JSNTSup 64; Sheffield: Sheffield Academic, 1991), 12: "The evidence we have been examining attests in itself a concern on the part of the earliest Christians to recall the ministry of Jesus, including not least his words and actions, and to preserve and pass on these traditions"; Hengel, "Eye-Witness Memory," 73: "One should not, however, weaken — let alone deny — the evangelists' basic intention to report about a historical person in space and time."

50. Stanley E. Porter, "Luke 17.11-19 and the Criteria For Authenticity Revisited," *JSHJ* 1 (2003): 204.

during the pre-Easter period as people asked who he was or who he said he was.[51] The older traditional view that the Gospels were written, at the broad level, to preserve the story of Jesus in literary form to tell the story for another generation is perhaps more plausible than it has often been thought in contemporary reckoning.[52]

Pedagogical and Rhetorical Devices

The ability of students to retain the information they receive orally from a teacher is conditioned on the utility of the verbal form carrying the instruction as well as the capacity for repetition of the subject content.

Rainer Riesner contends that around 80% of material in the Gospels attributed to Jesus contains features of Hebrew poetry such as parallelism and chiasmus which comprise a mnemonic device that renders such teachings quite memorable. The longer units that make up about 54% of the Synoptic tradition are entirely parabolic. Much of Jesus' teaching material appears to have been composed precisely in order to be wedged in memory.[53] Werner Kelber notes "the extraordinary degree to which sayings of Jesus have kept faith with heavily patterned speech forms, abounding in alliteration, paronomasia, appositional equivalence, proverbial and aphoristic diction, contrasts and antitheses, synonymous, antithetical, synthetic, and tautologic parallelism and the like."[54] Poetry with rhythm, rhyme, alliteration, and assonance

---

51. Cf. Stanton, *Jesus of Nazareth in New Testament Preaching*, 171: "Interest in the life and character of Jesus was already present *in nuce* in the ministry of Jesus. Jesus' proclamation drew critical questioning: Who is this Jesus? Why does he behave in this way?"

52. Cf. Donald Guthrie, *New Testament Introduction* (4th ed.; Leicester, England: Apollos, 1990), 21-24; Barnett, *Jesus and the Rise of Early Christianity*, 392-94; Dunn, *Living Word*, 27, 30.

53. Rainer Riesner, "Jesus as Preacher and Teacher," in *Jesus and the Oral Gospel Tradition*, ed. Wansbrough, 202; idem, *Jesus als Lehrer. Eine Untersuchung zum Ursprung der Evangelien-Überlieferung* (WUNT 2.7; Tübingen: Mohr, 1988), 302-404; idem, "From Messianic Teacher to the Gospels of Jesus Christ," in *HSHJ*, ed. T. Holmén and S. E. Porter (4 vols.; Leiden: Brill, 2011), 1:417-18. Cf. C. F. Burney, *The Poetry of Our Lord: An Examination of the Formal Elements of Hebrew Poetry in the Discourses of Jesus Christ* (Oxford: Clarendon, 1925); Matthew Black, *An Aramaic Approach to the Gospels and Acts* (3rd ed.; Oxford: Clarendon, 1967), 160-79; Ben Witherington, *The Christology of Jesus* (Minneapolis: Fortress, 1990), 8-9; Dunn, *Jesus Remembered*, 139-75; Hengel, "Eye-Witness Memory," 78; Dale C. Allison, *Constructing Jesus: Memory, Imagination, and History* (Grand Rapids: Baker, 2011), 24.

54. Werner Kelber, *The Oral and the Written Gospel* (Philadelphia: Fortress, 1983), 27.

probably has a greater chance of making a lasting cognitive impact on an audience than plain uninflected discourse.[55]

In my own experience, I can recite verbatim an amusing limerick about the late C. H. Dodd that I learned from D. A. Carson over ten years ago after hearing it only once.[56] I can also cite portions of several stanzas of Hamlet and Othello that I learned in high school over twenty years ago. Poetry has that ability to leave deep and enduring impressions on the depths of psyche due to the power of the imagery it evokes and the aural aesthetics experienced through the spoken word. Beyond poetry, several features of Jesus' didactic style were imprinted on the Jesus tradition and arguably made it more memorable. Dale C. Allison has identified eight "rhetorical strategies" prominent in the Jesus tradition, including parables, antithetical parallelism, rhetorical questions, the prefatory "amen," divine passives, exaggeration/ hyperbole, aphoristic formulations, and paradoxical remarks.[57] Such rhetorical techniques, if used often enough, would cement the distinctive character of the Jesus tradition as well as aid in its oral preservation. The poetic, parabolic, and pedagogical qualities of Jesus' teaching rendered the Jesus tradition naturally memorable and easily recalled in later contexts.

In the absence of mass media, Jesus probably broadcast his teachings through repetition from village to village in Galilee and Judea. Whereas the

55. An implication to be drawn from this is that material in the Gospels that is by nature "memorable" is all the more likely to be authentic. Stephen J. Patterson, *The God of Jesus: The Historical Jesus and the Search for Meaning* (Harrisburg: Trinity, 1998), 269, calls for the application of a "criterion of memorability." Patterson explains it: "This criterion takes into account the fact that all of what we have from Jesus would have circulated for many years orally and before (and after) it was included in an early Christian document. *That means special attention should be given to sayings, stories (or versions thereof) which appear to have certain memorable qualities:* they are brief, clever, structures in threes, use catch-phrases, etc." (italics original). If one grants the veracity of the description of the Jesus tradition as a memory, perhaps initially disseminated by eyewitnesses, then it is perfectly plausible that the memory of Jesus would be stamped with some kind of memorability in order to survive the attrition of time. A problem, of course, is that what is memorable may differ significantly from person to person or group to group. Nonetheless, Patterson's suggestion of a new index of authenticity is worthy of consideration, given the corporate remembrance of Jesus in the early church.

56. There once was a man called Dodd
Whose name was exceedingly odd
He spelt, if you please,
His name with three Ds
When one is sufficient for God.

57. Dale C. Allison, *Jesus of Nazareth: Millenarian Prophet* (Minneapolis: Fortress, 1998), 49-50; idem, *Constructing Jesus*, 15.

existence of multiple versions of sayings or discourses might give the impression of being doubled accounts by the Gospel authors, in fact they might be the result of Jesus teaching on a topic more than once.[58] For instance, the parable of the mustard seed exists in Mark, Q, and Thomas and could conceivably emanate from three separate oral performances of the same parable by Jesus.[59] The same could be said of the Sermon on the Mount/Plain and the variations on the Lord's Prayer. James Dunn urges that the default setting of trying to explain these variations entirely in terms of literary development needs to be abandoned in favor of a model that permits some degree of deviation emerging from continuing oral tradition.[60]

The presence of a host of verbal devices found consistently across the Jesus tradition is best explained as originating from the pedagogical technique of a single teacher who had a considerable impact on his audience. Where one finds these characteristic "strategies" in the Jesus tradition, it may be fair to offer the presumption of authenticity in the absence of extenuating factors that point to the contrary. This is not to discount, of course, the possibility that the disciples may have deliberately imitated Jesus' form and style in their own didactic methods. Nevertheless, it appears that Jesus taught and spoke in a manner that laid great emphasis upon mnemonic devices and was designed to leave a powerful impact on the minds of his audiences. If the disciples heard such poetry and pedagogy with some degree of frequency as they accompanied Jesus in his itinerant ministry, then their propensity for long-term memory retention would significantly increase.

Aramaic Sources

Beneath the Gospels lies a series of sources, oral and literary, some of which must have been in Aramaic at some point. Around two centuries ago there was speculation by G. E. Lessing and J. G. Eichhorn that behind the Gospels there was a proto-Gospel written in Aramaic or Hebrew which the Evange-

---

58. Gerhardsson, *Memory and Manuscript*, 334-35; Kelber, *Oral and the Written Gospel*, 30; Wright, *New Testament and the People of God*, 422-24; idem, *Jesus and the Victory of God*, 170-71; Craig Keener, *The Historical Jesus of the Gospels* (Grand Rapids: Eerdmans, 2009), 142.

59. Mark 4:30-32; Luke 13:18-19/Matt 13:31-32; *Gospel of Thomas* 20.

60. James D. G. Dunn, "Altering the Default Setting: Re-Envisaging the Early Transmission of the Jesus Tradition," *NTS* 49 (2003): 139-75, reprinted in *A New Perspective on Jesus: What the Quests for the Historical Jesus Missed* (Grand Rapids: Baker, 2005), 79-125; idem, *Living Word*, 32; idem, *Jesus Remembered*, 222-23, 237-38.

lists drew on (often called the "*Ur*-Gospel"). This theory was recently revised by James R. Edwards, who believes he can detect a Hebrew Gospel source used by Luke.[61] Others such as J. G. Herder and J. K. L. Giesler contended for a common pool of Aramaic oral tradition that the Evangelists had at their disposal.

Such theories may seem naive in view of the fairly wide acceptance of the two-source theory of Mark and "Q" as the primary springs for the Synoptic Gospels. Nevertheless, the notion of Aramaic sources undergirding parts of the Gospels is not entirely without merit. There are several instances where Aramaic words are used in the Gospels, and this indicates a Palestinian provenance for many of the stories (see Mark 5:41; 15:22, 34; John 4:25; 19:13; 20:16). Jesus' idiomatic self-reference to himself as "the Son of Man" is certainly based on an Aramaic idiom בר (א)נשא for "man" or "someone in my position."[62] Several scholars have called attention to the presence of Aramaisms, Semitic poetry, and pericopes easily retroverted into Aramaic within the Gospels.[63] For example, an ironic wordplay can be discerned in Matt 23:24, but only in Aramaic: "You blind guides, straining out a gnat (קמלא [*qamla*]) and swallowing a camel (גמלא [*gamla*])." This signifies a very probable Aramaic layer beneath the Gospel text.[64] So much so that Maurice Casey, hardly prone to any kind of conservatism, avers that in the case of the Gospel of Mark "our oldest Gospel is partly dependent on eyewitness accounts by Aramaic-speaking disciples."[65]

61. James R. Edwards, *The Hebrew Gospel and the Development of the Synoptic Tradition* (Grand Rapids: Eerdmans, 2009), 182-86, 260-61. See earlier Rainer Riesner, "Luke's Special Tradition and the Question of a Hebrew Gospel Source," *Mishkan* 20 (1994): 44-52.

62. Cf. for discussion Michael F. Bird, *Are You the One Who Is to Come? The Historical Jesus and the Messianic Question* (Grand Rapids: Baker, 2009), 78-98.

63. Burney, *Poetry of our Lord*; Black, *Aramaic Approach*; Joachim Jeremias, *New Testament Theology*, trans. John Bowden (London: SCM, 1971), 1.3-29; T. W. Manson, *The Teaching of Jesus: Studies in Its Form and Content* (Cambridge: Cambridge University Press, 1963), 45-56; Joseph A. Fitzmyer, *A Wandering Aramean: Collected Essays* (Missoula: Scholars, 1979), 1-27; Casey, *Aramaic Sources of Mark's Gospel*, 254-55; idem, "An Aramaic Approach to the Synoptic Gospels," *ExpT* 110 (1999): 275-78; idem, *Jesus of Nazareth* (London: Clark, 2010), 108-20; Dunn, *Jesus Remembered*, 225-26; see also M. O. Wise, "Languages of Palestine," in *DJG*, ed. J. B. Green, S. McKnight, and I. H. Marshall (Downers Grove: InterVarsity, 1992), 443-44.

64. For a list of Semitisms in the Gospel, see Jeremias, *New Testament Theology*, 1.4-7; Edwards, *Hebrew Gospel*, 125-53, 292-332. For indications of Semitisms beneath Greek texts in general, see G. Mussie, "Greek in Palestine and the Diaspora," in *The Jewish People in the First Century*, ed. S. Safrai and M. Stern (2 vols.; Amsterdam: Van Gorcum, 1974-76), 2.1048-49.

65. Casey, *Jesus of Nazareth*, 109.

A caveat is required, since there are several problems in trying to use signs of Aramaic as an index to authenticity. To begin with, many of the alleged Semitisms may simply result from bad *koine* Greek. A purported Semitism might derive from the influence of the Septuagint on the Gospels, or residual Semitisms in the Gospels might be products of Aramaic-speaking Christians and not derive from Jesus.[66] Still, the facts that numerous Semitisms are found in the Gospels and that large sections are capable of being retroverted back into Aramaic at least hint at the prospect of Aramaic sources as having a place in the Jesus tradition. Without postulating a single Aramaic source, one may conclude, with Barnabas Lindars, that "Careful analysis of the sayings shows again and again that the hypothesis of an Aramaic original leads to the most convincing and illuminating results."[67] The presence of an Aramaic substratum beneath the Gospels attests to a stage of Aramaic *formulation* and *preservation* of the Jesus tradition that also evidences an attempt to remember Jesus at a primitive stage of the tradition's development.

A further point needs to be made about the proper relationship between Aramaic and Greek forms of the Jesus tradition. Palestine was not immune from the Hellenization of the east since the time of Alexander the Great. The Greek language permeated Judean society especially among the political and literary elites. Quite expectedly, then, many of Jesus' followers, especially those engaged in trade and taxation, were probably bilingual, with competencies in both Aramaic and Greek. In addition, the early church appears to have been bilingual from the very beginning. Aramaic speakers among Jesus' disciples like Peter and John went into Greek cities, and we know that Greek-speaking disciples lived in Jerusalem. The first Gospel, the Gospel of Mark, seems to have been written by a bilingualist who was familiar enough with Greek but whose primary language was Aramaic. I deduce from this observation that Aramaic and Greek sources do not necessarily constitute two temporally removed stages of the Jesus tradition. Instead, Aramaic and Greek versions, translations, and editions

---

66. For recent evaluations of the criterion of Semitic language/environment, see Meier, *Marginal Jew,* 1.178-80; Stanley E. Porter, *The Criteria for Authenticity in Historical-Jesus Research: Previous Discussion and New Proposal* (JSNTSup 191; Sheffield: Sheffield Academic, 2000), 89-99; Craig A. Evans, "Life of Jesus," in *Handbook to Exegesis of the New Testament,* ed. S. E. Porter (Leiden: Brill, 2002), 445-46; Loren T. Stuckenbruck, "'Semitic Influence on Greek': An Authenticating Criterion in Jesus Research?" in *Jesus, Criteria, and the Demise of Authenticity,* ed. C. Keith and A. Le Donne (London: Clark, 2012), 73-94.

67. Barnabas Lindars, "The Language in Which Jesus Taught," *Theology* 86 (1983): 364.

of Jesus' teachings probably existed in the early church side-by-side and cross-pollinated from the very beginning.[68]

Notebooks

Sadly, most scholars are accustomed to explaining the complexities of the Synoptic Gospels purely in terms of literary relationships, while they account for the intricacy of the Jesus tradition exclusively with regard to oral transmission. But if the lines between orality and textuality were fluid — and they were — with oral material written down and written materials delivered orally — and if the Jesus tradition was carried in a mix of oral and textual media beginning in Jesus' own lifetime all the way through to the Gospels and beyond, then we need to take serious heed of the interface between oral and written forms. More specifically, we should take seriously the possibility of notebooks being used to aid in the remembrance and transmission of Jesus' teachings.[69]

I have to confess that I was originally skeptical about the prospect of notebooks being used to preserve Jesus' teachings. It struck me as a rather convenient way of preserving Jesus' words, and we do not actually have any surviving notebooks containing Jesus' words. I once regarded with incredulity Paul Barnett's claim: "In our view Jesus' disciples must have begun memorizing Jesus' teachings, and perhaps even writing them down, while he was still with them."[70] But my initial reservations have been assuaged.

---

68. For a brief summary of Greek in Palestine and bilinguality in the early church, see (with bibliography) Porter, *Criteria for Authenticity*, 127-41. Cf. too Catherine Hezser, *Jewish Literacy in Roman Palestine* (TSAJ 81; Tübingen: Mohr, 2001), esp. 237-47 on bilingualism. Note esp. Sang-Il Lee, *Jesus and Gospel Traditions in Bilingual Context: A Study in the Interdirectionality of Language* (Berlin: de Gruyter, 2012).

69. Cf. Heinz Schürmann, "Die vorösterlichen Anfänge der Logientradition. Versuch eines formgeschichtlichen Zugangs zum Leben Jesu," in *Der historische Jesus und der kerygmatische Christus*, ed. H. Ristow and K. Matthiae (Berlin: Evangelische Verlagsanstalt, 1962), 342-70; Gerhardsson, *Memory and Manuscript*, 202; Riesner, *Jesus als Lehrer*, 491-98; idem, "Messianic Teacher," 433-34; Graham Stanton, *Jesus and Gospel* (Cambridge: Cambridge University Press, 2004), 186; James D. G. Dunn, *Jesus, Paul, and the Gospels* (Grand Rapids: Eerdmans, 2011), 41; Keener, *Historical Jesus*, 148-49; Barnett, *Jesus and the Rise of Early Christianity*, 206-7, 380-81; Ellis, "Synoptic Gospels and History," 53-54; Bauckham, *Jesus and the Eyewitnesses*, 251-52, 287-89; Pheme Perkins, *Introduction to the Synoptic Gospels* (Grand Rapids: Eerdmans, 2007), 17; Tomas Bokedal, *The Scriptures and the Lord: Formation and Significance of the Christian Biblical Canon* (Lund: Lund University Press, 2005), 135-37.

70. Barnett, *Jesus and the Rise of Early Christianity*, 206.

It was quite common among literary elites of the Greco-Roman world to take notes (ὑπομνήματα, *commentarii*) as an aid to learning.[71] Greek *gnōmai* (sayings) and *chreiai* (short stories) collections provided short anthologies largely for didactic purposes.[72] The poet Martial recommended that persons carrying his poems on journeys should use a *membranae* or notebook for its convenience.[73] In Mediterranean schools of rhetoric, orators often used notes, and hearers of speeches often took notes to capture the gist of the delivery.[74] The notebook was regarded as a good alternative to the wax tablet.[75] The notes on lectures could even be published. Arrian in fact published an account of the lectures of his teacher Epictetus, saying: "[W]hatever I heard him say I used to write down, word for word, as best I could, endeavouring to preserve it as a memorial, for my own future use, of his way of thinking and the frankness of his speech."[76]

In the Jewish context, Birger Gerhardsson identified rabbinic evidence for the use of notebooks or "scrolls of secrets" to aid in pupils' memorization of their rabbis' words.[77] Though roughly criticized as reading later perspectives back into the first century, the thesis of Jewish notebooks has more going for it. Martin Jaffa has plotted the use of written sources in the redaction of the Mishnah well before 200 CE.[78] The Qumran scrolls provide first-century evidence of short prophetic *testimonia* collections (11QMelch) and halakhic collections (11QTemple) used in the community. Jacob Neusner proposes that Jewish communities often used a large body of manuscript material, teachers' notebooks, preachers' storybooks, exegetical catenae, and florilegia to maintain their traditions.[79] Early Christian *testimonia* collec-

---

71. Cf. George A. Kennedy, "Classical and Christian Source Criticism," in *The Relationship among the Gospels: An Interdisciplinary Dialogue,* ed. W. O. Walker (San Antonio: Trinity University Press, 1978), 130-37; C. H. Roberts and T. C. Skeat, *The Birth of the Codex* (London: Oxford University Press, 1987), 11-23.

72. Martin C. Albl, *And Scripture Cannot Be Broken: The Form and Function of the Early Christian Testimonia Collections* (Leiden: Brill, 1999), 77-79.

73. Martial, *Epigr.* 1.2.

74. See esp. Quintilian, *Inst.* 11.2.2, 24-26, 44-49 on taking notes from a speech in order to learn it and the dangers of orators being too reliant on written notes.

75. Quintilian, *Inst.* 10.3.30-32.

76. Epictetus, *Diatr.* 1, pref.

77. See *b. Shab.* 6b, 96b, and commentary in Gerhardsson, *Memory and Manuscript,* 160-62.

78. M. S. Jaffee, *Torah in the Mouth: Writing and Oral Tradition in Palestinian Judaism 200 BCE–400 CE* (Oxford: Oxford University Press, 2001), 100-125.

79. Jacob Neusner, *Method and Meaning in Ancient Judaism* (Missoula: Scholars, 1979).

tions, which provided a short extract of important Old Testament passages, were most likely used by Christians very early on, certainly by the time of Justin and Irenaeus.[80] Such a *testimonia* collection exists as P. Ryl. 460, a fourth-century codex.[81]

The notebook was ideal for a collection of Jesus' sayings to be used by teachers so they did not have to wade through scrolls and codices. The hypothetical document known to source critics as "Q" may have started out as such a notebook. The constant shadow of proto-Gospel theories in solutions to the Synoptic problem suggests at least the possibility of early notebooks/extracts/digests about Jesus before 70 CE. We find a reference to a "book" and "parchments" in 2 Tim 4:13, which might specifically designate a "notebook."[82] In the early second century, Papias's *Exposition of the Logia of the Lord* (Λογία κυριακῶν ἐξήγησις) was a collection of and commentary on sayings of Jesus, typical of notebooks.[83] Justin Martyr refers to twenty-six topically arranged sayings of Jesus in *Dial Tryph.* 15–17, which may have been based on a prior collection made by himself or someone else. Graham Stanton infers from the Christian "addiction" to the codex: "Even before Paul wrote his first 'canonical' letter c. AD 50, followers of Jesus were accustomed to use the predecessors of the codex-book format, various kinds of 'notebooks.' They used them for Scriptural excerpts and testimonies, for drafts and copies of letters, and probably also for collections of traditions of both the actions and teachings of Jesus."[84] According to C. H. Roberts, in the early church "No doubt the oral tradition was reinforced as it was in Judaism, with notes."[85] Thus, it is highly probable that notebooks were used

---

80. Cf. esp. Albl, *And Scripture Cannot Be Broken;* Bokedal, *Scriptures and the Lord,* 151-55.

81. Stanton, *Jesus and Gospel,* 183-84.

82. So Harry Gamble, *Books and Readers in the Early Church: A History of Early Christian Texts* (New Haven: Yale University Press, 1995), 64; Alan Millard, *Reading and Writing at the Time of Jesus* (New York: New York University Press, 2000), 63.

83. Eusebius, *Hist. Eccl.* 3.39.1. Cf. Ernst Bammel (*RGG* 5:48): "[Papias' *logia*] contained annotated reports about sayings and deeds of Jesus." We might also observe from "Gnostic" teachers, the *Exegetica* of Basilides consisting of twenty-four volumes (Eusebius, *Hist. Eccl.* 4.7.5-8; Clement, *Strom.* 4.81.1-83.1; called by Origen [*Homilies on Luke* 1] "Gospel according to Basilides") and Marcion's *Antitheses* and *Gospel of the Lord* (see Tertullian, *Adv. Marc.*), were books consisting of a mixture of agrapha, Synoptic tradition, and redaction of the canonical Gospels.

84. Graham Stanton, *Jesus and Gospel* (Cambridge: Cambridge University Press, 2004), 165.

85. C. H. Roberts, "Books in the Graeco-Roman World and the New Testament," in

by Jesus' own disciples and by later adherents in the early church to assist in memory retention by functioning as an aide-mémoire.

Eyewitnesses as Authenticators of the Jesus Tradition

An often underrated factor that undoubtedly contributed to a conserving of the Jesus tradition was the presence of eyewitnesses of Jesus within the earliest communities in the 30s-90s CE. The role of eyewitnesses in shaping the tradition has been emphasized in recent decades by three scholars, Samuel Byrskog, Richard Bauckham, and Martin Hengel. All three have drawn attention to the presence of eyewitnesses in the early church and the importance of eyewitnesses in ancient historiography.[86] A point validated by the observation that the only way one can affirm the Jesus tradition as both a living oral tradition that was constantly renegotiated and rehearsed anew as well as containing a stable core amid on-going performance of that tradition is through what Markus Bockmuehl says is "the (largely personal) apostolic vehicles of that stability."[87]

Before appealing to the existence of eyewitnesses as carriers of the Jesus tradition, it is important to preface such an argument with three observations. First, the role of witnesses in the New Testament, particularly the Johannine corpus and Luke-Acts, is largely a theological motif and not included for purely historical interests. Second, anyone who has been involved with interviewing eyewitnesses to an incident will know that participants do not always see the same thing: they often exhibit perspectives and, importantly, sometimes offer conflicting interpretations of what actually transpired. Thucydides

---

The Cambridge History of the Bible I: From the Beginnings to Jerome, ed. Peter R. Ackroyd and Craig F. Evans (Cambridge: Cambridge University Press, 1970), 55.

86. Samuel Byrskog, *Story as History — History as Story: The Gospel Tradition in the Context of Ancient Oral History* (WUNT 123; Tübingen: Mohr/Siebeck, 2000); Martin Hengel, *The Four Gospels and the One Gospel of Jesus Christ,* trans. J. Bowden (Harrisburg: Trinity, 2000), 141-45; idem, "Eye-witness Memory and the Writing of the Gospels," in *The Written Gospel,* ed. Bockmuehl and Hagner, 70-96; Richard Bauckham, "The Eyewitnesses and the Gospel Tradition," *JSHJ* 1 (2003): 28-60; idem, *Jesus and the Eyewitnesses* (Grand Rapids: Eerdmans, 2006). See in contrast, D. E. Nineham, "Eye-Witness Testimony and the Gospel Tradition," *JTS* 9 (1958): 13-25, 243-52.

87. Markus Bockmuehl, "Whose Memory? Whose Orality? A Conversation with James D. G. Dunn on Jesus and the Gospels," in *Memories of Jesus: A Critical Appraisal of James D. G. Dunn's Jesus Remembered,* ed. R. B. Stewart and G. R. Habermas (Nashville: Broadman & Holman, 2010), 42.

noted: "Different eyewitnesses give different accounts of the same events, speaking out of partiality for one side or the other or else from imperfect memories."[88] Third, there are examples in ancient literature of fictive eyewitnesses who purportedly guarantee the veracity of reports, and such is probably the case with the character of Damis in Philostratus's *Life of Apollonius of Tyana,* where Damis allegedly met Apollonius in Syria, became his disciple, and kept a memoir of Apollonius's words and deeds. Nonetheless, I wish to assert that there remains sufficient reason for appealing to eyewitnesses as persons who could transmit and verify elements of the Jesus tradition.

To begin with, we have good reasons for thinking that eyewitnesses to Jesus' ministry did inform, shape, and even to some extent "police" the developing oral and written traditions about him. Immediately following Jesus' execution there was in existence the group of the eleven disciples, an outer circle of followers, general supporters, and public spectators to Jesus' ministry. The implication to be drawn is that there were individuals and groups who could verbalize the impact Jesus had on them and offer authentication of the stories circulating about him.

The problem for those who argue for widespread variation and drastic inventiveness in the Jesus tradition is that they regularly fail to reckon with the presence of eyewitnesses to the ministry of Jesus in the formative Christian communities in Palestine and even in the Diaspora. As Vincent Taylor quipped, "If the Form Critics are right, the disciples must have been translated to heaven immediately after the Resurrection."[89] Taylor went on to affirm that the eyewitnesses "did not go into permanent retreat; for at least a generation they moved among the young Palestinian communities, and through preaching and fellowship their recollections were at the disposal of those who sought information."[90] Furthermore, "The principal agents who shaped the tradition were eyewitnesses and others who had knowledge of the original facts."[91] Similar is John Meier, who does not think that a wildly

---

88. Thucydides, *History of the Peloponnesian War* 1.22.

89. Taylor, *Formation of the Gospel Tradition,* 41. Cf. Dibelius (*From Tradition to Gospel,* 183), who believed that in the case of the young man who fled Gethsemane naked and Simon of Cyrene that "these remarks would draw the readers' attention to the actual eyewitnesses of the events." Stephen J. Patterson, "Can You Trust a Gospel? A Review of Richard Bauckham's *Jesus and the Eyewitnesses,*" *JSHJ* 6 (2008): 197: "Many stories told about Jesus certainly must have originated with people who actually witnessed the events themselves. This is the tacit assumption of anyone who would glean history from the Gospels."

90. Taylor, *Formation of the Gospel Tradition,* 42.

91. Taylor, *Formation of the Gospel Tradition,* 170.

creative oral tradition was then crowned by the Evangelists with their own redactional theology. He comments: "One would get the impression [from form critics] that throughout the first Christian generation there were no eyewitnesses to act as a check on fertile imaginations, no original-disciples-now-become-leaders who might exercise some control over the developing tradition, and no striking deeds and sayings of Jesus that stuck willy-nilly in people's memory."[92] Birger Gerhardsson inferred that the appeals to named figures in the Gospels was "a simple consequence of the fact that the message was presented as an eyewitness account."[93] Richard Bauckham states the same point, namely, that the "[E]yewitnesses were well-known figures in the Christian movement. Traditions derived from them did not develop independently of them; rather they remained throughout their lifetimes living and authoritative sources of the traditions that were associated with them as individuals, not just as a group."[94] This means that we have to countenance the influence of eyewitnesses as shapers and authenticators of the Jesus tradition.

These eyewitnesses were not restricted to Galilee and Judea. Many moved abroad, both east and west, into urban centers, and took their Jesus traditions with them. Paul probably gleaned information about Jesus when he persecuted Christ-believers, and he later met eyewitnesses of Jesus in Peter, James, and John (Gal 2:9).[95] Paul, I imagine, learned much of the Jesus tradition from Christ-believers in Syria and Judea, especially from his missionary companions Barnabas and John Mark, who were members of the Jerusalem church prior to his conversion. Several of the persons whom Paul names in Romans 16 may also have been from Judea and were known to the Roman churches, implying that eyewitnesses to Jesus' ministry traveled abroad (Rom 16:7-13). Paul also knows of the Lord's brothers who apparently had some kind of itinerant ministry, meaning that they traveled around sharing their message and testimony to Jesus with others (1 Cor 9:5). Peter traveled outside Jerusalem to Caesarea, Antioch, Corinth, and, according to tradition, eventually to Rome (Acts 10:1-48; Gal 2:11; 1 Cor

---

92. Meier, *Marginal Jew*, 1:170.

93. Gerhardsson, *Memory and Manuscript*, 283.

94. Bauckham, "Eyewitnesses and the Gospel Tradition," 30; idem, *Jesus and the Eyewitnesses*, 47.

95. Cf. Gerhardsson, *Memory and Manuscript*, 297-98; Bauckham, *Jesus and the Eyewitnesses*, 266, 271; James D. G. Dunn, *The Epistle to the Galatians* (BNTC; London: Black, 1993), 74; supported by Nicholas Taylor, *Paul, Antioch and Jerusalem* (JSNTSup 66; Sheffield: Sheffield Academic Press, 1992), 78-81.

9:5; 1 Pet 5:13; Irenaeus, *Adv. Haer.* 3.1.1; Eusebius, *Hist. Eccl.* 2.25.8; 3.3.1-3). John son of Zebedee is also associated in tradition with Ephesus in Asia Minor (*Adv. Haer.* 3.1; *Hist. Eccl.* 3.23.1). The oral dissemination of the Jesus tradition beyond Palestine by eyewitnesses or tradents of their testimony is highly probable.

The Evangelists were probably not eyewitnesses themselves, but were informed by eyewitness accounts.[96] This is the impression made by Luke's opening prologue:

> Since many have undertaken to set down an orderly account of the events that have been fulfilled among us, just as they were *delivered* to us by those who were, from the beginning, eyewitnesses and servants of the word, I too decided, after investigating everything carefully from the very first, to write an orderly account for you, most excellent Theophilus, in order that you may know the truth concerning the things about which you have been instructed.[97]

Several things can be ascertained from Luke's preface. First, the Lucan preface undoubtedly belongs to the genre of historiography as evidenced by a comparison with the prefaces written by Dionysius of Halicarnassus and Josephus, who employed similar terminology and stated analogous goals.[98] Second, the verb παραδίδωμι ("I deliver over") is often used in the New Testament in a technical sense for the transmission of traditions, and analogous terminology also appears in rabbinic and Greco-Roman literature.[99] It refers to a deliberate effort of handing on traditions to others as part of a process of instruction in the way of a particular teacher or school. Third, the traditions have been passed on "just as they were delivered to us" (καθὼς

96. Charlesworth, *Jesus within Judaism*, 19-20.

97. Luke 1:1-4 (NRSV). See for discussion, Loveday Alexander, "Luke's Preface in the Context of Greek Preface-Writing," *NovT* 28 (1986): 48-74; idem, *The Preface to Luke's Gospel* (SNTSMS 78; Cambridge: Cambridge University Press, 1993); Jacob Jervell, "The Future of the Past: Luke's Vision of Salvation History and Its Bearing on His Writing of History," in *History, Literature, and Society in the Book of Acts*, ed. Ben Witherington (Cambridge: Cambridge University Press, 1996), 104-26; David E. Aune, "Luke 1:1-4: Historical or Scientific *Prooimion?*" in *Paul, Luke and the Greco-Roman World: Essays in Honour of Alexander J. M. Wedderburn*, ed. A. Christophersen, C. Slaussen, J. Frey, and B. Longenecker (JSNTSup 217; Sheffield: Sheffield Univeòsity Press, 2002), 138-48.

98. Cf. Josephus, *Ant.* 5.1-9; *Against Apion* 1.1-5.

99. 1 Cor 11:1-23 (Lord's Supper); 15:3 (resurrection) Mark 7:13; Acts 6:14; (Pharisees' oral tradition); Jude 3 (body of Christian teaching); cf. BDAG, 762-73.

παρέδοσαν ἡμῖν), which implies a consciousness of the possibility of false transmission.[100]

Fourth, Luke's preface shows signs of what Byrskog defines as "autopsy," which is a visual means of gathering data about a certain object which can include direct means (being an eyewitness) or indirect means (access to eyewitnesses).[101] Byrskog claims that such autopsy is arguably utilized by Paul (1 Cor 9:1; 15:5-8; Gal 1:16), Luke (Luke 1:1-4; Acts 1:21-22; 10:39-41), and John (John 19:35; 21:24; 1 John 1:1-4).[102] These texts attest the inclusion of autopsy in the narrativizing process, and the paucity of references to eyewitnesses means the inclusion of such a feature cannot be reduced to an apologetic purpose.[103] By locating his Jesus-story in relation to eyewitness testimony, Luke was in accord with ancient historiography and was concerned with the historical veracity of his account. E. Earle Ellis writes, "The reference to 'eyewitnesses' is a calculated answer to an explicit concern. It reflects the conviction that the Christian faith is rooted not in speculative creation but in historical reality."[104]

Fifth, the grouping together of the "eyewitnesses" (αὐτόπτης) with the "servants" (ὑπηρέτης) in Luke 1:2 under one definite article and the word order indicate that both terms probably refer to the same group, which acted in two stages, viz. as witnesses and then as servants, rather than denoting two separate entities separated by time. Luke's remark here presupposes the existence and circulation of the first Christian leaders, who were Jesus' companions and then leaders of the early church. This group is also distinguished from the "many" (πολλοί) who have already made written accounts about Jesus (i.e., Mark, Q, and/or Matthew). In which case, Luke, as a second-generation Christian, anchors his Gospel in the initial group who testified, taught, and transmitted the message about Jesus to others.

It may be objected that it is precisely because Luke is a second or third-generation Christian, writing as late as the 90s CE perhaps, that his claim to

---

100. François Bovon, *Luke 1: A Commentary on the Gospel of Luke 1:1–9:40*, trans. Christine M. Thomas (Minneapolis: Augsburg, 2002), 21.

101. Byrskog, *Story as History,* 48.

102. Byrskog, *Story as History,* 223-42; see the evaluation of Bryskog's work in Peter M. Head, "The Role of Eyewitnesses in the Formation of the Gospel Tradition: A Review Article of Samuel Byrskog, *Story as History — History as Story,*" *TynBul* 52 (2001): 275-94.

103. Byrskog, *Story as History,* 246-49.

104. E. Earle Ellis, *The Gospel of Luke* (NCB; London: Thomas Nelson, 1966), 63; Byrskog (*Story as History,* 232) contends that Luke's preface claims that his tradition was "rooted in its entirety in the oral history of persons present at the events themselves."

eyewitness testimony cannot be taken seriously. There may be as much as sixty years between Jesus' death and when Luke wrote his two-volume work. Yet this may not be problematic, as Martin Hengel provides a fitting analogy.

> In the year 1990 I can still remember, sometimes very accurately, the portentous events of the years 1933-45 [in Germany], which I experienced between the ages of six and eighteen, and I know a good deal more from eye-witness reports. Can we completely deny Luke the use of such old reminiscences by eye-witnesses, even if he has reshaped them in a literary way to suit his bias?[105]

In addition, Hengel also conveys a cute piece of oral history about the nineteenth-century Tübingen scholar F. C. Baur (d. 1860), who was infamously known for his critical approach to the Bible. Apparently while teaching through Revelation, Baur came to Rev. 13:18 with the number of the beast as 666, and he quipped to a student: "As Hengstenberg [the spokesman of conservative Lutheranism] says in Berlin, that's me."[106] Hengel's source was his former teacher Otto Bauernfeind (1889-1972), whose own teacher was Eduard von der Goltz (1870-1939), who learned it from his father Hermann von der Goltz (1835-1906), who was himself Baur's student. Markus Bockmuehl also provides several vignettes passed on orally in his family from his late grandmother about her vivid recollections of imperial Germany pre–World War I and stories about her own grandparents from the mid-nineteenth century.[107] These are all anecdotal, but they also demonstrate the preservation of oral tradition over a period of more than a century. There is no reason why the living memory of the Apostles could not have continued on in the early church for a century and a half. Many of the early church fathers in fact maintained a real interest in memories from and about the Apostles well into the second century.[108] So if Luke had access to eyewitness

---

105. Martin Hengel, *The Pre-Christian Paul,* trans. John Bowden (Philadelphia: Fortress, 1991), 65.

106. Hengel, "Eye-Witness Memory," 86 n. 64.

107. Markus Bockmuehl, *Seeing the Word: Refocusing New Testament Study* (STI; Grand Rapids: Baker, 2006), 169-70.

108. Papias's quest to learn, interpret, and remember the sayings of Jesus from the Lord's disciples via their itinerant followers is not a unique phenomenon (*Fragment* 3.3). Quadratus's apology in the second century appealed to the fact that eyewitnesses of Jesus had "survived right up to our own time" (Eusebius, *Hist. Eccl.* 4.3.3). Irenaeus recounts how Polycarp and Papias were associates of the Apostle John (Irenaeus, *Adv. Haer.* 3.3.4; 5.33.4). Irenaeus also

testimony as he claims, then his belonging to a second or third generation of believers does not negate the veracity of those accounts.

One must still be cognizant of the fact that what a first-century author like Luke would understand by "historical reality" is perhaps not the same thing that a post-Enlightenment, hermeneutically suspicious, Jesus-questing New Testament scholar might understand by it. Even so, when Luke's prologue is milked for all its rhetorical appeal, literary guise, and theological significance, it still unpacks the assertion of the author that the Gospel traditions are rooted in eyewitness accounts and arguably anticipates the expectation of his readers that the narrative is duly authorized by those who recounted such things.

We might also consider the possibility of eyewitness testimony in the Gospel of John.[109] While the theme of "witness" is undoubtedly a major theological construct in John, the Evangelist (and quite possibly his redactors) emphasize the indebtedness of the Gospel to the eyewitness account of the Beloved Disciple: "The man who saw it has given testimony, and his testimony is true. He knows that he tells the truth, and he testifies so that you also may believe" (John 19:35) and "This is the disciple who testifies to these things and who wrote them down. We know that his testimony is true" (21:24). Now an appeal to eyewitness testimony for the Fourth Gospel might seem counterintuitive since the Gospel of John is generally regarded as the least historical of the four canonical Gospels. It has been scholarly dogma since David Strauss in the nineteenth century to maintain that the Gospel of John is not historical and has next to no historical worth. Clement of Alexandria labeled John's Gospel as a "spiritual gospel,"[110] while more recently

---

declares that Clement of Rome "had both seen the blessed apostles and associated with them, and had the teaching of the apostles still in his ears and the tradition before his eyes. And he was not alone: for at that time many who had been taught by the apostles were still alive" (Irenaeus, *Adv. Haer.* 3.3.3). Clement of Alexandria begins an account of the Apostle John with the words: "Listen to a story that is not a story but a true account of John the apostle preserved in memory" (Eusebius, *Hist. Eccl.* 3.23.6). François Bovon, "Apostolic Memories in Ancient Christianity," in *Studies in Early Christianity* (Grand Rapids: Baker, 2005), 1-2, was right to affirm that "there was a natural and distinct tendency to memorize the first generation of Christians, eyewitnesses and apostles, both men and women" and "As long as the Christians of antiquity tried to preserve the historicity of the revelation and the very real incarnation of their Lord, they could not avoid emphasizing the historical and human face of the communication of the gospel, that is to say, the actual value of the apostles themselves, including both their voices and their role as intermediaries."

109. Cf. Byrskog, *Story as History*, 235-38; Bauckham, *Jesus and the Eywitnesses*, 358-411.
110. Eusebius, *Hist. Eccl.* 6.14.7.

John Meier has regarded John's Gospel as an early "systematic theology."[111] Yet before we brazenly dismiss the possibility that the Gospel of John is based on eyewitness testimony, we need to take sufficient account of the claim in the Gospel that it draws from both the Beloved Disciple's own direct autopsy of events in the life of Jesus and also from the indirect autopsy of traditions he had directly received from individual disciples whose specific traditions did not enter the Synoptic tradition.[112] To reconcile the heavily theologized texture of the Fourth Gospel with its claims to eyewitness information we have to remember that historical testimony and interpreted memories are not mutually exclusive. There is no objective, unbiased, and uninterpreted Jesus. Clearly the Jesus of John is filtered through the grid of Jewish wisdom traditions, in view of a specific messianism, with midrashic expansions of sayings, and symbolism is detected in and even read into Jesus' deeds. Though John may be more theologically pronounced than the Synoptics, I believe that he plots an interpretive trajectory from similar traditions that sometimes parallel the Synoptics.

What is more, the Fourth Gospel possesses several historiographical characteristics.[113] The Evangelist exhibits an intimate awareness of Palestinian topography, including the pool of Siloam (9:7), the Kidron Valley (18:1), the Pool of Bethesda (5:2), and Gabbatha (19:13). John provides chronological markers concerning Jesus' movements to and from Jerusalem for the various feasts. The narrative is marked by selectivity, parenthetical remarks, and appeal to eyewitness testimony, which were traits of historiography. The dialogues and discourses are probably elaborations undertaken with fidelity to sources in respect to what was congruent with the narration of speeches in antiquity. Thus, in my reckoning, John takes up many authentic Jesus traditions and puts them on a theological and literary trajectory different from that of the Synoptic Gospels.[114]

111. John P. Meier, "The Present State of the 'Third Quest' for the Historical Jesus: Loss and Gain," *Bib* 80 (1999): 465.

112. Cf. Bauckham, *Jesus and the Eyewitnesses*, 403.

113. Richard Bauckham, "Historiographical Characteristics of the Gospel of John," *NTS* 53 (2007): 17-36.

114. On history and the Gospel of John, I have found the following studies useful: M. M. Thompson, "The Historical Jesus and the Johannine Christ," in *Exploring the Gospel of John*, ed. R. Alan Culpepper and C. Clifton Black (Louisville: Westminster/John Knox, 1996), 21-42; Craig L. Blomberg, *The Historical Reliability of John's Gospel* (Downers Grove: InterVarsity, 2002); Paul N. Anderson, *The Fourth Gospel and the Quest for Jesus: Modern Foundations Reconsidered* (London: Clark, 2006); Paul Barnett, *Finding the Historical Christ* (Grand Rapids: Eerdmans, 2009), 138-75; Dunn, *Jesus, Paul, and the Gospels*, 70-91; and see my earlier remarks

That the "Beloved Disciple" is invoked in several places as the source and authenticator of material (19:35; 20:2-9; 21:24) indicates that at some point in the Johannine tradition eyewitness testimony was involved. The claim to access to an eyewitness account, a direct autopsy, is analogous to what is found in other ancient authors.[115] Josephus, perhaps writing at the same time as John, comments about his testimony to the Jewish war that "My qualification as a historian of the war was that I had been an actor in many, and an eyewitness of most, of the events; in short, nothing whatever was said or done of which I was ignorant."[116] Although the Beloved Disciple is, narratively speaking, an ideal disciple, he is not purely a symbolic figure but is regarded as a real person who validates the historical message of the Gospel. The implied reader is assumed to be at a distance from Jesus, and that distance is traversed by the testimony of the Beloved Disciple. The faith in Jesus that the Evangelist aims to invoke or affirm is rooted in the history of the past by the testimony of the Beloved Disciple. This "faith" has the history of Jesus as its content. The more closely the theology of the Fourth Gospel is examined, the more clearly it is seen to possess a historical referent. Johannine christology has as its centerpiece the historical person and historical action of Jesus the Messiah. So, at a bare minimum, one could argue that the Fourth Gospel was indebted to the teaching of a Judean disciple of Jesus, who was an eyewitness to Jesus' mighty deeds, final meal, trial, and death and later led a Christian community in Asia Minor. In subsequent Christian tradition this person is identified as the Apostle John.[117]

We should also consider the value of Papias's testimony about the significance of eyewitness testimony even for those living into the second century.[118] Papias wrote:

> I will not hesitate to set down for you, along with my interpretations, everything I carefully learned then from the elders and carefully remembered, guaranteeing their truth. For unlike most people I did not enjoy

---

in Michael F. Bird and James Crossley, *How Did Christianity Begin? A Believer and Non-Believer Examine the Evidence* (London: SPCK, 2008), 110-13.

115. Cf. Byrskog, *Story as History*, 384-85.

116. Josephus, *Against Apion* 1.55.

117. Martin Hengel, *Johannine Question* (London: SCM, 1989), 124-35.

118. Bauckham, "Eyewitnesses and the Gospel Tradition," 31-44; idem, *Jesus and the Eyewitnesses*, 12-38; Byrskog, *Story as History*, 244-45. For a contrasting view of the value of Papias's testimony, see E. P. Sanders and Margaret Davies, *Studying the Synoptic Gospels* (London: SCM, 1989), 143.

those who had a great deal to say, but those who teach the truth. Nor did I enjoy those who recall someone else's commandments, but those who remember the commandments given by the Lord to the faith and proceeding from the truth itself. And if by chance someone who had been a follower of the elders should come my way, I inquired about the words of the elders — what Andrew or Peter said or Philip or Thomas or James or John or Matthew or any other of the Lord's disciples, and whatever Aristion and the elder John, the Lord's disciples, were saying. For I did not think that information from books would profit me as much as information from *a living and abiding voice.*[119]

Papias was bishop of Hierapolis, a small city in the Lycus Valley, and wrote a five-volume work known to us as *Exposition of the Logia of the Lord* sometime around the beginning of the second century.[120] In this controversial passage Papias is referring to two categories of persons as tradents of the tradition: (1) the Lord's disciples / the elders (Andrew, Peter, Philip, Thomas, James, John, Matthew, Aristion, and the elder John), and (2) those who were followers of the elders. The fact that Aristion and the elder John are mentioned apart from the other "Lord's disciples" could mean that they were alive at a time earlier in Papias's life. Indeed, Eusebius and Irenaeus both regard Papias as someone who had contact with Jesus' disciples John and Aristion.[121] Even though Papias does not claim as much, a trip from Hierapolis to Smyrna or Ephesus where Aristion and John are traditionally located was hardly unimaginable. Though Papias's own life very probably overlapped with that of the Lord's disciples, he describes himself mainly as a collector of traditions from the "elders." In any case, Papias lived at a time when he had intermediate access to the last few surviving members of Jesus' disciples and direct access to the closest associates of the elders as well. What he learned from the elders and their followers spans three generations of tradents, and the tradition seems to have been associated with certain key figures and eyewitnesses.

According to Bauckham, Papias's testimony can be utilized in conjunction with Luke's preface as evidence for the relationship between eyewitnesses and the Jesus tradition at the time the Gospels were composed.[122]

119. Papias, *Fragments* 3-4 (trans. M. Holmes).
120. Cf. on an early date, Robert W. Yarbrough, "The Date of Papias: Reassessment," *JETS* 26 (1983): 181-91; Charles E. Hill, "Papias of Hierapolis," *ExpT* 117 (2006): 309-15.
121. Eusebius, *Hist. Eccl.* 3.39.7; Irenaeus, *Adv. Haer.* 5.33.4.
122. Bauckham, *Jesus and the Eyewitnesses*, 20, 29-30.

Bauckham believes that Papias's preference for the "living voice" over written documents is repeating an ancient proverb.[123] Following Loveday Alexander, Bauckham cites several authors from antiquity, including Polybius, Galen, Quintilian, Seneca, and Pliny, who made similar remarks about the value of the "living voice" (Greek ζώσης φωνῆς, Latin *viva vox*).[124] The proverb refers not to the living voice conveyed in some kind of elongated oral tradition with nostalgic qualities but to the actual voice of the teacher from whose instruction one directly learns. Papias employed this proverb to emphasize his interest in getting firsthand information from informants who are the best sources. Polybius's use of the proverb is interesting because it occurs in the context of criticism of the work of the historian Timaeus, who relied exclusively on written sources for his account. In contrast, Polybius appeals to eyewitnesses and the value of access to direct experience for writing history. Bauckham locates Papias's use of the proverb in a similar historiographical context to that of Polybius. Papias urges the superiority of access to eyewitness accounts over written documents, not merely as a preference for oral over literary transmission, but for reliability of content. The historiographical setting for his statement is supported further by his critical evaluation of the reports he received from the disciples of the elders: "I *inquired* about the words of the elders (τοὺς τῶν πρεσβυτέρων ἀνέκρινον λόγους)." Polybius and Lucian both employ the word ἀνέκρίσις for their interrogation of eyewitnesses.[125] Like a good historian, Papias learned, remembered, and conveyed what he himself had received from informants who had access to eyewitness accounts of Jesus' words and deeds.

Papias also alters the proverb of the "living voice" by expanding it to the "living and surviving voice" (ζώσης φωνῆς καὶ μενούσης). The verb μένειν (to remain, endure, continue, abide, survive, etc.) is used by Paul and John in conjunction with eyewitnesses. Paul writes in 1 Cor 15:6 of the eyewitnesses to the resurrection, of whom "most are still alive" (οἱ πλείονες μένουσιν ἕως ἄρτι). Paul's point, perhaps even apologetic in motive, is that eyewitnesses to Jesus' resurrection are still around for questioning. In the Gospel of John, Jesus says about the fate of the Beloved Disciple, "If it is my will that he *remain* (μένειν) until I come, what is that to you?" (John 21:22-23). The passage explains why the Beloved Disciple lived for as long as he

---

123. Cf. Irenaeus, *Adv. Haer.* 3.2.1, who said against heretical groups that the truth "was not transmitted by means of writings, but rather through the living voice."

124. Polybius, 12.15d.6; Galen, *Compositione Medicamentorum Secundum Locus* 6; Quintilian, *Inst.* 2.2.8; Pliny, *Ep.* 2.3; Seneca, *Ep.* 6.5

125. Polybius, 12.27.3; 12.4c.3; Lucian, *Hist. Conscr.* 47.

did. It likewise refers to the continued existence in a Christian community of an eyewitness of Jesus to whom was attached particular authority. Thus, the "surviving" or "enduring" voice of eyewitnesses refers, then, to their continued presence and influence in the communities contemporary with Papias. In the case of the elder John and Aristion, they existed not merely as originators of oral tradition, but as "authoritative living sources of the traditions up to their deaths."[126] The corollary is that traditions of the sayings and deeds of Jesus were attached to specifically named eyewitnesses who transmitted the Jesus tradition in their own immediate settings and even saw it branch out beyond their own locations. This strongly diverges from the old form-critical assumption that the identity of the eyewitnesses would have been lost in a sea of anonymity during the time the Gospels were written. Papias does not regard the Jesus traditions as disengaged from the eyewitnesses who originated them, but he assumes that the authenticity of the tradition was based precisely on the surviving and remaining witnesses who gave their testimony to followers in the first place.

On the significance of named persons in the Gospels, Bauckham maintains the possibility that "in many cases named characters were eyewitnesses who not only originated the traditions to which their names are attached but also continued to tell these stories as authoritative guarantors of the traditions."[127] Bauckham questions the view of Bultmann that there was a tendency to increase detail in the oral tradition and to add the names of characters. On the contrary, Bauckham notes that the tendency of the Synoptic tradition is toward the opposite; that is, Matthew and Luke consciously eliminate the names of characters from Mark rather than (in all but a few brief instances) add them. It is in the extra-canonical traditions where one encounters the penchant to add names. One explanation for the inclusion of the characters is that, with a few exceptions, "all these people joined the early Christian movement and were well known at least in the circles in which these traditions were first transmitted."[128] The people named in the Gospels are, in fact,

> the kind of range of people we should expect to have formed these earliest Christian groups: some who had been healed by Jesus (e.g., Barti-

126. Bauckham, "Eyewitnesses and the Gospel Tradition," 35; idem, *Jesus and the Eyewitnesses*, 20.

127. Bauckham, "Eyewitnesses and the Gospel Tradition," 44; idem, *Jesus and the Eyewitnesses*, 39.

128. Bauckham, "Eyewitnesses and the Gospel Tradition," 49; idem, *Jesus and the Eyewitnesses*, 45.

maeus, perhaps Malchus), some who had joined Jesus in his itinerant ministry (certainly a larger group than the Twelve, and including the named women disciples, Levi, Nathanael, and Cleopas), some of Jesus' relatives (his mother and brothers, his uncle Cleopas/Clopas and aunt Mary, several residents of Jerusalem and its environs who had been sympathetic to Jesus' movement (Nicodemus, Joseph of Arimathea, Simon the Leper, Martha, and Mary).[129]

As evidence, Bauckham examines the examples of Cleopas, the women at the cross and the tomb, Simon of Cyrene and his sons, and the recipients of Jesus' healing miracles. These named figures are taken to refer to eyewitnesses in the early Christian communities who doubtless told and retold the stories in which their names appear. Bauckham surmises that the phenomenon of named characters is indicative of the "genuine possibility that many Gospel pericopes owe their main features not to anonymous community formation but to their formulation by the eyewitnesses from whom they derive."[130]

Several objections to the role of eyewitnesses can be made. First, it might be objected that the eyewitnesses only shaped the character of the tradition in its earliest stages, not in later decades across the Mediterranean: they were not ubiquitous.[131] True enough, but then again, eyewitnesses like Peter and John were active in the churches in the eastern Mediterranean and so too were their associates — such as John Mark, Barnabas, and Silas — who were also tradents of the Jesus tradition outside Palestine. Papias seemed to think that through disciples of the eyewitnesses he had in fact access to eyewitness testimony. While not every community had its own eyewitness authenticator of Jesus traditions, given the mobility of Christian leaders among the network of churches, plus the fact that most of the original eleven disciples appear to have left Jerusalem by the time of the Jerusalem council, it is quite reasonable to expect that eyewitnesses and tradents of eyewitness testimony were active and abundant within the relatively small Christian movement.[132]

129. Bauckham, "Eyewitnesses and the Gospel Tradition," 50; idem, *Jesus and the Eyewitnesses*, 46.

130. Bauckham, "Eyewitnesses and the Gospel Tradition," 60; idem, *Jesus and the Eyewitnesses*, 47.

131. Nineham, "Eye-Witness Testimony," 251; James D. G. Dunn, "On History, Memory, and Eyewitnesses: In Response to Bengst Holmberg and Samuel Byrskog," *JSNT* 26 (2004): 483.

132. On Jesus' closest followers engaging in a mission in the decades after his death, perhaps in Palestine, see Gerd Theissen, *Sociology of Early Palestinian Christianity*, trans. J. Bowden (Philadelphia: Fortress, 1978), 9.

Second, if the Gospels are based on eyewitnesses, then why are there so many differences within the Synoptic tradition and between the Synoptics and the Fourth Gospel?[133] This matter is relatively easy to answer. Bauckham himself noted several factors that explain the variations in the Jesus tradition even on the basis of a formally controlled oral tradition in which eyewitnesses played a key part. These include: (1) differences stemming from various versions of Jesus' sayings, (2) variations caused by translation from Aramaic to Greek, (3) variability in oral performance, (4) deliberate alterations or additions by tradents who sought to explain or adapt Jesus' teaching to post-Easter situations, and (5) changes made by the Evangelists to integrate the traditions into unified and connected narratives.[134] Byrskog also notes that eyewitnesses are not simply messengers of memory but also involved interpreters of events themselves.[135] The divergences in the Jesus tradition are attributable to the memory refraction by eyewitnesses, the rhetoricizing recital by later tradents, and theological redaction by the Evangelists. This is not irreconcilable with eyewitness testimony.[136]

The *Sitz im Leben* of the Jesus tradition is not among anonymous tra-

---

133. David Catchpole, "On Proving Too Much: Critical Hesitations about Richard Bauckham's *Jesus and the Eyewitnesses*," *JSHJ* 6 (2008): 169-81; Judith C. S. Redman, "How Accurate Are Eyewitnesses? Bauckham and the Eyewitnesses in Light of Psychological Research," *JBL* 129 (2010): 177-97.

134. Bauckham, *Jesus and the Eyewitnesses*, 285-87.

135. Byrskog, *Story as History*, 145-98. Cf. Peter Head, "The Role of Eyewitnesses in the Formation of the Gospel Tradition: A Review Article of Samuel Byrskog, *Story as History — History as Story*," *TynB* 52 (2005): 293: "The investigation [Byrskog's monograph] shows that eyewitness tradition was never uninterpreted brute fact. The eyewitness interprets what she sees even in the act of observing it, let alone when she speaks about it to someone else; the historian interprets what he hears from his informants, and then places it within a broader interpretive framework. This conclusion will have to moderate simple appeals to eyewitness sources from conservatives, just as it also takes the wind out of the sails of those who would point to the theological nature of the gospel traditions as proof that it could not have come from eyewitnesses."

136. Cf. Byrskog, *Story as History*, 304-5: "The gospel narratives, for all we know, are thus syntheses of history and story, of the oral history of an eyewitness and the interpretation and narrativizing procedures of an author . . . [T]he gospel narratives are themselves witnesses not of disruption and discontinuity, but of the same synthesis between history and story." Jens Schröter writes ("The Gospels as Eyewitness Testimony? A Critical Examination of Richard Bauckham's *Jesus and the Eyewitnesses*," *JSNT* 31 [2008]: 204): "Both perspectives — the obligation to historical events and early traditions as well as the shaping and theological interpretation at later stages — must not be played off against each other. 'Remembering Jesus' therefore cannot mean to invoke the trustworthiness of eyewitness accounts against interpretations in the transmission process and by the Gospel writers, but to correlate both aspects in an appropriate way."

dents who exercised wholesale invention over Jesus' deeds and words to meet the pressing needs of isolated communities, where the tradition was shaped according to impersonal laws of transmission. Instead, the setting was the preaching, apologetics, polemics, worship, and discipline of the early church. It was furthermore an orientation toward a mnemonic past — a past negotiated through the testimony of eyewitnesses — that was repeated and rehearsed and thereby exhibited a controlling force on the tradition.[137]

Jesus' Example

The early Christians may have preserved elements of the Jesus tradition by imitating Jesus. This is what Birger Gerhardsson calls the "behavioural tradition."[138] Social scientists have noticed how the transmission of traditions includes not merely learning what a teacher says but imitating how he or she said it.[139] Emulating the deeds of a teacher was practiced in philosophical schools.[140] In the Jewish world, a rabbi's particular interpretation of the Torah would lead to a specific halakhah, a distinctive "way of life." No surprise then to discover that in the New Testament the example of Jesus is a constituent element of ethics for the believing community (e.g., Rom 13:14; 1 Cor 11:1; Phil 2:5-11; 1 Thess 1:6; Heb 2:18-3:2; 12:3-4; 1 Pet 2:21). Particularly in Paul's epistles, the theme of "imitation" is telling and requires some detailed knowledge of Jesus' actions.[141]

Scholarship has gradually cottoned on to this point. John Dominic Crossan asserts that a study of mimetics shows how the early church replicated Jesus' deeds and praxis and thus contributed to the preservation of those traditions embodied in such memorable actions.[142] Gregory Ri-

137. Samuel Byrskog, "The Eyewitnesses as Interpreters of the Past: Reflections on Richard Bauckham's *Jesus and the Eyewitnesses,*" *JSHJ* 6 (2008): 159, 167.

138. Birger Gerhardsson, "The Gospel Tradition," in *The Interrelations of the Gospels,* ed. D. Dungan (Leuven: Leuven University Press, 1990), 501-2.

139. Jan Vansina, *Oral Tradition as History* (Madison: University of Wisconsin Press, 1985), 47.

140. Philostratus, *Lives of the Sophists* 5.21.

141. Cf. David Stanley, "Imitation in Paul's Letters: Its Significance for His Relationship to Jesus and to His Own Christian Foundations," in *From Jesus to Paul: Studies in Honor of F. W. Beare,* ed. P. Richardson and J. C. Hurd (Waterloo: Wilfred Laurier University, 1984), 127-41.

142. On the positive role of mimetics, see John Dominic Crossan, "Itinerants and Householders in the Earliest Jesus Movement," in *Whose Historical Jesus?* ed. W. E. Arnal and M. Desjardins (Waterloo: Wilfrid Laurier University Press, 1997), 15-16.

ley thinks that a greater source for the energy and fuel for the rise of the Christian movement came from Jesus' deeds.[143] More forthright is Samuel Byrskog, who contends that "The deepest continuity with the past was not in memory as such but in mimesis, not in passive remembrance but in imitation."[144]

A paradigm shift is therefore required in seeing the Jesus tradition not exclusively in terms of verbal transmission but also of praxis, deed, and behavior delivered on to others. This might include the practice of sharing meals, baptizing, healing, prayer, exorcism, itinerant preaching, foot washing, and so forth. Such actions have a history in Jesus' ministry and undoubtedly evoked some kind of symbolic significance when practiced. These practices provided the occasion for the deeds of Jesus to be remembered and interpreted. That is not to deny that new meanings could not be attached to these acts, but act and speech are likely to have been woven together.

Teachers as Custodians of the Jesus Tradition

The sayings of Jesus were not composed solely of short pithy remarks but were, in short, teachings. Jesus was recognized as a teacher and this implied a deliberate and structured impartation of knowledge as well as a concern for its subsequent transmission among his followers. It makes sense then that within the developing structures of the church teachers would emerge and naturally be assigned the role of preserving the integrity of these teachings. It would be true for Jesus as much as for the Teacher of Righteousness or even Pythagoras that the teachings of the master would be preserved and propagated by specialist teachers who were recognized by their ability to relay responsibly the way and wisdom of the movement founder. These teachers may not have necessarily been a "walking reference library,"[145] but were still guardians and guides to the instruction of one who was known to be both Rabbi and Redeemer.

The office of "teacher" (διδάσκαλος) emerged relatively quickly as

143. Gregory J. Riley, "Words and Deeds: Jesus as Teacher, Jesus as Pattern of Life," *HTR* 90 (1997): 427-36. It was E. P. Sanders (*Jesus and Judaism*, 3-13) who urged that more emphasis be placed on actions/deeds of Jesus than merely the sayings material. See also F. Scott Spencer, *What Did Jesus Do? Gospel Profiles of Jesus' Personal Conduct* (Harrisburg: Trinity, 2003).

144. Byrskog, *Story as History*, 107.

145. Vansina, *Oral Tradition as History*, 37.

seen in both the Pauline corpus and Acts.[146] As to what this office involves, Dunn comments, "These we may presume were responsible for retaining, passing on, and interpreting the congregation's foundation tradition, including interpretation of the prophetic scriptures and the Jesus tradition. What else would teachers teach?"[147] Over the course of time it would be natural for teachers to assume catechism and apologetics as well into their vocation, perhaps utilizing the Jesus tradition in these activities. As custodians of the traditions of their community, the teachers ensured the veracity of those very teachings either from Jesus or about Jesus. Therefore, it is altogether unsurprising that a document called the *Didache*, "teaching" (Διδαχή), should contain so many echoes of and allusions to the Jesus tradition, perhaps even independent of the Gospels.[148] This does not imply that the Jesus tradition was exclusively the property of a didactic elite within the church since elsewhere teaching is largely a function of the believing community (see Rom 15:14; Col 3:16). We are presented with a tradition preserved by believing communities and guided by eyewitnesses and teachers within that community. Important didactic figures were vital guarantors of the memory and traditions of Jesus.[149]

The Jesus Tradition as Community Possession

Jesus' closest followers, the eyewitnesses, and Christian teachers exhibited some control over the form and figure of the Jesus tradition. But it is also likely that, especially as time progressed, the Jesus tradition was

---

146. Rom 12:7; 1 Cor 12:28-29; Gal 6:6; Eph 4:11; cf. Acts 13:1; Jas 3:1; Heb 5:12; 1 Tim 2:7; *Did.* 15.1-2.

147. Dunn, *Theology of the Apostle Paul*, 582; cf. idem, *Living Word*, 28-30; idem, *Jesus Remembered*, 176-77.

148. On the possibility of independent oral traditions being preserved in the *Didache*, see R. Glover, "The *Didache's* Quotations and the Synoptic Gospels," *NTS* (1958): 12-29; J. S. Kloppenberg, "*Didache* 16:6-8 and Special Matthean Tradition," *ZNW* (1979): 54-67; Jonathan Draper, "The Jesus Tradition in the Didache," in *Gospel Perspectives 5*, ed. Wenham, 269-87; idem, "The Jesus Tradition in the Didache," in *The Didache in Modern Research*, ed. J. A. Draper (Leiden: Brill, 1996), 72-91; W. Rordorf, "Does the Didache Contain Jesus Tradition Independently of the Synoptic Gospels?" in *Jesus and the Oral Gospel Tradition*, ed. Wansbrough, 394-423; David Flusser and Huub van de Sandt, *The Didache: Its Jewish Sources and Its Place in Early Judaism and Christianity* (Compendia Rerum Iudaicarum Ad Novum Testamentum 5; Minneapolis: Fortress, 2002), 40-49.

149. Bockmuehl, *Seeing the Word*, 176.

democratized and became a possession of the community that looked to the words and deeds of Jesus as normative for its way of life. Thus greater stress needs to be placed on the Christian communities rather than merely on leaders as carriers of the tradition. Much scholarship has focused on the theological creativity of the Evangelists and assumed that the audience either naively accepted the picture of Jesus as authentic or were unconcerned with its historical liberties. If the Evangelists are situated in the context of "communities" or better yet "networks" of Christians spread across Palestine, Syria, and the Mediterranean, then one cannot assume either an uncritical acceptance of their presentation of Jesus or that the communities were entirely ignorant of the traditions that the Evangelists had re-presented.

Accuracy in oral transmission is guaranteed not by verbatim memorization but by habitual repetition in a community context where the community owns and secures the integrity of its traditions. The controlling factor was the community consensus that would stipulate, "Yes, that is how the story goes!"[150] This is in stark contrast to the view of Riesenfeld, who denied the role of the community as bearer of the tradition, seeing the tradition, rather, as entrusted exclusively to a defined group within the community.[151] I do not deny that specific teachers were designated in the church to safeguard the tradition, but the overall responsibility lay with the community as a whole. Graham Hughes states:

> [F]or those who lived as contemporaries with the transmission process, there was the genuine possibility of testing the information given by the writer . . . over against the traditions, [which are] the public property of the community within which the traditions have been received. . . . But this implies, in turn, that [the] picture of Jesus is not at [the Evangelists'] beck and call but is subject to some degree of historical scrutiny.[152]

Consideration for the role of the Christian communities in supplying and authenticating the integrity of the Jesus tradition should be taken seriously. Dunn quips:

150. Cf. Bailey, "Informal Controlled Oral Tradition," 6; idem, "Middle Eastern Oral Tradition," 364-65.

151. Riesenfeld, *Gospel Tradition*, 17.

152. Graham Hughes, *Hebrews and Hermeneutics: The Epistle to the Hebrews as a New Testament Example of Biblical Interpretation* (SNTSMS 36; Cambridge: Cambridge University Press, 1979), 92.

Where else did the Evangelists find the tradition? Stored up, unused, in an old box at the back of some teacher's house? Stored up, unrehearsed, in the failing memory of an old apostle? Hardly! On the contrary, it is much more likely that when the Synoptics were first received by the various churches, these churches *already* possessed (in communal oral memory or in written form) their own versions of much of the material. They would have been able to compare the Evangelist's version of much of the tradition with their own versions.[153]

The role of the community as participants in the teaching and remembering of the Jesus tradition is arguably present in Colossians. In Col 3:16, Paul's audience is urged to "Let the word of Christ dwell in you richly as you teach and admonish one another in all wisdom." "The word of Christ" (ὁ λόγος τοῦ χριστοῦ) may be a subjective genitive (words from Christ) or an objective genitive (words about Christ). Neither option should be pressed absolutely as both are likely to be meant, in which case, the Colossians are exhorted to impress on one another the words of Jesus.[154]

III. Conclusion

To put matters in brief, the cumulative weight of evidence supports the existence of a tendency in the early church to preserve the Jesus tradition. The memory of Jesus was pertinent and important to the early church and they were equipped with means of conserving it accordingly.

We have not arrived at a demonstrable blueprint outlining exactly how the Jesus tradition originated and metamorphosed into the Gospels. We have certain threads of evidence, some thicker than others, weaved together with historical detective work, to try to ascertain why this tradition circulated in the first place. Accordingly, I regard the evidence surveyed as constituting *moderate* grounds for identifying a conserving force in the transmission of the Jesus tradition, since the gaps in our knowledge are too vast to assert otherwise. At the end of the day most of what is said about the formation of the Jesus tradition is based on *a priori* assumptions, circumstantial evidence,

---

153. Dunn, *Jesus Remembered*, 250.

154. Cf. F. F. Bruce, *The Epistles to the Colossians, to Philemon, and to the Ephesians* (NICNT; Grand Rapids: Eerdmans, 1984), 157; James D. G. Dunn, *The Epistles to the Colossians and to Philemon* (NIGTC; Grand Rapids: Eerdmans, 1996), 236; Michael F. Bird, *Colossians and Philemon* (NCCS; Eugene: Cascade, 2009), 108-9.

inference, hypothesis, analogy, conjecture, and sheer guesswork. We will never arrive at a foolproof theory of how the Jesus tradition was handled and developed into the canonical Gospels, but the exercise remains necessary as a prolegomena to historical Jesus research.

Granted that qualification, I contend that one is still able to weave together several threads of evidence and excavate enough data to suggest that the Jesus tradition had a definite purpose in the early church and that several factors enabled the memory of Jesus to be preserved effectively.

Excursus
An Evangelical and Critical Approach to the Gospels

When it comes to studying the Gospels with a full assortment of scholarly tools like text criticism, source criticism, genre criticism, literary criticism, narrative criticism, redaction criticism, and social-science criticism, I find that many young evangelical students in their first few courses get rather edgy or even irritated. They seem very uneasy with things such as the Synoptic problem, textual suspicion about the story of the woman caught in adultery, Matthew's re-Judaizing of Mark, debates about the authenticity of this or that saying, discussing parallels between the birth narratives of Jesus and Alexander the Great, and so forth. I find that many of these students are happy to read Lee Strobel's popular apologetic book *The Case for Christ,* but often feel violated when they are asked to read B. H. Streeter's *The Four Gospels* or Albert Schweitzer's *The Quest of the Historical Jesus.* How does all this scholarly stuff square with a view of Scripture as inspired, infallible, containing a message of salvation, and embodying our Christian hopes? Good question![155]

There are two approaches to the Gospels that I ardently deride. First, some über-secularists want to read the Bible as nothing more than a deposit of silly ancient magic, mischievous myths, wacky rituals, and surreal superstitions. They engage in endless comparisons of the Bible with other mythic religions to flatten out the distinctive elements of the story. Added to that is advocacy of countless conspiracy theories to explain away any historical elements in the text. This approach is coupled with an inherent distaste for anything supernatural, pre-modern, and reeking of religion. Such skeptics become positively evangelical in their zealous fervor to prove

---

155. Of course, I have also lectured in university surroundings where students sometimes assumed that I would debunk all this Jesus nonsense as a load of fictitious hokum. Their consternation became quite evident when they discovered that Jesus is more historically accessible to us than are many other figures from antiquity. What is more, they were even more concerned to discover that everything they thought they knew about Jesus was based on ill-informed media hype and a biblically illiterate education, and owes more to *The Simpsons* than to sound historical investigation.

that nothing in the Bible actually happened. Second, then there are those equally ardent Bible-believers who want to treat the Bible as if it fell down from heaven in 1611, written in ye aulde English, bound in pristine leather, with words of Jesus in red, Scofield's notes, and charts of the end times. Such persons regard exploring topics like problems in Johannine chronology just as religiously affronting as worshiping a life-size golden statue of Barack Obama. Now I have to say that both approaches bore the proverbial pants off me. They are equally as dogmatic as they are dull. They are as uninformed as they are unimaginative. There is another way!

My own approach is what I would term "believing criticism."[156] This approach treats Scripture as the inspired and veracious Word of God, but contends that we do Scripture the greatest service when we commit ourselves to studying it in light of the context and processes through which God gave it to us. Scripture is trustworthy because of God's faithfulness to his own Word and authoritative because the Holy Spirit speaks to us through it. Nonetheless, God has seen fit to use human language, human authors, and even human processes as the means by which he has given his inscripturated revelation to humanity. To understand the substance of Scripture means wrestling with its humanity, the human face of God's speech to us in his Word. That requires that we can freely engage subjects such as how the text of the Gospels was transmitted (text criticism), sources that the Evangelists used (source criticism), when and where were the Gospels written (historical criticism), why the Gospels were written (literary criticism), what kind of literature they are (genre criticism), how the Evangelists edited and adapted their sources (redaction criticism), how the story in its current shape creates meaning (narrative criticism), how the stories of Jesus interacted with cultural values and modes of discourse (social-scientific criticism), and how the Gospels came to be accepted as the four official stories of Jesus sanctioned by the early churches (canonical criticism). These are legitimate inquiries, not in spite of but precisely in light of the faith communities who cherished the Gospels as testimonies to Jesus Christ.

What is more, when we say that the Gospels are historically reliable, we do not mean that they were intended to be judged by the standards of modern historiography or that they are the ancient equivalent of what it would have been like to follow Jesus around with a hidden video camera. They are historically rooted in the memories of the earliest eyewitnesses. Even if ancient writers did not have the apparatus of modern history writing — footnotes, plagiarism software, video footage, and editorial boards — they still knew the difference between events purported to have happened that did not happen and events purported to have happened that did happen. St. Luke, the Beloved Disciple, and the author of 2 Peter[157] all believed that

156. Cf. Mark Noll, *Between Faith and Criticism: Evangelicals, Scholarship, and the Bible in America* (Vancouver: Regent College, 1988), 163-80.

157. On 2 Peter, pseudonymity, and eyewitnesses, see Byrskog, *Story as History*, 242-44; Bockmuehl, *Seeing the Word*, 183.

the Jesus-story is not make-believe (Luke 1:1-4; John 19:35; 20:31; 2 Pet 1:16). After due allowances are made for artistic license, theological embellishment, and the inherent biases of the tradents of the tradition, our witnesses to Jesus remain steadfast in their conviction that the Jesus whom they narrate is historically authentic as much as he is personally confronting. All four canonical narratives render accounts about Jesus as a historical figure situated in first-century Palestine. The Gospels are not timeless myths or deliberate fictions spun for the purpose of spiritual nourishment. They make thick historical claims, though they are not merely historical reports.[158]

Let us remember, too, that all history, both ancient and modern, is interpreted. There is no unbiased reporting or purely objective history, whether by St. Matthew, Oxford University Press, or the New York Times. As such, the Gospels are not interested in brute facts about Jesus but in the unity between Jesus of Nazareth and the Lord worshiped in the church. The Gospels are unashamedly theologically oriented, to the point that "The story of Jesus is the continuation and actualization of the story of God."[159] As works of proclamation, the Gospels endeavor to present and interpret the story of Jesus in such a way that readers (and hearers) of the story will be moved to acknowledge him as the Son of God, the Lord Jesus, whose death and resurrection are the definitive means through which the God of Israel is rescuing the world.[160]

So although the Gospels have an interest in the back-then-ness of Jesus, his earthly life and pre-Easter ministry, they still tell the story from the perspective of people who believe that Jesus is the risen and exalted Lord. This is why the story of Jesus given in early Christian testimony is placed in a specific context that offers both a historical referent as well as explicating the life of Jesus in a religious narrative about God, Israel, and the kingdom of God. Larry Hurtado sets out wonderfully the dual historical reality and theological narrative of the Gospels:

> In short, this all amounts to a shared programmatic effort to locate Jesus in a spe-
> cific historical, geographical, and cultural setting. It represents an insistence that
> the Jesus whom the writers and intended readers of these Gospels reverenced (who
> include Gentile and Jewish believers in various locations in the Roman world), and
> were to see as linked with God's purpose in a unique way, is quite definitely *Jesus of*

158. Crossan's now famous remark (*Historical Jesus,* iii) that "Emmaus never happened. Emmaus always happens," expresses exactly the ahistorical faith that I think the Evangelists vehemently oppose. It was ancient pagan religions that treated religion as nothing more than timeless myths and metaphysical mystery concerning things that "never happened, but always are" as Sallustius, the friend of Emperor Julian the Apostate (361-63 CE), put it in his anti-Christian tractate for neo-platonic paganism (*On the Gods and the World,* 4).

159. Joel B. Green, "The Gospel according to Mark," in *The Cambridge Companion to the Gospels,* ed. Stephen C. Barton (Cambridge: Cambridge University Press, 2007), 147.

160. Beverly R. Gaventa and Richard B. Hays, "Seeking the Identity of Jesus," in *Seeking the Identity of Jesus: A Pilgrimage,* ed. Beverly R. Gaventa and Richard B. Hays (Grand Rapids: Eerdmans, 2008), 8.

Nazareth. He is not some timeless symbol, not a mythical figure of a "once upon a time," but instead very specifically a Jew whose life and activities are geographically and chronologically located in a particular place and period of Jewish history in Roman Judea. . . . [T]he canonical Gospels emphasize an explicit, larger "narrative world" or the story line into which they place their stories of Jesus. This narrative horizon extends both backward to include the story line of the Scriptures of Israel (Tanach/Old Testament) and forward chronologically to the eschatological triumph of God's purposes. . . . If the biblical sweep of the horizon "backward" in time gives the meaning-context of Jesus, the eschatological sweep of the horizon "forward" holds out the hope in which following Jesus is to be ventured, and the divine purpose that Jesus serves.[161]

Thus, the historical Jesus and the theologically significant Jesus are treated as one and the same by the Evangelists. Indeed, this is precisely why it is so difficult in the Gospels, even near impossible, to separate the Jesus of history from the Jesus of the church's faith. It is like trying to separate red from blue in the color purple.[162] The history of Jesus is available to us primarily, though perhaps not exclusively, through the theological testimony of the early church to Jesus. The Gospels are not just about what Jesus actually did and said but about who he is and will yet be in the grand purpose of the God of Israel to bring life and justice to his creation. Accordingly the historical task is not to cast aside the interpretive layer of the Gospels so that one can thereby scrounge through their underlying traditions in the hope of finding a pure and unadulterated image of Jesus in some textual relic. Rather, as Chris Keith says, "the first step in the critical reconstruction of the past that gave rise to the Gospels should be toward the interpretations of the Gospels in an effort to understand and explain them, not away from them, as was the case for form criticism and its outgrowth. . . ."[163]

This means that we are actually liberated to read the Gospels as they were intended to be read: as historically referential theological testimonies to Jesus as the exalted Lord. It does not matter then whether it was one demoniac (Mark 5:2; Luke 8:27) or two (Matt 8:28) that Jesus healed on the eastern shore of the Sea of Galilee. Jesus healed a demon-possessed man in the vicinity, and Matthew just likes doublets, making everything twos where he can! Similarly, trying to prove that mustard seeds really are the smallest seeds on earth (Mark 4:31) or that Peter denied Jesus

161. Larry Hurtado, *Lord Jesus Christ: Devotion to Jesus in Earliest Christianity* (Grand Rapids: Eerdmans, 2003), 266-68.

162. A point made recently and quite notably by Dale C. Allison, "The Historians' Jesus and the Church," in *Seeking the Identity of Jesus: A Pilgrimage,* ed. Gaventa and Hays, 79-95; idem, *The Historical Christ and the Theological Jesus* (Grand Rapids: Eerdmans, 2009).

163. Chris Keith, "The Indebtedness of the Criteria Approach to Form Criticism and Recent Attempts to Rehabilitate the Search for an Authentic Jesus," in *Jesus, Criteria, and the Demise of Authenticity,* ed. Keith and Le Donne, 39-40.

three times before the cock first crowed and then three times again afterward (Matt 26:69-74; Luke 22:56-60; John 18:16-27; Mark 14:66-68) is like trying to understand the *Magna Carta* by arguing about whether the commas are in the right position. John Calvin himself said: "We know that the Evangelists were not very exact as to the order of dates, or even in detailing minutely everything that Christ did or said."[164] The Evangelists give us the big picture about Jesus, the gist of his words, the major outlines of his career, they position him in relation to the prophetic promises, and they declare the all-important significance as to who he was and why he died. The details should not be treated with indifference, but they are not the focus of the stories we call "Gospels." While I think the overall historical reliability of the Gospels is vitally important, lest we treat them as religiously laden fiction, we should not import anachronistic and modernist criteria of historical reality into our treatment of the Gospels and make it a condition for theological validity. Martin Hengel lamented how an

> unbiblical, and ultimately rationalistic, apologetics remained the rule in Protestant orthodoxy until the beginning of historical criticism in the eighteenth century, and indeed in some evangelical fundamentalist circles to the present day. Such a "fundamentalistic rationalistic" exegesis which makes the New Testament a law book does little service to the real historical and theological understanding of the Gospels (the two cannot be separated) as the radical ahistorical scepticism which seeks to investigate the text only by a literary approach in terms of its aesthetic value or by a dogmatic approach in terms of its unalterable fixed "truth content" and prohibits any authentic historical investigation, or at least is not interested in it.[165]

The four canonical Gospels stand as a theological unity in their witness to Jesus and as a canonical authority for those who claim to follow Jesus as their Lord. To treat them as Scripture does not oblige us to explain away their distinctive narrations, to flatten out their individuality, to harmonize every apparent discrepancy, or to play down their unique portraits of Jesus. The Gospels should be studied and admired like four stained glass windows of Jesus in a cathedral, where each portrait displays the same person, but expresses his person in different ways. No single portrait is any "truer" than the others, but it is as a unity that they together provide us with the complete array of images that make up the Jesus of the church's faith. Along these lines the church father Augustine said:

> If you ask which of these different versions [of the Gospels] represent what was actually expressed by the voice, you may fix on whichever you wish, provided that

---

164. John Calvin, *Commentary on a Harmony of the Evangelists* (Grand Rapids: Eerdmans, 1989), 216.

165. Hengel, *Four Gospels and the One Gospel of Jesus Christ*, 23-24.

you understand that those of the writers who have not reproduced the identical form of speech have still reproduced the same sense intended to be conveyed. And these variations in the modes of expression are also useful in this way, that they make it possible for us to teach a more adequate conception of the saying than might been the case with only one form, and that they also secure it against being interpreted in a sense not consonant with the real state of the case.[166]

For Augustine it is the rich diversity in the portraits of Jesus given to us by the Evangelists that enable us to grasp more fully and more firmly who Jesus actually is!

So then, how do we as a believing and confessing community approach the critical questions that the texts of the Gospels present to us? First, we begin with a hermeneutic of trust. We trust Jesus, and he evidently trusts the Scriptures that point to him. God's Word is attested by God's Son and this Word is further validated by the inner witness of the Holy Spirit that it is always true and trustworthy. Second, we need to get our hands and feet dirty in the mud and muck of history. Jesus is not an ahistorical religious icon who can be deciphered entirely apart from any historical situation. On the contrary, he could not have been born as Savior of the world somewhere in the Amazon rainforest or in the Gobi Desert. He came to Israel and through Israel, to make good God's promises to save the world through a renewed Israel. So, whether we like it or not, we are obligated to study Jesus in his historical context. I would go so far to say that this is even a necessary task of discipleship.[167] For it is in the context of Israel's Scripture and in the socio-political circumstance of Roman Palestine that Jesus is revealed as the Messiah and Son of God. So unless we are proponents of a docetic christology in which Jesus only seems human, we are committed to a study of the historical person Jesus of Nazareth in his own context. That means archaeological, social-historical, and cultural studies of the extant sources as far as they are available to us. It requires immersing ourselves in as much of the primary literature of the first century as we can get our hands on — Jewish, Greek, and Roman — so that we can walk, talk, hear, and smell the world of Jesus. It entails that we go through the Gospels unit by unit and ask what exactly Jesus intended and how his hearers would have understood him. It equally involves asking why the Evangelists have told the story as they have and why they have the peculiarities that they do. Third, we have to explore the impact that the Gospels intended to make on their implied audiences and how the four Gospels as a whole intend to shape the believing communities who read them now.

So, when it comes to the hard and even treacherous "critical" questions, in the words of Bruce Chilton: "A primary evangelical and critical task is, not to peddle our

---

166. Augustine, *Harmony of the Gospels* 2.14.31.

167. N. T. Wright, *The Challenge of Jesus* (London: SPCK, 2000), 14-15; and see exploration of this point more fully in Michael F. Bird, "Should Evangelicals Participate in the 'Third Quest for the Historical Jesus'?" *Themelios* 29 (2004): 4-14.

assumptions, but to encourage the sort of open, detailed inquiry which will vindicate them."[168] Also, when it comes to reading the Gospels as a church community, we are not just mining for nuggets of devotional wisdom. Rather, we are striving to let the story of Jesus gradually shape our lives, enrich our worship, inspire us to mission, draw our community together, and impact our ministries, so that the evangelical vision of Jesus given to us in the Gospels becomes an evangelical project to make the story of Jesus known in all the world.

168. Bruce D. Chilton, "An Evangelical and Critical Approach to the Sayings of Jesus," *Themelios* 3 (1978): 85.

CHAPTER 3

The Formation of the Jesus Tradition

In twentieth-century New Testament studies the advent of several new types of critical study furthered the state of Gospels research. Form criticism recognized the oral setting of the early church, the social function of the Jesus tradition in certain settings, and the oral sub-genres that the tradition was carried in. Redaction criticism led to a heightened awareness of the theological activity of the Evangelists in adapting, shaping, and adding to their materials. More recently, narrative criticism has provided insights into the fundamentally storied nature of the Gospels and has demonstrated that meaning is created through characterization, plot, point of view, narration, and the like. This appreciation of the Gospels as *orality, theology,* and *story* has provided new avenues for exploration of the Gospels.

Whatever the benefits of these approaches, and they are many, one cannot help but feel that something has been lost in the avalanche of modern scholarship. Regardless of the precise "form" or "situation" in which traditions emerged, irrespective of what the Evangelists achieved theologically, or of what kind of intricate story the texts contain, one must remain cognizant of the fact that the Gospel texts have an extratextual referent beyond themselves in the historical figure of Jesus. Thus, it would be to the detriment of interpreters to displace the historical intentionality of the Gospels with entirely literary, narrative, or theological projections. As Seán Freyne comments: "A purely literary approach to Jesus the Galilean as he emerges in the various gospel portraits would be not be adequate, because it would lack a critical awareness in light of our modern historical self-consciousness, namely that as historical beings we make history, and cannot therefore ignore issues in evaluating our foundational texts and their extra-textual referent."[1] The purpose of the canonical Gospels is to proclaim good news about a historical figure and to set forth his enduring significance for their contemporaries.

As such, my aim in this chapter is to identify the factors that account for the formation of the Jesus tradition in the context of the early church. In the previous chapter I examined several reasons that the early church would have remained deliberately interested in the life of Jesus, and I also drew attention to several factors which explain how the Jesus tradition might have been preserved in the early church. What remains now is to plot the global coordinates of the Jesus tradition. Therefore, I intend to establish the model of transmission that best accounts for the form and character of Gospels. This will hopefully illuminate the process that moved, however complicated, from Jesus to tradition to text.

I. Models of Oral Tradition

Developing a working hypothesis of how the Jesus tradition originated and was transmitted is fraught with significant problems. Indeed, the gap in our historical knowledge about the precise details of the transmission of the Jesus tradition is roughly analogous to those medieval ocean maps which marked uncharted regions with "Here there be dragons!" We simply cannot know with any degree of certainty what is out there beyond and before the Gospels. E. P. Sanders and Margaret Davies comment, "We are left with questions which we cannot precisely answer: how was the material transmitted? Why were the diverse types either preserved or created?"[2] Yet these problems, dragons and all, may not be quite so perplexing. Such caveats are necessary, but many scholars still feel confident enough to posit some hypothesis about the formation of the tradition that has left its imprint on the Gospels.[3] There

---

1. Seán Freyne, *Galilee, Jesus and the Gospels: Literary Approaches and Historical Investigations* (Philadelphia: Fortress, 1988), 27.

2. E. P. Sanders and M. Davies, *Studying the Synoptic Gospels* (London: SCM, 1989), 136. Christopher Rowland, *Christian Origins* (London: SPCK, 1985), 130-31: "We have to face the fact that we are very much in the dark about the origin and development of the gospel tradition." James D. G. Dunn, *Jesus Remembered* (CITM 1; Grand Rapids: Eerdmans, 2003), 210: "We certainly do not know enough about oral traditioning in the ancient world to draw from that knowledge clear guidelines for our understanding of how the Jesus tradition was passed down in its oral stage."

3. Cf. Rowland, *Christian Origins*, 131; E. P. Sanders, *The Historical Figure of Jesus* (Lon-

are of course various models on offer and the question remains as to which one has the most explanatory power.

Irretrievably Lost

Some scholars believe that the entire enterprise of trying to postulate a theory about the oral transmission of the Jesus tradition is a dead end. For instance, Barry Henaut asserts that

> [T]he oral phase is now lost, hidden behind a series of Gospel texts and pre-Gospel sources that are full-fledged textuality — a textuality that does not intend to preserve an accurate account of the oral tradition but rather to convey a theological response to a new sociological situation. The oral phase is lost because after we employ form and redaction criticism we are left with a tradition that still bears the stamp of the post-resurrection church and which cannot be traced back through its prior oral transmission.[4]

According to Henaut, the problem is a textuality that forms an impregnable barrier to recovering anything of the oral tradition.[5] In response, Henaut's contention that the Gospels and their sources attempt to express a theological response to a social situation is true enough, yet his inference that an ideologically laden text renders its historical referent and mode of transmission as moot is not valid. This tacit assumption rests on an obviously false dichotomy between "history" and "theology." All Henaut has established is that there is no uninterpreted oral tradition, no objective oral history, and no control sample of the Jesus tradition — a conclusion that has the prosaic profundity of announcing that the pope is Catholic. Every text and tradition

---

don: Penguin, 1993), 60, posits a four-step process in the development of the Gospels: (1) units used in pedagogical contexts, (2) collection of related units into groups of pericopes, (3) proto-Gospels, and (4) Gospels. John Dominic Crossan, *The Historical Jesus: The Life of a Mediterranean Jewish Peasant* (San Francisco: HarperCollins, 1991), xxxi, identifies three layers in the Jesus tradition: (1) retention, recording the essential core of words, deeds, events, (2) development, applying the pre-Gospel data to new situations and circumstances, and (3) creation of new sayings, new stories, and large complexes that changed the contents in that very process.

4. Barry W. Henaut, *Oral Tradition and the Gospels: The Problem of Mark 4* (JSNTSup 82; Sheffield: Sheffield Academic, 1993), 14.

5. Henaut, *Oral Tradition and the Gospels*, 15, 190-91.

exhibits the imprint of its authors and tradents, but this does not mean that there is no history and no transmission process discernible in its content. Every historical account, whether oral or written, is embedded with the perspective of its originators and transmitters. It is as naive to think that the Jesus tradition remained woodenly fixed as much as it is to envisage some kind of creative free-for-all that evolved from simple folklore to complex Greco-Roman rhetoric.

Furthermore, Henaut remains rather selective in his skepticism. Whereas he is forthrightly cynical about being able to reconstruct the oral tradition behind the Gospels, he displays little to no reserve about his capacity to isolate Marcan sources from Marcan redaction, which strikes me as an equally formidable task. Henaut embodies an all too typical bias toward written texts over and against oral traditions. He is very confident in is his ability to peel back and identify layers of texts inside texts, but will not countenance the possibility that the Evangelists' oral sources have left their imprints on the Gospels. This is a peculiar prejudice to adopt, given the Jewish culture of "scribal orality" in which, according to Martin Jaffee, oral communication was the primary medium of textual knowledge.[6] In which case, we are very probably faced with the coexistence and coalescing of oral and written traditions about Jesus from the very beginning. Oral media (such as speeches) were often written down, while written media (such as letters) were often delivered orally.[7] What is more, the oral form of the Jesus tradition was not erased from memory as soon as Mark put quill to papyrus. The interface of oral and written sources existed from the beginning of the Jesus tradition and most probably continued for some time.

If one feels that I am naively lumping oral and written sources into a single clump, then I would point out that the New Testament, Gospels and Epistles, are the written expression of a largely oral phenomena. Our earliest

---

6. M. S. Jaffee, *Torah in the Mouth: Writing and Oral Tradition in Palestinian Judaism 200 BCE–400 CE* (Oxford: Oxford University Press, 2001), 61.

7. Cf. Hans von Campenhausen, *The Formation of the Christian Bible,* trans. J. A Baker (Philadelphia: Fortress, 1972), 121: "Written and oral traditions run side by side or cross, enrich or distort one another, without distinction or even the possibility of distinction between them." Harry Gamble, *Books and Readers in the Early Church* (New Haven: Yale University Press, 1995), 29-30: "Whatever may be said about the oral dimensions of the Jesus tradition or about the composition of the Gospel of Mark in particular, Christianity before 70 C.E. cannot be accurately described as an exclusively oral culture. Arising within the matrix of a broadly literate Judaism, early Christianity was never without a literary dimension, even though it did not immediately generate a large literature of its own."

Christian literature is the textual product of the oral activities of the early church, including proclamation, apologetics, exhortations, prayers, debates, hymns, creeds, and storytelling. As Ben Witherington comments: "Thus it is fair to say that when we tell the story of the New Testament, we are telling the story of a second-order phenomenon, the story of the literary residue of a largely oral movement which grew on the basis of preaching and teaching, praying and praising, and other forms of oral communication."[8] A letter like Romans was orally dictated and then, as far as we know, orally read out to Christians in Rome. Several scholars have drawn attention to the Gospel of Mark as a text designed to be orally performed and to be aurally penetrating.[9] The Fourth Evangelist assumes much of Mark's story, though not necessarily because he has a copy of the text sitting in front of him as he writes, but perhaps he has heard Mark aurally performed and has incorporated outlines from memory.[10] The words of Jesus found in the apostolic fathers may represent a mix of oral and written traditions.[11] Thus, the line between

---

8. Ben Witherington, *The New Testament Story* (Grand Rapids: Eerdmans, 2004), 5. Note also Paul Achtemeier, "*Omne Verbum Sonat:* The New Testament and the Oral Environment of Later Western Antiquity," *JBL* 109 (1990): 15: "The oral environment was so pervasive that *no* writing occurred that was not vocalized" (italics original). C. H. Dodd, *Historical Tradition in the Fourth Gospel* (Cambridge: Cambridge University Press, 1963), 8: "The early Church was not such a bookish community as it has been represented. It did its business in the world primarily through the medium of the living voice, in worship, teaching and missionary preaching, and out of these three forms of activity — liturgy, *didache, kergyma* — a tradition built up, and this tradition lies behind all literary production of the early period, including our written gospels."

9. Cf. Pieter J. J. Botha, "Mark's Story as Oral Traditional Literature: Rethinking the Transmission of Some Traditions about Jesus," *HTS* 47 (1991): 304-31; Joanna Dewey, "Mark as Aural Narrative: Structures and Clues to Understanding," *STR* 36 (1992): 45-56; idem, "Mark — A Really Good Oral Story: Is That Why the Gospel of Mark Survived?" *JBL* 123 (2004): 495-507; Christopher Bryan, *A Preface to Mark* (Oxford: Oxford University Press, 1993); Whitney Shiner, *Proclaiming the Gospel: First-Century Performance of Mark* (Harrisburg: Trinity, 2003). Richard A. Horsley, *Hearing the Whole Story: The Politics of Plot in Mark's Gospel* (Louisville: Westminster John Knox, 2001), 62: "It is important to recognize that, given the close relationship between text and performance in the ancient world, Mark was performed and heard in communities of people. Thus Mark was a 'text' that was recited repeatedly after it was written down in one or more copies."

10. As argued, in my mind convincingly, by Ian D. Mackay, *John's Relationship with Mark* (WUNT 2.182; Tübingen: Mohr, 2004).

11. Cf. recently Stephen E. Young, *Jesus Tradition in the Apostolic Fathers: Their Explicit Appeals to the Words of Jesus in Light of Orality Studies* (WUNT 2.311; Tübingen: Mohr, 2011); and still worth consulting is Helmut Koester, *Synoptische Überlieferung bei den apostolischen Vätern* (Berlin: Akademie, 1957).

orality and textuality was plastic and malleable.[12] As such, the complaint of Dunn should be heeded. The default mindset of thinking solely in terms of literary relationships between the Gospels and their sources needs to be seriously reexamined, and allowance needs to be made for the continuing effect of oral tradition on the composition of the Gospels.[13]

The quest for the Jesus tradition, by which I mean mapping the shape of the tradition in its pre-Gospel form, is not akin to chasing shadows. To begin with, we can probe the Gospels for telltale signs of orality, look for mnemonic devices, detect local coloring from Galilean or Judean settings, and identify stereotypical oral forms in the text. Next to that we can envisage the Jesus tradition as the continual verbalization of the impact of Jesus' instruction and mission on his disciples. The remembering, retelling, and rehearsing of Jesus' words and stories about him filled the earliest churches, a phenomenon attested by our earliest Christian sources from 1 Corinthians to 1 *Clement*. Therefore, analyzing the oral phase of the tradition that runs from Jesus through to the Gospels can be pursued at both ends — upward from the earliest phase of the primitive church and downward through the Gospels.[14]

Fluid, Free, and Flexible

The form-critical school claimed that the transmission process was largely fluid, with traditions minted in the "setting" of the early church (see the excursus at the end of this chapter on form criticism).[15] The most recent

12. A point emphasized at length by Jaffee, *Torah in the Mouth*, esp. 64-72. Richard Bauckham, *Jesus and the Eyewitnesses* (Grand Rapids: Eerdmans, 2006), 280: "Where books existed not so much to be read as to be heard and their contents to be held in memory and transmitted orally as well as in writing, we should not draw too sharp a distinction between memorizing of written and of oral material." See further, Tom Thatcher, ed., *Jesus, the Voice, and the Text: Beyond the Oral and Written Gospel* (Waco: Baylor University Press, 2008); Rafael Rodriguez, "Reading and Hearing in Ancient Contexts," *JSNT* 32 (2010): 151-78; Annette Weissenrieder and Robert B. Coote, eds., *The Interface of Orality and Writing* (WUNT 1.260; Tübingen: Mohr, 2010).

13. James D. G. Dunn, "Altering the Default Setting: Re-Envisaging the Early Transmission of the Jesus Tradition," *NTS* 49 (2003): 139-75; idem, *Jesus Remembered*, 222-23, 237-38; idem, "Remembering Jesus," 1:190-93.

14. Cf. James D. G. Dunn, "Remembering Jesus: How the Quest of the Historical Jesus Lost Its Way," in *Handbook for the Study of the Historical Jesus*, ed. T. Holmén and S. E. Porter (4 vols.; Leiden: Brill, 2011), 1:198.

15. Cf., e.g., Rudolf Bultmann, "The Study of the Synoptic Gospels," in *Form Criticism: A New Method of New Testament Research*, ed. F. C. Grant (New York: Harper & Row, 1962), 7-75.

exponents of this view are the members of the now defunct North American Jesus Seminar. According to the late Robert Funk, the seminar's main spokesperson, suspicion toward the historical integrity of Gospel traditions is warranted on the grounds that the Evangelists did a full and complete makeover on the Jesus tradition. They overlaid Jesus' sayings with interpretative comment, forced sayings to conform to their own viewpoints, lessened the force of difficult sayings, invented stories and sayings about Jesus as they wished, borrowed from commonly known cultural proverbs which they then attributed to Jesus, added glosses from the Septuagint at every opportunity, frequently engaged in a flagrant Christianizing of Jesus, credited him with knowledge of events after his death, and then projected the entire adulterated tradition back onto the lips of Jesus.[16] The end product is that the "Jesus of the gospels is an imaginative theological construct, into which has been woven traces of that enigmatic sage from Nazareth — traces that cry out for recognition and liberation from the firm grip of those whose faith overpowered their memories."[17] As analogy for oral transmission, Funk supposes that "Passing oral lore along is much like telling and retelling a joke"[18] which is never retold the same way. Funk also gives the example of the emergence of the urban myth of the alien landings at Roswell as indicative of how legends arise.[19] Both examples are given to underscore how quickly oral reports can either evolve or become distorted. Even so, Funk thinks that there is a core of authentic material in the Gospels consisting of sayings and anecdotes that are short, pithy, provocative, and memorable, viz., aphorisms and parables.[20]

The primary strength of this approach is that it accounts for the variety and variability in the Jesus tradition and rightly notes how the Evangelists have filtered the tradition through their own theological grids. The form critics and the participants in the Jesus Seminar are mostly correct about the propensity of performers and the Evangelists to theologize the tradition or to mold it to suit their own settings. We also know that well-intentioned religious people have a propensity to make up stuff to reinforce their religious

16. Robert W. Funk and Roy W. Hoover, *The Five Gospels: The Search for the Authentic Words of Jesus* (San Francisco: HarperCollins, 1993), 21-25.

17. Funk and Hoover, *Five Gospels,* 4.

18. Funk and Hoover, *Five Gospels,* 27.

19. Robert W. Funk, *The Acts of Jesus: The Search for the Authentic Deeds of Jesus* (San Francisco: HarperCollins, 1998), 5-6.

20. Funk and Hoover, *Five Gospels,* 28; Robert W. Funk, *Honest to Jesus: Jesus for a New Millennium* (San Francisco: HarperCollins, 1996), 40.

beliefs. Even so, I doubt that such a willful distortion of the Jesus tradition in fact occurred, at least not in the tradition's earliest phase.

First, one wonders if these scholars have gone too far in asserting a systematic contamination of the Jesus tradition and a complete lack of objection by anyone to such flagrant liberties being taken with the tradition. On the contrary, the early Christians appear to have cared a great deal about the precise type of Jesus who was announced by teachers (see 2 Cor 11:4; 1 John 4:2), which is also why the Jesus of the "other" Gospels was so reprehensible to many in the proto-orthodox churches of the second and third centuries. When we look at many of the traditions like the overlaps in the Marcan and Johannine feeding narratives (Mark 6–8 and John 6), possible double traditions like the Lord's Prayer (Matt 6:9-13/Luke 11:2-4), Paul's account of the Last Supper juxtaposed with the Synoptics (1 Cor 11:23-26; Luke 22:14-22), we find a mixture of variation and regularity,[21] but not absolute contradiction or massively inexplicable incongruities. This is what we should expect to find, viz., a mixture of adaptation and constancy. In other words: "Variability and stability, conservativism and creativity, evanescence and unpredictability all mark the pattern of oral transmission," and this seems to be equally true of the Jesus tradition.[22] Overall, I remain remarkably impressed about the consistency of the tradition across its various forms, in different locations, even when separated by some decades.[23] The memories of Jesus that circulated in the early church are markedly consistent in general outline and even in some detail.[24] John Knox, in his day hardly a doyen of historical conservatism, said

21. I am assuming that the similarities here cannot all be explained in terms of literary relationships.

22. E. A. Havelock, *Preface to Plato* (Cambridge: Harvard University Press, 1963), 92, 147, 184, cited from Dunn, *Jesus Remembered*, 200, who himself cites it from Werner Kelber, *The Oral and the Written Gospel* (Philadelphia: Fortress, 1983), 33.

23. Cf. C. H. Dodd, *The Founder of Christianity* (New York: Macmillan, 1970), 22: "When all allowance has been made for . . . limiting factors . . . the changes of oral transmission, the effect of translation, the interest of teachings in making the sayings 'contemporary' . . . it remains that the first three Gospels offer a body of sayings on the whole so consistent, so coherent, and withal so distinctive in manner, style and content that no reasonable critic should doubt, whatever reservation he may have about individual sayings, that we find reflected here the thought of a single unique teacher." A. E. Harvey, *Jesus and the Constraints of History* (London: Duckworth, 1982), 5: "Unless these authors [the Evangelists] were the most consummate and imaginative artists, able to create a striking and a consistent character out of scanty and unreliable sources, we have every reason to think that, in broad outline (whatever the case with some of the details), the Jesus whom they portray is the Jesus who actually existed."

24. Cf. Ernst L. Abel, "The Psychology of Memory and Rumor Transmission and Their Bearing on Theories of Oral Transmission in Early Christianity," *JR* 51 (1971): 275-76: "Contrary

that "The body of remembered fact and impression was throughout the first century substantial enough to prevent the wild growth of the tradition."[25]

Second, I would be prepared to argue that the Old Testament functioned as the *interpretive grid* rather than the *creative pool* for the Evangelists' handling of the Jesus tradition, particularly in the passion narratives.[26] All memory is filtered through the structures of pre-existing patterns, types, and categories.[27] The Old Testament provided a literary form and typological framework in which stories of Jesus as a prophet, miracle worker, and teacher could be retold. Yet the Old Testament types did not lead to a whole-scale manufacture of Jesus traditions.

Third, if the Jesus tradition was exploited and expunged in a way remotely akin to how Funk envisages it, then the entire field of historical Jesus studies is practically useless. It would be like trying to re-create a street map from the ashes of a city utterly annihilated by a thermal nuclear bomb. The general reliability of the Jesus tradition is a *sine qua non* for historical Jesus research. For if there was no real remembrance of Jesus by his followers, then all bets are off and the historical task becomes as pointless as booking a reggae band to play at a Klu Klux Klan convention.[28]

---

to the conclusions derived from Form Criticism, studies of rumor transmission indicate that *as information is transmitted, the general form or outline of a story remains intact, but fewer and fewer original details are preserved*" (italics original).

25. John Knox, *Jesus: Lord and Christ* (New York: Harper, 1958), 77.

26. Cf. J. B. Green, "Passion Narrative," in *DJG*, ed. Joel B. Green, Scot McKnight, and I. Howard Marshall (Downers Grove: InterVarsity, 1992), 602-3; N. T. Wright, *Jesus and the Victory of God* (COQG 2; London: SPCK, 1996), 60-61; Craig A. Evans, "The Passion of Jesus: History Remembered or Prophecy Historicized?" *BBR* 6 (1996): 159-65; Gerd Theissen and Annette Merz, *The Historical Jesus: A Comprehensive Guide*, trans. John Bowden (Minneapolis: Fortress, 1998), 106-8; Mark Goodacre, "Scripturalization in Mark's Crucifixion Narrative," in *The Trial and Death of Jesus: Essays on the Passion Narrative in Mark*, ed. G. van Oyen and T. Shepherd (Leuven: Peeters, 2006), 33-47; contra Crossan, *Historical Jesus*, 372; idem, *The Birth of Christianity: Discovering What Happened in the Years Immediately after the Execution of Jesus* (San Francisco: HarperCollins, 1998), 521.

27. Cf. Anthony Le Donne, *The Historiographical Jesus: Memory, Typology, and the Son of David* (Waco: Baylor University Press, 2009), esp. 52-64.

28. Cf. Seán Freyne, *Jesus, A Jewish Galilean: A New Reading of the Jesus-Story* (London: Continuum, 2005), 4: "Either we accept that the early followers of Jesus had some interest in and memory of the historical figure of Jesus as they began to proclaim the good news about him, or we must abandon the process entirely." Dale C. Allison, "The Historians' Jesus and the Church," in *Seeking the Identity of Jesus: A Pilgrimage*, ed. Beverly R. Gaventa and Richard B. Hays (Grand Rapids: Eerdmans, 2008), 84-85: "Either they [the Evangelists] tend to preserve pre-Easter memories or they do not. In the former case, we have some possibility of getting

Fourth, Funk's appeal to party jokes and urban myths about alien landings as analogies for the transmission process is plain spurious. Does anyone really think these are analogies to how the Jesus tradition was passed on? The earliest Christians appear to have attached more weight and authority to Jesus' words than Funk envisages. Jesus' words carried weight, they were freighted with eschatological fervor, they were narrated in preaching and teaching, and they inundated the churches wherever people were asking, "Who was this Jesus?"

Formally Controlled

Another approach to the early church's oral tradition has emerged from a group of scholars who argue for the fixation of the tradition according to rabbinic models of pupils memorizing the teachings of their instructor.[29] The rabbis taught with meticulous concern for reproduction of their in

---

somewhere. But in the latter case, our questing for Jesus is probably pointless and we should consider surrendering to ignorance. If the tradition is seriously misleading in its broad features, then we can hardly make much of its details." Sanders, *Historical Figure of Jesus,* 193: "The gospel writers did not wildly invent material. They developed it, shaped it and directed it in the ways they wished."

29. Harald Riesenfeld, *The Gospel Tradition* (Oxford: Blackwell, 1970); Birger Gerhardsson, *Memory and Manuscript: Oral Tradition and Written Transmission in Rabbinic Judaism and Early Christianity: With Tradition and Transmission in Early Christianity* (Grand Rapids: Eerdmans, 1998); idem, *The Origins of the Gospel Traditions* (Philadelphia: Fortress, 1979); idem, *The Gospel Tradition* (Lund: Gleerup, 1986); idem, "The Path of the Gospel Tradition," in *The Gospels and the Gospel,* ed. P. Stuhlmacher (Grand Rapids: Eerdmans, 1991), 75-96; idem, *The Reliability of the Gospel Tradition* (Peabody: Hendrickson, 2001); Rainer Riesner, *Jesus als Lehrer. Eine Untersuchung zum Ursprung der Evangelien-Überlieferung* (WUNT 2.7; Tübingen: Mohr, 1981); idem, "Jesus as Preacher and Teacher," in *Jesus and the Oral Gospel Tradition,* ed. H. Wansbrough (JSNTSup 64; Sheffield: Sheffield Academic, 1990), 185-210; idem, "From Messianic Teacher to the Gospels of Jesus Christ," in *HSHJ,* ed. T. Holmén and S. E. Porter (Leiden: Brill, 2011), 1:405-46; Samuel Byrskog, *Jesus the Only Teacher: Didactic Authority and Transmission in Ancient Israel, Ancient Judaism and the Matthean Community* (CBNT 24; Stockholm: Almquist & Wiksell, 1994). Cf. Peter H. Davids, "The Gospels and the Jewish Tradition: Twenty Years after Gerhardsson," in *Gospel Perspectives 1: Studies of History and Tradition in the Four Gospels,* ed. R. T. France and D. Wenham (Sheffield: JSOT, 1983), 75-99; Ben F. Meyer, "Some Consequences of Birger Gerhardsson's Account of the Origins of the Gospel Tradition," in *Jesus and the Oral Gospel Tradition,* ed. Wansbrough, 424-40; Paul Barnett, *Jesus and the Logic of History* (NSBT 3; Leicester: Apollos, 1997), 138-44; idem, *Finding the Historical Christ* (Grand Rapids: Eerdmans, 2009), 99-103.

struction and expected their students to memorize their teachings.[30] Rabbi Eliezer ben Hyrcanus announced: "I have never said in my life a thing that I did not hear from my teachers."[31] Exact recollection was treasured to the point that "whoever forgets a word of his mishnah, scripture accounts it as if he had lost his soul."[32] Mnemonic techniques and other controls were employed to minimize deviation from what had been learned by rote. Analogies between the rabbinic system of instruction and the transmission of the Jesus tradition date back as far as the early nineteenth century with J. K. L. Gieseler.[33] A number of continental scholars, especially from Scandinavia, have endeavored to utilize the rabbinic education model as a way of explaining how the Jesus tradition might have been passed on. According to Harald Riesenfeld, the teaching of Jesus was a "holy word" that was passed on much like the Jewish oral tradition later codified in the Mishnah, through "rigidly controlled transmission." Since the Jesus tradition was "entrusted to special persons" it was therefore "regulated by firmly established laws."[34] Riesenfeld admits that gradual elaboration of the tradition did indeed transpire, but he surmises that "The essential point is that the outlines, that is, the beginnings of the proper genus of the tradition of the words and deeds of Jesus, were memorized and recited as holy word. We should be inclined to trace these outlines back to Jesus' activity as a teacher in the circle of his disciples."[35]

Birger Gerhardsson, Riesenfeld's pupil, attempted to draw a more exact correlation between transmission of the Jesus tradition and proto-rabbinic methods of teaching, which laid strong emphasis on memorization. He asserts that memorization was a general feature of rabbinic and Hellenistic education: "The general attitude was that words and items of knowledge must be memorized: *tantum scimus, quantum memoria tenemus!*"[36] Memorization preceded comprehension in rabbinic pedagogy.[37] Repetition, condensation,

---

30. *m. 'Aboth* 1.2-12; *Sipre Deut* 48.1.1-4.

31. *b. Sukkoth* 28a.

32. *Pirqe 'Aboth* 3.9.

33. Riesner, "Messianic Teacher," 409-10. Note also that Martin Dibelius, *From Tradition to Gospel* (New York: Scribner, 1965), 39, also saw a genuine analogy between rabbinic models and the transmission of the Jesus tradition: "The Jew of Rabbinic education had had sufficient mnemonic practice to be able to quote such texts by heart."

34. Riesenfeld, *Gospel Tradition*, 15-16, 19.

35. Riesenfeld, *Gospel Tradition*, 26.

36. Gerhardsson, *Memory and Manuscript*, 123-24.

37. Gerhardsson, *Memory and Manuscript*, 126-27.

and use of mnemonic techniques were all part of the didactic toolbox.[38] Gerhardsson goes on to argue that if Jesus taught like a rabbi, then "He must have made his disciples learn certain sayings off by heart; if he taught, he must have required his disciples to memorize."[39]

The appeal to rabbinic parallels as providing the model for the transmission of the Jesus tradition has drawn severe criticism.[40] First, Martin Hengel has effectively argued that the rabbi-pupil model cannot be projected onto Jesus and his summons to discipleship. Jesus' leadership style is firmly oriented toward that of a charismatic prophet rather than that of a rabbi or scribe.[41] In fact, the Evangelists report that Jesus did not teach as the scribes did (Mark 1:22/Matt 7:29).[42] Second, a stringent and formally controlled tradition does not adequately explain the breadth of variation that has emerged in the Jesus tradition. Gerhardsson and company are aware of this charge, but explaining these variations the way they do through apostolic redaction or derivation from various schools is not entirely convincing. The fact remains that there was creativity in the formulation of the Jesus tradition.[43] Third, there is little evidence of an actual setting in which such systematic memorization occurred.[44] Riesenfeld's suggestion that Paul spent his three years

38. Gerhardsson, *Memory and Manuscript*, 136-70; idem, *Tradition and Transmission*, 17; idem, *Origins of the Gospel Tradition*, 19-20.

39. Gerhardsson, *Memory and Manuscript*, 328; idem, "Path of the Gospel Tradition," 85.

40. Morton Smith, "A Comparison of Early Christian and Early Rabbinic Tradition," *JBL* 82 (1963): 169-76; W. D. Davies, "Reflections on a Scandinavian Approach to the 'Gospel Tradition,'" in *Neotestamentica et patristica. Eine Freundesgabe, Herrn Professor Dr. Oscar Cullmann zu seinem 60. Geburtstag uberreicht* (NovTSup 6; Leiden: Brill, 1962), 14-34; Jacob Neusner, "The Rabbinic Traditions about the Pharisees before A.D. 70: The Problem of Oral Transmission," in *The Origins of Judaism, Volume II: The Pharisees and Other Sects* (New York: Garland, 1990), 160-62; Sanders, *Jesus and Judaism*, 15; Sanders and Davies, *Studying the Synoptic Gospels*, 129-32, Henaut, *Oral Traditions and the Gospels*, 41-53; Kelber, *Oral and Written Gospel*, 8-14, 17.

41. Martin Hengel, *The Charismatic Leader and His Followers*, trans. J. C. G. Greig (Edinburgh: Clark, 1981), 42-57; C. K. Barrett, *Jesus and the Gospel Tradition* (London: SPCK, 1967), 9-10.

42. Smith, "Comparison," 172.

43. See Gerhardsson, *Memory and Manuscript*, 334-35; idem, *Tradition and Transmission*, 37-40; idem, "Path of the Gospel Tradition," 78-79; idem, *Reliability*, 54; E. Earle Ellis, "The Synoptic Gospels and History," in *Authenticating the Activities of Jesus*, ed. B. D. Chilton and C. A. Evans (NTTS 28; Leiden: Brill, 1999), 56; Dunn, *Jesus Remembered*, 198.

44. Barrett, *Jesus and the Gospel Tradition*, 9-10; Sanders and Davies, *Studying the Synoptic Gospels*, 142.

in Arabia committing the Jesus tradition to memory seems far-fetched.[45] The same could be said of Riesner's suggestion that the reference to Jesus' house refers to Jesus' own school of teaching (Mark 2:1; 3:20; 9:33).[46] Byrskog posits a Matthean school that focused on Jesus as teacher and applied his teachings to community life with the result that the transmission was careful and controlled, but whether there even was a Matthean school should not be assumed.[47] Although some memorization very probably occurred during Jesus' teaching ministry, the urgent nature of Jesus' mission meant that there was no time to be wasted on systematic impartation of encyclopedic knowledge when other villages desperately had to hear the gospel of the kingdom.[48] Fourth, the notion that the post-resurrection apostles formed a *collegium* and thereafter controlled the tradition is clearly contestable since the apostles were not ubiquitous, and their authority was challenged often.[49]

Nevertheless, this perspective on the Jesus tradition has been dismissed somewhat prematurely. Many have wrongly criticized Gerhardsson for reading later rabbinic perspectives, which are post-135 CE, back into the pre-70 CE era.[50] Gerhardsson acknowledges that at the time he wrote there

45. Riesenfeld, *Gospel Tradition*, 17-18.

46. Riesner, *Jesus als Lehrer*, 33-39.

47. Byrskog, *Jesus the Only Teacher*, 235, 329, 401.

48. Crossan, *Historical Jesus*, xxxi: "Jesus left behind him thinkers not memorizers, disciples not reciters, people not parrots."

49. Gerhardsson, *Memory and Manuscript*, 214-25, 329-33; idem, *Tradition and Transmission*, 35-36; cf. Davies, "Reflections on a Scandinavian Approach," 25-27; Davids, "Gospels and the Jewish Tradition," 87-88; Kelber, *Oral and Written Gospel*, 17.

50. See Smith, "Comparison of Early Christian and Early Rabbinic Tradition," who has been (unfortunately) highly influential in attacking Gerhardsson's thesis for its anachronism. See similarly Shemaryahu Talmon, "Oral Tradition and Written Transmission, or the Heard and the Seen Word in Judaism of the Second Temple Period," in *Jesus and the Oral Gospel Tradition*, ed. Wansbrough, 132-33; Davids, "Gospels and the Jewish Tradition," 76-81. But note the penitent apology of Neusner for misrepresenting Gerhardsson in his initial review of *Memory and Manuscript*, as well as Neusner's scathing attack on Smith in the preface to the 1998 edition of *Memory and Manuscript*, xxv-xlvi. Neusner sees nothing wrong if, "[s]eeing the Rabbinic literature and the Gospels alike as models of phenomena, we then take the sources for what they are and value them for what they contain and exemplify" (xlvi). See also the sympathetic remarks by Bauckham (*Jesus and the Eyewitnesses*, 250) that, although Gerhardsson did assume too much continuity between Pharisaic and rabbinic Judaism, even so "Rabbinic Judaism could be an illuminating parallel despite being later than the New Testament period." Gerhardsson ("Path of the Gospel Tradition," 85) pleads: "I never pictured two four-cornered blocks, one rabbinical and the other early Christian, and said: these two are twins. I have never said that Jesus was only a rabbi, still less that he was a rabbi of the late Tannaitic type; that the disciples built a rabbinic academy in Jerusalem and that the gospel tradition was a ready-made entity which

was a more optimistic view of how far back the rabbinic traditions go. Even so, he maintained that the rabbinic methods of transmission in their mature form could not be traced back earlier than the destruction of Jerusalem (135 CE) or even to the destruction of the temple (70 CE). He always distinguished between Tannaitic and Amoraic rabbis (those before and after the compilation of the Mishnah in ca. 200 CE), mentioned the name of a rabbi to whom a text was attributed, and saw Rabbi Aqiba as a definite marker in the transitional period.[51] Gerhardsson's point is that although pedagogical techniques were refined after 70 and 135 CE, the essentials of the rabbinic method are traceable to an earlier period.[52] He urges that the "basic elements of pedagogics" were not broken in the revolutionary period of 65-135 CE. Rabbi Aqiba did not invent memorization.[53]

In support of Gerhardssson, we might add that memorization features significantly in Jewish education well-before the rabbinic era. A clear reference to the importance of memorization comes from 2 Maccabees: "we have aimed to please those who wish to read, to make it easy for those who are inclined to memorize, and to profit all readers" (2 Macc 2.25). Josephus emphasized memorization as a general feature of Jewish education.[54] Furthermore, the Gospels (Mark 7:1-15/Matt 15:1-11), Paul (Gal 1:14), Acts (6:14), and Josephus (*Ant.* 13.297-98) all attest that the Pharisees did indeed have an oral tradition independent of Scripture, and it was undoubtedly passed on through some form of memorization. Jacob Neusner has noted some mnemonic structures in pre-70 CE rabbinic materials.[55] Gerhardsson and Riesner were quite right to urge that pharisaic oral instruction possessed sufficient continuity with later rabbinic pedagogy. Consequently many scholars are taking seriously the view that, although the rabbinic didactic method

---

Jesus drilled into the disciples' memories and which they only had to repeat and to explicate." See also the cautionary but sympathetic remarks of Dale C. Allison, *Constructing Jesus: Memory, Imagination, and History* (Grand Rapids: Baker, 2011), 26 n. 105, toward Gerhardsson's thesis. A further positive evaluation of Gerhardsson's work is given by Werner Kelber, "The Work of Birger Gerhardsson in Perspective," in *Jesus in Memory: Traditions in Oral and Scribal Perspective*, ed. W. Kelber and S. Byrskog (Waco: Baylor University Press, 2009), 173-206.

51. Gerhardsson, *Memory and Manuscript*, xii, 77-78; idem, *Tradition and Transmission*, 14; idem, "Path of the Gospel Tradition," 85.

52. Gerhardsson, *Memory and Manuscript*, 76-78; idem, *Tradition and Transmission*, 16-21.

53. Gerhardsson, *Tradition and Transmission*, 14, 18; idem, "Path of the Gospel Tradition," 84-85.

54. Josephus, *Life* 8; *Against Apion* 1.60; 2.171-73, 204.

55. Neusner, "Rabbinic Traditions about the Pharisees before A.D. 70," 155-56.

belongs to a post-135 CE era, core elements of it probably existed in the pre-70 CE period.[56]

There is unequivocal evidence, not the least from Paul's letters, that early churches practiced a formal transmission of traditional material, "formal" in the sense that there was a deliberate effort to faithfully transmit traditions to others.[57] The New Testament and early Christian literature uses rabbinic-like terminology when it refers to the giving and receiving of traditional material. The references to a "tradition" (παράδοσις) that was handed on, as well the language of "delivering over" (παραδίδωμι) and "receiving" (παραλαμβάνω) a particular teaching transmitted to others, correspond to the rabbinic terms *māsar* (מסר) and *qibbēl* (קבל) used to describe the process of teachers delivering instruction to their pupils.[58] This provides at least one significant point of contact between the transmission of traditions in early Christianity and rabbinic Judaism.[59]

There is no reason to think that this process of transmitting a tradition is strictly a post-Easter phenomenon among followers of Jesus. The most frequent form of address for Jesus in the Gospels is "rabbi" (ῥαββί), and although Jesus transcends this category and fits partly into other leadership models (i.e., sage, healer, prophet, teacher, etc.), it is still an apt designation

---

56. Davids, "Gospels and the Jewish Tradition"; W. D. Davies, *The Setting of the Sermon on the Mount* (Cambridge: Cambridge University Press, 1964), 464-80; idem, "Reflections on a Scandinavian Approach," 10, 33-34; Sanders, *Jesus and Judaism*, 14-15; Philip S. Alexander, "Orality in Pharisaic-Rabbinic Judaism at the Turn of the Eras," in *Jesus and the Oral Gospel Tradition*, ed. Wansbrough, 159-84.

57. Cf. Bauckham, *Jesus and the Eyewitnesses*, 264.

58. παραδίδωμι: Mark 7:13 (traditions of elders); Luke 1:2; *Barnabas* 19.11 (Jesus tradition); Acts 6:14 (Pharisees and oral tradition); Rom 6:17 (pattern of teaching); 1 Cor 11:2, 23 (the Lord's Supper); 15:3-4 (the account of the resurrection); 2 Pet 2:21 (holy commandments); Jude 3 (the body of Christian teaching); cf. BDAG, 762-73. παράδοσις: Matt 15:2, 3, 6; Mark 7:3, 5, 8, 9, 13 (traditions of the elders); 1 Cor 11:2 (the Lord's Supper); Gal 1:14 (traditions of the fathers); Col 2:8 (traditions of men); 2 Thess 2:15; 3:6 (traditions taught to Christians). παραλαμβάνω: Mark 7:4 (traditions of the elders); 1 Cor 11:23 (the Lord's Supper); 15:1-3 (the account of the resurrection); Phil 4:9 (teachings from Paul); 1 Thess 2:13 (the word of God); 4:1-2 (Christian instruction); 2 Thess 3:6 (traditions from Paul); *Did.* 4.13 (commandments of the Lord). Note also the verbal connections between παραδίδωμι and παράδοσις in Mark 7:13 and 1 Cor 11:2 and between παραδίδωμι/παράδοσις and παραλαμβάνω in 2 Thess 3:6; 1 Cor 11:23; 15:3. See also, Riesenfeld, *Gospel Tradition*, 16; Gerhardsson, *Memory and Manuscript*, 290-91; idem, *Tradition and Transmission*, 7; BDAG, 763; Jaffee, *Torah in the Mouth*, 73-75.

59. Cf. Ben Witherington, *The Christology of Jesus* (Minneapolis: Fortress, 1990), 12; Paul W. Barnett, *Jesus and the Logic of History* (NSBT 3; Leicester: Apollos, 1997), 142-44.

for his didactic ministry.[60] As a rabbi, Jesus taught his disciples, and he expected them to learn what they had been instructed in. The Gospels also affirm that Jesus used his disciples to transmit his teachings to others during his lifetime (Mark 6:7-13; Luke 9:1-6; 10:1-16; Matt 9:36–10:15), which would have required his teaching to be retained and replicated by his closest followers.[61] The Jesus tradition had its rudimentary beginnings not in a rabbinic school, but in a "mission campaign" organized by Jesus himself.[62]

Memorization as an instructional tool was not limited to second- or third-century rabbinic practice, but was well known in the Greco-Roman world.[63] In Greek culture, professional bards could recite all of Homer by heart.[64] Students of rhetoric often memorized famous speeches.[65] Pliny the Younger praised orators who could repeat verbatim speeches he had delivered extemporaneously.[66] While the memorization of speeches was meant to be accurate, speeches learned by memory could also be revised or expanded.[67] In the philosophical schools, a teacher's disciples could collectively remember bits and pieces of speeches and sayings and bring them together to carry on their master's teachings.[68] The memorization of *chreiai* by repetition was practiced by children and adults.[69] When it comes to training by

---

60. Cf. Günther Bornkamm, *Jesus of Nazareth*, trans. Irene McLuskey, Fraser McLuskey, and James M. Robinson (London: Hodder & Stoughton, 1973), 57, 83, 96-97; Bruce D. Chilton, *Profiles of a Rabbi* (Atlanta: Scholars, 1989); idem, *Rabbi Jesus* (New York: Doubleday, 2000).

61. Davids, "Gospels and Jewish Tradition," 84; Riesner, *Jesus als Lehrer*, 453-75; idem, "Messianic Teacher," 422-23; Allison, *Constructing Jesus*, 25-26.

62. Gerd Theissen, *The New Testament: A Literary History*, trans. L. M. Maloney (Minneapolis: Fortress, 2012), 23, 25.

63. According to Libanius (*Autobiography* 11): "Now when I had committed to memory the works of those who were most renowned for their stylistic abilities, the urge for this way of life came over me." Cf. similarly Plato, *Euthydemos* 276D; Horace, *Ep.* 1.18.12-14; Quintilian, *Inst.* 1.3.1; 2.4.15; 11.2.1-51; Seneca, *Controversiae* 1. pref. 2; Plutarch, *De Liberis Educandis* 13; Philo, *De Vita Mosis* 1.48; Xenophon, *Symposium* 3.5-6; Diogenes Laertius, *Vitae* 10.1.12. See Gerhardsson, *Memory and Manuscript*, 123-26; Riesner, *Jesus als Lehrer*, 440-43; Craig S. Keener, *A Commentary on the Gospel of Matthew* (Grand Rapids: Eerdmans, 1999), 28; idem, *The Gospel of John: A Commentary* (2 vols.; Peabody: Hendrickson, 2004), 1:57-62; idem, *The Historical Jesus of the Gospels* (Grand Rapids: Eerdmans, 2009), 145-48; Bauckham, *Jesus and the Eyewitnesses*, 280-87.

64. Xenophon, *Symposium* 3.5-6.

65. Eunapion, *Vitae Sophistarum* 2.8; Cicero, *De Inventione* 1.9; Quintilian, *Inst.* 11.2.1-51.

66. Pliny, *Ep.* 2.3.3.

67. Seneca, *Ep.* 33.4.

68. Philostratus, *Vitae Sophistarum* 1.22.524.

69. Dio Chrysostom, *Orationes* 72.11; Seneca, *Ep.* 33.7.

memorization, there is no significant discontinuity between rabbinic and Greco-Roman evidence.[70] All of this means that learning by memory was simply part of ancient education. Memory was undoubtedly selective and imperfect, yet Riesner rightly comments: "Nevertheless, every scholar who tries to reconstruct to some degree the original wording of Jesus' sayings implicitly affirms that in the process of oral transmission there must have been some learning by heart."[71]

According to Jan Vansina, the conditions necessary for oral tradition to be transmitted reliably over time are: (1) the existence of fixed transmitters, and (2) the use of mnemonic techniques as aids to securing the traditions.[72] The memorability of Jesus' words, plus the ancient method of students memorizing the instruction of their teachers, combined with eyewitnesses and teachers as authenticators of the tradition, would seem to provide us with those two conditions. Granted now that memories are not infallible and are very much *constructed* on the basis of present experience, memories can also be *constrained* by the subject remembering something unusual or vivid, being emotionally involved in the event, and retaining outlines over details and by the memory becoming ingrained by the frequency of recall and tested by interaction with other rememberers.[73] While I do not think that the Scandinavian approach has the explanatory power to account for the diversity of the tradition and the somewhat more "informal" way it was often transmitted, nonetheless, it does have a genuine utility for accounting for the contours and content of the Jesus tradition in its Jewish context. So much so that Gerd Theissen comments, "Despite reservations concerning a direct transfer of rabbinic techniques of transmission to early Christianity, we must recognize that we have here a historical analogy to the process of tradition in Christianity's earliest phase."[74]

70. Keener, *Historical Jesus*, 150.

71. Riesner, "Jesus as Preacher and Teacher," 203.

72. Jan Vansina, *Oral Tradition as History* (Madison: University of Wisconsin Press, 1985), 31.

73. Cf. Bauckham, *Jesus and the Eyewitnesses*, 330-35, 341-46.

74. Gerd Theissen, *The Gospels in Context: Social and Political History in the Synoptic Tradition*, trans. Linda M. Maloney (Minneapolis: Fortress, 1991), 3 n. 3. Cf. Alexander, "Orality in Pharisaic-Rabbinic Judaism," 184: "Rabbinic models may be particularly relevant to elucidating how the early Christian groups elaborated and passed on their traditions. Comparison of the later rabbinic schools with the New Testament is, perhaps, all the more plausible because . . . rabbinic schools are not, broadly speaking, a distinctively rabbinic institution: they are an example of a cultural phenomenon widespread through the whole of the Middle East and the Mediterranean, a phenomenon established well before the rise of Christianity." Kelber, "Work

Between Orality and Textuality

Werner Kelber has attempted to demonstrate the relevance of folklore and anthropological studies for study of the Jesus tradition. He asserts a radical difference between oral and written communication. In written texts the author exercises exclusive hegemony over the communicative act.[75] Yet most unlike written texts, oral/aural communication results in an "oral synthesis" between speaker and audience.[76] In oral tradition the audience affects the oral performance and thereby participates in the construction of the message. This social process means, against Bultmann, that oral tradition about Jesus commenced during his life and is not strictly a post-Easter phenomenon.[77] Conversely, against Gerhardsson, Kelber maintains that "oral transmission is controlled by the law of *social identification* rather than by the technique of verbatim memorization."[78] The oral transmission that Kelber theorizes includes both formulaic stability and compositional variability.

Kelber's primary concern, however, is to argue for a sharp disjunction between the natures of oral performance and written texts. This leads him to postulate separate species of hermeneutics for the two forms of communication. Kelber supposes that "the very genre of the written gospel may be linked with the intent to provide a radical alternative to a preceding tradition."[79]

In criticism, many have responded that Kelber posits too great a chasm between oral and written media.[80] It is asked why and how Mark has retained features of oral communication in his text if the two mediums were so incompatible. One also gets the impression that the Gospel writers wrote their accounts in oral mode. Regardless of how significant Mark was in tex-

---

of Birger Gerhardsson," 177: Gerhardsson "advanced an explanatory model that was suited to demonstrate the historical concreteness of the traditioning processes and the actual techniques that were operative in the transmission and reception of the tradition."

75. Kelber, *Oral and the Written Gospel*, 14-15.

76. Kelber, *Oral and the Written Gospel*, 19.

77. Kelber, *Oral and the Written Gospel*, 20-21.

78. Kelber, *Oral and the Written Gospel*, 24, 21 (italics original).

79. Kelber, *Oral and the Written Gospel*, xvii.

80. Gerhardsson, *Gospel Tradition*, 113-43; Henaut, *Oral Tradition and the Gospels*, 73; Dunn, *Jesus Remembered*, 202-3. See also John Halverson, "Oral and Written Gospel: A Critique of Werner Kelber," *NTS* 40 (1994): 180-95; L. W. Hurtado, "Greco-Roman Textuality and the Gospel of Mark: A Critical Assessment of Werner Kelber's *The Oral and the Written Gospel*," *BBR* 7 (1997): 91-106. Gamble, *Books and Readers*, 30: "a strong distinction between the oral and the written modes is anachronistic to the extent that it presupposes both the modern notion of fixity of a text and modern habits of reading."

tualizing the Jesus tradition, we should not suppose that the composition of the Marcan Gospel led to a moratorium on oral performance of the Jesus tradition or that the appearance of Mark necessarily domesticated and froze the Jesus tradition, as a comparison of Mark with Matthew, Luke, and John indicates. The bifurcation between oral and textual transmission is also needless since any given pericope or logion may have oscillated from oral to written forms at various stages in its transmission and amid multiple streams of preservation. In which case, as Samuel Byrskog says, "There is no such thing as pure orality in early Christianity but various 'oralities' and interactions with scribal practices."[81] There also remains the question of applying folklore, Homeric rhapsodists, and socio-anthropological studies to the Jesus tradition. More appropriate parallels for the emergence and handling of the Jesus tradition are to be discovered in second temple Jewish and Greco-Roman sources.[82]

Informal Controlled Oral Tradition

Back in the mid-1990s, Kenneth Bailey made his own contribution to the debate by proposing an alternative theory of the transmission process.[83] Bailey rejects the form-critical view about a radical kerygmatizing of the tradition (informal uncontrolled tradition) and also the Scandinavian view of a rabbinic pedagogy (formal controlled tradition). Instead, he advocates a model that he labels informal controlled oral tradition.[84] On this model the tradition is transmitted informally: anyone in the community can theoretically participate in the retelling of stories and sayings. It is also controlled, however, since the traditions are owned by the community at large. The type of material transmitted in this setting includes proverbs, riddles, po-

---

81. Samuel Byrskog, "A New Perspective on the Jesus Tradition: Reflections on James D. G. Dunn's *Jesus Remembered*," in *Memories of Jesus: A Critical Appraisal of James D. G. Dunn's* Jesus Remembered, ed. R. B. Stewart and G. R. Habermas (Nashville: Broadman & Holman, 2010), 75.

82. Talmon, "Oral Tradition and Written Transmission," 121-58; Alexander, "Orality in Pharisaic-Rabbinic Judaism," 159-84; David E. Aune, "Prolegomena to the Study of Oral Tradition in the Hellenistic World," in *Jesus and the Oral Gospel Tradition*, ed. Wansbrough, 59-106.

83. Kenneth E. Bailey, "Informal Controlled Oral Tradition and the Synoptic Gospels," *AJT* 5 (1991): 34-54; reprinted in *Themelios* 20 (1995): 4-11 (all further references are from *Themelios*); idem, "Middle Eastern Oral Tradition and the Synoptic Gospels," *ExpT* 106 (1995): 363-67.

84. Bailey, "Informal Controlled Oral Tradition," 4; idem, "Middle Eastern Oral Tradition," 364.

etry, parables, and stories of important figures in the history of the village. Allowance is made for varieties of flexibility in the tradition, ranging from "no flexibility" for poems and proverbs, to "some flexibility" for parables and recollections of historical figures where the "central threads" of the story cannot be changed, but flexibility in detail is allowed. Finally there is "total flexibility" for jokes and casual news that is "irrelevant to the identity of the community and is not judged wise or valuable."[85] This model is close to Øivind Andersen's suggestion of oral transmission operating in a setting that is "structured but open."[86] Bailey produces a wonderful range of anecdotes and illustrations (ancient and modern) drawn from his own exposure to village life in thirty years of teaching in the Middle East.

When applied to Synoptic studies, Bailey suggests that his model functioned in the villages of Palestine up to the Jewish revolt against Rome in 70 CE. What is more, the types of material contained in the Synoptic Gospels include those forms preserved by informal controlled oral tradition, including proverbs, parables, poems, dialogues, conflict stories, and historical narratives. Bailey concludes that "the *informal* yet *controlled* oral tradition of the settled Middle Eastern village can provide a methodological framework within which to perceive and interpret the bulk of the material before us."[87]

Several factors count against Bailey's thesis:[88] (1) His anecdotes drawn

---

85. Bailey, "Informal Controlled Oral Tradition," 7-8; idem, "Middle Eastern Oral Tradition," 366.

86. Øivind Andersen, "Oral Tradition," in *Jesus and the Oral Gospel Tradition,* ed. Wansbrough, 19.

87. Bailey, "Informal Controlled Oral Tradition," 10 (italics original).

88. The strongest critique of Bailey has come from Theodore J. Weeden, "Kenneth Bailey's Theory of Oral Tradition: A Theory Contested by Its Evidence," *JSHJ* 7 (2009): 3-43, who questions whether Bailey's anecdotal evidence about Middle Eastern village life really does reflect an "informal controlled oral tradition," since many of the stories told by these communities are perpetuated not to preserve archaic historical facts but to validate the social identity of an oral society (33, 37). Weeden also contests the accuracy of Bailey's accounts of the career of the Scottish missionary John Hogg in Egypt, believing instead that the discrepancies between Bailey's oral account and the published biography written by Hogg's daughter Rena reflects instead an "informal uncontrolled oral tradition" (20). Weeden also protests that the *haflat samar* were not formal settings for preserving oral traditions but parties for entertainment by telling stories (38-42). In the end, Weeden concedes that Bailey's anecdotes do support "some form" of informal controlled oral tradition, but he doubts whether Bailey's theory of oral tradition represents a useful model for describing the transmission of the Jesus tradition (42-43).

In response, some of the differences that Weeden sees between Bailey's and Rena Hogg's account of John Hogg can easily be explained by her redaction of her sources and not by the wide-scale breakdown of the tradition (e.g., whether John Hogg's robbers were "converted"

from modern village life are just that, anecdotes. More rigorous socio-anthropological study is required to substantiate Bailey's theory. (2) For Bailey's hypothesis to work we must assume that the transmitters of the tradition, the kinds of material used, the controls exercised by the community, and the techniques for introducing new material used in Middle Eastern communities is virtually identical with what happened in the early church's handling of the Jesus tradition.[89] While analogies between Bailey's model and the early church can be imagined, we cannot be certain about them. (3) Even if Bailey's theory holds its own in a Palestinian environment, we still have the problem of what transpired when the Jesus tradition moved abroad to Syria, Greece, and Rome, where, most probably, the Gospels were actually written. (4) As Bailey admits, both *informal uncontrolled* and *formal controlled* models are extant in Middle Eastern settings.[90] By implication the same would be true also in first-century Palestine, in which case the Jesus tradition could have been preserved by different models, with different degrees of regulation, in different settings, depending on the context of the tradents and their attitude toward the tradition.

These drawbacks should not blind us to the relative strengths of Bai-

---

or were "convicted of their evil ways" and whether he had "urine" or "vile water" poured on his head while preaching hardly represents a distortion of the tradition!). More problematic is that Weeden seems to presume an original version preserved by Rena Hogg that then counts against Bailey's version. Apart from privileging Rena Hogg's written account, Weeden fails to grapple with the nature of oral tradition as a rehearsal of the same story, continuous in outline, but always with variation in detail. Oral tradition gives us variant versions of the same story, and Bailey posits a legitimate explanation for a mechanism to explain the flexibility and constancy in the retellings. Also, Rena Hogg's claim that stories about her father had begun to mix fact with fiction looks like a post-Victorian literary device to bring proper sensibility to popular rumors and to incline readers to adhere to her account. I would add that details of John Hogg's life never develop in a legendary direction. We do not see the band of a few robbers becoming a tribe of robbers, no miraculous elements are introduced, the needs of the Egyptian Protestant communities do not result in a rewrite of the history of John Hogg's life — in other words, everything that the form critics think happened to the Jesus tradition does not happen to the history of John Hogg's life.

Weeden is correct, however, that Bailey's anecdotes support a form of informal controlled oral tradition, one that has perhaps more flexibility and variation than Bailey noted but still retains a general accuracy in characterization, outline, sequence, geography, and significance. See, in defense of Bailey, James D. G. Dunn, "Kenneth Bailey's Theory of Oral Tradition: Critiquing Theodore Weeden's Critique," *JSHJ* 7 (2009): 44-62.

89. Bailey, "Informal Controlled Oral Tradition," 6.

90. Bailey, "Informal Controlled Oral Tradition," 6; idem, "Middle Eastern Oral Tradition," 364.

ley's proposal: (1) The model is far more analogous to Middle Eastern village life compared to other models which depend on studies of Homeric epics in ancient Greece or folklore studies from the early twentieth-century Balkans. (2) The type of material found in the Gospels resonates with the kind of material transmitted in an informal controlled environment. (3) Bailey also accounts for stability and flexibility in the Jesus tradition, whereas the form-critical and Scandinavian models tend to emphasize one over the other. (4) The proposal accentuates the role of "community" in handling the tradition. (5) Bailey's model is also garnering assent among Jesus scholars, who have found in it a suitable paradigm for oral transmission.[91]

II. A New Paradigm: Jesus in Social Memory

The theory of an "informally controlled" oral tradition looks like a plausible and realistic model for how the Jesus tradition might have been transmitted. However, it rests on largely anecdotal evidence and is at best analogous to

---

91. Wright, *Jesus and the Victory of God*, 135-36; Craig L. Blomberg, *Jesus and the Gospels: An Introduction and Survey* (Leicester: Apollos, 1997), 84; Dunn, *Jesus Remembered*, 205-10; idem, "Jesus in Oral Memory: The Initial Stages of the Jesus Tradition," in *Jesus: A Colloquium in the Holy Land*, ed. D. Donnelly (London: Continuum, 2001), 81-145; idem, *A New Perspective on Jesus: What the Quests for the Historical Jesus Missed* (Grand Rapids: Baker, 2005), 45-46; idem, "Remembering Jesus," 194-95; idem, *Jesus, Paul, and the Gospels* (Grand Rapids: Eerdmans, 2011), 37-38; Paul R. Eddy and Gregory A. Boyd, *The Jesus Legend: A Case for the Historical Reliability of the Synoptic Jesus Tradition* (Grand Rapids: Baker, 2007), 262-63 n. 84. Kelly R. Iverson, "Orality and the Gospels: A Survey of Research," *CBR* 8 (2009): 91, concludes that the "cumulative force of this work is compelling." Somewhat ambivalent is Allison, *Jesus of Nazareth*, 73 n. 280; note also the cautions of Markus Bockmuehl, *Seeing the Word: Refocusing New Testament Study* (STI; Grand Rapids: Baker, 2006), 175 n. 26, who regards Bailey's model as too unsubstantiated to support the burden of proof attributed to it. Birger Gerhardsson, "The Secret of the Transmission of the Unwritten Jesus Tradition," *NTS* 51 (2005): 6-7, believes that the relationship between modern Arab peasant culture and ancient Jewish customs is uncertain, making Bailey's comparisons "precarious." Bauckham, *Jesus and the Eyewitnesses*, 252-63, thinks that Bailey has not explained the precise mechanism for control of the tradition and that his account of stability and flexibility in informal controlled tradition is also applicable to a formally controlled tradition. According to Samuel Byrskog ("New Perspective on the Jesus Tradition," 68): "In order to work as an 'explanatory model' for the Jesus tradition, it [Bailey's model] needs to have some kind of link to texts that portray such practices in the ancient sociocultural setting. Moreover, it must account not only for the performance of a small village gathering but also for the urban setting of early Christian house meetings. It does neither of these things."

how the Jesus tradition could have been transmitted in the early churches. Therefore, it needs to be supplemented or perhaps even supplanted by a theory that accounts for the selectivity and subjectivity involved in passing on the tradition. If Jesus was "remembered" by eyewitnesses and if much of the Jesus tradition was "memorized" within the earliest churches, then we need to develop a theory of memory to account for the transmission of the tradition.[92] We are not dealing simply with the memories of key individuals but are pursuing instead the individual, collective, and cultural memories that acquired currency in the early churches. When a memory is shared within a group it becomes in some sense a corporate memory, since others can now rehearse the same memory in new performances, and similarly the group can also regulate and correct the factuality of any new recital by common consent, especially if the originators of the memory are still present.[93]

92. According to Jens Schröter ("Remarks on James D. G. Dunn's Approach to Jesus Research," in *Memories of Jesus*, ed. Stewart and Habermas, 130-31): "History . . . therefore [does not give] an image of the past as it 'really' was but as it appears under the circumstances of the present. Consequently, the idea of recovering 'real' events of the past should be replaced by a model of history as 'remembered past.' Consequently, the idea of recovering 'real' events of bygone times should be replaced by an understanding of history as remembered past. To put it in my own words, history, as image of the past, is always due to revisions and modifications." Accordingly, we might say that a lack of reflection on the concept of memory in relation to orality is a major lacuna in the work of the early form critics. See Wolfgang Schadewaldt, "Die Zuverlässigkeit der synoptischen Tradition," *Theologische Beiträge* 13 (1982): 220; Werner H. Kelber, "The Case of the Gospels: Memory's Desire and the Limits of Historical Criticism," *Oral Tradition* 17 (2005): 65; Judith C. Redman, "How Accurate Are Eyewitnesses? Bauckham and the Eyewitnesses in Light of Psychological Research," *JBL* 129 (2010): 193.

93. In my mind, Bauckham (*Jesus and the Eyewitnesses*, 310-18; cf. Samuel Byrskog, "A New Perspective on the Jesus Tradition: Reflections on James Dunn's *Jesus Remembered*," *JSNT* 26 [2004]: 464-68) plays down too much the collective aspect of memory in favor of the individual memories of eyewitnesses (in implicit dialogue with Dunn's *Jesus Remembered*). Bauckham is concerned that a focus on collective memory forgoes the role of eyewitnesses as individual owners of their memory even when shared with a group (313-16), that it does not take into account the role of eyewitnesses as spokespersons for the group's attempt to make sense of the present by remembering the past, and that emphasis on collective memory could lead to the kind of erroneous model proposed by the form critics where the Jesus tradition was manufactured largely out of community needs (317-18). Though Dunn, "On History, Memory and Eyewitnesses: In Response to Bengt Holmberg and Samuel Byrskog," *JSNT* 26 (2004): 482, believes otherwise: "I have no desire to play down the importance of individuals in the process. I may not have given them the emphasis and attention that S[amuel]B[yrskog] thinks necessary, but I do emphasize the role of teachers, of 'apostolic custodians' and church-founding apostles, I stress not least the function of Jesus' disciples generating tradition by sharing their personal 'eyewitness' experiences, and I envisage assemblies dependent on such individuals

The model I am espousing here, which I have labeled "Jesus in social memory," takes its cue from James Dunn's work *Jesus Remembered*. Dunn attempts to establish a hermeneutic for study of the historical Jesus that avoids the futile pursuit of objective history and evades the jaws of historical skepticism. The Jesus tradition bears traces of the impact that Jesus had on his disciples. That "impact" includes a hermeneutical circle that oscillates between authentic recollection of Jesus in tandem with the ongoing cognitive processing of that encounter in the subsequent experience of the disciples. He states, "What we actually have in the earliest retellings of what is now the Synoptic tradition, then, are the memories of the first disciples — not Jesus himself, but the remembered Jesus."[94] The central tenet is that who Jesus is can be determined only by his effect on his followers. Because an impact

---

and 'senior disciples' retelling again particular elements of the tradition. But on the other hand, it is not really possible to speak of *tradition* except as community tradition." I. Howard Marshall, "A New Consensus on Oral Tradition? A Review of Richard Bauckham's *Jesus and the Eyewitnesses*," 6 (2009): 190-91, shows that Bauckham's and Dunn's views are not mutually exclusive: "We are dealing with comparatively minor differences between allies who form a solid phalanx against the mistaken view of the tradition that they are opposing." Similar is Iverson, "Orality and the Gospels," 94: "their competing models should not obscure a shared view of oral tradition." Byrskog ("New Perspective on the Jesus Tradition," 71) could later say that "the corporate activity of a group in no way should deter the attention from the role of specific persons behind the tradition or within the traditioning group."

94. Dunn, *Jesus Remembered*, 130-31; see also idem, *The Living Word* (Philadelphia: Fortress, 1987), 27-44; idem, *New Perspective*, 35-56; idem, *Jesus, Paul, and the Gospels*, 7-8, 22-44. Note Dahl's similar comment ("Anamnesis: Memory and Commemoration in Early Christianity," in *Jesus in the Memory of the Early Church* [Minneapolis: Augsburg, 1976], 28-29): "The historical critic will conclude from this that what is to be sought in the gospels is first of all the disciples' memory of Jesus, not the life of Jesus." Le Donne, *The Historiographical Jesus*, 76: "For those disciples of the first generation, the real Jesus was the Jesus of their memory." Francis Watson, "Veritas Christi: How to Get from the Jesus of History to the Christ of Faith without Losing One's Way," in *Seeking the Identity of Jesus*, ed. Hays and Gaventa, 108: "We hear of Jesus only what the first Christians wanted us to hear. That is the grain of truth in the claim that the Gospels give us direct access only to the early Christian communities and not to Jesus himself. But it would be better to say that the Gospels give us direct access to Jesus as he was received within the early communities." See also N. A. Dahl, "The Problem of the Historical Jesus," in *Jesus the Christ: The Historical Origins of Christological Doctrine* (Minneapolis: Fortress, 1991), 94; Jens Schröter, *Erinnerung an Jesu Worte. Studien zur Rezeption der Logienüberlieferung in Markus, Q und Thomas* (Neukirchen-Vluyn: Neukirchener, 1997), 1-5, 462-66, 482-86; Luke Timothy Johnson, *The Writings of the New Testament: An Interpretation* (rev. ed.; London: SCM, 1999), 125-55; Gerhardsson, *Memory and Manuscript*, 329-33; idem, *Tradition and Transmission*, 43; idem, *Origin of the Gospel Tradition*, 46; Stephen Hultgren, *Narrative Elements in the Double Tradition: A Study of their Place within the Framework of the Gospel Narrative* (BZNW 113; Berlin: de Gruyter, 2002), 354.

happened, a tradition was a created, a tradition that bore the marks of Jesus' influence and the disciples' memory. Consequently the gap between Jesus and the Gospels was not an empty space but was inhabited by people influenced by Jesus. Since Jesus said and did memorable things, the memory of such sayings and deeds filled that space. These memories of Jesus, when verbalized or inscribed, became the Jesus tradition. The memories were shared, circulated, and elaborated, often material was grouped together differently, with conclusions drawn to show the relevance of the stories for the current situation of the audience.[95] Though many will quibble over the details of Dunn's paradigm (especially its failure to engage actual social memory theory!), it remains a heuristically valuable approach to the formation of the Jesus tradition and a profitable model for explaining the development of the Gospels.

Unsurprisingly, in the aftermath of Dunn's volume there has been an explosion of interest in studies related to the Jesus tradition and memory theory. The sociology and psychology of memory have been increasingly mapped onto the fields of Gospel studies.[96] The result has led to a more so-

---

95. Dunn, *Jesus, Paul, and the Gospels*, 44.

96. Cf. *before* Dunn, W. S. Taylor, "Memory and the Gospel Tradition," *TT* 14 (1959): 470-79; Nils A. Dahl, "Anamnesis: Memory and Commemoration in Early Christianity," in *Jesus in the Memory of the Early Church* (Minneapolis: Augsburg, 1976), 11-29 (and 167-75); G. M. Keightley, "The Church's Memory of Jesus: A Social Science Analysis of 1 Thessalonians," *BTB* 17 (1987): 149-56; Jens Schröter, "The Historical Jesus and the Sayings Tradition: Comments on Current Research," *NeoT* 30 (1996): 151-68; idem, *Erinnerung an Jesu Worte*; Werner H. Kelber, "The Case of the Gospels: Memory's Desire and the Limitations of Historical Criticism," *Oral Tradition* 17 (2002): 55-86; Richard Horsley, "Oral Tradition in New Testament Studies," *Oral Tradition* 18 (2003): 34-36; and *after* Dunn especially Alan Kirk and Tom Thatcher, "Jesus Tradition as Social Memory," in *Memory, Tradition, and Text: Uses of the Past in Early Christianity*, ed. Kirk and Thatcher (Semeia 52; Leiden: Brill, 2005), 25-42; P. J. J. Botha, "New Testament Texts in the Context of Reading Practices of the Roman Period: The Role of Memory and Performance," *Scriptura* 90 (2005): 621-40; Werner Kelber, "The Generative Force of Memory: Early Christian Traditions as Processes of Remembering," *BTB* 36 (2006): 15-22; Bauckham, *Jesus and the Eyewitnesses*, 310-57; Tom Thatcher, *Why John Wrote a Gospel: Jesus — Memory — History* (Louisville: Westminster John Knox, 2006); Richard A. Horsley, Jonathan A. Draper, and John Miles Foley, eds., *Performing the Gospel: Orality, Memory, and Mark: Essays Dedicated to Werner Kelber* (Minneapolis: Fortress, 2006); Scot McKnight and Terence C. Mournet, eds., *Jesus in Early Christian Memory* (LNTS 359; London: Clark, 2007); Stephen C. Barton, Loren T. Stuckenbruck, and Benjamin G. Wold, eds., *Memory in the Bible and Antiquity: The Fifth Durham-Tübingen Research Symposium* (WUNT 212; Tübingen: Mohr, 2007); Werner Kelber and Samuel Byrskog, eds., *Jesus in Memory: Traditions in Oral and Scribal Perspectives* (Waco: Baylor University Press, 2009); Rafael Rodriguez, *Structuring Early Christian Memory: Jesus in Tradition, Performance, and Text* (LNTS 407; London: Clark, 2010); Yoon-Man Park, *Mark's Memory Resources and the Controversy Stories (Mark 2:1–3:6)*:

phisticated and thicker description of the Jesus tradition as "memory" using the social-science field of social memory studies (e.g., Tom Thatcher, Jens Schröter, Alan Kirk, Chris Keith, Anthony Le Donne, and Rafael Rodriguez). In social memory theory, the past is not something that is purely a matter of a cognitive store-and-retrieve function; rather, past memories are mounted on mental artifacts that are reconstructed in light of the needs of the present. Social memory theory allows us to see past memories as something that continue to shape the present, and their social nature means that they will always transcend or even correct any individual recital. At the same time, the past is refracted or reconstructed in light of the present, and the present situation even imposes itself on the past. In which case, "memory" is the constant renegotiation of past and present in social and cultural frameworks. Social memory provides a way of conceptualizing how groups like the early church appropriate the past in light of and with respect to their present contexts.

What validates this model of Jesus in social memory is the frequent reference to the Jesus tradition as *memory* or the repeated description of Jesus being *remembered* in the earliest churches.[97] To begin with, there are clear indications in the Gospel that the impetus to remember Jesus began during his own lifetime.

The story of the anonymous woman who anointed Jesus in Bethany at the house of Simon the Leper has her deed memorialized because Jesus tells his disciples, "wherever the gospel is preached throughout the world, what she has done will also be told, *in memory of her* (εἰς μνημόσυνον αὐτῆς)" (Matt 26:13/Mark 14:9). This *chreia* illustrates precisely Mark's own under-

---

An Application of the Frame Theory of Cognitive Science to the Markan Oral-Aural Narrative (Leiden: Brill, 2009); Kelly R. Iverson, "Orality and the Gospels: A Survey of Research," *CBR* 8 (2009): 71-106; Robert Stewart and Gary R. Habermas, eds., *Memories of Jesus: A Critical Appraisal of James D. G. Dunn's Jesus Remembered* (Nashville: Broadman and Holman, 2010); Ruben Zimmermann, "Memory and Form Criticism: The Typicality of Memory as a Bridge between Orality and Literality in the Early Christian Remembering Process," in *The Interface of Orality and Writing,* ed. Weissenrieder and Coote, 130-43; Le Donne, *Historiographical Jesus;* Allison, *Constructing Jesus,* 1-30; Redman, "How Accurate Are Eyewitnesses?" 177-97; Dennis C. Dulling, "Social Memory and Biblical Studies: Theory, Method, and Application," *BTB* 26 (2006): 2-3; idem, "Memory, Collective Memory, Orality and the Gospels," *HTS* 67 (2011): 103-13; William D. Shiell, *Delivering from Memory: The Effect of Performance on the Early Christian Audience* (Eugene: Pickwick, 2011); Chris Keith, "Memory and Authenticity: Jesus Tradition and What Really Happened," *ZNW* 102 (2011): 155-77; idem, *Jesus' Literacy: Scribal Culture and the Teacher from Galilee* (LNTS 413; London: Clark, 2011), 27-70; Robert K. McIver, *Memory, Jesus, and the Synoptic Gospels* (Atlanta: Society of Biblical Literature, 2011).

97. Cf. Dahl, "Anamnesis," 25-29.

standing that the individual stories representing the pre-Easter life of Jesus are vehicles for the announcement of the good news in his own time.[98]

At Jesus' Passover meal with his disciples, one of his symbolic gestures was that "he took bread, gave thanks and broke it, and gave it to them, saying, 'This is my body given for you; *do this in remembrance of me* (τοῦτο ποιεῖτε εἰς τὴν ἐμὴν ἀνάμνησιν)'" (Luke 22:19). The Lucan words of institution were known to Paul and became a living memory that was duly handed on and received by others (1 Cor 11:23-25). The notion of remembrance was pivotal to celebration of the Passover.[99] Yet in Jesus' "Last Supper" the call for remembrance is not merely affective, that is, a cognitive recall of prior events; instead, the meal was fundamentally about mimesis (i.e., "do this"). That is, imitation and replication of the act in the future was for the purpose of remembrance. We have here a perfect example of a pre-Easter story, crucially important for understanding Jesus' death, laden with rich symbolic import, in which imitation of Jesus results in commemoration of his death.

During Jesus' trial, when Peter denied Jesus for the third time, a cock again crowed, and we are told that "*Peter remembered the words* (ἀνεμνήσθη ὁ Πέτρος τὸ ῥῆμα) that Jesus had spoken to him" (Matt 26:75/Mark 14:72/Luke 22:61). The words in question are Jesus' prediction of Peter's imminent denial of him (Matt 26:34-35/Mark 14:30-31/Luke 21:31-34). Peter's failure is built on a remembrance of Jesus' words; these memorable words provide the sting for his failure and the pain behind his remorse. Since readers or hearers of Mark also know of Peter's restoration (Mark 16:7; cf. John 21:15-19), they also know that the denial was not the end of the story for Peter. In fact, the memory of Peter's failure here might well have encouraged believers, perhaps in Rome, who also felt the temptation to lapse under pressure. In which case, remembrance of the words of Jesus and of the failure and restoration of Peter were intertwined in the social memory of the church.

In the Johannine farewell discourse, Jesus informs his disciples that future persecution will provide an occasion to recall his warnings to them. Jesus urges his disciples to *remember* his words that a servant is not greater than his master, explaining why it is that in the future they will be persecuted just as he was (John 15:20). Later Jesus tells his disciples that when they are persecuted, they need to *remember* his words, and recall that he warned them about this in advance (16:4). The Johannine tradition witnesses to the importance of "remembering" (μνημονεύω) as a way of explaining a post-

---

98. M. Eugene Boring, *Mark* (NTL; Louisville: Westminster John Knox, 2006), 384.
99. Cf. Exod 12:14; Deut 16:3; *m. Pesaḥim* 10.5.

Easter situation of persecution by way of a pre-Easter dominical tradition that warned of its eventual occurrence.

A further interesting phenomenon is how pre-Easter words of Jesus are not simply recalled but accentuated by remembering them in a post-Easter setting. The Fourth Gospel provides two prime examples of a post-Easter remembrance of a pre-Easter episode. First, when Jesus issues his parabolic challenge to the Judeans to destroy the temple, which he will then raise in three days, the enigmatic words are explained by the Evangelist in an editorial remark: "After he was raised from the dead, his disciples recalled (ἐμνήσθησαν) what he had said. Then they believed the scripture and the words that Jesus had spoken" (John 2:22). Second, the Johannine Jesus' fulfillment of Scripture at his triumphal entry (i.e., Zech 9:9) is only grasped by his disciples much later, hence the explanation: "At first his disciples did not understand all this. Only after Jesus was glorified did they remember (ἐμνήσθησαν) that these things had been written about him and that these things had been done to him" (John 12:16).

Shifting to Luke, the Easter experience included an impetus to "remember" that Jesus taught his disciples that he would rise again. The angel tells the women at the tomb, "He is not here; he has risen! Remember how he told you (μνήσθητε ὡς ἐλάλησεν ὑμῖν), while he was still with you in Galilee . . . 'The Son of Man must be delivered over to the hands of sinners, be crucified and on the third day be raised again.'" Immediately following we are told, "Then they remembered his words (καὶ ἐμνήσθησαν τῶν ῥημάτων αὐτοῦ)," indicating that in Luke's telling the Easter experiences induced and underlined pre-Easter memories (Luke 24:6-8).

Luke and John did not fuse the pre- and post-Easter horizons together; rather, Easter experiences instilled a new framework in which to remember the pre-Easter history of Jesus. According to John, the soon-to-be-sent Holy Spirit "will teach you all things and will remind you (ὑπομνήσει ὑμᾶς) of everything I have said to you," with specific respect to obeying Jesus' teaching and acknowledging that he was sent by the Father (John 14:26). Analogously, in Luke's resurrection narrative, a proper "remembering" of Jesus' mission and understanding of Scripture takes place only after Jesus has "opened their minds so they could understand the scriptures" (Luke 24:45). The post-Easter period is represented as a time that brings noetic illumination and scriptural interpretation to bear on remembrance of Jesus. Thus, the Easter experience did not wipe memories or facilely fabricate memories; instead, it provided an impetus for real memories to be recalled and reinterpreted along the lines of a new messianic hermeneutic created by faith in Jesus as the risen Lord.

In the rest of the New Testament and early Christian literature, remembering Jesus' words and deeds constituted the pinnacle of exhortation since there was no higher authority that one could turn to for instruction. In Peter's speech in Jerusalem, explaining why he chose to enter the house of the Gentile Cornelius in Joppa, he recounts how, upon his preaching the good news, the Gentiles received the Holy Spirit just as the Jerusalem church had, leading to Peter's justification of his actions with a recollection of Jesus' words: "Then I remembered what the Lord had said (ἐμνήσθην δὲ τοῦ ῥήματος τοῦ κυρίου): 'John baptized with water, but you will be baptized with the Holy Spirit.' So if God gave them the same gift he gave us who believed in the Lord Jesus Christ, who was I to think that I could stand in God's way?" (Acts 11:16-17). Here charismatic experience and breaking perceived norms is explained and justified with reference to the Jesus tradition. Later in Acts, in Paul's farewell speech to the Ephesian elders, the Apostle vouches for his good example to them and the necessity of pastoral care, and he justifies this with reference to an otherwise unknown saying from the Jesus tradition: "In everything I did, I showed you that by this kind of hard work we must help the weak, remembering the words the Lord Jesus himself said (μνημονεύειν τε τῶν λόγων τοῦ κυρίου Ἰησοῦ): 'It is more blessed to give than to receive'" (Acts 20:35).[100] In one of the Pastoral Epistles, Paul gives a tweet-length definition of his gospel: "Remember Jesus Christ (Μνημόνευε Ἰησοῦν Χριστὸν), raised from the dead, descended from David" (2 Tim 2:8). Notably this definition of the evangel is rooted in recalling an evangelical narrative, indicating that recollection of Jesus' messianic career was the central focus of an early creed, deployed in this instance as an encouragement for Christian leaders. Finally, in 2 Peter (avoiding for now debates about its authorship and provenance), the whole of the letter is built on an exhortation to remember scriptural injunctions, apostolic instruction, and the Jesus tradition: "I want you to remember the words spoken in the past (μνησθῆναι τῶν προειρημένων ῥημάτων) by the holy prophets and the command given by our Lord and Savior through your apostles" (2 Pet 3:2). On two occasions Clement of Rome (ca. 70-100 CE) included two otherwise unknown sayings in his letter to the Corinthians: "Most of all, let us remember the words of the Lord Jesus (μεμνημένοι τῶν λόγων τοῦ κυρίου Ἰησοῦ), which he spoke as he taught with gentleness and patience. For he said this: 'Show mercy so that you may receive mercy; forgive, so that you may be forgiven. As you do, so shall it be done to you. As

100. On the Jesus tradition in Acts, see W. A. Strange, "The Jesus-Tradition in Acts," *NTS* 46 (2000): 59-74.

you give, so shall it be given to you. As you judge, so shall you be judged. As you show kindness, so shall kindness be shown to you. With the measure you use it will be measured to you.'"[101] As an injunction against schism, Clement wrote: "Remember the words of Jesus our Lord (μνήσθητε τῶν λόγων Ἰησοῦ τοῦ κυρίου ἡμῶν), for he said: 'Woe to that person! Rather than cause one of my elect to sin, it would have been good for that one not to have been born. It would have been better for that person to have been tied to a millstone and cast into the sea, rather than pervert one of my elect.'"[102] The appeals to "remember" might be all the more pertinent for sayings such as this one not found in the Gospels (i.e., the agrapha) since there was no written deposit that we know of containing it, so it could only be preserved in corporate memory.

The advent of the year 100 CE did not cause instantaneous and widespread amnesia: memories of Jesus and the Apostles continued into the early second century. Papias claimed that he "carefully learned and carefully remembered" (καλῶς ἔμαθον καὶ καλῶς ἐμνημόνευσα) everything from the elders, not from those who "remember (μνημόνευσιν) someone else's commandments," but tradents who "remember the commandments given by the Lord."[103] The living voice of the Jesus tradition was a living memory. Papias also provides attestation of a tradition, obviously debatable, about the origins of the Gospel of Mark as based on Petrine testimony and written by John Mark:

> And the elder used to say this: "Mark, having become Peter's interpreter (ἑρμηνευτὴς), wrote down accurately everything he remembered (ἐμνημόνευσεν), though not in order, of the things either said or done by Christ. For he neither heard the Lord nor followed him, but afterward, as I said, followed Peter, who adapted his teachings as needed but had no intention giving an ordered account of the Lord's sayings. Consequently Mark did nothing wrong in writing down some things as he remembered (ἀπεμνημόνευσεν) them, for he made it his one concern not to omit anything that he heard or to make any false statement in them."[104]

The Marcan tradition is thus said to be based on Mark's memory of the teaching of Peter. Clement of Alexandria, via Eusebius, narrates the same

101. *1 Clem.* 13.1-2.
102. *1 Clem.* 46.7-8.
103. Papias, *Fragments* 3.3.
104. Papias, *Fragments* 3.15.

story, where Peter's Roman audience was not satisfied with "a single hearing or with the unwritten teaching of the divine proclamation," and so exhorted Mark to give them a "written statement of the teaching given to them verbally." Clement's language highlights the trajectory taken by living memory, transmitted as oral tradition, shaped by repetition, used for teaching and preaching, and ending up as a written record.[105]

Polycarp's letter to the Philippians draws on an almost identical agraphon as Clement of Rome does in *1 Clem.* 13.2. Rather than commit immoral deeds, the Philippians are exhorted instead to engage in "remembering (μνημονεύοντες) what the Lord said as he taught: 'Do not judge, so that you may not be judged; forgive, and you will be forgiven; show mercy, so that you may be shown mercy; with the measure you use, it will be measured back to you.'"[106] The Jesus tradition was regarded as an object for rhetorical appeal to authenticate certain patterns of belief and behavior and was identified as a corporate memory, which authors expected their audiences to know about.

Even well into the second century the importance of remembering Jesus continued. The Christian author Hegessipus (ca. 110-80 CE) wrote five books of "memoirs" (ὑπομνήματα) about the early church, which is a deposit of apostolic instruction and a history of the early church.[107] In the Pseudo-Clementine *Recognitions,* Peter is portrayed "recalling and repeating the words of the Lord" in order "to keep them in memory."[108] Although the Pseudo-Clementines are secondary, late, and even fictitious, they still celebrate the importance of memory and also resonate with ancient practices for preserving the memory of a movement founder. In the *Epistula Apostolorum* is a depiction of the Apostles as self-conscious tradents of memory: "When we heard it [the word of the gospel], we both committed it to memory and wrote it for all the world."[109] It is surely pertinent to studies for both the genre and tradition-history of the Gospels that they are labeled by Justin Martyr as the "memoirs of the Apostles" (τὰ ἀπομνημονεύματα τῶν ἀποστόλων).[110] It is apparent that "memory" was an important category in determining *what* the Gospels contained and also *how* they preserved a tradition about Jesus. Justin's claim is more than a stereotypical genre for the recollection of the

105. Eusebius, *Hist. Eccl.* 2.15.
106. Polycarp, *Philippians* 2.3.
107. Eusebius, *Hist. Eccl.* 2.23.3.
108. *Pseudo-Clementine Recognitions* 2.1.
109. *Epistula Apostolorum* 1.
110. *Dial. Trypho.* 100.4; 101.3; 102.5; 103.6, 8; 104.1; 105.1, 5, 6; 106.1, 3; 107.1; *Apologia I* 33.5; 66.3; 67.3.

traditions about an ancient sage, but specifically places apostolic accounts of Jesus within a period of living memory.[111] We might note as well that Irenaeus says that Polycarp "remembered" and "taught" about what he had gained from "eyewitnesses" about the Lord. Irenaeus himself "made notes of them, not on paper but in my heart" and could "recall them faithfully."[112] He contributed to a tradition whereby eyewitness testimony was preserved in later memory, even late into the second century. Finally, when Gnostic writers composed their respective works, they equally claimed that their documents were based on apostolic memory. The *Apocryphon of James* narrates how "the twelve disciples [were] all sitting together at the same time and remembering what the Savior had said to each one of them, whether in secret or openly, and [putting it] in books."[113] Debates in the early church over who was the custodian of the true apostolic tradition were ultimately debates over who possessed the apostolic memory of Jesus.[114]

Taking all this together, the sway of evidence from the first and second centuries suggests that a key task of the early church was to faithfully recall the words and deeds of Jesus.[115] It would seem inescapable that "The evidence we have been examining attests in itself a concern on the part of the earliest Christians to recall the ministry of Jesus, including not least his words and actions, and to preserve and pass on these traditions."[116]

If this is the case, then the goal of source criticism and tradition criticism needs to be radically overhauled. It can no longer be defined in terms of separating history from theology or identifying layers of tradition, but should be conceived as tracing the impact of a memory in the formation of early Christianity. The historical event of Jesus cannot be safely stripped from the subsequent narrative representations of Jesus given in the Gospels.[117]

111. Bockmuehl, *Seeing the Word*, 185.

112. Eusebius, *Hist Eccl.* 5.20.6-7.

113. *Apocryphon of James* 2.1-15.

114. Cf. Helmut Koester, *Ancient Christian Gospels: Their History and Development* (London: SCM, 1990), 34.

115. James H. Charlesworth, *Jesus within Judaism: New Light from Exciting Archaeological Discoveries* (London: SPCK, 1989), 20.

116. Henry Wansbrough, "Introduction," in *Jesus and the Oral Gospel Tradition*, ed. Wansbrough, 12.

117. Cf. Jens Schröter, "Von der Hostorizität der Evangelien. Ein Beitrag zur gegenwärtigen Diskussion um den historischen Jesus," in *Der historische Jesus. Tendenzen und Perspektiven der gegenwärtigen Forschung*, ed. J. Schröter and R. Brucker (BZNW 114; Berlin: de Gruyter, 2002), 205-6: "Das Ergebnis ist nicht der 'wirkliche' Jesus *hinter* den Evangelien. Das Ergebnis ist eine historische Konstruktion, die den Anspruch erhebt, unter gegenwärtigen

The Jesus tradition cannot be reduced to an onion with layers of ecclesiastical dogma to be peeled away before an authentic core of Jesuanic sayings can be found. On the contrary, the Jesus tradition is the contingent recollection of the memory of Jesus which shaped the early church. Bruce Chilton correctly infers what this means for Gospels research: "An exegesis of the Gospels must be generative exegesis. We need to trace how things Jesus did and said generated a movement and produced a memory. That movement and memory then generated successive phases, each with its own social context, until the time the Gospels were written."[118]

A further qualification should be made since remembering Jesus never happened in a vacuum, but transpired in a social setting. Memories are not cherished in the vault of one's private mind, but are sorted, shared, and spread throughout a community that equally cherishes the memory of a collective past. The memory of Jesus became, in a sense, "intersubjective."[119] This is, for the historian, a good thing, since the sharing of a memory with others and subsequent social dialogue can correct imagination and misremembering to a reasonable extent.[120] The memory of Jesus was cultivated in a community context where key individuals and the group consensus determined the veracity and continuity of the memory against prior acts of remembering and in comparison with other memories of Jesus.[121] The sociology of memory is one of the best factors to account for its preservation and integrity.[122]

Erkenntnisbedingungen plausible zu sein." Keith, "Memory and Authenticity," 170: "[F]rom the perspective of social memory theory, scholars in search of authentic Jesus traditions might as well be in search of unicorns, the lost city of Atlantis, and the pot of gold at the end of the rainbow. Not only are there no longer Jesus traditions that reflect solely the actual past, there never were. All tradition — all memory — is an indissoluble mix of past and the present. The present would have nothing to remember if it were not for the past; the past would not be capable of being remembered if it were not for the frameworks of the present."

118. Bruce D. Chilton, *Pure Kingdom: Jesus' Vision of God* (Grand Rapids: Eerdmans, 1996), 51.

119. Cf. Bauckham, *Jesus and the Eyewitnesses*, 311-13.

120. Le Donne, *Historiographical Jesus*, 47-48.

121. Cf. Redman ("Eyewitnesses," 186): "As one would expect, a group of people working together will be able to retrieve more details of a particular event than any one member of the group working alone. If, however, the individual memories of each person are pooled, the sum of items and details remembered is higher than the sum of the times and details remembered by a collaborative group. Group memory appears to be more stable over time than individual memory, though, and there are differences in the way in which material is organized within the group."

122. For this reason, the hesitations about "social memory" by Bauckham (*Jesus and the Eyewitnesses*, 291), Dunn (*New Perspective on Jesus*, 43-44), Gerhardsson ("Secret of the

However, memories are not just memorials of the past recalled for the sake of posterity. Memory makes the past come alive in order to impact the present, defines the present by spelling out the past, and cues the present by informing audiences of a heritage that they subscribe to. It is not simply a retrieval of past information from dormant brain cells. Rather, the past is constructed on the basis of mnemonic processes and shaped in light of the social framework of one's community. The reason for this is quite straightforward. In order for images of the past to make sense in the present, memories must be localized for the context of remembering and manufactured to fit with existing structures of plausible belief when that memory is shared. Memory is continued from the past and contingently constructed on the basis of the present. The past is synchronically constructed for the present, while memory concurrently retains its diachronic depth in the past. The past is constituted by acts of recollection — through commemoration, mimesis, and performance. These recollections instantiate the past in a wider narrative known to and accepted by a community. The communal narrative serves as a cognitive–linguistic key for deciphering the recollection, while recollection engrains the past into the narrativized history of the community. Recollection and communal narrative become fused, so that the past shapes the social reality of the present and the recollection of the past itself is shaped by the social situation of the community. Social memory, then, constitutes a negotiation between relics of the past and the contingencies of the present.[123] Thus, the memory of Jesus is a mixture of past recollection and present imposition accounting for the stability and variance in the tradition itself. The Jesus tradition may accordingly be conceived as the artifact of memory, a continual negotiation and semantic engagement between a memorialized past and a dynamic present.[124] The history of Jesus is constructed in the remembering process and democratized in that diverse memories of Jesus are fused together to the point of forming a single communally validated remembrance of Jesus.

This social memory model diverges from the Scandinavian approach

---

Transmission," 8-9), and Byrskog (*Story as History,* 255) are unfounded because social memory does not collapse oral history into a bed of anonymity or deny other controls like eyewitnesses and teachers. The point is that social memory refuses to treat individuals as isolated entities, analyzable apart from social contexts. Individual and collective memory are mutually and simultaneously influencing (Rodriguez, *Structuring Early Christian Memory,* 44-47).

123. Kirk, "Memory Theory and Jesus Research," 1:817-18.

124. Schröter, *Erinnerung,* 463. According to Keith (*Jesus' Literacy,* 58), in social memory theory, "The present does not simply run roughshod over the past; the present acts on the past while the past simultaneously acts on the present."

since no appeal is made to systematic memorization. The memory is repeated informally and the control is located in the community corporately and exercised by the community's authorized teachers. Transmission is attributable to the impact of the memory on Jesus' followers rather than to a perception of Jesus' teaching as holy word or to rote memorization. The memory of Jesus is never replayed in entirely fixed or fluid form, but is performed in order to (re)produce a dramatic effect in the audience.[125] It is the corporate dimension, however, that provides the main control.[126] When we analyze the Jesus tradition in the Gospels, we are not dealing with a single "chain" of transmission based on a single person's memory, prone to flounder, but rather a "net" transmission of a community, which helps guarantee that larger amounts of tradition are preserved.[127]

Alternatively, doubts about whether the disciples or the early church accurately remembered Jesus have been raised by many. Dale Allison offers the caveat that "The frailty of human memory should distress all who quest for the so-called historical Jesus."[128] According to the late Robert Funk, "Much of the lore recorded in the gospels and elsewhere in the Bible is folklore, which means that it is wrapped in memories that have been edited, deleted, augmented, and combined many times over many years."[129] Although John Dominic Crossan does not doubt that people can remember things accurately, he is at pains to emphasize that memory is not always a reliable mechanism. He states, "Memory is as much or more creative reconstruction as accurate recollection, and, unfortunately, it is often impossible to tell where one ends and the other begins."[130] Crossan adds, "fact and fiction,

---

125. Cf. Kelber, *Oral and Written Gospel,* 24, 27: "Remembrance and transmission depended on the ability to articulate a message in such a way that it found an echo in people's hearts and minds." The Jesus tradition "is typecast in a fashion that lends itself to habitual, not verbatim, memorization."

126. I would point out that in the Mishnah there is a story about the deathbed advice of Aqavya ben Mehalelel, a sage who regretted defying the traditions of his contemporaries: "I insisted on what I heard and they insisted on what they heard. But you have heard from an individual and from the multitude. It is best to leave the teachings of an individual and to hold fast to the teachings of the multitude" (*m. Eduyoth* 5.7). Jaffee, *Torah in the Mouth,* 68, sees here an example of how "[It] was the consensus of collective memory that defined the authentic contour of the transmitted tradition over against the insistence of an individual."

127. Keener, *Historical Jesus,* 146, 149; Kirk, "Memory Theory and Jesus Research," 839-40.

128. Allison, *Constructing Jesus,* 1.

129. Funk, *Acts of Jesus,* 6; cf. Funk and Hoover, *Five Gospels,* 28-29.

130. Crossan, *Birth of Christianity,* 59.

memory and fantasy, recollection and fabrication are intertwined in remembering. . . . nobody, including ourselves, can be absolutely certain which is which, apart from independent and documented verification."[131] Crossan goes on to cite several psychological case studies which underscore the inadequacies of memory.

It should be conceded to Crossan and Funk that experience alone teaches us that people are inclined to remember outlines or frameworks rather than details.[132] Memory is not an infallible guide, and one cannot romanticize the effectiveness of oriental memory as a fallback. There are, however, several cogent reasons for dismissing the thesis that the early Christians did not "accurately" remember Jesus:

1. The examples that Crossan cites as indications of the failure of memory (e.g., someone wrongly remembering where he or she was when the *Challenger* shuttle crashed) pertain to events that, for the individuals in question, are merely incidental and not tied to their core beliefs and identity.[133] The subjects were not emotionally involved in the past event, nor was the past event even vaguely connected to the founding of a community with a traceable story. So these examples represent an implausible analogy with recollection of the Jesus tradition. We should take into account that the sayings and deeds of Jesus comprised the bedrock for the self-understanding of the early Christian communities. We are not dealing with forgettable and trivial details of general knowledge. The faith, ethics, symbols, and praxis of early Christian communities were all defined and oriented around the impact that Jesus had upon them, an impact that was embodied in memories about Jesus.

2. If one envisages Jesus' closest disciples and general supporters attempting to conjure up recollections of Jesus only decades later and independent of one another, then studies about the fragility and failure of memory obviously gain traction. However, we know that the Jesus movement formed networks and clusters of believers together in Galilee, Jerusalem, Judea, Syria, and Asia Minor and that their memories of Jesus were retrieved in a "net" context. These groups of Christians remembered Jesus not as indi-

---

131. Crossan, *Birth of Christianity*, 60.

132. Cf. Robert McIver and Mark Carroll, "Experiments to Determine Distinguishing Characteristics of Orally Transmitted Material When Compared to Material Transmitted by Literary Means, and Their Potential Implications for the Synoptic Problem," *JBL* 121 (2002): 667-87.

133. See Abel, "Psychology of Memory and Rumor," 280, who noted a study by Schachter and Burdick which demonstrated that rumors are only remembered when the information was of interest and relevance to the subject observed.

viduals, but as a community. Moreover, it was the community context that provided certain controls and parameters for the extent to which memories could be augmented or developed. Ironically, Crossan proves exactly that. For he provides instances of memories that were shown to be flawed and were corrected by contemporaries to the subject who had access to witnesses within living memory.[134]

3. Remembering Jesus was not an isolated instance like remembering what one was doing at 7:15 p.m. exactly twelve days ago. Key to memory consistency is the frequency of memory retrieval. According to Jeffrey Olick: "Genuine communities are communities of memory that constantly tell and retell their constitutive memory."[135] During his own lifetime, Jesus probably taught and said the same things in multiple instances, in various locations, over the course of three years. His itinerant ministry would require that much the same thing be said from place to place as he urgently broadcast the message of the kingdom to the string of villages he entered.[136] So much so that Theissen surmises: "The origins of the Jesus tradition can thus be seen in Jesus' teaching and itinerant existence."[137] This repetition would have reinforced memories of sayings — not of original sayings, since there can be no "original" when there are multiple performances, where each performance is in a sense an original — among his closest disciples and wider circle of supporters. But even beyond Jesus' followers, recounting and rehearsing what Jesus did and said began well and truly before Easter. We can easily imagine a recipient of healing telling his neighbors what had happened to him, a fisherman telling his sons about the ruckus Jesus caused in the synagogue, and a wife telling her husband an amusing parable she heard that day.[138] Then, in the early church, this retrieval happened even more regularly

---

134. Bockmuehl, *Seeing the Word*, 174.

135. Jeffrey K. Olick, "Collective Memory: The Two Cultures," *Sociological Theory* 17 (1999): 344, cited by Kirk, "Memory Theory and Jesus Research," 815.

136. Gerhardsson, *Memory and Manuscript*, 334-35; Kelber, *Oral and the Written Gospel*, 30; N. T. Wright, *The New Testament and the People of God* (COQG 1; Minneapolis: Fortress, 1992), 422-24; idem, *Jesus and the Victory of God*, 51, 170-71; Keener, *Historical Jesus*, 142; Dunn, *Jesus Remembered*, 239-45; idem, "Remembering Jesus," 197-98; idem, *Jesus, Paul, and the Gospels*, 43-44; Bauckham, *Jesus and the Eyewitnesses*, 345-46; Allison, *Constructing Jesus*, 24; Redman, "Eyewitnesses," 189; Theissen, *New Testament*, 23.

137. Theissen, *New Testament*, 25.

138. Dunn, *Jesus Remembered*, 240; Bauckham, *Jesus and the Eyewitnesses*, 345-46. See also the fictitious yet realistic account of the beginnings of oral transmission of the Jesus tradition in Galilean villages according to Gerd Theissen's *The Shadow of the Galilean*, trans. J. Bowden (Philadelphia: Fortress, 1987), esp. 97-107. Elsewhere Theissen (*New Testament*, 26)

and formally. In diverse didactic, apologetic, liturgical, and even polemical settings, memories of Jesus were constantly recalled, not merely by an individual but by a community, and not merely by one community but by many communities spread across Palestine and the Mediterranean cities. Indeed, where we find these repetitive patterns in the Gospels, we are on fairly solid ground to conclude that we are encountering the literary deposit of an oral tradition based on solid memory.[139]

4. Those who suggest that the disciples forgot Jesus may effectively give fantasy free rein.[140] Skepticism fosters a rather convenient vacuum in which to grow theories of divergent Jesuses and internecine conflicts among multifarious communities being played out in these biographical narratives about Jesus. It means that the Gospels are not really about "Jesus" but about something else, such as a Thomasine community versus a Johannine community. More likely, oral performances wedged the Jesus tradition in the collective memory of the early Christians and became a vital component of the traditional milieux in which Jesus' followers lived. It cannot be otherwise, unless of course we suppose that the Jesus tradition was initially performed, promptly released from memory, without impact on any community, only to be later written down, detached from any enduring impact of Jesus' memory on the early church.[141] Yet this postulates that the earliest followers of Jesus suffered from some kind of "radical amnesia," which I find unlikely.[142]

IV. Conclusion

It is essential for understanding the Gospels to observe that the intention of the texts is to tell the story of Jesus for readers spread throughout the Greco-

---

declares: "Thus, after Jesus' death his traditions were handed down in three social contexts: among disciples, in communities, and by the general public." A more concerted study is Heinz Schürmann, "Die vorösterlichen Anfänge der Logientradition. Versuch eines formgeschichtlichen Zugangs zum Leben Jesu," in *Der historische Jesus und der kerygmatische Christus,* ed. H. Ristow and K. Matthiae (Berlin: Evangelische Verlaganstalt, 1962), 342-70.

139. Cf. Allison, *Constructing Jesus,* 15-24.

140. Dahl, "Problem of the Historical Jesus," 94.

141. Rodriguez, *Structuring Early Christian Memory,* 4.

142. Witherington, *Christology of Jesus,* 14. Cf. too Meier, *Marginal Jew,* 1:169-70, who thinks that next to a "creative thrust" there was also a "conservative force" in the Jesus tradition that did not permit a "convenient amnesia." Allison, *Constructing Jesus,* 9 n. 47, despite his general reservations about the reliability of memory, refuses to castigate the Evangelists as "amnesiacs."

Roman world. The Gospels arose out of networks of professing Christ-believers, they are intensely theological documents in their own right, and they are stamped with the faith of the early church. Yet the Gospels do not come across as fictitious formulations utterly ridden with theological impositions, making access to the past of Jesus impossible. They are biographical accounts about a historical figure, set in the coordinates of Israel's religious history and narrated in light of the situation of Christians in the Greco-Roman cities of the eastern Mediterranean.

After examining all the proposed models for the oral transmission of the Jesus tradition, noting the pros and cons of each one, I want to suggest that no single model possesses the explanatory power to account completely for the shape of the Gospels. While I resonate with the general "vibe" of Kenneth Bailey's model of "informal controlled oral tradition," drawn especially to its social realism, which fits so neatly into Palestinian village life and the urban chatter of the synagogues and agoras in Greco-Roman cities, in the end it is anecdotal rather than based on social anthropological evidence. Similarly, the Scandinavian model, with its appeal to rabbinic pedagogy, is undoubtedly our closest analogy to how the Jesus tradition was initially transmitted in Palestine. But again, while the Scandinavian model explains some things, it does not explain all things, and we simply cannot root the transmission in a pre-70 CE oral culture for which our knowledge is scant at best. Models like these, Bailey's and the Scandinavians', are heuristic insofar as they provide us with ways of imagining, often with good reasons, how it might well have happened. They lack, however, the ability to comprehensively account for the forms, content, stability, and variability of the tradition.

In which case, rather than try to identify the least problematic model of the oral tradition, perhaps what we really need is something more fundamental like a mnemonic hermeneutic for explaining how oral history is transmitted through oral tradition along with a fluid exchange between orality and textuality. In other words, any view about the Jesus tradition needs to be sustained with an underlying theory of social memory, that is, a theory that characterizes the Gospels as the memory of Jesus interpreted and applied to the context of the early Christians in the both oral and scribal culture of their day, a way of accounting for the intersubjective nature of the remembrance of Jesus as shaped by individual, collective, and cultural forces across a variety of oral and written media.

I am suggesting that the term "Jesus in social memory" is a useful signifier for this enterprise since it highlights that the tradition is ultimately a memory and that memory is transmitted and transformed by a mnemonic process of both individuals and groups. Such a model also enables us to unify the elements of bias and biography, to uncover a memory that is reliable but also refracted. Aided by eyewitnesses, teachers, a discernible process of handing-on and receiving traditions, and a rich mix of oral mnemonics and textual aide-mémoire, the early church remembered Jesus, recounting him as a Judean sage as much as a divine Savior. The tradition oscillated between fixity and flexibility depending on the type of material in question and whether its tradents controlled the tradition in a formal or informal manner; there is no reason to think that this was uniform. This does not yield a Jesus who can be clinically separated from the devotion of his later followers, but gives us instead the Jesus who impacted his peers and pupils alike.

What the Gospels produce is not the Christ of faith superimposed onto the historical Jesus. Rather, the Gospels offer a striking representation, much like a docu-drama, of Jesus' actions in the past and his voice for the present available through the corporate memory of Jesus. Consequently, the memory of Jesus deposited in the Gospels bequeaths to us both authenticity and artistry, fact and faith, history and hermeneutic. The objective of the Evangelists is not to write a life of Jesus to satisfy a positivistic epistemology, but neither is it to offer an image of Jesus concocted out of thin air to be a weapon of intra-Christian or inter-Jewish polemics. The Gospels intend to narrate a back-then story and to evoke the right-now significance of one called Jesus, Israel's Messiah, and the world's rightful Lord.

Excursus
The Failure of Form Criticism

A dominant approach in twentieth-century Gospels scholarship was form criticism *(Formgeschichte)*. The object of form criticism was to conceptualize and explain the pre-literary oral phase behind the Synoptic tradition. New Testament form critics built on the work of their erstwhile colleagues in Old Testament such as Hermann Gunkel and Julius Wellhausen in the early twentieth century. By the 1920s, a trio of German scholars, K. L. Schmidt, Martin Dibelius, and Rudolf Bultmann, were pioneering a form-critical approach to the Gospels.[143] In the British Isles during the 1930s and 40s, scholars like Vincent Taylor and R. H. Lightfoot cautiously appropri-

---

143. K. L. Schmidt, *Der Rahmen der Geschichte Jesu. Literarkritische untersuchungen zur Altesten Jesuberlieferung* (Berlin: Trowitzsch, 1919); Martin Dibelius, *From Tradition to Gospel*, trans. Bertram Lee Woolf (Cambridge: Clarke, 1971 [1919]); Rudolf Bultmann, *History of the Synoptic Tradition*, trans. J. Marsh (2nd ed.; New York: Harper & Row, 1963 [1921]).

ated and applied the principles of form criticism.[144] According to Rudolf Bultmann, the objective of form criticism was to discover "what the original units of the Synoptics were, both sayings and stories, to try to establish what their historical setting was, whether they belonged to a primary or secondary tradition or whether they were the product of editorial activity."[145]

Form criticism proceeded by identifying various "forms" or sub-genres in the Gospels, then assigning a given unit to a particular form, inferring a *Sitz im Leben* ("life setting") in the early church behind that form, and then plotting the development of the unit through its pre-literary stages. The operating assumption was that the Gospels are a form of folk literature that evolved from simple forms into complex rhetoric units by the accretion of a tradition that had imposed itself over the various units. The achievement of each Evangelist was to link together these individual units (sayings, stories, etc.) into a singular narrative. In approaching the Gospels, form criticism was much like peeling an onion, tearing off layer upon layer, and getting back to the original saying or story. What is more, just like peeling an onion, watching a form critic cut and tear his way through the alleged layers of tradition in Gospels also makes one want to cry because it is so painful to watch (more criticism anon).

While there was no agreement on what these forms actually were, the most widely attested taxonomy of forms included: (1) individual logia (sayings), (2) pronouncement stories, also called apophthegms or paradigms (short stories climaxing in punchy sayings), (3) parables and similitudes (short metaphorical narratives), (4) discourses (speeches), (5) miracle stories (containing supernatural deeds), and (6) historical narratives (usually based on myths). These forms carried the oral tradition and were contaminated by the accretion of layers to the tradition. The Gospels took their final shape from forms that corresponded to settings within the early church.

The value of form criticism was in recognizing that Jesus' teaching was couched in extant oral forms, postulating an oral component to the Jesus tradition, and it made a valiant effort to trace the origins and shape of that tradition in the early church. However, it is no exaggeration to say that virtually every single presupposition and procedure in form criticism has been thoroughly discredited. While form criticism faded from the scholarly scene around the same time that disco died, it is still necessary, much like what the Romans did to Carthage, to salt the earth to make sure that nothing ever grows from it again. Thus, in what follows

---

144. Vincent Taylor, *The Formation of the Gospel Tradition* (London: Macmillan, 1933); R. H. Lightfoot, *History and Interpretation in the Gospels* (London: Hodder & Stoughton, 1935). Not to be neglected either are the later studies by B. S. Easton, *The Gospel before the Gospels* (London: Allen & Unwin, 1928); C. K. Barrett, *Jesus and the Gospel Tradition* (London: SPCK, 1967); and C. F. D. Moule, *The Birth of the New Testament* (London: Black, 1981 [1962]).

145. Bultmann, *History of the Synoptic Tradition*, 2-3.

I list the major failings of the form-critical paradigm for mapping the origins of the Jesus tradition.[146]

The Distinction between Palestinian and Hellenistic Settings

It is important to remember that the form-critical paradigm for tracing the development of the tradition is tied very closely to the form critics' view of Christian origins. Rudolf Bultmann followed the lead of Wilhelm Bousset in seeing Christianity as evolving through different tiers. "The early church" is just an umbrella term for a number of different Christian groups, each with their own distinct situation and outlook. While Christianity began in a Palestinian Jewish Christian setting, it promptly moved into the Diaspora and took root in a Hellenistic Jewish Christian setting, and then finally Christianity shifted beyond its Jewish context into a Gentile Christian setting. These "settings" are really "stages" through which the tradition passed through on the way to taking their place in the Gospels. Some material was created at a later stage, while some passed through several stages with embellishments made along the way. So Bultmann could say that the controversy stories came from a Palestinian setting, the miracle stories and "I-sayings" from a Hellenistic setting, and so forth. These various "settings" become pigeonholes that one can slot various units from the Gospels into so as to attribute the units' origins to particular settings. Now it has to be said that this framework is just so problematic that it is impossible to find anyone today who would adhere to it.

First, it is no longer historically possible to pry Judaism and Hellenism absolutely apart. Martin Hengel has carefully shown the complex relationship the Jewish world had with Hellenistic influences in the Greek and Roman periods. The Judeans under the Ptolemaic and Seleucid regimes, then during the post-Maccabean era and under the Herodian client rulers, just like other peoples of the ancient Near East, experienced a degree of acculturation and integration with Hellenism. Whether in commerce, education, culture, or literature, Hellenistic influences permeated Judean society at all levels. So much so that by the middle of the third century BCE all Juda-

---

146. See other evaluations and critiques of form criticism in Graham N. Stanton, "Form Criticism Revisited," in *What about the New Testament?* ed. M. Hooker and C. Hickling (London: SCM, 1975), 13-27; S. H. Travis, "Form Criticism," in *New Testament Interpretation: Essays on Principles and Methods,* ed. I. Howard Marshall (Grand Rapids: Eerdmans, 1977), 153-64; Reiner Blank, *Analyse und Kritik der formgeschichtlichen Arbeiten von Martin Dibelius und Rudolf Bultmann* (Basel: Reinhardt, 1981); Martin Hengel, *Four Gospels and the One Gospel of Jesus Christ,* trans. J. Bowden (Harrisburg: Trinity, 2000), 143-45; Robert H. Stein, *Studying the Synoptic Gospels: Origin and Interpretation* (2nd ed.; Grand Rapids: Baker, 2001), 173-94; Bauckham, *Jesus and Eyewitnesses,* 241-49; Craig Blomberg, *The Historical Reliability of the Gospels* (2nd ed.; Downers Grove: InterVarsity, 2007), 50-66; Eddy and Boyd, *Jesus Legend,* 237-306; Keener, *Historical Jesus,* 153-61.

ism must be designated as forms of Hellenistic Judaism, so that one cannot separate a Palestinian Judaism from a Hellenistic Judaism.[147]

Second, the early church did not have woodenly insulated Jewish, Hellenistic, and Gentile tiers. As far as we know from Acts 1–6 and Paul's letters, the Palestinian church had Aramaic-speaking and Greek-speaking members existing together side by side from the very beginning. Persons such as Barnabas and John Mark were linguistically competent enough to move between both groups fairly freely as they worked in Judea, wider Palestine, and the Jewish Diaspora of the eastern Mediterranean. Gentile converts were probably made from the start, from Nicolaus the proselyte in Jerusalem (Acts 6:5) to other converts in Damascus, Antioch, and Caesarea (Acts 8–11). Paul dealt with issues relating to Jewish and Gentile fellowship in his letters to churches in Galatia, Corinth, Philippi, and Rome in the 50s and 60s CE, leaving no evidence for an exclusively Gentile religious space in the early churches. The Gospel of Mark is arguably the work of a bilingual and thus digests the Jesus tradition in its Aramaic and Greek forms.[148] The Gospels of Matthew and John, exhibiting as they do a strong familiarity with Greek language and culture, still express themselves in a robustly Jewish idiom and worldview. Evidently the early church was ethnically, culturally, and linguistically mixed from the very beginning with degrees of hybridity fluctuating depending on the location and composition of the resident Christ-believers.

Third, we have to take into account that the early church was a fairly small movement, with perhaps no more than 20,000 adherents by 70 CE, and very mobile as leaders moved around a lot, with close interaction and sharing of literature and traditions between various communities.[149] The Jesus tradition circulated back and forth between various linguistic and cultural settings as materials like letters and Gospels were shared between churches in both Palestinian and Diaspora settings. *If* the Jesus traditions textualized in Mark (in, say, Rome) found their way eastward to be utilized by Matthew (in, say, Syria), and *if* Mark and Matthew were both taken up by Luke (in, say, Achaia), and *if* Mark and Luke were incorporated somewhat indirectly by John (in, say, Ephesus), *then* this is a clear example of a fluctuation between eastern and western spheres concerning the textual and perhaps even oral form of the Jesus tradition. So the idea that the tradition took a one-way path comprising Palestinian → Hellenistic → Gentile setting is naively simplistic to say the least.

Therefore, much of the form-critical enterprise was based on an attempt to

---

147. Martin Hengel, *Judaism and Hellenism: Studies in Their Encounter in Palestine during the Early Hellenistic Period* (2 vols.; Philadelphia: Fortress, 1974), 1:103-6.

148. On the significance of bilinguality for the transmission of the Jesus tradition, see Sang-Il Lee, *Jesus and Gospel Traditions in Bilingual Context: A Study in the Interdirectionality of Language* (Berlin: de Gruyter, 2012).

149. On this, see Michael B. Thompson, "The Holy Internet: Communication between Churches in the First Christian Generation," in *The Gospels for All Christians: Rethinking the Gospel Audiences*, ed. R. Bauckham (Grand Rapids: Eerdmans, 1998), 49-70.

explain the tradition by attributing the development of the tradition to entities such as "Hellenistic Christianity" that did not even exist.

An Erroneous View of the Oral Tradition

The form-critical practitioners can be faulted for their mistaken understanding of the nature of the oral tradition. Despite their grasp of the importance of orality in the early church, they over-freighted the value of forms in originating the tradition, they neglected the tradents of the tradition, and they relied on literary models to explain a largely oral phenomenon.

First, deep and troubling questions are raised by how the form critics imagined the Jesus tradition to have emerged. In essence, they advocated that stories about Jesus were "generalized and stereotyped by the pressures of community need and use,"[150] but with little actual reference to Jesus and the impact he had on his earliest followers. The Gospels are, according to form critics, the result of a bare memory overlaid with extant layers of oral tradition and then configured theologically into written documents. Bultmann is adamant that the Gospels cannot be explained by way of reference to "memory" but are accounted for in terms of a literary form that creatively erupted in the early church. Memories might have played a part in the early church, yet not in determining the final shape of the Gospels themselves.[151] The problem here is that the Gospels are seen as shaped by every contingent factor except that of the past itself.[152] But memory has to play a more important part if we are to properly grasp the shape and substance, not only of the Gospels, but of the early Christian context in which the Gospels were written. Martin Hengel wrote:

> A further neglected factor in form criticism, therefore, is personal memory, which can hold fast what is seen and heard for decades. It is closely connected with the phenomenon of the "eye-witnesses." To begin with, everyone had individual memory. Particular "eye-witnesses" may observe the same process rather differently and only in a limited way. Of course, there was simultaneously a constant exchange, which was then "institutionalized" in primitive Christian worship through the community of witnesses, in that "the memory of Jesus" from his baptism by John to his passion and its interpretation was narratively proclaimed. There arose thus a "treasure of memory," which could be supplemented but also controlled.[153]

150. Nineham, "Eyewitness Testimony and the Gospel Tradition," 243.

151. Bultmann, *History of the Synoptic Tradition*, 48 n. 2.

152. Kirk, "Memory Theory and Jesus Research," 813.

153. Martin Hengel, "Eye-Witness Memory and the Writing of The Gospels," in *The Written Gospel*, ed. M. Bockmuehl and D. A. Hagner (FS Graham Stanton; Cambridge: Cambridge University Press, 2005), 86. See similarly Kirk and Thatcher, "Jesus Tradition as Social

Second, the form-critical appeal to forms as an explanation for the origin of the tradition is contestable. Here the form critics made two mistaken assumptions. (a) They assumed that the stories began as "pure forms" and were then adulterated with additions in the course of transmission, leaving us with the quest for an original form to be found under the layers of ecclesial accretion. But there is no reason why oral forms could not have been modified or mixed from the very beginning. In fact, Vincent Taylor supposed the opposite of Bultmann and Dibelius, namely, that the tradition began in a messy and muddled form with extraneous details that were then gradually refined into more standard and discernible forms.[154] (b) The form critics assumed that that there was a one-to-one correspondence between a particular form and a particular setting. So one type of material derived from one setting, while another type of material derived from another setting. Now it should be self-evident that the same traditions can be performed in a variety of settings. Standard types of oral or even literary forms are not monopolized by singular settings. For instance, what might have passed as an apophthegm in a Jewish context could easily be regarded as a *chreia* in a Greco-Roman context. This evacuates the argument that form corresponds to setting.

Third, notably absent from the form-critical paradigm are the tradents of the tradition. Where are the eyewitnesses and teachers in this process? If the form critics are right, the eyewitnesses of Jesus must have been raptured away not long after the resurrection, and all teachers about the Jesus tradition must have been swallowed up by the earth soon after the Day of Pentecost. This, of course, is hyperbolic, but even so the role of designated custodians of the tradition, acting either formally or informally, is neglected in form criticism. Indeed, the absence of such figures seems a necessity if the form critics' postulation of a fluid and creative tradition is to have any credibility. Absences of this kind are just not defensible given appeals to memory, the persistence of eyewitnesses, and the presence of teachers. The more we locate the Jesus tradition in the context of social memory, not in a deposit of anonymous recollection but in coordinates of a tradition that fluctuated between informal and formal controls, the more the entire form-critical approach to the tradition becomes grossly improbable.

Fourth, form critics were guilty of viewing the development of the oral tradition in the same way as the development of written documents. Bultmann believed that Matthew's and Luke's use of Mark's written text is analogous to how tradents handled and modified pre-Marcan oral traditions.[155] There are a number of problems here. For a start, the tendency of the Synoptic tradition was not simply toward addi-

---

Memory," 29: "'The disappearance of memory as an analytical category in biblical research may be attributed to a number of factors, most significantly the effects of form criticism."

154. Vincent Taylor, *The Formation of the of the Gospel Tradition* (London: Macmillan, 1933).

155. Bultmann, *History of the Synoptic Tradition*, 6.

tion and growth. E. P. Sanders demonstrated that the Synoptic tradition could grow and contract depending on a given unit.[156] He states: "The form critics were right in thinking that the material changed; they were wrong in thinking that they knew how it changed."[157] In addition, whereas form critics applied literary models to the study of oral traditions and imagined oral tradition as a series of sequential layers, each building on the one before, it is much more appropriate to think of oral tradition as a series of performances, a stream of interactive tradition, capable of correction just as much as embellishment. According to Rodriguez, performance *actualized* the tradition. Each performance is different, in wording and sequence, but it is basically the *same thing* that is transmitted by the performance. The performance is a living tradition, the tradition is embedded in a social story, and the story is the memory.[158] Furthermore, the fact that the Jesus tradition followed stereotypical patterns drawn from the Old Testament or existing oral forms in Rabbinic and Hellenistic literary types is not to say that the story was invented on the basis of the form. Rather, the use of pre-existing categories and patterns are an indispensable part of our cognitive mechanisms for the maintenance and dissemination of reminiscences.[159]

The Role of Christian Prophets Adding to the Dominical Tradition

A popular image in form criticism is that of Christian prophets adding to the dominical tradition by speaking oracles on behalf of the risen Jesus, oracles which then became intermingled with sayings of the historical Jesus.[160] There are indeed several passages in the New Testament, such as 1 Thess 4:15-17, that comprise prophetic "word[s] of the Lord." Likewise, in Rev 16:15 it looks as if a saying of the historical Jesus has been prophetically expanded (see Matt 24:43-44). The idea that prophetic material has accidentally become fused with sayings of the historical Jesus must remain a genuine possibility, but once more, I am not convinced that things are quite so straightforward.

156. E. P. Sanders, *The Tendencies of the Synoptic Tradition* (SNTS 9; Cambridge: Cambridge University Press, 1969), 272.

157. Sanders, *Jesus and Judaism*, 16.

158. Rodriguez, *Structuring Early Christian Memory*, 85.

159. Le Donne, *Historiographical Jesus*, 52-64.

160. Cf. Bultmann, *History of the Synoptic Tradition*, 127-28: "The Church drew no distinction between such utterances by Christian prophets and the sayings of Jesus in the tradition, for the reason that even the dominical sayings in the tradition were not the pronouncements of a past authority, but the sayings of the risen Lord, who is always a contemporary for the Church." See further M. Eugene Boring, *The Continuing Voice of Jesus: Christian Prophecy and the Gospel Tradition* (Louisville: Westminster John Knox, 1991); and esp. Dale C. Allison, *Jesus of Nazareth: Millenarian Prophet* (Minneapolis: Fortress, 1998), 7-10, with his imaginative story about a Jewish prophetess named "Faustina."

Bultmann argued that the assimilation of oracles of the risen Christ with sayings of the Jesus tradition occurred "gradually,"[161] and according to Boring it occurred "finally."[162] Similarly, Gerald Hawthorne thinks that the mingling of the two materials happened at times "unconsciously."[163] This implies that a demarcation between the words of the risen Lord and the sayings of the historical Jesus did originally exist.[164] Boring concedes that by the time of the book of Revelation a distinction was again made between pre- and post-Easter sayings of Jesus.[165] This probably occurred even earlier and was facilitated by the writing of the Gospels, which set forth a clear distinction between the historical and post-Easter/prophetic sayings of Jesus. This implies that at both the commencement of the Christian movement (ca. 30 CE) and by the time of the Gospel of Mark (ca. 70 CE), a distinction was made between the prophetic voice of the risen Christ and the sayings of the historical Jesus. If so a shift is envisaged, within the interim period of 40 years, from a differentiation between historical sayings and prophetic utterances, to no differentiation between prophetic utterances and historical Jesus sayings, and then back again to a differentiation between prophetic utterances and the Jesus tradition. Such radical changes within so short a time frame, occurring simultaneously in a variety of Christian settings, seem improbable.

Dunn has argued that the New Testament, Jewish literature, and later Christian writings all show a healthy degree of skepticism toward prophecy.[166] Luke is always careful to name the prophet who utters an oracle (see Luke 1:67-79; Acts 11:27-28; 13:1-2; 21:9-12). This should lead us to question the notion that there ever was a period when a collection of "the sayings of the risen Christ circulated without reference to who gave utterance to them."[167] Additionally, despite the plea for

161. Bultmann, *History of the Synoptic Tradition*, 127.

162. Boring, *Continuing Voice of Jesus*, 31.

163. G. F. Hawthorne, "Christian Prophets and the Sayings of Jesus: Evidence of and Criteria for," *SBL Seminar Papers* 8 (Missoula: Scholars, 1975), 117.

164. Hawthorne, "Christian Prophets and the Sayings of Jesus," 110; David Hill, *New Testament Prophecy* (Atlanta: John Knox, 1979), 162; David E. Aune, *Prophecy in Early Christianity and the Ancient Mediterranean World* (Grand Rapids: Eerdmans, 1983), 234.

165. Boring, *Continuing Voice of Jesus*, 112-13.

166. James D. G. Dunn, "Prophetic 'I'–Sayings and the Jesus Tradition: The Importance of Testing Prophetic Utterances within Early Christianity," *NTS* 24 (1977-78): 179. Dunn states on the same page, *"Wherever we look in the comparative material of the time the distinctive character of the prophetic utterances as the saying of a* prophet, *or as the words of the* exalted *Christ is maintained, and some sort of distinction between the words of the earthly Jesus and the prophetic inspiration of the present is implicit or explicit"* (italics original). Byrskog, *Jesus the Only Teacher*, 360: "It is indeed possible that prophets did utter new and independent oracles. But Matthew did apparently not allow them to enter into the Jesus tradition as pre-Easter Jesus-sayings. There was no entirely free incorporation and integration of new and independent oracles into the Jesus tradition. Within the creativity, there was the aim to preserve."

167. Dunn, "Prophetic 'I'–Sayings and the Jesus Tradition," 179.

a stalemate by Boring,[168] many scholars still assert that in 1 Cor 7:10, 12, 25, and 40 Paul clearly distinguishes his own inspired utterances from sayings of Jesus.[169] In light of that, a satisfactory reconstruction of the development of the Jesus tradition must account for both the Jewish context of the transmission of oral traditions and the charismatic dimension of early Christianity.[170]

The Link between Text Form and *Sitz im Leben*

The form-critical assumption about the formation of the Gospels was that the Gospels tell us more about the situation of the primitive church than they do about the historical Jesus. By implication, though the outward expression of the Gospels is a story about Jesus, their actual referent is the earliest church's expression of its own self-understanding and concerns. According to Bultmann, "What the sources offer us is first of all, the message of the early Christian community, which for the most part the Church freely attributed to Jesus."[171] Similar is Perrin: "[W]e must take as our starting point the assumption that the Gospel writers offer directly information about the theology of the early church and not about the teaching of the historical Jesus."[172] For case in point, the controversy stories, such as the one concerning fasting in Mark 2:18-22, do not tell of events that happened in Jesus' life, but of how the early church defended its own practice of not fasting against questions raised by Pharisaic and Baptist sectarian contemporaries, by appeal to a story about Jesus that somebody made up. Bultmann thought that Jesus may well have healed on the Sabbath and avoided fasting, but did not regard that as the point of such stories. The controversy stories are simply the apologetics and polemics of the early Palestinian church. They comprise imaginary scenes illustrating a principle that the early church ascribed to Jesus.[173]

However, many of the debates within the early Christian movement, partic-

---

168. Boring, *Continuing Voice of Jesus*, 28-29.

169. Cf. Ben Witherington, *Jesus the Seer: The Progress of Prophecy* (Peabody: Hendrickson, 1999), 325. For other cautious assessments of the function of Christian prophets in shaping the tradition, see Theissen and Merz, *Historical Jesus*, 110-11; Rowland, *Christian Origins*, 131; Byrskog, *Jesus the Only Teacher*, 360.

170. Ellis, "Synoptic Gospels and History," 56.

171. Rudolf Bultmann, *Jesus and the Word*, trans. Louise Pettibone Smith (London: Ivor Nicholson & Watson, 1935), 12. More restrained and believable is Helmut Koester, "Written Gospels or Oral Tradition?" *HTR* 113 (1994): 297: "Form criticism begins with the presupposition that the beginning and the continuation of the tradition were the early Christian community and that therefore the oral use of materials from and about Jesus in ritual, instruction, and missionary activity of this community was the congenial life situation of everything that was remembered from and about Jesus."

172. Norman Perrin, *What Is Redaction Criticism?* (London: SPCK, 1970), 69.

173. Bultmann, *History of the Synoptic Tradition*, 18, 40-41.

ularly those stemming from the Pauline circle, are entirely absent from the Gospels: justification by faith, circumcision, speaking in tongues, baptism, the status of Gentiles, criteria of apostleship, and food sacrificed to idols. All these topics are candidates for being written onto the lips of Jesus but are significantly missing from the Gospels. N. T. Wright notes: "The synoptic tradition shows a steadfast refusal to import 'dominical' answers to or comments on those issues into the retelling of the stories about Jesus. This should put us firmly on our guard against ideas that the stories we do find in the synoptic tradition were invented to address current needs in the 40s, 50s, 60s or even later in the first century."[174] Wright's judgment is confirmed by Acts, Galatians, and 1 Peter, where one observes a distinct reluctance to produce texts attributable to Jesus to resolve recurring problems.[175] It is in a much later esoteric document such as *Gospel of Thomas* 53 where one finds a statement about circumcision placed on the lips of Jesus.[176]

It would seem, then, that the form critics failed to distinguish between *use* of Jesus traditions in the early church and *origins* of Jesus traditions in the early church. Though Bultmann effectively collapsed the two issues together, this was an illegitimate move, as was his correlation of a form with a setting. As T. W. Manson wrote: "We can list these stories in the Gospels. We can label them. . . . But a paragraph in Mark is not a penny the better or the worse as historical evidence for being labeled, 'Apophthegm,' or 'Pronouncement Story' or 'Paradigm.'"[177]

There is also a feeling of circularity to the arguments that many passages in the Gospels are allegories of a church's *Sitz im Leben*. To give one example, Matt 10:5-6 ("Do not go into the way of the Gentiles, nor enter a city of the Samaritans, but go rather to the lost sheep of the house of Israel") is often seen as a creation by a Jewish Christian group opposed to the Gentile mission.[178] Even E. P. Sanders acknowledges that no primitive Christian group opposed the Gentile mission; only the basis of the Gentiles' entry into the church was disputed. Yet in the very next sentence Sanders remarks that behind Matt 10:5-6 stands a group, not mentioned in Galatians or Acts, which did oppose the Gentile mission.[179] So Matt 10:5-6 is the product of an

---

174. Wright, *New Testament and the People of God*, 422; cf. C. F. D. Moule, *The Phenomenon of the New Testament* (London: SCM, 1967), 43-81; Theissen and Merz, *Historical Jesus*, 104-6.

175. Sanders and Davies, *Studying the Synoptic Gospels*, 132.

176. It seems unlikely that these disputes were resolved by the time the Gospels were written. This is evidenced by the apostolic fathers and Justin Martyr, who demonstrate that Jewish-Christian interaction continued to be volatile and the developing church continued to wrestle with the implications of its Jewish heritage; cf. Ignatius, *Magn.* 8.1; 10.3; *Phld.* 6.1; Justin, *Dial. Tryph.*

177. T. W. Manson, "The Quest of the Historical Jesus — Continued," in *Studies in the Gospels and Epistles* (Manchester: Manchester University Press, 1962), 5.

178. Bultmann, *History of the Synoptic Tradition*, 155-56, 163.

179. Sanders, *Jesus and Judaism*, 220.

anti-Gentile Christian group, and the evidence for the existence of this group is Matt 10:5-6! The argument is viciously circular, but somehow it finds wide adherence.[180] This hypothetical and unattested Jewish group which was resolutely opposed to the inclusion of the Gentiles becomes a rather convenient source to which all the particularistic tendencies of the Jesus tradition can be attributed. In addition, one is still stuck with explaining why Matthew, who is clearly in favor of a Gentile mission, has retained such an ethnocentric logion.

It is worth repeating the dictum that there is no such thing as uninterpreted history.[181] All history-telling is a mixture of fact and interpretation, a fusion of past and present perspectives.[182] Communal needs and contemporary events may have *colored* the Jesus tradition, but they did not *create* it.[183] The corollary is that the theological substance of the Gospels does not necessarily negate their historical value. For it is likely that the historical referent and theological interpretation of the Jesus tradition were molded together from the beginning rather than one being abandoned for the other at a later date by the Evangelists or their sources. There never was a "once upon a time" when there was a historical Jesus separate from the faith of Jesus' followers. Howard Marshall writes:

> It is clear that the basic tradition of the sayings of Jesus was *modified* both in the tradition and by the Evangelists in order to re-express its significance for new situations; it is by no means obvious that this basic tradition was *created* by the early church. Similarly, it is unlikely that the stories about Jesus and the narrative settings for his teachings are the products of the church's *Sitz im Leben*. The fact

---

180. Richard Bauckham, foreword in James LaGrand, *The Earliest Christian Mission to "All Nations" in the Light of Matthew's Gospel* (Grand Rapids: Eerdmans, 1999), comments: "it has also become reasonably clear in recent scholarship that there is no evidence for a group in the early church which opposed taking the Christian gospel to the nations. Not even the most conservative Jewish Christians are elsewhere represented as saying what Matthew 10:5-6 says, while even those in the Jerusalem church who insisted that converts be circumcised and obey the whole Torah (a crucially different policy from Matthew 10:5-6) were only briefly influential at all. We are left hypothesizing a Jewish Christian group who could plausibly have originated the saying of Jesus in Matthew 10:5-6 solely on the evidence of this text itself."

181. Cf. Wright, *New Testament and the People of God*, 94-96; idem, *Jesus and the Victory of God*, 87-89; Charlesworth, *Jesus within Judaism*, 166.

182. Bauckham, *Jesus and the Eyewitnesses*, 3. Cf. Chris Keith ("The Indebtedness of the Criteria Approach to Form Criticism and Recent Attempts to Rehabilitate the Search for an Authentic Jesus," in *Jesus, Criteria, and the Demise of Authenticity*, ed. C. Keith and A. Le Donne [London: Clark, 2012], 39): "The notion that there is a past entity — a personal memory, unit of gospel tradition, historical figure, etc. — that one can detach from the interpretations that gave it meaning to a person or group, is simply erroneous."

183. Gerhardsson, *Origins of the Gospel Traditions*, 46.

that such material was found to be congenial for use in the church's situation is no proof that it was created for this purpose.[184]

I am not denying that the Gospels were written out of particular settings. Like all literature, they have contexts for both authors and readers that are embedded in the text. All narration tells us something about the setting of the storyteller. Although I am skeptical about using the Gospels to plot the interior debates and internecine rivalries of various isolated and introspective communities that purportedly stand behind the Gospels, nonetheless I do recognize that the Gospels were written amid networks or clusters of Christians and the Gospels were composed to speak to those settings. The memory of Jesus in the Gospels is designed to impact the beliefs, behavior, and identity of followers of Jesus in the Greco-Roman world. So while the Gospels are not simply mirrors of a singular community's beliefs, they do indeed reflect the setting of their authors and audiences to some extent. We might say that the *Sitz im Leben* is the synchronic horizon of the mnemonic event of remembering Jesus in the early church. Samuel Byrskog is right when he posits the *Sitz im Leben* as having to do with the "social dynamics of mnemonically relating to the past in the present" with a tradition that attempted to negotiate "between the two temporal horizons" of past and present.[185]

---

184. I. Howard Marshall, *The Gospel of Luke* (NIGTC; Grand Rapids: Eerdmans, 1978), 33.

185. Samuel Byrskog, "A Century with the *Sitz im Leben:* From Form-Critical Setting to Gospel Community and Beyond," *ZNW* 98 (2007): 22.

CHAPTER 4

The Literary Genetics of the Gospels:
The Synoptic Problem and Johannine Question

We know that Jesus traditions were carried in oral and written sources in the early church and we can reasonably infer that these various sources shaped the four canonical Gospels (see Luke 1:2). For example, it is quite possible that Mark 2–3, with its strong thematic coherence, was based on an early written collection of conflict stories about Jesus that were grouped together. The Olivet Discourse of Mark 13 is thought to have taken on concrete form by ca. 40 CE in light of the crisis caused by Caligula's desire to place a statue of himself in the Jerusalem temple. Mark 14–16 might draw on a well-known passion narrative extant in written form sometime before Mark wrote his Gospel. Either all or some of the sayings of Jesus common to Luke and Matthew could stem from a short document that both Evangelists incorporated into their respective Gospels.[1] The Gospel of John might have utilized a document which highlighted the prominence of Jesus' "signs" as vehicles of faith.[2] More hypothetically, some scholars have proposed that there could

---

1. Cf., e.g., H. W. Kuhn, *Ältere Sammlungen im Markusevangelium* (Göttingen: Vandenhoeck & Ruprecht, 1971); Yoon-Man Park, *Mark's Memory Resources and the Controversy Stories (Mark 2:1–3:6): An Application of the Frame Theory of Cognitive Science to the Markan Oral-Aural Narrative* (Leiden: Brill, 2010); N. H. Taylor, "Palestinian Christianity and the Caligula Crisis, Part II: The Markan Eschatological Discourse," *JSNT* 62 (1996): 13-41; Gerd Theissen, *The Gospels in Context: Social and Political History in the Synoptic Tradition* (Minneapolis: Fortress, 1991), 125-65; Marion L. Soards, "The Question of a PreMarkan Passion Narrative," *Bible Bhashyam* 11 (1985): 144-69; idem, "Oral Tradition before, in, and outside of the Canonical Passion Narratives," in *Jesus and the Oral Gospel Tradition*, ed. H. Wansbrough (Sheffield: JSOT, 1991), 334-50; John S. Kloppenborg, *Excavating Q: The History and Setting of the Sayings Gospel* (Minneapolis: Fortress, 2000); James M. Robinson, Paul Hoffman, and John S. Kloppenborg, eds., *The Critical Edition of Q* (Minneapolis: Fortress, 2000).

2. Cf. Robert Fortna, *The Fourth Gospel and Its Predecessor: From Narrative Source to*

have even been first and second editions of the Gospels before achieving their canonical form, such as an early Hebrew edition of Matthew, an *Ur-Mark*, a deutero-Mark, or a proto-Luke.[3]

It goes without saying that all of this talk of pre-Gospel sources is somewhat speculative. It is like attempting to figure out how many pieces of a jigsaw puzzle make up the picture on the cover of the box. There is no doubt that the Gospels were based on a variety of oral and written sources, but whether we are able to isolate and identify these sources in the Gospels with any precision is a matter of debate among Gospel scholars. Consequently, a critical task in Gospel studies is to identify as far as we can the precise sources used by the Evangelists and to describe how they used them. Source criticism of this order attempts to discern the history, unity, and shape of these sources in the Gospels.[4]

A primary feature of source criticism of the Gospels is examination of their literary relationships. The four canonical Gospels are similar but different at the same time. More specifically, the three Synoptic Gospels (Matthew, Mark, and Luke) have a particular affinity in their shared narrative framework and verbal content, while the Gospel of John represents a more independent branch of the Gospel tradition and therefore has its

---

Present Gospel (Philadelphia: Fortress, 1988), 219-20; J. L. Martyn, *History and Theology in the Fourth Gospel* (rev. ed.; Nashville: Abingdon, 1979), 12, 24, 65, 93-94, 164-66. See evaluation in Craig L. Blomberg, *The Historical Reliability of John's Gospel* (Downers Grove: InterVarsity, 2002), 44-46.

3. For several of these theories, see B. H. Streeter, *The Four Gospels: A Study of Origins* (London: Macmillan, 1930), 199-222; Vincent Taylor, *Behind the Third Gospel: A Study of the Proto-Luke Hypothesis* (Oxford: Oxford University Press, 1926); Albert Fuchs, *Sprachliche Untersuchungen zu Matthäus und Lukas. Ein Beitrag zur Quellenkritik* (Analecta Biblica 49; Rome: Biblical Institute Press, 1971); idem, *Spuren von Deuteromarkus* (5 vols.; SNTU 5; Münster: Lit, 2004-7); M.-É. Boismard and P. Benoit, *Synopses des quatre Évangiles en Français avec parrallèles des apocrypes et des pères* (Paris: Cerf, 1972); M.-É. Boismard, "The Two-Source Theory at an Impasse," *NTS* 26 (1979): 1-17; Ralph P. Martin, *New Testament Foundations* (2 vols.; Grand Rapids: Eerdmans, 1975-78), 1:152-56; Philippe Rolland, "Les prédécesseurs de Marc. Les sources présynoptiques de Mc, II, 18-22 et parallèles," *RB* 89 (1982): 370-405; idem, "Marc, première harmonie évangélique?" *RB* 90 (1983): 23-79; idem, "A New Look at the Synoptic Question," *EJTh* 8 (1999): 133-44; Helmut Koester, "History and Development of Mark's Gospel (From Mark to Secret Mark and 'Canonical' Mark)," in *Colloquy on New Testament Studies: A Time for Reappraisal and Fresh Approaches,* ed. B. Corley (Macon: Mercer University Press, 1991), 35-57; Delbert Burkett, *Rethinking the Gospel Sources: From Proto-Mark to Mark* (London: Clark, 2004).

4. For a decent introduction, see David Wenham, "Source Criticism," in *New Testament Interpretation,* ed. I. H. Marshall (Grand Rapids: Eerdmans, 1977), 139-52.

own unique relatedness to the other Gospels. The similarities between the Synoptic Gospels are of such a nature that it is highly probable that one Evangelist has borrowed from one or more of the others. The big questions are: who borrowed from whom, when, how, and to what extent? Then when we come to Gospel of John, because of its distinctive character we are left with the question of whether John is entirely independent of the Synoptics, or does the Gospel of John possess some kind of indirect dependence on Synoptic tradition? These questions are known as the "Synoptic Problem" and "Johannine Question" respectively.

I. The Synoptic Problem

The first three Gospels have been called the "Synoptic Gospels" because they offer a similar picture of the events of Jesus' life and can be viewed together, that is, syn-optically. The "problem" in the Synoptic problem is why Matthew, Mark, and Luke are so remarkably similar to each other and yet diverge in the ways that they do.[5] Of the 661 verses in Mark, roughly 500 recur in Matthew in parallel form and around 350 in Luke. Put statistically, about 85% of Mark's verses are found in Matthew and 65% in Luke (the "triple tradition"). There are also around 220 to 235 verses of non-Marcan material shared by Matthew and Luke (the "double tradition"). Then there are small pockets of material found exclusively in each Gospel that is not replicated in the other Gospels (often called "special" tradition in the case of Matthew and Luke). Over the course of church history much attention was given to harmonizing these differences. However, toward the middle of the nineteenth century concerted efforts were made to explain the similarities in terms of common sources and literary relationships. In order to demon-

---

5. The best introduction to the Synoptic problem is Mark Goodacre, *The Synoptic Problem: A Way Through the Maze* (London: Sheffield Academic, 2001). For a history of the debate, see David L. Dungan, *The History of the Synoptic Problem: The Canon, the Text, the Composition, and the Interpretation of the Gospels* (New York: Doubleday, 1999) and the bibliographic survey in Thomas R. W. Longstaff and Page A. Thomas, *The Synoptic Problem: A Bibliography, 1716-1968* (Macon: Mercer University Press, 1988). A collection of important essays on the subject can be found in Arthur J. Bellinzoni, ed., *The Two-Source Hypothesis: A Critical Appraisal* (Macon: Mercer University Press, 1985). For the *status quaestionis*, see the recent volume by Paul Foster, Andrew Gregory, John Kloppenborg, and Jozef Verheyden, eds., *New Studies in the Synoptic Problem: Oxford Conference, April 2008* (FS Christopher Tuckett; BETL 239; Leuven: Peeters, 2011).

strate the textual complexity of the Synoptic problem we will consider below similarities in wording, order, parenthetical and redactional material, and biblical quotations, since these exemplify the need for a solution to explain the similarities and divergences.

	unshared material	shared material[6]
Mark (661 verses)	7%	93%
Matthew (1068 verses)	42%	58%
Luke (1149 verses)	59%	41%

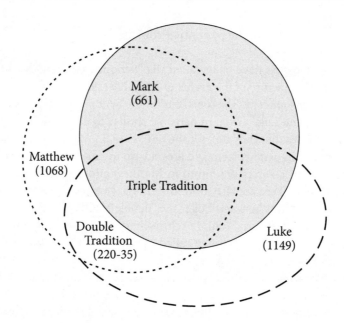

Why There Is a Synoptic Problem

1. Similarities in Wording

Viewing a pericope that occurs in all three Gospels synoptically (laid out side-by-side) is a good way of visibly observing the strong similarities in verbal content among the Gospels.[7] The exact degree of verbal correspondence

6. Adapted from B. F. Westcott, *Introduction to the Study of the Gospels* (8th ed.; London: Macmillan, 1895), 179.

7. The English translation used here is from the New Revised Standard Version (NRSV)

varies from unit to unit with, predictably, more similarities in sayings material than in narrative material. What is more, the verbal agreements oscillate among Mark-Matthew, Mark-Luke, and Matthew-Luke. The agreements are at different points in words, phrases, grammar, and/or order. It is possible to demonstrate these verbal agreements with any number of pericopes, but here I focus on the account of Jesus blessing the little children and the riddle of how the Messiah can be a Son of David.

Key to Wording Similarities

Plain	Unique Material
Shaded	Triple Agreement
Underlined	Mark-Matthew Agreement
Italics	Mark-Luke Agreement
Bold	Matthew-Luke Agreement

Jesus Blesses the Little Children

Mark 10:13-16	Matt 19:13-15	Luke 18:15-17
¹³People *were bringing* little children to him in order that he might touch *them;* and the disciples spoke sternly to them.	¹³Then little children were being brought to him in order that he might lay his hands on them and pray. The disciples spoke sternly to those who brought them;	¹⁵People *were bringing* even infants to him that he might touch *them;* and when the disciples saw it, they sternly ordered them not to do it.
¹⁴But when Jesus saw this, he was indignant and said to them, "Let the little children *come* to me; do not stop them; for it is to such as these that the kingdom *of God* belongs. ¹⁵*Truly I tell you, whoever does not receive the kingdom of God as a little child will never enter it.*" ¹⁶And he took them up in his arms, laid his hands on them, and blessed them.	¹⁴but Jesus said, "Let the little children come to me, and do not stop them; for it is to such as these that the kingdom of heaven belongs." ¹⁵And he laid his hands on them and went on his way.	¹⁶But Jesus called for them and said, "Let the little children *come* to me, and do not stop them; for it is to such as these that the kingdom *of God* belongs. ¹⁷*Truly I tell you, whoever does not receive the kingdom of God as a little child will never enter it.*"

and the Greek is from United Bible Society's fourth edition of the Greek New Testament (UBS⁴). I have also marked the similarities according to the Greek text based on shared wording, which is not always reflected in the English text.

Mark 10:13-16	Matt 19:13-15	Luke 18:15-17
¹³Καὶ προσέφερον αὐτῷ παιδία ἵνα αὐτῶν ἅψηται· οἱ δὲ μαθηταὶ ἐπετίμησαν αὐτοῖς.	¹³Τότε προσηνέχθησαν αὐτῷ παιδία ἵνα τὰς χεῖρας ἐπιθῇ αὐτοῖς καὶ προσεύξηται· οἱ δὲ μαθηταὶ ἐπετίμησαν αὐτοῖς.	¹⁵Προσέφερον δὲ αὐτῷ καὶ τὰ βρέφη ἵνα αὐτῶν ἅπτηται· ἰδόντες δὲ οἱ μαθηταὶ ἐπετίμων αὐτοῖς.
¹⁴ἰδὼν δὲ ὁ Ἰησοῦς ἠγανάκτησεν καὶ εἶπεν αὐτοῖς· ἄφετε τὰ παιδία ἔρχεσθαι πρός με, μὴ κωλύετε αὐτά, τῶν γὰρ τοιούτων ἐστὶν ἡ βασιλεία τοῦ θεοῦ. ¹⁵ἀμὴν λέγω ὑμῖν, ὃς ἂν μὴ δέξηται τὴν βασιλείαν τοῦ θεοῦ ὡς παιδίον, οὐ μὴ εἰσέλθῃ εἰς αὐτήν. ¹⁶καὶ ἐναγκαλισάμενος αὐτὰ κατευλόγει τιθεὶς τὰς χεῖρας ἐπ᾽ αὐτά.	¹⁴ὁ δὲ Ἰησοῦς εἶπεν· ἄφετε τὰ παιδία καὶ μὴ κωλύετε αὐτὰ ἐλθεῖν πρός με, τῶν γὰρ τοιούτων ἐστὶν ἡ βασιλεία τῶν οὐρανῶν. ¹⁵καὶ ἐπιθεὶς τὰς χεῖρας αὐτοῖς ἐπορεύθη ἐκεῖθεν.	¹⁶ὁ δὲ Ἰησοῦς προσεκαλέσατο αὐτὰ λέγων· ἄφετε τὰ παιδία ἔρχεσθαι πρός με καὶ μὴ κωλύετε αὐτά, τῶν γὰρ τοιούτων ἐστὶν ἡ βασιλεία τοῦ θεοῦ. ¹⁷ἀμὴν λέγω ὑμῖν, ὃς ἂν μὴ δέξηται τὴν βασιλείαν τοῦ θεοῦ ὡς παιδίον, οὐ μὴ εἰσέλθῃ εἰς αὐτήν.

Here Mark's is the longest account and Matthew's is the shortest. Note that the major verbal connections between all three versions pertain principally to the words of Jesus about not preventing the children coming to him. Only Mark and Luke retain the "amen" saying about the positive example of children for entering the kingdom, which is absent from Matthew. While there are a couple of Mark-Matthew agreements, there are no Matthew-Luke agreements here.

How Can the Messiah Be a Son of David?

Mark 12:35-37	Matt 22:41-46	Luke 20:41-44
³⁵While Jesus was teaching in the temple, he said, "How can the scribes say that the Messiah is the son of David?	⁴¹Now while the Pharisees were gathered together, Jesus asked them this question: ⁴²"What do you think of the Messiah? Whose son is he?" They said to him, "The son of David."	⁴¹Then he said to them, "How can they say that the Messiah is David's son?
³⁶David himself, by the Holy Spirit, declared, 'The Lord said to my Lord, "Sit	⁴³He said to them, "How is it then that David by the Spirit calls him Lord, saying, ⁴⁴'The Lord said to	⁴²For David himself says in the book of Psalms, 'The Lord said to my Lord, "Sit

Mark 12:35-37	Matt 22:41-46	Luke 20:41-44
at my right hand, until I put your enemies under your <u>feet</u>." '	my Lord, "Sit at my right hand, until I put your enemies under your <u>feet</u>" '?	at my right hand, ⁴³until I make your enemies your footstool." '
³⁷David himself calls him Lord; so how can he be his son?" And the large crowd was listening to him with delight.	⁴⁵If David thus **calls** him Lord, **how** can he be his son?"	⁴⁴David thus **calls** him Lord; so **how** can he be his son?"
	⁴⁶No one was able to give him an answer, nor from that day did anyone dare to ask him any more questions.	
³⁵Καὶ ἀποκριθεὶς ὁ Ἰησοῦς ἔλεγεν διδάσκων ἐν τῷ ἱερῷ· πῶς λέγουσιν οἱ γραμματεῖς ὅτι ὁ χριστὸς υἱὸς Δαυίδ ἐστιν;	⁴¹Συνηγμένων δὲ τῶν Φαρισαίων ἐπηρώτησεν αὐτοὺς ὁ Ἰησοῦς ⁴²λέγων· τί ὑμῖν δοκεῖ περὶ τοῦ χριστοῦ; τίνος υἱός ἐστιν; λέγουσιν αὐτῷ· τοῦ Δαυίδ.	⁴¹Εἶπεν δὲ πρὸς αὐτούς· πῶς λέγουσιν τὸν χριστὸν εἶναι Δαυὶδ υἱόν;
³⁶αὐτὸς Δαυὶδ εἶπεν ἐν τῷ πνεύματι τῷ ἁγίῳ· εἶπεν κύριος τῷ κυρίῳ μου· κάθου ἐκ δεξιῶν μου, ἕως ἂν θῶ τοὺς ἐχθρούς σου ὑποκάτω τῶν ποδῶν σου. ³⁷αὐτὸς Δαυὶδ λέγει αὐτὸν κύριον, καὶ πόθεν αὐτοῦ ἐστιν υἱός; Καὶ [ὁ] πολὺς ὄχλος ἤκουεν αὐτοῦ ἡδέως.	⁴³λέγει αὐτοῖς· πῶς οὖν Δαυὶδ ἐν πνεύματι καλεῖ αὐτοῦ κύριον λέγων· ⁴⁴εἶπεν κύριος τῷ κυρίῳ μου· κάθου ἐκ δεξιῶν μου, ἕως ἂν θῶ τοὺς ἐχθρούς σου ὑποκάτω τῶν ποδῶν σου; ⁴⁵εἰ οὖν Δαυὶδ **καλεῖ** αὐτὸν κύριον, πῶς υἱὸς αὐτοῦ ἐστιν; ⁴⁶καὶ οὐδεὶς ἐδύνατο ἀποκριθῆναι αὐτῷ λόγον οὐδὲ ἐτόλμησέν τις ἀπ᾽ ἐκείνης τῆς ἡμέρας ἐπερωτῆσαι αὐτὸν οὐκέτι.	⁴²αὐτὸς γὰρ Δαυὶδ λέγει ἐν βίβλῳ ψαλμῶν· εἶπεν κύριος τῷ κυρίῳ μου· κάθου ἐκ δεξιῶν μου, ⁴³ἕως ἂν θῶ τοὺς ἐχθρούς σου ὑποπόδιον τῶν ποδῶν σου. ⁴⁴Δαυὶδ οὖν κύριον αὐτὸν **καλεῖ**, καὶ πῶς αὐτοῦ υἱός ἐστιν;

We can see here how what is clearly the same story is framed somewhat differently by the three Evangelists. Matthew's is the longest, Luke's is the shortest; there are many shared words, not least in the citation of Ps 110:1. Beyond the triple agreements, there is a mix of Mark-Luke, Mark-Matthew, and Matthew-Luke agreements on particular words.

This phenomenon of verbal agreement is best explained by reference to a literary relationship among the Synoptic Gospels. Such close verbal and compositional similarities are best explained in literary terms. One Gospel's content was copied into another Gospel. We can postulate either a common literary source known to the Synoptic Evangelists, or, and more likely I think, we must posit a literary relationship between the Synoptic Gospels to account for these verbal and compositional agreements. But if this is indeed the case, then we can naturally ask which Gospel has the *original wording* that was followed, adapted, and supplemented by the other two Evangelists.

2. Similarities in Outline and Order

A further feature of the Gospels that suggests a literary relationship is their shared narrative outline and agreements in order of pericopes.

The Synoptic Gospels share an outline that begins with Jesus' baptism, his Galilean ministry, his journey to Jerusalem, and then his arrest, trial, death, and resurrection in Jerusalem. The narratives are organized differently by each Evangelist. The Gospel of Mark is very much a story in two parts divided by events leading up to Peter's confession at Caesarea-Philippi (Mark 1:1–8:30) and the events following after it (8:31–16:8). Matthew's Gospel is dominated by five large discourses (Matt 5:1–7:29; 10:1-42; 13:1-53; 18:1-35; 24:1–25:46), each followed by narratives that explicate Jesus' teachings. The Gospel of Luke is structured around the journey to Jerusalem, where the bulk of Jesus' teaching material can be found (Luke 9:51–19:10). There are also significant amounts of material unique to Matthew (often labeled "M") and material unique to Luke (often labeled "L") interspersed throughout their respective Gospels. If the Synoptic Gospels were written independently or even semi-independently of each other, then it would have been possible to have outlines that were, for whatever reason, rather different from what they are now. For example, the Gospel of John places Jesus' demonstration in the Jerusalem temple at the beginning of his ministry (John 2:13-22), while the Synoptic Gospels place it at the end of his ministry (Mark 11:15-18/Matt 21:12-13/Luke 19:45-46). Yet the Synoptic Gospels follow the same outline very closely and provide what is recognizably the same story with the same basic plot.

In addition to a shared general outline, the Synoptic Gospels narrate the same stories often in the same order. A complete list of the order of every pericope in the Gospels can be found in an appendix to Kurt Aland's

Synopsis, and reading it is a most illuminating exercise.[8] Of all the imaginable ways to set out the various sub-stories of Jesus' activities, the fact that healing stories, sayings, narrative descriptions, and the like frequently follow a common order suggests a literary relationship of some kind. For instance, Mark 2:1–3:6 contains a sequence of controversy stories involving Jesus and the Judean leaders without indicating the order in which the confrontations took place. Matthew and Luke both contain the same sequence of individual units, although Matthew does insert additional intervening material (see Luke 5:17–6:11; Matt 9:1-17; 12:1-14). The most likely scenario is that this order has been established by one of the Evangelists, who was followed in this sequence by the others. In addition, we may also consider two lists of units from early and late stages of Jesus' ministry as indicative of the shared order among the Synoptics.

Jesus' Ministry in Galilee

Episode	Mark	Matthew	Luke
Jesus teaches in the synagogue in Capernaum	1:21-22		4:31-32
Jesus heals the demoniac in Capernaum	1:23-28		4:33-37
Jesus heals Peter's mother-in-law	1:29-31	8:14-15	4:38-39
Jesus heals in the evening	1:32-34	8:16-17	4:40-41
Jesus departs from Capernaum	1:35-38		4:42-43
Summary of Jesus' preaching in Galilee	1:39	4:23	4:44
Jesus, Peter, and the miraculous catch of fish			5:1-11
Jesus heals a leper	1:40-45	8:1-4	5:12-16
Jesus heals a paralytic	2:1-12	9:1-8	5:17-26
The calling of Levi	2:13-17	9:9-13	5:27-32
Controversy about fasting	2:18-22	9:14-17	5:33-39
Controversy about plucking grain on the Sabbath	2:23-28	12:1-8	6:1-5
Controversy about healing on the Sabbath	3:1-6	12:9-14	6:6-11
Healing by the seashore	3:7-12	4:24-25; 12:15-16	6:17-19
Choosing of the twelve apostles	3:13-19	10:1-4	6:12-16

8. Kurt Aland, *Synopsis of the Four Gospels: Greek-English Edition of the Synopsis Quattuor Evangeliorum* (12th ed.; Stuttgart: German Bible Society, 2001), 341-55. The other synopsis of choice for most scholars is A. Huck and H. Greeven, *Synopse der drei ersten Evangelien mit Beigabe der johanneischen Parallelstellen* (Tübingen: Mohr, 1981).

Mark and Luke share a common outline at this point, the only disagreement between them being that Luke includes the story of the call of Peter with the miraculous catch of fish, which is not found in Mark (Luke 5:1-11). Matthew picks up this outline at spasmodic points, especially in chapters 8, 9, and 12, but intersperses other material, and places summaries of Jesus' activities at different points.

Jesus' Last Night in Jerusalem

Episode	Mark	Matthew	Luke
Jesus' death is premeditated	14:1-2	26:1-5	22:1-2
Jesus is anointed in Bethany	14:3-9	26:6-13	
Betrayal by Judas	14:10-11	26:14-16	22:3-6
Preparations for Passover	14:12-17	26:17-20	22:7-14
Jesus predicts his betrayal	14:18-21	26:21-25	
The Last Supper	14:22-25	26:26-29	22:15-20
Jesus predicts his betrayal			22:21-23
Honor among the disciples and rewards for discipleship			22:24-30
Jesus predicts Peter's denial	14:26-31	26:30-35	22:31-34

In the Synoptic accounts of the night that Jesus was betrayed, the order of events is remarkably similar in all three Gospels, especially the agreement between Mark and Matthew. Luke digresses from this order only slightly since he does not have the account of Jesus' anointing in Bethany. Instead, he has a story about Jesus being anointed at the house of a Pharisee earlier in his ministry (Luke 7:36-50). Luke also moves the prediction of Jesus' betrayal to *after* the Last Supper rather than *before* it as Mark and Matthew have it. Even so, there is a remarkable concord of the order of events surrounding the messy day that Jesus was betrayed. All this is too coincidental to be based on an orally remembered record. The explanation for this similarity has to be literary.

3. Similarities in Parenthetical and Redactional Material

It is very illuminating when we find intrusive and unnecessary editorial comments shared among one or more of the Synoptics. A sure indicator of a genetic literary relationship between the Synoptics is the presence of shared parenthetical remarks that were obviously inserted editorially at the written level but shared across two or more Gospels. Let me give two examples:

Parenthetical Remarks for the "Reader"

Mark 13:14-16	Matt 24:15-17	Luke 21:20-22
[14]"But when you see the desolating sacrilege set up where it ought not to be (let the reader understand), then those in Judea must flee to the mountains; [15]the one on the housetop must not go down or enter the house to take anything away; [16]the one in the field must not turn back to get a coat."	[15]"So when you see the desolating sacrilege standing in the holy place, as was spoken of by the prophet Daniel (let the reader understand), [16]then those in Judea must flee to the mountains, [17]the one on the housetop must not go down to take what is in the house, [18]the one in the field must not turn back to get a coat."	[20]"When you see Jerusalem surrounded by armies, then know that its desolation has come near. [21]Then those in Judea must flee to the mountains, and those inside the city must leave it, and those out in the country must not enter it; [22]for these are days of vengeance, as a fulfillment of all that is written."
[14]Ὅταν δὲ ἴδητε τὸ βδέλυγμα τῆς ἐρημώσεως ἑστηκότα ὅπου οὐ δεῖ, ὁ ἀναγινώσκων νοείτω, τότε οἱ ἐν τῇ Ἰουδαίᾳ φευγέτωσαν εἰς τὰ ὄρη, [15]ὁ [δὲ] ἐπὶ τοῦ δώματος μὴ καταβάτω μηδὲ εἰσελθάτω ἀραί τι ἐκ τῆς οἰκίας αὐτοῦ, [16]καὶ ὁ εἰς τὸν ἀγρὸν μὴ ἐπιστρεψάτω εἰς τὰ ὀπίσω ἀραι τὸ ἱμάτιον αὐτοῦ	[15]Ὅταν οὖν ἴδητε τὸ βδέλυγμα τῆς ἐρημώσεως τὸ ῥηθὲν διὰ Δανιὴλ τοῦ προφήτου ἑστὸς ἐν τόπῳ ἁγίῳ, ὁ ἀναγινώσκων νοείτω, [16]τότε οἱ ἐν τῇ Ἰουδαίᾳ φευγέτωσαν εἰς τὰ ὄρη, [17]ὁ ἐπὶ τοῦ δώματος μὴ καταβάτω ἀραι τὰ ἐκ τῆς οἰκίας αὐτοῦ, [18]καὶ ὁ ἐν τῷ ἀγρῷ μὴ ἐπιστρεψάτω ὀπίσω ἀραι τὸ ἱμάτιον αὐτοῦ	[20]Ὅταν δὲ ἴδητε κυκλουμένην ὑπὸ στρατοπέδων Ἰερουσαλήμ, τότε γνῶτε ὅτι ἤγγικεν ἡ ἐρήμωσις αὐτῆς. [21]τότε οἱ ἐν τῇ Ἰουδαίᾳ φευγέτωσαν εἰς τὰ ὄρη καὶ οἱ ἐν μέσῳ αὐτῆς ἐκχωρείτωσαν καὶ οἱ ἐν ταῖς χώραις μὴ εἰσερχέσθωσαν εἰς αὐτήν, [22]ὅτι ἡμέραι ἐκδικήσεως αὗταί εἰσιν τοῦ πλησθῆναι πάντα τὰ γεγραμμένα.

The phrase "let the reader understand" is enigmatic and baffling. Does it mean let the reader of the *book of Daniel* understand, or does it mean let the reader of the *Gospel* understand? In either case, it is even more amazing that this aside made by either Mark or Matthew has found its way into the text of the other Gospel, and yet is noticeably absent from Luke.

Editorial Remarks about the Plot to Seize Jesus

Mark 14:1-2, 10	Matt 24:4-5, 14	Luke 22:1-3
[1]It was two days before the Passover and the festival of *Unleavened Bread*. The *chief priests and the scribes were looking* for *a way* to arrest Jesus by stealth and kill him; [2]for they said, "Not during the festival, or there may be a riot among the people."	[4]and they conspired to arrest Jesus by stealth and kill him. [5]But they said, "Not during the festival, or there may be a riot among the people."	[1]Now the festival of *Unleavened Bread*, which is called the Passover, was near. [2]*The chief priests and the scribes were looking* for *a way* to put Jesus to death, for they were afraid of the people.
[10]Then Judas Iscariot, who was one of the twelve, went to the chief priests in order to betray him to them.	[14]Then one of the twelve, who was called Judas Iscariot, went to the chief priests . . .	[3]Then Satan entered into Judas called Iscariot, who was one of the twelve.
[1]Ἦν δὲ τὸ πάσχα καὶ τὰ ἄζυμα μετὰ δύο ἡμέρας. καὶ ἐζήτουν οἱ ἀρχιερεῖς καὶ οἱ γραμματεῖς πῶς αὐτὸν ἐν δόλῳ κρατήσαντες ἀποκτείνωσιν· [2]ἔλεγον γάρ· μὴ ἐν τῇ ἑορτῇ, μήποτε ἔσται θόρυβος τοῦ λαοῦ.	[4]καὶ συνεβουλεύσαντο ἵνα τὸν Ἰησοῦν δόλῳ κρατήσωσιν καὶ ἀποκτείνωσιν· [5]ἔλεγον δέ· μὴ ἐν τῇ ἑορτῇ, ἵνα μὴ θόρυβος γένηται ἐν τῷ λαῷ.	[1]Ἤγγιζεν δὲ ἡ ἑορτὴ τῶν ἀζύμων ἡ λεγομένη πάσχα. [2]καὶ ἐζήτουν οἱ ἀρχιερεῖς καὶ οἱ γραμματεῖς τὸ πῶς ἀνέλωσιν αὐτόν, ἐφοβοῦντο γὰρ τὸν λαόν.
[10]Καὶ Ἰούδας Ἰσκαριὼθ ὁ εἷς τῶν δώδεκα ἀπῆλθεν πρὸς τοὺς ἀρχιερεῖς ἵνα αὐτὸν παραδοῖ αὐτοῖς.	[14]Τότε πορευθεὶς εἷς τῶν δώδεκα, ὁ λεγόμενος Ἰούδας Ἰσκαριώτης, πρὸς τοὺς ἀρχιερεῖς . . .	[3]Εἰσῆλθεν δὲ σατανᾶς εἰς Ἰούδαν τὸν καλούμενον Ἰσκαριώτην, ὄντα ἐκ τοῦ ἀριθμοῦ τῶν δώδεκα·

What we have here is some scene setting for Jesus' arrest, in no way part of the oral tradition but remarks made by an omniscient narrator who knows what Jesus' opponents were fearful of and plotting about. There is agreement across all three Synoptic Gospels in the outline and details regarding the chief priests' fear of the people and how Judas, one of the twelve, agreed to betray Jesus to them. But note also the Mark-Matthew verbal agreements and the Mark-Luke verbal agreements. It would seem that one Evangelist's attempt to build up the picture pertaining to Jesus' final day in Jerusalem has found its way into the version of the other two Synoptic Evangelists.

4. Similarities in Old Testament Citations

A further phenomenon to explore is how the Synoptics agree on the precise wording of Old Testament citations that are different from all extant Hebrew and Greek Old Testament texts.

A Voice in the Wilderness

Isa 40:3 (MT)	Isa 40:3 (LXX)	Mark 1:3	Matt 3:3	Luke 3:4
A voice cries out: "In the wilderness prepare the way of the LORD, make straight in the desert a highway for **our God**."	The voice of one crying in the wilderness, "Prepare the way of the Lord, make straight the paths of **our God**."	The voice of one crying out in the wilder-ness: "Prepare the way of the Lord, make **his** paths straight."	"The voice of one crying out in the wilder-ness: 'Prepare the way of the Lord, make **his** paths straight."	"The voice of one crying out in the wilder-ness: 'Prepare the way of the Lord, make **his** paths straight.'"
קוֹל קוֹרֵא בַמִּדְבָּר פַּנּוּ דֶּרֶךְ יהוה יַשְּׁרוּ בָּעֲרָבָה מְסִלָּה לֵאלֹהֵינוּ	φωνὴ βοῶντος ἐν τῇ ἐρήμῳ ἑτοιμάσατε τὴν ὁδὸν κυρίου εὐθείας ποιεῖτε τὰς τρίβους τοῦ **θεοῦ ἡμῶν**.	φωνὴ βοῶντος ἐν τῇ ἐρήμῳ· ἑτοιμάσατε τὴν ὁδὸν κυρίου, εὐθείας ποιεῖτε τὰς τρίβους **αὐτοῦ**.	φωνὴ βοῶντος ἐν τῇ ἐρήμῳ· ἑτοιμάσατε τὴν ὁδὸν κυρίου, εὐθείας ποιεῖτε τὰς τρίβους **αὐτοῦ**.	φωνὴ βοῶντος ἐν τῇ ἐρήμῳ· ἑτοιμάσατε τὴν ὁδὸν κυρίου, εὐθείας ποιεῖτε τὰς τρίβους **αὐτοῦ**.

Mark, Matthew, and Luke all agree *against* the MT (Hebrew) and LXX (Greek) versions of Isa 40:3 in using the pronoun "his" for "his paths" in contrast to the pronoun "our" for "our God." It is possible that the Synoptic version is based on an Aramaic targumic tradition, a Hebrew midrash, or even a loose Greek paraphrase from a source otherwise unknown to us but accessible to all three Evangelists. But that such a distinct translation of Isa 40:3 in Greek should be found across all three Synoptic Gospels is surely a sign of a shared literary relationship between them. We are left asking, though, which Evangelist first introduced this creative rendering of the pronouns into the Synoptic tradition? This is not an isolated instance. Many other examples could be given, such as the citation of Deut 6:5 in Mark 12:30/ Matt 22:37/Luke 10:27 with its distinctive four-part "heart, soul, mind, and strength," which is unique when compared to the MT and LXX versions. Now not all Old Testament citations agree across the Synoptic Gospels, but there are often singular renderings of Old Testament passages that are shared by all three Synoptic Gospels. It is a factor that warrants explanation as to how the unique wording in these citations was introduced into the Synoptic tradition.

5. Conclusion

From all of this we can see that the Synoptic problem is indeed a problem when we attempt to explain exactly *why* there are these widespread verbal agreements between the Synoptic Gospels, why the Synoptics follow the same outlines, why they share parenthetical remarks and redactional arrangements, and why they appear to jointly employ unique Greek translations of Old Testament texts. This all points to some kind of interrelationship between the Synoptic Gospels, but the root of the riddle remains: Who used whom first?

Various Options for Solving the Synoptic Problem

Now that we have briefly dipped into the textual phenomenon of the Synoptic tradition in order to experience firsthand the complexity of the Synoptic problem, it is time to look at the various theories that try to explain the similarities and differences between the Synoptic Gospels. Although there is a proliferation of solutions, the views I shall focus on are the Augustinian, Griesbach, *Ur*-Gospel, common oral tradition, two-(four-)source theory, and Farrer varieties.[9]

1. The Augustinian View

The Augustinian order of the Gospels proposes that Matthew wrote first, followed by Mark, then Luke, and finally John. This ordering was the dominant view of Christian theologians until even after the Reformation.[10]

---

9. In favor of Lucan priority is Robert L. Lindsey, "A Modified Two-Document Theory of the Synoptic Dependence and Interdependence," *NovT* 6 (1963): 239-63; and in favor of Matthean posteriority is Ronald V. Huggins, "Matthean Posteriority: A Preliminary Proposal," *NovT* 34 (1992): 1-22; Martin Hengel, *The Four Gospels and the One Gospel of Jesus Christ*, trans. J. Bowden (Harrisburg: Trinity, 2000), 68-70; Bartosz Adamczewski, *Q or not Q? The So-Called Triple, Double, and Single Traditions in the Synoptic Gospels* (Frankfurt am Main: Lang, 2010). See evaluation of Matthean posteriority in Paul Foster, "Is It Possible to Dispense with Q?" *NovT* 45 (2003): 333-36.

10. On Augustine and the Synoptic problem, see Dungan, *History of the Synoptic Problem*, 112-41.

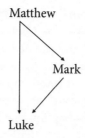

Matthew

Mark

Luke

Augustine took time out from composing his massive *On the Trinity* to write up a response to Manichaean allegations that the Gospels were contradictory. The allegation was of course not a new one, it was a key argument of pagan critics of Christianity from Celsus to Porphyry, and its bite was felt by Christian exegetes. Augustine wrote *Harmony of the Gospels* as his response to these criticisms, not a historical-critical work, but fundamentally a theological reading of the Gospels that offered a rejoinder to critics of Christianity. Augustine was concerned with preserving the special authority of the four canonical Gospels and accounting for the differences in the Gospels by means of a harmonious explanation. The African bishop wrote:

> So these four evangelists, well-known through the entire world (and perhaps they are four because of this, since there are four parts of the world, through the whole of which, they have proclaimed, in a certain manner by the very sacrament of their own number, that the church of Christ has spread) are regarded to have written in this order: first Matthew, then Mark, third Luke, and last John. Hence, there is one order to them in learning and preaching, and another in writing.[11]

Augustine's *Harmony* was the most ambitious project ever undertaken to demonstrate the textual, historical, and theological consistency of the Evangelists. Augustine was not the first to posit Matthean priority. The view undoubtedly preceded him. In all manuscripts with the four Gospels, Matthew is always placed first, with a few western texts (W and D) placing John second.[12] Matthew was also by far the most popular and prominent of the four Gospels in the early church, which explains in part why people just as-

---

11. Augustine, *Harmony of the Gospels* 1.3.

12. Beyond the assumption of Matthean priority, the patristic consensus about the order of the Gospels broke down as to where the non-apostolic authors of Luke and Mark fitted into the sequence of composition.

sumed it must have been written first. Augustine appears then to be simply following popular tradition in putting Matthew first.

Obviously patristic evidence can be ignored only at one's own peril. However, the case for Matthean priority needs to be established textually, not just assumed on the basis of tradition in order to be reasonably warranted. It is evident that patristic authors were duly influenced in their view of Matthean priority on the assumption that the "Matthew" of the "Gospel according to Matthew" was the same Matthew who was a tax collector and then apostle and eyewitness to Jesus' ministry (see Matt 9:9). Yet the authorship of Matthew is an open question. It is no surprise, then, that as Protestant scholasticism applied critical methods to the study of the Gospels, the Augustinian view had to be either modified (as by J. J. Griesbach) or rejected (as by H. J. Holtzmann and B. H. Streeter).

2. The Griesbach Hypothesis

The Griesbach hypothesis, named after Johann Jakob Griesbach (1745-1812), is distinguished by its emphasis on Matthean priority, Marcan posterity, and

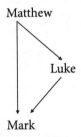

Matthew

Luke

Mark

Lucan intermediacy. Unlike the Augustinian view, which also places Matthew first, it is Mark rather than Luke that is last among the Synoptic Gospels. When Griesbach wrote, Matthean priority was largely assumed based on the popularity of the Augustinian tradition and had already been argued in Henry Owen's *Observations on the Four Gospels* (1764), which Griesbach may have encountered on his trip to England. Griesbach contributed two essays on the Synoptic problem in which he advocated that Matthew was the first Gospel written, that it was utilized by Luke, and that Mark summarized both Matthew and Luke. In a lecture delivered in 1783, Griesbach argued that the Synoptic resurrection narratives indicate that Mark used both Matthew and Luke as his sources and that Luke also used Matthew. Then, in another essay delivered in 1789, Griesbach argued in greater depth that Mark summarized both Luke and Matthew in order to compose a shorter and more succinct Gospel.[13]

The Griesbach thesis fell out of favor by the late nineteenth century, being supplanted by the two-source theory with Marcan priority. Though many Roman Catholic scholars retained adherence to Matthean priority due to its traditional pedigree, in the wake of Pope Pius XII's encyclical *Divino Afflante Spiritu* (1943) and after Vatican II (1962-65), Catholic biblical scholars have increasingly embraced Marcan priority.[14] In nineteenth-century Germany, the Griesbach theory enjoyed support in the Tübingen school, conducive as it was to F. C. Baur's Hegelian dialectic of the "thesis" of Jewish Christianity (Matthew), followed by its "antithesis" in Pauline Christianity (Luke), resulting in a "synthesis" of Catholic Christianity (Mark). This Tübingen framework was largely rejected by critical analysis of the sources, which demonstrated that the dates assigned to the sources to make the thesis work did not stand up to scrutiny. Consequently, German support for the Griesbach hypothesis began to crumble, even more so in the wake of H. J. Holtzmann's and Paul Wernle's case for Marcan priority at the approach of the twentieth century. However, there has been resurgence in the Griesbach hypothesis in some quarters, led principally by William Farmer.[15] The primary strengths of the Griesbach hypothesis are: (1) the argument from order can be accounted for not only on the basis of the two-source hypothesis, but also on the basis of the Griesbach hypothesis;[16] and (2) the Luke-Matthew

13. William Farmer, *The Synoptic Problem: A Critical Analysis* (New York: Macmillan, 1964), 7-9; William Baird, *History of New Testament Research* (3 vols.; Minneapolis: Fortress, 1992-2003), 1:138-48; Dungan, *History of the Synoptic Problem*, 309-26.

14. Cf., e.g., Raymond E. Brown, *Introduction to the New Testament* (ABRL; New York: Doubleday, 1997), 111-24; Joseph A. Fitzmyer, "The Priority of Mark and the 'Q' Source in Luke," in *Jesus and Man's Hope*, ed. D. G. Buttrick (Pittsburgh: Pittsburgh Theological Seminary, 1970), 1:131-70.

15. Farmer, *Synoptic Problem*, chapter 3, reprinted as "A New Introduction to the Synoptic Problem," in Bellinzoni, ed., *The Two-Source Hypothesis*, 163-97; idem, *Jesus and the Gospel: Tradition, Scripture, and Canon* (Philadelphia: Fortress, 1982), 1-11; idem, *The Gospel of Jesus: The Pastoral Relevance of the Synoptic Problem* (Louisville: Westminster John Knox, 1994); idem, "The Case for the Two-Gospel Hypothesis," in *Rethinking the Synoptic Problem*, ed. D. A. Black and D. R. Beck (Grand Rapids: Baker, 2001), 97-135; see esp. Christopher M. Tuckett, *The Revival of the Griesbach Hypothesis: An Analysis and Appraisal* (SNTSMS 44; Cambridge: Cambridge University Press, 1983).

16. Farmer, "New Introduction," 177-80, idem, *Jesus and the Gospel*, 4-5; idem, "Two-

minor agreements against Mark in the triple tradition and the so-called Q-Mark overlaps all raise serious questions about the independence of Luke from Matthew.[17]

The arguments against the Griesbach hypothesis are really those following on from the case for Marcan priority and for the existence of the Q source known to both Matthew and Luke (more on both below). The real Achilles' heel of the Griesbach hypothesis has been its prejudice against Mark. Griesbach was committed to the traditional authorship of the Gospels, stating that "Very far from the truth is the opinion of some who think that the Evangelists are not the true authors of the books that are circulated under their names."[18] Consequently, he found it very unlikely that Matthew, an apostle and an eyewitness to Jesus, would depend upon the non-eyewitness testimony of Mark. Yet that is an assumption about authorship on which an inference concerning inter-Synoptic relations is made, not something demanded by the phenomenon of the texts. Griesbach is scathing in his regard for the Gospel of Mark in other ways: "Those who argue that Mark wrote under the influence of divine inspiration must surely regard it as being a pretty meager one!"[19] Mark is also relegated by Farmer to the early second century, beyond the apostolic era.[20] Moreover, we are left wondering on the Griesbach hypothesis why Mark would abbreviate and conflate Luke and Matthew the way that he did. Why leave out the birth narratives, the Sermon on the Mount/Plain, and so many parables? Sanders and Davies put it this way:

> Mark could have done what the Griesbach proposal has him do. The question is, why would he? The strongest arguments against the Griesbach hypothesis are general, not technical. Why would anyone write a shorter version of Matthew and Luke, carefully combining them, and leaving out so much — such as the Lord's prayer and the beatitudes —

Gospel Hypothesis," 111-13; see discussion of the argument from order in David J. Neville, *Arguments for Order in Synoptic Source Criticism* (Macon: Mercer University Press, 1993); idem, *Mark's Gospel — Prior or Posterior? A Reappraisal of the Phenomenon of Order* (JSNTSup 222; London: Sheffield Academic, 2002); Malcolm Lowe, "The Demise of Arguments from Order for Marcan Priority," *NovT* 24 (1982): 27-36; but see criticism of Farmer in Tuckett, *Griesbach Hypothesis*, 26-40.

17. Farmer, "New Introduction," 181-82; idem, *Jesus and the Gospel*, 5-6; idem, "Two-Gospel Hypothesis," 113-14; but see criticism of Farmer in Tuckett, *Griesbach Hypothesis*, 61-93.

18. Cited in Baird, *History of New Testament Research*, 1:146 n. 102.

19. Cited in Baird, *History of New Testament Research*, 1:147.

20. Farmer, "New Introduction," 191-92.

while gaining nothing except perhaps room for such trivial additions as the duplicate phrases and minor details ("carried by four" and the like)?[21]

No discernible purpose for Mark on the Griesbach hypothesis seems evident.[22]

3. A Hebrew/Aramaic Ur-Gospel

Another solution to the Synoptic problem has been to posit an underlying written source, a Hebrew or Aramaic *Ur*-Gospel, perhaps identifiable with one of the early Jewish Christian Gospels referred to by the church fathers, as a means of accounting for the similarities and differences between the Gospels.[23]

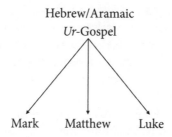

G. E. Lessing, in his *Neue Hypothese über die Evangelisten* (1778), believed that the Gospels were based on a single Aramaic or Hebrew Gospel that was utilized differently by each Evangelist. He identified this with the *Gospel of the Nazarenes* or *Gospel of the Hebrews* known to the church fathers. This *Ur*-Gospel underwent modifications in the early church so that different versions of this Aramaic/Hebrew Gospel were utilized by the Evangelists, who also adapted the materials to suit their point and purpose. Lessing's proposal was taken up and developed further by J. G. Eichhorn in his *Einleitung in das Neue Testament* (1804), which suggested that an original *Ur*-Gospel was revised in different versions. But unlike Lessing, Eichhorn

---

21. Sanders and Davies, *Studying the Synoptic Gospels*, 92.

22. Cf. Tuckett, *Griesbach Hypothesis*, 12-13, 52-60; Robert H. Stein, *Studying the Synoptic Gospels: Origin and Interpretation* (2nd ed.; Grand Rapids: Baker, 2001), 146-48.

23. Farmer, *Synoptic Problem*, 3-5, 10-11, 14; Baird, *History of New Testament Research*, 1:150-51; Dungan, *History of the Synoptic Problem*, 323-24.

had a way of accounting for the double tradition of Matthew-Luke agreements. Eichhorn suggested that the *Ur*-Gospel was revised in four forms: *A* the basis of Matthew, *B* the basis of Luke, *C* a version made out of *A* and *B* and used by Mark, and finally *D* which was used by both Matthew and Luke.

Soon after, J. G. von Herder, a German pastor and literary critic, also writing at the end of the eighteenth century, argued that the Synoptic tradition derived from a common Aramaic *Ur*-Gospel that was independently taken up by the Synoptic Evangelists.[24] Herder had initially believed in a more traditional scheme of Matthean priority but by 1797 had changed his mind and postulated a process of oral tradition leading to the Aramaic *Ur*-Gospel. The early oral tradition had been structured into an Aramaic oral Gospel in Palestine by "ministers of the word" (Luke 1:2) sometime between 35 and 40 CE and shared with their preaching assistants. It included a sketch of the life of Jesus, beginning with his baptism and ending with his ascension (Acts 1:22). These assistants committed the *Ur*-Gospel to writing for their convenience, and it became the basis for the canonical Gospels. According to Herder, Mark took the *Ur*-Gospel to Rome where he published it there in Greek. Luke also used the *Ur*-Gospel, supplemented with his own outline. Later the *Ur*-Gospel was published in Palestine in two forms, in Hebrew as the *Gospel of the Nazarenes* and then in Greek as the Gospel of Matthew.

More recently, James Edwards has argued that a Hebrew Gospel was authored by Matthew, translated into Greek, and used by Luke and by the authors of the *Gospel of the Ebionites* and the *Gospel of the Nazarenes*.[25] Stephen Hultgren has proposed that the traditional framework known to Mark encompassed all Jesus traditions, even those ordinarily ascribed to Q, in "a common, coherent, and primitive narrative-kerygmatic framework that ran from the baptism of Jesus to his passion, death and resurrection." The result is that the triple and double traditions are dependent on a preexisting narrative framework rather than compartmentalized into a dichotomy of narrative-kerygmatic and sayings traditions.[26]

While the Gospels may have incorporated a variety of Palestinian and

24. See the overviews of J. G. Herder's contribution to the Synoptic problem in Farmer, *The Synoptic Problem,* 30-34; Baird, *History of New Testament Research,* 1:181.

25. James R. Edwards, *The Hebrew Gospel and the Development of the Synoptic Tradition* (Grand Rapids: Eerdmans, 2009); idem, "The Gospel of the Ebionites and the Gospel of Luke," *NTS* 48 (2002): 568-86.

26. Stephen Hultgren, *Narrative Elements in the Double Tradition: A Study of Their Place within the Framework of the Gospel Narrative* (BZNW 113; Berlin: de Gruyter, 2002), 310, 316.

Aramaic sources, there are a number of problems with the theory of an original Aramaic or Hebrew *Ur*-Gospel which purportedly underlies the Synoptic tradition. First, if the Synoptic Gospels were based on a single underlying Aramaic *Ur*-Gospel, then one would expect to find far more variability in the tradition than what we currently find, since translation from Aramaic to Greek would introduce a breadth of variety in the content, order, and wording of the Synoptic materials. Second, although we do have the statement from Papias that "Matthew composed the oracles [of the Lord] in the Hebrew language and each person interpreted them as best he could (Ματθαῖος μὲν οὖν Ἑβραΐδι διαλέκτῳ τὰ λόγια συνετάξατο, ἡρμήνευσε δ' αὐτὰ ὡς ἦν δυνατὸς ἕκαστος)," the remark is ambiguous as to whether the Gospel of Matthew was initially written in a Judean language or with a Jewish idiom and style.[27] In any case, Matthew appears to stand within the Hellenistic Judaism of the Diaspora, even if its tradition, author, and audience have connections to Palestinian Judaism.[28] Third, the Septuagintal nature of the Old Testament citations in the Gospels is indicative of a Greek rather than Hebrew literary context for the final compilation of the Synoptic Gospels.[29] Fourth, the existence and precise number of Jewish Christian Gospels is disputed (i.e., *Gospel according to the Hebrews, Gospel of the Nazarenes, Gospel of the Ebionites*). Regardless, it is more likely the case that the *Gospel according to the Hebrews* and/or *of the Nazarenes* is a second-century revision of Matthew or Luke, perhaps supplemented with sayings of Jesus not represented in the canonical Gospels, rather than representing the original Aramaic Gospel used by the canonical Greek Matthew.[30] Fifth, the more that a pre-Gospel source document resembles either Mark or Matthew, the more superfluous it becomes as an explanation for the canonical Mark or Matthew, hence the demise of the once popular *Ur*-Mark theory.

---

27. Papias, *Fragment* 3.16 (= Eusebius, *Hist. Eccl.* 3.39.16). See for discussion W. R. Schoedel, *Polycarp, Martyrdom of Polycarp, Fragments of Papias* (Camden: Nelson, 1967), 109-10; Josef Kürzinger, *Papias von Hierapolis und die Evangelien des Neuen Testament* (Regensberg: Pustet, 1983), 10-11; Robert H. Gundry, *Matthew: A Commentary on His Handbook for a Mixed Church under Persecution* (2nd ed.; Grand Rapids: Eerdmans, 1994), 619-20; Armin Baum, "Ein aramäischer Urmatthäus im kleinasiatischen Gottesdienst. Das Papiaszeugnis zur Entstehung des Matthäusevangelims," *ZNW* 92 (2001): 257-72; Edwards, *Hebrew Gospel*, 3-7.

28. Cf., e.g., Joachim Gnilka, *Das Matthaüsevangelium II* (HTK; Freiberg: Herder, 1988), 533-34.

29. Gundry, *Matthew*, 617-20.

30. Andrew Gregory, "Prior or Posterior? The Gospel of the Ebionites and the Gospel of Luke," *NTS* 51 (2005): 344-60, argues, contra James Edwards, that the *Gospel of the Ebionites* known to us from citations in Epiphanius's *Panarion* is probably a post-Synoptic harmony.

4. Common Oral Traditions

Beyond theories about an original *Ur*-Gospel, others have advanced proposals that the Gospels are based on a common pool of oral and/or written sources, but still written independently of each other.[31]

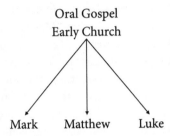

Oral Gospel
Early Church

Mark   Matthew   Luke

J. K. L. Gieseler's critical study of the Gospels (1818) preferred an *oral* rather than *written* Aramaic Gospel as the central source for the Synoptic Gospels. The famous British New Testament scholar B. F. Westcott regarded the Gospels as chiefly derived from the oral context of Palestine and the apostolic preaching about Jesus. The first Gospel was an oral message, not a written document, and its influence extended as far as the New Testament epistles. According to Westcott, the Gospels can be connected with the oral cycle of evangelic facts about Jesus. Mark was composed on the basis of Peter's preaching. Matthew was based on a Hebrew archetype. Luke derived from the preaching of the Pauline circle. Westcott concluded that "Hitherto all the evidence which can be gathered from the circumstances of the early Church, and the traditions of the origin of the Gospels, has tended to establish the existence of an original oral Gospel, definite in general outline and even in language, which was committed to writing in the lapse of time in various special shapes, according to the typical forms which it assumed in the preaching of different Apostles."[32] Westcott also thinks that the many agreements in the Gospels have been overstated as they apply predominantly to dominical sayings and not so much to narrative material. He rejects "mutual use" of the Gospels since that would imply that the divergences were deliberately designed, but no such design is detectable. Likewise, Westcott rejects

31. Farmer, *Synoptic Problem*, 30-35.
32. Westcott, *Introduction to the Study of the Gospels*, 174-75 (see for the entire argument 165-93).

a Greek or Aramaic written source for the Synoptics as no such sources are extant. Westcott maintained that "The general form of the Gospels points to an oral source."[33] Though the Gospels were written independently according to the needs of different audiences, he thinks that Mark "in essence, if not in composition, is the oldest."[34]

John M. Rist advocated the view that Mark and Matthew were written separately from each other on the basis of similar traditions. In his view, just because one version seems more primitive is no reason to presume that it formed the source for the other. Also, if Matthew was working from a copy of Mark in front of him, then he was needlessly careless in a number of his adaptations of Marcan material (e.g., the death of John the Baptist, Jairus's daughter, blind Bartimaeus).[35] An analogous thesis was argued by J. W. Scott: Luke wrote independently of both Mark and Matthew. He takes Luke 1:1-4 to mean that Luke was entirely dependent on oral sources. Scott sees two main bodies of tradition: a narrative tradition including Mark and half of the "Q" material and a body of independent tradition of apostolic origins.[36]

Eta Linnemann, a student of Rudolf Bultmann, renounced the historical-critical method at her conversion at age 60. She asserted that the Synoptic Gospels came into being without any direct dependence on each another. She relied heavily on the notions of eyewitnesses, memory, and patristic traditions to account for the origins of the Synoptics, which arose in a span of three or four years in three different locations and thus independently.[37] Similarly, Bo Reicke dated all three Gospels to the 60s CE and attributed their similarities to shared oral traditions, a theory he found preferable to the "artificial source theories" posed by literary dependence.[38]

John Wenham set forth a case for verbal independence with a measure of structural dependence. The Gospels' verbal similarities are based on inde-pendent use of primitive oral tradition, but generic and structural likenesses imply a literary relationship. In Wenham's scenario, the Evangelists utilized

---

33. Westcott, *Introduction to the Study of the Gospels*, 189.

34. Westcott, *Introduction to the Study of the Gospels*, 190.

35. John M. Rist, *On the Independence of Matthew and Mark* (SNTSMS 32; Cambridge: Cambridge University Press, 1978).

36. James M. Scott, *Luke's Preface and the Synoptic Problem* (unpublished dissertation, University of Aberdeen, 1985).

37. Eta Linnemann, *Is There a Synoptic Problem? Rethinking Literary Dependence of the First Three Gospels*, trans. R. Yarbrough (Grand Rapids: Baker, 1992).

38. Bo Reicke, *The Roots of the Synoptic Problem* (Philadelphia: Fortress, 1986), 169.

Jerusalem oral traditions, but did so while remaining aware of the other Gospels, resulting in basically an Augustinian view supplemented with oral tradition. He dates the Synoptics very early, opting for dates of Matthew by 40, Mark by 45, and Luke by the mid-50s.[39]

Several conservative scholars, writing out of a deep antipathy toward biblical criticism, have argued that the independence of the Synoptic Gospels is an important article of evangelical faith that has been brazenly compromised by scholars who postulate literary relationships between the Gospels.[40] They call any postulation of a literary relationship a result of "satanic blindness" that results in the "deterioration of the Gospel records."[41]

The theory of literary independence runs amiss for several reasons. First, if the Synoptic Gospels are based on general oral traditions, then we still have a hard time detailing their close verbal agreements. The fact is, as any experienced translator will tell you, that three independent translations of Jesus' Aramaic words into Greek — and Greek was a very flexible language in word order and grammar — would be unlikely to reproduce so often a verbatim concurrence in wording or even a majority agreement. Second, there is the gross improbability of three authors independently summarizing the diverse body of oral tradition in the same order and with the same sentence constructions, the same narrative framing, and the same intrusive editorial commentary. These must be explained, in part at least, by means of literary connections. Third, given the mobility and literacy of Christian leaders in the first century, it would not be odd if a copy of Mark found its way into the hands of Matthew or Luke. So we are not dealing with three independent accounts that have been written up in near-identical fashion, but an interlocking tradition.

---

39. John Wenham, *Redating Matthew, Mark, and Luke: A Fresh Assault on the Synoptic Problem* (Downers Grove: InterVarsity, 1992). Bruce Chilton, *Profiles of a Rabbi: Synoptic Opportunities in Reading about Jesus* (Atlanta: Scholars, 1989), has argued for a position analogous to Wenham's though deliberately situated between Westcott and Streeter, that accepts Marcan priority but sees Luke and Matthew utilizing Mark's same oral sources. Along this line is also Armin Baum, *Der mündliche Faktor und seine Bedeutung für die synoptische Frage. Analogien aus der Antiken Literatur, der Experiemtnalpsychologie, der Oral Poetry-Forschung und dem rabbinischen Traditionswesen* (TANZ 49; Tübingen: Francke, 2008); idem, "Matthew's Sources — Written or Oral? A Rabbinic Analogy and Empirical Insights," in *Built upon the Rock: Studies in the Gospel of Matthew*, ed. J. Nolland and D. Gurtner (Grand Rapids: Eerdmans, 2008), 1-23.

40. Robert L. Thomas and F. David Farnell, eds., *The Jesus Crisis: The Inroads of Historical Criticism into Evangelical Scholarship* (Grand Rapids: Kregel, 1998); Robert L. Thomas, ed., *Three Views on the Origins of the Synoptic Gospels* (Grand Rapids: Kregel, 2002).

41. Thomas, "Epilogue," in *Jesus Crisis*, 380.

5. *The Two- (Four-)Source Theory*[42]

The two- (four-)source theory postulates two primary sources in Mark and a hypothetical document utilized independently by Matthew and Luke called

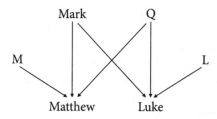

Mark   Q

M   L

Matthew   Luke

"Q." In addition, Matthew also had access to unique and special material labeled "M," while Luke had access to unique and special material labeled "L,"[43] hence the idea of a "four"-source theory. The most significant element in this theory is that traditional Matthean priority is exchanged for Marcan priority.[44]

Although there were a number of scholars who intimated this approach (such as C. G. Storr in 1786, K. Lachmann in 1835, and C. H. Weisse in 1838), it was really Heinrich Julius Holtzmann in his celebrated work *Die synoptischen Evangelien* (1863) which set the bar for arguments for Marcan priority and for the existence of Q (precise arguments for this position will be given later). Initially Holtzmann maintained that Matthew and Luke were

---

42. Not all two-source theorists would accept B. H. Streeter's view of four sources, but I take two- and four-source theories together here simply because the latter depends on the former.

43. See the convenient summary and discussion in Brice C. Jones, *Matthean and Lukan Special Material: A Brief Introduction with Texts in Greek and English* (Eugene: Wipf & Stock, 2011), and a brief précis of the materials in Goodacre, *Synoptic Problem*, 42-47. Notable studies are provided by Gerd Petzke, *Das Sondergut des Evangeliums nach Lukas* (ZWB; Zurich: Theologischer, 1990); Bertram Pittner, *Studien zum lukanischen Sondergut* (ETS 18; Leipzig: Benno, 1991); Kim Paffenroth, *The Story of Jesus According to L* (JSNTSup 147; Sheffield: Sheffield Academic, 1997); Stephenson H. Brooks, *Matthew's Special Community: The Evidence of His Special Sayings Material* (JSNTSup 16; Sheffield: JSOT, 1987); Hans-Theo Wrege, *Das Sondergut des Matthäus-Evangeliums* (ZWB; Zurich: Theologischer, 1991); Hans Klein, *Bewährung im Glauben. Studien zum Sondergut des Evangelisten Matthäus* (Neukirchen-Vluyn: Neukirchener, 1996).

44. Farmer, *Synoptic Problem*, 36-177; Dungan, *History of the Synoptic Problem*, 326-41; Baird, *History of New Testament Research*, 2:115-16, 265-66.

not directly dependent on canonical Mark but on a lost original *Ur-Mark*, though he eventually abandoned this position in favor of the priority of canonical Mark. Holtzmann's achievement was that he provided an account of the Synoptic tradition that attacked the skepticism of David Strauss, F. C. Baur, and the Tübingen school concerning the historicity of the Synoptic Gospels, while also impugning the argument for Matthean priority long treasured in Roman Catholic dogma, since Matthew supports the preeminence of Peter in the church. Holtzmann's views won the day in Germany, even persuading Albrecht Ritschl and Adolf von Harnack to change their minds on the matter. Then in England, B. H. Streeter's *The Four Gospels* (1924), building on the research of others like F. C. Burkitt, John Hawkins, and E. A. Abbott, presented a robust case for the four-source theory that has dominated Gospel scholarship for the last hundred years (the so-called "Oxford Hypothesis"). It remains the preferred option for most Gospel scholars today, even if it has not gone unchallenged.[45]

Dominant as the two- (four-)source theory is, it is not without weaknesses.[46] (1) Just as Matthean priority is often preferred for ideological reasons, so too the case for Marcan priority is said to be theologically prejudiced. Farmer points out that in Albert Schweitzer's analysis the "Marcan hypothesis" (i.e., Marcan priority) was the "creed and catechism" of liberal theology's life of Jesus research.[47] Herbert Stoldt and Hajo Uden Meijboom both surveyed the Marcan hypothesis and argued that it is based on theological agendas and not supported by the textual evidence.[48] (2) The so-

---

45. Cf., e.g., Stein, *Synoptic Gospels*, 143-52; Craig Blomberg, *Jesus and the Gospels: An Introduction and Survey* (Downers Grove: InterVarsity, 1997), 86-92; Scot McKnight, *Interpreting the Synoptic Gospels* (Grand Rapids: Baker, 1993), 33-44; Mark Goodacre, *The Case Against Q* (Harrisburg: Trinity, 2002), 19-45; Darrell L. Bock, *Studying the Historical Jesus: A Guide to Sources and Methods* (Grand Rapids: Baker, 2003), 163-79; Craig A. Evans, "Sorting Out the Synoptic Problem: Why an Old Approach Is Still Best," in *Reading the Gospels Today*, ed. S. E. Porter (Grand Rapids: Eerdmans, 2004), 1-26; Mark L. Strauss, *Four Portraits, One Jesus: An Introduction to Jesus and the Gospels* (Grand Rapids: Zondervan, 2007), 43-55.

46. Cf. esp. the collection of classic essays in Bellinzoni, ed., *Two-Source Hypothesis*, against Marcan priority (95-217) and against the existence of Q (319-433).

47. Farmer, *Pastoral Relevance*, 207, citing Albert Schweitzer, *The Quest of the Historical Jesus*, trans. W. Montgomery (New York, Macmillan, 1948), 203-4.

48. Hans-Herbert Stoldt, *History and Criticism of the Marcan Hypothesis*, trans. D. Niewyk (Macon: Mercer University Press, 1980); Hajo Uden Meijboom, *A History and Critique of the Origin of the Marcan Hypothesis, 1835-1866*, trans. J. J. Kiwiet (Macon: Mercer University Press, 1993).

called minor agreements between Matthew and Luke against Mark have always been deeply troubling for the two-source theory as such agreements make better sense on the assumption that Luke used Matthew or vice-versa. (3) The Q theory has always been the chink in the armor of the two-source theory. The Q theory is beset with problems like explaining Mark-Q overlaps, why Q material in Luke and Matthew does not appear in the same order, the problem of verbal differences between Matthew and Luke on allegedly Q material, and the fact that the double tradition as a whole can be explained by other factors like continuing oral traditions and Luke's use of Matthew. Even Holtzmann eventually capitulated to Luke's use of Matthew, leaving the Q theory in a historical-critical limbo.[49] According to Clayton Sullivan:

> The arguments of the Stoldts and Farmers *against* Marcan priority are as convincing as arguments of the Holtzmanns and Streeters *for* Marcan priority. Thus the primitivity of the second gospel has become an open question, not a closed one, and Marcan priority can no longer be assumed by exegetes as an "unquestionable" hermeneutical tool. . . . Likewise, in recent years scholars have appraised the Q hypothesis. This theory, like Belshazzar, has been weighed in the balances and found wanting.[50]

6. The Farrer Theory

A final hypothesis for our consideration is the "Farrer Theory" named after Austin Farrer (the theory is also closely associated with Michael Goulder and Mark Goodacre). On this account, Mark was written first and was subsequently used by the author of Matthew, and later again Mark and Matthew were both used by the author of Luke. A key distinctive here is that Marcan priority is maintained (contra the Griesbach hypothesis), but the existence of a Q document is dispensed with (contra the two- [four-] source hypothesis).

---

49. Dungan, *History of the Synoptic Problem*, 330-31, citing H. J. Holtzmann, *Lehrbuch der historisch-kritischen Einleitung in das Neue Testament* (Freiburg: Siebeck, 1892), 2:339, 350.

50. Clayton Sullivan, *Rethinking Realized Eschatology* (Macon: Mercer University Press, 1988), 23 (italics original).

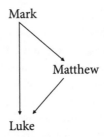

In what is now a classic article on the Synoptic problem, Farrer attempted to remove the apparent need for Q by positing Luke's use of Matthew.[51] He proposed that the Q hypothesis rests on the alleged incredibility of Luke's use of Matthew.[52] Against Q, he finds nothing distinctive from the theology of the two Evangelists in the so-called Q material, nor any apparent order that indicates that Q was a self-contained entity. Q was not a proper "Gospel" and does not resemble any document we know about from Christian antiquity. It would seem, then, "To postulate Q is to postulate the unevidenced and the unique."[53] Farrer also questions why a purported sayings document like Q would contain so much narrative material as well.[54] He then responds to Streeter's explanations for the Matthew-Luke minor agreements (e.g., scribal errors of assimilation of one Gospel to the other, various coincidences of style and substance, and shared doctrinal interests) and to arguments that Luke could not have used Matthew (e.g., Luke would not have omitted so much, Luke's wording of Q often seems more primitive than Matthew's, Luke's supposed use of Matthew would have to proceed differently from how he used Mark, Luke's placing common material in less appropriate places and in different Marcan contexts than Matthew).[55] When it comes to the composition of Luke, Farrer asserts that Luke intended to begin his Gospel with a narrative (1:10–10:24), followed by a large block of Jesus' teachings (10:25–18:30), and returned to narrative for the events

51. Austin M. Farrer, "On Dispensing with Q," in *Studies in the Gospels: Essays in Memory of R. H. Lightfoot*, ed. D. E. Nineham (Oxford: Blackwell, 1955), 55-58, repr. in Bellizoni, ed., *The Two-Source Hypothesis*, 321-56 (subsequent citations of this article are from the reprint). Note the earlier study of E. W. Lummins, *How Luke Was Written: Considerations Affecting the Two-Document Theory with Special Reference to the Phenomena of Order in the Non-Markan Matter Common to Luke* (Cambridge: Cambridge University Press, 1915).

52. Farrer, "Dispensing with Q," 323.

53. Farrer, "Dispensing with Q," 324-26 (quotation at 326).

54. Farrer, "Dispensing with Q," 327-29.

55. Farrer, "Dispensing with Q," 329-33.

in Jerusalem (18:31–24:53). Luke wrenches Matthew's non-Marcan material away from its Marcan context simply because he can flesh out his story on only one skeleton, and he chose Mark.[56] Farrer concludes: "Once rid of Q, we are rid of a progeny of nameless chimaeras, and free to let St. Matthew write as he is moved."[57]

Other scholars have come to Farrer's aid. Michael Goulder attempted a systematic reading of Luke in the new paradigm of the Farrer theory of Luke's use of Mark and Matthew. Central to his arguments were the absence of Q from patristic literature, the alleged appearance of Matthean vocabulary in Luke, and the presence of minor agreements outside the sayings material, such as the triple tradition of the passion story. For Goulder these all indicate Luke's use of Matthew.[58] Mark Goodacre has been a robust advocate for the Farrer theory and has also pointed to apparent "editorial fatigue" where Luke makes initial changes to his source document (i.e., Matthew) but then lapses into docile reproduction of the text before him with diminished augmentation as a given unit proceeds.[59] There has been an industry of Q skepticism in the last few years, gradually finding its way into various publications so that the hegemony that the two-source theory once nearly enjoyed is being slowly eroded.[60]

The strength of the Farrer thesis is that it avoids the need for Q and presents us with a simple and succinct theory of literary relationships between the Synoptic Gospels. In particular, it explains the minor agreements

56. Farrer, "Dispensing with Q," 333-53.

57. Farrer, "Dispensing with Q," 353.

58. Michael Goulder, *Midrash and Lexicon, the Evangelist's Calendar: A Lectionary Explanation of the Development of Scripture* (London: SPCK, 1978); idem, *Luke: A New Paradigm* (2 vols.; JSNTSup 20; Sheffield: JSOT, 1989); idem, "Luke's Compositional Options," *NTS* 39 (1993): 150-52; idem, "Is Q a Juggernaut?" *JBL* 115 (1996): 667-91; idem, "Self-Contradiction in the IQP?" *JBL* 118 (1999): 506-17. See evaluations of Goulder (positively) by Mark S. Goodacre, *Goulder on the Gospels: An Examination of a New Paradigm* (JSNTSup 133; Sheffield: Sheffield Academic, 1996), and (negatively) John S. Kloppenborg, "Is There a New Paradigm?" in *Christology, Controversy, and Community: New Testament Essays in Honour of David Catchpole*, ed. D. Horrell and C. M. Tuckett (NovTSup 99; Leiden: Brill, 2000), 23-47.

59. Goodacre, *Synoptic Problem*, 154-56; idem, *Case against Q*, 40-43; idem, "Fatigue in the Synoptics," *NTS* 44 (1998): 45-58.

60. Cf., e.g., David L. Dungan, Allan J. McNicol, and David B. Peabody, eds., *Beyond the Q Impasse: Luke's Use of Matthew* (Valley Forge: Trinity, 1996); Mark Goodacre and Nicholas Perrin, eds., *Questioning Q: A Multi-Dimensional Critique* (Downers Grove: InterVarsity, 2004); and Bartosz Adamczewski, *Q or not Q? The So-Called Triple, Double, and Single Traditions in the Synoptic Gospels* (Frankfurt am Main: Lang, 2010); John C. Poirier, "The Synoptic Problem and the Field of New Testament Introduction," *JSNT* 32 (2009): 179-90.

of Luke and Matthew against Mark and the so-called Mark-Q overlaps. The lingering doubts are that perhaps it is just too neat. If Luke had other sources beyond Mark and Matthew, especially in the sayings material, and if those other sources (written or oral) overlapped with Matthew in some cases, then the riddle of the double tradition cannot be solved by simply positing Luke's use of Matthew.[61]

A Fresh Look at the Old Problem

The above survey has been necessary to demonstrate that the Synoptic problem is indeed very complicated. It is exacerbated by a number of circumstances of which we need to be soberly aware:

1. Synoptic research often naively operates on an assumption of a correlation between the eclectic texts of the Nestle-Aland Greek New Testament with the original autographs of the Evangelists. While I am reasonably confident that the eclectic texts developed over the last two hundred years are probably very close to what the Evangelists actually wrote (or at least as close as we can critically reconstruct them), we cannot automatically assume that our neatly printed Greek New Testaments are identical to what the Evangelists actually wrote. Our UBS[4] version of Mark might not have been identical to a text of Mark utilized by Matthew or Luke.[62]

2. It needs to be borne in mind that the synopses which are used to

---

61. Cf. John C. Poirier, "The Composition of Luke in Source-Critical Perspective," in *New Studies in the Synoptic Problem*, ed. Foster, Gregory, Kloppenborg, and Verheyden, 210: "In my view, the FH [Farrer hypothesis] can (and should) be pursued with as much openness to hypothetical documents as the 2DH [two-document hypothesis] displays." Note also the criticism of Foster, "Is It Possible to Dispense with Q?" 321: "If Goodacre is willing to admit that alternative sources are being used in some of these cases, (and this seems to be the implication of his statement about 'other traditions'), how is he able to determine with such confidence that such material was oral and not written?"

62. Cf. Gordon D. Fee, "A Text-Critical Look at the Synoptic Problem," *NovT* 22 (1980): 12-28; J. K. Elliott, "The Relevance of Textual Criticism to the Synoptic Problem," in *The Interrelations of the Gospels*, ed. D. L. Dungan (BETL 95; Leuven: Leuven University Press, 1990), 348-59; idem, "Which Is the Best Synopsis?" *ExpT* 102 (1991): 200-204; idem, "Printed Editions of Greek Synopses and their Influence on the Synoptic Problem," in *The Four Gospels 1992*, ed. F. Van Segbroeck, C. M. Tuckett, G. Van Belle, and J. Verheyden (FS F. Neirynck; BETL 100; Leuven: Leuven University Press, 1992), 337-57; Peter Head, "Textual Criticism and the Synoptic Problem," in *New Studies in the Synoptic Problem*, ed. Foster, Gregory, Kloppenborg, and Verheyden, 115-56.

work on the Synoptic problem are not hypothesis-neutral but tend to bias toward one particular solution for the Synoptic problem. David Dungan and Bernard Orchard complain that the two most commonly used synopses, those of Huck-Greeven and Aland, are biased toward the two-source theory in the paragraphing and presentation of Synoptic parallels.[63] Orchard responded to this bias by compiling his own synopsis deliberately geared toward the Griesbach theory.[64] Though the alleged bias of the various synopses may be overstated, even so, a critical evaluation of all synopses is required.[65]

3. There may be factors beyond our knowledge that contributed to the rise of the Synoptic Gospels that we are simply ignorant about. Theories about *Ur*-Mark, deutero-Mark, or proto-Luke are problematic: Why would someone bother to reissue a book in only slightly revised form? And such theories are ultimately impossible to prove given the nature of our extant sources. But if one of these theories were true then all bets would be off regarding our ability to accurately map the origins of the Synoptic Gospels.[66] But that is unlikely to happen unless someone actually finds one of these hypothetical Gospel sources in some future archaeological discovery. Similarly, if the Synoptic Gospels were influenced by non-literary sources (i.e., oral sources), then, once more, they were shaped by factors that we simply have no chance of recovering or integrating into a solution.

4. At the end of the day there remains a great deal of subjectivity in positing any solution to the Synoptic problem. One might want to develop "laws" explaining the development of the tradition, but, even if those laws

63. Bernard Orchard, "Are All Gospel Synopses Biased?" *TZ* 34 (1978): 157-61; idem, "The 'Neutrality' of Vertical-Column Synopses," *ETL* 62 (1986): 155-56; David L. Dungan, "Theory of Synopsis Construction," *Bib* 61 (1980): 305-29; idem, "Synopses of the Future," *Bib* 66 (1985): 457-92; idem, "Synopses of the Future," in *The Interrelations of the Gospels,* ed. Dungan, 317-47.

64. Bernard Orchard, *A Synopsis of the Four Gospels in Greek: Arranged According to the Two-Gospel Hypothesis* (Macon: Mercer University Press, 1983).

65. John Kloppenberg claims that while some synopses can elucidate or obscure certain aspects of a Synoptic theory, there is no widespread and systematic bias: see John S. Kloppenborg, "Synopses and the Synoptic Problem," in *New Studies in the Synoptic Problem,* ed. Foster, Gregory, Kloppenborg, and Verheyden, 51-86.

66. To tease that out further, what if Mark wrote an earlier draft of his Gospel that Matthew and Luke used before Mark or someone else rehashed it into its current canonical form? What if Matthew wrote a version of his Gospel in Aramaic (used by Luke) and then another in Greek (used by the church fathers)? What if Luke wrote a version of his Gospel based on Mark and then updated it after he came across Matthew (with Marcion utilizing the proto-Luke)? How would we know? How would we prove it? Where would the evidence take us in resolving the Synoptic problem?

were actually true, which cannot really be demonstrated, such an approach wrongfully assumes that the laws are constant and consistent across the entire breadth of the Synoptic tradition. Yet experience tells us that people are rarely so woodenly constant and inflexibly consistent when they incorporate written and oral materials into their own work. Furthermore, a variety of explanations for agreement and differentiation can be given, often with some degree of cogency for each case, and it can be very difficult to adjudicate between them.

Indeed, the Synoptic problem is so complicated and challenging that it can make the most determined researcher want to escape from the frustration somehow. Such respite has eluded every Synoptic researcher apart from the most self-assured.

After stating the case for skepticism, I now wish to optimistically put forward a tentative solution. Nearly half a century ago, E. P. Sanders proffered his opinion on the future of the Synoptic problem: "I rather suspect that when and if a new view of the Synoptic problem becomes accepted, it will be more flexible and complicated than the tidy two-document hypothesis. With all due respect for scientific preference for the simpler view, the evidence seems to require a more complicated one."[67] I think that is indeed the case. While I think that the two- (four-)source hypothesis is basically correct, there are several features of the theory that need to be tweaked in order to accommodate what I believe to be the slightly more complex nature of the problem, specifically, that Luke used Mark, Q, and Matthew.

I call this position the Holtzmann-Gundry hypothesis (though it has also been called the "three-source theory"). It is named after the German scholar H. J. Holtzmann, its first proponent, and American scholar Robert H. Gundry, its best-known proponent. In a nutshell, this view is (1) Marcan priority; (2) Matthew used Mark and Q; (3) Luke used Mark and Q; and (4) at a later point, Luke incorporated Matthew into his own work.

To give a brief history of this position, Holtzmann argued for Marcan priority and postulated the existence of Q (or Λ as he called it, for "logia"),[68] but he modified his view in a journal article published fifteen years later that tacitly suggested that Luke reproduced Matt 5:18 in Luke 16:17.[69] Holtzmann

67. E. P. Sanders, *Tendencies of the Synoptic Tradition* (SNTSMS 9; Cambridge: Cambridge University Press, 1969), 279.

68. H. J. Holtzmann, *Die synoptischen Evangelien. Ihr Ursprung und geschichtlicher Charakter* (Leipzig: Engelmann, 1863).

69. H. J. Holtzmann, "Zur synoptischen Frage," *Jahrbücher für protestantische Theologie* 4 (1878): 145-88, 328-82, 533-68, esp. 552-62.

afterward declared in his *Einleitung* that he had come to change his mind on several areas of the Synoptic problem:[70]

1. Not everything in Matthew and Luke that goes beyond Mark can be accommodated in the sayings collection. At times elements from the collection are more highly modified by Luke than they are by Matthew. It is possible that it contained narrative sketches that formed undetachable frames for the sayings of the Lord.
2. Other sources for Matthew are unprovable, but such a question remains open for Luke.
3. *Luke knew Mark and Matthew even if he might not have used them.*
4. Consequently, at least most of the motives for distinguishing between an *Ur*-Mark and Mark are eliminated.[71]

Holtzmann's student, Eduard Simons, put forward the case for Luke's use of Matthew as well as Q.[72] Although Luke's main sources were Mark and Q, Luke still made periodic use of Matthew, not necessarily in the same way that he used Mark, but more in a secondary sense, with Matthean expressions sometimes filtering into Luke. According to Simons, if we imagine that Luke had much of the Gospel of Matthew in his head from some exposure to it, then it makes sense that he recalled and utilized Matthew in greater and lesser ways and sometimes even with involuntary echoes. He writes, "We have to formulate our view as meaning that canonical Matthew is for Luke

---

70. Some, such as Farmer, *Synoptic Problem*, 20, 40, 47, think that Holtzmann was influenced by his doctoral student Eduard Simons's dissertation *Hat der dritte Evangelist den kanonischen Matthäus benutzt?* (Bonn: Georgi, 1880) in coming to this conclusion. Edward C. Hobbs, "A Quarter-Century without 'Q,'" *Perkins School of Theology Journal* 33 (1980): 11, points out that Holtzmann more probably influenced Simons, since Holtzmann published such a view two years before Simons's dissertation was submitted and taught Simons for a number of years earlier.

71. The original German reads: "1) In der Spruchsammlung lässt sich nicht Alles unterbringen, was Mt und Lc von Redegehalt über Mc hinaus darbieten; ihre Elemente sind zuweilen von Lc noch mehr überarbeitet als von Mt; sie enthielt möglicher Weise auch skizzenhafte Erzählungen als Umrahmungen davon unabtrennbarer Herrnssprüche. 2) Weitere Quellen sind für Mt unerweislich; dagegen bleibt für Lc die Frage nach solchen offen. 3) Lc hat neben Mc auch Mt, wenn nicht benutzt, so doch gekannt. 4) In Folge dessen kommen wenigstens die Meisten Motive zur Unterscheidung eines Urmarcus von Mc in Wegfall." H. J. Holtzmann, *Lehrbuch der historisch-kritischen Einleitung in das Neue Testament*, 2:350. The English translation is from Stoldt, *History and Criticism of the Marcan Hypothesis*, 92, with my own adjustments.

72. Simons, *Hat der dritte Evangelist den kanonischen Matthäus benutzt?* esp. 11-13, 104-12.

a tertiary source, used with a critical distance that was uneven and free."[73] But once more there is a reticence against totally eliminating Q. Simons concedes that it is not possible that all the material shared by Matthew and Luke beyond Mark corresponds to the content of the Λ source (i.e., Q). Be that as it may, the place of Q as the second main source of Luke is preserved as the postulated sayings collection he drew on.[74]

Simons's approach mostly passed away unnoticed, but it was cited and affirmed by Edward Y. Hincks in the U.S. in the late nineteenth century.[75] Hincks noted the main rival hypotheses of the time including the *Ur*-Mark theory (H. J. Holtzmann) and the theory that Mark used Matthew's Logia source (B. Weiss) and rejected them as problematic and inadequate. Instead, Hincks found Simons's argument compelling since Matthew's Gospel circulated widely, Luke was written later and so could have had access to Matthew, and the divergences between Matthew and Luke can be accounted for without requiring Luke's independence of Matthew.[76] Furthermore, for Hincks, Luke's use of Matthew explains the Luke-Matthew agreements against Mark. He also posits that Mark and the Logia source (Q) may have had independent reports of the same account that were used by Luke and Matthew. This is said to explain the contours of the mission discourses and the accusation of Jesus' alliance with Satan (i.e., the Mark-Q overlaps).[77]

Robert Morgenthaler's study of the statistics in the Synoptic Gospels led him to regard the view that *either* Luke used Mark and Matthew *or* that Luke used Mark and Q as a "false alternative." He preferred instead the "three-source theory" with Luke using Mark, Q, and Matthew *(Dreiquellentheorie)*. According to Morgenthaler, the minor agreements between Luke

73. "Vielmehr müssen wir unsere Auffassung dahin formuliren, dass der kanonischen Mt. für Lc. eine Nebenquelle, die Benutzung eine mit Kritik verbundene . . . ungleichmässige und freie war." Simons, *Hat der dritte Evangelist den kanonischen Matthäus benutzt?* 108.

74. Simons, *Hat der dritte Evangelist den kanonischen Matthäus benutzt?* 112.

75. Edward Y. Hincks, "The Probable Use of the First Gospel by Luke," *JBL* 10 (1891): 92-106.

76. On the Matthew-Luke divergences, Hincks argued ("Use of the First Gospel," 96-97): (1) Luke used the Logia source (i.e., Q) differently from Matthew. (2) In the infancy narrative, Luke shows the influence of Matthew's genealogy, but otherwise follows different sources. (3) Luke uses Mark differently from how Matthew used Mark because Luke esteemed Mark more than Matthew. (4) On Luke's omission of material from Matthew, if the materials were in the Logia source where Matthew found them, the problem of omission still remains. (5) Luke does not use Matthew's pragmatic way of referencing the Old Testament because of Luke's independent "doctrinal conception." (6) Luke used different sources for his resurrection accounts.

77. Hincks, "Use of the First Gospel," 99-101.

and Matthew, although they point to Luke's use of Matthew, do not eliminate the existence of Q.[78] The fact that the percentage of agreements vary in the double and triple traditions show that it is theoretically possible that "Luke used Mark and Q and secondarily Matthew, or he used Mark and Matthew and secondarily Q."[79] Since Matthew is the younger document it is therefore likely to be more secondary. Luke strove to keep the latent Matthew in mind as he built a new combination of the older sources of Mark, Q, and his special material.[80]

Robert Gundry has been the most recent advocate for a three-source approach, although his views have largely gone unnoticed among those outside the field of Synoptic problem studies. Gundry has written major commentaries on Matthew and Mark and has explored the presence of so-called Matthean "foreign bodies" in Luke.[81] According to Gundry, both Matthew and Luke used Mark and the non-Marcan tradition held in common. The non-Marcan tradition included material usually designated Q, but also other material like the nativity story. While this sounds like the standard two-source theory, Gundry adds:

> Because Mattheanisms occasionally appear as foreign bodies in Luke, we also have to think of Luke's using Matthew as an overlay on his primary sources. That Matthew's gospel did not provide one of those sources is shown by the disarrangement of Matthean material we would otherwise have to suppose. But that the Matthean foreign bodies come from our present Gospel of Matthew, not from an earlier source, is shown by their conforming to Matthew's distinctive diction, style, and theology as evident elsewhere and by their frequently depending for their point on Matthew's context (often stemming from Mark), whereas in Luke they lack contextual point. Therefore we need not fret over the numerous minor agreements of Matthew and Luke that do not fall into the cate-

78. Robert Morgenthaler, *Statistische Synopse* (Zurich: Gottelf, 1971), 300-305.

79. "Lk neben Mk und Q auch noch Mt, oder neben Mk und Mt auch noch Q benützete." Morgenthaler, *Statistische Synopse*, 300.

80. Morgenthaler, *Statistische Synopse*, 301.

81. Gundry, *Matthew*; idem, *Mark: A Commentary on His Apology for the Cross* (Grand Rapids: Eerdmans, 1993); idem, "Matthean Foreign Bodies in Agreements of Luke with Matthew against Mark: Evidence That Luke Used Matthew," in *The Four Gospels 1992*, ed. van Segbroeck et al., 2:1466-95; idem, "A Rejoinder on Matthean Foreign Bodies in Luke 10,25-28," *ETL* 71 (1995): 139-50; idem, "The Refusal of Matthean Foreign Bodies to Be Exercised from Luke 9,22; 10,25-28," *ETL* 75 (1999): 104-22.

gory of Mattheanism. . . . They, too, may represent a Matthean overlay in Luke, though apart from the Matthean foreign bodies we would not have known so with any confidence.[82]

Gundry still remains convinced of the existence of Q on the grounds that "Luke's borrowing wholesale from Matthew" remains problematic because it leads to "Luke's equally wholesale disarrangement of Matthew's materials."[83] The postulation of Q does not prevent Gundry from arguing that Luke used Matthew because doing so accounts for the presence of a number of Matthean foreign bodies in Luke.

1. Marcan Priority

In want of a solution to the Synoptic problem, Marcan priority seems to be the one nearly indubitable premise we can build on. Though the subsequent scaffolding may not join Matthew and Luke in the right place and in the right order, the foundation of Marcan priority seems to hold firm. It rests on the following arguments:[84]

1. *Content Absorption.* Not only is Mark the shortest Gospel, but Matthew possesses about 85% of Mark and Luke in the vicinity of 65% of Mark. Mark also has the least amount of unique material.[85] These statistics make the most sense on the assumption of the absorption of Mark into Matthew and Luke. In any given section of the triple tradition, the actual words of Mark are essentially reproduced by Matthew and Luke, either jointly or alternately (e.g., see the question about fasting in Mark 2:18-22/Matt 9:14-17/Luke 5:33-39). Mark is normally the middle term or common denominator among the Synoptics in the triple tradition. If Mark had Luke and Matthew in front of

---

82. Gundry, *Matthew*, 5.

83. Gundry, *Matthew*, xvi.

84. Cf. Streeter, *Four Gospels*, 151-52; Werner G. Kümmel, *Introduction to the New Testament* (Nashville: Abingdon, 1966), 56-63; Stein, *Synoptic Gospels*, 49-96 (esp. 94-96); essays contained in Bellizoni, ed., *Two-Source Hypothesis*, 21-29; Scot McKnight, "A Generation Who Knew Not Streeter: The Case for Markan Priority," in *Rethinking the Synoptic Problem*, ed. D. A. Black and D. R. Beck (Grand Rapids: Baker, 2001), 65-95.

85. The only Marcan material not found in Matthew and Luke is Mark 7:33-36 (healing of a deaf mute); 8:22-26 (healing of a man in Bethsaida); and 14:51-52 (man fleeing Gethsemane naked). These units make better sense as units omitted by Matthew and Luke than they do added by Mark since they provide no new dimension or dynamic to the Synoptic tradition.

him when he wrote, then it is harder to explain the Marcan disagreements with the Luke/Matthew minor agreements (e.g., see the Beelzebul controversy story in Mark 3:22-27/ Matt 12:24-30/Luke 11:15, 17-23). Marcan posteriority leaves too many unanswered questions, such as: Why did Mark exclude so much material and why would he omit the concurrent testimony from Matthew and/or Luke on certain passages that he included in his Gospel?

2. *Order.* The order of units and sections in Mark is normally supported by Matthew and Luke. When either Matthew or Luke departs from Mark, the other is usually found supporting Mark. The argument from order by itself can fall prey to the "Lachmann fallacy,"[86] but, when combined with cogent explanations as to why Luke and Matthew depart from Mark's order the way they do (such as Matthew inserting major discourses and Luke shelving Mark's pro-Gentile material until his second volume, Acts), then the case for the priority of the Marcan order remains.

3. *Improvement and Redaction.* The priority of Mark is further supported by improvements to Mark's grammar and editorial adjustments to his narrative made by Matthew and Luke. For instance, in Mark 1:13, we read that "the Spirit expelled him [Jesus] into the wilderness." Mark uses the word ἐκβάλλω, which means "drive" or "expel" and is normally used to describe how Jesus "drives out" demons from the demon-possessed. Luke and Matthew both change Mark's imprecise word to the more nuanced and accurate ἄγω, "lead," (Matt 4:1/Luke 4:1). It is more likely that Matthew and Luke have improved Mark's somewhat clunky word-choice than that Mark introduces ἐκβάλλω into Matthew's or Luke's account. Much of Matthew also makes better sense on the assumption that he used Mark as his source. Matthew has a propensity to re-Judaize Mark so as to remove any potential offense or misunderstanding caused by Mark's narration, especially for a Jewish Christian audience. For instance, a juxtaposition of Mark 7:19c with Matt 15:17-18

---

86. The Lachmann fallacy — so-named after Karl Lachmann, although it refers to scholars after Lachmann who make a misstep in their logic for Marcan priority — is basically presupposing what one proves. Scholars like Lachmann posited an *Ur*-Mark document on which the three Synoptic authors were dependent for the order of their pericopes. Canonical Mark was the intermediate link between *Ur*-Mark and Matthean/Lukan agreements in order because canonical Mark stood as the closest to the order of *Ur*-Mark. However, if one eliminates the distinction between *Ur*-Mark and canonical Mark (as did C. H. Weisse, P. Wernle, and eventually H. Holtzmann), then the chronological priority of canonical Mark does not follow since Mark could be second or third and still be the intermediary link between Matthew and Luke. See B. C. Butler, *The Originality of St. Matthew* (Cambridge: Cambridge University Press, 1951), 62-71; William R. Farmer, "The Lachmann Fallacy," *NTS* 14 (1968): 441-43.

shows how Matthew omits Mark's editorial aside "Thus he declared all foods clean," since Mark probably reflects Pauline instruction for Gentiles, and Matthew may well have expected his Jewish Christian audience to continue to observe the Jewish dietary laws. From all this, Streeter complains: "How anyone who has worked through those pages with a Synopsis of the Greek text can retain the slightest doubt of the original and primitive character of Mark I am unable to comprehend."[87]

4. *Old Testament Citations.* The citation of Old Testament texts in the Synoptics lends itself toward Marcan priority. Matthew includes the most explicit citations of Old Testament texts in his Gospel. Matthew also includes the highest number of singular and unparalleled renderings of Old Testament texts. David New has proposed that Matthew's quotation of these particular readings implies Marcan priority rather than Marcan posteriority. For if Mark depended on Matthew it would seem odd that he chose only to include quotations that have text-forms closely related to extant text-forms of the Septuagint. It is more likely that Matthew has used minority text-forms of the Old Testament whenever he was not relying on Mark.[88]

5. *Christology.* The diverse christological portraits of the Evangelists provide further grounds for Marcan priority. Peter Head's dissertation utilized a christological argument to contend for Marcan priority over Matthew. Head argues that selected features of Matthew's christology, especially his use of important titles like "Lord," "Teacher," "Messiah," "Son of Man," and "Son of David," make better sense on the assumption that Matthew was using Mark rather than vice-versa.[89] For example, Mark's account of Peter's confession at Caesarea-Philippi, "You are the Messiah" (Mark 8:29), is quite subdued compared to Matthew's "You are the Messiah, the Son of the Living God" (Matt 16:16), and even Luke's "Messiah of God" is more emphatic than Mark.[90]

2. Q-Lite

Approximately 220 to 235 verses are shared between Matthew and Luke and not present in Mark, which amounts to a quarter of Matthew and a

---

87. Streeter, *Four Gospels,* 164.

88. David S. New, *Old Testament Quotations in the Synoptic Gospels and the Two-Document Hypothesis* (SBLSCS 37; Atlanta: Scholars, 1993).

89. Peter M. Head, *Christology and the Synoptic Problem: An Argument for Markan Priority* (SNTSMS 94; Cambridge: Cambridge University Press, 1997).

90. Cf. Head, *Christology and the Synoptic Problem,* 174-86.

fifth of Luke. This "double tradition," in whole or part, is often regarded as belonging to the hypothetical Q document. Discussion of Q dates as far back as 1794, when Johann Eichhorn proposed Matthew's and Luke's independent use of pre-Synoptic sources.[91] In England, Herbert Marsh posited the existence of a proto-Gospel source (א) and a sayings source (ב) in 1798.[92] Friedrich Schleiermacher (1832) thought that Papias's "oracles of the Lord" might refer to a common source shared between Matthew and Luke, a theory subsequently taken up by K. A. Credner (1836). Christian Hermann Weisse (1838) labeled this logia source with the Greek letter Λ, and it was probably Johannes Weiss (1890) who first signified this source with the letter Q, from the German *Quelle*, "source." The notion of a sayings source used by Luke and Matthew was popularized later mainly through H. J. Holtzmann (1863) and Paul Wernle (1899) in Germany and by B. H. Streeter (1924) in the British Isles.

The double tradition contains several types of material:[93]

N   Narratives, which recount the deeds of Jesus.

Par   Parables, which consist of figurative language about the kingdom of God.

JOr   Judgment Oracles, which warn of conflict and punishment for the wicked.

Beat   Beatitudes, declaration of blessings for those in God's special favor.

PP   Prophetic Pronouncements, which foretell what God intends to do for his people.

WS   Wisdom Sayings, which are proverbial utterances about the divine intent.

Exh   Exhortations, which focus on the shared life of the community of the kingdom.

Scholars debate which units actually belong to Q and the precise extent of the parallels; nonetheless, the scope of the double tradition (and therefore of "Q") includes approximately the following texts:

---

91. Kümmel, *Introduction to the New Testament*, 50; Farmer, *Synoptic Problem*, 9-11.

92. Farmer, *Synoptic Problem*, 11-15.

93. Adapted from Howard Clark Kee, *The Beginnings of Christianity: An Introduction to the New Testament* (London: Clark, 2005), 85-86.

The Double Tradition (Lucan Sequence)[94]

Lucan Order	Luke			Matthew	Matthean Order
1	3:7-9, 16-17	PP	John the Baptist's preaching	3:7-12	1
2	4:1-13	N	the temptation of Jesus	4:1-11	2
3	6:20-23, 27-30, 32-36	Beat, WS	Sermon on the Plain (part 1)	5:3-6, 11-12, 39-42, 45-48	3
4	6:37-38, 41-49	WS, Par	Sermon on the Plain (part 2)	7:1-5, 16-21, 24-27	7
5	7:1-10	N	the centurion from Capernaum	8:5-13	9
6	7:18-35	N, PP	sayings about the Baptist	11:2-19	13
7	9:57-60	PP	sayings about discipleship	8:19-22	10
8	10:1-12	PP	the Mission Discourse	9:37–10:15	11
9	10:13-15, 21-24	JOr, Beat	woes and blessings	11:21-23, 25-26	14
10	11:1-4	Exh	the Lord's Prayer	6:9-13	5
11	11:9-13	WS	on prayer	7:7-11	8
12	11:14-23	N, PP	the Beelzebub controversy	12:22-30	15
13	11:24-26	JOr	sayings about apostasy	12:43-45	17
14	11:29-32	PP	against a request for miracles	12:38-42	16
15	11:33-35	Par	sayings about light	5:15; 6:22-23	4
16	11:39-52	JOr	against the Pharisees	23:4, 23-25, 29-36	20
17	12:2-10	PP, JOr, Par	summons to confession	10:26-33	12
18	12:22-34	Par	cares and treasures	6:25-33, 19-21	6
19	12:39-46	Par	watchfulness	24:43-51	23
20	13:18-21	Par	mustard seed and leaven	13:31-33	18
21	13:34-35	PP	lament over Jerusalem	23:37-39	21
22	14:15-24	Par	the great supper/wedding feast	22:1-14	19
23	17:22-37	JOr	discourse on the coming Son of Man	24:26-28, 37-41	22
24	19:11-28	Par	parable of the talents	25:14-30	24

94. Adapted from Kümmel, *Introduction to the New Testament*, 65-66. See lists, synopses, and commentary in T. W. Manson, *The Sayings of Jesus* (London: SCM, 1937), 39-148; John S. Kloppenborg, *Q Parallels: Synopsis, Critical Notes and Concordance* (Sonoma: Polebridge, 1988); Dale C. Allison, *The Jesus Tradition in Q* (Harrisburg: Trinity, 1997); James M. Robinson, John S. Kloppenborg, and Paul Hoffman, eds., *The Critical Edition of Q* (Herm.; Minneapolis: Fortress, 2000).

The postulation of Q makes sense on both source-critical and genre grounds. To begin with, it explains the double tradition, in whole or part, without having to resort to the thesis that Luke used Matthew or vice-versa, which many see as problematic.[95] The Q source also makes sense in the literary milieu of the first-century Greco-Roman world. A convenient collection of Jesus' sayings, parables, pronouncements, and warnings put together by either his immediate followers or disciples in the early church is entirely conceivable.[96] The abundant echoes of dominical sayings from the Synoptic tradition found in the epistle of James and the anthology of Jesuanic logia presented in the *Gospel of Thomas* are clear instances of the sayings of Jesus, whatever their authenticity and origins, being venerated and utilized in Christian literature. Furthermore, a sayings document like Q would exhibit an affinity in genre with extant literature of the period, resembling the collected utterances of a revered sage as found in Jewish wisdom literature like Sirach, possessing a likeness to the sayings of the rabbis codified in the Mishnah, and being somewhat analogous to Greek anthologies of gnomic sayings such as Pseudo-Isocrates's *To Demonicus* or Cyprian's *To Quirinius*. Q is thus an entirely plausible thesis, since such a document would meet the didactic needs of the early church for catechetical material about Jesus and resonate with analogous literature that provided collections of sayings of venerated leaders.[97]

The main problem with Q is not the notion of a written source used by both Matthew and Luke. The problem is that Q theorists sometimes make seemingly extraordinary speculations about the origins, layers, redaction, and community behind Q. I suspect that around 70% of Q scholarship is doing little more than building castles in the air. Attempts to determine the redaction and composition history of Q from the texts of Luke and Matthew are about as futile as trying to determine the redaction and composition history of Mark

---

95. On reasons for Luke's non-use of Matthew, see Streeter, *Four* Gospels, 183; Joseph A. Fitzmyer, *The Gospel According to Luke* (2 vols.; AB; Garden City: Doubleday, 1981), 1:73-75; Stein, *Synoptic Gospels,* 99-112; Christopher Tuckett, "Synoptic Problem," in *ABD,* 4:268.

96. Cf. study of ancient sayings collections by John S. Kloppenborg, *Formation of Q: Trajectories in Ancient Wisdom Collections* (Philadelphia: Fortress, 1987), 263-316; cf. the same point in abbreviated form in Foster, "Is It Possible to Dispense with Q?" 322-24.

97. I would tend to think along the lines of the proposal of Larry Hurtado, *Lord Jesus Christ: Devotion to Jesus in Earliest Christianity* (Grand Rapids: Eerdmans, 2003), 256-57: "If Q was composed by Hellenist believers such as the Jerusalem circles linked with Stephen in Acts, this would account satisfactorily for how it came to embody such a sizable collection of Jesus tradition with good claims to authenticity."

from the texts of Luke and Matthew. Furthermore, Q scholarship is so much at odds with itself that it is often schizophrenic. E. Earle Ellis commented:

> Q is a single document, a composite document, several documents. It incorporates earlier sources; it is used in different redactions. Its original language is Greek; it is Aramaic; Q is used in different translations. It is the Matthean *logia;* it is not. It has shape and sequence; it is a collection of fragments. It is a Gospel; it is not. It consists wholly of sayings; it includes narrative. It is all preserved in Matthew and Luke; it is not. Matthew's order of Q is correct; Luke's is correct; neither is correct. It is used by Mark; it is not used by Mark.[98]

I propose that all Gospel researchers rise early every day and recite the words of John Meier: "Q is a hypothetical document whose exact extension, wording, originating community, strata, and stages of redaction cannot be known," and he adds, "This daily devotion might save us flights of fancy that are destined, in my view, to end in skepticism."[99]

Attempts, however, to altogether eliminate Q by appealing to Luke's possible use of Matthew, though warranting due consideration, seem less probable.

1. The word-for-word agreements between Matthew and Luke in their common text are so thorough as to warrant the postulation of a shared written source. For example, Matt 6:24 and Luke 16:13 (serving two masters) have 27 out of 28 words in common; Matt 11:21-23 and Luke 10:13-15 (woe oracles) have 43 out of 49 words in common.[100]

2. The doublet sayings in Matthew and Luke also favor the existence of Q. The doublets are two forms of a saying, one Marcan and the other non-Marcan, such as the sayings on divorce (Mark 10:11-12/Matt 19:9 and Matt 5:32/Luke 16:18) and the sign of Jonah (Mark 8:11-12/Matt 16:1-2 and Matt 12:38-42/Luke 11:29-32). Sometimes the doublets appear in both Luke and Matthew. Other times the doublet is found in only one. On the two-source theory the doublets emerge from Matthew's and Luke's use of two different sources, Mark and Q.

98. E. Earle Ellis, *The Making of the New Testament Documents* (Leiden: Brill, 2002), 17-18.

99. John P. Meier, *A Marginal Jew: Rethinking the Historical Jesus* (ABRL; New York: Doubleday, 2001), 2:178.

100. Cf. further lists of statistics in J. A. Fitzmyer, "Luke's Use of Q," in *Two-Source Hypothesis,* ed. Bellinzoni, 251-52.

The Double Sayings in the Synoptic Tradition

Saying	Version	Mark	Matthew	Luke
in Mark and Luke				
Whoever wants to be first must be last of all.	Mark	9:35		9:48
	Mark	10:43-44	20:26-27	22:24-27
in Matthew and Luke				
To those who already have, more will be given.	Mark	4:25	13:12	8:18
	double tradition		25:29	19:26
If anyone wants to be my disciple let them take up their cross.	Mark	8:34	16:24	9:23
	double tradition		10:38	14:27
Whoever wants to save their life will lose it.	Mark	8:35	16:25	9:24
	double tradition		10:39	17:33
Whoever welcomes a child in my name welcomes me.	Mark	9:37	18:5	9:48
			10:40	10:16
in Matthew				
By the prince of demons he casts out demons.	Mark	3:22	9:34	
	double tradition		12:24	11:15
No sign will be given except the sign of Jonah.	Mark	8:11-12	16:1-2	
	double tradition		12:38-42	11:29-32
Whoever divorces his wife and marries another . . .	Mark	10:11-12	19:9	
	double tradition		5:32	16:18
Many who are first will be last and the last will be first.	Mark	10:31	19:30	
	double tradition		20:16	13:30
If you say to this mountain . . .	Mark	11:22-23	21:21	
	double tradition		17:19-20	17:5-6
in Luke				
Is a lamp brought in to be placed under a bushel?	Mark	4:21		8:16
	double tradition		5:15	11:33
There is nothing hidden, except to be revealed.	Mark	4:22		8:17
	double tradition		10:26	12:2
Whoever is ashamed of me and my words . . .	Mark	8:38		9:26
	double tradition		10:32-33	12:9
It is not you who speaks, but the Holy Spirit.	Mark	13:9-11		21:12-15
	double tradition		10:19	12:11-12

Luke's use of Matthew might account for some of these doublets, especially when Luke follows the version found in Mark and another version found in Matthew. However, since Q is reckoned to be a sayings source, it is expected that it would potentially include sayings that parallel Marcan sayings. In addition, if Luke used Matthew, then we are left wondering why Luke kept four of these Matthean doublets, eliminated five by dropping the Marcan version, and then created five more by augmenting units he had inherited from Matthew and Mark. Luke's dual elimination and formulation of doublets looks more complex than selectively following Matthew as he is dependent somewhere on a further source of sayings that influenced his inclusion of sayings material.

3. Luke is sufficiently different from Matthew in the double tradition to posit some degree of independence as well. A juxtaposition of the saying about the kingdom of God suffering violence (Matt 11:12/Luke 16:16), the parable of the talents/minas (Matt 25:14-30/Luke 19:11-27), and the parable of the lost sheep (Matt 18:12-14/Luke 15:3-7) demonstrate these differences with respect to the details of the given unit. While this differentiation could be explained by way of Lucan redaction of Matthew, it is also explainable by Luke accessing a parallel tradition that he has deployed differently, especially in regard to the Sermon on the Plain, a couple parables, and several sayings. This independence would also explain why Luke does not reference Matthean expansion of speeches in Mark or incorporate features said to be indicative of Matthean redaction in the triple tradition (e.g., on Peter's confession compare Mark 8:29-30; Matt 16:15-19; and Luke 9:20-21).[101]

4. Luke also appears on many occasions to possess the more primitive version of a unit in the Q parallels.[102] What is meant by "more primitive" can be very slippery. Does it mean more authentic and closer to what Jesus actually said? Does it mean an earlier form in the tradition history? Does it mean permeated with less redaction by the Evangelists? At several points Luke does indeed seem to have the more primitive version if we judge primitiveness in terms of being simple, succinct, and less embellished. For instance, some of the Beatitudes (Matt 5:3, 6/Luke 6:20-21), judgment oracles (Matt 23:24/Luke 11:49), the Lord's Prayer (Matt 6:9-13/Luke 11:2-4), and the sign of Jonah (Matt 12:40/Luke 11:30) do look more primitive in Luke's presentation. To give more specific examples, in the Beelzebul debate (Matt 12:28/Luke 11:20) Luke's "finger of God" is probably more original than

---

101. Note, however, the response by Goodacre, *Synoptic Gospels*, 128-31.

102. Cf. further Streeter, *Four Gospels*, 183; Foster, "Is It Possible to Dispense with Q?"

Matthew's "Spirit of God" since Luke has a special interest in the Holy Spirit (e.g., Luke 10:21; 11:13) and would probably have added it had he known it from Matthew. Similarly, in the story of the faithful and unfaithful stewards (Matt 24:51/Luke 12:46), Luke's "unfaithful" is probably more original than Matthew's "hypocrites." Although Luke is not averse to using "hypocrite," Matthew tends to use it far more often, probably adding it here.[103] While Luke and Matthew alternate in their apparent "primitivity" in the double tradition, Luke preserves more primitive versions more often, indicative of access to a separate source.

5. A juxtaposition of the macro-outlines of Luke and Matthew demonstrates that their shared material occurs in very different locations. For a start, with all but two exceptions (Luke 3:7-9, 17 and 4:2-13), Luke never inserts material from the double tradition into a Marcan context as Matthew does. Luke basically follows the Marcan outline, with several peculiar omissions (Mark 1:16-20 and 6:45–8:26) and seems to add in material shared with Matthew primarily — though not exclusively — in two main blocks (Luke 6:20–7:35 and 9:57–13:34) and in ways that depart from Matthew's own order. So, for instance, the parable about watchfulness and the parable of the wedding feast/great supper occurs halfway through Luke (Luke 12:39-46; 14:15-24), but the same two parables occur much later in Matthew (Matt 24:43-51; 22:1-14). Furthermore, material found in the Matthean discourses is broken up and distributed somewhat unevenly across Luke. Christopher Tuckett asks, "If Luke knew Matthew, why has he changed the Matthean order so thoroughly, disrupting Matthew's clear and concise arrangement of the teaching material into five blocks, each concerned with a particular theme?"[104] Kloppenborg thinks that Luke's usage of Matthew would mean that "Luke rather aggressively dislocated sayings from the context in which he found them in Matthew."[105] Streeter goes so far as to state that this would

---

103. To be fair we might also consider that: (1) Sometimes Matthew looks like the more primitive source, such as the saying about the kingdom suffering violence (Matt 11:12/Luke 16:16), where Luke's account is redacted with his salvation-historical perspective and includes one of his favorite words, εὐαγγελίζω. (2) Sometimes Matthew looks more primitive than Mark, too, even though Matthew very definitely used Mark (e.g., see the conclusion to Jesus healing a paralytic and forgiving his sins in Matt 9:8 and Mark 2:12, since Matthew seems to recognize the generic connotations of "Son of Man" as implying mankind in general). (3) Lucan primitivity could be Luke simplifying Matthew's language and cleansing it of Matthean vocabulary. See further Goodacre, *Synoptic Problem*, 133-40.

104. Tuckett, "Synoptic Gospels," 4:268.

105. Kloppenborg, *Excavating Q*, 39.

turn Luke into a "crank."[106] If Luke used Matthew, then this cite and scatter approach to the Sermon on the Mount is compositionally odd and disassembles one of the greatest religious speeches of history: Why would anyone do that?[107] It is more likely, then, that Luke and Matthew have in many instances used the same source differently than it is for Luke to have moved back and forth through Matthew and inserted Matthean material into his Marcan outline in such a disconnected fashion. For many scholars, the two-source theory is a better explanation for the arrangement of Luke's order.[108]

Despite my affirmation of Q, I am not convinced that everything in the double tradition can be safely attributed to Q. The double tradition may constitute a array of sources, oral and written, some of which found their way into Q. I remain inclined to think therefore that additional sources, especially for the narrative material in the double tradition, were also shared by Luke and Matthew.[109] B. H. Streeter soberly admitted that "a substantial proportion of the 200 verses in question were probably derived from some other source than Q."[110] Terence Mournet has argued that less than 70% verbatim parallelism between sources means that there is a good chance that oral tradition is in operation, and this may apply to much of the Q material as verbal correspondence between Matthew and Luke range between nearly 100% to 8%.[111] In a peculiar alliance, advocates of both the Griesbach and Farrer theories have appealed to Luke's use of other oral and written traditions beyond Mark and Matthew to help explain some of the overlaps.[112] It is entirely plausible,

106. Streeter, *Four Gospels*, 183; see response in Michael Goulder, "The Order of a Crank," in *Synoptic Studies: The Ampleworth Conferences of 1982 and 1983*, ed. C. M. Tuckett (JSNTSup 7; Sheffield: JSOT, 1984), 111-30; Goodacre, *Synoptic Gospels*, 123-28.

107. But see Goodacre, *Synoptic Gospels*, 123-28.

108. Cf. Sanders and Davies, *Synoptic Gospels*, 112, 114; Foster, "Is It Possible to Dispense with Q?" 316-19.

109. I profess to having lingering doubts about the Q provenance of John the Baptist material (Matt 3:7-12/Luke 3:7-9, 16-17; Matt 11:2-19/Luke 7:18-35), the temptation story (Matt 4:1-11/Luke 4:1-13), the story of the centurion (Matt 8:5-13/Luke 7:1-10), and anything in the Mark-Q overlaps.

110. Streeter, *Four Gospels*, 185.

111. Terence C. Mournet, *Oral Tradition and Literary Dependency: Variability in the Synoptic Tradition and Q* (WUNT 2.195; Tübingen: Mohr, 2005), following James D. G. Dunn, *Jesus Remembered* (CITM 1; Grand Rapids: Eerdmans, 2003), 147-49, 173-254.

112. Farmer "Two-Gospel Hypothesis," 100, 116; Allan James McNicol, "The Composition of the Synoptic Eschatological Discourse," in *The Interrelations of the Gospels: A Symposium*, ed. D. Dungan (BETL 95; Leuven: Leuven University Press, 1990), 162; Farrer, "Dispensing with Q," 332-33; Goodacre, *Synoptic Problem*, 94-96, 138-40; idem, *Case against Q*, 65-66, 133-51; Poirier, "Composition of Luke," 210.

if not likely, that some other written and oral sources may have been jointly shared by Luke and Matthew. The result may be a Q-lite. An examination of Matt 8:5-13 and Luke 7:1-10; 13:28-29 will help demonstrate this point.

Sayings Material and Narrative Elements in the Double Tradition

Healing of the Centurion's Servant

Matt 8:5-10	Luke 7:1-10
⁵When he entered **Capernaum, a centurion** came to him, appealing to him ⁶and saying, "Lord, my servant is lying at home paralyzed, in terrible distress." ⁷And he said to him, "I will come and cure him."	¹After Jesus had finished all his sayings in the hearing of the people, he entered **Capernaum**. ²**A centurion** there had a slave whom he valued highly, and who was ill and close to death. ³When he heard about Jesus, he sent some Jewish elders to him, asking him to come and heal his slave. ⁴When they came to Jesus, they appealed to him earnestly, saying, "He is worthy of having you do this for him, ⁵for he loves our people, and it is he who built our synagogue for us." ⁶And Jesus went with them, but when he was not far from the house, the centu-
⁸The centurion answered, "**Lord, I am not worthy to have you come under my roof; but only speak the word, and my servant** will be **healed.**	rion sent friends to say to him, "**Lord**, do **not** trouble yourself, for **I am not worthy to have you come under my roof;** ⁷therefore I did not presume to come to you. But only **speak the word**, and let my servant be **healed.**
⁹**For I also am a man under authority, with soldiers under me; and I say to one, 'Go,' and he goes, and to another, 'Come,' and he comes, and to my slave, 'Do this,' and the slave does it."** ¹⁰**When Jesus heard him, he was amazed** and **said** to those who followed him, "Truly **I tell you**, in no one **in Israel have I found such faith."**	⁸**For I also am a man set under authority, with soldiers under me; and I say to one, 'Go,' and he goes, and to another, 'Come,' and he comes, and to my slave, 'Do this,' and the slave does it."** ⁹**When Jesus heard** this **he was amazed** at him, and turning to the crowd that followed him, **he said, "I tell you**, not even **in Israel have I found such faith."** ¹⁰When those who had been sent returned to the house, they found the slave in good health.
⁵Εἰσελθόντος δὲ αὐτοῦ **εἰς Καφαρναοὺμ προσῆλθεν αὐτῷ ἑκατόνταρχος παρακαλῶν αὐτὸν** ⁶**καὶ** λέγων· κύριε, ὁ παῖς μου βέβληται ἐν τῇ οἰκίᾳ	ⁱἘπειδὴ ἐπλήρωσεν πάντα τὰ ῥήματα αὐτοῦ εἰς τὰς ἀκοὰς τοῦ λαοῦ, εἰσῆλθεν **εἰς Καφαρναούμ**. ²Ἑκατοντάρχου δέ τινος **δοῦλος κακῶς ἔχων ἤμελλεν τελευτᾶν**, ὃς ἦν αὐτῷ ἔντιμος. ³ἀκούσας δὲ περὶ τοῦ Ἰησοῦ ἀπέστειλεν

Matt 8:5-10	Luke 7:1-10
παραλυτικός, δεινῶς βασανιζόμενος. ⁷καὶ λέγει αὐτῷ· ἐγὼ ἐλθὼν θεραπεύσω αὐτόν.	πρὸς αὐτὸν πρεσβυτέρους τῶν Ἰουδαίων ἐρωτῶν αὐτὸν ὅπως ἐλθὼν διασώσῃ τὸν δοῦλον αὐτοῦ. ⁴οἱ δὲ παραγενόμενοι πρὸς τὸν Ἰησοῦν παρεκάλουν αὐτὸν σπουδαίως λέγοντες ὅτι ἄξιός ἐστιν ᾧ παρέξῃ τοῦτο· ⁵ἀγαπᾷ γὰρ τὸ ἔθνος ἡμῶν καὶ τὴν συναγωγὴν αὐτὸς ᾠκοδόμησεν ἡμῖν. ⁶ὁ δὲ Ἰησοῦς ἐπορεύετο σὺν αὐτοῖς. ἤδη δὲ αὐτοῦ οὐ μακρὰν ἀπέχοντος ἀπὸ τῆς οἰκίας ἔπεμψεν φίλους ὁ ἑκατοντάρχης
⁸καὶ ἀποκριθεὶς ὁ ἑκατόνταρχος ἔφη· **κύριε, οὐκ εἰμὶ ἱκανὸς ἵνα μου ὑπὸ τὴν στέγην εἰσέλθῃς, ἀλλὰ μόνον εἰπὲ λόγῳ, καὶ ἰαθήσεται ὁ παῖς μου.**	λέγων αὐτῷ· **κύριε,** μὴ σκύλλου, **οὐ γὰρ ἱκανός εἰμι ἵνα ὑπὸ τὴν στέγην μου εἰσέλθῃς**· ⁷διὸ οὐδὲ ἐμαυτὸν ἠξίωσα πρὸς σὲ ἐλθεῖν· **ἀλλὰ εἰπὲ λόγῳ, καὶ ἰαθήτω ὁ παῖς μου.**
⁹**καὶ γὰρ ἐγὼ ἄνθρωπός εἰμι ὑπὸ ἐξουσίαν, ἔχων ὑπ' ἐμαυτὸν στρατιώτας, καὶ λέγω τούτῳ· πορεύθητι, καὶ πορεύεται, καὶ ἄλλῳ· ἔρχου, καὶ ἔρχεται, καὶ τῷ δούλῳ μου· ποίησον τοῦτο, καὶ ποιεῖ.** ¹⁰**ἀκούσας δὲ ὁ Ἰησοῦς ἐθαύμασεν** καὶ εἶπεν τοῖς ἀκολουθοῦσιν· ἀμὴν **λέγω ὑμῖν,** παρ' οὐδενὶ **τοσαύτην πίστιν ἐν τῷ Ἰσραὴλ εὗρον.**	⁸**καὶ γὰρ ἐγὼ ἄνθρωπός εἰμι ὑπὸ ἐξουσίαν** τασσόμενος **ἔχων ὑπ' ἐμαυτὸν στρατιώτας, καὶ λέγω τούτῳ· πορεύθητι, καὶ πορεύεται, καὶ ἄλλῳ· ἔρχου, καὶ ἔρχεται, καὶ τῷ δούλῳ μου· ποίησον τοῦτο, καὶ ποιεῖ.** ⁹**ἀκούσας δὲ** ταῦτα **ὁ Ἰησοῦς ἐθαύμασεν** αὐτὸν καὶ στραφεὶς τῷ ἀκολουθοῦντι αὐτῷ ὄχλῳ εἶπεν· **λέγω ὑμῖν,** οὐδὲ ἐν τῷ **Ἰσραὴλ τοσαύτην πίστιν εὗρον.** ¹⁰Καὶ ὑποστρέψαντες εἰς τὸν οἶκον οἱ πεμφθέντες εὗρον τὸν δοῦλον ὑγιαίνοντα.

Judgment Oracle and Great Reversal

Matt 8:11-13	Luke 13:28-29
¹¹I tell you, many **will come from east and west** and will eat with **Abraham and Isaac and Jacob in the kingdom** of heaven, ¹²while the heirs of the kingdom will be thrown into the outer darkness, where **there will be weeping and gnashing of teeth."** ¹³And to the centurion Jesus said, "Go; let it be done for you according to your faith." And the servant was healed in that hour.	²⁸**There will be weeping and gnashing of teeth** when you see **Abraham and Isaac and Jacob** and all the prophets **in the kingdom** of God, and you yourselves thrown out. ²⁹Then people **will come from east and west**, from north and south, and will eat in the kingdom of God.

Matt 8:11-13	Luke 13:28-29
¹¹λέγω δὲ ὑμῖν ὅτι πολλοὶ ἀπὸ ἀνατολῶν καὶ δυσμῶν ἥξουσιν καὶ ἀνακλιθήσονται μετὰ Ἀβραὰμ καὶ Ἰσαὰκ καὶ Ἰακὼβ ἐν τῇ βασιλείᾳ τῶν οὐρανῶν, ¹²οἱ δὲ υἱοὶ τῆς βασιλείας ἐκβληθήσονται εἰς τὸ σκότος τὸ ἐξώτερον· ἐκεῖ ἔσται ὁ κλαυθμὸς καὶ ὁ βρυγμὸς τῶν ὀδόντων. ¹³καὶ εἶπεν ὁ Ἰησοῦς τῷ ἑκατοντάρχῃ· ὕπαγε, ὡς ἐπίστευσας γενηθήτω σοι. καὶ ἰάθη ὁ παῖς [αὐτοῦ] ἐν τῇ ὥρᾳ ἐκείνῃ.	²⁸ἐκεῖ ἔσται ὁ κλαυθμὸς καὶ ὁ βρυγμὸς τῶν ὀδόντων, ὅταν ὄψησθε Ἀβραὰμ καὶ Ἰσαὰκ καὶ Ἰακὼβ καὶ πάντας τοὺς προφήτας ἐν τῇ βασιλείᾳ τοῦ θεοῦ, ὑμᾶς δὲ ἐκβαλλομένους ἔξω. ²⁹καὶ ἥξουσιν ἀπὸ ἀνατολῶν καὶ δυσμῶν καὶ ἀπὸ βορρᾶ καὶ νότου καὶ ἀνακλιθήσονται ἐν τῇ βασιλείᾳ τοῦ θεοῦ.

Several things can be observed about these two units:[113]

1. Both units are placed in very different contexts by the two Evangelists. Matthew joins the story of the healing of the centurion's servant (Matt 8:5-10) with the saying about the eschatological banquet (vv. 10-11) by way of a concluding editorial remark (v. 13). But Luke has the story of the healing of the centurion's servant after the Sermon on the Plain (Luke 7:1-10) and places the saying about the eschatological banquet amid a later section of exhortation and teaching about the kingdom of God (13:28-29).

2. The two versions of the healing of the centurion's servant exhibit verbal correspondences only in the setting in Capernaum at the beginning and in the subsequent dialogue between Jesus and the centurion. The two versions disagree on whether Jesus met the centurion in person or through a Judean delegation.

3. The two version of the saying about the eschatological banquet are verbally very close. The key difference is Luke's enlargement of the logion and the inversion of the order of the saying between the warning of weeping and gnashing of teeth (first in Luke, second in Matthew) and the promise of reclining at the banquet (first in Matthew, second in Luke).

There are three possible explanations for this: (1) The Griesbach and Farrer theory: Luke has reordered Matthew's material. (2) The two-source theory: both units were contained in Q and either (i) Matthew joined the story and saying together to create a pro-Gentile picture, or (ii) Luke pulled apart the saying and story that were originally united in Q. (3) The Holtzmann-Gundry theory: the saying originally belonged in Q while Luke either received the story from a separate source or took it over from Matthew.

113. See further analysis in Michael F. Bird, *Jesus and the Origins of the Gentile Mission* (LNTS 311; London: Clark, 2006), 83-93; idem, "Who Comes from the East and the West? The Historical Jesus and Matt 8.11-12/Luke 13.28-29," *NTS* 52 (2006): 441-57.

I think option (3) has the most going for it. First, if the only version of the saying and story that Luke knew was that of Matt 8:5-13, he would be more inclined to keep them together, since Luke is, on the Griesbach and Farrer theories, more of a mover and conflater of Matthean material than a divider of Matthean material.[114] Or Luke might have omitted the story of the centurion found in Matthew in the same way that he omitted the story of the Syro-Phoenician woman from Mark because he intended to play his big Gentile inclusion trump card later. I do not envisage Luke retaining yet partitioning and reordering a unit like Matt 8:5-13 because we have no real example of him doing anything like that. So it is unlikely that he received *both* units in their current form from Matthew, implying that either one or both parts were drawn from Q or other traditions.[115]

Second, the saying about many coming from the east and the west fits naturally into the proposed theology of the Q document. Originally the eschatological saying was intended as a statement that Israel's exile was ending in Jesus' kingdom ministry and that those who scorned it would miss out on vindication at the patriarchal banquet of the eschaton, a motif completely in accord with other Q material concerning Israel's restoration (e.g., Matt 19:28-29/Luke 22:28-30; Matt 23:37-39/Luke 13:34-35).

Third, the story of the centurion sticks out like a sore thumb in Q. Scholars have always found the presence of narrative traditions in Q to be something of an anomaly, an intrusive presence in a document containing predominantly sayings material about John the Baptist, discipleship, and judgment. I suspect that is the case, that Q originally did not have any narrative material and was indeed a pure collection of sayings. The Matthean and Lucan versions of the story of the centurion have less than 50% verbal agreement and may therefore derive from a common oral tradition or from different source documents, or Luke took up the story from Matthew. In any case, Matthew and Luke probably received the saying from Q and the narrative from a different source. Matthew joined them together, and Luke kept them separate.[116]

Thus far I have argued for the priority of Mark, more tentatively argued

114. For instance, Luke 16:16-17 is a combination of Matt 11:12-13 and 5:18.

115. Simons, *Hat der dritte Evangelist den kanonischen Matthäus benutzt?* 11-12, thinks that this passage proves that Luke drew directly from Q and not from Matthew since the Lucan version is inexplicable if Luke knew only Matthew.

116. Matthew's combination of Matt 8:5-10 and 8:11-12 still remains quite apt because several Old Testament passages and second temple texts that predict the end of Israel's exile are frequently combined with hopes for the eschatological pilgrimage of the Gentiles. See discussion in Bird, *Jesus and the Origins of the Gentile Mission*, 90-92.

for the existence of a Q-lite, with the double tradition containing a mixture of Q and independent traditions, and opened up the possibility of Luke using Matthew, a possibility that needs to be explored further.

3. Luke's Use of Matthew

The presumption of Marcan priority in conjunction with the postulation of Q would seem to put much of the Synoptic problem to rest. But, alas, I do not think it does. I will contend that the minor agreements between Luke and Matthew in the triple tradition plus the Mark and Q overlaps strongly suggest Lucan usage of Matthew in addition to Luke's and Matthew's incorporation of Q material.

a. Minor Agreements in the Triple Tradition

A slight hitch in the two-source theory has always been the number of Matthew-Luke agreements against Mark.[117] If one single occurrence of Luke's use of Matthew can be demonstrated, then the two-source theory falls into disarray. Exactly how many of these minor agreements there are is a matter of debate, and estimates range considerably from 200 to over 1000.[118] What is more, these agreements take different forms and include shared omissions, revisions, extensions, and additions.[119] Some of these minor agreements are also more impressive than others, though cumulatively they are very impressive, especially when Matthean redactions ("foreign bodies") seemingly find their way into Luke.[120]

---

117. Cf. the cogent introduction in M. E. Boring, "The 'Minor Agreements' and Their Bearing on the Synoptic Problem," in *New Studies in the Synoptic Problem*, ed. Foster, Gregory, Kloppenborg, and Verheyden, 227-51.

118. E. A. Abbott, *The Corrections of Mark Adopted by Matthew and Luke* (London: Black, 1901), 300-324 (230); J. C. Hawkins, *Horae Synopticae* (Oxford: Clarendon, 1909), 210-11 (239); Josef Schmid, *Mathäus und Lukas. Eine Untersuchung des Verhältnisses ihr Evangelien* (Freiburg: Herder, 1930), 175 (250); Stoldt, *Marcan Hypothesis*, 11-21 (272); Frans Neirynck, *The Minor Agreements of Matthew and Luke against Mark* (Leuven: Leuven University Press, 1974), 55-195; idem, *The Minor Agreements in a Horizontal-Line Synopsis* (SNTA 15; Leuven: Leuven University Press, 1991) (770); Andreas Ennulat, *Die "Minor Agreements" Untersuchungen zu einer offenen Frage des synoptischens Problems* (WUNT 2.62; Tübingen: Mohr, 1994), 35-416 (1187).

119. Cf. Stoldt, *Marcan Hypothesis*, 11-21; Stein, *Synoptic Gospels*, 125-36.

120. Cf. Goodacre, *Goulder and the Gospels*, 89-131; idem, *Case against Q*, 154-60; Gundry, "Matthean Foreign Bodies," 1467-95.

However, what is especially troubling for the two-source theory is the presence of many peculiar agreements in the passion story, clearly outside the range of the Q material. Here are two examples from the Synoptic version of the trial of Jesus:

Two Minor Agreements in the Passion Narrative

Jesus Predicts the Coming Son of Man

Mark 14:62	Matt 26:64	Luke 22:69
Jesus said, "I am; and 'you will see the Son of Man seated at the right hand of the Power,' and 'coming with the clouds of heaven.'"	Jesus said to him, "You have said so. But I tell you, From now on you will see the Son of Man seated at the right hand of Power and coming on the clouds of heaven."	But from now on the Son of Man will be seated at the right hand of the power of God.
ὁ δὲ Ἰησοῦς εἶπεν· ἐγώ εἰμι, καὶ ὄψεσθε τὸν υἱὸν τοῦ ἀνθρώπου ἐκ δεξιῶν καθήμενον τῆς δυνάμεως καὶ ἐρχόμενον μετὰ τῶν νεφελῶν τοῦ οὐρανοῦ.	λέγει αὐτῷ ὁ Ἰησοῦς· σὺ εἶπας. πλὴν λέγω ὑμῖν· ἀπ' ἄρτι ὄψεσθε τὸν υἱὸν τοῦ ἀνθρώπου καθήμενον ἐκ δεξιῶν τῆς δυνάμεως καὶ ἐρχόμενον ἐπὶ τῶν νεφελῶν τοῦ οὐρανοῦ.	ἀπὸ τοῦ νῦν δὲ ἔσται ὁ υἱὸς τοῦ ἀνθρώπου καθήμενος ἐκ δεξιῶν τῆς δυνάμεως τοῦ θεοῦ.

Jesus Is Mocked as a Prophet

Mark 14:65	Matt 26:67-68	Luke 22:64
Some began to spit on him, to blindfold his face, and to strike him, saying to him, "Prophesy!" The guards also took him over and beat him.	Then they spat in his face and struck him; and some slapped him, saying, "Prophesy to us, you Messiah! Who is it that struck you?"	they also blindfolded him and kept asking him, "Prophesy! Who is it that struck you?"
Καὶ ἤρξαντό τινες ἐμπτύειν αὐτῷ καὶ περικαλύπτειν αὐτοῦ τὸ πρόσωπον καὶ κολαφίζειν αὐτὸν καὶ λέγειν αὐτῷ· προφήτευσον, καὶ οἱ ὑπηρέται ῥαπίσμασιν αὐτὸν ἔλαβον.	Τότε ἐνέπτυσαν εἰς τὸ πρόσωπον αὐτοῦ καὶ ἐκολάφισαν αὐτόν, οἱ δὲ ἐράπισαν λέγοντες· προφήτευσον ἡμῖν, χριστέ, τίς ἐστιν ὁ παίσας σε;	καὶ περικαλύψαντες αὐτὸν ἐπηρώτων λέγοντες· προφήτευσον, τίς ἐστιν ὁ παίσας σε;

In the first agreement (Mark 14:62/Matt 26:64/Luke 22:69), Jesus' response to Caiaphas conflates Ps 110:1 and Dan 7:13. Mark and Matthew are the closest in sharing the future verb "you will see" (ὄψεσθε) and the subsequent description of the Son of Man coming on the clouds of heaven. Luke in contrast is more succinct and less descriptive, almost terse. Mark's statement could be understood as a straightforward parousia prediction, given the future tense of ὄψεσθε, though I am not convinced of this because Psalm 110 and Daniel 7 are about exaltation, not a descent to earth. Proof that the main point is Jesus' exaltation, not his future parousia, is found in the peculiar Matthew-Luke gloss: both add "from now on," indicating that the exaltation of Jesus has already begun! It would be courageous to argue that Matthew and Luke made this gloss independently as a clarification to Mark's statement. Moreover, Matthew's Greek phrasing ἀπ' ἄρτι is his distinctive reference to the age of the church (Matt 23:39; 26:29), which Luke has followed with a slight linguistic variation (ἀπὸ τοῦ νῦν).[121] A likely scenario here is that Mark was composed first, that Matthew followed Mark fairly closely but clarified Mark's reference to Jesus' "coming," and that Luke followed Matthew's gloss while both abbreviating and moving the saying in his own version of the trial.

In the second agreement (Mark 14:65/Matt 26:67-68/Luke 22:64) Jesus is mocked as a prophet and physically attacked. Only Matthew and Luke add "Who is it that struck you?" (τίς ἐστιν ὁ παίσας σε;) to explain the cruel humor of Jesus' tormentors.[122] Goulder says that "most defenders of Q disappear into the smokescreen" here because there seems to be no reason that Matthew and Luke would both add this verse independently and with identical wording.[123] Neirynck and Tuckett are forced to explain the agreement by means of a conjectural emendation, the last refuge of a Synoptic solution with no material evidence.[124]

---

121. Cf. Gundry, *Matthew*, 545.

122. Strangely, Gundry (*Matthew*, 547) thinks that despite the agreement "probably we should not think of Matthean influence [on Luke], but of Matthew's conflating two historical traditions — the Marcan and the pre-Lukan." See also Streeter, *Four Gospels*, 199-222; Marion L. Soards, *The Passion According to Luke: The Special Material of Luke 22* (JSNTSup 14; Sheffield: JSOT, 1987), 102-3.

123. Goulder, "Juggernaut," 675.

124. Frans Neirynck, "The Minor Agreements and the Two Source Theory," in *Minor Agreements: Symposium Göttingen, 1991*, ed. G. Strecker (Göttingen: Vandenhoeck & Ruprecht, 1993), 49-51; Christopher Tuckett, "The Minor Agreements and Textual Criticism," in *Minor Agreements*, ed. Strecker, 135-41.

There are a number of ways that these minor agreements can be explained. Some have been impressed with them and wondered if Q might in fact have had a passion story.[125] Such arguments, though, have largely been dismissed by Q scholars because there is no reason to think that the special Lucan material in the passion story was from Q and because Q was more probably a strict sayings collection.[126] Others have argued that Matthew and Luke used a different version of Mark than the one we have. William Sanday proposed that Matthew and Luke used "a recension of the text of Mark different from that from which all the extant MSS of the Gospel are descended."[127] Similarly, Stein claims that Matthew and Luke did not use Mark's "autograph"; instead their copy arose from a " 'family' of the autograph that was somewhat different from the 'family' from which we today derive our 'Mark.' "[128] The notion of different recensions of Mark is also entertained by Ennulat and Boring.[129] Albert Fuchs has even written a mammoth five volumes arguing that the minor agreements stem from an earlier form of Mark than our canonical Mark, which is really a deutero-Mark, an edition of Mark that was linguistically revised and enlarged with the addition of several sayings.[130] Ulrich Luz has proposed a mix of Marcan priority, deutero-Mark, and oral tradition variants to account for the minor agreements.[131] The problem is that while theories of Ur-Mark and deutero-Mark are certainly possible, they still remain purely hypothetical. In addition, if one appeals to divergent editions and diverse textual recensions then we have to ask why, amid all the textual variations in our manuscripts for Mark, none can be found in the manuscript tradition supporting the presence of these minor agreements in Mark. Moving on, proponents of the Farrer and Griesbach theories have found in the minor agreements good evidence for their claim that Luke used Matthew, a point I would not

---

125. Cf. E. Hirsch, *Frühgeschichte des Evangeliums* (Tübingen: Mohr, 1941), 1:243-48 (who suspects that Luke 22:48, 62, 64, 69; 22:47 were from a Mark-like Q-passion story); E. Earle Ellis, "Gospel Criticism: A Perspective on the State of the Art," in *The Gospel and the Gospels*, ed. P. Stuhlmacher (Grand Rapids: Eerdmans, 1991), 36.

126. Cf., e.g., Kloppenborg, *Formation of Q*, 85-87.

127. William Sanday, "The Conditions under Which the Gospels Were Written, in Their Bearing upon Some Difficulties of the Synoptic Problem," in *Oxford Studies in the Synoptic Problem*, ed. W. Sanday (Oxford: Clarendon, 1911), 21.

128. Stein, *Synoptic Gospels*, 138.

129. Ennulat, *Die "Minor Agreements,"* 418; Boring, "'Minor Agreements,'" 246-49.

130. Fuchs, *Spuren von Deuteromarkus*.

131. Ulrich Luz, "Korreferat zu W. R. Farmer, The Minor Agreements of Matthew and Luke against Mark and the Two-Gospel Hypothesis," in *Minor Agreements*, ed. Strecker, 209-20.

contest except that the Farrer and Griesbach theories have other issues that potentially undermine them.[132] Finally, Morgenthaler contends that while these minor agreements do not necessarily eliminate the existence of Q, they do call for a framework that requires an extension of the two-source theory, namely, the three-source theory, to account for the word and sentence agreements.[133]

Quite naturally the strongest response to the minor agreements comes from two-source advocates, beginning above all with Streeter.[134] Streeter attempted to explain the minor agreements as irrelevant and derived from coincidence, deceptive agreements that are really editorial improvements of Mark by two independent editors and evidence of textual corruption effected by scribal assimilation of Matthew. I think Streeter's case is certainly possible and remains consistent with the view that Matthew and Luke used Mark and Q independently of each other. For instance, in the story of Jesus healing a man with leprosy (Mark 1:40-42/Matt 8:2-3/Luke 5:12-13), the fact that Matthew and Luke both add to Mark's account the words "Behold!" (ἰδού) and "Lord!" (Κύριε) and amend the form of the adverb "immediately" (εὐθέως) is hardly a smoking gun for dependence and could well be coincidental changes made by two editors to a text written in rough Greek. Similarly, some of the agreements between Matthew and Luke against Mark are plausibly accounted for on the assumption that both editors have found need to clarify Mark's text in the same manner. This explains why Matthew and Luke specify that the healed paralytic who was told to go home by Jesus really did go home, hence changing Mark's "He went out before them all" (ἐξῆλθεν ἔμπροσθεν πάντων) to "He went home" (ἀπῆλθεν εἰς τὸν οἶκον αὐτοῦ) (Mark 2:12/Matt 9:7/Luke 5:25). Moreover, we know that in the Gospels, assimilation and harmonization was the primary form of textual corruption. For instance, concerning Jesus' journey to the Decapolis

132. Cf., e.g., Farrer, "Dispensing with Q," 329-30; Michael D. Goulder, "Luke's Knowledge of Matthew," in *Minor Agreements*, ed. Strecker, 142-62; Goodacre, *Goulder and the Gospels*, 89-131; idem, *Case against Q*, 152-69; and William R. Farmer, "The Minor Agreements of Matthew and Luke against Mark and the Two Gospel Hypothesis," in *Minor Agreements*, ed. Strecker, 163-208; David B. Peabody, *One Gospel from Two: Mark's Use of Matthew and Luke: A Demonstration by the Research Team of the International Institute for Renewal of Gospel Studies* (Harrisburg: Trinity, 2002), 4-7.

133. Morgenthaler, *Statistische Synopse*, 305.

134. Cf., e.g., Streeter, *Four Gospels*, 293-331; Robert H. Stein, "The Matthew-Luke Agreements against Mark: Insight from John," *CBQ* 54 (1992): 482-502; idem, *Synoptic Gospels*, 125-42; Neirynck, "Minor Agreements and the Two Source Theory"; Ennulat, *Die "Minor Agreements."*

(Mark 5:1/Matt 8:28/Luke 8:26), scribes had a propensity to force Matthew's "Gadara" (Γαδαρηνός) onto Luke and Mark despite their witness to "Gerasa" (Γαρασηνός).[135] Streeter even goes so far as to suggest that the agreement in Matt 26:67-68/Luke 22:64 — "Who is it that struck you?" — may derive from a similar corruption evidenced by the fact that the same phrase occurs in some manuscripts of Mark (W f^{13} 579 700). Just as the phrase was interpolated into Mark so it might have been interpolated into Matthew.[136]

In the end, Streeter's explanation for the minor agreements is possible, but not convincing. Coincidences do happen, but, when textual coincidences pile up, then one gets the suspicion that we are no longer dealing with coincidences but with deliberate duplication. Likewise, any theory that has to resort to Ur-Mark or conjectural emendations to explain the minor agreements is engaging in acts of desperation caused by evidence that points to the contrary. Finally, while Streeter's explanations might account for many of the minor agreements, there are still literally dozens of places where Matthean foreign bodies — Matthean and un-Lucan materials — find their way into Luke.[137] These foreign bodies cannot be brushed aside as they constitute an eminently superior case for Luke's use of Matthew than they do for denying it on the basis of conjectures about documents and variants that nobody has ever seen or heard about.

b. Mark-Q Overlaps

The Mark-Q overlaps are those places where there is clear triple tradition but are also characterized by even stronger Matthew-Luke agreements against Mark. These passages are among the trickiest because they blur the distinction between the triple and double traditions.[138] Advocates of the two-source theory have generally explained these agreements as Mark and Q having recorded the same event and then been independently conflated by Luke and Matthew. Alternatively, supporters of the Farrer and Griesbach theories detect a sliding scale of Matthew's influence on Luke ranging from slight cosmetic changes (minor agreements) to fuller and

---

135. Cf. Michael F. Bird, "Textual Criticism and the Historical Jesus," *JSHJ* 6 (2008): 133-56.

136. Streeter, *Four Gospels*, 326-27.

137. Among Gundry's list of "foreign bodies," particularly persuasive is his examination of Mark 6:7/Matt 10:1/Luke 9:1; Mark 9:1/Matt 16:28/Luke 9:27; Mark 9:40/Matt 12:30/Luke 11:23; and Mark 15:39/Matt 27:54/Luke 23:34 for Matthean influence on Luke.

138. Goodacre, *Synoptic Problem*, 53.

more substantive additions by Matthew to Mark carried over into Luke (major agreements).

Materials Identified as Mark-Q Overlaps

	Mark	Matthew	Luke
the preaching of John the Baptist	1:7-8	3:11-12	3:15-17
the baptism of Jesus	1:9-11	3:13-17	3:21-22
the temptation story	1:12-13	4:1-11	4:1-13
the Beelzebub controversy	3:22-30	12:22-37	11:14-23
the parable of the mustard seed	4:30-32	12:31-32	13:18-19
the disciples' mission	6:6-13	10:1-15	9:1-6; 10:1-12

Assuming the two-source theory, the relationship between Mark and Q has been strenuously debated. Some have concluded that Mark is entirely independent of Q on the grounds that Mark and Q oscillate in their primitiveness.[139] For others, Mark is secondary to and dependent on Q, given the overlaps and doublets of sayings.[140] Some prefer even more complex solutions, such as Mark dependent on Q and Q dependent on pre-Marcan tradition.[141] The fact that these Marcan and Q passages overlap presents us with a conflation of material at some point in the Synoptic tradition, and the challenge is to identify what sources were actually conflated.

A good example of these "Mark-Q overlaps or "major agreements" is the parable of the mustard seed:[142]

---

139. Rudolf Laufen, *Die Doppelüberlieferungen der Logienquelle und des Markusevangeliums* (BBB 54; Bonn: Hanstein, 1980); Joachim Schüling, *Studien zum Verhältnis von Logienquelle und Markusevangelium* (FB 65; Würzburg: Echter, 1991); Harry T. Fledderman, *Mark and Q: A Study of the Overlap Texts* (BETL 122; Leuven: Leuven University Press, 1995); Joel Marcus, *Mark 1-8* (AB; New York: Doubleday, 2000), 51-53.

140. T. E. Floyd Honey, "Did Mark Use Q?" *JBL* 62 (1943): 319-31; John Pairman, "Mark as Witness to an Edited Form of Q," *JBL* 80 (1961): 29-44; Jan Lambrecht, "Q Influence on Mark 8,34–9,1," in *Logia: Les paroles de Jésus — The Sayings of Jesus*, ed. J. Delobel (BETL 59; Leuven: University of Leuven, 1982), 277-304; Hultgren, *Narrative Elements in the Double Tradition*, 328-29.

141. Wolfgang Schenk, "Der Einfluß der Logienquelle auf das Markusevangelium," *ZNW* 70 (1979): 145-46.

142. See the excellent survey article by Zeba Antonin Crook, "The Synoptic Parables of the Mustard Seed and the Leaven: A Test-Case for the Two-Document, Two-Gospel, and Farrer-Goulder Hypotheses," *JSNT* 78 (2000): 23-48.

The Parable of the Mustard Seed

Mark 4:30-32	Matt 13:31-32	Luke 13:18-19
³⁰*He said,* "With what can we compare the kingdom of God, or *what* parable will we use for *it*? ³¹It is like a mustard seed, which, when sown upon the ground, is the smallest of all the seeds on earth; ³²yet when it is sown it grows up and becomes the greatest of all shrubs, and puts forth large branches, so that the birds of the air can make nests in its shade."	³¹*He put before them another parable:* "The kingdom of heaven is like a mustard seed that some-one took and sowed in his field; ³²it is the smallest of all the seeds, but when it has grown it is the greatest of shrubs and becomes a tree, so that the birds of the air come and make nests in its branches."	¹⁸*He said* therefore, "What is the kingdom *of* God like? And to *what* should I compare *it*? ¹⁹It is like a mustard seed that someone took and sowed in the garden; it grew and became a tree, and the birds of the air made nests in its branches."
³⁰Καὶ ἔλεγεν· πῶς ὁμοιώσωμεν τὴν βασιλείαν τοῦ θεοῦ ἢ ἐν τίνι αὐτὴν παραβολῇ θῶμεν; ³¹ὡς κόκκῳ σινάπεως, ὃς ὅταν σπαρῇ ἐπὶ τῆς γῆς, μικρότερον ὃν πάντων τῶν σπερμάτων τῶν ἐπὶ τῆς γῆς, ³²καὶ ὅταν σπαρῇ, ἀναβαίνει καὶ γίνεται μεῖζον πάντων τῶν λαχάνων καὶ ποιεῖ κλάδους μεγάλους, ὥστε δύνασθαι ὑπὸ τὴν σκιὰν αὐτοῦ τὰ πετεινὰ τοῦ οὐρανοῦ κατασκηνοῦν.	³¹Ἄλλην παραβολὴν παρέθηκεν αὐτοῖς λέγων· ὁμοία ἐστὶν ἡ βασιλεία τῶν οὐρανῶν κόκκῳ σινάπεως, ὃν λαβὼν ἄνθρωπος ἔσπειρεν ἐν τῷ ἀγρῷ αὐτοῦ· ³²ὃ μικρότερον μέν ἐστιν πάντων τῶν σπερμάτων, ὅταν δὲ αὐξηθῇ μεῖζον τῶν λαχάνων ἐστὶν καὶ γίνεται δένδρον, ὥστε ἐλθεῖν τὰ πετεινὰ τοῦ οὐρανοῦ καὶ κατασκηνοῦν ἐν τοῖς κλάδοις αὐτοῦ.	¹⁸Ἔλεγεν οὖν· τίνι ὁμοία ἐστὶν ἡ βασιλεία τοῦ θεοῦ καὶ τίνι ὁμοιώσω αὐτήν; ¹⁹ὁμοία ἐστὶν κόκκῳ σινάπεως, ὃν λαβὼν ἄνθρωπος ἔβαλεν εἰς κῆπον ἑαυτοῦ, καὶ ηὔξησεν καὶ ἐγένετο εἰς δένδρον, καὶ τὰ πετεινὰ τοῦ οὐρανοῦ κατεσκήνωσεν ἐν τοῖς κλάδοις αὐτοῦ.

This is a clear instance in the Synoptic Gospels where Mark is not the middle term. We have here triple agreements (shaded gray), Mark-Matthew agreements (underlined), Mark-Luke agreements (italics), and Luke-Matthew agreements (bold). The parable is, viewed source-critically, a very vexing text to explain.

Streeter believed that Matthew conflated Mark and Q and that Luke followed the Q version.[143] Tuckett similarly thinks that a strong case can be made for the independence of the two versions, given that Mark and Luke,

143. Streeter, *Four Gospels*, 209, 246-48, 306.

apart from the form and the opening double question, have almost no words in common.[144] McNicol proffers the view that Luke delved into the discourse of Matthew 13 for a third time and used the twin parables of the mustard seed and the leaven to introduce the theme of the kingdom of God.[145] Gundry thinks that Matthew's only source here is Mark, not Q, and that Luke follows Mark in retaining the two opening questions. Luke may show Matthew's influence in the use of "like" (ὁμοία) and the reference to "someone took" (ὅν λαβὼν ἄνθρωπος).[146] Goulder's explanation is that Luke simply favored the Matthean version of the story.[147] Rudolf Pesch proposed that the Marcan extensions to the parable imply that Mark's version is secondary to Q's.[148]

Many of the source-critical explanations for the parable of the mustard seed are problematic. The problem with the Griesbach explanation is that it means that Mark has conflated Luke and Matthew by a fastidious process of removing anything on which they agreed but leaving Matthew intact where they differed, and doing so in a very awkward style of Greek. On this perspective Mark has also arbitrarily excluded the parable of the leaven, which is umbilically connected to the parable of the mustard seed in Luke and Matthew (Matt 13:33/Luke 13:20-21). The puzzle with the two-source theory is that if Luke wrote the parable with Q before him, then we are at a loss to explain why Luke retains Mark's double question. It would seem that Luke rather than Matthew is the one conflating Mark with another source on the parable. The most plausible theory then is one that posits Marcan priority, Matthew's augmentation of Mark, and Luke adopting Mark's form while filling it with abbreviated Matthean content.

I have no *prima facie* problem with the concept of sources overlapping. The fact that sayings and stories of Jesus are multiply attested in different sources in early Christian literature proves that overlaps are indeed possible (e.g., versions of the words of institution). It would make sense for two documents, like Mark and Q, both written about Jesus within 40 years of his death, to overlap in their content at some points since they were focused on the same subjects. Even advocates of the Griesbach and Farrer theories still assume the existence of "other" sources to account for variations in the double tradition, and the prospect that these other sources might overlap occasionally is expected. So the notion of overlaps is not peculiar to the two-

144. Tuckett, *Griesbach Hypothesis*, 80-81.
145. McNicol in *Beyond the Q Impasse*, 204-5.
146. Gundry, *Matthew*, 264-67.
147. Goulder, *Luke*, 566.
148. Rudolf Pesch, *Das Markusevangelium 1,1-8,26* (HTK; Freiburgh: Herder, 1976), 260.

source theory or implausible as an explanation.[149] But the Mark-Q overlaps are a rather convenient blessing for two-source theorists as they fortuitously explain conjunctions between Marcan material and the double tradition without implying Luke's use of Matthew.[150]

Yet this coincidence may yield a critical curse because the simpler explanation of Luke's usage of Matthew is both possible and preferable. As an explanation of the phenomenon, Luke's use of Matthew and Mark is materially simpler, requiring as it does the postulation of fewer sources with less complex relationships. We are also absolved of answering further questions as to why the overlaps are in these texts only and not elsewhere, such as in the Lord's Prayer, the Sermon on the Mount, the Lord's Supper, or the passion story, places where one might expect to find a multiplicity of versions of Jesus traditions. The Mark-Q overlaps maintain Luke's independence of Matthew only by speculating that the reason for Mark's surprising congruence with the double tradition is by way of an independent convergence of Mark with Q. Yet the surprise is shattered and the independence is compromised when one realizes that Luke may well be the middle term in conflating Mark with Matthew, as is arguably the case in the parable of the mustard seed. Furthermore, while it is plausible enough to suppose that Mark and Q overlapped, to suppose that Matthew and Luke both independently thought to conflate them and to do so in the Marcan order (presumably looking at Mark when writing these units) makes one a tad suspicious and pushes us toward another solution: Luke knew Matthew.[151] There is gravity in the judgment of E. P. Sanders who noted that the Mark-Q overlaps are the "Achilles' heel" of the two-source theory.[152]

If the minor and major agreements can be accounted for — notwithstanding the possibility of some oral tradition influences too — by Luke's use of Matthew, does this eliminate the need for Q in toto? I think it certainly questions it and maybe shrinks it, but does not entirely eliminate it. Morgenthaler surmised that "it would be a fundamental mistake to put Q in doubt on the basis of these 'minor agreements.'"[153] Tuckett believes that in light of the

149. Tuckett, Griesbach Hypothesis, 77-78; Poirier, "Composition of Luke," 210.

150. David Dungan, "Mark — The Abridgement of Matthew and Luke," in Jesus and Man's Hope (Pittsburgh: Pittsburgh Theological Seminary, 1970), 73.

151. Poirier, "Composition of Luke," 215.

152. Sanders and Davies, Synoptic Gospels, 79; E. P. Sanders, "The Overlaps of Q and Mark and the Synoptic Problem," NTS 19 (1973): 453.

153. "Es wäre ein prinzipieller Fehler, anhand dieser 'minor agreements' Q in Frage zu stellen." Morgenthaler, Statistische Synopse, 301.

minor agreements it is still possible that "Luke used Q for most of the 'double tradition' but that he also knew Matthew's gospel and used it occasionally."[154] In a later study Tuckett adds: "[T]he MA's [minor agreements] might show at most a subsidiary use of Matthew by Luke in the Markan material; from this one might perhaps deduce a subsidiary use of Matthew in non-Markan material. But the MA's themselves cannot show . . . that Luke used Matthew alone where Mark was not available."[155] Similar is Neirynck, who concedes that even if Luke used Mark and Matthew in the triple tradition a further source is not impossible in the double tradition, so that "the inference could only be that elsewhere, where Luke is using another source [like Q], a similar subsidiary influence of Matthean reminiscences can be expected."[156]

Also, while the Mark-Q overlaps are best accounted for by Luke's use of Matthew and Mark, overlaps in sources remain a genuine possibility, irrespective of whether the sources are Mark, Q, or other Jesus traditions. In other words, Luke's use of Matthew need not eliminate Q since Matthew could have a subsidiary influence on Luke in both the triple and double traditions. That leads to Tuckett's truism: Matthean subsidiary influence on Luke does not necessitate primary Lucan dependence on Matthew.[157] Construed this way, Luke need not have used Matthew the same way that he used Mark or Q. For example, Gundry thinks that "Luke used Matthew by way of reminiscence rather than by way of using a copy of Matthew at hand less often than he used such copies of Mark and Q," or, if he did have a copy of Matthew, "he followed Mark and Q more closely than he followed Matthew and Q."[158] Or, as Morgenthaler put it, "Luke had all three sources in front of him and in principle holds to the primacy of Mark and Q, but occasionally took into account the Matthean text.'"[159] As such, scholars have referred to Matthew as a *Nebenquelle* (Simons), an "overlay" (Gundry), or a possible "subsidiary" influence on Luke (Tuckett, Neirynck).

154. Christopher M. Tuckett, "On the Relationship Between Matthew and Luke," *NTS* 30 (1984): 130.

155. Christopher M. Tuckett, "The Existence of Q," in *The Gospel behind the Gospels: Current Studies on Q*, ed. R. A. Piper (Leiden: Brill, 1995), 32-33.

156. Frans Neirynck, "Recent Developments in the Study of Q," in *Evangelica II. 1982-1991*, ed. F. van Segbroeck (BETL 99; Leuven: Leuven University Press, 1991), 414.

157. Christopher Tuckett, *Q and the History of Early Christianity* (Edinburgh: Clark, 1996), 17-18 n. 43.

158. Gundry, "Foreign Bodies," 1494.

159. "Lk hatte alle 3 vor sich, gab grundsätzlich Mk und Q den Primat, berücksichtigte aber gelegentlich den Mt-Texten. So entstanden die 'minor agreements.'" Morgenthaler, *Statistische Synopse*, 301.

This approach will probably raise a few eyebrows, and some will wonder why I do not just assent to Luke's use of Matthew to account for all or most of the double tradition and dispense with Q entirely (i.e., the Farrer hypothesis).[160] Jack Poirier thinks that Holtzmann-Gundry advocates' postulation of Luke's simultaneous use of Q and Matthew is "a failure of nerve."[161] Several factors, however, compel me toward this more difficult course.

First, positing Luke's use of Mark, Q, and Matthew is not unprecedented, with arguments from Holtzmann, Simons, Hincks, Morgenthaler, and Gundry put forward and deserving further consideration. Given some of the lingering problems surrounding the two-source theory and the Farrer hypothesis, I think a new front in the Synoptic problem, Q studies, and source criticism can be opened up here if some brave souls fancy writing Ph.D. theses on such ambitious topics.

Second, I retain the existence of Q and other sources used by Luke because the double tradition as a whole cannot be accounted for just on the postulation of Luke's use of Matthew any more than it can be accounted for just on the postulation of Q. The essential premise for Q is not Luke's independence from Matthew; it is, rather, the possibility of Matthew and Luke sharing a source beyond Mark to account for elements of the double tradition, irrespective of a literary connection between Matthew and Luke.[162] Why would Mark be the only source that Luke and Matthew shared in common given the mobility of Christian leaders who traveled fairly widely and disseminated in their movements the literature in their possession?[163] Even Farrer and Griesbach theorists think Luke had other sources beyond Mark and Matthew, something that opens the door for a Q-like theory. In fact, E. P. Sanders and Margaret Davies sympathetically wrote of the (Farrer-) Goulder thesis: "Goulder has not persuaded us that one can give up sources

160. Cf. Goulder, *Luke*, 10; Goodacre, *Case against Q*, 60-61, 165-69; Jeffery Peterson, "Order in the Double Tradition and the Existence of Q," in *Questioning Q*, ed. Goodacre and Perrin, 41-42.

161. John C. Poirier, "The Q Hypothesis and the Role of Pre-Synoptic Sources in Nineteenth-Century Scholarship," in *Questioning Q*, ed. Goodacre and Perrin, 17.

162. Cf. Foster, "Is It Possible to Dispense with Q?" 326, contra Goodacre, *Case against Q*, 167.

163. This is the impression I get from the Acts of the Apostles, Paul's letters, *1 Clement*, and Papias's own testimony about the itinerant movements of the Lord's disciples and the elders. See further Michael Thompson, "The Holy Internet: Communication between Churches in the First Century," in *The Gospels for All Christians*, ed. R. Bauckham (Grand Rapids: Eerdmans, 1998), 49-70.

for the sayings material. With this rather substantial modification, however, we accept Goulder's theory: Matthew used Mark and Luke used them both." That is probably a good summation.

The riddle that I admit to being unable to solve is knowing precisely when the double tradition is a feature of Luke's use of Matthew or when Luke and Matthew have shared oral or written sources beyond Mark. For a rule of thumb I am willing to attribute *most* of the sayings material to a document known to both Matthew and Luke (Q-lite), attribute the narrative material in the double tradition to other traditions accessed by Luke and Matthew, and suggest that Luke's use of Matthew was at a latent stage and sparing, perhaps even as a first revision to the Lucan text.

Conclusion

In sum, I believe in a *literary relationship* between the Gospels, because oral tradition does not account for the strong verbal and structural correspondences that we find in the Gospels and because proto-Gospel theories are speculative and lack solid evidence. I believe in *Marcan priority,* because it explains why Mark is the middle term between Luke and Matthew and why Mark's roughness in language is smoothed over by the other two Evangelists. I believe in *Q* because, despite its potential misgivings, it allows us to hold together a literary connection between Matthew and Luke that is indirect enough to explain their varied order and divergent utilization of the double tradition. I believe that *Luke used Matthew* because it accounts for the minor agreements and erases the anomaly of the so-called Q-Mark overlaps. This leaves us, finally, with a solution to the Synoptic problem rendered in the following diagram:

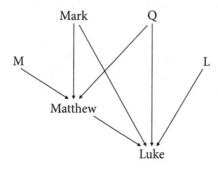

II. The Johannine Question

The Fourth Gospel is definitely a Gospel. It is about Jesus, it climaxes in his death and resurrection, and it calls for faith in Jesus as the Messiah. But the Gospel of John is also very different from the other three canonical Gospels. It has much unique material, a different theological texture, much dissimilar content, and even a divergent narrative structure. It constitutes a deviation or even a deliberate departure from the Synoptic tradition. Leaving the Synoptics for John is a bit like putting down a detective novel and taking up a sci-fi thriller. If the Synoptic Gospels were a movie it would have to be *The Bourne Identity*, whereas the Gospel of John would have to be *The Matrix*.

The "Johannine Question" (or *Johanneische Frage* as the Germans call it) is about the origins of the Johannine corpus, that is, the Gospel according to John, the epistles of John, and for some the Apocalypse of John. The primary set of questions pertains to their authorship, background, and origin.[164] In terms of the genetics of the Fourth Gospel, we are here concerned with its sources and relationship to the Synoptic Gospels. However, it is impossible to address the relationship of the Fourth Gospel to the Synoptic Gospels without first commenting on the authorship of the Fourth Gospel.

Authorship

The Gospel of John, just like the Synoptics, is formally anonymous as it is not directly attributed to a named author. The title, "Gospel according to John" (P^{66} P^{75} A D L W 33) or "According to John" (ℵ B), in our manuscripts was probably added to scrolls and codices by copyists on the basis of local knowledge of the Gospel's origins.[165] The name "John" most likely originated among disciples of the community leader who wrote the Gospel, who added it to the document sometime shortly after his death. The title was probably added in deliberate imitation of other Gospel titles found in manuscripts of Mark, Matthew, and Luke, which were already widespread in Christian circles by 100 CE. It thereafter circulated in the Johannine net-

---

164. Cf., e.g., Holtzmann, *Einleitung,* 497-53; Martin Hengel, *The Johannine Question,* trans. J. Bowden (London: SCM, 1989).

165. See chapter 6 on the Gospel titles more generally.

work and beyond with reference to "John" as its originator. But "John" is one of the commonest names for Palestinian Jewish males, so which "John" is the author?

There are internal references to an enigmatic figure called the "Beloved Disciple," who sat next to Jesus at the Last Supper, was a friend of the high priest, and personally witnessed Jesus' crucifixion and resurrection (John 13:23; 18:15-16; 19:26-27; 20:2-8; 21:7, 20). This disciple provides the authoritative testimony on which the Gospel is based (John 1:14; 21:24; cf. 1 John 1:1-3). In the second and third centuries, this Beloved Disciple is normally equated with John the son of Zebedee, one of the twelve, an apostle, and the brother of James. The early second-century figures Polycarp and Papias were thought to have been students of the Apostle John.[166] According to Irenaeus, Polycarp celebrated Easter in the Quartodeciman reckoning "along with John the disciple of our Lord and the rest of the Apostles with whom he associated."[167] Irenaeus also declared that "John the disciple of the Lord, who leaned back on his breast, published the Gospel while he was resident at Ephesus in Asia."[168] Clement of Alexandria claimed that "John, last of all, conscious that the outward facts had been set forth in the Gospels, urged by his disciples, and divinely moved by the Spirit, composed a spiritual Gospel."[169] Bishop Polycrates of Ephesus asserted that the Apostle John was the beloved disciple who "was both a witness and a teacher, who reclined on the breast of the Lord."[170] The Valentinian teachers Ptolemaeus and Heracleon both identified John the Apostle as the author of the Fourth Gospel.[171] The anti-Marcionite prologue narrates that John dictated his Gospel to his disciple Papias while still "in the body," that is, while still living. The Muratorian canon refers to the author as "John, one of the disciples," and narrates the circumstances of its composition as follows: "To his fellow disciples and bishops, who had been urging him [to write], he said, 'Fast with me from today for three days, and what will be revealed to each one of us let us tell it to each other.' In the same night it was revealed to Andrew, among the apostles,

---

166. Irenaeus claimed that Polycarp knew John (Eusebius, *Hist. Eccl.* 5.20.5-6) and that Papias knew John (Irenaeus, *Adv. Haer.* 5.33.4), but Eusebius claimed that Papias did not know John (*Hist. Eccl.* 3.39.2).

167. Eusebius, *Hist. Eccl.* 5.24.

168. Irenaeus, *Adv. Haer.* 3.1.2.

169. Eusebius, *Hist. Eccl.* 6.14.7.

170. Eusebius, *Hist. Eccl.* 5.24.3.

171. Irenaeus, *Adv. Haer.* 1.8.5; Origen, *Commentary on John* 6.13.

that John should write down all things in his own name while all of them should review it." The dating of both the anti-Marcionite prologues and the Muratorian canon are debated (estimates range from the second to the fourth centuries), but their legendary stories do not lend themselves to historical veracity. In any case, the identification of John the disciple, the son of Zebedee, one of the apostles, as the author of the Fourth Gospel, writing in the city of Ephesus in Roman Asia,[172] is strongly attested among proto-orthodox and "other" forms of Christianity.[173]

However, despite the weight of tradition, another good candidate for the authorship of the Fourth Gospel is a figure whom Papias calls "John the Elder."[174] The testimony of Papias is that "And if by chance anyone who had been in attendance on the elders should come my way, I inquired about the words of the elders — what Andrew or Peter said, or Philip or Thomas, or James, or John, or Matthew, or any other of the Lord's disciples, and

172. Irenaeus, *Adv. Haer.* 3.1.1; 3.3.4; Clement of Alexandria apud Eusebius, *Hist. Eccl.* 3.23.6; *Acts of John.*

173. The exception is a group called the *Alogoi,* the "anti-Logosites" or "irrationalists," who attributed the Gospel and Apocalypse of John to the heretic Cerinthus (Epiphanius, *Panarion* 51.3-4). A mid-second-century Roman elder named Gaius also rejected the authenticity and authority of the Apocalypse of John and probably the Gospel (Eusebius, *Hist. Eccl.* 3.28; Dionysius Bar-Salibi). After the death of the Roman church leader Hippolytus in the early third century, a statue was set up in honor of him, and its inscription listed among his achievements a work known as "A Defense of the Gospel and Apocalypse of John," which assumes that people like Gaius were opposing them (Streeter, *Four Gospels,* 437). The reason for the doubt and dismissal of John in some quarters was probably due to the late date of its composition (ca. 90-100 CE). The Gospel was also conducive to certain heresies such as Montanism due to its mention of the Paraclete and Gnosticism due to its reference to the Logos. There are plenty of echoes of Johannnine themes in the Nag Hammadi writings, and the first commentary on John that we know of was written by the Valentinian Gnostic Heracleon. The proto-orthodox reclamation of John was led by not only Hippolytus but also Irenaeus, who suggested that John wrote his Gospel to put the Gnostic doctrines of Cerinthus and Valentinus to an end and to establish "the rule of truth in the church" (*Adv. Haer.* 3.11.1, 7). The Fourth Gospel was evidently quite popular among Christians in Egypt given that all of our earliest manuscript witnesses to it come from Egypt. See further F. F. Bruce, "Some Notes on the Fourth Evangelist," *EQ* 16 (1944): 101-9; Charles Hill, *The Johannine Corpus in the Early Church* (Oxford: Oxford University Press, 2004); Kyle Keefer, *The Branches of the Gospel of John: The Reception of the Fourth Gospel in the Early Church* (LNTS 332; London: Clark, 2006); Tuomas Rasimus, ed., *The Legacy of John: Second-Century Reception of the Fourth Gospel* (NovTSup 132; Leiden: Brill, 2010); Dan Batovici, "The Second-Century Reception of John: A Survey of Methodologies," *CBR* 10 (2012): 396-409.

174. Cf. Hengel, *Johannine Question,* 76-80; Bauckham, *Jesus and the Eyewitnesses,* 412-71.

whatever Ariston and the elder John, the Lord's disciples, were saying."[175] Papias is referring to his direct encounter with eyewitness tradition through disciples of the elders who knew the Apostles. Yet he also singles out two figures among "the Lord's disciples," differentiated from the Apostles, and identifies them as the elder John and Ariston. This "elder" John may be the Beloved Disciple and the author of the Johannine letters (see the reference to the "elder" in 2 John 1, 3 John 1, and reference to eyewitness testimony in 1 John 1:1-3). This view is strengthened because (1) the reliance on eyewitness testimony and relative lateness of the Gospel of John require an older follower of Jesus as its author, someone like this "John the Elder"; (2) Eusebius himself makes clear that it was not John son of Zebedee but John the Elder who wrote the book of Revelation, implying that authorship of at least some of the Johannine corpus was attributed to John the Elder;[176] and (3) the Beloved Disciple is not mentioned in the Fourth Gospel until John 13, so he was probably not one of the twelve who accompanied Jesus in his itinerant ministry, but was a Judean follower of Jesus with priestly connections.[177] Furthermore, (4) could a member of Jesus' inner circle really compose a Gospel so completely different from another Gospel known or suspected to be based on the recollections of the Apostle Peter, namely, the Gospel of Mark?

The most compelling conclusion is that the Fourth Gospel is indebted to the testimony of a Judean disciple of Jesus who later led a Christian community in Ephesus. In later tradition this disciple is identified as John the Apostle, though the identification may not be certain. The Fourth Gospel is based on this disciple's testimony, even if its final form was redacted by his pupils to emphasize the validity of his witness and to cope with his unexpected death prior to the parousia.[178]

---

175. Papias, *Fragment* 3.4 (Eusebius, *Hist. Eccl.* 3.39.3-4).

176. Eusebius, *Hist. Eccl.* 3.39.5-7. Though admittedly this might constitute Eusebius's attempt to exonerate the Apostle John of authorship of a book that many, including Eusebius, regarded as spurious.

177. I remain unconvinced that the Beloved Disciple is intimated in John 1:35-41 since there are no explicit indicators of his presence at this point.

178. Armin Baum, "The Original Epilogue (John 20:30-31), the Secondary Appendix (21:1-23), and the Editorial Epilogues (21:24-25) of John's Gospel," in *Earliest Christian History,* ed. M. F. Bird and J. Maston (WUNT 2.320; Tübingen: Mohr, 2012), 227-70, puts forward a good case for John 20:30-31 as the original ending of the Fourth Gospel with editorial matter added secondarily.

The Synoptic Gospels and the Gospel of John[179]

1. Differences between John and the Synoptics

The relationship between the Fourth Gospel and the Synoptic Gospels has been discussed since the second century. All four Gospels share the same basic setting, characters, genre, and plot. In particular, the overlapping material includes the ministry of John the Baptist, the cleansing of the temple, Jesus' walking on the water, the multiplication of the loaves, the anointing of Jesus, the triumphal entry, Jesus' last night with his followers, and his passion, death, and resurrection. Yet the Synoptics differ from John's Gospel in several substantial ways.

First, there are narrative differences between John and the Synoptics in their respective accounts of Jesus' ministry.[180] While the Synoptic Gospels locate the beginning of Jesus' ministry in Galilee after the arrest of John the Baptist (Mark 1:14; Matt 4:12; Luke 3:20), in the Fourth Gospel Jesus' ministry overlaps for a time with that of John the Baptist, and it begins in Judea (John 1:28-37; 3:23-36; 4:1-2). Whereas the Synoptic Gospels recall Jesus ministering in Galilee and Judea and then making a final visit to Jerusalem which climaxed in his crucifixion, the Fourth Gospel presents Jesus spending the majority of his time in Judea and relatively little time in Galilee (John 2:1-11; 4:43-54; 6:1; 7:1-9), attending several festivals in Jerusalem, including Passover (John 2:13; 12-19), Pentecost (ch. 5), Tabernacles (chs. 7–8), and Dedication (ch. 10). In the Synoptic Gospels, the antagonism of the scribes, Pharisees, and priestly leaders toward Jesus gradually builds throughout the narrative (e.g., Mark 3:6) and reaches its climax after Jesus' action in the temple (e.g., Mark 11:18; Matt 26:3-5; Luke 19:47). John's Gospel also contains a progressive building of opposition against Jesus by the Judean leadership, but their determination to kill him was driven by the raising of Lazarus from the dead (John 11:47-53). In terms of chronology, John and the Synoptics sometimes present a different sequence of events, not least in connection with the temple action and the Last Supper. The temple action occurs in the

---

179. What follows is largely an expansion of my preliminary thoughts on the subject in "Synoptics and John," in *Dictionary of Jesus and the Gospels,* ed. J. B. Green, N. Perrin, and J. K. Brown (2nd ed.; Downers Grove: InterVarsity, 2013), 920-24.

180. The synopsis of H. F. D. Sparks conveniently lays out the parallels largely following the Johannine order and is useful for identifying where the Fourth Gospel does and does not parallel the Synoptics. H. F. D. Sparks, *A Synopsis of the Gospels, Part 2: The Gospel According to St. John with the Synoptic Parallels* (London: Black, 1974).

Synoptics at the end of Jesus' ministry (Mark 11:15-18; Matt 21:12-13; Luke 19:45-46), whereas in John it appears at the beginning of his ministry (John 2:1-12). The Synoptics specify that the final meal that Jesus had with his disciples was a Passover meal (Mark 14:12; Matt 26:17-19; Luke 22:15). Yet the Fourth Gospel states that the meal took place on the eve of Passover (John 13:1; 18:28) and that Jesus died immediately prior to Passover (19:31).

Second, there are discrepancies in the style and message of Jesus' ministry. Whereas all four Gospels identify Jesus with divine activity, in the Fourth Gospel Jesus is more acutely aware of his divine identity. There are intimations in the Synoptics that Jesus bears divine authority (e.g., Matt 1:21; 28:18), but in the Fourth Gospel Jesus is explicitly identified as the incarnation of the God of Israel (John 1:1, 14; 8:58; 20:28), and he even claims equality with God (5:18). Moreover, Jesus' message in the Synoptics focuses on the kingdom of God (e.g., Mark 1:15; Luke 4:43, etc.), but in John the thrust of Jesus' message pertains to receiving "eternal life" (e.g., John 3:15-16, 36; 4:14, 36; 5:24, 39). A common feature of Jesus' teaching ministry according to the Synoptics is his use of parables (e.g., Mark 4:34). Yet in the Fourth Gospel, Jesus' teaching is parabolic and figurative, but lacks the more explicit eschatological narrative and social polemics of the Synoptic parables.

Third, John omits major Synoptic themes and contains much unique material. John has no parables, exorcisms, tax collectors, temptation account, Transfiguration, or institution of the Lord's Supper. The Fourth Gospel is filled with unique and unparalleled material such as the "I am" sayings, the dialogues with Nicodemus and the Samaritan woman, stories of female disciples, healing stories like the crippled man at the pool of Siloam and the man born blind, miracle stories like turning the water into wine in Cana and the raising of Lazarus, the footwashing episode, the promise of the coming of the Paraclete or "Comforter," and Jesus' high priestly prayer. There are distinctive themes such as truth, witness, world, love, abiding, faith, light versus darkness, and the Father-Son relationship.

The Fourth Gospel is obviously different and this raises a host of questions about its sources. While comparing it with the Synoptics may not be quite like comparing apples to oranges, it certainly is like comparing oranges to mandarins. Rather than crassly harmonizing or explaining away these differences, we may choose to act with a higher respect for our canonical Gospels by letting John be John without trying to Synopticize him.[181] I will have much

---

181. Cf. in this regard James D. G. Dunn, "Let John Be John: A Gospel for Its Time," in *The Gospel and the Gospels*, ed. Stuhlmacher, 293-322.

more to say about the unity of the fourfold Gospel in the final chapter and so show the essential resonance of their narrative and theological masterpieces. Suffice it for now to say that the Fourth Gospel possesses its own unique vision of Jesus and that this raises acute source-critical questions. The most pressing of those questions pertains to the relationship of John to the Synoptics.

2. A Possible Literary Relationship between John and the Synoptics?

There are a number of different ways that the Fourth Gospel has been related to the Synoptic Gospels and the Synoptic tradition. The following analysis is by no means exhaustive, but presents the major options for consideration.[182]

1. *Supplement.* Awareness of and even discomfort at the differences between the Synoptics and John have long been evident. Pagan critics of Christianity from Celsus to Porphyry saw the cracks of discord between John and the Synoptics and attempted to drive a chariot of criticism through them. Gospel harmonies from Tatian to Augustine to Calvin endeavored to resolve these tensions and to smooth out the apparent conflicts in chronology and content. Along the way, a primitive and pervasive response has been to regard the Gospel of John as a conscious supplement to the work of the other three Evangelists.

According to the Muratorian canon, John's Gospel was written at the behest of the other disciples and at the petition of the bishops when it was revealed to the Apostle Andrew that John should write down his own Gospel, which in turn would be reviewed by his colleagues. Thus the most individual of the Gospels becomes a community project authorized by an apostolic college of leaders.

Clement of Alexandria saw John's Gospel as possessing a unique temperament and operating on a different spiritual plane. He wrote: "But that

---

182. Cf. Dwight Moody Smith, *John among the Gospels* (2nd ed.; Columbia: University of South Carolina Press, 2001); Adelbert Denaux, ed., *John and the Synoptics* (BETL 101; Leuven: Leuven University Press, 1992); James D. Dvorak, "The Relationship between John and the Synoptic Gospels," *JETS* 41 (1998): 201-13; Raymond E. Brown, *An Introduction to the Gospel of John*, ed. F. J. Moloney (ABRL; New York: Doubleday, 2003), 94-104; Ian D. Mackay, *John's Relationship with Mark* (WUNT 2.182; Tübingen: Mohr, 2004), 9-54; Tom Thatcher, "The New Current through John: The Old 'New Look' at the New Critical Orthodoxy," in *New Currents through John: A Global Perspective*, ed. T. Thatcher and F. Lozada (Atlanta: Society of Bibilical Literature, 2006), 1-26; Francis J. Moloney, "Recent Johannine Studies: Part Two: Monographs," *ExpT* 123 (2012): 421-24.

John, last of all, conscious that the outward facts had been set forth in the Gospels (τά σωματικά ἐν τοῖς εὐαγγελίοις δεδήλωται), urged by his disciples, and divinely moved by the Spirit, composed a spiritual Gospel (πνευματικόν ποιῆσαι εὐαγγέλιον)."[183] In other words, the Gospel of John is not a mere outward or historical account, but was composed as a deliberate supplement heavily infused with spiritual insight about Jesus.

The spiritual-symbolic interpretation of John goes back even earlier, as far as the Valentinian teacher Heracleon in the second century, who first subjected the Gospel to a symbolic interpretation.[184] A thorough spiritual interpretation of the Fourth Gospel was undertaken by Origen in the third century. Origen regarded the historical tensions between John and the Synoptics as irreconcilable and strove systematically to attribute to John's Gospel a deeper mystical and spiritual sense.

Eusebius of Caesarea suggested that John wrote to fill in the gaps in the Synoptic Gospels largely pertaining to an earlier phase of Jesus' ministry prior to the Baptist's death.

> One who understands this can no longer think that the Gospels are at variance with one another, inasmuch as the Gospel according to John contains the first acts of Christ, while the others give an account of the latter part of his life. And the genealogy of our Saviour according to the flesh John quite naturally omitted, because it had been already given by Matthew and Luke, and began with the doctrine of his divinity, which had, as it were, been reserved for him, as their superior, by the divine Spirit.[185]

For much of church history, the Gospel of John was regarded as a supplement to the other Gospels, written to complement them, by adding details that they omitted, and turning attention to the spiritual plane of Jesus' message.[186] Even modern scholarship has continued to propound the perspective that the Fourth Gospel was written as an interpretation or an additional extra to the Synoptic Gospels.[187]

---

183. Eusebius, *Hist. Eccl.* 6.14.7.

184. Cf. Elaine H. Pagels, *The Johannine Gospel in Gnostic Exegesis: Heracleon's Commentary on John* (Nashville: Abingdon, 1973).

185. Eusebius, *Hist. Eccl.* 3.24.7-13.

186. Cf. Maurice Wiles, *The Spiritual Gospel: The Interpretation of the Fourth Gospel in the Early Church* (Cambridge: Cambridge University Press, 1960), 13-21.

187. Streeter, *Four Gospels,* 393-426; R. H. Lightfoot, *St. John's Gospel: A Commentary,*

The problem with the traditional view is that it assumes something like a pact among the apostles that John would write a supplementary Gospel. The story was contrived out of apologetic interests and mixed with legendary embellishment to account for John's uniqueness. In addition, far from supplementing the Synoptics, a juxtaposition of John and the Synoptics creates many chronological dilemmas (e.g., when did Jesus cleanse the temple?) and some theological obscurities (e.g., was John the Baptist the eschatological Elijah or not?).

2. *Complement.* A modern variation of the "supplement" thesis is given by Richard Bauckham, who argues that John was written with readers of Mark in mind.[188] Whereas much of Johannine scholarship assumed the oral and literary independence of the Gospel of John from the Synoptic Gospels, so too have many assumed that the Gospel of John derived from an isolated and introspective "Johannine community" removed from other Christian networks. Yet if Mark's Gospel circulated beyond its own immediate constituency — hence its use by Luke and Matthew — perhaps it circulated as far as the "Johannine community" and perhaps the Johannine author and editors intended their Gospel to circulate just as widely as the Gospel of Mark did. Rather than query sources used by John, Bauckham takes a narrative-critical approach, arguing instead that the text tacitly assumes some knowledge of Mark's story on the part of the implied readers (i.e., the picture of the readers that emerges from the text) in places. Bauckham acknowledges that John is a self-contained story with its own narrative integrity that does not need any inter-texts like Mark to be coherent. But John still caters to readers who were familiar with the Marcan story. As examples, Bauckham points to the parenthetical remarks in John 3:24 (John the Baptist had not yet been thrown into prison = Mark 1:14) and 11:2 (Mary of Bethany was the one who anointed Jesus = Mark 14:3-9) as

---

ed. C. F. Evans (Oxford: Clarendon, 1956), 26-42; R. V. G. Tasker, *John: An Introduction and Commentary* (TNTC; London: Tyndale, 1960), 32-33; Andrew T. Lincoln, *The Gospel According to Saint John* (BNTC; Peabody: Hendrickson, 2005), 39.

188. Richard Bauckham, "John for Readers of Mark," in *The Gospels for All Christians,* ed. Bauckham, 147-71. See also Andreas Köstenberger, "John's Transposition Theology: Retelling the Story of Jesus in a Different Key," in *Earliest Christian History,* ed. Bird and Maston, 191-226. Köstenberger's view is a cross between the "complement" and "interlocking tradition" views. Also along similar lines to Bauckham is Jörg Frey, "Das Vierte Evangelium auf dem Hintergrund der älteren Evangelientradition. Zum Problem Johannes und die Synoptiker," in *Johannesevangelium, Mitte oder Rand des Kanons? Neue Standortbestimmungen,* ed. T. Söding (Freiburg im Bresgau: Herder, 2003), 60-118. Frey thinks that John presupposes Mark and perhaps Luke (but not Matthew). The Fourth Gospel is not a replacement or supplement of Mark but a critical reception and independent adaptation of the Marcan storyline.

well as John's elaboration of certain characters (John the Baptist, Andrew, the twelve, Judas Iscariot, and Pontius Pilate) as evidence that John assumes that some of his readers are familiar with the Marcan tradition. For Bauckham, the Fourth Gospel is not a correction or a mere supplement to Mark, but is complementary and intended to enhance and extend the Marcan account of Jesus with a more reflective interpretation. Bauckham avers that "the Fourth Gospel was written, not for a Johannine community isolated from the rest of the early Christian movement, but for general circulation among the churches in which Mark's Gospel was already being widely read."[189]

Bauckham's thesis is both refreshing and in many ways compelling. However, it does have several perceptible weaknesses: (1) While the postulation of hypothetical sources underlying John does not always evoke great confidence in source critics (*à la* Bultmann!), the attempt to infer a source from an implied reader, not a real reader, is equally perilous, as narrative worlds and real worlds do not always correspond. (2) Rendering John's Gospel as both self-contained and yet intertextually reliant on Mark, though not impossible, perhaps makes too much of too little; for if John was intended to evoke and extend Mark, one might expect this to occur far more often than it does. While all texts are intertextual to some degree, on a literary perspective, the Fourth Gospel is a largely independent account of Jesus. (3) Bauckham seems to imagine readers/hearers mentally inserting Johannine material into a Marcan outline that is embedded in their minds, like noting how the events in John 1:19–4:43 would fit between Mark 1:13 and 1:14. We might ask if anyone except perhaps Christian scribes attempting to construct a Gospel harmony would have made that connection. (4) That John presupposes a tradition about Jesus is one thing, but that he specifically presupposes Mark's Gospel is quite another, since the account of John the Baptist being put into prison before Jesus starts his ministry is known elsewhere (Matt 11:2; Luke 3:19-20; perhaps Acts 11:16), and likewise material about the anointing of Jesus and material about the Bethany sisters is known to Luke, even if he did not join them as John did (Luke 7:36-50; 10:38-52).[190] While Bauckham's narrative-critical perspective is a new avenue for consideration, and he rightly points out that John assumes a tradition known to his audience, the questions remain, "which tradition" and "in what form" did John and his readers/hearers know it?

---

189. Bauckham, "John for Readers of Mark," 171.

190. Bauckham, "John for Readers of Mark," 153-54, 164, attempts to show the Marcan character of the material assumed by John and that it is not simply shared oral tradition.

3. *Displacement.* Hans Windisch, building on the work of others before him, regarded the Fourth Gospel not as a supplement to the Synoptics, but as a deliberate attempt to displace them. Windisch saw the main rivals to the displacement theory as the supplementation theory, the interpretation theory, and the independence theory, and he endeavored to refute them in the course of his study. He was certain that John at least knew Mark, given some precise parallels with Mark in the narrative tradition and that some Marcan sayings appeared in John albeit in new Johannine forms (e.g., the saying about saving one's life and losing it in Mark 8:35 and John 12:25). He found it probable that John knew Matthew and Luke as well, given points of contact with the Synoptic tradition in non-Marcan material, such as John the Baptist not claiming to be the Messiah. Given John's knowledge in some form of all three other Gospels, Windisch believed that there is nothing in John's Gospel that looks complementary to the Synoptics since it is an autonomous and self-sustaining narrative, not a gap-filler. Indeed, the author appears at most to present an alternative account of Jesus or in the very least to snub the Synoptics entirely.[191]

There are many problems with Windisch's theory. He anticipated many of them, but his responses were inadequate. For a start, the Fourth Gospel nowhere cites, criticizes, or rejects other Jesus stories, hardly indicative of a critical effort at displacement. Windisch's reply was that John's refutation was subtle or indirect, but I find John's alleged critique of the Synoptics to be so subtle and so indirect as to be virtually undetectable. I think it certainly possible that the author and editors of the Fourth Gospel thought their Gospel could meet the needs of Christians, both local and universal, in a way that the Synoptics did not. They achieved this by writing an evangelistic narrative geared toward Jews of the Diaspora, composed in light of rancorous polemics between non-Christ-believing Jews and Christ-believing Jews, providing additional insights into Jesus and appealing to a different pool of tradition, but again that sounds more like supplementation than subrogation. Yet perhaps the biggest problem with the displacement theory is, despite the limited amount of Synoptic parallels, that John's Gospel is still like the Synoptic Gospels in genre, narrative outline, characterization, and key Jesuanic themes. If we accept the

---

191. Hans Windisch, *Johannes und die Synoptiker. Wollte der vierte Evangelist die älteren Evangelien ergänzen order ersetzen?* (Leipzig: Hinrich, 1926). See also Ernest C. Colwell, *John Defends the Gospel* (Chicago: Willet, Clark, 1936); Robert M. Grant, "The Fourth Gospel and the Church," *HTR* 35 (1942): 95.

maxim that *imitation is the highest form of admiration* then it is almost impossible to see John as a critique of the Synoptic tradition without it also operating with a feature of literary respect and theological regard of the highest quality.

Examples of Parallel Sayings in John and the Synoptics

Jesus answered them, "Destroy this temple, and in three days I will raise it up." (John 2:19)	"We heard him say, 'I will destroy this temple that is made with hands, and in three days I will build another, not made with hands.'" (Mark 14:58) "This fellow said, 'I am able to destroy the temple of God and to build it in three days.'" (Matt 26:61)
When the two days were over, he went from that place to Galilee (for Jesus himself had testified that a prophet has no honor in the prophet's own country). (John 4:43-44)	Then Jesus said to them, "Prophets are not without honor, except in their hometown, and among their own kin, and in their own house." (Mark 6:4) And they took offense at him. But Jesus said to them, "Prophets are not without honor except in their own country and in their own house." (Matt 13:57) And he said, "Truly I tell you, no prophet is accepted in the prophet's hometown." (Luke 4:24)
Those who love their life lose it, and those who hate their life in this world will keep it for eternal life. (John 12:25)	He called the crowd with his disciples, and said to them, "If any want to become my followers, let them deny themselves and take up their cross and follow me. For those who want to save their life will lose it, and those who lose their life for my sake, and for the sake of the gospel, will save it." (Mark 8:34-35) Then Jesus told his disciples, "If any want to become my followers, let them deny themselves and take up their cross and follow me. For those who want to save their life will lose it, and those who lose their life for my sake will find it." (Matt 16:24-25) Then he said to them all, "If any want to become my followers, let them deny themselves and take up their cross daily and follow me. For those who want to save their life will lose it, and those who lose their life for my sake will save it." (Luke 9:23-24)

Very truly, I tell you, servants are not greater than their master, nor are messengers greater than the one who sent them. (John 13:16)	"A disciple is not above the teacher, nor a slave above the master." (Matt 10:24)
Remember the word that I said to you, "Servants are not greater than their master." If they persecuted me, they will persecute you; if they kept my word, they will keep yours also. (John 15:20)	"A disciple is not above the teacher, but everyone who is fully qualified will be like the teacher." (Luke 6:40)

4. *Dependence.* Although the mid-twentieth century was dominated by the views of P. Gardner-Smith and C. H. Dodd on the essential independence of John from the Synoptics, C. K. Barrett successfully reinvigorated the case for dependence, but without judging that dependence to merely supplemental or necessarily polemical.[192]

Barrett is careful in where he attempts to find dependence. He acknowledges that it has rarely been argued that John knew Matthew.[193] John's borrowing from Luke is a stronger possibility given that only John and Luke mention Mary and Martha of Bethany (John 11:1–12:8; Luke 10:38-42) and the former high priest Annas (John 18:13, 24; Luke 3:2; Acts 4:6). Some narrative details are shared too, such as the entrance of the Satan into Judas (John 13:2, 27; Luke 22:3), the prediction of Peter's denial at the Supper (John 13:38; Luke 22:34), and the servant of the high priest whose ear was cut off during Jesus' arrest (John 18:10; Luke 22:50), and they both have two angels at the tomb on Easter morning (John 20:12; Luke 24:4). These are suggestive, though hardly definitive for a Johannine and Lucan literary relationship, since they could stem from common knowledge of the Jesus tradition.[194]

Barrett more confidently contended for Johannine dependence on Mark. He was impressed by agreements between John and Mark in order and in selected instances even in wording. Barrett saw John as occasionally

192. C. K. Barrett, "John and the Synoptics," *ExpT* 85 (1974): 228-33; idem, *The Gospel According to St. John: An Introduction with Commentary and Notes on the Greek Text* (2nd ed.; London: SPCK, 1978), 42-56.

193. Streeter, *Four Gospels*, 396 and 408-16, summarizes what many believe: "Between Matthew and John the points of contact are, on any view, extremely slight." But see H. F. D. Sparks, "St. John's Knowledge of Matthew: The Evidence of John 13:16 and 15:20," *JTS* 3 (1952): 58-61; Lincoln, *Saint John*, 26-39; Paul N. Anderson, *The Fourth Gospel and the Quest for Jesus: Modern Foundations Reconsidered* (London: Clark, 2006), 119-25.

194. Cf. survey in Smith, *John among the Gospels*, 85-110. Barbara Shellard, *New Light on Luke: Its Purposes, Sources, and Literary Context* (London: Clark, 2004), 148-88, thinks that it was Luke who used John.

correcting traditions embodied in Mark such as the timing of Jesus' ministry in relation to John the Baptist's imprisonment (John 3:24; Mark 1:14-15) and about who carried Jesus' cross to Golgotha (John 19:17; Mark 15:21). Barrett recognized that this is not incontestable proof that John knew and used Mark. However, it does render the thesis sufficiently plausible that John had at least read Mark, used its basic outline, and perhaps involuntarily echoed Mark's phrases when writing about certain events. While one could infer from this evidence that John knew Mark's tradition or Mark-like traditions rather than Mark, we do not have Mark's tradition beyond Mark itself. So the simpler hypothesis is to posit that John accessed Mark. The historical and theological differences between the two Gospels are then due to John's peculiar interest and presuppositions and do not negate a potential literary relationship.[195]

Barrett has not been alone. Many others have joined his side advocating Johannine dependence on one or more of the Synoptics. The close links to the Synoptics in the Johannine passion and resurrection accounts have come under close scrutiny by the "Leuven school" led by Frans Neirynck.[196] Thomas Brodie envisages John as reflective of the Synoptics like a form of midrash.[197] Urban C. van Wahlde creatively proposes that the first edition of the Fourth Gospel was independent of the Synoptics, while the editor of the third edition attempted to bring elements of the Johannine Gospel into line with the Synoptics.[198]

Doubts linger about the literary dependence of John on Mark because the similarities are often vague, could be coincidences, and can be explained in other ways such as by parallel or interlocking traditions rather than by literary dependence. The criteria for isolating source material from the Synoptics allegedly used in John is not exactly self-evident either. What is more, whereas 93% of Mark can be found in Matthew and Luke, only 8% of the Synoptics parallels John, hardly a strong case for Johannine dependence on Mark in the same way that Luke or Matthew depended on Mark.[199] Finally,

---

195. Barrett, *St. John*, 42-45.

196. Cf., e.g., M. Sabbe, "The Johannine Account of the Death of Jesus and Its Synoptic Parallels (Jn 19,16b-42)," *ETL* 70 (1994): 34-64; Frans Neirynck, "John and the Synoptics: The Empty Tomb Stories," *NTS* 30 (1984): 161-87.

197. Thomas L. Brodie, *The Quest for the Origin of John's Gospel: A Source-Oriented Approach* (Oxford: Oxford University Press, 1993).

198. Urban C. von Wahlde, *The Gospel and Letters of John* (ECC; 3 vols.; Grand Rapids: Eerdmans, 2010), 1:130-31.

199. Gary M. Burge, *Interpreting the Gospel of John* (Grand Rapids: Baker, 1992), 23.

this view also requires that every difference can be explained as a result of a deliberate change of Synoptic material by the Fourth Evangelist, which is hard to sustain uniformly, especially in sections like the narratives of John the Baptist and the trial of Jesus.

5. *Aural Influence.* The Johannine dependence theory died in the mid-twentieth century, but was resurrected almost as quickly.[200] But dependence does not have to be conceived of as literary influence. John did not necessarily sit at a desk with codices of Matthew, Mark, and Luke in front of him. Some have argued that one or more of the Synoptic Gospels influenced John through either performance or secondary orality.[201]

Ian Mackay embarked on a comparative study of Mark 6–8 and John 6 and he concluded that the remarkable reverberations between the two accounts make it more likely that John worked certain elements of Mark's feeding narrative into his own account. But he wonders whether John's dependence on Mark is not so much direct but free, pragmatic, and at some remove from the actual text. This leads Mackay to suggest that the Evangelist knew Mark as a performance that he drew from (and perhaps even performed himself).[202] He surmises: "If Mark's gospel had taken root in the evangelist's imagination and memory, notwithstanding the fact that the evangelist intended to continue to work on and expand the community's own independent story with its particular perspective and thrust, the puzzling combination of exactitude and freedom would be adequately explained."[203] The Evangelist wrote or rewrote the Gospel of the Beloved Disciple for a community with its own traditions and needs.

Michael LaBahn has appealed to first-century media culture to explain the origins of the Fourth Gospel.[204] LaBahn identifies the Fourth Gospel as a product of secondary orality with written material from the Synoptic Gospels reentering the pool of oral tradition, from which the Johannine Evangelist

---

200. George R. Beasley-Murray, *John* (WBC; Dallas: Word, 1987), xxxvi-xxxvii.

201. Cf. Kümmel, *Introduction*, 204, who thinks that John used Mark and Luke "from memory and cited them as seemed useful, according to his recollection." See similarly C. Goodwin, "How Did John Treat His Sources?" *JBL* 73 (1954): 61-75.

202. Mackay distinguishes the Beloved Disciple from the Evangelist who redacted the Beloved Disciple's testimony.

203. Mackay, *John's Relationship with Mark*, 302.

204. Michael LaBahn, *Jesus als Lebensspender. Untersuchungen zu einer Geschichte der johanneischen Tradition anhand ihrer Wundergeschichten* (BZNW 98; New York: de Gruyter, 1999); cf. Anthony Le Donne and Tom Thatcher, eds., *The Fourth Gospel in First-Century Media Culture* (LNTS 426; London: Clark, 2011).

then drew. According to LaBahn, the Fourth Gospel is independent of the Synoptics but dependent on a stream of tradition that the Synoptics generated.

These appeals to memory, performance, and secondary orality are very good models for explaining the same-yet-different relationship John has to the Synoptics. The problem is that, as good as they are, they remain unproven and unprovable.

6. *Mutual Influence*. A number of scholars have advocated that, while the Gospel of John is textually independent of the Synoptic Gospels, the traditions underlying both mutually influenced each other.

M.-E. Boismard, with his penchant for positing complex pre-literary traditions, argued that all four canonical Gospels underwent several stages of development, with each drawing materials from the others at various stages. He proposed intermediate versions of Mark and Luke drawing on preliminary versions of John, with later redactions of John in turn drawing on intermediate versions of Mark and Luke by both the Evangelist and the final editor.[205]

Paul Anderson envisaged a series of "interfluential" relationships between John and the Synoptics. According to Anderson, the Johannine tradition is autonomous and independent of the Synoptics, but also shows evidence of engagement with various elements of the Synoptic Gospels and their traditions at an earlier phase. Simply because John was written last does not mean that it is dependent on the Synoptics, as the traditions underlying the four Gospels might have been interwoven at several points. John's Gospel can be seen as influential, augmentive, and corrective (toward Mark), formative, orderly, and theological (toward Luke), and reinforcing, dialectical, and corrective (toward Matthew).[206]

The problem with Boismard's proposal is that every difference between John and the Synoptics seems to require a separate source with these sources multiplied without much restraint. Yet the more complex the solution postulated to our Johannine Question the less confident we should be that we can really trace the development of pre-Synoptic and pre-Johannine traditions in any serious way. Anderson's proposal is far more viable and makes a lot of sense. In an oral culture, with Christian leaders moving about fairly freely, influence between traditions was not restricted to the level of literary

---

205. M.-E. Boismard and A. Lamouille with G. Rochais, *L'Evangile Jean. Commentaire* (Paris: Cerf, 1977).

206. Anderson, *Fourth Gospel and the Quest for Jesus*, 40, 101-25. See also Raymond E. Brown, *The Gospel According to John* (AB; 2 vols.; New York: Doubleday, 1966), 1:lxvi-lxvii, who earlier referred to "cross-influences" between the Synoptic and Johannine traditions.

composition but took place at an early and largely oral phase of the Jesus tradition's formation. However, we are still left haggling over at what point the Synoptic tradition has influenced John or vice-versa; which stories were influenced, when, where, and by whom; and at what stage the influence occurred, oral or literary stage, first edition of John or second, and so forth. Answers for these questions are not really possible, and many will suggest that positing a straightforward literary relationship is the simpler solution.

A good example of a place where John and Mark are fairly close is in the miraculous feeding story. Here there are strong structural similarities (shared basic outline, both follow the feeding story with the account of Jesus walking on water), close verbal connections (esp. Mark 6:36-37 with John 6:5-7), curious agreements with John 6 and Mark 8 against Mark 6 (Jesus gives thanks for the bread), and yet also some key differences, John having divergent details and including some non-Synoptic material (e.g., John 6:14 on Jesus as the coming prophet). It is a good test passage to try out any theory of Johannine and Synoptic relationships.[207]

Johannine and Marcan Accounts of the Miraculous Feeding Story

John 6	Mark 6	Mark 8
[1]After this Jesus went to the other side of the Sea of Galilee, also called the Sea of Tiberias. [2]A large crowd kept following him, because they saw the signs that he was doing for the sick. [3]Jesus went up the mountain and sat down there with his disciples. [4]Now the Passover, the festival of the Jews, was near. [5]When he looked up and saw a large crowd coming toward him, Jesus said to Philip, "Where are we to buy bread for these people to eat?" [6]He said this to test him, for he	[30]The apostles gathered around Jesus, and told him all that they had done and taught. [31]He said to them, "Come away to a deserted place all by yourselves and rest a while." For many were coming and going, and they had no leisure even to eat. [32]And they went away in the boat to a deserted place by themselves. [33]Now many saw them going and recognized them, and they hurried there on foot from all the towns and arrived ahead of them. [34]As he went ashore,	[1] In those days when there was again a great crowd without anything to eat, he called his disciples and said to them, [2]"I have compassion for the crowd, because they have been with me now for three days and have nothing to eat. [3]If I send them away hungry to their homes, they will faint on the way — and some of them have come from a great distance." [4]His disciples replied, "How can one feed these people with bread here in the desert?" [5]He asked them, "How

207. Cf. further Paul N. Anderson, *The Christology of the Fourth Gospel: Its Unity and Disunity in Light of John 6* (Valley Forge: Trinity, 2006), 98-102; Mackay, *John's Relationship with Mark*, 111-58.

John 6	Mark 6	Mark 8
himself knew what he was going to do. ⁷Philip answered him, "Six months' wages would not buy enough bread for each of them to get a little." ⁸One of his disciples, Andrew, Simon Peter's brother, said to him, ⁹"There is a boy here who has five barley loaves and two fish. But what are they among so many people?" ¹⁰Jesus said, "Make the people sit down." Now there was a great deal of grass in the place; so they sat down, about five thousand in all.	he saw a great crowd; and he had compassion for them, because they were like sheep without a shepherd; and he began to teach them many things. ³⁵When it grew late, his disciples came to him and said, "This is a deserted place, and the hour is now very late; ³⁶send them away so that they may go into the surrounding country and villages and buy something for themselves to eat." ³⁷But he answered them, "You give them something to eat." They said to him, "Are we to go and buy two hundred denarii worth of bread, and give it to them to eat?"	many loaves do you have?" They said, "Seven." ⁶Then he ordered the crowd to sit down on the ground; and he took the seven loaves, and after giving thanks he broke them and gave them to his disciples to distribute; and they distributed them to the crowd. ⁷They had also a few small fish; and after blessing them, he ordered that these too should be distributed. ⁸They ate and were filled; and they took up the broken pieces left over, seven baskets full. ⁹Now there were about four thousand people. And he sent them away.
¹¹Then Jesus took the loaves, and when he had given thanks, he distributed them to those who were seated; so also the fish, as much as they wanted. ¹²When they were satisfied, he told his disciples, "Gather up the fragments left over, so that nothing may be lost." ¹³So they gathered them up, and from the fragments of the five barley loaves, left by those who had eaten, they filled twelve baskets. ¹⁴When the people saw the sign that he had done, they began to say, "This is indeed the prophet who is to come into the world."	³⁸And he said to them, "How many loaves have you? Go and see." When they had found out, they said, "Five, and two fish." ³⁹Then he ordered them to get all the people to sit down in groups on the green grass. ⁴⁰So they sat down in groups of hundreds and of fifties. ⁴¹Taking the five loaves and the two fish, he looked up to heaven, and blessed and broke the loaves, and gave them to his disciples to set before the people; and he divided the two fish among them all. ⁴²And all ate and were filled; ⁴³and they took up twelve baskets full of broken pieces and of the fish. ⁴⁴Those who had eaten the loaves numbered five thousand men.	

205

Similarities and Differences

Texts	Similarities	Differences
John 6:1-3; Mark 6:32	Jesus and the disciples cross the sea.	Solitary place (Mark 6), ascending the mountain (John)
John 6:2; Mark 6:33; 8:1	Large crowd comes to Jesus.	The crowd recognized him (Mark 6); the crowd is hungry (Mark 8); the crowd saw Jesus' signs (John).
John 6:4	Unparalleled	The Passover was near (John).
John 6:5a; Mark 6:34; 8:2-3	Jesus is moved with compassion for the crowd.	The crowd is like sheep without a shepherd (Mark 6); they have nothing to eat (Mark 8); they have no bread (John).
John 6:5-6; Mark 6:35-39; 8:2-5	Jesus talks to his disciples about feeding the crowd.	The disciples initiate the conversation with Jesus (Mark 6); Jesus initiates the conversation (Mark 8); Jesus speaks to Philip (John 6).
John 6:7; Mark 6:37; 8:4	The problem of feeding the crowd is posed.	Two hundred denarii (Mark 6), six months wages (John 6)
John 6:8-9; Mark 6:38; 8:7	Five loaves and two fishes are produced.	No young boy (Mark 6); few small fish (Mark 8); food comes from a young boy (John 6)
John 6:10; Mark 6:39, 44; 8:6, 9	Jesus makes the crowd sit down.	5000 in groups on the green grass (Mark 6), 4000 with no groups or grass (Mark 8), 5000, no groups, much grass (John 6)
John 6:11; Mark 6:41; 8:6-7	Jesus takes the loaves and fishes, prays over them, and distributes them to the crowd.	Jesus blesses the bread (Mark 6), gives thanks for the bread (Mark 8 and John 6), blesses the fish (Mark 8).
John 6:12-13 (cf. 6:26); Mark 6:42-43; 8:8	The crowd eats and is satisfied; the leftover pieces are gathered.	Twelve baskets of broken pieces (Mark 6), seven baskets of broken pieces (Mark 8), Jesus gives the command to collect broken pieces and there are twelve baskets (John 6).
John 6:14	Unparalleled	Jesus is the prophet who has come into the world (John 6).
John 6:17; Mark 6:45; 8:10	Getting into a boat	The disciples go to Bethsaida by boat (Mark 6); Jesus and his disciples go to Dalmanutha (Mark 8); the disciples get into the boat to get to Capernaum (John 6).

7. *Interlocking tradition.* According to another cohort of scholars, John represents a largely independent tradition based on eyewitness accounts. However, there are also several "interlocking traditions" between John and the Synoptics that contain partial parallels with subtle differences that mu-

tually reinforce and explain each other, though without implying a strict literary dependence.[208]

Leon Morris pointed out that John sometimes agrees with Matthew and Mark against Luke, sometimes with Luke against Matthew and Mark, sometimes with Matthew alone, and sometimes with Mark alone. For Morris this suggests not dependence, but interlocking connections with Synoptic traditions behind the Fourth Gospel. In places, John provides information that explains and coheres with many elements in the Synoptics, creating an intermeshing of material, which indicates that, although their respective portraits are different, it is the same personal subject that is presented by the Evangelists.[209]

From the examples that Morris gives, the most convincing is the saying about "destroying this temple."[210] In the Marcan version of Jesus' trial, some witnesses report: "We heard him say, 'I will destroy this temple that is made with hands, and in three days I will build another, not made with hands'" (Mark 14:58; cf. Matt 26:60-61). The charge is repeated by those who mock Jesus while he hangs on the cross (Mark 15:29; cf. Matt 27:40). The problem is that nowhere in the Synoptics does Jesus actually say that he will destroy the temple and build another. However, there is a tradition found in John where Jesus does say something like that. The Johannine temple demonstration climaxes with Jesus' claim: "Destroy this temple and in three days I will raise it," and we are informed by an editorial comment that this is a cryptic reference to Jesus' resurrection body (John 2:19, 21). It is a clear instance of John clarifying something found in the Synoptic tradition but without necessarily relying on the Synoptic Gospels.

Likewise several elements of the Gospel of John seem odd and intrusive on their own, such as the saying that a prophet is without honor in his own country (John 4:44), which gains traction when read beside a near-identical saying in Mark 6:4/Matt 13:57 as a way of expressing the Galilean ambivalence toward Jesus. These interlocks seem incidental rather than contrived and testify to a complex tradition history.[211] From this Morris concludes that there is a relationship with the Synoptic tradition but not

208. Leon Morris, *Studies in the Fourth Gospel* (Grand Rapids: Eerdmans, 1969), 40-63; D. A. Carson, *The Gospel According to John* (Pillar; Grand Rapids: Eerdmans, 1990), 51-58; Craig Keener, *The Gospel of John: A Commentary* (Peabody: Hendrickson, 2003), 1:40-42; Köstenberger, "John's Transposition Theology," 191-226.

209. Morris, *Studies in the Fourth Gospel*, 41-42.

210. Morris, *Studies in the Fourth Gospel*, 46; cf. Carson, *Gospel According to John*, 53.

211. Carson, *Gospel According to John*, 54-55.

necessarily a literary one. The traditions found in both bodies of Jesus tradition are resonant and reinforcing.[212]

One can still posit these interlocking traditions even if one does not think that John is entirely independent of the Synoptics. Carson, for example, thinks that John has probably read Mark if not Luke, but that John still wrote his own book.[213] Similarly, Köstenberger believes that John drew on eyewitness recollections as well as Mark and Luke, but engaged in a deliberate theological transposition of Synoptic materials. The result is a creative reworking of existing texts which realizes their hidden potential and extends their message in a new and distinctive context. John had read Mark and possibly Luke. While John's relationship with them is indirect and fairly subtle, John nonetheless worked from the literary plan and theological character of Mark if not Luke as well.[214] For instance, Köstenberger sees a transposition in exchanging Peter's confession of Jesus as the Messiah at Caesarea Philippi (Mark 8:29; Matt 16:16; Luke 9:20) with Peter's confession of Jesus as the "Holy One of God" (John 6:69) and further indirect reflection of Marcan material in Martha's confession of Jesus as the Messiah, Son of God (John 12:27), which in turn foreshadows the purpose statement of the Fourth Gospel (20:31).[215]

The proposal of interlocking traditions certainly has a lot of explanatory power for the seeming concord of the Johannine and Synoptic materials without resorting to full-fledged independence. Even so, some of the apparent Johannine clarifications could be simply Johannine harmonizations of Synoptic material. Also, we are left wondering if the final result is simply literary dependence with a somewhat weaker, indirect, and flexible uptake of the Synoptics by John.

8. *Synoptic-Like Sources.* Rudolf Bultmann influenced much of continental European scholarship with his view that the Synoptics had little if any direct influence on John's Gospel. He saw the Gospel of John as based on a number of sources including a miracle source, a discourse source heavily influenced by Gnostic themes, a passion and resurrection source, and an ecclesiastical redactor who created and rearranged materials. Bultmann envisaged John drawing from parallel sources that often described the same events in the Synoptics, such as the passion story. For the most part, the

212. Morris, *Studies in the Fourth Gospel,* 61-62.

213. Carson, *Gospel According to John,* 51.

214. Köstenberger, "John's Transposition Theology," 197-201.

215. Köstenberger, "John's Transposition Theology," 205.

John-Synoptic similarities are due to sources that are similar and parallel yet independent of each other. The few verbatim agreements are due to a final redactor who did in fact know the other Gospels.[216] So, for example, Bultmann regarded John 1:26 ("I baptize you with water"), which verbally agrees with Mark 1:8, as an addition by an editor because it is intrusive to the context. He also regarded the feeding miracle of John 6:1-26, which like Mark 6:30-51 combines the feeding miracle with Jesus walking on the water, as containing considerable agreements in details, yet also possessing many divergent characteristics indicative of independence.[217]

Though Bultmann had a profound grasp of the source-critical, literary, and theological questions of the Fourth Gospel, especially its unities and disunities, his own solution is dissatisfying. To begin with, other than a possible signs source, none of his proposed sources for the Fourth Gospel have survived the day, and even the signs source has not won universal consent among Johannine scholars.[218] On top of that, projecting the similarities between John and the Synoptics either to parallel pre-Gospel sources or to post-Gospel redactional activity seems to posit similarity at every level other than that of the original Evangelist. While Bultmann rightly understood the literary and theological independence of the Fourth Gospel, he did not give a compelling account of the reasons for its similarity to the Synoptic tradition.

9. *Independence.* When it had been simply assumed that John was dependent on the other Gospels as a supplement or replacement, along came Percival Gardner-Smith with a Johannine thunderbolt, arguing for John's independence from the Synoptics.[219] According to Gardner-Smith, the widespread dissemination and interpretation of the oral tradition about Jesus can account for much of John and the Synoptics. The number of verbal agreements are very few and the structural similarities might be based on a widely known kerygma rather than on literary dependence. Not only that, but he pointed out that the problem is not just explaining the similarities but

---

216. Rudolf Bultmann, *The Gospel of John: A Commentary*, trans. G. R. Beasley-Murray, R. W. N. Hoare, and J. K. Riches (Philadelphia: Westminster 1971), esp. the introduction by Walter Schmithals, 6-7. For summaries of Bultmann's view, see Smith, *John among the Gospels*, 48, 65-66; Mackay, *John's Relationship with Mark*, 16-19.

217. Bultmann, *Gospel of John*, 91 n. 1, 210-11.

218. Cf. D. A. Carson, "Current Source Criticism of the Fourth Gospel," *JBL* 97 (1978): 411-29.

219. P. Gardner-Smith, *Saint John and the Synoptic Gospels* (Cambridge: Cambridge University Press, 1938).

accounting for the differences too. After moving systematically albeit briefly through the Fourth Gospel, Gardner-Smith thinks it better to account for the sameness-yet-difference between John and the Synoptics on the basis of Johannine independence.

Gardner-Smith was somewhat of a John the Baptist to C. H. Dodd, who prosecuted the thesis of Johannine independence with even greater verve and gusto in his landmark study *Historical Tradition in the Fourth Gospel.*[220] Dodd engaged in a near-exhaustive comparison and analysis of similarities between John and the Synoptics and offered a point-by-point case for seeing the Johannine material as largely oral in character and some-how distinguishable from the Synoptic parallels. Dodd stated:

> In comparing, therefore, a given passage in the Fourth Gospel with a parallel passage in the other gospels, we have to inquire whether the co-incidences of language or content go beyond what might be reasonably expected in works having behind them the general tradition of the early Church, and next whether any marked difference might be accounted for (supposing he were copying the Synoptics) by known mannerisms of the evangelist, or his known doctrinal tendencies. If not, then there is a *prima facie* case for treating the passage as independent of the Synoptics, and we have to ask whether it has characteristics, in form or substance, or possible indications of a *Sitz im Leben,* which would associate it with traditional material so far as it is known to us.[221]

There are several problems with Gardner-Smith and Dodd's thesis of Jo-hannine independence. For a start, they over-appealed to oral tradition as an explanation for the shape of the Johannine tradition. Yes, the Gospel of John does have an oral tradition behind it, but it is not clear at what point John's overlapping with Synoptic material can be attributed to inde-pendent oral tradition rather than to redaction of a Synoptic Gospel just because some element is distinctive.[222] Dodd was also writing back in the mid-twentieth century when form criticism was still in its heyday, but in-creasingly the form-critical perspective (and Dodd was more involved in the form-critical perspective than the form-critical method) has crumbled

---

220. C. H. Dodd, *Historical Tradition in the Fourth Gospel* (Cambridge: Cambridge University Press, 1963).

221. Dodd, *Historical Tradition in the Fourth Gospel,* 9.

222. An issue of which Dodd was fully aware (see *Historical Tradition in the Fourth Gospel,* 9).

from its rooftop to its foundations. Thus appealing to the oral dissemination of the Jesus tradition as form critics understood it now lacks the argumentative weight it once had. What is more, Dodd also bought into the premise that dependence must be explained in purely literary terms — one scribe copying the work of another — yet, as we have seen, there are other categories for us to consider, such as memory, secondary orality, and performance, different ways in which John might have known the other Gospels. Finally, and what I regard as most problematic of all, it is simply unlikely that a document like Mark, which circulated fairly widely (as far as the setting of Matthew and Luke at least), would have been unknown and unused by John, writing at the end of the first century. If John knew or knew of Mark, then somehow it probably influenced him, even if only at the level of genre and framework.

Conclusion: *The Johannine Question Revisited*

The question of the origins of the Fourth Gospel and its sameness-yet-difference compared to the Synoptics continues to baffle all and sundry. D. A. Carson observes the stalemate: "The thesis that John is *literarily* dependent on one or more of the Synoptics has not been demonstrated beyond reasonable doubt, but neither has the thesis that John is literarily *in*dependent of the Synoptics."[223] If we are to move the debate forward then we simply have to develop new categories and frameworks for understanding the development of the Johannine tradition vis-à-vis the Synoptic tradition beyond dependent *or* independent because the relationship is more complex than this dichotomy allows.

In pursuit of a solution, it seems to me that John is independent in that his Gospel is very different from the Synoptics, mostly drawn on different traditions, and has its own unique goals and purposes. Yet John clearly knows something of the Synoptic tradition and the Synoptic Gospels. He seems to assume his readers' familiarity with elements of the Synoptic storyline, hence his frequent parenthetical remarks. There are also some strong verbal connections with Synoptic material in places like John 6 and 18–20. The widespread movement of Christian leaders and the mutual interest that churches had in each other's affairs make it unlikely that the Evangelist, writing presumably in Ephesus, had not come across a reading of Mark

223. Carson, *Gospel According to John,* 51 (italics original).

or Luke.[224] Regardless of how John "knows" the Synoptics, he applies that knowledge in a way that makes his Gospel look somewhat removed and distant from them. Irrespective of whether John's Gospel and its sources are pre-Synoptic or post-Synoptic, the Evangelist tells these stories freely without direct dependence on the Synoptics.[225] The Fourth Gospel exhibits continuity with the earlier accounts but also a strong degree of freedom from them.[226]

To explain this, I suggest that we envisage the spasmodic interpenetration of Synoptic and Johannine tradition across each other in pre-literary stages, recognize the independent nature of many of John's sources, and imagine also John's exposure to the Synoptic tradition through either a prior reading or from observing an oral performance of a Synoptic text, probably Mark and perhaps also Luke. This accounts for the Fourth Gospel's overall differentiation from the Synoptics in conjunction with its conscious adoption of the Marcan framework, the presence of interlocking traditions, and John's deliberate transposition of Synoptic units. When that complex relationship is combined with the fourth Evangelist's somewhat maverick approach in telling the Jesus story encoded with symbolic meanings, amplifying a christology of sonship and messiahship, engaging in a midrashic interpretation of the sayings tradition, and richly interweaving Jewish sapiential motifs, then I submit that we have a plausible explanation as to why the Gospel of John is what it is.

III. Conclusion

The Gospels emerged from a pool of oral tradition and from the gradual textualization of the Jesus tradition. Whereas oral traditions interfaced between various witnesses and groups, each with its respective pool of material and school of followers, so too the Gospels appear to have influenced each other in some way at the literary level. These literary genetics, by which I mean the interior relationships among the Gospels, have been explained as follows.

224. Cf. Brown, *Gospel According to John*, 1:xlvi; Smith, *John among the Gospels*, 241; Keener, *Gospel of John*, 1:41-42.

225. Keener, *Gospel of John*, 1:42.

226. Cf. Manfred Lang, *Johannes und die Synoptiker. Eine redaktionsgeschichtliche Analyse von Johannes 18–20 vor dem markanischen und lukanischen Hintergrund* (FRLANT 192; Göttingen: Vandenhoeck & Ruprecht, 1999), 56-60. Though I demur from Lang that John essentially redacts Mark and Luke to produce his passion story.

In the Synoptic Gospels we detect clear traces of a literary relationship between them with one or more of the Gospels borrowing from the others. But the relationship is not simple, complicated as it is by continuing oral tradition, secondary orality, parallel traditions, and perhaps even earlier and later editions. What seems almost certain is the priority of the Gospel of Mark and its subsequent use by Luke and Matthew. After that we are entering into the realm of conjecture. Even so, what I take to be very likely is that Matthew and Luke shared some materials beyond Mark (i.e., perhaps a document we call "Q" and other miscellaneous traditions) and that Luke at a later point has incorporated elements of Matthew into his Gospel (i.e., the Holtzmann-Gundry thesis). Luke then stands as the apex of the development of the Synoptic tradition.

In regard to the Gospel of John, its origins are truly enigmatic, and it defies neat categorization as "dependent on" or "independent of" the Synoptics in any absolute way. My overall impression is that it is indebted to the testimony of a Judean disciple of Jesus, the Beloved Disciple, who wrote a Gospel in Ephesus, which was later appended with an appendix by his followers. It seems unlikely that either the Evangelist or his followers were isolated from the rest of the early churches. At some point he has come across Mark, perhaps Luke, and, who knows, maybe even Matthew. A Synoptic text, however it was known to him, has provided the framework and genre for his own creative narration of the Jesus tradition and has left a soft fingerprint creating a close resemblance in a few places, yet his story remains literarily independent and relies predominantly on non-Synoptic tradition for its account.

We have given an account here of the literary genetics of the four Gospels. The danger of source criticism is that while we do our best to figure out how the jigsaw puzzle of the Gospels was put together, we often forget the literary beauty of the story and the theological shape of the narrative, which is after all why people still bother to read the Gospels today. One does not appreciate the Gospels by comprehending the source-critical questions that they present to us. Certainly source-critical studies can help, especially in identifying how each Evangelist has edited or redacted his sources, and this enables us to see their precise purposes and unique perspectives in a given instance. Yet to appreciate any of the Gospels one must enter the Evangelist's narrative world and look at how stories create meaning through characterizations, plots, tensions, mood, themes, and the like. It is the textures of the story — theological, rhetorical, historical, and cultural — that exert the most influence on readers. It is thus the Gospels as literary works to which we must now turn.

Excursus
Patristic Quotations on the Order of the Gospels

The following collection of patristic quotations about the origins of the Gospels is not an exhaustive listing of traditions and speculations about where the four Gospels came from in the opinion of Christian writers. Due to limitations of length, the collection includes the better known references to the origins of the Gospels according to Christian tradition.[227]

Papias (ca. 70-155)

In his writing he also passes along other accounts of the sayings of the Lord belonging to Aristion, who has been mentioned above, and the traditions of John the Elder, to which we refer those interested. For our present purpose we must add to this statement already quoted above a tradition concerning Mark, who wrote the Gospel, that has been set forth in these words: "And the elder used to say this: 'Mark, having become Peter's interpreter, wrote down accurately everything he remembered, though not in order, of the things either said or done by Christ. For he neither heard the Lord nor followed him, but afterward, as I said, followed Peter, who adapted his teachings as needed but had no intention of giving an ordered account of the Lord's sayings. Consequently, Mark did nothing wrong in writing down some things as he remembered them, for he made it his one concern not to omit anything that he heard or to make any false statement in them.'" Such, then is the account given by Papias with respect to Mark. But with respect to Matthew the following is said: "So Matthew composed the oracles in the Hebrew language and each person interpreted them as best he could." The same writer utilized testimonies from the first letter of John and, likewise from that of Peter. He has related another account about a woman accused of many sins before the Lord, which the *Gospel according to the Hebrews* contains. And these things we must take into account, in addition to what has already been stated.[228]

Irenaeus (d. 202)

So Matthew published a written Gospel among the Hebrews in their own language, while Peter and Paul were preaching at Rome and founding the church. After their

---

227. For a more thorough account of patristic evidence, see Bernard Orchard, "The Historical Tradition," in *The Order of the Synoptics: Why Three Gospels?* ed. B. Orchard and H. Riley (Macon: Mercer University Press, 1987), 111-214.

228. Papias, *Fragment* 3.15-17 = Eusebius, *Hist. Eccl.* 3.39.

departure, Mark, the disciple and interpreter of Peter, did also hand down to us in writing what had been preached by Peter. Luke also, the companion of Paul, recorded in the book the Gospel preached by him [Paul]. Then John, the disciple of the Lord, the one who leaned back on the Lord's breast, himself published a Gospel while he resided in Ephesus.[229]

Clement of Alexandria (ca. 150-215)

This extract from Clement I have inserted here for the sake of the history and for the benefit of my readers. Let us now point out the undisputed writings of this apostle [John]. And in the first place his Gospel, which is known to all the churches under heaven, must be acknowledged as genuine. That it has with good reason been put by the ancients in the fourth place, after the other three Gospels, may be made evident in the following way. Those great and truly divine men, I mean the apostles of Christ, were purified in their life, and were adorned with every virtue of the soul, but were uncultivated in speech. They were confident indeed in their trust in the divine and wonder-working power which was granted unto them by the Saviour, but they did not know how, nor did they attempt to proclaim the doctrines of their teacher in studied and artistic language, but employing only the demonstration of the divine Spirit, which worked with them, and the wonder-working power of Christ, which was displayed through them, they published the knowledge of the kingdom of heaven throughout the whole world, paying little attention to the composition of written works. And this they did because they were assisted in their ministry by one greater than man. Paul, for instance, who surpassed them all in vigor of expression and in richness of thought, committed to writing no more than the briefest epistles, although he had innumerable mysterious matters to communicate, for he had attained even unto the sights of the third heaven, had been carried to the very paradise of God, and had been deemed worthy to hear unspeakable utterances there. And the rest of the followers of our Saviour, the twelve apostles, the seventy disciples, and countless others besides, were not ignorant of these things. Nevertheless, of all the disciples of the Lord, only Matthew and John have left us written memorials, and they, tradition says, were led to write only under the pressure of necessity. For Matthew, who had at first preached to the Hebrews, when he was about to go to other peoples, committed his Gospel to writing in his native tongue, and thus compensated those whom he was obliged to leave for the loss of his presence. And when Mark and Luke had already published their Gospels, they say that John, who had employed all his time in proclaiming the Gospel orally, finally proceeded to write for the following reason. The three Gospels already

229. Irenaeus, *Adv. Haer.* 3.1.1 = Eusebius, *Hist. Eccl.* 5.8.2-4.

mentioned having come into the hands of all and into his own too, they say that he accepted them and bore witness to their truthfulness; but that there was lacking in them an account of the deeds done by Christ at the beginning of his ministry. And this indeed is true. For it is evident that the three evangelists recorded only the deeds done by the Saviour for one year after the imprisonment of John the Baptist, and indicated this in the beginning of their account. For Matthew, after the forty days' fast and the temptation which followed it, indicates the chronology of his work when he says: "Now when he heard that John was delivered up he withdrew from Judea into Galilee." Mark likewise says: "Now after that John was delivered up Jesus came into Galilee." And Luke, before commencing his account of the deeds of Jesus, similarly marks the time, when he says that Herod, "adding to all the evil deeds which he had done, shut up John in prison." They say, therefore, that the apostle John, being asked to do it for this reason, gave in his Gospel an account of the period which had been omitted by the earlier evangelists, and of the deeds done by the Saviour during that period; that is, of those which were done before the imprisonment of the Baptist. And this is indicated by him, they say, in the following words: "This beginning of miracles did Jesus"; and again when he refers to the Baptist, in the midst of the deeds of Jesus, as still baptizing in Aenon near Salim; where he states the matter clearly in the words: "For John was not yet cast into prison." John accordingly, in his Gospel, records the deeds of Christ which were performed before the Baptist was cast into prison, but the other three evangelists mention the events which happened after that time. One who understands this can no longer think that the Gospels are at variance with one another, inasmuch as the Gospel according to John contains the first acts of Christ, while the others give an account of the latter part of his life. And the genealogy of our Saviour according to the flesh John quite naturally omitted, because it had been already given by Matthew and Luke, and began with the doctrine of his divinity, which had, as it were, been reserved for him, as their superior, by the divine Spirit. These things may suffice, which we have said concerning the Gospel of John. The cause which led to the composition of the Gospel of Mark has been already stated by us. But as for Luke, in the beginning of his Gospel, he states himself the reasons which led him to write it. He states that since many others had more rashly undertaken to compose a narrative of the events of which he had acquired perfect knowledge, he himself, feeling the necessity of freeing us from their uncertain opinions, delivered in his own Gospel an accurate account of those events in regard to which he had learned the full truth, being aided by his intimacy and his stay with Paul and by his acquaintance with the rest of the apostles.[230]

Again, in the same books [*Hypotyposeis* 6], Clement gives the tradition of the earliest presbyters, as to the order of the Gospels, in the following manner: The Gospels

230. Eusebius, *Hist. Eccl.* 3.24.1-15.

containing the genealogies, he says, were written first. The Gospel according to Mark had this occasion. As Peter had preached the Word publicly at Rome, and declared the Gospel by the Spirit, many who were present requested that Mark, who had followed him for a long time and remembered his sayings, should write them out. And having composed the Gospel he gave it to those who had requested it. When Peter learned of this, he neither directly forbade nor encouraged it. But, last of all, John, perceiving that the external facts had been made plain in the Gospel, being urged by his friends, and inspired by the Spirit, composed a spiritual Gospel. This is the account of Clement.[231]

Anti-Marcionite Prologues (ca. 150-250)

Mark recorded, who was called stubby-fingered, because he had fingers that were too small for the height of the rest of his body. He himself was the interpreter of Peter. After the death of Peter himself, the same man wrote this gospel in the parts of Italy.

Indeed Luke was an Antiochene Syrian, a doctor by profession, a disciple of the apostles: later however he followed Paul until his martyrdom, serving the Lord blamelessly. He never had a wife, he never fathered children, and died at the age of eighty-four, full of the Holy Spirit, in Boetia. Therefore — although gospels had already been written — indeed by Matthew in Judaea but by Mark in Italy — moved by the Holy Spirit he wrote down this gospel in the parts of Achaia, signifying in the preface that the others were written before his, but also that it was of the greatest importance for him to expound with the greatest diligence the whole series of events in his narration for the Greek believers, so that they would not be led astray by the lure of Jewish fables, or, seduced by the fables of the heretics and stupid solicitations, fall away from the truth. And so at once at the start he took up the extremely necessary [story] from the birth of John, who is the beginning of the gospel, the forerunner of our Lord Jesus Christ, and was a companion in the perfecting of the people, likewise in the introducing of baptism and a companion in martyrdom. Of this disposition the prophet Malachi, one of the twelve, certainly makes mention. And indeed afterwards the same Luke wrote the Acts of the Apostles. Later the apostle John wrote the Apocalypse on the island of Patmos, and then the Gospel in Asia.

The Gospel of John was revealed and given to the churches by John while still in the body, just as Papias of Hieropolis, the close disciple of John, related in the

---

231. Eusebius, *Hist. Eccl.* 6.14.5-7.

exoterics, that is, in the last five books. Indeed he wrote down the Gospel, while John was dictating carefully. But the heretic Marcion, after being condemned by him because he was teaching the opposite to him [John], was expelled by John. But he [Marcion] had brought writings or letters to him [John] from the brothers which were in Pontus.[232]

Origen (ca. 184-254)

The first written [Gospel] was that according to Matthew, who was once a tax-collector but later an apostle of Jesus Christ. He published it for those who became believers from Judaism, since it was composed in the Hebrew language. The second was that according to Mark, who wrote it according to Peter's instructions. Peter also acknowledged him as his son in his general letter, saying in these words: "She who is in Babylon chosen with you, sends you greetings; so does my son Mark" [1 Pet 5:13]. And the third was that according to Luke who wrote for those who were from the Gentiles, the gospel that was praised by Paul [2 Cor 8:18]. And after them all, that according to John.[233]

Augustine (354-430)

So these four evangelists, well-known through the entire world (and perhaps they are four because of this, since there are four parts of the world, through the whole of which, they have proclaimed, in a certain manner by the very sacrament of their own number, that the church of Christ has spread) are regarded to have written in this order: first Matthew, then Mark, third Luke, and last John. Hence, there is one order to them in learning and preaching, and another in writing.[234]

Of these four, it is true, only Matthew is reckoned to have written in the Hebrew language; the others in Greek. And however they may appear to have kept each of them a certain order of narration proper to himself, this certainly is not to be taken as if each individual writer chose to write in ignorance of what his predecessor had done, or left out as matters about which there was no information things which another nevertheless is discovered to have recorded. But the fact is, that just as they received each of them the gift of inspiration, they abstained from adding to their several labours any superfluous conjoint compositions. For Matthew is

232. Found in several pre-Vulgate Old Latin mss. (trans. R. Pearce).
233. Eusebius, *Hist. Eccl.* 6.25.
234. Augustine, *Harmony of the Gospels* 1.2.3.

understood to have taken it in hand to construct the record of the incarnation of the Lord according to the royal lineage, and to give an account of most part of His deeds and words as they stood in relation to this present life of men. Mark follows him closely, and looks like his attendant and epitomizer. For in his narrative he gives nothing in concert with John apart from the others: by himself separately, he has little to record; in conjunction with Luke, as distinguished from the rest, he has still less; but in concord with Matthew, he has a very large number of passages. Much, too, he narrates in words almost numerically and identically the same as those used by Matthew, where the agreement is either with that evangelist alone, or with him in connection with the rest. On the other hand, Luke appears to have occupied himself rather with the priestly lineage and character of the Lord. For although in his own way he carries the descent back to David, what he has followed is not the royal pedigree, but the line of those who were not kings. That genealogy, too, he has brought to a point in Nathan the son of David, which person likewise was no king. It is not thus, however, with Matthew. For in tracing the lineage along through Solomon the king, he has pursued with strict regularity the succession of the other kings; and in enumerating these, he has also conserved that mystical number of which we shall speak hereafter.[235]

And in this way, Mark, who seems to answer to the figure of the man in the well-known mystical symbol of the four living creatures, either appears to be preferentially the companion of Matthew, as he narrates a larger number of matters in unison with him than with the rest, and therein acts in due harmony with the idea of the kingly character whose wont it is, as I have stated in the first book, to be not unaccompanied by attendants; or else, in accordance with the more probable account of the matter, he holds a course in conjunction with both [the other Synoptists]. For although he is at one with Matthew in the larger number of passages, he is nevertheless at one rather with Luke in some others. And this very fact shows him to stand related at once to the lion and to the steer, that is to say, to the kingly office which Matthew emphasizes, and to the sacerdotal which Luke introduces, wherein also Christ appears distinctively as man, as the figure which Mark sustains stands related to both these.[236]

Jerome (347-420)

I am now speaking of the New Testament. This was undoubtedly composed in Greek, with the exception of the work of Matthew the Apostle, who was the first

---

235. Augustine, *Harmony of the Gospels* 1.2.4.
236. Augustine, *Harmony of the Gospels* 4.10.11.

to commit to writing the Gospel of Christ, and who published his work in Judea in Hebrew characters.[237]

Muratorian Fragment (ca. 150-450)

. . . at which nevertheless he [Peter] was present, and so he [Mark] placed [them in his narrative]. The third book of the Gospel is that according to Luke. Luke, the well-known physician, after the ascension of Christ, when Paul had taken with him as one zealous for the law, composed it in his own name, according to [the general] belief. Yet he himself had not seen the Lord in the flesh; and therefore, as he was able to ascertain events, so indeed he begins to tell the story from the birth of John. The fourth of the Gospels is that of John, [one] of the disciples. To his fellow disciples and bishops, who had been urging him [to write], he said, "Fast with me from today to three days, and what will be revealed to each one let us tell it to one another." In the same night it was revealed to Andrew, [one] of the apostles, that John should write down all things in his own name while all of them should review it. And so, though various elements may be taught in the individual books of the Gospels, nevertheless this makes no difference to the faith of believers, since by the one sovereign Spirit all things have been declared in all [the Gospels]: concerning the nativity, concerning the passion, concerning the resurrection, concerning life with his disciples, and concerning his twofold coming; the first in lowliness when he was despised, which has taken place, the second glorious in royal power, which is still in the future. What marvel is it then, if John so consistently mentions these particular points also in his Epistles, saying about himself, 'What we have seen with our eyes and heard with our ears and our hands have handled, these things we have written to you? For in this way he professes [himself] to be not only an eye-witness and hearer, but also a writer of all the marvelous deeds of the Lord, in their order. Moreover, the acts of all the apostles were written in one book. For "most excellent Theophilus" Luke compiled the individual events that took place in his presence — as he plainly shows by omitting the martyrdom of Peter as well as the departure of Paul from the city [of Rome] when he journeyed to Spain.[238]

---

237. Jerome, *Preface to the Four Gospels* (to Damasus).
238. *Muratorian Fragment* 1-39 (trans. B. Metzger).

CHAPTER 5

The Genre and Goal of the Gospels:
What Is a Gospel and Why Write One?

When the second-century pagan philosopher Celsus, who felt compelled to write a refutation of the Christian religion, took up and read the Gospels for the first time, what kind of literature did he think he was reading? Was it a Christian version of ancient biography, or was it some new-fangled form of literature uniquely devised by Christians themselves? Or if someone donated a copy of the Gospel of Mark to the great library of Alexandria, in what part of the library would the librarians store it: among tragedies, comedies, histories, biographies, letters, prophecies, or where? Exploring the genre of the Gospels and comparing them to analogous Greco-Roman and Jewish writings enables us to place them in their ancient literary environment better and to understand their literary parameters and purposes.[1]

The question of the Gospel genre is an essential historical and herme-neutical exercise.[2] Genre consists of an identifiable literary pattern that marks out a text's relationship to a family of texts. Literary critics debate to what extent genre is normative or descriptive and how genre constrains readers and readings. In any case, genre creates a communicative framework for authors

---

1. I owe this illustration to Scot McKnight.

2. Cf. Adela Yarbro Collins, *The Beginning of the Gospel: Probings of Mark in Context* (Minneapolis: Fortress, 1992), 2: "The decision about the genre of Mark is not merely a matter of taxonomy or academic scholarship. One's assumptions about the literary form of Mark affect the way this work is allowed to function in the lives of readers, in the life of the church, and in society." On theological agendas connected to the investigation of Gospel genre, see esp. Robert H. Gundry, "The Symbiosis of Theology and Genre Criticism of the Canonical Gospels," in *The Old Is Better: New Testament Essays in Support of Tradition Interpretations* (WUNT 178; Tübingen: Mohr, 2005), 18-48. See also the survey by Judith A. Diehl, "What Is a 'Gospel'? Recent Studies in Gospel Genre," *CBR* 20 (2010): 1-26.

to encode communicative acts in a form that is readily decoded by readers. For instance, when we come across a story that begins "Once upon a time," we identify it with the fairytale genre and immediately have been given a clue as to what to expect in the story and how to understand the story's relationship to reality. Similarly, if we come across a document that begins with "Act One" we know that we are reading the script for a play and we should regard it as a dramatized narrative. Or if we pick up a tabloid and read the words, "President Falls Behind in Recent Poll," the physical medium and type of content makes us realize that we are reading a news story with a mixture of fact and journalistic opinion, something to be read as information, yet digested critically. Genre matters because genre creates a framework of expectation between an author and readers by appealing to known literary frames of reference.

Given the power of genre to create and delineate specific frameworks for understanding literature, we are right to explore what set of literary expectations the Evangelists attempted to activate in people who read their respective Jesus stories. What is more, if we can determine what type of literature the Gospels are intended to be, then we are also a step toward understanding what kind of impact the Evangelists intended their works to achieve. In communication the medium is often the message because how something is said is just as important as what is said. Genres are accordingly selected and developed to provide suitable literary vehicles that will enable authors to achieve their purposes, whether that is to entertain, inform, debate, shame, or provoke. Thus, matters of literary genre and authorial intent are closely interrelated. Only when we grasp "what" the Gospels are can we really know "why" the Gospels were written.

Therefore, the objective of this chapter is to examine the genre and goal of the Gospels as a way of determining their place in ancient literature and their purpose in the Greco-Roman world of the first Christian communities.

I. The Genre of the Gospels

Most scholarship of the modern era has regarded the Gospels as a unique literary genre in the Greco-Roman world. However, the consensus wore away by the early 1980s with the Gospels being increasingly compared to a variety of literary forms known from antiquity.[3] The primary options for

---

3. Cf. Richard Burridge, *What Are the Gospels? A Comparison with Graeco-Roman Biography* (2nd ed.; Grand Rapids: Eerdmans, 2004), 78-100.

consideration are to regard the Gospels as a distinct Christian literary production; or as analogous to forms of Jewish sacred literature, to aretalogies, or to novels; or as a form of Greco-Roman biography.

Options

1. Distinct Christian Writing

The most popular perspective about the genre of the Gospels in the twentieth century was that the Gospels reflect a new and distinctive literary form, a *sui generis*, a unique type of Christian literature. The Gospels' external shape is much like the Greek *bios* or Roman *vita*, but its narrative mode and theological framework is strongly indebted to the Old Testament, and its precise content is determined by Christian preaching about Jesus.[4]

The distinctive nature of the Gospels emerges because they represent the end point in the evolution of the Christian kerygma and the formation of the Jesus tradition. In the form-critical paradigm the Gospels were essentially oral folklore pressed into a literary form, thus a new, specifically Christian type of oral folk literature. Besides the passion story, the various units of traditional material, complete with their oral forms, were arranged and selected by the Evangelists much like pearls on a string.[5]

The luminaries of the form-critical school were foremost in promoting a view of the Gospels as a distinct type of Christian oral folk literature. In the case of Karl L. Schmidt, the framework of the Gospels was largely an artificial creation by the Evangelists, not constrained by historical memory or by the conventions of a literary form, creating a loose and somewhat arbitrary collection of anecdotes about Jesus. The Gospel of Mark is, for instance, a simple and artless sketch.[6] According to Martin Dibelius, the Gospels are products of the early church's eschatology, its missionary preaching about Jesus' death and resurrection (i.e., the kerygma), and tertiary recollections about Jesus. Dibelius regarded the Synoptic Gospels as "unliterary writings," more than notebooks but less than literary achievements, unlearned collec-

---

4. Loveday Alexander, "What Is a Gospel?" in *The Cambridge Companion to the Gospels,* ed. S. C. Barton (Cambridge: Cambridge University Press, 2006), 29.

5. Karl L. Schmidt, "Die Stellung der Evangelien in der allegemeinen Literaturgeschichte," in *EUCHARISTERION,* ed. H. Schmidt (FS H. Gunkel; 2 vols.; FRLANT 19; Göttingen: Vandenhoeck & Ruprecht, 1923), 2:127.

6. Karl L. Schmidt, *Der Rahmen der Geschichte Jesu* (Berlin: Trowitzsch, 1919).

tions of materials about Jesus. He writes: "The composers are only to the smallest extent authors. They are principally collectors, vehicles of tradition, editors. Before all else their labour consists in handing down, grouping, and working over the material which has come to them."[7] The Evangelists had a very limited role in forming the literary character of the Synoptic tradition. All they did was join together units that had been independent of each other.[8] Rudolf Bultmann took it as axiomatic that there was a definable boundary between oral and written tradition. He proceeded to argue that Mark was not a real biography but an expansion and illustration of the Christian kerygma in its Hellenistic setting.[9] The Gospels are expanded cult legends shaped by Christian preaching of the risen Christ. Bultmann stated: "Mark was the creator of this sort of Gospel; the Christ myth gives his book, the book of secret epiphanies, not indeed a biographical unity, but an unity [sic] based upon the myth of the kerygma."[10] He does not think the Gospels are really comparable to Greek biography, popular oriental books, or even an apocalypse. A juxtaposition of the Gospels with other literature serves only to highlight the uniqueness of the Gospels all the more. Consequently the Gospels represent an original literary creation of Christianity, formed out of Christian faith and worship.[11]

C. H. Dodd regarded the Gospels not as an evolution of the Jesus tradition but as an exposition of the early kerygma.[12] Early Christian preaching focused on Jesus' death and resurrection in its eschatological coordinates of fulfilled promises and an imminent apocalyptic consummation. However, as anticipation of an imminent end declined, interest in an eschatological interpretation of Jesus' life and teaching increased. This is why the Gospels were written. The Gospel of Mark is really a narrative expansion of the historical section of the early kerygma that culminates in Jesus' death. Evidence for this is the remarkable correspondence between the Marcan outline and the sketch of gospel preaching in Acts 10 and 13, indicating a well-known gospel framework. As such, "Mark serves as a commentary

---

7. Martin Dibelius, *From Tradition to Gospel*, trans. B. L. Woolf (Cambridge: Clarke, 1971), 3.

8. Dibelius, *From Tradition to Gospel*, 3-4.

9. Rudolf Bultmann, *History of the Synoptic Tradition*, trans. J. Marsh (2nd ed.; New York: Harper & Row, 1963), 321.

10. Bultmann, *History of the Synoptic Tradition*, 371.

11. Bultmann, *History of the Synoptic Tradition*, 371-74.

12. C. H. Dodd, *The Apostolic Preaching and Its Developments* (London: Hodder & Stoughton, 1936), 36-56.

on the *kerygma.*"[13] The Evangelist Mark, by focusing the second half of his work on Jesus' journey to Jerusalem, composed a large introduction to the passion story. Matthew followed suit, but contracted the passion story to add further emphasis to the fulfillment motif, infused more futurist eschatology, and combined kerygma (preaching) with *didachē* (teaching), with *didachē* predominating. Luke's narrative account (διήγησις) is more subtle in giving increased attention to Jesus' prophetic pronouncements and compassionate acts as an ideal for Christian conduct. Resultantly, for Dodd, a Gospel is not a biography but an expression of the early church's kerygma.[14]

Parallels between Peter's Speech in Acts 10 and the Gospel of Mark[15]

Acts 10:36-41	Mark's Gospel
[36]"You know the message he [God] sent to the people of Israel, preaching peace by Jesus Christ — he is Lord of all.	"The beginning of the gospel about Jesus Christ" (1:1).
[37] That message spread throughout Judea, beginning in Galilee after the baptism that John announced:	Jesus' ministry begins after his baptism by John (1:14-15).
[38] how God anointed Jesus of Nazareth with the Holy Spirit and with power; how he went about doing good and healing all who were oppressed by the devil, for God was with him.	Jesus is baptized and receives the Holy Spirit (1:9-11). The subsequent narratives ascribe healings, exorcisms, and miracles to Jesus (1:16–10:52).
[39] We are witnesses to all that he did both in Judea and in Jerusalem. They put him to death by hanging him on a tree;	The apostles accompany Jesus in the final phase of his Judean ministry, climaxing in his arrest and crucifixion in Jerusalem (chs. 11–15).
[40] but God raised him on the third day and allowed him to appear,	There are reports of Jesus' resurrection at the end of Mark's Gospel (16:1-8).
[41] not to all the people but to us who were chosen by God as witnesses, and who ate and drank with him after he rose from the dead. [42] He commanded us to preach to the people and to testify that he is the one ordained by God as judge	The Lucan tradition of the risen Jesus eating with the disciples, the summary of how the Scriptures point to the Messiah's passion and resurrection, and the commissioning of the disciples to be witnesses to Jesus (Luke 24:41-53).

13. Dodd, *Apostolic Preaching*, 48-49 (italics original).

14. Dodd, *Apostolic Preaching*, 50-55.

15. Adapted from William L. Lane, *The Gospel of Mark* (NICNT; Grand Rapids: Eerdmans, 1974), 10-11.

Acts 10:36-41	Mark's Gospel
of the living and the dead. [43] All the prophets testify about him that everyone who believes in him receives forgiveness of sins through his name."	

Viewing the Gospels as a distinct form of Christian literature — even if we dismiss the literary analysis of the form critics and reject Dodd's equation of "kerygma" and "Gospel" — remains a valid hypothesis as it explains several distinguishing features about the Gospels.

1. The Gospels are strictly anonymous at the literary level. The authors are never mentioned and first-person narrative is altogether missing. While the authorship and origins of the Gospels was probably known to Christian leaders who commissioned, copied, and kept these works, even so, the lack of explicit authorial identification does push us away from the category of historiography and biography somewhat.

2. The Gospels are rooted in the Jewish Scriptures. They explicitly function as the continuation and fulfillment of the story of Israel. That is why they are replete with citations, allusions, and echoes of the Old Testament. The religious content and theological texture of the Gospels is heavily indebted to the worldview, socio-political landscape, and sacred texts of Judaism. Roman biography and Greek legends could refer to various religious literary works such as Delphic oracles or Homer's *Iliad*. But for the Gospels, the story and worldview of Israel's Scriptures are very much what the Gospels are about, namely, the God of Israel inaugurating his kingdom through Jesus the Messiah. It should not raise anyone's eyebrows to say that the Gospels comprise a form of post-biblical Jewish literature with messianic faith in Jesus as its primary content.

3. The Gospels reflect early Christian preaching and teaching about Jesus. Against Dodd, I do not think that the division between kerygma and *didachē* was particularly thick, but what many Christians preached and taught about Jesus certainly found its way into the Gospels. That preaching and teaching were eventually put into a unified biographical narrative. This explains the episodic quality of the Gospels, rooted as they are in brief sayings and anecdotes about Jesus, but always with a view to climaxing in Jesus' death and resurrection. Concerning the first Evangelist to compose a Gospel, Mark, his literary achievement was selecting, arranging, and bringing together narratives and sayings about Jesus, integrating them into a

framework of gospel preaching, and then placing the resultant product in written form.[16]

It is unassailable that there are characteristics of the Gospels that make them highly unique within the literary environment of the Greco-Roman world. They are, in view of their contents, a distinct form of Christian writing. However, it is very difficult to maintain the proposition that the Gospels are simply a textualized form of Christian preaching that evolved out of oral tradition. First, there is no such thing as oral traditional literature in the absolute sense. While writings can remain hugely influenced by their oral sources and reflect characteristics of their prior oral performances, no writing is purely "oral" since the process of textualizing an oral tradition impacts the content in an irreversible way. A piece of oral composition is changed when its content is transferred from verbal media to written media. In oral performance the actor is the center of the process of creating meaning, which he directly controls through the performance, whereas in written media the author communicates his intent indirectly through a text that must be decoded by a reader.[17] So, whereas oral tradition is by nature flexible and no reproduction of a speech is ever strictly the same, the transfer of oral speech to a written medium in effect freezes the content to some degree.[18] Second, written texts are more susceptible to intertextuality. Obviously written texts can influence oral performance as well, but in the hands of authors, there is more capacity to relate a text to other known texts. Writing is the ideal place for a synthesis between oral and written sources. In fact, Luke's prologue reports exactly this, composed as it was after a careful investigation of "eyewitnesses" and written in direct imitation of earlier attempts "to set down an orderly account" of the events of Jesus' life. Luke's Gospel is not oral literature, but reflects a mix of oral and literary sources. Thus, "oral traditional literature" is more of a mode of composition and performance,

---

16. Robert Guelich, "The Gospel Genre," in *The Gospel and the Gospels*, ed. P. Stuhlmacher (Grand Rapids: Eerdmans, 1991), 202.

17. I think this is where Werner Kelber makes a good point (*The Oral and the Written Gospel* [Philadelphia: Fortress, 1983]) in identifying the differences between oral and written mediums. However, it does not mean that oral materials and written materials are two vastly different modes of communication requiring different hermeneutical strategies. As I have argued earlier, written texts can exhibit the characteristics of oral performance, and written texts can also create an oral phenomenon.

18. Of course, the written texts of the Gospels took on a life of their own in the development of their respective textual histories. See David C. Parker, *The Living Text of the Gospels* (Cambridge: Cambridge University Press, 1997).

not an actual genre, and we should hesitate to regard "oral literature" as the determinative genre of the Gospels.[19]

At the end of the day, the Gospels cannot be a *sui generis* because they simply contain too many affinities with Greco-Roman literature. Regardless of whether we compare the Gospels to historiography, biography, or novels, there are a variety of motifs shared between the Gospels and Greco-Roman writings.[20] Moreover, the element of the Gospels thought to be most unique, their focus on Jesus' passion, turns out to be not so unique after all. According to Tacitus, Gaius Fannius wrote about the deaths of famous men who were killed or exiled under Nero. Gnaeus Octavius Titinius Capito's work *Passing of Famous Men* memorialized the memory of the republican martyrs.[21] Plutarch also has two biographies that could be described as passion narratives with extended introductions since they climax in the death of the hero, *Cato the Younger* and *Eumenes*. A biography composed of anecdotes and sayings and closing with the exemplary death of its protagonist can be found in Lucian's *Demonax,* a portrayal of a revered Cynic philosopher who starved himself to death in later life.[22]

2. Jewish Literature

While many have highlighted the specifically Christian form and content of the Gospel genre, others have found grounds to emphasize their Jewish characteristics. The "Christian" Gospels are said to most closely resemble literary forms found in the Old Testament, second temple literature, or rabbinic biography of revered leaders.

Jewish literature has a long biographical tradition. Historical books like 1 and 2 Samuel include a strong focus on key characters like Samuel, Saul, and David amid the socio-political fortunes and religious climate of the united Israelite monarchy. Similarly, the prophetic careers of Elijah and

---

19. Alexander, "What Is a Gospel?" 20.

20. F. Gerald Downing, "Contemporary Analogies to the Gospels and Acts: 'Genres' or 'Motifs'?" in *Synoptic Studies,* ed. C. M. Tuckett (JSNTSup 7; Sheffield: JSOT, 1984), 51-64.

21. Tacitus, *Ep.* 5.5; 8.12.

22. Martin Hengel, "Eye-Witness Memory and the Writing of the Gospels: Form Criticism, Community Tradition and the Authority of the Authors," in *The Written Gospel,* ed. M. Bockmuehl and D. A. Hagner (FS Graham Stanton; Cambridge: Cambridge University Press, 2005), 72 n. 11; Christopher Bryan, *A Preface to Mark: Notes on the Gospel in Its Literary and Cultural Setting* (Oxford: Oxford University Press, 1993), 42.

Elisha, complete with divine messages and miraculous deeds, are a center of attention in 1 and 2 Kings. The prophetic books are partly biographies of particular prophets, including their calling and ministry and its impact on the Judean and Israelite kingdoms amid the struggle with foreign powers. Nehemiah is a memoir, often in the first person, concerned with the rebuilding of the Judean nation under the aegis of the Persian Empire. Books about Jewish heroines such as Ruth, Esther, and Judith are powerful stories about the struggle of unassuming women for justice, often bound up with the fate of the Jewish people. Authors like Philo appear to have adopted Greco-Roman biographical forms for a specific Jewish style of biography for figures like Abraham, Joseph, and Moses, resulting in a hybrid of Greek biography and rewritten Bible. Then there are works that are largely narrative encomia, literary praises for Jewish heroes, as is arguably the case with 4 Maccabees and *The Lives of the Prophets*. The rabbinic *haggadot* are another potential point of contact with the Gospels, containing as they do short anecdotes about the Judean holy men and rabbinic leaders, figures like Eliezer ben Hyrcanus, Rabbi Akiba, and Honi the Circle Drawer.

The main point of contact with the Gospels is that Jewish biographical literature contains a theography, a story about Israel's God, working through an agent of deliverance, such as a prophet, king, or teacher. The protagonist leads the Jewish people at a time of national crisis or performs some miraculous deed at an important moment in Israel's history. The Gospels possess a theological worldview, a geopolitical setting, didactic content, and a deliberate replication of Old Testament literary types that make some kind of connection with Jewish sacred literature irrefutable.

Proponents of such a perspective have pressed the similarities between the Gospels and Jewish writings. Mark in particular has come under particular consideration. John Bowman believes that the Marcan Gospel is a form of *haggadah,* a midrashic exposition of Jesus' death, modeled after the exodus narrative.[23] Eduard Schweizer regarded Mark as more like a volume of sermons than a biography. Even so, he regarded the historical books of the Old Testament and the prophetic book of Jonah as the only real literary parallels.[24] According to Michael E. Vines, Mark resembles not a biography but a Jewish novella. Mark employs a narrative tradition

---

23. J. W. Bowman, *The Gospel of Mark: The New Christian Jewish Passover Haggadah* (Leiden: Brill 1965); see also on the Gospels and the exodus narrative, Meredith G. Kline, "The Old Testament Origins of the Gospel Genre," *WTJ* 38 (1975): 1-127.

24. Eduard Schweizer, *The Good News According to Mark,* trans. D. H. Madvig (London: SPCK, 1970), 24.

ordinarily used to subvert the ideological profile of foreign oppressors and uses it to frame an antagonistic perspective against the Jewish leaders who opposed Jesus.[25]

There is a deliberate intertextual relationship between the Old Testament and the Gospels since the Evangelists appear to be writing a story that is an extension of Israel's sacred history. However, the connections between the Gospels and other Jewish writings remain fairly superficial. Even the largely biographical books of Jonah and Nehemiah are still somewhat removed from the literary style and narrative construction that we find in the Gospels. Similarities with other forms of Jewish literature are even more tenuous. For instance, *The Lives of the Prophets*, probably written in the first century CE, is rather terse, with some prophets' lives given only a couple lines, and focus resides exclusively on each prophet's birth, a précis of his prophetic work, his death, and his place of burial. Neither do the rabbinic anecdotes of famous sages contain anything the length of the Gospels, nor do they exhibit a chronological structure and theological framework as employed by the Evangelists. That is because no rabbi ever occupied a place in Judaism analogous to the place Jesus holds in Christianity.[26] What is more, just as Jewish literature shows signs of influence from the ancient Near East on their literary forms, so too do the Gospels exhibit influence from the dominant literary culture of the Greco-Roman world on their genre and content.

3. Aretalogy

Shifting to Greco-Roman literary types, some have argued that the Gospels are analogous to aretalogy.[27] Aretalogy is alleged to be a form of Greek biography that provides an account of a "divine man" (θεῖος ἀνήρ) who was an impressive teacher, performed miraculous deeds, and died a heroic death at the hands of the tyrants he opposed.[28]

25. Michael E. Vines, *The Problem of Markan Genre: The Gospel of Mark and the Jewish Novel* (Leiden: Brill, 2002).

26. Philip S. Alexander, "Rabbinic Biography and the Biography of Jesus: A Survey of the Evidence," in *Synoptic Studies*, ed. Tuckett, 40-44; cf. Burridge, *What Are the Gospels?* 19-21.

27. For a brief history of comparison of the Gospels to aretalogies, see Morton Smith, "Prolegomena to a Discussion of Aretalogies, Divine Men, and the Gospels and Jesus," *JBL* 90 (1971): 74-99.

28. Moses Hadad and Morton Smith, *Heroes and Gods: Spiritual Biographies in Antiquity* (New York: Harper & Row, 1965), 3; Helmut Koester, "The Structure and Criteria of

The most noted example of an aretalogy is a work by the Athenian sophist Philostratus, his *Life of Apollonius of Tyana*, written sometime around the 220s CE. In this work, Philostratus describes the career of a first-century Neo-Pythagorean philosopher from Cappadocia, alleged to be based on the memoirs of Apollonius's follower Damis. Apollonius is described as having a miraculous birth, developing philosophical genius from youth, practicing ascetic behavior, traveling to foreign lands like India, discoursing with Roman emperors, speaking wise sayings, reforming cultic practices in various regions, performing miraculous deeds like ridding Ephesus of a plague, experiencing imprisonment, and being assumed into the heavens after his death. Philostratus's biography is largely apologetic and seeks to discount the claim that Apollonius was a magician and instead portrays him as a great philosopher. In later literature, Apollonius is regarded as a pagan antitype to Jesus Christ. Pagan critics of Christianity such as Hierocles and Celsus made comparisons between Jesus and Apollonius in order to deny the uniqueness of Jesus and to urge the superiority of paganism. Justin earlier had noted the similarities between Jesus and legendary demigods and explained them as demonic imitations of Christianity.[29] Others, including Origen, Eusebius, and Lactantius, replied in kind that Philostratus was a populist author of fiction and Apollonius a magician.[30] In any event, it is claimed by some that a juxtaposition of the Gospels of Jesus and the *Life of Apollonius* is really a comparison of aretalogies. Effectively it becomes possible on this account to change "the Gospel of Jesus" to the "the aretalogy of Jesus."

The root of this perspective is that the Gospels are really "cult legends," lacking historical reference and written on the basis of Hellenistic hero motifs.[31] Ascribing the Gospels to the genre of aretalogy is said to explain in literary terms why they present Jesus as the divine hero par excellence. It is even claimed by some that one of the earliest christologies of the early church was a "divine man" christology which focused on Jesus as a divine miracle-worker.[32] According to Helmut Koester: "Gospels in the form of

---

Early Christian Beliefs," in *Trajectories through Early Christianity* (Eugene: Wipf & Stock, 2011 [1971]), 216-19.

29. Justin, *1 Apol.* 21-27.

30. Origen, *Contra Celsum* 6.41; Eusebius, *Contra Hieroclem*; Lactantius, *Divine Institutes* 5.3.

31. Cf., e.g., Bultmann, *History of the Synoptic Tradition*, 371-72.

32. Cf., e.g., Siegfried Schulz, *Die Stunde der Botschaft* (Hamburg: Furche, 1967); Thomas Weeden, *Mark — Traditions in Conflict* (Philadelphia: Fortress, 1971); Dieter Georgi, *The Op-*

aretalogies, such as the miracle sources of Mark and John, proclaim that a particular divine power is present and available in these powerful acts of Jesus. Belief in this 'gospel' implies that the benefits of such miraculous acts are accessible, or even that these acts can be repeated in the religious experience of the believer. Jesus is the 'divine man' (θεῖος ἀνήρ); he can be imitated by his apostle, who thereby incorporates and represents the revelation in his missionary activity."[33] This christology of the divine man was, in Koester's opinion, held by Paul's opponents in 2 Corinthians, simultaneously absorbed and criticized by John and Mark, adopted into the structure of Luke, amplified further in the apostolic preaching of Acts, and continued in apocryphal Gospels such as the infancy Gospels.

In more recent times Lawrence Wills has argued that the Gospels, especially Mark and John, find their generic origins in the "cult of the dead hero."[34] He derives this conclusion from a comparison of Mark and John to the *Life of Aesop*. Wills avers that the Aesop narrative constitutes an aretalogical biography that forms the basis for a hero cult paradigm with devotion given to a deceased hero. Mark and John agree with *Aesop* in genre as an "aretalogical biography — that is, an account of the great deeds of a god or hero — which is attached to the cult, and they develop the same theme of the opposition of the protagonist to his people (and perhaps to his god, or at least his temple), the antagonism that results from opposition, and the resolution of the antagonism through an expiatory death."[35]

The first of many problems with this thesis is that aretalogy is not really a fixed literary genre as much as it is a vague Hellenistic literature form about miracle-working heroes.[36] The mere presence of miracle stories in a biography does not in itself indicate aretalogy, unless one chooses to define aretalogy simply as a biography featuring a collection of miracle stories, which would constitute a hopelessly broad and vague definition.[37] In addition, it is vastly more probable that the miracle stories in the Gospels were influenced by Old Testament narratives about the exploits of Moses and

---

ponents of Paul in Second Corinthians: A Study of Religious Propaganda in Late Antiquity (Philadelphia: Fortress, 1986); Helmut Koester, "One Jesus and Four Primitive Gospels," in *Trajectories through Early Christianity*, 187-93.

33. Koester, "One Jesus and Four Primitive Gospels," 188.

34. Lawrence Wills, *The Quest of the Historical Gospel* (London: Routledge, 1997).

35. Wills, *Quest*, 10.

36. Cf. H. C. Kee, "Aretalogy and Gospel," *JBL* 92 (1973): 402-22; Burridge, *What Are the Gospels?* 18-19.

37. Guelich, "Gospel Genre," 182-83.

Elijah than by stories of Hellenistic divine man figures, given the manifold Old Testament allusions in Gospel miracle stories.

Second, the designation θεῖος ἀνήρ is exceedingly rare in ancient Greek literature and lacks precise definition, and the features of the "divine man" in later antiquity, such as Porphyry's Pythagoras or Philostratus's Apollonius, cannot be confidently traced back to an earlier era.[38] As such, several scholars have convincingly argued that there was no single "divine man" portrait ready and waiting in the wings to be superimposed onto Jesus by the Evangelists. According to David Tiede, the divine man heroes of the third and fourth centuries were not monolithic and could be divided into two categories: miracle-workers and virtuous philosophers.[39] Carl Holladay has demonstrated that the "divine man" can have a huge range of functions and that miracles represent only one tier of them. A divine man can be an "inspired man" or an "extraordinary man" or even a "man related to God." In addition, it is not the case that Hellenistic Jewish Christians would have moved inevitably toward a "divine man" christology, because there was no clear tendency in Hellenistic Jewish literature to amplify the thaumaturgical abilities attributed to Jewish heroes by Jewish authors like Philo, Artapanus, and Josephus.[40] Barry Blackburn concludes that a miracle-working "divine man" is "really a twentieth century abstraction encompassing a wide array of figures, mythical and historical, whose diversity becomes apparent when one analyzes their social roles, the nature of their divinity, and the types and techniques of the miracles or miracle working powers ascribed to them." Furthermore, there is no need to appeal to Hellenistic traditions to account for the portrait of Jesus in Mark, since the representation of Jesus, even with his miraculous deeds, can be accounted for on the basis of a Jewish Christian Palestinian setting.[41] Consequently it would be notoriously naive to expect that the title "Son of God" in early Christian writings from the first century could automatically be read as a cipher for a "divine man" figure.[42]

---

38. Wülfing von Mauritz in *TDNT* 8:339.

39. David Tiede, *Charismatic Figure as Miracle Worker* (Missoula: Scholars, 1972), 289-91.

40. Carl R. Holladay, *Theios Anēr in Hellenistic Judaism: A Critique of the Use of This Category in New Testament Christology* (Missoula: Scholars, 1977).

41. Barry Blackburn, *Theios Anēr and the Markan Miracle Traditions: A Critique of the Theios Anēr Concept as an Interpretive Background of the Miracle Traditions Used by Mark* (WUNT 2.40; Tübingen: Mohr, 1991), 263.

42. Martin Hengel, *The Son of God: The Origin of Christology and the History of Jewish-Hellenistic Religion,* trans. J. Bowden (Philadelphia: Fortress, 1976), 31.

Third, the "divine man" as depicted in Philostratus's account of Apollonius seems to have been deliberately intended and marketed as a pagan rival to the Gospels. So later pagan notions of a "divine man" should be understood in light of the christology of the Gospels, rather than vice-versa.

Fourth, a major problem with Wills's thesis about the influence of the *Life of Aesop* is that, apart from a few episodic parallels (e.g., Aesop and Jesus both have humble origins; Aesop tells fables comparable to Jesus' parables; Aesop and Jesus both experience opposition from the city leaders), the similarities between *Aesop* and the Gospels remain rather superficial. Wills's proposal proves the maxim that partial analogy is hardly grounds for literary genealogy, especially when it comes to genre. In light of those criticisms, it is more likely that the mature shape of aretalogy represents a pagan literary scheme created in response to the widespread dissemination of the Gospels than it does that the Gospels were composed in replication of a recognizable genre of aretalogy with a widely known and well-defined concept of a "divine man" (θεῖος ἀνήρ).

4. Tragedies and Novels

Others have attempted to situate the Gospels in relation to Greek tragedy or ancient novels. Gilbert Bilezikian plotted points of intersection between Aristotle's six criteria for a tragedy in his *Poetics* and the literary form of the Gospels.[43] Mary Ann Tolbert likened Mark to a Greek romance novel.[44] Dennis R. MacDonald believes that Mark is a deliberate imitation of Homeric epics, especially the *Odyssey* and the ending of the *Iliad*.[45]

Again, there is much to commend in a comparison of the Gospels to Greco-Roman novels and tragedies. The Gospels, especially Mark and John, have a dramatic structure that climaxes in tragic circumstances, which naturally evokes empathy in the reader or hearer. I do think it possible that Greco-Roman literary works, such as ancient epics, that were part of the general literary landscape could have shaped the way that traditional material was cast into literary form.[46] One could imagine a Jewish reader from Alexandria com-

---

43. Gilbert Bilezikian, *The Liberated Gospel: A Comparison of the Gospel of Mark and Greek Tragedy* (Grand Rapids: Baker, 1977).

44. Mary Anne Tolbert, *Sowing the Gospel: Mark's World in Literary-History Perspective* (Philadelphia: Fortress, 1996).

45. Dennis R. MacDonald, *The Homeric Epics and the Gospel of Mark* (New Haven: Yale University Press, 2000).

46. Cf., e.g., Marianne Palmer Bonz, *The Past as Legacy: Luke-Acts and Ancient Epic*

paring Mark to the romantic Jewish novella *Joseph and Aseneth*. Or a Greek reader of Mark might be reminded of imagery and themes from Homer. The Evangelists, writing in a prestige language like Greek, were unlikely to have been ignorant of ancient novels, epics, and tragedies.

The chief problem here is appealing to general parallels for the inspiration of a new literary genre. Bilezikian emphasizes the character of Mark as a "passion play" comparable to Greek tragedy, but that hardly accounts for the didactic portions of the Marcan Gospel. MacDonald's Mark-imitating-Homer thesis relies on several superficial parallels. MacDonald infers that once Mark characterized Jesus as one who "suffered much," like Odysseus, he then "found in the epic a reservoir of landscapes, characterizations, type-scenes, and plot devices useful for crafting his narrative." That is a momentous logical and literary leap of faith.[47] Similarly, to think that Mark's naming the two sons of Zebedee "boanerges" or "sons of thunder" based on Homer's two "sons of Zeus," with Zeus being the god of thunder, is an imaginative connection but not a literary one.[48] Things found in Mark might remind readers of Homer, but in the absence of Homeric quotations, there is no reason to think that Mark is modeled after the Homeric epics.[49] So I doubt that the Gospels are religious fictions written up on the back of Homer. We must remember as well, as Burridge reminds us, that the presence of dramatic, comic, and tragic elements in the Gospels does not therefore make the Gospels drama, comedy, or tragedy any more than the presence of parabolic stories in the Gospels makes the Gospels a parable. The dramatic and tragic features of the Gospels are more a mode of presentation than a genre against which the Gospels can be placed.[50]

5. Greco-Roman Biography

An increasing number of scholars have regarded the Gospels as most analogous to Greco-Roman biographies.[51] The genre of "lives" (βίοι or *vitae*)

(Minneapolis: Fortress, 2000), who argues that Luke has shaped his traditional material in light of Virgil's epic works.

47. MacDonald, *Homeric Epics and the Gospel of Mark*, 19.

48. Cf. criticism of MacDonald by Karl Olav Sandnes, "*Imitatio Homeri?* An Appraisal of Dennis R. MacDonald's 'Mimesis Criticism,'" *JBL* 124 (2005): 715-32.

49. Pheme Perkins, *Introduction to the Synoptic Gospels* (Grand Rapids: Eerdmans, 2007), 24.

50. Burridge, *What Are the Gospels?* 239-40.

51. On ancient biography more generally, see Arnaldo Momigliano, *The Development*

emerged in the fifth century CE and was one of the more complex literary forms of antiquity. Subjects ordinarily included political leaders, philosophers, emperors, generals, authors, and orators. Emphasis was placed on the career, virtues, deeds, sayings, instruction, and legacy of the protagonists. Since Friedrich Leo's study in 1901, Greco-Roman biographies have been divided into two groups: (1) peripatetic biography, typified by chronological arrangement with a deliberate posturing by the author about the subject, conducive to a treatment of politicians and generals, and (2) Alexandrian biography, characterized by a topical arrangement, conducive to a treatment of authors and artists.[52] Such a taxonomy of biographies is not a foreign imposition but was recognized by Quintilian, who noted that one could praise a man by a biography written in a "chronological order," while on other occasions it was appropriate to deal with the virtues of a man's life separately or thematically.[53] As to a specific definition of the genre, Aune writes: "Biography may be defined as *a discrete prose narrative devoted exclusively to the portrayal of the whole life of a particular individual perceived as historical.*"[54]

It was primarily in the twentieth century that Greco-Roman biography came to the fore as a possible genre for the Gospels. Johannes Weiss argued that Mark has some features reminiscent of the peripatetic biographies written by Plutarch. Mark, like Plutarch, emphasized a person's deeds as a window into his or her character.[55] Clyde Votaw's famous article, which compared the Gospels with Greco-Roman literature, concluded that the Gospels were a form of propagandistic literature in biographical form. They were not "historical biography" but "popular biography," closest in style to the Socratic tradition of biographies written by Plato and Xenophon.[56]

---

of Greek Biography (Cambridge: Harvard University Press, 1993); M. J. Edwards and Simon Swain, eds., *Portraits: Biographical Representation in Greek and Latin Literature of the Roman Empire* (Oxford: Clarendon, 1997).

52. Friedrich Leo, *Die Griechisch-römische Biographie nach ihrer literischen Form* (Leipzig: Teubner, 1901).

53. Quintilian, *Inst.* 3.7.17.

54. David E. Aune, *The New Testament in Its Literary Environment* (Philadelphia: Westminster, 1987), 29 (italics original).

55. Johannes Weiss, *Das älteste Evangelium. Ein Beitrag zum Verständnis des Markus-Evangeliums und der ältesten evangelischen Überlieferung* (Göttingen: Vandenhoeck & Ruprecht, 1903), 11-15.

56. Clyde H. Votaw, *The Gospels and Contemporary Biographies in the Greco-Roman World* (Philadelphia: Fortress, 1970); repr. from *American Journal of Theology* 19 (1915): 45-73, 217-49.

Bultmann protested at a comparison of the Gospels to Greco-Roman biography. He insisted that unlike ancient biographies the Gospels had no biographical or historical interest and no pretensions about comprising a form of prestige literature. He advocated instead that the Gospels were cult legends that marry the Hellenistic divine man with the Jesus tradition.[57] Bultmann's criticism of attributing a biographical genre to the Gospels was met with a devastating point-by-point refutation by Charles Talbert. Talbert showed that, even granting Bultmann his criteria, cultic and mythic elements can be detected in Greco-Roman biography and are not unique to the Gospels. Moreover, the Gospels can be correlated with specific types of biography. Mark and John belong to that subtype of biography that aims to dispel a false image of a teacher and to provide an authentic model to follow. Luke is a subtype of biography that focuses on the protagonist as a movement founder, with Acts best described as a historical succession narrative about Jesus' disciples. Matthew belongs to the subtype of biography that endeavors to validate the hermeneutical key to a teacher's doctrine.[58]

Several others have followed suit in comparing the Gospels with ancient Greco-Roman biography. Philip L. Shuler advocated that the Gospels were a form of "laudatory biography," similar to the rhetorical form known as an encomium. He detects this especially in Matthew, as Matthew narrates Jesus' birth, message, and death with a view to eliciting praise for Jesus and showing how Jesus is a paradigm for emulation by followers.[59] The encomiastic element of the Gospels was also noted by Klaus Berger, who asserted that the Gospels were much like the *Lives* of philosophers.[60] David Aune has done more than most to situate the New Testament, not least the Gospels, in the wider literary context of the ancient world. His conclusion is that although the Gospels do not correspond to any exact literary form of antiquity, they are most like ancient biographies in their language, structure, and stereotypical presentation of the main character, creating in effect a paradigmatic and propagandistic account of Jesus in biographical form.[61]

---

57. Bultmann, *History of the Synoptic Tradition*, 373-74.

58. Charles H. Talbert, *What Is a Gospel? The Genre of the Canonical Gospels* (Philadelphia: Fortress, 1977).

59. Philip L. Shuler, *A Genre for the Gospels: The Biographical Character of Matthew* (Philadelphia: Fortress, 1982).

60. Klaus Berger, "Hellenistische Gattung im NT," *ANRW* 2.25.2 (1984), 1031-1432 (esp. 1259-64).

61. David E. Aune, "The Problem of the Genre of the Gospels: A Critique of C. H. Talbert's *What Is a Gospel?*" in *Gospel Perspectives 2: Studies of History and Tradition in the Four*

The singularly most successful effort at connecting the Gospels with Greco-Roman biography has come from Richard Burridge. The similarities between the Gospels and Greco-Roman biography are clear, he says, in their structural affinities and shared topics such as the hero's ancestry and birth, anecdotes about his upbringing and debut into public life, accounts of his sayings and deeds, his death, and his legacy.[62] Among the chief similarities are that the Gospels all present the stylized career of a public leader, written in a narrative of medium length, with a chronological framework of his life from birth to death, with some topical inserts and similar subunits of stories and sayings, and exhibiting the same function of honoring the protagonist and defending him from shameful accusations.[63]

Readers might complain that the Gospels do not exactly resemble biographies by Xenophon, Plutarch, and Suetonius. The Gospels are in many ways unique: they have a strong Jewish ambience, their primary content is Jewish Christian teaching and preaching about Jesus, they exhibit signs of a very specific theological worldview, and they engage in an explicit intertextual dialogue with the Old Testament.[64] However, the case for ascribing a biographical genre to the Gospels is enhanced when we remember that ancient biography was a diverse and fluid genre. Greco-Roman biography was a single genre exhibiting great breadth and variety. Adaptation in biography was the norm.[65] Plutarch's parallel lives of great Greeks and Romans

---

Gospels, ed. R. T. France and D. Wenham (Sheffield: Sheffield Academic, 1981), 9-60; idem, *The New Testament in Its Literary Environment* (Philadelphia: Westminster, 1987), 17-76; idem, "The Gospels as Hellenistic Biography," *Mosaic* 20 (1987): 1-10; idem, "Gospels, Literary Genre of," in *The Westminster Dictionary of New Testament and Early Christian Literature and Rhetoric* (Louisville: Westminster John Knox, 2003), 204-6.

62. In this sense, one could argue that Matthew and Luke are more like the biographical genre given their exploration of Jesus' ancestry, birth, childhood, and early life, than are Mark and John, which have no account of Jesus' birth and upbringing.

63. Burridge, *What Are the Gospels?*; idem, "About People, by People, for People: Gospel Genre and Audiences," in *The Gospels for All Christians: Rethinking the Gospel Audiences,* ed. R. Bauckham (Grand Rapids: Eerdmans, 1998), 113-45; idem, "Gospel," in *A Dictionary of Biblical Interpretation,* ed. R. Coggins and J. L. Houlden (London: SCM, 1990), 266-68.

64. Cf. Jonathan T. Pennington, *Reading the Gospels Wisely: A Narrative and Theological Introduction* (Grand Rapids: Baker, 2012), 27-31, for several qualifications to Burridge's thesis. Pennington himself stands between Burridge (Greco-Roman biography) and Collins (eschatological history) on the matter of genre by regarding the Gospels as "eschatological kerygmatic biblical historical biographies" (35). N. T. Wright (*The New Testament and the People of God* [COQG 1; London: SPCK, 1992], 418) says that the Gospels are "a unique combination of Hellenistic biography and Jewish history."

65. Aune, *New Testament in Its Literary Environment,* 32, 46.

epitomizes their character traits, while Suetonius shows an eclectic interest in anecdotes about his subjects.[66] Biography was, according to Burridge, a "diverse and flexible genre, yet still one with a recognizable family resemblance in both form and content."[67] There was considerable cross-pollination among biographical forms, so it is methodologically unsound to link the Gospels with a specific type of ancient biography. The Gospels are a subtype of Greco-Roman biography, marrying the Jewish Christian message of Jesus with a Hellenistic literary form.

Among the diverse biographies of antiquity, the Gospels appear to resonate most closely with "Lives" of great philosophers, especially the Socratic tradition. It is true of course that the Gospels do not present doctrines of a philosophical school or portray Jesus as the founder of a new philosophy.[68] But we must keep in mind that philosophy had a quasi-religious function in the ancient world and that the lives of philosophers were the lives of holy sages. That is why Xenophon, for instance, focuses so much on defending Socrates from accusations that he failed to honor the gods or that he was impious.[69] Given the sacred texture of many biographies of ancient philosophers, it is perfectly plausible for the Evangelist Mark to integrate Jewish prophetic traditions with biographical forms.[70] A recognizable difference is, of course, that the Gospels are not just encomia in praise of Jesus, though they certainly include that, but they are fundamentally apologetic, kerygmatic, and socially formative.

The triumph of the biographical thesis in scholarship for the genre of the Gospels is well stated by Graham Stanton in his preface to the second edition of Burridge's work: "I do not think it is now possible to deny that the Gospels are a sub-set of the broad literary genre of 'lives,' that is, biographies. Even if the evangelists were largely ignorant of the tradition of Greek and Roman 'lives,' that is how the Gospels were received and listened to in the

---

66. Perkins, *Introduction to the Synoptic Gospels*, 9.

67. Burridge, "About People," 121. Cf. similarly Larry Hurtado, *Lord Jesus Christ: Devotion to Jesus in Earliest Christianity* (Grand Rapids: Eerdmans, 2003), 282: "[T]he flexibility of the *bios* genre was such that the authors apparently saw it as a literary form they could successfully adapt in their individual ways to serve the profound, christologically driven, and ecclesiologically orientated concerns that moved them to write."

68. Perkins, *Introduction to the Synoptic Gospels*, 11.

69. The fact that Lucian of Samosata (*Peregrinus* 13) called Jesus a "crucified sophist" is indicative of a perceived connection between Jesus and the lives of other philosophers in the late second century by a pagan author.

70. Vernon K. Robbins, *Jesus the Teacher: A Socio-Rhetorical Interpretation of Mark* (Philadelphia: Fortress, 1984), 53-55, 68; Bryan, *Preface to Mark*, 37-38.

first decades after their composition."[71] The consensus is that the Gospels are broadly a type of biography. We might even call them, as Burridge does, βίοι Ἰησοῦ ("Lives of Jesus"). The next step is to marry them to the phenomenon of their content, production, and usage.

Literary Phenomena of the Gospels

Any attempt to identify the literary genre of the Gospels must take into account their literary phenomena. An examination of various facets of the Gospels — their openings, contents, reception, and media — will go some way toward helping us understand what kind of literature they are. These things we now explore.

1. The "Beginnings" of the Gospels as Clues to Their Literary Form

Despite the fact that all four Gospels lack any kind of biographical title, their opening features — such as genealogy (Matthew), historical preamble (Mark), preface (Luke), and prologue (John) — are all appropriate for an ancient biography.

Mark's incipit creates a type of "evangelical biography" by introducing his life of Jesus with an announcement of "The Beginning of the Gospel of Jesus the Messiah" (Mark 1:1).[72] Moreover, the incipit also heads up Mark's introduction, which runs from 1:1 to 1:15, creating a deliberate *inclusio* based on the appearance of "gospel" in 1:1 and 1:15. Commencing in this manner, Mark frames his opening with his definition of his book in the incipit and his summary of Jesus' message as "proclaiming the gospel of God" in relation to the "kingdom of God."[73]

---

71. Graham Stanton, "Foreword," to Burridge, *What Are the Gospels?* ix.

72. I am assuming here that Mark 1:1 is the author's title for the whole book; see M. Eugene Boring, "Mark 1:1-15 and the Beginning of the Gospels," *Semeia* 52 (1990): 43-82; John G. Cook, *The Structure and Persuasive Power of Mark: A Linguistic Approach* (Atlanta: Scholars, 1995), 138-40, 173; Petr Pokorný, *From the Gospel to the Gospels: History, Theology and Impact of the Biblical Term "Euangelion"* (BZNW 195; Berlin: de Gruyter, 2013), 196-97.

73. Scholars do some incredibly odd things with the noun εὐαγγέλιον in the Gospel of Mark. Adolf von Harnack, "Gospel: History of the Conception in the Earliest Church," in *The Constitution and Law of the Church in the First Two Centuries* (London: Williams & Norgate, 1910), 278-84, was desperate to make Jesus solely the *proclaimer* of the gospel, not its subject,

Mark's incipit could lead an ancient audience to expect next something like a speech in praise of Jesus as Messiah or a record of his great achievements as found in inscriptions to the emperor.[74] Or else, one might anticipate, as per most biographies, something about Jesus' birth, prestigious ancestry, education, and upbringing. Mark has none of these, but then again they are also absent from the anonymous *Life of Secundus*, which includes no reference to its hero's lineage or birth. Mark has other features that are congruent with the biographical tradition. Mark's preamble is an entirely appropriate biographical beginning given the Jewish ambience of his Gospel. Mark's association of "the beginning of the gospel" with Israelite prophecy and John the Baptist's prophetic message in 1:2-8 creates a historical context for his subsequent narrative much in the same way that Tacitus begins his *Histories* with the year of the three emperors (69 CE) and with a brief summary of the mixed fortunes of Rome's preceding 820-year history.[75] Mark's opening sequence, with the baptismal scene, the temptation story, and the beginning of Jesus' Galilean ministry (1:9-15), provides

---

so he took every reference to the εὐαγγέλιον in Mark to designate a gospel proclaimed by Jesus, not a gospel about Jesus. While that holds true enough in Mark 1:14-15, later on the cause of Jesus and the cause of the gospel are one and the same (Mark 8:35; 10:29). Elsewhere the εὐαγγέλιον is connected with Jesus' prophetic word against the temple and with the mission to all nations (Mark 13:10), and news of Jesus' passion is something to be transmitted to others as part of the gospel (Mark 14:9). In direct contrast, Helmut Koester, *Ancient Christian Gospels: Their History and Development* (London: SCM, 1990), 12-14, endeavors to make Jesus solely the *proclaimed* of the gospel by arguing that εὐαγγέλιον in Mark always refers to Jesus' death and resurrection. He argues that the exceptions to this, the uses of εὐαγγέλιον in Mark 1:15b; 8:35; 10:29 for Jesus' message, are interpolations, due to their omission in parallel passages in Matt 4:17; 16:25; 19:29. That allows him to suggest that Mark 1:1, although also a later addition, means no more than that the proclamation of Jesus Christ's death and resurrection began with the preaching of repentance by John the Baptist and by Jesus. The upshot is that the earliest text of Mark witnesses to no tradition that Jesus preached a gospel and that Mark did not think "Gospel" was an appropriate title for his work. However, Koester's textual conjectures are unsupported. Mark was a much neglected Gospel in the first four centuries, and creative copyists would be more likely to interpolate εὐαγγέλιον into Matthew than into Mark, as Matthew was the default Gospel for most of the proto-orthodox churches. Also, it is not certain either that Mark's usage of εὐαγγέλιον is always redactional and strictly Pauline. While adherence to τό εὐαγγέλιον is characteristic of Paul, it is not unique to Paul. At any rate, Mark's sources were probably eclectic and included influences other than Paul, and many do argue for traditional sources behind units like Mark 1:14-15 and 14:9 at a cautious minimum.

74. Perkins, *Introduction to the Synoptic Gospels*, 3.

75. Tacitus, *Historiae* 1.1.1. The *Gospel of the Ebionites* begins (1-2) with reference to the reign of King Herod, the high priest Caiaphas, and the baptism of John, most likely drawn from Luke 1:5; 3:1-3 — a beginning also suitable for an ancient biography.

an appropriate way to introduce Jesus' divine sonship, his prophetic call, and his messianic credentials. These incidents perform the same narrative function as a list of the youthful exploits of the hero in other biographies as they the mark Jesus' debut into public life and show what kind of man he is.[76] As such, the opening sequence of Mark would probably suggest to readers that they are about to read a "life of the sage," though, as the story develops, particularly in the passion story in chapters 14–15, it becomes clear that it is really a "life of the king."[77]

Matthew opens with "The Scroll of the Origins of Jesus the Messiah, Son of David."[78] The change from Mark's is made most likely because Matthew intends to launch into a genealogy about Jesus, a deliberate choice to make Mark's awkward biographical format more acutely biographical since ancestry was a common beginning point in ancient biographies.[79] And I suspect that Matthew thought that Mark's incipit was not a good starting point for moving into a genealogy.[80] In addition, Matthew's opening, also reminiscent of the Old Testament as βίβλος γενέσεως ("scroll of origins"), is right out of Gen 2:4 and 5:1 (LXX), and the Matthean genealogy is littered with heroes from Israel's sacred history. Matthew has thus performed an intensification of Mark's biographical form and brought together Greco-Roman and Jewish literary patterns in the process.

Luke differs from Mark, beginning not with an incipit, but with a preface in Luke 1:1-4. The preface of Luke obviously brings us to the question of genre, and the genre of Luke cannot be studied in isolation from Acts. Given the literary connections between Luke and Acts, especially in the prefaces (Luke 1:1-4 and Acts 1:1-2), some have argued that Luke-Acts constitutes one genre, a type of "general history,"[81] while others identify two distinct genres of biography and historical monograph.[82] Promising is Charles Talbert's claim that Luke-Acts is a succession narrative, espousing

76. Aune, *New Testament in Its Literary Environment*, 48; Collins, *Beginning of the Gospel*, 17; Bryan, *Preface to Mark*, 51-52.

77. Berger, "Hellenistische Gattungen im NT," 1245.

78. On Matthew's introduction, see further Matthew F. Bird, *Jesus Is the Christ: The Messianic Testimony of the Gospels* (Downers Grove: InterVarsity, 2012), 58-60.

79. Cf., e.g., Diogenes Laertius, *Lives of Eminent Philosophers* 3.1-2, 45 (Plato); Plutarch, *Parallel Lives* 2.1-3.2 (Alexander the Great); Suetonius, *Lives of the Caesars* 2.94.1-7 (Augustus).

80. Graham Stanton, *Jesus and Gospel* (Cambridge: Cambridge University Press, 2004), 56.

81. Aune, *New Testament in Its Literary Environment*, 77.

82. Cf. Richard I. Pervo and Mikael C. Parsons, *Rethinking the Unity of Luke and Acts* (Minneapolis: Fortress, 2007), 20-44.

a pattern that provides the life of the founder, a story about his disciples and successors, and a summary of the teachings of the school.[83] We should, however, be mindful that the borders between biography, historiography, and monograph were flexible and blurred.[84] Plutarch even uses the term βίος ("Life") and ἰστορία ("History") interchangeably to describe the same literary activity.[85] More to the point, Luke's preface puts him firmly in line with the classic biographer.[86] The preface operates rhetorically as an *exordium* for his two-volume work. Luke's prefaces also remain remarkably similar to those in Josephus's works and Philo's *Life of Moses*.[87] Luke stands, then, as the pinnacle of the Christian *Life of Jesus* tradition, building on Mark (and I believe Matthew) in improving, not supplanting, his literary predecessors in order to underscore the role of Jesus as a movement founder.[88]

The riddle of the Fourth Gospel is that it is both like and unlike the Synoptic Gospels, and this applies equally so to the question of genre. Still, for all its distinctiveness, such as the discourses, John remains closer to the Synoptics than it does to the *Gospel of Thomas* or the *Pistis Sophia* from the Nag Hammadi codices, since it embarks on a biographical narrative based on historical memories about Jesus. James Dunn says that John composed his Gospel with "greater freedom than we find in the Synoptics, but greater restraint than we find in the Gnostic equivalents."[89] John's aim is to provide testimony to Jesus with a view to awakening and/or affirming faith in Jesus as the Messiah and Son of God (John 20:30-31). John takes over Mark's biographical genre, even if his mode of presentation is more dramatic, even edging into a mixture of Jewish midrash and Greek tragedy.[90] John's prologue, running approximately 1:1-18, is a strange way to begin a biographical

---

83. Charles Talbert, *Reading Acts: A Literary and Theological Commentary on the Acts of the Apostles* (New York: Crossroad, 1997), ix-xxvii; but note criticism in Aune, *New Testament in Its Literary Environment*, 78-79.

84. Burridge, *What Are the Gospels?* 237.

85. Thatcher, "Gospel Genre," 133.

86. Burridge, *What Are the Gospels?* 188.

87. Josephus, *Ant.* 1.1-17; *Against Apion* 1.1-5; 2.1-4; Philo, *De Vita Mosis* 1-4.

88. In this sense, I sharply disagree with Aune's conclusion (*New Testament in Its Literary Environment*, 17) that Luke and Matthew were unimpressed with Mark, simply because they seek positively to emulate him for the most part.

89. James D. G. Dunn, "Let John Be John: A Gospel of Its Time," in *The Gospel and the Gospels*, ed. P. Stuhlmacher (Grand Rapids: Eerdmans, 1991), 322.

90. Cf. Burridge, *What Are the Gospels?* 213-32, 279-81; Warren Carter, *John: Storyteller, Interpreter, Evangelist* (Peabody: Hendrickson, 2006), 4-20.

narrative, and some might think that reason enough to reject the idea of John as a biography. But I am not so sure.

The first section of an ancient biography normally answered two questions about the subject: who is he and where is he from? John does this, though not like the Synoptics, but with his own distinct poem of praise to underscore Jesus' heavenly origins, his divine identity, and his role in creation and new creation. The Johannine prologue also functions much like an operatic overture in providing a summary of the various motifs soon to follow: life, light, witness, glory, Israel, grace, truth, etc. In addition, John introduces the basic plot of his Gospel in the prologue. The Son comes to a hostile world, some reject him, and others receive him. "Thus," as Burridge comments, "despite the divine heights and the cosmic scale of this gospel, the essential storyline is the same: the mission of Jesus, how he was rejected by the Jewish leaders, and accepted by the disciples."[91] Furthermore, by prefacing his narrative with a poem of praise to Jesus, an epideictic device to heighten the prestige of Jesus, the Fourth Evangelist is simply doing what Matthew and Luke also did to Mark: providing further grounds for esteeming the biographical hero by setting Jesus' career into the context of Israel's sacred history. As Morna Hooker writes:

> John's prologue begins and ends with references to the wider narrative: the story he is about to tell has its origins "in the beginning," and it is the crucial turning point in the continuing story of God's dealings with the world which he has made. Within that wider narrative, God's self-revelation to his people Israel is a vital factor; how, then, does the story the evangelist is about to tell relate to the Torah, and to the promises made to Israel? John's answer is that Jesus Christ is the fulfilment of those promises because he is the fulfilment of the Torah itself — the true embodiment of God's self-revelation which was glimpsed by Moses on Sinai.[92]

In sum, it would seem that all four canonical Gospels, in their literary form and openings, are best located in the context of Greco-Roman biography.

---

91. Richard A. Burridge, *Four Gospels, One Jesus? A Symbolic Reading* (2nd ed.; Grand Rapids: Eerdmans, 2005), 137.

92. Morna D. Hooker, "Beginnings and Endings," in *The Written Gospel*, ed. Bockmuehl and Hagner, 188.

2. Designations for Jesus Books in the Early Church

A further indication as to what type of literature the Gospels are can be ascertained by investigating the designations that were used in the early church to refer to the sources of information about Jesus. In many cases, we cannot always neatly determine whether authors are referring to oral Jesus traditions, quoting pre-Gospel written sources, or recalling the Gospels from a text before them or by memory. But the gospel tradition as a whole, in either oral or written forms, comes to be identified with several designations which are worth exploring.

a. Sayings (λόγια)

In Greek usage, λόγια usually refers to short sayings of a religious nature like those given by priests or prophets in pagan temples.[93] In the Septuagint, λόγια is first used with reference to the oracle of Balaam and his revelation from the Lord (Num 24:4, 16 LXX), but elsewhere it is used for divine instruction more generally (e.g., Deut 33:9; Pss 11:7; 17:31; 106:11). In the New Testament, λόγια is used of divine words given to persons in the Old Testament. For example, in Stephen's speech in Acts, Moses received "living oracles" (λόγια ζῶντα) to give to the Israelites (Acts 7:38). One of the advantages of Jewish identity, according to Paul, is that the Jews were entrusted with "the oracles of God" (τὰ λόγια τοῦ θεοῦ) as one of their inherited privileges (Rom 3:2). The writer to the Hebrews opines that his audience still needs to be instructed in the "oracles of God" (λογίων τοῦ θεοῦ) as a way to maturity (Heb 5:12). What that means is ambiguous and it is not clear whether we are to understand λογία as instruction in the Jewish Scriptures with its proto-gospel (4:2) or as a reference to "teaching about Christ" (6:1). Or, having a bet both ways, the "oracles of God" might signify the Jewish Scriptures underlying the audience's new covenant faith. A more explicitly Christian content for λόγια can be found in 1 Peter, where it refers to a speaking-gift used by Christian leaders which is as authoritative as Israel's sacred Scriptures (1 Pet 4:11). Polycarp's letter to the Philippians demonstrates a similar Christian content for λόγια, referring in close succession to "the testimony of the cross" (τὸ μαρτύριον τοῦ σταυροῦ), "the sayings of the Lord" (τὰ λόγια τοῦ κυρίου), and "the word delivered to us from the beginning" (τὸν ἐξ ἀρχῆς ἡμῖν παραδοθέντα λόγον), rounded off with a citation of a saying

93. BDAG, 598.

of the Lord drawn from Matt 26:41.[94] Polycarp's λόγια proves to be the Christian message about Jesus.

For the most part, however, Christian usage of λόγια represented a close integration of Jewish Scriptures and Gospel traditions. In *1 Clement*, written from Rome at the end of the first century, Clement utilizes λόγια to refer to Israel's Scriptures.[95] But he elsewhere presents an interesting collocation of λόγος and λόγια in relation to the Jewish Scriptures and the Jesus tradition. He refers to "the words of the Lord Jesus" (τῶν λόγων τοῦ κυρίου Ἰησοῦ) to introduce an agraphon that is analogous to Matt 5:7; 6:14; 7:1-2, 12 and Luke 6:31, 36-38.[96] This commandment and similar precepts comprise Jesus' "holy words" (ἁγιοπρεπέσι λόγοι) and are to be obeyed because another "holy word" (ὁ ἅγιος λόγος), namely Isa 66:2, says: "Upon whom shall I look, except upon the one who is gentle and quiet and who trembles at my words (τά λόγια)."[97] Here the words of Jesus and the words of Isaiah are placed on par with each other as sacred, divine, and authoritative λόγια.

Among other writers we observe a similar phenomenon where scriptural texts and Gospel traditions are mingled together as part of the Christian λόγια. The second call to repentance in *2 Clement* contains an exhortation for the audience to live righteously before outsiders lest the Lord's name be "blasphemed among all the nations" (Isa 52:5). For even if Gentiles hear from one's mouth "the oracles of God" (τὰ λόγια θεοῦ) and "marvel at their beauty and greatness," if actions are not matched with words, then the Gentiles will denounce the marvel as a myth. A citation of Luke 6:32, 35 is then introduced with the expression "God says" (λέγει ὁ θεός), giving Jesus' words a divine quality and divine authority.[98] The divine oracles here include elements drawn from the Jewish Scriptures, the Christian message, and the words of Jesus as part of a single divine discourse.

Further correlation of Gospel traditions with λόγια reaches as far back as Papias of Hierapolis (ca. 110 CE). According to our sources, Papias had access to oral tradition from the disciples of the Lord such as Aristion and John the Elder[99] and also knew of traditions related to the origins of the Gospels of Mark, Matthew, and John.[100] His usage of λόγια for all that Jesus

---

94. Polycarp, *Philippians* 7.1-2.
95. *1 Clem.* 19.1; 53.1.
96. *1 Clem.* 13.1-2.
97. *1 Clem.* 13.3-4.
98. *2 Clem.* 13.2-4.
99. Papias, *Fragment* 3.2-3, 14.
100. Papias, *Fragment* 3.15-16; 19–20; 21.1-2, 23.

did and said is genuinely illuminating. He wrote a five-volume work called "Expositions of the *Oracles* of the Lord" (ἐπιγέγραπται λογίων κυριακῶν).[101] His exposition was a collection of sayings and stories about Jesus and the Apostles, much of which, as far our limited sources tell us, are not paralleled in the canonical Gospels.[102] Unfortunately we cannot be sure if Papias's material was sourced from oral tradition, written texts, pious invention, secondary orality, or a mix of all of the above.

It is interesting that Papias refers to Mark as Peter's interpreter who recorded Peter's somewhat disordered account of "the Lord's sayings" (κυριακῶν . . . λογίων).[103] About Matthew, Papias says: "Matthew composed the oracles (τά λόγια) in the Hebrew language and each person interpreted them as best he could."[104] Note that for Papias, λόγια is not what Matthew and Mark's Gospels are but what they contain, a collection of Jesus material, to which Papias's own *Exposition* is organically related to in a consciously post-apostolic context.

Moving toward the mid-second century, Justin Martyr noted how Trypho claimed to have read the "doctrines taught by our Savior" (τὰ ὑπ' ἐκείνου τοῦ Σωτῆρος ἡμῶν διδαχθέντα), and Justin presumes to argue by adding to Jesus' "short sayings" (βραχέα λόγια τῶν ἐκείνου λόγια) some "prophetic statements" (προφητικοῖς ἐπιμντσθείς) in order to make his point.[105] Irenaeus declares in his preface to *Against Heresies* that his purpose is to confute the errors of those who falsify "the oracles of the Lord" (τὰ λόγια κυρίου). It appears that he uses λόγια to signify the sacred texts that are revered by believers and yet grossly misused by false teachers. Further to that, Irenaeus assails the unscriptural mode of argument used by the Valentinians, and along the way he places due emphasis on the λόγια as part of a coordinated set with the prophetic word and apostolic message:

> Such, then, is their system, which neither the prophets announced, nor the Lord taught, nor the apostles delivered (Προφῆται ἐκήρυξαν, οὔτε ὁ Κύριος ἐδίδαξεν, οὔτε Ἀπόστολοι παρέδωκαν), but of which they boast

---

101. Papias, *Fragment* 3.1.

102. Cf. Papias, *Fragment* 3.11-12; 14.6-8. Importantly, as Hans von Campenhausen, *The Formation of the Christian Bible*, trans. J. A. Baker (Philadelphia: Fortress, 1972), 134, observed, Papias collected not only sayings about Jesus but anything from the earliest days of the early church that might help in understanding them.

103. Papias, *Fragment* 3.15.

104. Papias, *Fragment* 3.16.

105. Justin, *Dial. Tryph.* 18.1.

that beyond all others they have a perfect knowledge. They gather their views from other sources than the Scriptures (ἐξ ἀγράφων, literally "from unwritten things"); and, to use a common proverb, they strive to weave ropes of sand, while they endeavour to adapt with an air of probability to their own peculiar assertions the parables of the Lord, the sayings of the prophets, and the words of the apostles (παραβολὰς κυριακὰς, ἢ ῥήσεις προφητικὰς, ἢ λόγους ἀποστολικούς), in order that their scheme may not seem altogether without support. In doing so, however, they disregard the order and the connection of the Scriptures (τὴν μὲν τάξιν καὶ τὸν εἱρμὸν τῶν γραφῶν ὑπερβαίνοντες), and so far as in them lies, dismember and destroy the truth. By transferring passages, and dressing them up anew, and making one thing out of another, they succeed in deluding many through their wicked art in adapting the oracles of the Lord (κυριακῶν λογίων) to their opinions. . . . In like manner do these persons patch together old wives' fables, and then endeavour, by violently drawing away from their proper connection words, expressions, and parables whenever found, to adapt the oracles of God (τὰ λόγια τοῦ θεοῦ) to their baseless fictions.[106]

In Irenaeus's mind, it seems that "Scripture" and the "oracles of God" are synonymous. But a subset thereof includes prophetic preaching, the words of Jesus, and the apostolic tradition.

Evidently when many Christian authors spoke about the "oracles of God" (τά λόγια θεοῦ) they had in mind several sacred texts including Israel's Scriptures, the words of Jesus, and in some cases the apostolic writings. The attention given to the "words of the Lord" (τὰ λόγια κυρίου/λογίων κυριακῶν) was a frequent way of referencing the literature that contained Jesus' teaching. At one level, this classification is merely descriptive, in that it describes any writing which contains the words and teachings of Jesus. In many instances, "the words of the Lord" encompasses the content of what we would call "non-canonical" writings like Papias's *Exposition* and even "agrapha" of Jesus from otherwise unknown sources. Where the true words of Jesus could be found, there were the "words of the Lord."[107] But in another sense, for authors like Irenaeus, the classification is more precise, as it

---

106. Irenaeus, *Adv. Haer.* 1.8.1.

107. This explains why many of the church fathers were interested in "other" Gospels, because (1) positively, they may have offered access to authentic words of Jesus, and (2) negatively, they rivaled the Jesus presented in the tetraevangelium, which was regarded as the authoritative account of the "words of the Lord" used in the proto-orthodox churches.

designates those particular Jesus books containing the words of Jesus which constitute a form of sacred literature for Christians since they are thought to be in accordance with Israel's Scriptures and the apostolic teaching (i.e., the *regula fidei*).

b. Memoirs of the Apostles
(ἀπομνημονεύματα τῶν ἀποστόλων)

In chapter 3 we explored the concept of the Gospels as based on social memory, specifically, the living memories of Jesus' followers. Now we point out how the Gospels came to be described as the "memoirs of the Apostles" (ἀπομνημονεύματα τῶν ἀποστόλων) and determine the significance of that designation for the genre of the Gospels.

Papias regarded the Gospel of Mark as based on the teachings of Peter. He considered it rhetorically unpolished because it was based on Peter's anecdotal manner of teaching as Mark remembered it (ἐμνημόνευσεν/ ἀπεμνημόνευσεν).[108] That the Gospel was based on Mark's "memory" of Peter (ἀπομνημονεύματα) and that it lacked literary sophistication, combined with its paratactic and asyndetic style, indicated to many that Mark had composed a "notebook" (ὑπομνήματα), meaning a "rough draft," in the sense of possessing an unfinished feel.[109] Similarly, Eusebius recounts from Clement of Alexandria a story about how Peter's audience in Rome urged Mark to give them a "written statement" (γραφῆς ὑπόμνημα) of the teaching that they had received orally from Peter, which thus became the "Scripture called the Gospel of Mark" (κατὰ Μάρκον εὐαγγελίου γραφῆς). Although Mark's Gospel was essentially Peter's preaching notes, it remained both "Gospel" and "Scripture."[110]

Justin Martyr was probably aware of the Papian tradition that associated Peter with the Gospel of Mark.[111] In any case, Justin's access to Jesus traditions is mostly written rather than oral. He knows of the Gospel as a book, something written and to be read.[112] The "free" nature of his quotations of the Gospels is largely attributable to his employment of "secondary

---

108. Papias, *Fragment* 3.15.

109. Aune, *New Testament in Its Literary Environment,* 66-67.

110. Eusebius, *Hist. Eccl.* 2.15.

111. Justin, *Dial. Tryph.* 106.3, with respect to Mark 3:16-17. The genitive phrase ἀπομνημονεύμασιν αὐτοῦ ("his memoirs") could refer to the memoirs of Peter, Christ, or perhaps Mark.

112. Cf. Justin, *Dial. Tryph.* 10.2; 18.1; 88.3; 2 *Apol.* 3.6;

orality," that is, citing texts from memory or from long-term oral use.[113] His preferred way of referring to the Gospels is as "the memoirs of the Apostles," which he uses over a dozen times (τὰ ἀπομνημονεύματα τῶν ἀποστόλων).[114] By this he means something along the lines of the Apostles' testimony and memory about Christ.[115] The content of these memoirs includes records about Jesus written by the Apostles and "those who followed them,"[116] and he cites principally Matthew and Luke, Mark on one occasion, and very probably John.[117]

Justin calls them "Gospels" three times, twice in close proximity to the "apostolic memoirs," making it clear that he is referencing a written account and not just citing oral traditions. He introduces the words of institution of the Lord's Supper from Luke 22:10 with "For the apostles, in the memoirs composed by them (οἱ γὰρ ἀπόστολοι ἐν τοῖς γενομένοις ὑπ' αὐτῶν), which are called Gospels (ἃ εὐαγγέλια καλεῖται), have thus delivered unto us what was enjoined upon them."[118] When referring to Jesus as the true Israelite, he comments: "Also in the Gospel it is written that he said (ἐν τῷ εὐαγγελίῳ γέγραπται εἰπών): 'All things are delivered unto me by my Father;' ... since we find it recorded in the memoirs of His apostles (ἐν τοῖς ἀπομνημονεύμασι τῶν ἀποστόλων αὐτοῦ) that He is the Son of God."[119] Justin describes his interlocutor Trypho as claiming that "I am aware that your precepts in the so-called Gospel (ἐν τῷ λεγομένῳ εὐαγγελίῳ) are so wonderful and so great, that I suspect no one can keep them; for I have carefully read them."[120]

---

113. Eric Osborne, *Justin Martyr* (Tübingen: Mohr, 1973), 132, argued that as late as 155 CE, "we have to do with oral tradition; but it is not the kind of oral tradition which Köster postulates for the Apostolic Fathers. It is much more a secondary or tertiary growth. Between the original oral and synoptic tradition and Justin's oral tradition stands the written gospels. Oral tradition in Justin in largely the transmission in unwritten form of what had been written in the Synoptic gospels."

114. Justin, *Dial. Tryph.* 100.4; 101.3; 102.5; 103.6, 8; 104.1; 105.1, 5, 6; 106.1, 3; 107.1; *1 Apol.* 66.3; 67.3; cf. 33.5.

115. Justin, *Dial. Tryph.* 88.3; *1 Apol.* 33.5.

116. Justin, *Dial. Tryph.* 103.8; *1 Apol.* 33.5.

117. Charles Hill, "Justin and the New Testament Writings," in *Studia Patristica* 30, ed. D. A. Livingstone (Leuven: Peeters, 1997), 42-48; Joseph Verheyden, "Justin's Text of the Gospels: Another Look at the Citations in *1 Apol.* 15.1-8," in *The Early Text of the New Testament*, ed. C. E. Hill and M. J. Kruger (Oxford: Oxford University Press, 2012), 313-35.

118. Justin, *1 Apol.* 66.3.

119. Justin, *Dial. Tryph.* 100.4.

120. Justin, *Dial. Tryph.* 10.2.

Justin was acquainted with the Socratic tradition. He explicitly cites Plato and Xenophon[121] and could well have known Xenophon's *Memoirs of Socrates*[122] and Plato's Socratic dialogues as they were highly esteemed among the philosophers whom Justin debated. This is hardly unexpected given that many biographies were disseminated widely, not just in the Socratic tradition, but Pythagorean memoirs too, as circulated by the prominent historian Alexander Polyhistor in the middle of the first century in Rome. The philosopher Favorinus of Arelate (d. ca. 160), a friend of Emperor Antoninus Pius, published his own "memoirs" around the same time that Justin was in Rome.[123] By using the term ἀπομνημονεύματα, Justin is the first, as far as we can tell, to liken the Gospels to the biographical tradition.[124] His

121. Cf. Justin, *2 Apol.* 10.5 (Plato's *Apology* for Socrates); 10.8 (Socrates had some knowledge of Christ); 11.2-3 (Xenophon's story of Herakles at the crossroads).

122. Koester, *Ancient Christian Gospels*, 38-39, points out that the Latin designation for Xenophon's biography of Socrates as *Memorabilia* was not used until Johann Lenklau's 1569 edition of Xenophon. Even so, the Greek title for the work, Ξενοφῶντος Σωκράτους ἀπομνημονευμάτων βιβλίον πρῶτον ("First Book of Xenophon's Memoirs of Socrates") was extant in some manuscripts, and such a title, or a source like it, is probably what influenced Justin.

123. David L. Dungan, *A History of the Synoptic Problem: The Canon, the Text, the Composition, and the Interpretation of the Gospels* (ABRL; New York: Doubleday, 1999), 31-32.

124. Koester, *Ancient Christian Gospels*, 37-40, is of the opinion that Justin regarded the written Gospels as a more reliable account of Jesus' words and deeds than extant oral traditions about Jesus. Indeed, in Koester's perception, Justin sought to "replace" the oral Gospel with the written Gospels. Several problems count against this proposal: (1) Justin nowhere delineates a distinction between oral and written accounts of Jesus, so any attempt to regard him as implicitly supplanting a continuing oral tradition with written texts is a mistake. He does not even appear to differentiate authorized and unauthorized accounts of Jesus, and cites "other" Jesus traditions in isolated instances (see *Dial. Tryph.* 47.5; 78.5; 88.3). Justin argues, in fact, that the traditions of sayings and deeds of Jesus found in the "memoirs" are based on what Christ taught and transmitted to his followers, clearly aligning the "memoirs" with oral tradition (*1 Apol.* 4.7; 6.2; 8.3; 65.5; 66.1-3: note the repeated use of παραδίδωμι for "handing over" traditions). (2) Justin appears to know the Papian tradition of Mark's association with Peter in composing his Gospel and yet speaks no ill of the tradents of the tradition (*Dial. Tryph.* 106.3). (3) Koester thinks Justin's designation of the Gospels as "memoirs" was not influenced by the Greco-Roman biographical tradition but derives instead from a view of the Gospels as based on ancient memory, as in Papias. In which case, it is surely odd that Justin is somehow critical of oral tradition, while using a key term from oral tradition, i.e., "memory," to designate the Gospels. (4) Koester thinks that Justin coined the term "memoirs" from Papias, but with a view to eclipsing the "living voice" esteemed by Papias. Equally strange is Koester's claim that Justin was aware of appeals to memory in Gnostic documents like *Apocryphon of James* 2.1-15, but was unaware of the use of "memoirs" by the Second Sophistic. Would Justin have been more likely to have encountered the *Apocryphon of James* than Xenophon's biography of Socrates? Is it not more likely that Justin's use of "memoirs" was influenced by knowledge of the

attempt to approximate the Gospels to another known literary genre is without doubt our best clue to the type of literature the Gospels were perceived as by their early readers. That is not to say that the Gospels are exactly modeled on any particular type of the biographical tradition, but they belonged to the same literary family.[125] I suggest that Justin's equating the Gospels with the biographical memoirs of great philosophers is an apologetic ploy designed to show that Christianity is a genuine philosophy and that Christian accounts of Jesus contained cultural sophistication, but without sophistry.[126]

Justin also regarded the Gospels as a form of sacred literature. Aune is correct to a point when he writes that: "For Justin the Gospels are *apomnēmoneumata* because they preserve the authentic teachings of Jesus, the true master of philosophy."[127] Likewise, Koester's contention is generally valid that "memoirs" designates the Gospels as "true recollections of the apostles, trustworthy and accurate. . . ."[128] But the Gospels are more than that. The Gospels are not simply deposits of apostolic memory but part of a revelatory history in the process of fulfillment. The primary context in which Justin refers to the "memoirs" is in the *Dialogue with Trypho* 97–107 in a systematic exposition of Psalm 22, which is correlated with Gospel material.[129] There the emphasis falls on reference to the fulfillment of scriptural prophecy, pertaining to Jesus' birth, and especially to Jesus' death. Unlike Justin's contemporary Marcion, who tried to drive a wedge between the Jewish Scriptures and the written Gospel, Justin attempted to tighten the con-

---

Jesus tradition as based on apostolic memory and also by the Socratic biographical tradition (so also Dungan, *History of the Synoptic Problem*, 33; Martin Hengel, *The Four Gospels and the One Gospel of Jesus Christ*, trans. J. Bowden [Harrisburg: Trinity, 2000], 212 n. 13)?

125. Note the words of Martin Hengel, *Acts and the History of Earliest Christianity* (Philadelphia: Fortress, 1980), 29: "The ancient reader will probably have been well aware of the differences in style and education, say, between Mark and Xenophon; but he will also have noticed what the gospels had in common with the literature of biographical 'reminiscences' — and unlike the majority of German New Testament scholars today, he did not mind at all regarding the evangelists as authors of biographical reminiscences of Jesus which went back to the disciples of Jesus themselves."

126. Justin calls Christianity "philosophy safe and simple" (*Dial. Tryph.* 8.1), he extols Christians as those "who have lived in accordance with the Divine Reason" (*1 Apol.* 46), and he regards Jesus as a great philosophical teacher by drawing attention to the brevity rather than bombastic nature of Jesus' teaching (*Dial. Tryph.* 18.1; *1 Apol.* 14.4). See Stanton, *Jesus and Gospel*, 103-5; Dungan, *History of the Synoptic Problem*, 32.

127. Aune, *New Testament in Its Literary Environment*, 67.

128. Koester, *Ancient Christian Gospels*, 39-40.

129. Luise Abramowski, "The 'Memoirs of the Apostles' in Justin," in *The Gospel and the Gospels*, ed. P. Stuhlmacher (Grand Rapids: Eerdmans, 1990), 323-25.

nection by tying prophecy to its fulfillment in the Gospels.[130] The appeal to the apostolic memoirs highlights the most theologically significant moments of Jesus' career, including his birth, temptation, and death. Justin locates the content of the Gospels as part of a wider story, the *regula fidei*, writing: "For I have already proved that He was the only-begotten of the Father of all things, being begotten in a peculiar manner Word and Power by Him, and having afterwards become man through the Virgin, as we have learned from the memoirs. . . ."[131] In a significant section of the *First Apology*, Justin introduces twenty-six topically organized sayings of Jesus, claiming that "his word was the power of God" (δύναμις θεοῦ ὁ λόγος αὐτοῦ ἦν).[132] The divine origin of the Apostles' words is emphasized elsewhere, for in the same way that Abraham heard the voice of God, so are Christians those who have "believed God's voice spoken by the apostles of Christ."[133] Time and time again, Justin moves so seamlessly between citing the Jewish Scriptures and citing the Gospels that he clearly puts them on a par.[134] Furthermore, his famous description of Christian worship includes: "And on the day called Sunday, all who live in cities or in the country gather together to one place, and the memoirs of the apostles or the writings of the prophets are read, as long as time permits; then, when the reader has ceased, the president verbally instructs, and exhorts to the imitation of these good things."[135] Some like Koester think that Justin regarded the Gospels as historical documents testifying to Jesus but not actually as "Scripture,"[136] and Stanton cautiously

---

130. Cf. "Whence we become more assured of all the things He taught us, since whatever He beforehand foretold should come to pass, is seen in fact coming to pass; and this is the work of God, to tell of a thing before it happens, and as it was foretold so to show it happening" (*1 Apol.* 12.9-10).

131. Justin, *Dial. Tryph.* 105.1.

132. Justin, *1 Apol.* 14.4.

133. *Dial. Tryph.* 119.6.

134. Cf., e.g., Justin, *1 Apol.* 61–63; *Dial. Tryph.* 18.1; 78.1; 113–14.

135. Justin, *1 Apol.* 67.3-4; cf. Philo, *Hypothetica* 7.13 and synagogue worship in Alexandria.

136. Koester (*Ancient Christian Gospels,* 41-43) proposes that Justin thought of the Gospels as informative "written records," but not "Scripture." On Koester's perspective, the Gospels are testimony to the fulfillment of prophecy, a historical record of the same value as accounts written under Quirinius and Pilate to which Justin also appeals (*1 Apol.* 34.2; 35.9; 48.3). I have three objections: (1) The fact that the Gospels are corroborated with Roman historical accounts does not entail that they are mere historical accounts. (2) As Koester admits, the Gospels are sometimes introduced with the formula γέγραπται (e.g., ἐν τῷ εὐαγγελίῳ γέγραπται εἰπών, "in the Gospel, it is written, saying . . . ," *Dial. Tryph.* 100.1; cf. also 49.5; 105.6), and, taking the perfect tense as aspectually stative, this would indicate an authoritative state of writtenness

surmises that Justin "comes within a whisker" of calling the Gospels "Scripture."[137] I would urge, in contrast, that Justin provides ample evidence for the use of the Gospels in worship, teaching, and theological discourse in connection to Israel's sacred writings, all of which strongly indicates that the Gospels *function* very much as Scripture for the communities that Justin reflects to us.

Justin, then, is among the surest evidence that the Gospels are identifiable with a form of biographical literature, but also that the Gospels were equally regarded as possessing a sacred texture, and quickly became part of the "Scriptures" of the early church.

c. Gospel (ΕΥΑΓΓΕΛΙΟΝ)

We come now to a primary matter on which our regard for the genre of the Gospels depends. When was the title "Gospel" (Εὐαγγέλιον) first given to our four "Jesus books," and what was it meant to signify?[138]

In the manuscript tradition there is a degree of flexibility in the shortening and lengthening of the titles for the Gospels in both superscriptions and subscriptions. One of the earliest attested titles for the Gospels comes from P.[75] (ca. 200 CE) with witnesses to the titles for Luke and John:[139]

ΕΥΑΓΓΕΛΙΟΝ
ΚΑΤΑ
ΛΟΥΚΑΝ

ΕΥΑΓΓΕΛΙΟΝ
ΚΑΤΑ
ΙΩΑΝΗΝ

The evidence from the major codices of the fourth and fifth centuries for the titles is somewhat mixed. Codex Sinaiticus (א) has in all cases a header or

---

that is used for sacred literature. (3) We need to remember that γραφή does not mean "canon" or "Bible," but is an elastic term to designate literature that is religiously significant to its users.

137. Stanton, *Jesus and Gospel*, 105.

138. Necessary reading on this topic is Simon J. Gathercole, "The Titles of the Gospels in the Earliest New Testament Manuscripts," *ZNW* 104 (2013): 33-76.

139. In other contemporary witnesses, P.[66] (ca. 200 CE) has Εὐαγγέλιον κατά [I]ωάννην on a flyleaf title page, while P.[4] (ca. 200 CE) has Εὐαγγέλιον καταμαθ'θιον also on a flyleaf title page.

superscript in the shorter form Κατά + Name, but at the end of each Gospel is a subscription with the longer form of Εὐαγγέλιον κατὰ + Name.[140] In contrast, Codex Vaticanus (B) is the more consistent of the great uncials in its presentation of the titles by consistently using Κατά + Name in both superscriptions and subscriptions. Later codices, fourth to fifth centuries, like Bezae (D), Washingtonianus (W), and Alexandrinus (A), with some minor variations, overwhelmingly prefer the longer form of Εὐαγγέλιον κατὰ + Name in headings, superscriptions, and subscriptions. Despite wider attestation of the longer form, Κατά + Name is preferred in the printed editions NA28 and UBS4, on the basis of being the shorter reading. The upshot is that "*Gospel* according to Matthew" (Εὐαγγέλιον κατὰ Μαθθαῖον), etc., are not regarded by many as the original titles but represent a lengthening of the earlier titles "According to Matthew," "According to Mark," and so forth. On such a view, "Gospel" (Εὐαγγέλιον) was probably added to the titles in the late second or early third century, while B and א preserve the earliest form with the simple Κατά + Name.[141]

While a prevalent opinion is that the earliest title for the Gospels was the short form Κατά + Name, there are also solid reasons as to why the names of the Evangelists were probably not part of the original compositions either.

First, the Gospels are strictly speaking anonymous; there is no direct self-reference to the authors in these works.[142] Accordingly, many scholars regard the Gospel titles as based on a mix of tradition and legend, added to

140. Though א has the longer form in the subscription, except in Matthew, where the subscription is missing.

141. Cf. Aune, *New Testament in Its Literary Environment*, 18: "Since ancient book titles usually consisted of a short title and the author's name in the genitive (at the end of the papyrus roll), the old titles of the Gospels appear unusual. Yet since the Greek preposition *kata* with the accusative can function as a genitive of possession, the titles reflect colloquial usage. The simple two-word titles [e.g., 'According to Mark'] were soon expanded to, for example, 'the Gospel according to Mark,' which should be understood as 'the Gospel *by* Mark.'"

142. The fact that the Gospel of Matthew specifically names Mark's "Levi" as "Matthew" (Mark 2:14/Matt 9:9) is not a substantive argument for Matthean authorship. Attempts to identify Mark as the young man who fled the Garden of Gethsemane naked (Mark 14:52) are speculative. It is true that the author of Luke-Acts may have been a traveling companion of Paul, hence the "we passages" in Acts (e.g., 16:10-17), but there is no explicit evidence that the companion was "Luke the physician," and some regard the "we" passages as narrative device rather than eyewitness report. The identity of the "Beloved Disciple" in the Fourth Gospel has been questioned for centuries, and many believe that the "John" in question was "John the Elder" of Ephesus, not the Apostle "John son of Zebedee."

give the documents apostolic authority, probably at the end of the second century when the fourfold Gospel collection was given its definitive textual form.[143] As will become clear below, I am relatively confident about both the antiquity and authenticity of the names used in the titles, but an honest approach means recognizing that the superscriptions may represent a form of aetiological development.

Second, assuming the received names in our titles, it would have appeared rather self-aggrandizing for Mark and Luke, who were not Apostles, to put their own names in the titles of their work, when their subject was Jesus and their sources were apostolic testimony set in the matrix of corporate memory. Obviously authors, both ancient and modern, are hardly averse to self-promotion through self-titling their works.[144] Still, a book titled something like "According to Mark" remains in some respect odd when the author never writes in the first person, nor is the author a character in the narrative that follows. When Eusebius provides a story about the circumstances of the composition behind the Gospel of Mark, he presents the Roman church as begging Mark to write an account of Jesus. Even so, in the story it remains clear that it is Peter's teaching and not simply Mark's unique version of it that the church wanted. In fact, for our earliest Gospel, Mark, it would have made perfect sense for him to title his work with any number of headings such as "The *Logia* of the Lord," which was a common way of referring to sayings of Jesus as evidenced from Papias and onward; "The Gospel of Peter"[145] if it was really sourced in Peter's reminiscences; "The Life of Jesus" in direct imitation of Greco-Roman biographies; "The Memoirs of the Apostles" as we find in Justin; "The Gospel of our Lord" as the *Didache* arguably regards Matthew as representing;[146] or "The Gospel of the Apostles," which is how Irenaeus describes the sum of the Gospels.[147] So one would not naturally expect a self-named title by John Mark for a book about Jesus based on the memories of Peter when a plethora of other titles might more naturally spring to mind.

Third, if Mark and John were written independently or semi-independently of each other, it would be a rather strange coincidence if

---

143. David Trobisch, *The First Edition of the New Testament* (Oxford: Oxford University Press, 2000), 41-44.

144. In walking through airport bookshops, I am amazed at the number of biographical titles that take the form: Name + "My Story."

145. There is in fact a Gospel named "Gospel of Peter," found in the *Akhmîm Fragment* and known to the early church fathers (Eusebius, *Hist. Eccl.* 3.3.2; 6.12.1-6).

146. *Did.* 15.4.

147. Irenaeus, *Adv. Haer.* 3.11.9 (juxtaposed with the Valentinian "Gospel of Truth").

they both just happened to have titled their Jesus books with the unique and unprecedented headings "According to Mark" and "According to John."

To briefly recap, there are longer and shorter versions of the titles for the Gospels. Many think that the shorter titles are the earliest form. It is also very unlikely that the names of the Evangelists were originally at the head of the documents. However, in contrast to the received scholarly orthodoxy, I want to argue that Εὐαγγέλιον was probably used in the title of the earliest recoverable text of the Gospels and that the attribution of named authors emerged very early in the first collections of the Gospels. In other words, "Gospel according to Mark" is probably the earliest title for the earliest Gospel, but how did we get it?

My starting point is that our earliest witnesses to the titles, namely, P.[4], P.[66], and P.[75], are the ones that read, "Gospel according to John" and "Gospel according to Luke." While these titles might constitute an expansion of a simpler and earlier "According to X" it is equally likely that B and ℵ have abbreviated the longer form. The secondary character of the Gospel titles in B and ℵ is suggested by the observation that the majuscules are a century older than the earliest papyri attesting the longer form. Not only that, but κατά + accusative is not the equivalent to a genitive of authorship but implies, rather, conformity to a type. For instance, some titles for the LXX have "The Old Covenant *according to* the seventy" (ἡ παλαιὰ διαθήκη κατὰ τοὺς ἑβδομήκοντα), and Diodorus refers to Herodotus's work as "The histories *according to* Herodotus" (ἡ καθ' Ἡρόδοτον ἱστορία).[148] A title like κατὰ Μαθθαῖον lacks a literary type against which the author is identified by the preposition, and one must mentally insert one. The "type" in question known from our sources is Εὐαγγέλιον. In which case, κατὰ Μαθθαῖον must assume something like Εὐαγγέλιον κατὰ Μαθθαῖον. Thus, we have text-critical and literary grounds for envisaging the longer title as the earliest.[149]

148. Alfred Plummer, *The Gospel According to St. Luke* (ICC; Edinburgh: Clark, 1896), 1. Gathercole ("Titles," 71) writes: "One might also make the common-sense point that titles such as κατα μαθθαιον and κατα λουκαν would sound like gibberish at least to outsiders, rather as talking of 'the Browning version' (which Browning? version of what?) or 'the Authorised Version' (of what? authorised by whom?) would to those unfamiliar with these short-hands."

149. Cf. David Trobisch (*First Edition of the New Testament*, 126 n. 142): "The short form is not representative for the tradition; in my opinion, it should be interpreted as an editorial characteristic of the Codex Vaticanus and not of the original form." Gathercole ("Titles," 71): "[T]he longer version appears to have been closer to a 'real' title, and the shorter version an abbreviation, rather as scholarly footnotes today first cite a title in full and thereafter abbreviate it." David Aune ("The Meaning of Εὐαγγέλιον in the *Inscriptiones* of the Canonical Gospels," in *Jesus, Gospel Traditions and Paul in the Context of Jewish and Greco-Roman Antiquity: Collected*

Coming now to the origins of the named authors in the titles, for the reasons given earlier, I do not think that Mark himself titled his work "Gospel according to Mark." The book was probably intended initially for local use by Mark and his network of fellow believers, and so no title was needed as its contents and origins were known. However, when the need or opportunity arose to copy the book, to share it with others, or to place it in some private library — what the author and patrons of the project probably well envisaged — it became necessary to add a title to the work. I suggest that at this stage the title "Gospel" was added as a heading to Mark on the basis of his incipit, "The Beginning of the Gospel of Jesus Christ" (Mark 1:1),[150] while the authorial designator "according to Mark" was added later by the scribes who began copying the book based on their local knowledge of the book's origins. The title was taken over by other scribes who knew Mark and also copied Matthew, Luke, and John, where the same format was also used.[151] Certainly, the unique titling was necessary to distinguish each book once two or more of the Gospels began to be collected together, probably sometime around 90-110 CE during the time of Clement, Ignatius, and Papias.

Largely following Martin Hengel, I contend that there is good reason to think that this attribution of names to the Gospels occurred very early, perhaps as early as the last decade of the first century. (1) Papias's statements about the origins of the Gospels in the first years of the second century already identify the Gospels with certain personalities and locations, a tradition probably reaching back into the late first century.[152] (2) Marcion's preference for Luke by the mid-second century presupposes that the third Evangelist was named "Luke" and was regarded as a traveling companion of Paul. (3) Justin refers to "Gospels" in the plural (εὐαγγέλια) as writings derived from the Apostles and their followers, hinting at the names already attributed to these Jesus books. Otherwise, how would he know that some authors were followers of the Apostles?[153] (4) The non-canonical Gospels of the late second century such as the *Gospel of Thomas* and *Gospel of Peter* probably imitated the names already used to label the canonical Gospels. (5) If the Gospels had circulated for a lengthy period of time with no names

---

Essays II [WUNT 303; Tübingen: Mohr, 2013], 24) is similar: "These shorter forms make sense only if they are understood as abbreviations implying the antecedent EYAΓΓΕΛΙΟΝ in a codex containing all four Gospels."

150. Cf. also Trobisch, *First Edition of the New Testament*, 127 n. 146; Aune, "Meaning," 7.

151. Cf. Hengel, *The Johannine Question* (London: SCM, 1989), 75.

152. Papias, *Fragment* 3.5, 15-16; 19; 20; 21.

153. Justin, *Dial. Tryph.* 103.8; *1 Apol.* 66.3; cf. Irenaeus, *Adv. Haer.* 2.22.3; 3.11.7-9.

of authorship ascribed, then one would expect to find a multiplication of titles ascribed to them (as is the case with some of Galen's works), yet there is an absolute uniformity in the authors attributed to the four canonical Gospels. Matthew is always called "Matthew," and Luke is always called "Luke," and so forth. (6) Anonymous works in antiquity were actually quite rare, mainly because buyers would normally only purchase books written by esteemed authors, hence the rise of pseudepigraphy. Tertullian went so far as to say that a Gospel not bearing the name of its author should not be received, because the only Gospels he knew had titles and the single exception of a Gospel without a title was Marcion's mutilated text of Luke.[154]

So while an untitled Jesus book was possible in its original setting where the network of people who used the document already knew its author and the circumstances of its composition, once the document was shared or copied, it would be necessary to label it for ease of use. In a library of scrolls or codices, a collector would need to inscribe a designation of some kind on the document to indicate something of its contents. I suggest that it is in these markings on the verso side of a scroll or on the cover of a codex that the Gospels were first given titles on the basis of the knowledge of copyists concerning the origin of the Gospels.[155] So rather than a "big bang" approach to the titles for the Gospels emerging in the late second century as part of a hefty redaction of the tetraevangelium, I have argued that the titles were probably first used by the end of the first century.

In order to underscore the early recognition of the Gospels precisely as "Gospel," we may now examine the many possible references to "Gospel" as a type of literature known to Christian authors in the first and second centuries. The problem is, of course, that when Christian authors mention an εὐαγγέλιον it is not always clear whether they mean a written document, an oral proclamation, or an authoritative deposit of teaching.[156] I would

154. Tertullian, *Adv. Marc.* 4.2.4.

155. Martin Hengel, *Studies in the Gospel of Mark*, trans. J. Bowden (London: SCM, 1985), 64-85; idem, *Four Gospels*, 48-56; cf. Stanton, *Jesus and Gospel*, 78-79.

156. For texts among the apostolic fathers that identify the εὐαγγέλιον as an oral message, see *1 Clem.* 42.1, 3; 47.1; *Barnabas* 5.9; 8.3; 14.9; Polycarp, *Philippians* 6.3; *Martyrdom of Polycarp* 1.1; 19.1; 22.1. Campenhausen, *Formation*, 129, states: " 'The Gospel', to which appeal is normally made, remains an elastic concept, designating the preaching of Jesus as a whole in the form in which it lives on in church tradition." Similar is Aune ("Meaning," 12), who writes: "Τὸ εὐαγγέλιον in these texts [apostolic fathers] refers to an authoritative complex of traditional teachings and activities of Jesus with an implicit indifference toward the issue of whether this complex was transmitted in oral or written form." See also, with respect to

even suggest that a clear and crisp division between an oral and written εὐαγγέλιον would have been foreign to many.[157] In the first two centuries, εὐαγγέλιον was an elastic concept, designating the preaching about Jesus and the teaching of Jesus, with no specific preference for oral or written media. There are, however, several texts that in various degrees of probability suggest that a reference to a book as a "Gospel" is intended.[158]

The *Didache* is a document containing moral exhortation, instructions on church order, and a brief apocalyptic section. It could be dated anywhere from ca. 70 to 150 CE and in its current form could be a composite document. Debate rages on whether its Jesus traditions derive from independent oral tradition or from dependence on the Synoptic Gospels, especially Matthew and Luke. The *Didache* refers to the εὐαγγέλιον in three places. First, a version of the Lord's Prayer is introduced as, "pray like this, just as the Lord commanded in his Gospel (ἐν τῷ εὐαγγελίῳ αὐτοῦ)."[159] We can hardly expect Jesus' pattern for prayer to be known only from the text of Matthew. Prayers are among the most widely shared types of oral material, so oral tradition might be in play here.[160] However, given the closeness of the

---

Irenaeus, Annette Yoshiko Reed, "ΕΥΑΓΓΕΛΙΟΝ: Orality, Textuality, and the Christian Truth in Ireaneus' *Adversus Haereses*," *VC* 56 (2002): 11-46.

157. We can note how Irenaeus uses both senses of "gospel" as oral and written fluidly (*Adv. Haer.* 3.11; cf. Praef. 3; 3.1.1; 3.11.7). Cf. Origen, *Commentary on John* 1.1-9 on various usages of "gospel."

158. Some scholars (e.g., Koester) think that the "free" or "loose" nature of Jesus' sayings cited in the post-apostolic church indicates that what is cited is oral tradition rather than a Gospel text. However, many of the church fathers were probably citing texts from memory (e.g., Ignatius of Antioch), and there are also many "loose" citations of Old Testament texts in the church fathers, yet we would never propose that such citations are due to Hebrew oral tradition when the Old Testament was undoubtedly a fixed written document in the patristic era (see John Barton, *Holy Writings, Sacred Scripture: The Canon in Early Christianity* [Louisville: Westminster John Knox, 1997], 92). Charles Hill, "The Debate over the Muratorian Fragment and the Development of the Canon," *WTJ* 57 (1995): 442-44, undertakes an amusing exercise where he gives similar summaries from Gamble and Hahneman about the nature of oral tradition in the apostolic fathers, obviously dependent on Koester, and facetiously asks questions such as whether Hahneman borrowed from Gamble, whether Hahneman and Gamble derived their material from the same oral lecture, if they used an *Ur-kanonsgeschichtebuch*, and even whether Hahneman and Gamble are in fact the same person!

159. *Did.* 8.2.

160. Cf. Koester, *Synoptische Überlieferung bei den apostolischen Vätern* (Berlin: Akademie, 1957), 103-9; idem, *Ancient Christian Gospels*, 16; idem, *From Jesus to the Gospels: Interpreting the New Testament in Its Context* (Minneapolis: Fortress, 2007), 62-63; Gundry, "ΕΥΑΓΓΕΛΙΟΝ: How Soon a Book?" *JBL* 115 (1996): 322-23; Stephen E. Young, *Jesus Tradition*

Didache's version of the Lord's Prayer to Matthew's — and the affinity of the *Didache* with Matthew in general — [161] it is very probable that there is dependence on the Gospel of Matthew or a Matthean-like text, a text explicitly designated as εὐαγγέλιον as the source of the prayer.[162] Second, concerning itinerant apostles and prophets, the *Didache* urges that they be treated "in accordance with the rule of the Gospel" (κατὰ τὸ δόγμα ὑμᾶς εὐαγγελίου), which is largely reminiscent of the Matthean mission discourse.[163] Third, with regard to community life, the author urges the audience to "correct one another not in anger but in peace, as you find in the Gospel" (ὡς ἔχετε ἐν τῷ εὐαγγελίῳ), and prayer and mercy should be undertaken "just as you find it in the Gospel of our Lord" (ὡς ἔχετε ἐν τῷ εὐαγγελίῳ τοῦ κυρίου ἡμῶν), material that appears to allude to Matthean exhortation to intra-community relations.[164] While the first appearance of εὐαγγέλιον is admittedly ambiguous as to whether its source was oral or textual,[165] the second and third are very likely to be based on the Gospel of Matthew, given their allusions to distinctively Matthean material.[166] The author writes from a time when the words of Jesus have been located under the aegis of an εὐαγγέλιον, and that could only occur after the textualization of the Jesus tradition and its inclusion in a document known as εὐαγγέλιον. Further to that, the general

---

in the Apostolic Fathers: Their Explicit Appeals to the Words of Jesus in Light of Orality Studies (WUNT 2.311; Tübingen: Mohr, 2011), 219-21.

161. Cf. esp. Christopher M. Tuckett, "Synoptic Tradition in the Didache," in *The New Testament in Early Christianity*, ed. J.-M. Sevrin (Leuven: Peeters, 1989), 173-230; idem, "The Didache and the Writings That Later Formed the New Testament," in *The Reception of the New Testament in the Apostolic Fathers*, ed. C. Tuckett and A. Gregory (Oxford: Oxford University Press, 2005), 83-127; but see a recent alternative in Huub van de Sandt, "Matthew and the Didache," in *Matthew and His Christian Contemporaries*, ed. D. C. Sim and B. Repschinski (LNTS 333; London: Clark, 2008), 123-38.

162. Cf. Harnack, "Gospel," 313; Edouard Massoux, *The Influence of the Gospel of Saint Matthew on Christian Literature before Saint Irenaeus* (2 vols.; trans. A. J. Bellinzoni and N. J. Belval; Macon: Mercer University Press, 1990), 3.145, 155; Stanton, *Jesus and Gospel*, 55, 79; James A. Kelhoffer, "'How Soon a Book' Revisited: EYAΓΓΕΛΙΟΝ as a Reference to 'Gospel' Materials in the First Half of the Second Century," *ZNW* 95 (2004): 17-22; Tuckett, "The Didache and the Writings That Later Formed the New Testament," in *Reception of the New Testament in the Apostolic Fathers*, ed. Tuckett and Gregory, 104-5; Murray J. Smith, "The Gospels in Early Christian Literature," in *The Content and Setting of the Gospel Tradition*, ed. Mark Harding and Alanna Nobbs (Grand Rapids: Eerdmans, 2010), 186.

163. *Did.* 11.3; Matt 10:5-13, 40-41; cf. Luke 11:49.

164. *Did.* 15.3-4; cf. Matt 5:22; 6:1-6; 18:15-17.

165. *Did.* 8.2.

166. *Did.* 11.3; 15.3-4.

Matthean character of the sayings would suggest that it is either Matthew or a Matthew-like text that is being cited as εὐαγγέλιον. The author also presumes that the audience possesses and knows the εὐαγγέλιον that he is referring to and knows it as a written document.[167]

Ignatius of Antioch (d. ca. 110 CE), the martyr-bishop, wrote several letters to Christian congregations en route to his execution in Rome, making notable mention of εὐαγγέλιον in these texts.[168] In one case, he appears to refer to εὐαγγέλιον as an oral proclamation. Writing to the Philadelphians, the bishop claimed to have taken refuge in the "gospel as the flesh of Jesus." He professes love for the prophets because they "anticipated the gospel in their preaching and set their hope on him and waited for him" to the point that they are "included in the gospel of our shared hope."[169] Ignatius's "gospel" here is a preached message that accords with the preaching of the prophets. Elsewhere, however, he describes the εὐαγγέλιον in terms that make it probable that a written document is intended.[170]

Ignatius also urges the Philadelphians not to be contentious about Jewish matters and to act instead in accordance with "the teaching of Christ" (κατὰ Χριστομαθίαν).[171] The neologism Χριστομαθίαν can be rendered loosely as "Christ's way of discipleship," an apt summary of the Gospel of

---

167. In order to avoid this conclusion, Koester (*Synoptische Überlieferung*, 10-11; *Ancient Christian Gospels*, 17; *From Jesus to the Gospels*, 63) is forced to plead that even if a written document is alluded to in *Did.* 15.3-4 (and in 11.3), it is not necessarily a Gospel that is cited, but simply Gospel-like traditions in written form. He also believes that the designation εὐαγγέλιον is not original and was added by a later redactor to identify the Jesus material designated here as deriving specifically from the "Gospel." But Koester fails to recognize the allusion and echo of material from Matthew that is found in these passages, and there is no evidence internally or externally to suggest that εὐαγγέλιον is an interpolation in *Did.* 11.3; 15.3-4.

168. We have to remember that Ignatius was unlikely to have had a copy of the Gospels with him en route to Rome, nor was he concerned to make his sources known to his readers. Thus his many allusions to and echoes of the Gospels were based on either memory or a secondary orality. The inexactness of his replication of Synoptic material does not rule out his knowledge of them as literary sources. On Ignatius and the Gospels, see further Paul Foster, "The Epistles of Ignatius of Antioch and the Writings That Later Formed the New Testament," in *Reception of the New Testament in the Apostolic Fathers*, ed. Gregory and Tuckett, 173-84.

169. Ignatius, *Phild.* 5.1-2.

170. Cf. Hengel, *Four Gospels*, 64, 134, 248 n. 247; Stanton, *Jesus and Gospel*, 55, 79; Charles E. Hill, "Ignatius, 'the Gospel,' and the Gospels," in *Trajectories through the New Testament and the Apostolic Fathers*, ed. A. Gregory and C. Tuckett (Oxford: Oxford University Press, 2005), 267-85; Smith, "Gospels in Early Christian Literature," 186-87.

171. Ignatius, *Phild.* 8.2; cf. *Magn.* 13.1: "Be eager, therefore, to be firmly grounded in the precepts of the Lord (δόγμασιν τοῦ κυρίου) and the apostles. . . ."

Matthew validated by the significant number of allusions to and echoes of Matthew in the Ignatian corpus.[172] Following that, when some are purported to have said that unless they find something "in the archives" (ἐν τοῖς ἀρχείοις) of the Jewish Scriptures, they will not believe it "in the Gospel" (ἐν τῷ εὐαγγελίῳ), Ignatius appears to be contrasting two sets of written documents as deposits of a community's faith. According to Michael Goulder, Ignatius refers to "a written εὐαγγέλιον to balance the written ἀρχεία."[173] Ignatius's argument at this point is opaque. He seems to emphasize that the gospel is indeed "written" in Christian sources (γέγραπται), but, rather than enter a hermeneutical row that plays off the Jewish ἀρχεία against the Christian εὐαγγέλιον, he short-circuits the debate by declaring that his "archives" are Jesus Christ and that the "unalterable archives are his cross and death and his resurrection and the faith that comes through him."[174] Though Ignatius does not cite a text per se, these are the subjects of the Gospels and could be regarded as a salient summary of their contents, found presumably in the same place as "the teaching of Christ" mentioned a few lines earlier.[175]

In the developing argument of the same letter, Ignatius argues for the distinctive and superior nature of εὐαγγέλιον over the former Jewish dispensation.[176] The εὐαγγέλιον pertains to "the coming of the Saviour, our Lord Jesus Christ, his suffering, and the resurrection." The fact that he mentions Jesus' coming (τὴν παρουσίαν) implies that Ignatius has an outline of Jesus' career in mind as part of the εὐαγγέλιον, confirmed by his use elsewhere of creedal summaries that encompass Jesus' birth and baptism as well as his death and resurrection.[177] These were not supplemental topics to the kerygma of Jesus' death and resurrection but constituent parts of the εὐαγγέλιον understood as the story of Jesus that Ignatius knew in both oral and written forms.[178] Ignatius next softens the contrast between Judaism and Christianity by noting that the prophets preached

---

172. Cf. Ignatius, *Smyrn.* 1.1 (= Matt 3:15); 6.1 (= Matt 19.12); *Trall.* 11.1, *Phild.* 3.1 (= Matt 15:13); *Polycarp* 1.2-3 (= Matt 8:17); 2.2 (= Matt 10:16); *Magn.* 9.1 (= Matt 23:8); *Eph.* 5.2 (= Matt. 18:19-20); 6.1 (= Matt 10:40); 14.2 (= Matt 12:33).

173. Michael Goulder, "Ignatius' 'Docetists,'" *VC* 53 (1999): 17.

174. Ignatius, *Phild.* 8.2.

175. Cf. Hill, "Ignatius," 273. I would add that Ignatius's logic appears to be something like this: (1) Jesus Christ is the true "archive"; (2) Jesus Christ is the subject of the Gospels; therefore (3) the Gospels, by virtue of setting forth Christ, hold the same authority as the "archive" of the Jewish Scriptures.

176. Ignatius, *Phild.* 9.1-2.

177. Cf. Ignatius, *Eph.* 18.2; *Smyrn.* 1.1-2; *Trall.* 9.1-2.

178. Contra Koester, *Ancient Christian Gospels,* 7; idem, *From Jesus to the Gospels,* 57-58.

in anticipation of Jesus, but the εὐαγγέλιον remains an "imperishable finished work."[179] In his letter to the Philadelphians, Ignatius thus sets out the εὐαγγέλιον as a type of written archive, embodying the message about Jesus, eclipsing the prophets in some regard, and encompassing Jesus' life, death, and resurrection.

Ignatius's letter to the Smyrnaeans is slightly more lucid on this account with its reference to εὐαγγέλιον as a Jesus book. The letter opens with a creedal summary that includes a clear Mattheanism with Jesus baptized by John "in order to fulfill all righteousness," meaning that Ignatius knew the text of Matthew and not simply the Jesus tradition (though by what route is admittedly an open question).[180] He might also know of Luke's Gospel given the inclusion of the words of the risen Jesus in a saying close to Luke 24:39.[181] Thus, when describing what unbelievers are not persuaded by, Ignatius sets the εὐαγγέλιον as coordinate to the prophets and the law of Moses in a triplet of written documents.[182] That is confirmed by what he says later, when he urges the Smyrnaeans to "pay attention to the prophets and especially to the Gospel (τοῖς προφήταις, ἐξαιρέτως δὲ τῷ εὐαγγελίῳ) in which the passion has been made clear to us and the resurrection has been accomplished."[183] He envisages a study of written documents that, through their textual interconnectedness, expound and clarify Jesus' death and resurrection.[184] One of these documents he knows as a "Gospel."[185]

Second Clement is a sermon composed by an anonymous presbyter to a Gentile congregation probably in Corinth. Dating the document has proved

179. Ignatius, *Phild.* 9.2.

180. Ignatius, *Smyrn.* 1.1 (= Matt 3:15). See the brief but sober discussion in Foster, "Ignatius of Antioch," 174-76. Another significant Mattheanism is where Ignatius calls Jesus "our only teacher" (*Magn.* 9.1), a clear allusion to Matt 23:8 not discussed by Foster.

181. Ignatius, *Smyrn.* 3.2.

182. Ignatius, *Smyrn.* 5.1.

183. Ignatius, *Smyrn.* 7.2.

184. Hill ("Ignatius," 269) shows that Ignatius consistently places "Gospel" in a sequence with other written documents called the apostles, prophets/prophecies, and the law of Moses.

185. Contra Helmut Koester (*Synoptische Überlieferung*, 6-10; *Ancient Christian Gospels*, 7-8; *From Jesus to the Gospels*, 57-58) and Charles Thomas Brown (*The Gospel and Ignatius of Antioch* [SBL 12; New York: Lang, 2000]) it is impossible that for Ignatius the εὐαγγέλιον is simply a Paulinesque preached message of salvation with no tangible connections to the canonical Gospels. References to Jesus' birth, his life under Herod and Pilate, his "coming," and his status as teacher, descriptions of his "teachings," and the various allusions to and echoes of Gospel texts in the Ignatian corpus provide a solid cache of evidence for Ignatius's knowledge of the Synoptics, probably Matthew. Ignatius is no less Pauline for that fact. He is, indeed, Pauline with a Matthean slant.

notoriously difficult, but a date in the first half of the second century has proved to be the most popular position.[186] The author works with several texts, principally Isaiah and Ezekiel, and he very probably knows Matthew and Luke as well.[187] Ps.-Clement (as we can call the sermon's author) refers to several sayings of Jesus, some of which are not fully identical to Synoptic sayings and may come from other sources.[188] One particular saying is attributed to the Lord "in the εὐαγγέλιον." The author urges his audience to purity by appealing to a saying given in 2 *Clem.* 8.5: "For the Lord says in the Gospel (λέγει γὰρ ὁ κύριος ἐν τῷ εὐαγγελίῳ): 'If you did not guard something small, who will give you something great? For I say to you, whoever is faithful with very little is also faithful with much.'" While some take this to be an independent logion stemming from oral tradition,[189] it more likely comprises an expansive rendering of Luke 16:10-11, given the identical wording in part of the saying (ὁ πιστὸς ἐν ἐλαχίστῳ καὶ ἐν πολλῷ πιστός ἐστιν). That Ps.-Clement uses εὐαγγέλιον for a book is confirmed when he quotes Synoptic material (Matt 8:32/Mark 2:17/Luke 5:32) and calls it "Scripture" (γραφή) on par with a quotation from Isa 54:1 mentioned a few verses earlier.[190] Also, when arguing about the living church as the body of Christ, appeal is made to "the books and the Apostles" (τὰ βιβλία καὶ οἱ ἀπόστολοι) who declare such things.[191] The "books

---

186. Kelhoffer, "ΕΥΑΓΓΕΛΙΟΝ as a Reference to 'Gospel,'" 15-16, dates 2 *Clement* to the second quarter of the second century and notes that εὐαγγέλιον is used in a context devoid of debate about authoritative writings or canon, making it independent of and prior to Marcion.

187. Andrew F. Gregory and Christopher M. Tuckett, "2 *Clement* and the Writings That Later Formed the New Testament," in *Reception of the New Testament in the Apostolic Fathers*, ed. Gregory and Tuckett, 252-78. Even Koester (*Ancient Christian Gospels*, 18) affirms that "Several of the sayings of Jesus quoted in 2 *Clement* indeed reveal features which derive from the redactional activities of the authors of Matthew and Luke." That of course leads him to date 2 *Clement* after Marcion because the harmonizing collection on which the Jesus sayings in 2 *Clement* are drawn can only have been assembled after Gospel collections had been formed and Jesus books had been called "Gospel," a designation that Marcion was allegedly the first to undertake. The problem is, however, that such harmonizing collections bringing together more than one Gospel came into being in the first half the second century, as evidenced by the longer ending of Mark (16:9-20), the *Epistula Apostolorum*, and perhaps even John 21 (see Kelhoffer, "ΕΥΑΓΓΕΛΙΟΝ as a Reference to 'Gospel,'" 10-13).

188. 2 *Clem.* 3.2 (= Matt 10:32); 4.2 (= Matt 7:21); 6.1 (= Luke 16:13); 9.11 (= Mark 3:35); 12.2 (= *Gospel of Thomas* 22 and *Gospel of the Egyptians* according to Clement of Alexandria, *Strom.* 3.13.92).

189. Gundry, "ΕΥΑΓΓΕΛΙΟΝ," 324.

190. 2 *Clem.* 2.4.

191. 2 *Clem.* 14.2.

and Apostles" may mean the Jesus books (i.e., Gospels) and apostolic writings (i.e., the New Testament epistles).[192]

The Gnostic teacher Basilides was active in Alexandria ca. 120-60 CE and may have had an influence on Valentinus before the latter came to Rome sometime between 136 and 140. Basilides composed a twenty-four-volume *Exegetica* as a commentary on "the Gospel" (τό εὐαγγέλιον), and Origen knows of a "Gospel according to Basilides" (κατὰ βασιλείδην εὐαγγέλιον).[193] Basilides was writing at a time roughly concurrent with Papias and Ignatius. Indeed, his *Exegetica* may belong to a genre similar to that of Papias's *Logia* as a multivolume effort to exposit sayings of Jesus with added commentary. His adaptation of the title εὐαγγέλιον for his work probably rests on imitation of other Jesus books that he had access to.

It is at the feet of Marcion that many lay the responsibility for designating a Jesus book as εὐαγγέλιον. Marcion came to Rome from Pontus sometime around 140, and his project was to launch a reformation of the Christian faith by returning the church to its Pauline roots and extricating it from Judaizing corruptions. His role in influencing both the text and canon of the New Testament has been much debated since the mid-nineteenth century. He understood those passages where Paul spoke of "my gospel" (e.g., Rom 2:16; 16:25; 2 Cor 4:3) to refer to one particular Jesus book, namely that of Luke, which was allegedly at the Apostle's disposal.[194] According to Campenhausen, Marcion selected the Gospel of Luke as his preferred Gospel, not because it was from "Luke," a traveling companion of Paul, but simply because it was the least problematic and the most conducive to Marcion's conception of the original gospel.[195] Marcion provided no attribution to his Gospel, the corrected text of Luke, but described it simply as "Gospel." He was allegedly the first to label a Jesus book with such a designation.[196] Koester concurs with this assessment that Marcion "introduces this novel

192. Cf. further discussion on 2 *Clement* in Kelhoffer, "ΕΥΑΓΓΕΛΙΟΝ as a Reference to 'Gospel,'" 5-16.

193. Clement, *Strom.* 4.81.1-83.1; Eusebius, *Hist. Eccl.* 4.7.7 (from Agrippa Castor); Origen, *Commentary on Luke* 1.1; cf. Irenaeus, *Adv. Haer.* 1.23.3-7.

194. Cf. Origen, *Commentary on John* 5.7; Tertullian, *Adv. Marc.* 3.5.4; 4.2-4; *Muratorian Fragment* 4-5; cf. Eusebius, *Hist. Eccl.* 3.4.6-7, which assumes a similar correlation of "my Gospel" with "Luke."

195. Sebastian Moll, *The Arch-Heretic Marcion* (WUNT 250; Tübingen: Mohr, 2010), 90: "It seems more likely that Marcion, using only one Gospel, simply saw no need to attribute an author's name to it since he did not have to distinguish it from others."

196. Campenhausen, *Formation*, 157-60, 170-77.

usage [of εὐαγγέλιον] in conscious protest against the still undefined and mostly oral traditions to which the churches of his day referred as their dominical and apostolic authority."[197]

It seems grossly unlikely that Marcion was the first to call a Jesus book an εὐαγγέλιον for a number of reasons. First, we have already seen widespread attestation of Jesus traditions in their written form going under the heading εὐαγγέλιον in the *Didache,* Ignatius, and 2 *Clement.* That is not to assume that all Jesus literature referred to as εὐαγγέλιον was identical to the canonical four Gospels — quotations of agrapha rule this out. Nonetheless, citations of and allusions to passages known to be found in the four Gospels, when explicitly said to be part of the εὐαγγέλιον, strongly suggest that one or more Gospels were known as εὐαγγέλιον prior to Marcion. If we add to that the early traditions about the names of the Evangelists attached to particular Gospels, which are as early as Papias, then we have good reasons to infer that designations approximating to "Gospel according to Matthew" or "Gospel according to Luke" were used as titles before Marcion came on the scene. In fact, this explains why Marcion chose Luke, since Luke was known to be a traveling companion of Paul, even if Marcion thought that Luke had adulterated Paul's gospel.

Second, although Marcion was excommunicated by the Roman church ca. 144, he remained active in Rome and promoted his Marcionite Gospel, quite effectively it would seem since Marcionite churches spread widely and endured for some time.[198] However, by 150, two other significant Christian teachers were also leading schools in Rome, and their teachings differed markedly from Marcion's version of the Christian faith, the two teachers being Valentinus and Justin.

The Valentinians were opposed to many teachings of both Marcion and the proto-orthodox, as evidenced by Ptolemy's *Letter to Flora* written in the 150s.[199] The Valentinians also produced their own Gospels. According to Irenaeus, the Valentinians had a "Gospel of Truth" (ἀληθείας εὐαγγέλιον, *veritatis Evangelium*),[200] and this document could well be genetically related

---

197. Koester, *Ancient Christian Gospels,* 36.

198. Justin, *1 Apol.* 26.5; 58.1; *Dial. Tryph.* 35.6 (?); Tertullian, *Adv. Marc.* 1.19; Epiphanius, *Panarion* 42.1.1. As late as the fifth century, a Syrian bishop boasted about the conversion of eight Marcionite villages to the true faith: see Marco Frenschkowski, "Marcion in arabischen Quellen," in *Marcion und seine kirchengeschichtliche Wirkung,* ed. G. May and K. Greschat (Berlin: de Gruyter, 2002), 39-63.

199. Cf. esp. Ptolemy, *Letter to Flora* 2 (= Epiphanius, *Against Heresies* 33.3.1-33.7.10).

200. Irenaeus, *Adv. Haer.* 3.11.9. *Muratorian Fragment* 81 also rejects the writings of Valentinus.

to the "Gospel of Truth" in the Nag Hammadi codices.[201] It is unlikely, however, that the Valentinian *Gospel of Truth* was titled in imitation of Marcion. The impression one gets from Irenaeus is that it was intended as a kind of supplement to the other Gospels. That makes sense since the Valentians used what was basically the proto-orthodox canon. Valentinius's sermon *On Friends* refers to how non-Christian wisdom can be found in "the writings of God's church," an affirmation of some corpus of Christian writings.[202] There are also quotations from Matthew and John that run throughout Ptolemy's *Letter to Flora*.[203] Irenaeus sets the Valentinian "Gospel of Truth" in opposition to the "Gospel of the Apostles," not to the "Gospel" of Marcion. He sees it as a challenge to the proto-orthodox church, not to the Marcionite churches. The Valentinian "Gospel of Truth" probably took over its title from the names of the four Gospels, which were already in circulation in Rome. Justin knew about Marcion and his theology.[204] Clearly for Justin the apostolic "memoirs" are the same as the apostolic "Gospel." He refers explicitly to "the Gospel" three times, once in the plural, with no apologetic indication that he has taken over the term from Marcion.[205] All in all, the existence of Jesus books known as εὐαγγέλια in mid-second century Rome does not appear to be dependent on Marcion.

Looking toward the non-canonical Gospels, we find further evidence for a relatively early date for the canonical Gospels being labeled as εὐαγγέλια. The various other Gospels composed in the second century such as the *Gospel of Thomas, Gospel of Peter, Gospel of Judas,* and *Gospel according to the Hebrews* were at some point in their textual transmission probably titled in imitation of the four canonical Gospels. Finally, we might add that Irenaeus and the Muratorian fragment also know of the canonical four named as Gospels and attached to certain apostles or apostolic companions.[206] Combined with our earliest manuscript evidence

---

201. Though the *Gospel of Truth* in the NHC is not titled as such, modern authors infer this title from the opening line ("The gospel of truth is a joy for those who have received grace from the father of truth") and the general Valentinian ambience of the document. Also in the NHC, the *Gospel of Philip* is another document potentially of Valentinian stock (see Epiphanius, *Panarion* 26.12.2-3).

202. Clement, *Strom.* 6.52.3-4 (fragment G in Bentley Layton, *The Gnostic Scriptures: A New Translation with Annotations and Introductions* [London: SCM, 1987], 243).

203. Layton, *Gnostic Scriptures*, xxiii.

204. Justin, *1 Apol* 26.5; 58.1; *Dial. Tryph.* 35.6.

205. Justin, *1 Apol.* 66.3; *Dial. Tryph.* 10.2; 100.1.

206. *Muratorian Fragment* 2, 9, 17; Irenaeus, *Adv. Haer.* 3.1.1.

for the Gospel titles in the late second century (P.[75], P.[66]) we can effectively put a ceiling on evidence for Jesus books labeled as εὐαγγέλιον by 180 CE at the latest.

We have surveyed evidence from the *Didache* (70-150 CE), Ignatius of Antioch (ca. 110), *2 Clement* (ca. 125-50), Basilides (120-60), Marcion (140), and Justin Martyr (150-60), briefly noted several late second-century literary artifacts, and seen that εὐαγγέλιον referred to a written document beginning early in the second century.[207]

Truth be told, this should be entirely unsurprising. The εὐαγγέλιον of the earliest church was a story about the salvation that comes through Jesus as the fulfillment of Israel's Scriptures. The story began with his birth and baptism and ended in his redemptive death and glorious resurrection. The shift in medium from oral to written was a natural and necessary progression for the continued promulgation of the εὐαγγέλιον and for its augmentation with further biographical and didactic material about Jesus. This is why no one was ever scandalized by the labeling of a book as εὐαγγέλιον and why no one ever defended or sanctioned this innovation in the use of εὐαγγέλιον. In the beginning, εὐαγγέλιον was primarily a matter of content rather than media, be it oral or written.[208] However, in the developing churches, the four Gospels were so prominent, so widely used, and so esteemed that εὐαγγέλιον came to be largely defined as the books themselves. The εὐαγγέλιον became a literary prestige label to provide authority to a variety of Jesus books, in the hope of legitimating and authorizing the Jesus presented therein. The debates about the authenticity of Jesus books were partly about which "Gospel" accurately conveyed the Jesus of the apostolic faith and accorded with the Jewish Scriptures, which "Gospel" reflected the worship, prayer, and beliefs of believers, and which "Gospel" agreed with a broadly accepted creedal tradition.

---

207. Other definite references to εὐαγγέλιον as a writing are *Epistle to Diognetus* 11.6, even though it comes from the homily section, which is secondary, and probable also is *Martyrdom of Polycarp* 4.1 (ca. 160-190 CE).

208. Cf. Collins, *Beginning of the Gospel*, 7. Scot McKnight, "Matthew as 'Gospel,'" in *Jesus, Matthew's Gospel and Early Christianity*, ed. D. M. Gurtner, R. Burridge, and J. Willitts (FS Graham Stanton; LNTS 435; London: Clark, 2011), 67-75, regards Matthew as functioning as "gospel," good news about the liberating and victorious story of Israel's Messiah. Pennington, *Reading the Gospels Wisely*, 31, affirms the biographical genre of the Gospels, but notes as well a major difference: they are *good news*, not just biography.

The Gospels as Biographical Kerygma

Thus far we have embarked on a long discussion about the literary form of the Gospels. We have explored and evaluated the various genre categories that the Gospels have been compared to and have favored the identification with Greco-Roman biography. We have also located the meaning of "Gospel" in its Greco-Roman and Jewish contexts, linked it to the preaching of Jesus, examined the beginnings of the Gospels, and surveyed second-century designations for Jesus books (sayings of the Lord, memoirs of the Apostles, and Gospels). This has been necessary to establish what kind of literature the Gospels are, but also to determine what it actually means in this context to call a Jesus book a "Gospel."

The Gospels are the textual imprint of the oral phenomena of Christian preaching and teaching about Jesus. Viewed this way, they are Christian documents related to the needs of Christians in corporate reading, worship, apologetics, and proclamation. So in that sense they are a unique genre with no precise literary counterparts. However, their uniqueness is in many ways inconsequential because they remain largely analogous to Greco-Roman biography, and the biographical genre was typified by innovation and adaptation. The content of the Gospels is singularly determined by Jewish Christian content, while the literary form of the Gospels is a clear subtype of Greco-Roman biography.[209]

It would seem that Mark has, perhaps unconsciously, adopted Greco-Roman biography as the literary vehicle to produce the first Gospel, narrating Jesus' career, teaching, and death. Composing a biography may not have been Mark's specific aim, and the resultant literary form was perhaps more indebted to the general literary climate than to anything else, but his decision to make his pioneering literary work a biography-like narrative was likely not made without awareness of the biographical genre itself.[210] Matthew and

---

209. Aune, *New Testament in Its Literary Environment*, 46. Note also that Guelich, "Gospel Genre," 174, 205, questions the *sui generis* designation for the Gospels since genre is premised on a "context of expectation," implying that no genre can be so unique as to be inexplicable and that any genre's intelligibility is based on prior and analogous reading experiences; and all genres are by definition unique, so the statement "unique literary genre" is redundant. Similar also is Burridge, *What Are the Gospels?* 247, who puts it abruptly that "an idea of the gospels as unique, *sui generis* works is a nonsense: authors cannot create, and readers cannot interpret, a total novelty."

210. Larry Hurtado, "Gospel (Genre)," in *DJG*, ed. J. B. Green, S. McKnight, and I. H. Marshall (Downers Grove: InterVarsity, 1992), 280-82; Burridge, *What Are the Gospels?* 245-46; Bryan, *Preface to Mark*, 61-62.

Luke deliberately develop Mark so as to clarify and accentuate the literary form of a Gospel as an ancient biography. John exhibits variations on the themes, but is basically the same genre, albeit projected across a different theological trajectory. Thus the Gospels can be likened to Greco-Roman biography, but also form a distinctive family within that body of ancient writings.

Several things make the Gospels a distinct adaptation of the biographical genre. *Theologically*, while Jesus is the main character, God is the subject and source of Jesus' work. As Joel Green puts it: "The story of Jesus is the continuation and actualization of the story of God."[211] So although the Gospels are indebted to the Greco-Roman genre of biography, their narrative mode and ideological orientation is clearly indebted to Israel's sacred traditions.[212] Furthermore, *christologically*, the Gospels promote the story of Jesus, a story derived from Christian preaching, and they articulate who Jesus is precisely in their story. Terence Donaldson rightly asserts: "The narrative of any one of the Gospels is not merely a convenient receptacle for that Gospel's christology, something that might be discarded once the christological contents have been extracted from it. Rather, christology is narratively constituted."[213] Finally, *intertextually*, the Gospels are a continuation of the Old Testament narration of the great acts of God toward his people in their history. The Gospels deliberately extend a scriptural story, so much so that, as Martin Hengel put it: "The Gospels are simply not understood if one fails to appreciate their fundamental 'salvation-historical' direction, which presupposes the 'promise history' of the Old Testament, equally narrative in character."[214] Given these specific features of the Gospels, features completely defensible within the genre of ancient biography, I choose to label the Gospels as "biographical kerygma."

A few implications follow on from this observation. First, the Gospels must be studied in light of both orality and textuality rather than opting for either one. Matters of orality, performance, and book culture all shaped the context for the origin and reception of the Gospels. Second, the Gospels are historically referential. Suspending for now the question of how much "history" was in Greco-Roman biography, the Gospels narrate the career

---

211. Joel B. Green, "The Gospel According to Mark," in *The Cambridge Companion to the Gospels*, ed. S. C. Barton (Cambridge: Cambridge University Press, 2007), 147.

212. Cf. Alexander, "What Is a Gospel?" 27-28.

213. Terence L. Donaldson, "The Vindicated Son: A Narrative Approach to Matthean Christology," in *Contours of Christology in the New Testament*, ed. R. N. Longenecker (Grand Rapids: Eerdmans, 2005), 105.

214. Hengel, "Eye-Witness Memory," 71.

of a historical figure and show concern for his historical message and his impact on his earliest followers.[215] Third, the use of biography, as opposed to discourses of the risen Jesus or a mere collection of sayings, suggests that the Gospels are about Jesus — not about theological ideas behind the text nor about communities in front of the text. The Gospels are about Jesus.[216]

III. The Purpose of the Gospels

After identifying the genre of the Gospels as a type of Christian biography we may now infer something of their overall purposes, both general and specific.

Ancient biographies could serve a number of purposes. Some biographies could aim to exonerate the protagonist from certain charges (Xenophon on Socrates), highlight the exemplary qualities of a great leader (Plutarch and Xenophon on Agesilaus), serve didactic purposes as an illustration of key virtues (the biographies written by Satyrus), preserve the memory of a great man (Tacitus on Agricola), insist on the social legitimation of a leader and his followers (Porphyry on Plotinus and Eusebius on Origen), or in some cases even entertain (those written by Lucian).[217]

The Gospels can be correlated with several of these purposes. Mark appears to be an apology for the notion of a crucified Messiah. Matthew highlights the didactic qualities of Jesus for an audience under social distress. Luke emphasizes Jesus' noble death and legitimates the movement of his followers by drawing unities between the God of Israel, the Messiah of Israel, and the followers of "the Way." John preserves a unique memory of the Jesus tradition filtered through mystical and midrashic lenses and explicitly attempts to recruit followers to the Jesus who embodies God's glory, wisdom, law, and life.[218]

---

215. See Hengel, "Eye-witness Memory," 70-71: "In reality, however, the Synoptic Gospels consciously intend to narrate *a temporally removed event of the past, i.e., Jesus' unique history, which, of course, has fundamental significance for the present time of the evangelists* and the communities addressed through them, indeed for all humanity, since what is narrated is already for Mark *euangelion* which wishes to convey saving faith in Jesus as Messiah and Son of God. The closing statement of John 20.31 basically applies to all four Gospels" (italics original).

216. On this last point, see Burridge. "About People," 124; idem, *What Are the Gospels?* 248-50.

217. Burridge, *What Are the Gospels?* 297.

218. Cf. Bird, *Jesus is the Christ*, passim; Bryan, *Preface to Mark*, 58-61.

It is surely not without significance that the Gospels were written at the end of the first generation and at the beginning of the second generation of Christians. While written notes about Jesus undoubtedly preceded the composition of the Gospels, the Gospels endeavor to produce a kind of authorized account of the apostolic witness to Jesus. As first-generation figures in the Jesus movement either aged or died (Peter, James, John, and others) it was thought necessary to have written accounts of their testimony in lieu of their physical presence. In this sense, Bauckham and others are correct that the Gospels were written at the death of key eyewitnesses in order to maintain access to the apostolic eyewitness testimony to Jesus. This understanding resonates with the Peter-Mark tradition known to Papias and the epilogue of the Fourth Gospel regarding the Beloved Disciple.[219]

It is very probable that the Evangelists intended from the beginning that their accounts be read aloud in churches.[220] Paul encouraged the corporate reading of his letters for exhortation (1 Thess 5:27; Col 4:16), and Mark and Matthew both include an editorial aside for readers of the Olivet Discourse (Mark 13:14; Matt 24:15). Justin's famous account of a Christian worship service describes an occasion whereby believers "gather together to one place, and the memoirs of the apostles or the writings of the prophets are read, as long as time permits; then, when the reader has ceased, the president verbally instructs, and exhorts to the imitation of these good things."[221] The Gospels corporately functioned as a mixture of both doxology and discipleship, a Christ-centered narrative read aloud in order to create a Christ-shaped community. According to Martin Hengel: "The Gospels, at least Mark, Matthew and John, were written in the first place for worship. The hearers and — in the second place — the readers should place themselves in 'the story of Jesus,' should become 'simultaneous' with it, should make his cause their own, although one always remained conscious of the uniqueness and singularity of Jesus and thus also of the historical distance."[222]

The Gospels were read and taught in worship not simply with a view to entertainment or imparting propositions for assent. The hortatory element was meant to move audiences toward imitation of Jesus. The imitation of

---

219. Richard Bauckham, *Jesus and the Eyewitnesses* (Grand Rapids: Eerdmans, 2006), 308-10; cf. similarly Paul Barnett, *Jesus and the Logic of History* (NSBT 3; Leicester: Apollos, 1997), 137; Gundry, "Symbiosis of Theology and Genre Criticism," 39; Edward Adams, *Parallel Lives of Jesus: A Guide to the Four Gospels* (Louisville: Westminster John Knox, 2011), 16.

220. Cf. *inter alia* Campenhausen, *Formation of the Christian Bible*, 122-23.

221. Justin, *1 Apol.* 67.

222. Hengel, "Eye-Witness Memory," 92.

Christ was a core and constituent element of early Christian ethics.[223] Paul belabors the theme far more than most modern readers are often aware (1 Cor 11:1; Phil 2:5-11; 1 Thess 1:6). The Gospels are filled with repeated calls to follow Jesus and to emulate his practice and ethos (e.g., Luke 9:23; John 13:15). The theme is also prevalent in the apostolic fathers.[224] The importance of imitating Jesus is not something merely derived from figuring out how to use the Gospels pastorally, but probably was deliberately part of their authors' intention as to how the books were to function for audiences. The biographical genre illuminates not only the life of a particular individual but the particular way of life that he founded.[225] As David Capes has argued, the move from oral to written Gospel narratives reflects the desire to provide Jesus' followers with mimesis by which they could imitate Jesus' life and obey his teachings.[226]

The use of the Gospels in early worship is evidence that by the mid-second century, if not earlier, the Gospels were functioning as Scripture. By the end of the second century the Gospels were part of a series of sources including Prophets, Gospels/Lord, and Apostles that comprised a uniquely authoritative body of writings.[227] It would be incredibly naive to suggest an active consciousness on the part of the Evangelists that they were writing something that was to be considered part of a "New Testament," a "canon," or a book of the "Bible." Even so, it is not incredulous to suppose that the Evangelists were conscious of writing a form of sacred literature for their communities. Some have speculated that the Gospels were, much in line with Jewish synagogue readings, meant for year-long public readings in worship.[228]

223. Cf. Richard Burridge, *Imitating Jesus: An Inclusive Approach to New Testament Ethics* (Grand Rapids: Eerdmans, 2007); Jason B. Hood, *Imitating God in Christ: Recapturing a Biblical Pattern* (Downers Grove: InterVarsity, 2013).

224. Ignatius, *Eph.* 3.2; 4.2; 10.3; *Trall.* 8.1; *Rom.* 6.3; *Phild.* 3.5; Polycarp, *Philippians* 1.1; 8.2; *Martyrdom of Polycarp* 19.1; 22.1.

225. Adela Yarbro Collins, *Mark* (Hermeneia; Minneapolis: Fortress, 2007), 31. Also, Pennington, *Reading the Gospels Wisely,* 33, comments, "Any interpretation that neglects this aspect [emulation of Jesus] is missing a major function of the genre."

226. David G. Capes, "*Imitatio Christi* and the Gospel Genre," *BBR* 13 (2003): 1-19. According to Aune ("Greco-Roman Biography," in *Greco-Roman Literature and the New Testament* [Atlanta: Scholars, 1988], 122; cf. idem, *The New Testament in Its Literary Environment,* 25, 59-63) the Gospels function as "the legitimation of present beliefs and practices of Christians by appealing to the paradigmatic role of the founder, just as the cultural values of the Hellenistic world were exemplified by the subjects of Greco-Roman biographies."

227. Law, Prophets, Gospel, Apostles (*Epistle to Diognetus* 11.6); Gospel and Apostles (Irenaeus, *Adv. Haer.* 1.3.6); Prophets, Gospel, blessed Apostles (Clement, *Strom.* 7.16.95.3, 7.16.97.2), Prophets, Lord, Apostles (Hippolytus, *Commentary on Daniel* 4.49).

228. Cf., e.g., Michael Goulder, *Midrash and Lexicon, The Evangelist's Calendar: A Lec-*

Luke's composition of his Gospel and Acts looks like a New Testament in miniature, a singular narrative account of Jesus and the Apostles deliberately written as the fulfillment of Israel's Law, Prophets, and Psalms.[229] D. Moody Smith makes a nuanced and sober claim:

> In the case of the earliest Christian Gospels we observed already that the initial and fundamental impulse for their composition came with the proclamation of Jesus as the fulfillment of scripture. The use of the Gospels alongside the older, Jewish scriptures in worship, certainly as early as the mid-second century, probably much earlier, was likely a continuation of the use to which the earlier Gospel traditions had already been put. Matthew and Luke particularly, if in different ways, adopted biblical genres and styles as they also continued the biblical story. This is nowhere clearer than in their infancy narratives. In his own independent mode, John rewrites the story of creation from Genesis, like many of his Jewish contemporaries retelling the biblical narrative, but in a revolutionary way.[230]

The Gospels were written in order to produce authoritative guides to the story of Jesus as a companion to Israel's sacred literature. The Evangelists intended to continue the sacred story about God and his people and so, consciously or not, imputed scriptural status to the writings that they set forth.

A further purpose of the Gospels is to comprise a form of missionary literature for the earliest congregations (i.e., *Missionsschriften*). That purpose is made quite explicit in the Gospel of John, even without pleading a special case for the significance of present and aorist tense forms, that it was written in order that its audience might believe (John 20:31).[231] The Synoptic Gospels, even without any overt evangelistic statement of purpose, in the very least can function as evangelistic writings simply by virtue of the fact that they present Jesus as an attractive figure to be trusted, followed, and emulated. The Gospels appear to assume a context of preaching and teaching, intra-sectarian polemics, and interreligious apologetics. Many have even suggested that the Gospels can be located within the mission of key

---

tionary Explanation of the Development of Scripture (London: SPCK, 1978); Philip Carrington, *The Primitive Christian Calendar: A Study in the Making of the Marcan Gospel* (Cambridge: Cambridge University Press, 1952).

229. Cf. C. K. Barrett, "The First New Testament?" *NovT* 38 (1996): 94-104.

230. D. Moody Smith, "When Did the Gospels Become Scripture?" *JBL* 119 (2000): 19.

231. Cf. discussion in Bird, *Jesus Is the Christ*, 135-38.

personalities from the first generation of Christian leaders.[232] The Gospels were made available to outsiders in the second century like Trypho the Jew and the pagan philosopher Celsus.[233] Historians of ancient biography have identified the Gospels as "religious tracts intended to promote the Christian movement" and "evangelistic tracts" to commend Jesus as "Christ, Lord, Savior and Teacher to the Mediterranean world."[234] That is plausible, as some Greco-Roman biographies endeavored to promote the achievements, personality, and virtues of their protagonists. Aune is right to argue that in the competitive marketplace of religious ideas "Rhetorically, the Gospels are primarily persuasive literature, using various strategies to persuade their audiences that the crucified risen Jesus is the Messiah, the Son of God. The Gospels, then, are fundamentally Christian literary propaganda."[235]

Finally, a further issue is what audiences the Gospels were intended for. For much of the twentieth century it was assumed that the Gospel of Mark was intended for a "Marcan community," Matthew for a "Matthean community," Luke for a "Lucan community," and John for a "Johannine community." These communities were not merely receptive audiences for the Gospels, but the Gospels were very much about these communities. The Gospels were regarded as mirrors of the events and episodes taking place in these communities. A history of each community was even discernible at some subtextual level if one delved into the tradition history behind the text. Many pericopes were thought to be literary fabrications, reflecting not events in the life of Jesus but debates within the community that were seamlessly projected into the lifetime of Jesus.

However, this entire approach of perceiving the Gospels as creations about and for particular isolated and introspective communities has been seriously undermined by Richard Bauckham and his associates in the book *The Gospels for All Christians*.[236] Bauckham provocatively argues that the

---

232. Cf., e.g., Barnett, *Jesus and the Rise of Early Christianity: A History of New Testament Times* (Downers Grove: InterVarsity, 1999), 394; E. Earle Ellis, *The Making of the New Testament Documents* (Leiden: Brill, 2002), 32-47.

233. Justin, *Dial. Tryph.* 10; Origen, *Contra Celsum* 2.16, 34, 37.

234. Votaw, *Gospels and Contemporary Biographies*, 1, 4.

235. Aune, *New Testament in Its Literary Environment*, 59.

236. Bauckham, ed., *Gospels for All Christians*. See similar views propounded earlier by H. F. Gamble, *Books and Readers in the Early Church* (New Haven: Yale University Press, 1995), 102; Hengel, *Four Gospels*, 106-15; Stanton, *Jesus and Gospel*, 193; Burridge, *What Are the Gospels?* 294-99. See my defense of Bauckham against his critics in Michael F. Bird, "Bauckham's *The Gospels for All Christians* Revisited," *EJTh* 15 (2006): 5-13. Further dialogue on the matter

Gospels were not written for any single community but for all Christians or as many as might read them.

In the opening essay Bauckham begins by questioning why the community hypothesis is so widely assumed when, in fact, so little argumentation has been offered to substantiate it.[237] He proposes a wider audience for the Gospels based on several arguments. First, the Gospels are not like the Pauline epistles in that they lack the particularity exhibited in Paul's correspondence with his churches. If the Gospels are analogous in genre to a *bios*, then a more generalized audience is implied since a *bios* was not meant for internal consumption by small communities but propagated political, philosophical, and religious viewpoints further afield.[238] Second, Bauckham asserts that the early Christian movement did not comprise isolated enclaves of believers, but made up "a network of communities with constant, close communication among themselves."[239] The mobility of Christians in the Roman Empire, especially among its leaders, meant that authors would have known, if not expected, their works to come into contact with several Christian groups. The wide circulation of literature and exchanges of communication between churches lends credence to this proposal, as does the fact that Mark quickly circulated in the regions where Matthew, Luke, and John were composed.[240] Bauckham concludes that "the idea of writing a Gospel purely for the members of the writer's own church or even for a few neighboring churches is unlikely to have occurred to anyone."[241] To that I would add that some of the hypothetical reconstructions of these so-called Gospel "communities" are just so speculative and almost ephemeral. The Gospels may well owe part of their impetus and shape to their community settings, but being able to derive and describe that setting from the texts of the Gospels is quite another matter. Even if the Gospels were written from the evolving perspectives of particular Christian communities — which undoubtedly they were — we are still a long way from establishing that such an experience is limited to one location. In the case of, say, John Mark, according to canonical and traditional accounts, his travels took him from Jerusalem to Antioch to

can be found in Edward W. Klink, ed., *The Audience of the Gospels: The Origin and Function of the Gospels in Early Christianity* (LNTS 353; London: Clark, 2010).

237. Richard Bauckham, "For Whom Were the Gospels Written?" in *The Gospels for All Christians*, ed. Bauckham, 9-48.

238. Bauckham, "For Whom Were the Gospels Written?" 26-30.

239. Bauckham, "For Whom Were the Gospels Written?" 30.

240. Bauckham, "For Whom Were the Gospels Written?" 30-44.

241. Bauckham, "For Whom Were the Gospels Written?" 44.

Cyprus to Rome to Alexandria. For which community did he write his Gospel, and which church's experiences shaped it?[242] In the end, we should no more assume a single community behind each Gospel than we would assume that Tacitus wrote on Agricola for a "Tacitean community" or that Plutarch wrote his *Parallel Lives* for a "Plutarchian community."[243] It might be better to proffer the view that the Gospels were intended for local digestion within a broad network of like-minded churches with a deliberate and conscious intent of disseminating the document further afar.[244]

Further evidence for the intended audiences of the Gospels can be gleaned from a study of ancient Christian writing materials. Greco-Roman reading culture was generally elitist. High-quality Greek prose manuscripts were intended to reflect and validate the elite nature of the persons and groups who read them. The use of *scriptio continua* (continuous and uninterrupted text with no breaks between words or grammatical markers), written in elaborate script, usually on scrolls that had to be held open with two hands, often inscribed with ornate artwork, were designed not for ease of reading but to inculcate the prestige of the textual artifact and the special competency of its readers.[245]

In contrast, Christian book culture was more open and enfranchising as literary materials were prepared for a spectrum of persons with non-elite reader competences. For a start, as opposed to the use of scrolls, Christians overwhelmingly preferred the user-friendly codex, especially for sacred

242. Cf. further Michael F. Bird, "The Marcan Community, Myth or Maze?" *JTS* 57 (2006): 474-86.

243. Smith, "About Friends," 67, points out that Greco-Roman biographies were normally written to be read widely and, in light of that, "It should also come as no surprise that they [the Evangelists] expected their biographies of Jesus to be copied, spread, read, and discussed by Christians within their immediate reference group and by others as well." Burridge (*What Are the Gospels?* 295-96) contends that biographies of philosophers were "written for a wider audience — to attract people outside the author's own group," and in the case of biographies of politicians "while the book is written within one group ([e.g.,] Tacitus and his family) it is aimed at others involved in Roman politics." On the plasticity of a division between private and public "publication" of books, see Gamble, *Books and Readers,* 85; Loveday Alexander, "Ancient Book Production and the Circulation of the Gospels," in *Gospels for All Christians,* ed. Bauckham, 99-104.

244. Cf. Craig L. Blomberg, "The Gospels for Specific Communities *and* All Christians," in *Audience of the Gospels,* ed. Klink, 111-33. See also Alexander, "Ancient Book Production," 104, on the interweaving of "local" and "general" circulation of texts within the churches.

245. William A. Johnson, "Towards a Sociology of Reading in Classical Antiquity," *AJP* 121 (2000): 593-627; idem, *Readers and Reading Culture in the High Roman Empire: A Study of Elite Communities* (Oxford: Oxford University Press, 2010).

writings like Gospel collections. Of the forty-one Christian manuscripts from the second century, 76% are codices; of one hundred and ninety manuscripts from the third century, 77% are codices. Frequently the scribal hands appear to be clear and crisp as opposed to calligraphic or artistic. Lettering is often larger and spaces often greater than in contemporary writings. Compared to pagan codices, Christian codices have fewer lines per page and less letters per line. The use of punctuation in second-century mss. like P.[75] (Gospels of Luke and John) and P.[66] (Gospel of John) to delineate sense-units was probably intended to signal when a reader should pause. Similarly, the widespread use of paragraph indentation helped the reader to delineate units. The use of *nomina sacra* (abbreviations for sacred names) hint at a mix of pious abbreviation and aids for the readers. Christian literature, at least before the fourth century, was usually pragmatic rather than aesthetic. The various helps for readers might even denote a deliberate attempt to make texts accessible to a wider range of readers with diverse competences and constitute a conscious effort to turn away from the elitist format of high-quality manuscripts.[246]

It would be an over-exaggeration to say that all Gospel codices were "utilitarian handbooks," since it is possible to detect manuscripts with upmarket scribal features, and some manuscripts do look like they were intended for private rather than public use.[247] That caveat aside, Christian manuscripts exhibit traits of workmanlike qualities rather than elitist elegance. That observation carries weighty significance for the question of the intended readers of these manuscripts. In the words of Graham Stanton: "Taken together, addiction to the codex and addiction to the use of *nomina sacra* suggest that Christian communities around the eastern Mediterranean were in closer touch with one another than is usually supposed to have been the case."[248] That would mean that copies of the Gospels were meant to

---

246. Larry Hurtado, *The Earliest Christian Artifacts: Manuscripts and Christian Origins* (Grand Rapids: Eerdmans, 2006), 155-89; idem, "Manuscripts and the Sociology of Early Christian Reading," in *The Early Text of the New Testament,* ed. Hill and Kruger, 55-59; cf. also C. H. Roberts, *Manuscript, Society and Belief in Early Christian Egypt* (London: Oxford University Press, 1979); Gamble, *Books and Readers,* 79-80; Alexander, "Ancient Book Production," 84-86; Harry Gamble, "The Book Trade in the Roman Empire," in *Early Text of the New Testament,* ed. Hill and Kruger, 31-35.

247. Stanton, *Jesus and Gospel,* 192-206, and esp. Kim Haines Eitzen, *Guardians of Letters: Literacy, Power, and the Transmitters of Early Christian Literature* (Oxford: Oxford University Press, 2000).

248. Stanton, *Jesus and Gospel,* 190.

disseminate widely around the "Holy Internet" as Michael Thompson called it, the worldwide movement of churches who had mutual interest in each other's affairs and each other's literature.[249]

IV. Conclusion

This lengthy chapter has surveyed the various proposals to establish the genre of the four canonical Gospels. While the Gospels remain in many respects unique — deliberately tied as they are to Jewish sacred literature, exhibiting the characteristics of Jewish Christian oral tradition and the formal elements of Hellenistic rhetoric, and largely theological in content — all the same, the Gospels are most identifiable against the Greco-Roman literary type of ancient biography.

That observation was confirmed further by a brief investigation of the beginnings of the Gospels, where the opening sequences utilized forms that were either indicative of or compatible with ancient biography. Furthermore, the various designations for media carrying Jesus traditions in the second century ("logia," "memoirs of the Apostles," and "Gospel") indicate no uniform way of designating Jesus traditions in either oral or written forms. However, by the end of the first century, or at least by the first quarter of the second century, it would appear that the Jesus books which we call Matthew, Mark, Luke, and John were very probably first called εὐαγγέλιον as a recognizable and revered literary type. In the end, then, the Gospels are a form of biographical kergyma, which narrate the story of Jesus in the mode of Greco-Roman biography.

A corollary of this conclusion is that the purposes of the Gospels are just as multivalent as Greco-Roman biography. In a general sense, the Gospels are purposed for a mixture of apologetics, instruction, social legitimation, worship, and evangelism. Their audiences were most likely an immediate network of co-believers and benefactors, but they were also written with a view to widespread dissemination among wider circles who shared similar beliefs, a point underscored by the quality and character of early Christian manuscripts.

---

249. Michael B. Thompson, "The Holy Internet: Communication between Churches in the First Christian Generation," in *Gospels for All Christians*, ed. Bauckham, 49-70.

Excursus
WHAT ABOUT THE "OTHER" GOSPELS?

In this volume we have focused on the origins of the four canonical Gospels because they comprise the Jesus books that came to be regarded as Scripture and were later formally included as part of the biblical canon for the ancient catholic church. In the next chapter we will explore the reason and rationale behind a fourfold Gospel collection. Suffice it to say now that the reason for their inclusion and for the exclusion of other writings from the canon is that these four Jesus books were regarded as deriving from the Apostles and their companions (apostolicity), they constituted the Jesus literature that was the most widely used among the churches (catholicity), and they were believed to teach that which accords with the church's rule of faith (orthodoxy).

However, the four Gospels were not the only Gospels written, celebrated, and used in the ancient church. William Petersen quips that in the second century there was a "sea of multiple gospels" and that during this period "gospels were breeding like rabbits."[250] There are as many as forty or fifty "other" Gospels known to us from ancient manuscripts, papyrus fragments, and references in patristic sources.[251] Before the promulgation of an authoritative biblical canon in the fourth century, Christian authors were quite happy to cite Jesus traditions and Jesus books that did not find their way into the biblical canon. Although the fourfold Gospel won the day for the orthodox churches, it was not necessarily the earliest and universally agreed register of Jesus books for all Christ-believers in the early decades of the second century. Throughout the second century other Gospels were playing in town, often with big billing and drawing big crowds. The reason these "other" Gospels were written was, generally, to supplement or supplant the canonical Gospels.[252] For example, the *Gospel of Peter* could be read as a supplement to Matthew, whereas the *Gospel of Thomas* is a very deliberate effort to articulate an alternative conception of Jesus in direct competition to that of the Synoptics and probably also of the Fourth Gospel.

Part of the problem in the study of these "other" Gospels — I will not refer to them as "non-canonical" because it is anachronistic for the period we are looking at, nor refer to them as "apocryphal" because such a description presumes a tertiary

---

250. William L. Petersen, "The Diatessaron and the Fourfold Gospel," in *The Earliest Gospels: The Origins and Transmission of the Earliest Christian Gospels,* ed. C. Horton (London: Clark, 2004), 51.

251. For a useful and accessible introduction, see Rick Brannan, *Greek Apocryphal Gospels, Fragments, and Agrapha: Introductions and Translations* (Bellingham: Logos Bible Software, 2013), idem, *Greek Apocryphal Gospels, Fragments, and Agrapha: Texts and Transcriptions* (Bellingham: Logos Bible Software, 2013).

252. Johan Ferreira, "The Non-Canonical Gospels," in *Content and Setting of the Gospel Tradition,* ed. Harding and Nobbs, 209.

quality to them — is that many studies often fall into one of two extremes. Some approach the "other" Gospels with purely apologetic interest to disprove their authenticity and their worth, but often do so with ill-informed historical judgments. For instance, it is often assumed that all the "other" Gospels are Gnostic, and authors often operate with an erroneous view of Gnosticism, that they were written and used only by heretical groups, and that they are historically useless for understanding the historical Jesus. These claims are patently false when one studies these "other" Gospels closely. Contemporary apologists, often well-intentioned and sometimes making genuine points of note, tend to read their own canonical consciousness into the minds of the developing church.

Then there are those studies that utilize the "other" Gospels for conspiracy-fueled revisionist histories of Christian origins. The new narrative is one in which the early church was initially characterized by a deep diversity, where proto-orthodox and proto-Gnostic Christians existed side-by-side from the beginning, where there were no official heresies, heretics, or hierarchical orders and no single dominant theology of Christ's person. It was a time of innocent pluralism. But this blissful pluralism ended sometime in the second and third centuries when a vociferous minority of proto-orthodox leaders sought to silence alternative voices within the Christian movement and to impose their own narrow theology, sexual asceticism, sacred texts, and ecclesial hierarchy on a religious movement that was blessedly diverse. Now there is a valid correction here to tellings of Christian history, which are monolithic and recount the triumphal rise of orthodoxy over heretical minorities, but the revisionist narration is hardly any more compelling. In the end such approaches, both apologetic and revisionist, are historically inaccurate, theologically prejudiced, and largely misleading to the general public.

In what follows below I will (1) provide a brief tabulated summary of several of the "other" Gospels, (2) inquire as to what makes a Gospel a Gospel, and (3) explain why the "other" Gospels did not make the canonical cut.

The "Other" Gospels

The "other" Gospels can be grouped in several different ways. I have chosen below to categorize them either by likeness or by the sources in which they are extant. Other taxonomies are possible and the listing here is not exhaustive. An important caveat to make is that our evidence for these Gospels is often fragmentary and ambiguous. As a result the dating and provenance of these Gospels are contested.

Jewish Christian Gospels

Gospel	Sources	Date and Provenance	Description
Gospel of the Nazarenes	Jerome Epiphanius Marginal readings in mss. 4, 273, 566, 899, 1414, 1424.	Mid-second century. Used by Jewish Christians in the vicinity of Berea, proximate to Aleppo in Syria.	Written in Aramaic and closely connected with the Gospel of Matthew.
Gospel according to the Hebrews	Clement of Alexandria Origen Didymus the Blind Jerome Eusebius	Mid-second century. Used by Jewish Christians living in Egypt.	Composed in Greek, contained Synoptic-like materials.
Gospel of the Ebionites	Epiphanius	Mid-second century. Used by Jewish Christian groups east of the Jordan River.	Greek Gospel harmony with adoptionist christology.

Nag Hammadi Gospels

Gospel	Sources	Date and Provenance	Description
Gospel of Truth	NHC I Irenaeus	Second quarter of second century. Originally from Rome but redacted in Egypt.	Valentinian Gnostic document containing a mixture of teaching and exhortation.
Gospel of Thomas	NHC II P. Oxy 1 P. Oxy 654 P. Oxy 655 Hippolytus Origen Cyril of Jerusalem Eusebius	Mid-second century. Probably deriving from Jewish Christian circles in Edessa, Syria.	An esoteric collection of sayings of Jesus that lean in a Gnostic direction.
Gospel of Philip	NHC II Epiphanius	Late second century.	An eclectic collection of materials with sayings, parables, narratives, parenesis, exegetical remarks, and theological assertions based on Gnostic themes.
Gospel of the Egyptians (Coptic)	NHC III	Third-century Egypt.	Mythic stories about Seth and his descendants in the wider span of a saving history.
Gospel of Mary	BG 8502 P. Ryl 463 P. Oxy 3525	Late second century.	Contains a dialogue between the risen Jesus and his disciples, especially Mary.

Pseudo-Apostolic Gospels

Gospel	Sources	Date and Provenance	Description
Gospel of Judas	Codex Tchacos Epiphanius Irenaeus Theodoret	Mid-second century.	Gnostic document with emphasis on Judas's receipt of secret knowledge about the nature of the world.
Gospel of Matthias	Eusebius Gelasian Decree	Unknown.	Unknown.

Death and Resurrection Gospels

Gospel	Sources	Date and Provenance	Description
Gospel of Peter	P. Cair 10759 (Akhmim) P. Oxy 2949 (?) P. Oxy 4009 (?) Eusebius	First half of second century. Possibly from Asia Minor.	Possibly part of a larger work, but the extant text focuses on Jesus' death and resurrection with some legendary embellishments.
Gospel of Nicodemus	Also known as the *Acts of Pilate*. Extant in many Greek, Latin, and other language versions and divided into A and B recensions. Justin (?)	Fourth or fifth century.	A and B describe Jesus' trial before Pilate, his crucifixion and resurrection, and the fate of Joseph of Arimathea. B then includes Jesus' descent into Hades.
Gospel of Bartholomew	Also known as the *Questions of Bartholomew*. Extant in Greek, Latin, and Old Slavonic mss. Jerome Gelasian Decree	Second to fifth century, probably composed in Egypt.	A cross between a dialogue Gospel and an apocalypse. The questions pertain to descent into hell, the annunciation, the origins of Satan, and the nature of sin.
Gospel of the Egyptians (Greek)	Clement of Alexandria Hippolytus Origen	Mid-second century. Originally in Egypt but perhaps redacted in Rome.	Contains statements of the risen Jesus to a Salome about the afterlife and sexuality.

Infancy Gospels

Gospel	Sources	Date and Provenance	Description
Protevangelium of James	Over 140 mss. are extant. P. Bodmer V is the oldest Greek witness (fourth century). Gelasian Decree	Second half of second century.	Presents the story of the birth of Mary, a synthesis of the Lucan and Matthean birth stories, the death of John the Baptist's father, and in an epilogue the author identifies himself as James.
Infancy Gospel of Thomas	Available mss. give the work many titles, and it exists in three recensions (A, B, and C). Irenaeus (?)	Second to fifth century.	Contains several episodes from the childhood of Jesus where Jesus performs miracles and debates teachers.
Gospel of Ps.-Matthew	Extant in several Latin mss.	Early seventh century.	A Latin reworking of the *Protevangelium of James* and the *Infancy Gospel of Thomas*

Dialogues with the Risen Jesus

Gospel	Sources	Date and Provenance	Description
Sophia Jesu Christi	BG 8502 NHC III P. Oxy 1081	Late second or early third century, probably from Egypt.	Based on another NHC text, *Eugnostos the Blessed,* and narrates the wisdom instruction of the risen Jesus to his disciples, with affirmation of Sophia as a consort of the Savior.
Apocryphon of John	Found in shorter and longer recensions in NHC II.1, III.1, IV.1, and BG 8502.	Late second century.	Depicts a revelation given by Jesus to John featuring a mythological interpretation of the early chapters of Genesis and focusing on salvation from evil.
Epistula Apostolorum	Extant in several Ethiopic and Copic mss. and a Latin fragment.	Middle third of the second century, possibly from Asia Minor or Syria.	Anti-Gnostic document that begins as a letter then turns into an apocalypse in which the risen Jesus gives a series of revelations to the eleven disciples.

Some Gospel Fragments

Gospel	Sources	Date and Provenance	Description
P. Egerton 2 (P. Köln 255)		Second half of second century.	Contains Gospel-like material with an unparalleled account of a miracle by Jesus near the Jordan River.
Papyrus Oxyrhyn-chus 840		Third or fourth century.	Synoptic-like woe oracles given by Jesus to Judean leaders.
Papyrus Oxyrhyn-chus 1224		Fourth century.	Synoptic-like material featuring controversy stories, an exhortation to pray for enemies, and an account of the author's dream.
Fayûm Fragment		Third century.	A few verses parallel to Matt 26:30-35 and par.

What Makes a Gospel a Gospel?

One starting point is to consider what qualifies for inclusion in the large domain of Gospel literature. The problem is that these ancient Gospels are notoriously diverse. Not only are many of them fragmentary, known only indirectly, and often incomplete, but they do not reflect any kind of homogeneity in literary structure, form, or content. For instance, the Nag Hammadi *Gospel of the Egyptians* says little about Jesus and deals with the origins and redemptive activity of Seth. The *Protevangelium of James* is more interested in Mary than Jesus. The *Gospel of Philip* is a disorganized collection of instructions on sacraments and ethics. The *Gospel of Thomas* is a collection of esoteric sayings of Jesus. The *Gospel of Mary* is a revelation discourse of the risen Lord with his disciples. Many of the "other" Gospels represent a "tertiary stage of reinterpretation and sophistication away from the basic generic patterns of βίοι Ἰησοῦ."[253] In which case, it is impossible to compress the various "other" Gospels into a single literary type.[254]

One might hold up the canonical Gospels as a type of gold standard and regard "other" Gospels as Gospels only insofar as they resemble the canonical Gospels with their narrative climax in Jesus' death and resurrection. In other words, a Gospel is exclusively a kerygma-narrative.[255] Such a narrow definition would restrict

---

253. Burridge, *What Are the Gospels?* 243.

254. Cf. further Stephen Gero, "Apocryphal Gospels: A Survey of Textual History and Literary Problems," *ANRW* 2.25.5 (1988): 3969-96.

255. Cf., e.g., F. F. Bruce, "When Is a Gospel Not a Gospel?" *BJRL* 45 (1963): 319-39. In

us to the canonical Gospels, the *Gospel of Peter*, and perhaps the Jewish Christian Gospels. However, Koester opines a prevailing prejudice against the "other" Gospels when a Gospel is defined narrowly around a theological commitment to the kerygma of Jesus' death and resurrection. He alleges that such a definition is based on dogmatic assumptions and serves to reinforce ancient prejudices — prejudices as old as the anti-heretical polemicists — that the "other" Gospels are secondary, derivative, and speculative, while the canonical Gospels are original, historical, and replete with theological insights. For Koester, traditional classifications of Gospel as a kerygma-narrative fail to engage the complex and diversified corpus of Gospel literature produced in the early church. He also thinks that the canonical Gospels are, ironically, not all that kergymatic, since the Evangelists focus on Jesus' teaching rather than his death for most of their content. In addition, Koester points out that the very sources behind the canonical Gospels themselves do not fit into the genre of kerygmatic Gospels. The characteristic features of these pre-Gospel sources also appear in several of the "other" Gospels, entailing that both canonical and non-canonical Gospels were based on a similar array of sources, so to partition them is arbitrary.[256]

By way of an alternative, Koester takes a historical approach and defines Gospel literature as follows: "This corpus should include all those writings which are constituted by the transmission, use and interpretation of materials and traditions from and about Jesus of Nazareth."[257] He calls writings "Gospel" if they stand within a trajectory of the continuing development of sources that derive from Jesus. A Gospel then is a source of information about the historical Jesus. Such a definition consciously excludes "other" Gospels that show dependence on the canonical Gospels or are not thought to be authentic carriers of Jesus traditions (e.g., Jewish Christian Gospels, *Epistula Apostolorum, Gospel of Philip, Gospel of Truth, Gospel of the Egyptians,* or fragments of Gospel writings in papyri).[258]

Koester's historical approach is problematic. For a start, some writings actually called "Gospel" are excluded from his definition of Gospel literature, which seems odd. On top of that, he also redefines "Gospel" as a Jesus source rather than as a proper genre so that a "Gospel" can encompass multiple subgenres. But that is precisely the issue: Gospel as a genre. The four canonical Gospels, for all their diver-

---

the same vein Stanton (*Jesus and Gospel*, 4) asks, "When is a gospel not Gospel? When it is a set of Jesus traditions out of kilter with the faith of the church."

256. Koester, *Ancient Christian Gospels*, 43-44.

257. Koester, *Ancient Christian Gospels*, 46. Cf. similarly Philipp Vielhauer, *Geschichte der urchristlichen Literatur. Einleitung in das Neue Testament, die Apokryphen und die Apostolischen Väter* (Berlin: de Gruyter, 1975), 614; Christopher M. Tuckett, "Forty Other Gospels," in *The Written Gospel*, ed. Bockmuehl and Hagner, 243; Andrew Gregory, "The Non-Canonical Gospels and the Historical Jesus — Some Reflections on Issues and Methods," *EQ* 81 (2009): 3-22.

258. Koester, *Ancient Christian Gospels*, 47-48.

sity, do belong to a single and recognizable literary class.[259] Beyond that, Koester is somewhat overconfident in his ability to determine which documents give us reliable access to a historical layer of Jesus traditions. Koester includes the *Infancy Gospel of Thomas* as part of Gospel literature even though it contains a legendary and fanciful narration of Jesus' childhood. While it might be analogous to the Synoptic infancy narratives, one would be pushing a large rock up a steep hill to argue that it contains earlier or more authentic traditions. John P. Meier thinks that the *Infancy Gospel of Thomas* is about as useful for reconstructing the historical Jesus as *Alice in Wonderland*.[260] Moreover, if one could prove that the *Gospel of Thomas* was dependent on the canonical Gospels — and I believe it was — then it would be ejected from the company of Gospel literature.[261] Irrespective of its sources or historicity, the *Gospel of Thomas* is a vitally important document for the study of second-century Christianity.

Now one could say that Gospel literature broadly pertains to any writing where the label "Gospel" is referenced or attached to a source. Evidently various writings about Jesus and numerous sources for sayings from Jesus were regularly called "Gospel" in the early church, a point that holds true from the apostolic fathers through to the Nag Hammadi codices. The label "Gospel" is so prevalent because "Gospel" became a prestige tag to commend the contents of a document as containing valued information and insightful perspectives about Jesus, irrespective of the document's literary form, historical source, or theological orientation. On a literary definition, a Gospel is a document that is identified by someone somewhere as a "Gospel."

The problem with this literary approach is that many of the writings regarded as "Gospel" do not actually use the word "Gospel" in their title or contents. For instance, the *Infancy Gospel of Thomas* is not actually titled as a "Gospel" in its extant manuscripts even though it is a narrative about Jesus' childhood. The title is given by scholars as a summary of its content and to distinguish it from the Coptic *Gospel of Thomas*. Some Jesus books were labeled as "Gospels" only later by editors. The colophon at the end of the *Gospel of Philip* may have been added secondarily.

---

259. John P. Meier, *A Marginal Jew* (ABRL; 4 vols.; New York/New Haven: Doubleday/Yale University Press, 1991-2009), 1:144 n. 15.

260. John P. Meier, "The Present State of the 'Third Quest' for the Historical Jesus: Loss and Gain," *Bib* 80 (1999): 464.

261. I do think that *Gospel of Thomas* 82, 97, and 98 might have pre-Synoptic origins, but on the whole *Gospel of Thomas* is dependent on the Synoptic Gospels, perhaps even on John and Paul. See recently Nicholas Perrin, *Thomas: The Other Gospel* (Louisville: Westminster John Knox, 2007); Simon Gathercole, *The Composition of the Gospel of Thomas: Original Language and Influences* (SNTSMS 151; Cambridge: Cambridge University Press, 2012); Mark Goodacre, *Thomas and the Gospels: The Making of an Apocryphal Text* (Grand Rapids: Eerdmans, 2012); John P. Meier, "The Parable of the Wicked Tenants in the Vineyard: Is the Gospel of Thomas Independent of the Synoptics?" in *Unity and Diversity in the Gospels and Paul*, ed. C. W. Skinner and K. R. Iverson (FS Frank Matera; Atlanta: Society of Biblical Literature, 2012), 129-45.

Similarly, the *Gospel of Truth*, known to Irenaeus and used by Valentinians,[262] is not titled as *Gospel of Truth* in the NHC, but the title is inferred from the incipit, which reads "The gospel of truth is joy for those who have received from the Father of truth the grace of knowing him."[263] The many Gospel fragments, though perhaps parts of larger works that were called "Gospel," are not themselves identified as a "Gospel" in their extant texts. So even a literary approach can be somewhat narrow in what it excludes.

The kerygmatic, historical, and literary definitions of Gospel are all problematic in that they are all restrictive toward other Jesus books and fragments to some degree. In want of a resolution, I propose that all books and writings pertaining to Jesus should go under the heading "Ancient Jesus Literature" and thereby leave the question of "What is a Gospel?" as a secondary question once all the ancient materials about Jesus are properly grouped together. All these writings, irrespective of form and content, regardless of their dependence on or independence of the canonical Gospels, whatever titles they have or are given, are a type of Jesus *Festschriften* (i.e., celebratory writing about a person). They carry traditions of various antiquity and authenticity as well as provide insights into the effective-history of Jesus among his diverse bodies of followers in the first, second, and third centuries with their manifold writings about him.

It would be appropriate, then, to think of a "Gospel" as a distinct type of Jesus literature based on a kerygmatic narrative account of Jesus' life, death, and resurrection. The best criterion for what amounts to a "Gospel" is the "gospel." That is after all the definition that became the dominant position in the ancient church. A Gospel is an announcement of good news, a message of salvation in the story of Jesus' ministry, cross, and exaltation, to be received by faith. The Jesus literature that qualifies as "Gospel," then, would be restricted to the canonical Gospels, arguably include some other writings like Jewish Christian Gospels, many Gospel harmonies, and perhaps even the *Gospel of Peter* if it is a fragment of a larger work.

I did originally toy with the idea of "Gospel" as a broad class of literature that either contains content that is similar to the canonical Gospels or else uses the title "Gospel" at some point. But, while large portions of Jesus literature, whether logia, discourses, deeds, or fragments, resemble parts of the canonical Gospels, the fact remains that a single piece of text does not necessarily possess the same quality and function as the whole document which the piece of text is drawn from or compared to. The fallacy of composition warns us against attributing the qualities of a part to the whole of something. In which case, the observation that a document contains sayings attributed to Jesus does not thereby mean the document constitutes a "Gospel" because the four Gospels also have sayings attributed to Jesus (I am thinking here especially of the presence of sayings of Jesus in the *Gospel of*

---

262. Irenaeus, *Adv. Haer.* 3.11.9.
263. *Gospel of Truth* 16.31-35.

Thomas or P. Oxy 840). The generic similarities between two documents must be mapped globally and not piecemeal. Furthermore, putting the heading "Gospel" on a document does not really determine its genre any more than inscribing "Recent Observations on Nocturnal and Hematophagic Humanoids" on the cover of a *Twilight* novel turns it into a scientific research paper. When people added the word "Gospel" to a book that is unlike the four Gospels, they were not so much telling us what they thought about its genre as communicating something about the prestige and importance which they thought the book deserved. At the end of the day the four canonical Gospels, as the first writings to be called "Gospel" and as the most popular type of Jesus literature in the ancient church according to citations and extant manuscripts, constitute the archetype against which all designations and definitions of Gospel are determined, whether by ideological deference or by historical default. So, whether one likes it or not, the holy quartet of Matthew–Mark–Luke–John will inevitably become the standard for determining what it means for a document to be a "Gospel."

In which case, the *Gospel of Thomas* is "Jesus literature," but it is not a "Gospel" per se. The Thomasine Jesus is dispensing esoteric and elitist advice, not bringing Israel's prophetic promises to their climax. The *Gospel of Thomas* as a whole hardly declares good news about the crucified and risen Lord who promises deliverance from sin and calls people to follow him as part of a renewed Israel, to participate in this-worldly kingdom-work, and to live forever in the age to come. That definition will seem prejudiced to some, but all definitions are inherently prejudicial.[264] So it is simply a question of whether one accepts or rejects the proto-orthodox definition of "gospel." I submit that defining "Gospel" by "gospel" coordinates the contents of the canonical Gospels with the apostolic preaching of Jesus, a preaching which covered Jesus' baptism, preaching, message, healings, and passion (e.g., Acts 10:34-43) and which also identifies the Gospels as community-forming narratives that shaped, by way of imitation or even refutation, the subsequent history of Jesus literature.

Why the "Other" Gospels Lost Out

The proto-orthodox and orthodox churches rejected the "other" Gospels in favor of the four Gospels that are now regarded as canonical. In polemical writings of the patristic period, some Christ-believing groups were criticized for using "other"

264. While Koester is rather quick to protest against any theological prejudice that heralds the religious qualities of the canonical Gospels over the non-canonical Gospels, he has his own theological predilection for certain sources, preferring sources that point away from the prophetic fulfillment of Israel's Scriptures, omit reference to the redemptive suffering of the cross, and present Jesus as the conveyor of Hellenistic wisdom traditions that are cosmopolitan rather than in any way theologically "conservative." For Koester, "Gospel" is what stands in historical proximity to Jesus, even if it stands opposed to the apostolic message about Jesus.

Gospels, either singularly or in addition to the canonical Gospels.[265] For example, Irenaeus fervently argued unswervingly for the unchallenged authority of the "Gospel of the Apostles" understood as the fourfold Gospel.[266] This creates the impression for many that the proto-orthodox church was notoriously intolerant toward other Christ-believing groups and their Jesus books. Elaine Pagels believes that alternative groups like the Gnostics were "forced outside" the church to the "impoverishment of the Christian tradition."[267] Helmut Koester regards the canonization of the New Testament as a process geared toward the exclusion and oppression of minorities. Koester claims: "The canon was the result of a deliberate attempt to exclude certain voices from the early period of Christianity: heretics, Marcionites, Gnosticism, Jewish Christians, perhaps also women. It is the responsibility of the New Testament scholar to help these voices to be heard again."[268]

However, while theological minorities did not always get a fair hearing from their critics, the decision not to include their writings was not born out of *realpolitik*. The canon of the orthodox church was not designed principally for oppression and promulgated out of a quest for ecclesiastical power. Rather, it was driven by a desire to be faithful to the apostolic faith and to define the consensus of the worldwide church on the writings that make up its register of sacred books. We find numerous examples of the early church willing to include and take seriously other Jesus literature even if it was not believed to possess the same quality and authority as texts regarded as Scripture. The second century attests both an inquisitiveness toward all forms of Jesus literature in tandem with a desire to affirm those writings that are congruent with the apostolic tradition. While the proto-orthodox churches very quickly venerated the four Gospels, this never seems to have meant restricting themselves to reading only those Gospels.

First, the papyri available from the second century attest the popularity of Mat-

---

265. Origen, *Homilies on Luke* 1: "The Church has Four Gospels, but the heretics have many . . . So also today 'many' have wanted to write gospels, but not all [of them] have been sanctioned [by the Assembly]. Indeed, everyone knows that not four gospels alone but very many have been written, from which these which *we* have were selected and handed down in the Assembly. . . . So the Assembly has four gospels, the heretics many. They have such titles as 'Gospel according to the Egyptians,' and another one is entitled 'According to the Twelve Apostles.' Indeed Basilides dared to write a 'Gospel according to Basilides.' Many have 'undertaken' [to write gospels]. I also know of a 'Gospel according to Thomas,' and another called 'According to Matthias' and many others. These are those which [the heretics] have 'undertaken' [to write], but the Assembly of God has granted authority only to four" (trans. Dungan, *History of the Synoptic Problem*, 70).

266. Irenaeus, *Adv. Haer.* 3.11.9.

267. Elaine H. Pagels, *The Gnostic Gospels* (New York: Random, 1979), 27, 149.

268. Helmut Koester, "Epilogue: Current Issues in New Testament Scholarship," in *The Future of Early Christianity: Essays in Honor of Helmut Koester,* ed. B. A. Pearson (Minneapolis: Fortress, 1991), 472.

thew (P.^{64} + ^{67}, P.^{77}, P.^{103}, P.^{104}), then Luke, and especially John (P.^{4}, P.^{5}, P.^{52}, P.^{66}, P.^{75}, P.^{90}, P.^{108}, P.^{109}),[269] in addition to an interest in other Jesus traditions given the residual remains of "other" Gospel fragments (P. Oxy 1, 654, and 655 [*Gospel of Thomas*]; P. Eg. 2 [Gospel-like materials]; P. Oxy 4009 and 2949 [*Gospel of Peter* ?]).[270]

Second, evidence of further openness to "other" Jesus traditions is attested by the presence of agrapha in proto-orthodox sources. Proto-orthodox Christians were interested in what Jesus is reported to have said irrespective of the source his words were found in.[271] The travel and close networking of persons between Jerusalem, Syria, Egypt, and Rome meant there was a constant interchange of oral and written Jesus traditions.[272]

Third, the use of "free sayings" for Gospel citations — deriving from a mixture of memory, harmonization, and alternate traditions — by proto-orthodox authors like Ignatius, Papias, Clement, Pseudo-Clement, Justin, and the authors of the *Epistula Apostolorum* and the longer ending of Mark 16 prove that the proto-orthodox did not see themselves as living in a textual straitjacket, even while they argued for the apostolicity and integrity of their sacred texts.

Fourth, and similar to the last point, the willingness of authors to cite "other" Gospels and their traditions, not polemically but as anecdotal evidence about some point of interpretation of events of Jesus' life, suggests a serious openness to other Jesus literature when it was deemed illuminating to the author's literary tasks. Justin shares the tradition found in infancy Gospels about Jesus being born in a cave and the tradition of the great light that shone around at his baptism found in the *Diatessaron* and the *Gospel of the Ebionites*.[273] The chronicler Hegesippus quotes from the *Gospel according to the Hebrews* and from a Syriac Gospel.[274] Irenaeus preserves three agrapha that he received from Papias, believing them to be authentic.[275] Clement of Alexandria

---

269. Roger Bagnall (*Early Christian Books in Egypt* [Princeton: Princeton University Press, 2009], 1-24) has recently questioned the dating of many of these papyri to the second century, but see Larry Hurtado's review at *Review of Biblical Literature*, http://www.bookreviews.org/pdf/7755_9195.pdf.

270. On doubt as to whether P. Oxyrhynchus 4009 and 2949 were originally part of the *Gospel of Peter*, see Paul Foster, "Are There Any Early Fragments of the So-Called *Gospel of Peter?*" *NTS* 52 (2005): 1-28.

271. Cf. W. D. Stroker, *Extracanonical Sayings of Jesus* (Atlanta: Scholars, 1989); John K. Elliott, *The Apocryphal New Testament* (Oxford: Clarendon, 1993), 26-30; Bart Ehrman and Ziatko Pleše, *The Apocryphal Gospels: Texts and Translations* (Oxford: Oxford University Press, 2011), 351-67.

272. Cf. Hengel, *Four Gospels and the One Gospel of Jesus Christ*, 112-13.

273. Cf. *Protevangelium of James* 18-19; *Arabic Gospel of the Infancy* 2-3; (and Origen, *Contra Celsum* 1.51) with Justin, *Dial. Tryph.* 78.7-8 and Tatian, *Diatessaron* 4.40; *Gospel of the Ebionites* 2 with Justin *Dial. Tryph.* 88.3.

274. Eusebius, *Hist. Eccl.* 4.22.8.

275. Irenaeus, *Adv. Haer.* 5.33.3-4.

utilized the *Gospel of the Egyptians,* the *Gospel according to the Hebrews,* and the *Traditions of Matthias* without any query as to their scriptural status.[276] Later Origen, for all his polemic in his Luke homily against "other" Gospels, is quite comfortable citing non-canonical texts in his Gospel commentaries, even if they are not quite authoritative.[277] Eusebius divided Christian writings into the categories of canonical, disputed, spurious, and heretical. He points out that the *Gospel according to the Hebrews,* though not canonical, was both familiar to and held in fondness by some writers.[278]

Fifth, this openness to other Jesus books was not restricted to Christian book collections, but even extended to corporate worship. Bishop Serapion of Antioch in the 180s initially permitted believers at Rhossus to use the *Gospel of Peter.* He only later forbade it when the book was deemed conducive to docetic teachers and because its content was not authentically Petrine.[279] Bishops like Irenaeus and Serapion, despite their mixture of caution and condemnation of "other" Jesus literature, could only call for the rejection of certain writings with the consent of their church bodies. Thus, one searches in vain for some kind of top-down episcopal authority that excised the diversity of Christian literature in proto-orthodox churches in the second and even the third centuries.[280]

The rejection of "other" Gospels by the proto-orthodox and orthodox churches was neither arbitrary nor merely political. The reasons for rejecting them were cogent and compelling. Among the main criticisms raised against the "other" Gospels and their authors were that (1) the "Jesus" they set forth was not recognizable as the Jesus known in other sacred writings or congruent with apostolic tradition, (2) the "other" Gospels are often esoteric, elitist, and erroneous in what they affirm about God, creation, sin, holiness, ethics, and redemption, and (3) they do not properly have origins among Jesus' earliest followers and are late and tendentious.

---

276. Cf. Ehrman and Pleše, *Apocryphal Gospels,* 218-19, 226-29 for these citations.

277. Origen cites the *Gospel according to the Hebrews (Commentary on John* 2.6), the *Gospel of Peter,* and the *Protevangelium of James (Commentary on Matthew* 10.17) among others.

278. Eusebius, *Hist. Eccl.* 3.25.

279. Eusebius, *Hist. Eccl.* 6.12.4.

280. Hurtado, *Lord Jesus Christ,* 521: "There was, after all, no real means of 'top-down' coercive success for any version of Christianity over others until after Constantine, when imperial endorsement and power could be brought to bear. Second-century bishops elected by Christians of the locale in which they were to serve. So, for example, if the bishop did not have (or could not win) sufficient support from the local Christians, he could hardly impose on them some version of faith contrary to the preferences of the majority. Thus, if any version of Christianity enjoyed success and became more prominent in the first three centuries (whether locally or translocally), it was largely the result of its superior ability to commend itself to sufficient numbers of adherents and supporters. To reiterate the point, the apparent success of what I am calling 'proto-orthodox' Christianity was probably the result of the teaching and behavior that were more readily comprehended and embraced by larger numbers of ordinary Christians of the time than were the alternatives."

It was not the fault of Christian censors or a theological thought-police that the "other" Gospels were criticized and rejected. The "other" Gospels were not recognizable as "gospel," and they failed to capture the hearts, minds, and imaginations of Christians in the worldwide church. The proof of this is the limited number of extant manuscripts for many of these "other" Gospels and the fact that many Jesus books were not known beyond their own immediate circles. The exclusion of other Gospels was not the result of the victory of the orthodox. It was rather based on an objective claim as to who more properly transmitted the teaching of Jesus and the Apostles. In the end, the reason the "other" Gospels lost out is that they simply failed to convince the majority of their antiquity and authenticity as stories of Jesus. According to Arland Hultgren:

> In spite of the diversity of early Christianity, an expression of Christian faith arose in the first three centuries that claimed continuity with the faith of the apostles and is exhibited in the classic texts that come to make up the New Testament. Alternative expressions of faith, such as Marcionism, Montanism, Ebionitism, and Gnosticism, arose and made — to one degree or another — the same or similar claims. But there were factors within them — confessional and communal — that made those claims difficult to sustain.[281]

The early heresiologists wrote works that summarized the concerns and criticisms that many had about alternative Jesuses, fringe groups, and their literature. In the context of discussing these "other" Gospels, Irenaeus put forth an eloquent though sometimes peculiar argument for the authority of the fourfold Gospel over and against alternative approaches.[282] First, he identifies in the four Gospels a singular narrative, analogous to the *regula fidei,* which affirms God the creator, Moses and the prophets, and the dispensation of Jesus Christ. Second, he points out that certain deviant groups gravitate toward one particular Gospel and ignore the other three because it suits their peculiar (mis)claims and enables them to set aside the wider witnesses to God and Jesus.[283] Similarly, those who add more Gospels do so because of an audacious claim to have discovered more than the truth revealed in the Gospels, a truth that does not accord with the teachings of the Evangelists or the Apostle Paul.[284]

Eusebius is forthright in his account as to why certain books were rejected from the canon. In the case of the Gospels of *Peter, Thomas,* and *Matthias,* Eusebius

---

281. Arland J. Hultgren, *The Rise of Normative Christianity* (Eugene: Wipf & Stock, 1994), 4.

282. Irenaeus, *Adv. Haer.* 3.11.7-9.

283. The examples are Marcion with Luke, the Ebionites with Matthew, the Docetists with Mark, and the Valentinians with John.

284. The example is the Valentinians and the *Gospel of Truth.*

declares that "the type of phraseology used contrasts with apostolic style, and the opinions and thrusts of their contents are so dissonant from true orthodoxy that they show themselves to be forgeries of heretics. Accordingly, they ought not be reckoned even among the spurious books [like the *Gospel according to the Hebrews*] but discarded as impious and absurd."[285] This is not a groundless theological rant against other writings; rather, Eusebius weighs them against an objective criterion: apostolic authenticity and catholic consensus. These "other" Gospels are esoteric rather than evangelical, oddities rather than orthodox. The plethora of alternative Gospels were not squeezed out by a power-hungry episcopal oligarchy hell-bent on erasing other stories of Jesus from history to consolidate their own power base. Eusebius acknowledges the broad discussions about which sacred texts should be used, and the debate was more than "in" or "out." There was a reasonable attempt to be wide-ranging in the adoption of books into the canon. Hence the inclusion of disputed books like Revelation and 2 Peter, while books like the *Shepherd of Hermas* came within a bee's whisker of being included,[286] and there was even recognition of a class of books that were not considered canonical but were still valued and esteemed by many.

The "other" Gospels were neither persuasive nor popular and were never really serious contenders for inclusion in the canon.[287] As Augustine wrote:

> All those other individuals who have attempted or dared to offer a written record of the acts of the Lord or the apostles, failed to commend themselves in their own times as men of character which would induce the Church to yield them its confidence, and to admit their compositions to the canonical authority of the Holy Books. [Instead] they were condemned by the catholic and apostolic rule of faith and by sound doctrine.[288]

The alternative accounts of Jesus did not correspond with the faith, worship, prayer, and devotion of Christians — a valid point since in the Gnostic Gospels, Jesus is not a historical figure, but a timeless symbol of redemption from the material world. The sayings tradition and stories about his life are ostentatiously converted into mythical signs and images, encoded for elite insiders, and then deciphered in a

---

285. Eusebius, *Hist. Eccl.* 3.25.

286. The *Shepherd of Hermas* is in fact included in Codex Sinaiticus and is named in several ancient canonical lists.

287. It is worth noting that from the second and third centuries that there are approximately thirteen fragments from non-canonical texts and thirty-eight fragments of canonical texts. The upshot is that the ratio of non-canonical to canonical texts in this period is roughly 1:3. See Bart Ehrman, *Lost Christianities: The Battle for the Scripture and the Faiths We Never Knew* (Oxford: Oxford University Press, 2003), 22-23; Hurtado, *Early Christian Artifacts*, 20-23; Charles E. Hill, *Who Chose the Gospels? Probing the Great Gospel Conspiracy* (Oxford: Oxford University Press, 2010), 18.

288. Augustine, *Harmony of the Gospels* 1.1.2.

Gnostic key. Simon Gathercole points out that the *Gospel of Judas* presents us with a disembodied Jesus, a loveless Jesus, and a Jesus without suffering.[289] Basilides, who had his own Jesus book, professed a Jesus who was not even crucified, but escaped by taking the form of Simon of Cyrene.[290] The Jesus of the *Gospel of Thomas* is not a Jewish Messiah but more like a beatified beatnik dispensing amorphous aphorisms and even advocating salvation by androgyny.[291] For many others, Jesus was not actually human and was not even born but merely appeared so as some kind of phantasm. These "other" Gospels, regardless of their tradition history, are not historically oriented and regard Jesus as a cipher for a host of mythic realities, things that in a sense never were but always are.[292] In fact, they are anachronistic to a ridiculous degree, akin to finding a document purportedly about Napoleon giving orders to his officers on tactics, but where he discusses nuclear submarines and B52 bombers therein.[293] These other Jesuses are neither the bearers nor the subjects of good news and were accordingly rejected by the proto-orthodox.

The reasons for rejecting the "other" Gospels were not incidental or based on minutiae of religious dogma but concerned the very nature of Christian faith and what it meant to be a human being. The proto-orthodox movement, diverse as it was, could not accommodate views where: (1) the Father of Jesus is not the creator of heaven and earth, (2) there is a division between the man Jesus and an astral entity called "Christ," (3) the human problem is fundamentally a lack of self-awareness of the cosmic origins of humanity, (4) salvation exists only in the spiritual plane and does not pertain to the material world or bodily existence, and (5) Jesus is a revealer of truth rather than a redeemer by virtue of his incarnation, passion, and resurrection.[294]

A number of "Ivy League Gnostics," as Rodney Stark calls them,[295] seem to think that, had Gnosticism or any of its theological cousins prevailed, then Christianity would somehow have been more tolerant, accepting, and fuzzier toward women, ethnic minorities, and gays. But nothing could be further from the truth. The Christ-believing groups who produced these Jesus books often had sectarian beliefs that were far from conducive to an inclusive and humanitarian philosophy. Many regarded sexuality with disdain, denigrated bodily human existence, were virulently anti-Semitic,

---

289. Simon Gathercole, *The Gospel of Judas* (Oxford: Oxford University Press, 2007), 162-71.

290. Irenaeus, *Adv. Haer.* 1.24.4; cf. *Apocalypse of Peter* 81; *Qur'an* 4.157-58. In the *Gospel of Barnabas* (twelfth century), Judas morphs into Jesus and is crucified instead.

291. Cf. esp. *Gospel of Thomas* 22, 114.

292. To echo Sallustius, *On the Gods and the World* 4.9.

293. N. T. Wright, *Judas and the Gospel of Jesus: Have We Missed the Truth about Christianity?* (Grand Rapids: Baker, 2006), 63.

294. Cf. Darrell L. Bock, *The Missing Gospels: Unearthing the Truth behind Alternative Christianities* (Nashville: Nelson, 2006), 208.

295. Rodney Stark, *Cities of God: Christianizing the Urban Empire* (San Francisco: HarperSanFrancisco, 2006), 154.

demonized the Old Testament, rejected marriage, saw women as symbolic of the human failure to be all one could be, engaged in speculative cosmology, multiplied semi-divine intermediaries to nonsensical degrees, insisted on a narrower selection of sacred texts as authoritative, regarded themselves as the sole possessors of a "true" revelation of Jesus, were so spiritually superior that sometimes they had to separate from others, and lacked any sense of social concern beyond their own introspective group.

One should entirely admit that, in some cases, dissident groups were simply magnifying what we might call the unseemly side of proto-orthodoxy such as the penchant for sexual asceticism, authoritative patriarchy, and a tendency toward anti-Judaism. But several of these dissident groups also appear to have been operating outside the margins of a broad church and to have moved into an alien religious framework and adopted an eclectic arrangement of religious symbology. Some "other" Christ-believing groups were simply variations on a proto-orthodox theme. Their peculiar matrix of christological and soteriological configurations yielded a very different praxis, but in many cases the resultant body of beliefs and behaviors were still genetically "Christian." Yet other Christ-believing groups look as if they have retained a vague Christian grammar of discourse but redefined its lexicon with alternative and even adversarial accounts of the nature of God, Christ, redemption, and the self, accounts which were hard to square with even the most broadly defined version of Christian faith. The various species of Gnostic belief, testified to principally by the Nag Hammadi codices, yield a neo-Platonic religion of self-discovery and self-redemption, but nothing that can be described as authentically "Christian," and with good reason. A religion of this order might have given us a guru like Deepak Chopra, who urges people to look for the god or divine spark within themselves, but it would not have given us figures like Augustine, Martin Luther, William Wilberforce, Dietrich Bonhoeffer, or Desmond Tutu.

That is not to say that the "other" Gospels are without value. They are vitally important for our study of early Christianity for several reasons. These writings prove the elastic way that "gospel" could be defined, plot the various trajectories that Jesus traditions followed in some groups, constitute rigorous intellectual efforts to make faith in Christ more palatable in a pagan context, indicate the diverse expressions of faith in Christ in different regions, and demonstrate how images of Jesus continued to be shaped in the second and third centuries. Furthermore, the various fragments, however many there actually are out there, might not have been part of whole Gospels, but been more like *marginalia,* an extra tradition spliced into a Synoptic framework, or perhaps even a deliberate attempt at an oral synthesis of text and sermon. Many such texts were arguably "para-canonical" and possibly attest to efforts to imaginatively retell — rather than reform or replace — some treasured pericopes from the canonical Gospels.[296] In addition, Clement of Alexandria provides a prime

---

296. I owe this thought to correspondence with Prof. Markus Bockmuehl (January 22, 2013).

example of how "other" Gospel traditions can be dealt with generously and even used in a creative dialogue with canonical accounts in order to explicate the story of Jesus and its relevance for one's own immediate situation.[297] Many of the church fathers made room for additional writings, writings that were not canonical but were not dismissed as apocryphal and were considered "useful," the classic case being hagiographical narratives like the *Protevangelium of James* and martyrologies such as *The Passion of Perpetua and Felicitas*. Indeed, artwork and iconography from the Middle Ages and the Byzantine period show how a few non-canonical texts inspired artistic imaginations, the *Protevangelium of James* in particular.[298] The non-canonical writings can still have great utility for exploring the development and density of the broad Christian tradition as it emerged in the early centuries.

297. Cf. Hengel, *Four Gospels and the One Gospel of Jesus Christ*, 139-40.

298. François Bovon, "Canonical, Rejected, and Useful Books," in *New Testament and Christian Apocrypha*, ed. G. E. Snyder (Grand Rapids: Baker, 2009), 321.

CHAPTER 6

The Fourfold Gospel of Jesus Christ: Why Four Gospels?

The fact that the ancient catholic church settled on four Gospels rather than choosing a single Gospel or adopting any gaggle of Gospels is a curious historical eventuality. It is a decision that requires a historical explanation as much as a theological justification: Why *four* Gospels and why *these four* Gospels?

Many have long pondered that the Christian faith would, in some ways, have been a lot simpler if it had only one Gospel. For a start, we would not be confronted with dizzying source-critical matters like the "Synoptic Problem" or "Johannine Question" as intra-canonical quandaries. Second, adoption of a single Gospel would be convenient because we would not have to deal with the alleged contradictions that arise when the various accounts in the Gospels are juxtaposed. By using only one authorized book of Jesus' life, ancient critics like Celsus and Porphyry would immediately forfeit one of their main criticisms of the Christian faith, namely, that its four biographies of Jesus do not always agree. Third, opting for a single Gospel would enable us to avoid the question of theological diversity, whether we have two "Jesuses" in the canon — the Synoptic Jesus and the Johannine Jesus — or even four "Jesuses" given the unique narration and texture of each of the four Gospels. Thus, one can imagine critical, apologetic, and theological reasons for preferring one Gospel over many.

Alternatively, rather than settle for one Gospel to rule them all, why not exploit the multiplicity of Gospels as a deliberate feature of Christian diversity? Why stop at four? Why not have five or six or even forty Gospels? Everyone can have their own Gospel and *vive la différence*. Anyone and everyone who is keen on Jesus can put up their own Gospel, cast the net for Jesus literature wide, and let the creative juices flow into the composition of manifold Jesus books. We could have a plethora of Jesus books from a Gospel of Adam to a Gospel of Zacchaeus with room made for Marcionites, Mormons, Moonies, and even a Michael Moore Appreciation Society. The big four and all the more!

I should also point out, and I will unpack this later, that the adoption of the fourfold Gospel was not a foregone conclusion.[1] The early church could well have adopted a single Gospel, perhaps limited itself to two, produced a harmony of the four as its definitive Jesus book, or even added a fifth or sixth to the collection. The fourfold Gospel emerged triumphantly from the rigorous debate about which Jesus literature was authored by the Holy Spirit and authorized by the church. But a fourfold Gospel was not in any way inevitable *at the opening of the second century* given the various forms that Jesus traditions took at this time. According to Martin Hengel:

> It is almost a miracle that the church preserved the four earliest Gospels we have, so often differing in part, despite their striking discrepancies, indeed contradictions, and resisted any attempt at harmonization or radical selection along the lines of Marcion. On the one hand in so doing it created for itself a permanent cause of offence and theological controversy, indeed, a direct occasion for the contradiction by its opponents. The temptation to expand the series of four partially contradictory Gospels by constantly new narratives about Jesus and collections of sayings especially with additional revelations, like secret teachings from the risen Christ to his disciples, was further increased by the plurality of these four which were already in existence shortly after AD 100.[2]

Therefore, it is the aim of this chapter to plot the origins of the fourfold Gospel collection (i.e., the tetrevangelium), to evaluate the theological rationale for the fourfold Gospel, and to explicate the significance of a fourfold Gospel collection for the wider biblical canon.

---

1. Cf. similarly Francis Watson, "The Fourfold Gospel," in *The Cambridge Companion to the Gospels*, ed. S. C. Barton (Cambridge: Cambridge University Press, 2006), 35, 46.

2. Martin Hengel, *The Four Gospels and the One Gospel of Jesus Christ* (Harrisburg: Trinity, 2000), 106.

I. Emergence of the Fourfold Canon

Alternatives to a Fourfold Gospel Collection

Before we can describe the emergence of the fourfold Gospel collection, we have to explore the literary rivals that were real alternatives to the fourfold Gospel collection.

First, it is possible that that the proto-orthodox church could have opted for a single Gospel. To begin with, it probably took a while for the fourfold Gospel collection to get together and to get around. Mark, written ca. 70 CE, circulated immediately and widely — enough to be used by Matthew, Luke, and John in their diverse locations — but for a long time many churches would have known no written Gospel, only one, or perhaps only two. So the churches knew how to get by as it were with a limited number of Gospels. Other Christ-believing groups, however, deliberately chose to have just one Gospel.

Marcion's choice of a single Gospel, a Lucan text excised of Jewish traits,[3] is tangible evidence that holding to a single Gospel was a possible and preferential option for some. His choice of Luke, though he disdained Luke's distortion of Paul,[4] was probably driven by the fact that Luke was known to be a companion of Paul, though we have to seriously canvass the possibility that Luke might have been the only Gospel that Marcion knew since his younger days in Pontus.[5] Marcion's *Euangelion* was the prolegomena to his *Apostolikon,* and together they provided a collection of authoritative sacred writings for his followers.[6] Marcion's literary project involved a refurbishment of Jesus literature and a revisioning of the Christian faith. To that end, an edited version of Luke severed from the Old Testament proved to be a simple and attractive option, an attraction that even extended to nineteenth-

---

3. Cf. Tertullian, *Adv. Marc.* 4.4.4; 4.6.2; Irenaeus, *Adv. Haer.* 1.27.2; 3.11.7; 3.12.12.

4. Hans von Campenhausen, *The Formation of the Christian Bible,* trans. J. A. Baker (Philadelphia: Fortress, 1972), 158.

5. One wonders why Marcion did not choose John or even Matthew, for besides their Jewish "feel," they also engage in some vehement intra-Jewish polemics toward Judean groups. See Campenhausen, *Formation,* 159-60.

6. Cf. Sebastian Moll, *The Arch-Heretic Marcion* (WUNT 250; Tübingen: Mohr, 2010), 89-102, though we should point out that a literary compilation of *euangelion* plus *apostolikon* was not unique to Marcion. It is very probable that Luke and Acts initially circulated together, and the Gospel and Letters of John form a distinct literary body. Also, 2 Peter assumes the existence of Matthew, Paul's Letters, and Jude (*euangelion, Paulus, Apostolos*).

and early twentieth-century German Protestants with their fascination with or admiration of Marcion.[7]

Irenaeus pointed out that certain groups gravitated toward one particular Gospel to establish their peculiar doctrines. Marcion chose Luke, the Montanists and Valentinians used John, the Docetists preferred Mark, and the Ebionites claimed Matthew.[8] That is not to say that these groups were always ignorant of or adamantly opposed to the other Gospels,[9] but a single Gospel was much easier to use to justify a particular theological framework. The resident framework — be it Gnostic, Docetic, or Christian Judaic — was easier to sustain when the other three "canonical" Gospels were distanced from it, and when the framework was reinforced with the composition of freshly minted "other" Gospels like the *Gospel of the Ebionites,* the *Gospel of Truth,* or the *Gospel of Judas.* Many Christ-believing groups of the second century preferred a single Gospel with supporting literature as opposed to accepting the authority of a fourfold Gospel collection.[10]

However, this trend of preferring one particular Gospel was not the exclusive prerogative of dissenting Christ-believing groups. Even the proto-orthodox were not immune from preferring in practice one particular Gospel. Irenaeus, for all his arguments for the "fourfold Gospel,"[11] overwhelmingly prefers Matthew as his go-to Gospel, and Matthew is the Gospel that sets up his own theological framework and hermeneutical strategies.[12] He was not alone in this preference for Matthew. Justin too had a disposition to cite Matthew more than any other Gospel. Clement of Alexandria, who knew all four canonical Gospels and several of the "other" Gospels, cited

---

7. Hengel, *Four Gospels and the One Gospel of Jesus Christ,* 33.

8. Irenaeus, *Adv. Haer.* 3.11.7, 9.

9. The Valentinian teacher Ptolemy's *Letter to Flora* contains numerous citations of Matthew, the *Gospel of the Ebionites* appears to incorporate many Lucan elements, and there is evidence that later Marcionite groups employed Matthew in some form (see Moll, *Arch-Heretic Marcion,* 109-10 nn. 9, 20; Lee Martin McDonald, *The Formation of the Christian Biblical Canon* [Peabody: Hendrickson, 1995], 154-61).

10. For example, Basilides had his Gospel with his *Exegetica,* Marcion had his shortened Luke with his *Antitheses,* and Tatian had his *Diatessaron* with his *Problemata.* According to Tomas Bokedal, *The Scriptures and the Lord: Formation and Significance of the Christian Biblical Canon* (Lund: Lund University Press, 2005), 176, Marcion's *Antitheses* functioned as a "hermeneutic manual to his gospel."

11. Irenaeus, *Adv. Haer.* 3.1.1-2; 3.11.8-9.

12. Cf. Dwight J. Bingham, *Irenaeus' Use of Matthew's Gospel in Adversus Haereses* (Leuven: Peeters, 2010).

Matthew proportionately far more than the other Gospels.[13] Edouard Massoux's study on the use of Matthew in the early church, though maximalist in where it detects Matthean citations or allusions, shows the widespread prominence of the first Gospel in the time before Irenaeus.[14] The patristic evidence is also confirmed by papyri, where witnesses to Matthew in the second and third centuries far outnumber witnesses to Luke and Mark. The attestation of witnesses to Matthew's text is rivaled only by witnesses to John, who comes in second.[15] It would seem that Matthew was first among equals even among those who knew, used, and had a high regard for a fourfold Gospel.

In sum, many groups, either by choice or by practice, converged around one Gospel. As such, a one Gospel collection stood a good chance of turning into the single Gospel of a New Testament canon.

Second, a further option that was pursued by several Christian authors was the development of a Gospel harmony that drew primarily on the four Gospels but also from other tertiary Jesus traditions. The impetus for this emerged very early. It appears that Matthew, Luke, and John all engaged in an incorporation and harmonization of Mark with their own tradition by writing their own Gospels based on Mark's outline and content.[16] The longer ending of Mark, probably written in the second quarter of the second century,[17] can be understood as someone filling in a perceived gap in Mark's Gospel by inserting a harmonized account of the resurrection narrative that drew on Matthew, Luke, John, and perhaps even Acts.[18] Several sayings in

13. Cf. statistics in Charles E. Hill, *Who Chose the Gospels? Probing the Great Gospel Conspiracy* (Oxford: Oxford University Press, 2010), 70-75.

14. Edouard Massoux, *The Influence of the Gospel of Saint Matthew on Christian Literature before Saint Irenaeus* (2 vols.; trans. A. J. Bellinzoni and N. J. Belval; Macon: Mercer University Press, 1990). For precise figures on patristic citations of the Gospels, see *Biblica Patristica. Index des citations et allusions bibliques dans la littérature patristique* (3 vols; Paris: CNRS, 1975-80), where Matthew proves time and again to be the most popular Gospel.

15. Cf. Larry Hurtado, *The Early Christian Artifacts: Manuscripts and Christian Origins* (Grand Rapids: Eerdmans, 2006), 20.

16. The epilogue to the Fourth Gospel is probably secondary (esp. 21:24 with the switch to the plural "we"), and some have argued that it shows an awareness of Luke and Matthew. See Theo K. Heckel, *Vom Evangelium des Markus zum Viergestaltigen Evangelium* (WUNT 120; Tübingen: Mohr, 1999), 105-218, followed by James A. Kelhoffer, "'How Soon a Book' Revisited: ΕΥΑΓΓΕΛΙΟΝ as a Reference to 'Gospel' Materials in the First Half of the Second Century," *ZNW* 95 (2004): 10-13.

17. Cf. external attestation in *Epistula Apostolorum* 30.1 (ca. 140 CE); Justin, *1 Apol.* 45.5 (ca. 155 CE); Tatian, *Diatessaron* 55.4-11 (ca. 172 CE).

18. Cf. esp. James A. Kelhoffer, *Miracle and Mission* (WUNT 2.112; Tübingen: Mohr,

2 *Clement* might be derived from either "free" quotations or a harmonization of several Synoptic sayings.[19] A number of scholars have argued that Justin Martyr used a harmony of sorts for his Gospel citations.[20] The *Gospel of the Ebionites* (mid-second century) also possesses traits that make it a likely post-Synoptic harmony used by a Jewish Christian group.[21] Jerome reports that Theophilus of Antioch, bishop and apologist (d. ca. 183), "put together into one work the words of the four Gospels."[22] According to Eusebius, the Alexandrian theologian Ammonius (third century) "has left us the Gospel *Diatessaron* (διὰ τεσσάρων), in which he placed beside a section of the Gospel according to Matthew the same pericope of the rest of the Evangelists, with the inevitable result that the order of events of the other three was eliminated as far as the coherence of the text was concerned."[23] The existence and acceptance of so many harmonies tells us something of the attitude toward Jesus literature of the second century, namely, that the four Gospels were largely accepted but could be utilized in different ways.[24]

The thing to remember about harmonies is that they are not just homiletical tools but hermeneutical exercises. What one includes or excludes, augments or deletes, pushes to the front or pushes to the back inevitably shapes the final form of the text. No harmony is theologically neutral since it rests on a prioritization of texts and passages and lends itself to the opportunity to give the book a particular "spin."[25]

2000), 48-156; and similarly Heckel, *Vom Evangelium des Markus zum Viergestaltigen Evangelium*, 279-86.

19. Helmut Koester, *Ancient Christian Gospels: Their History and Development* (London: SCM, 1990), 351-60.

20. Cf. Arthur J. Bellinzoni, *The Sayings of Jesus in the Writings of Justin Martyr* (Leiden: Brill, 1967), 139-43 (Justin used a written catechetical source that harmonized Matthew, Luke, and possibly Mark); Koester, *Ancient Christian Gospels*, 360-402 (Justin wrote his own harmony of the Gospels of Matthew, Luke, and possibly Mark). Oskar Skarsaune, "Justin and His Bible," in *Justin Martyr and His Worlds*, ed. S. Parvis and P. Foster (Minneapolis: Fortress, 2007), 53-76, concludes that Justin used a harmonized source in his *First Apology* but relies on individual Gospels in his *Dialogues with Trypho*.

21. Andrew Gregory, "Prior or Posterior? The *Gospel of the Ebionites* and the Gospel of Luke," *NTS* 51 (2005): 344-60.

22. Jerome, *Ep.* 121.6 (to Aglasius).

23. Eusebius, *Letter to Carpianus* 1 (my trans.), though it is unclear if Ammonius's work was a genuine harmony or more like a synopsis based on Matthew.

24. Cf. further William L. Petersen, "From Justin to Pepys: The History of the Harmonized Gospel Tradition," *Studia Patristica* 30 (1997): 71-96.

25. Ronald A. Piper, "The One, the Four, and the Many," in *The Written Gospel*, ed. M. Bockmuehl and D. A. Hagner (Cambridge: Cambridge University Press, 2005), 262-63.

By far the most influential harmony was Tatian's *Diatessaron,* written ca. 170 and composed in the first instance in Syriac (*Diatessaron* means literally "through the four").[26] Tatian based his harmony largely on Matthew and supplemented it with the others, especially John. He may have adopted his harmony from his teacher Justin. The work was highly influential in the Syriac church up until the fifth century. While Old Syriac translations certainly go back to the mid-second century,[27] the *Diatessaron* was probably the only Jesus book many congregations used, and it persisted even after the formalization of a Syriac canon with the *Peshitta.* In fact, the earliest type of Jesus literature translated into Latin, Syriac, Armenian, and Georgian might even have been the *Diatessaron.*[28] The *Diatessaron* gradually fell out of favor, not because it contained anything spurious but on account of Tatian's lapse

---

26. Witnesses for the *Diatessaron* are sparse, and no actual copies appear to have survived antiquity in their original language. A small fourteen-line Greek fragment was discovered at Dura Europos in 1933. For the most part, however, the text is reconstructed based on various witnesses that either quote the text or were thought to be influenced by it. The most important is Ephraem the Syrian (d. ca. 373) whose commentary on the Syriac survives in an Armenian translation. Also important are an Arabic translation of the *Diatessaron,* a Persian harmony of the Gospels that largely resembles the *Diatessaron,* the Syriac versions of the Gospels, which attest readings that appear to have been influenced by the *Diatessaron,* and many Gospel citations from the eastern fathers of Diatessaronic character (e.g., Ephrem, Aphrahat, Rabbula of Edessa, Isho'dad of Merv, et al.). The primary western witness to the *Diatessaron* is Codex Fuldensis, a sixth-century Latin Gospel harmony, which seems to preserve many Diatessaronic readings, despite being conformed to the language of the Vulgate and put into Matthew's order by a Latin scribe. See William Petersen, "Tatian's *Diatessaron*" in Koester, *Ancient Christian Gospels,* 403-30.

It is not certain that Tatian himself titled his harmony a *Diatessaron* since the first mention of this name is not until Eusebius, *Hist. Eccl.* 4.39.6. Ephraem the Syrian wrote a commentary on Tatian's work and called it "The Gospel of the Mixed." There is also a good chance that Tatian incorporated some "apocryphal" traditions not found in the four Gospels, such as the shining light visible at Jesus' baptism (*Diatessaron* 4.40; *Gospel of the Ebionites* 2; Justin, *Dial. Tryph.* 88.3). See James H. Charlesworth, "Tatian's Dependence upon Apocryphal Traditions," *HeyJ* 15 (1974): 5-17. Tatian undoubtedly utilized the four Gospels as his main sources, and, though he was willing to mix them up with a few other traditions at several isolated points, it is not clear that he incorporated "other" Gospels into his harmony such as the *Gospel of Peter* or the *Gospel of the Hebrews,* as some allege (Petersen in Koester, *Ancient Christian Gospels,* 403). It is only the Persian version of the *Diatessaron* that might have been influenced by the *Infancy Gospel of James* (Craig D. Allert, *A High View of Scripture* [Grand Rapids: Baker, 2007], 117-18). McDonald (*Formation,* 214) thinks that Tatian's followers might have inserted clauses from the *Gospel of the Hebrews* and *Protevangelium of James.*

27. Cf. Eusebius, *Hist. Eccl.* 4.22 where Hegesippus allegedly used a Syriac Gospel.

28. Petersen, "Tatian's *Diatessaron*," 403-4.

into Encratism.[29] Theodoret of Cyrus in the fourth century had 200 copies of the work destroyed and replaced by the canonical Gospels. Theodoret's contemporary, Rabbula of Edessa, also took active measures to expunge the *Diatessaron* from his region, ordering the Gospel of the "separated" replace the Gospel of the "mixed."[30] But in the West, the non-canonical status of the *Diatessaron* was the key to its survival. Prior to the European Reformation there was great resistance against translating the Vulgate into vernacular languages, yet no such prohibition existed for Gospel harmonies. As such, the *Diatessaron* became a para-liturgical text and provided a template for Gospel harmonies for the burgeoning middle classes in Italy, Germany, and the low countries (hence the large number of Diatessaronic readings in the Liège, Tuscan, Pepsian, and Venetian harmonies of the Middle Ages).[31]

William Petersen argues that Tatian's *Diatessaron* was a forthright rejection of the fourfold Gospel collection and was composed in a deliberate attempt to supersede them.[32] While that is certainly possible, it is by no means certain. The harmonies of Theophilus and Ammonius (and even later ones from John Calvin to Loraine Boettner) were not intended to rival or replace the Gospels as much as they were designed to be didactic tools for readers to be able to access the contents of the Gospel in a helpful arrangement.[33] As David Dungan comments, Gospel harmonies "are, properly understood, *missionizing tools,* not replacements for the canonical Gospels."[34]

It is worth considering as well that a harmony could only be written if one first believed that it was possible to bring the sources into a harmonious

---

29. Cf. Irenaeus, *Adv. Haer.* 1.28.1; 3.23.8; Hippolytus, *Refutatio* 8.9; 10.14; Clement, *Strom.* 13; Eusebius, *Hist. Eccl.* 4.28-29; Epiphanius, *Panarion* 46.1.8.

30. Theodoret, *Haereticarum fabularum compendium* 1.20; Rabbula of Edessa, *Canon* 43; see William L. Petersen, *Tatian's Diatessaron: Its Creation, Dissemination, Significance, and History in Scholarship* (Leiden: Brill, 1994), 42-43.

31. Karl Gerlach, *The Antenicene Pascha: A Rhetorical History* (Leuven: Peeters, 1998), 173.

32. William L. Petersen, "The Diatessaron and the Fourfold Gospel," in *The Earliest Gospels: The Origins and Transmission of the Earliest Christian Gospels,* ed. C. Horton (London: Clark, 2004), 67-68.

33. Hill, *Who Chose the Gospels?* 108-9. It is also worth pointing out that Theophilus and Augustine, in addition to their works that harmonize the Gospels, also wrote commentaries on the individual Gospels, so that harmonization and treating each Evangelist in turn were not mutually exclusive.

34. David Dungan, *History of the Synoptic Problem* (ABRL; New York: Doubleday, 1999), 39 (italics original).

accord.[35] Thus a harmony, far from undermining the fourfold Gospel, does the exact opposite. The fact that the four Gospels were chosen to be part of the harmony tells us something of the high regard in which they were held. That they were regarded as harmonizable indicates a perception of their coherence and unity when put together.[36]

That said, we have to countenance the possibility that, as happened in Syria, a Gospel harmony could function as a substitute for the fourfold Gospel collection. The *Diatessaron* is called a "Gospel" on several occasions, the "Gospel called *Diatessaron*" in the west or the "Gospel of the mixed" in the east. The subscriptions laud the work as a Gospel compiled by Tatian and the Vatican ms. makes the work a point of praise to God. One must also wonder whether, if Tatian had not taken to Encratism, the *Diatessaron* could have potentially become a fifth Gospel or been chosen as an alternative to the fourfold Gospel collection. Sadly, we will never know.[37]

A final word on Gospel harmonies and harmonization is necessary. Composing a harmony was not the only way of addressing apparent disparities in the Gospel accounts. Eusebius composed both his *Proof of the Gospel* and *Gospel Problems and Solutions* to tackle many of the apparent contradictions case-by-case. Eusebius also produced his *Gospel Canons* so that, rather than rearranging the Gospel pericopes in a new order, one could identify which occurred in which Gospels. In addition, Augustine's prestigious *Harmony of the Four Gospels* stands out as a near definitive effort to demonstrate the harmonious agreement of the Evangelists in the matters

---

35. That would also explain why it would have been impossible to incorporate documents like the *Gospel of Thomas* or the *Gospel of Truth* in their entirety (one might possibly include fragments, I suppose) into a harmony based largely around the four Gospels. One could at best achieve a fusion of sources, but not an actual harmony, not a single coherent thread, because the materials would be too disparate.

36. This would seem to count against the claim of William Petersen, "The Genesis of the Gospels," in *New Testament Textual Criticism and Exegesis*, ed. A. Denaux (FS J. Delobel; Leuven: Peeters, 2002), 43, that "The *Diatessaron* is evidence that, by 172 or so, there appears to have been neither an established text of the gospels nor a reverential attitude towards their text; rather, the traditions we now regard as part of the canonical gospels were malleable, rearrangeable, and subject to the whims of any writer, editor, or harmonist." A more modest claim is that of McDonald, *Formation*, 214-15, who thinks that Tatian saw the four Gospels as "responsible and faithful documents, but not as inviolable texts." Then again Pheme Perkins, *Introduction to the Synoptic Gospels* (Grand Rapids: Eerdmans, 2007), 29, believes that "the *Diatessaron* represents an alternative way of preserving the traditional apostolic canon, not a challenge to its authority."

37. Petersen, *Tatian's Diatessaron*, 35-67.

over which they differ, a book that had long-lasting significance in the medieval church. Thus, defending the concord of the Gospels did not have to be undertaken by compiling a "jumbo-Gospel," and evangelical harmony could be argued without forfeiting the fourfold apostolic witness to Jesus.[38]

A third possibility was to compose a new Jesus book to rival extant Jesus books. Although much Jesus literature is supplementary to the four Gospels, some documents seem intended to supplant one or more of the four Gospels.

The *Gospel of Thomas* contains traits oriented toward an inward looking sectarianism but also an impetus toward sharing its beliefs with similarly minded Christ-believers and even supplanting rival Jesus literature.[39] The translation of it from Syriac into Greek made wider dissemination in the eastern Mediterranean area possible. It spread from its original provenance in Edessa to Rome, where it was known to Hippolytus, and to Egypt, where it eventually became part of the Nag Hammadi codices, which suggests that it was deliberately carried with a view to promulgating its contents.[40] The identification of Thomas in the incipit is a self-authenticating authorial device that legitimates the work by appealing to readers/hearers who venerate the Apostle Thomas. Moreover, the *Gospel of Thomas* might contain so much Synoptic material, carefully reinterpreted and interwoven with new material, so that it would get a fair hearing from groups where the Synoptic tradition was known. Along this line Mark Goodacre suggests, "The Synoptic sayings are, in other words, the necessary baggage that *Thomas* chose to carry to make the voice of his newly constructed 'living Jesus' sound sufficiently similar to the known voice of Jesus familiar to his audience."[41]

Much of the content of the *Gospel of Thomas* hints at a deliberate attempt to compete with other Christ-believing groups and to supplant their

38. Jonathan T. Pennington, *Reading the Gospels Wisely: A Narrative and Theological Introduction* (Grand Rapids: Baker, 2012), 54.

39. Cf. Michael F. Bird, "Sectarian Gospels for Sectarian Christians? The Non-Canonical Gospels and Bauckham's *The Gospels for All Christians*," in *The Audience of the Gospels: Further Conversation about the Origin and Function of the Gospels in Early Christianity*, ed. Edward W. Klink (LNTS 353; London: Clark, 2010), 37-42.

40. On a Syrian setting and initial Syriac edition of the *Gospel of Thomas*, see Nicholas Perrin, *Thomas and Tatian: The Relationship between the Gospel of Thomas and the Diatessaron* (Atlanta: Society of Biblical Literature, 2002).

41. Mark Goodacre, *Thomas and the Gospels: The Case for Thomas's Familiarity with the Synoptics* (Grand Rapids: Eerdmans, 2012), 180.

Jesus literature. For example, in logion 13, where Thomas trumps Simon Peter and Matthew at best describing Jesus, the episode arguably reflects an intramural debate designed to ridicule the christological beliefs of other Christ-believing groups in favor of the esoteric perspective of Jesus in the *Gospel of Thomas*. The Thomasine aim appears to be to denigrate the Jesus of the Jesus literature belonging to the proto-orthodox churches by criticizing the leaders who were associated with such literature, including Simon Peter (i.e., the Gospel of Mark) and Matthew (i.e., the Gospel of Matthew).[42] Or again the "chosen ones" referred to in the document may not be a local "community" but those with similar beliefs living among the myriads of proto-orthodox believers.[43] The two references to what others "say" and say in error imply a polemical interaction with other Christ-believing groups in regard to their eschatology and their suspicion toward the Thomasine teaching.[44] Indeed, the *Gospel of Thomas* addresses contentious topics among the proto-orthodox concerning fasting, apostolic succession, christology, eschatology, Scripture, and circumcision, and the Thomasine Jesus offers answers to these questions over against proto-orthodox affirmations.[45] Bruce Lincoln puts it this way:

> On the one hand, it [the *Gospel of Thomas*] proclaims itself to be secret, or to contain secrets, as in the Prologue. . . . But on the other hand, the text was widely circulated, and states that this is as it should be. . . . This contradiction, however, can be accounted for by recognizing that *Thomas*, like Ptolemaeus' *Letter to Flora* and numerous other religious documents, is a text that is addressed at the same time to initiates and non-initiates alike. Thus, the *fact* that the *Thomas*-community possessed secret knowledge was proclaimed loudly to outsiders, but the *nature* of that knowledge and its true meaning were disclosed only within the community itself in a program of detailed instruction which must have lasted over a period of several years.[46]

42. Larry Hurtado, *Lord Jesus Christ: Devotion to Jesus in Earliest Christianity* (Grand Rapids: Eerdmans, 2003), 462; Watson, "Fourfold Gospel," 37-39; Nicholas Perrin, *Thomas: The Other Gospel* (Louisville: Westminster John Knox, 2007), 107-24; Goodacre, *Thomas and the Gospels,* 178-79.

43. *Gospel of Thomas* 23; cf. 49, 50.

44. *Gospel of Thomas* 3, 50.

45. *Gospel of Thomas* 6, 12, 18, 20, 24, 37, 43, 51, 52, 53, 99, 113.

46. Bruce Lincoln, "Thomas-Gospel and Thomas-Community: A New Approach to a Familiar Text," *NovT* 19 (1977): 68-69.

The *Gospel of Thomas* shows that there was always the option of writing an alternative Gospel if one did not like the Gospels that were around, and many took the time to engage in such a literary activity, even with some degree of success and attracting notoriety among proto-orthodox authors.[47]

To briefly recap, a fourfold Gospel was not the only possibility or the preference for all Christ-believing groups. Some opted for a single Gospel, others used a harmony in conjunction with or as an alternative to the four Gospels; and others still composed their own Gospels based on received tradition and a belief in their own revelation about the true Jesus. While the fourfold Gospel triumphed among the proto-orthodox, it was certainly not an uncontested rise, nor an inevitable victory. The rise and reasoning behind the fourfold Gospel collection thus still needs an explanation.

Early Witnesses to a Fourfold Gospel Collection

In regard to the emergence of the fourfold Gospel, as a preliminary remark we have to discern the difference between a "collection" and a "canon." Or, as Bruce Metzger put it, there is a difference between a collection of author-itative books and an authoritative collection of books.[48] The four Gospels became part of the canon (i.e., an authoritative collection of books) in the fourth century when the twenty-seven New Testament documents were rati-fied as the church's official list of sacred writings. The Synod of Carthage first

---

47. Goodacre (*Thomas and the Gospels,* 179) thinks that "It would be well nigh impos-sible for the author of Thomas to think of replacing the Synoptic Gospels at this point, and he does not try that. Instead, his best bet is to accept their existence but to attempt to transcend them by means of the fiction of special revelation and hidden sayings to a key figure, Judas Thomas the twin." True enough, but when I say that the authors and disseminators of *Thomas* were trying to "supplant" the Synoptics, that does not mean instantly and universally. Rather, I think that they were trying to edge out the Synoptics and to commend their own work among disenfranchised persons and within sympathetic groups among the proto-orthodox, who might take their Synoptic tradition plus new revelations of the living Jesus as their primary (though perhaps not exclusive) Jesus book.

48. Bruce M. Metzger, *The Canon of the New Testament: Its Origin, Development, and Significance* (Oxford: Clarendon, 1987), 283. François Bovon, *New Testament and Christian Apocrypha* (Grand Rapids: Baker, 2011), 320: "One must distinguish a collection's birth from its formal canonization. The creation of the corpus of four Gospels or of Pauline letters was a work of second-century piety, recognizing the authority of these documents. Not yet a formal canon validated by official decision, its existence was common opinion shared by those who considered themselves to be the orthodox church."

promulgated such a list in 397 CE, but that was little more than a regional council with no universal authority, and its decisions were hardly innovative. Similar lists about the register of authoritative Christian books had been around since the late second century as in the Muratorian canon and lists set forth by Clement of Alexandria, Eusebius, Cyril of Jerusalem, and Athanasius.[49] While the fourfold Gospel did not become an authoritative canonical collection until the fourth century, in any event the widespread use of the Gospels in the preceding centuries indicates that the fourfold Gospel was certainly a collection of authoritative books for many churches.

The broad circulation and widespread use of the four Gospels was hardly random. According to McDonald, the reason for the immense popularity of the four Gospels was because they told the story of Jesus, the Lord of the church, and they conveyed popular tradition about him.[50] That is why they were so frequently deployed in the "church's worship and catechetical instruction, its defense of the 'gospel' in the pagan world, and in its response to the heretical challenges it faced by the end of the first century and beyond."[51] As far as manuscript evidence for Christian writings goes, it is not too much to say that the fourfold Gospel codex was the most popular book among Christians and the proverbial bestseller.

But how did this collection come to be? Who first thought to put Matthew, Mark, Luke, and John into one codex? Why was it done? What has one created, literarily and theologically, by putting together this kind of "Gospel-boy-band"?

The impetus (or blame!) for the fourfold Gospel collection is often left at the feet of the second-century bishop of Lyons, Irenaeus. It was Irenaeus who wrote:

> It is not possible that the Gospels can be either more or fewer in number than they are, for, since there are four zones of the world in which we live, and four principal winds [Ezek 37:9], while the Church is scattered throughout the world, and the "pillar and ground" of the Church is the Gospel and the spirit of life; it is fitting that she should have four pillars, breathing out immortality on every side, and vivifying men afresh. From which fact, it is evident that the Word, the Artificer of all, He that sitteth

---

49. Cf. discussion in Geoffrey M. Hahneman, *The Muratorian Fragment and the Development of the Canon* (Oxford: Clarendon, 1992), 134-35.

50. Lee Martin McDonald, "The Gospels in Early Christianity: Their Origin, Use, and Authority," in *Reading the Gospels Today,* ed. S. E. Porter (Grand Rapids: Eerdmans, 2004), 155.

51. McDonald, "Gospels in Early Christianity," 150.

upon the cherubim, and contains all things, He who was manifested to men, has given the Gospel under four aspects, but bound together by one Spirit. As also David says, when entreating His manifestation, "Thou that sittest between the cherubim, shine forth" [Ps 80:1]. For, [as Scripture says], "The first living creature was like a lion" [Rev. 4:7], symbolizing His effectual working, His leadership, and royal power; the second [living creature] was like a calf, signifying [His] sacrificial and sacerdotal order; but "the third had, as it were, the face as of a man," — an evident description of His advent as a human being; "the fourth was like a flying eagle," pointing out the gift of the Spirit hovering with His wings of the Church. And therefore the Gospels are in accord with these things, among which Christ Jesus is seated.[52]

By insisting on four Gospels, Elaine Pagels says that "Irenaeus resolved to hack down the forest of 'apocryphal and illegitimate' writings . . . and leave only four 'pillars' standing."[53] Others think that Irenaeus was a bit of a loner in his reasoning. McDonald believes that "Irenaeus' acceptance of the four canonical Gospels was not generally shared by his contemporaries or even by many Christians at a later time" and "Although Irenaeus may have seen the need for four 'pillars' of gospels for the church, it is difficult to establish that the evangelists themselves or anyone before Irenaeus saw such a need."[54] Campenhausen is even more emphatic: "All that can be said without fear of contradiction is that in fact not the slightest trace has survived to suggest that these four 'canonical' Gospels already possessed special status, as is often alleged, and were formally grouped together. All speculations about the emergence of a Four-Gospel canon, whether in Asia Minor or in Rome, prior to the time of Marcion, are without foundation, and rest simply on the arbitrary retrojection onto this period of an anachronistic idea."[55] But does the skepticism hold up? A study of our sources suggests otherwise.

Papias, bishop of Hierapolis, is our first author to demonstrate an awareness of more than one written Gospel.[56] He is aware of traditions

---

52. Irenaeus, *Adv. Haer.* 3.11.8; cf. 3.1.1.

53. Elaine Pagels, *Beyond Belief: The Secret Gospel of Thomas* (New York: Random, 2003), 111.

54. McDonald, "Gospels in Early Christianity," 172; idem, *Formation*, 168.

55. Campenhausen, *Formation*, 142.

56. I prefer to date Papias's writings in 110 CE rather than the usual 130, convinced as I am by the fine arguments of Robert Yarbrough, "The Date of Papias: Reassessment," *JETS* 26

concerning the origin of the Gospel of Mark based on Mark's "memory" of Peter's preaching and of the Hebraic texture of Matthew.[57] Some allege that he also knew the Gospel of John.[58] His preference for oral testimony should not be construed as a denunciation of written texts.[59] Like many ancient historians, Papias simply preferred to get his information from eyewitnesses when possible. His exposition of the sayings of the Lord was likely a commentary based on the Jesus traditions and Jesus literature that he knew, in which two or more of the Gospels probably figured prominently.[60]

Other early second-century literature also attests a widespread usage of the four Gospels. The longer ending of Mark 16:9-20, composed by the time of Justin in 150 CE, is very likely an attempt to fill a gap in Mark's Gospel by inserting a resurrection narrative that was, deliberately or accidentally, lacking in extant witnesses. The insertion deliberately imitates Mark's style, but is also based on a coagulation of materials from Matthew, Luke, John, and Acts. It is no "novel composition" but an "intentional imitation of all four of the NT Gospels."[61] That assumes of course that the four Gospels were in circulation and usage in some locations by this time (ca. 125-50). In addition, someone thought that a Gospel could be legitimately augmented with new material as long as the supplementary material was connected to the other Gospels. While the Gospels evidently held authority for the author of Mark's longer ending, it was still possible in the mind of the author to handle the texts with some degree of evangelically inspired creativity.

Another text roughly contemporaneous with Mark's longer ending is the *Epistula Apostolorum,* or "Letter of the Apostles." The document is framed as a letter from the eleven Apostles, and its opening chapters recount much of Jesus' ministry and resurrection, but it is primarily a dialogue between the risen Jesus and his Apostles. The text is extant in Ethiopic, Coptic, and a single Latin sheet. It is a proto-orthodox writing that attempts to refute Docetic and Gnostic christologies. Hill has argued persuasively that it is an Asian tract, specifically from Smyrna, going back to the time of Polycarp

---

(1983): 181-91. The date 110 is accepted also by Graham Stanton, *Jesus and Gospel* (Cambridge: Cambridge University Press, 2004), 79. Recently Heckel, *Vom Evangelium des Markus zum Viergestaltigen Evangelium,* 221, 265, opts for a date of 120-30.

57. Papias, *Fragment* 3.15-16 (= Eusebius, *Hist. Eccl.* 3.39.15-16).

58. Cf. Charles E. Hill, "What Papias Said about John (and Luke)," *JTS* 49 (1998): 582-629; idem, *Who Chose the Gospels?* 210-22.

59. Papias, *Fragment* 3.3-4 (= Eusebius, *Hist. Eccl.* 3.39.4).

60. Cf. Heckel, *Vom Evangelium des Markus zum Viergestaltigen Evangelium,* 261-65.

61. Kelhoffer, *Miracle and Mission,* 121.

(ca. 70-156), and is best dated around the 140s.[62] Hill surmises that "The *Ep. Apost.* may be viewed as an Asian author's attempt, through the medium of an openly fictional but seriously purposed pseudepigraphon, to provide edificatory resources to his Christian community in its struggle with false teaching, outside persecution, and tribulation common to the Asian situation."[63] The document's form was probably influenced by other resurrection dialogues like the *Apocryphon of James*, and it is also incorporates a tradition found in the *Infancy Gospel of Thomas* about Jesus' boyhood.[64] That said, the *Epistula Apostolorum* draws the vast bulk of its material from all four Gospels with a clear preference for the Gospel of John. Understood this way, it is evidence of the widespread usage and synthesis of the four Gospels up to half a century before Irenaeus.[65] Hannah outlines its significance: "The *Epistula*, then, knew and used all four of the canonical gospels. The author explicitly names the apostles as authors and places their writings alongside the Old Testament, thereby attributing to them a certain authority even if not quite stating unambiguously that they possess the same authority of the earlier Scriptures (*Ep. Apost.* 31)."[66]

The Valentinians are further witnesses to the fourfold Gospel. Valentinus himself may have drawn much impetus for his approach to Jesus books from Basilides in Alexandria. Basilides had his own Gospel and wrote a twenty-four-volume commentary on it. Information about Basilides' Gospel from Hippolytus, Epiphanius, and Clement of Alexandria shows connections with John, Matthew, and perhaps Luke.[67] The Nag Hammadi *Gospel of Truth*, perhaps authored by Valentinus himself, contains echoes of Matthew and John as well as Romans, 1-2 Corinthians, Ephesians, Colossians, Hebrews, 1 John, and Revelation. The Valentinian teachers Ptolemy and Heracleon both wrote commentaries on John, with Heracleon also writing on Luke.[68] Ptolemy's *Letter to Flora* also cites Matthew, John, and Paul's letters. It would

---

62. Charles E. Hill, "The *Epistula Apostolorum*: An Asian Tract from the Time of Polycarp," *JECS* 7 (1999): 1-53; and similarly Darrell D. Hannah, "The Four-Gospel 'Canon' in the *Epistula Apostolorum*," *JTS* 58 (2007): 628-32.

63. Hill, "*Epistula Apostolorum*," 53.

64. *Epistula Apostolorum* 4-5; cf. critical remarks by Irenaeus, *Adv. Haer.* 1.20.1.

65. Cf. esp. Hannah, "Four-Gospel 'Canon,'" 598-633.

66. Hannah, "Four-Gospel 'Canon,'" 632.

67. Cf. Campenhausen, *Formation*, 139 n. 159.

68. Ptolemy's comments on John 1:1-4 are found in Irenaeus, *Adv. Haer.* 1.8.5, while Heracleon's commentaries are extant throughout Origen's commentary on John, and see Clement of Alexandria, *Strom.* 4.9; *Eclogae Propheticae*.

seem that the Valentinian "canon" was essentially identical to the proto-orthodox one.[69] The Valentinians differed primarily in their claim to be able to detect in Scripture an underlying Gnostic narrative, especially in John. When Tertullian contrasted Marcion and Valentinus, he noted that Marcion perverted the Scriptures with a knife, but Valentinus more cunningly perverted them with the pen.[70]

Marcion's role as a catalyst for the canonization of the Gospels and the wider New Testament is ordinarily overstated.[71] His "canon" of Luke plus Paul allegedly forced church leaders to start thinking once and for all about what the agreed register of sacred books comprised.[72] Irenaeus, however, asserts that Marcion's co-opting and correction of Luke was in fact a response to the fourfold Gospel. The bishop writes: "He likewise persuaded his disciples that he himself was more worthy of credit than are those apostles who have handed down the Gospel to us, furnishing them not with the Gospel, but merely a fragment of it."[73] There is no doubt that Marcion forced church leaders like Tertullian and Irenaeus to delve into deep questions about texts, hermeneutics, and authority, but in no way can the fourfold canon simply be a response to Marcion.

Justin Martyr provides further witness to a fourfold Gospel collection. He clearly knows the texts of Matthew and Luke, he may even have made his own harmony of the two in a notebook, and there are isolated instances that show he was aware of both Mark and John.[74] Justin is also the first to our

---

69. Bentley Layton, *The Gnostic Scriptures* (New York: Doubleday, 1987), xxii-xxiii.

70. Tertullian, *De praescriptione hereticorum* 38.

71. Cf. Campenhausen, *Formation*, 142, 147-209; see the sympathetic but more nuanced approach in McDonald, *Formation*, 160-61.

72. It seems doubtful that Marcion thought of himself as creating a "canon," and if he did it was ineffective because his later follower Miltiades composed a book of Psalms for the Marcionite churches (*Muratorian Fragment* 81-83). Hahnemen, *Muratorian Fragment*, 90-91, shows that later Marcionite communites were not limited to the Marcionite canon and Marcion may have used other Christian writings and edited them too. It is probable, as John Barton contends ("Marcion Revisited," in *The Canon Debate*, ed. L. M. McDonald and J. A. Sanders [Peabody: Hendrickson, 2002], 342-43) that Marcion was not assembling a collection of Christian books but making a very restricted selection from a corpus of texts which already existed and were recognized by many in the church as Scripture.

73. Irenaeus, *Adv. Haer.* 1.27.2.

74. Justin, *Dial. Tryph.* 106.3 (Mark 3:16-17) and *1 Apol.* 61.4 (John 3:3-5). That Justin knew John is the most contested claim. Several scholars think that Justin cites a free-floating baptismal liturgy mentioning new birth rather than John's Gospel (so Bellinzoni, *The Sayings of Jesus in the Writings of Justin Martyr*, 136-37; Koester, *Ancient Christian Gospels*, 257-58), but others point out that while the verbal parallel is not exact, there is enough continuity to

knowledge to use the plural "Gospels" (εὐαγγέλια), certainly substantiating the claim that he knew more than one.[75] As I argued in the previous chapter, for Justin the Gospels are not just records of Jesus but sacred narratives, on a par with the Jewish Scriptures, and they are revelatory documents.[76]

To recap from earlier, the harmonies of Theophilus of Antioch and Tatian the Syrian and the synopsis of Ammonius the Alexandrian are additional proof for the wide reception of and high regard for the four Gospels. Their works were most likely intended as didactic supplements rather than as attempts to supplant the fourfold Gospel. Even if Tatian or his disciples added a few isolated traditions from "other" Gospels, there is no doubt that the overwhelming body of his harmony is composed of the four canonical Gospels.

The testimony of the Muratorian fragment is another block in the wall of a solid fourfold Gospel collection in the second century. It was discovered in 1738-40 by Lodovico Antonio Muratori in a Latin codex that contains a miscellaneous collection of Latin fragments of church fathers. The fragment contains eighty-five lines of text, normally regarded as a Latin translation of a Greek original, giving a list of New Testament books. The fragment runs:

> . . . at which nevertheless he [Peter] was present, and so he [Mark] placed [them in his narrative]. The third book of the Gospel is that according to Luke. Luke, the well-known physician, after the ascension of Christ, when Paul had taken with him as one zealous for the law, composed it in his own name, according to [the general] belief. Yet he himself had not seen the Lord in the flesh; and therefore, as he was able to ascertain events, so indeed he begins to tell the story from the birth of John. The fourth of the Gospels is that of John, [one] of the disciples. To his fellow disciples and bishops, who had been urging him [to write], he said, "Fast with me from today to three days, and what will be revealed to each one let us tell it to one another." In the same night it was revealed to Andrew, [one] of the apostles, that John should write down all things in his own

---

envisage knowledge of the Fourth Gospel, and other echoes of Johannine materials can be found in Justin. See John Pryor, "Justin Martyr and the Fourth Gospel," *The Second Century* 9 (1992): 165; Charles Hill, "The Fourth Gospel in the Second Century: The Myth of Orthodox Johannophobia," in *Challenging Perspectives on the Gospel of John*, ed. J. Lierman (WUNT 2.219; Tübingen: Mohr, 2006), 153-56; idem, *Who Chose the Gospels?* 135-40; Heckel, *Vom Evangelium des Markus zum Viergestaltigen Evangelium*, 320-24.

75. Justin, *1 Apol.* 66.3.

76. Cf. esp. Justin, *Dial. Tryph.* 119.6; *1 Apol.* 42.4; 67.

name while all of them should review it. And so, though various elements may be taught in the individual books of the Gospels, nevertheless this makes no difference to the faith of believers, since by the one sovereign Spirit all things have been declared in all [the Gospels]: concerning the nativity, concerning the passion, concerning the resurrection, concerning life with his disciples, and concerning his twofold coming; the first in lowliness when he was despised, which has taken place, the second glorious in royal power, which is still in the future. What marvel is it then, if John so consistently mentions these particular points also in his Epistles, saying about himself, 'What we have seen with our eyes and heard with our ears and our hands have handled, these things we have written to you?' For in this way he professes [himself] to be not only an eye-witness and hearer, but also a writer of all the marvelous deeds of the Lord, in their order. Moreover, the acts of all the apostles were written in one book. For "most excellent Theophilus" Luke compiled the individual events that took place in his presence — as he plainly shows by omitting the martyrdom of Peter as well as the departure of Paul from the city [of Rome] when he journeyed to Spain.[77]

The fragment begins toward the end of a section about Mark writing down a record of Peter's preaching about Jesus, then moves into an account of the origins of the Gospels of Luke and John, and presumably it also had an account of Matthew's Gospel. Most likely the fragment is simply a rehearsal of Papias's comments about the origins of the Gospels with supplementary material about Luke gleaned from Paul's letters and Acts.

Dating the Muratorian fragment has proved contentious. The early consensus was that it was composed sometime between 180 and 200 CE, probably in Rome. Others, however, proffer that it came from the east sometime in the 300s.[78] In favor of an early date is the observation that the fragment stems from a time when several writings are still very much debated as to their status in the churches. The fragment refers to the reception of the Apocalypses of John and Peter, noting that some are not willing to admit the latter. It also presents a forthright case for not accepting the *Shepherd of Hermas* on the grounds that it is has only been around "very recently, in our

---

77. *Muratorian Fragment* 1-39 (trans. B. Metzger). Quite notable is the switch between singular *evangelium* and plural *evangeliorum* in 2, 9, and 17.

78. Cf. Albert C. Sundberg, "Canon Muratori: A Fourth Century List," *HTR* 66 (1973): 1-41; Hahneman, *Muratorian Fragment*; McDonald, *Formation*, 209-20.

times" *(nuperrime et temporibus nostris),* coming from Rome, during the Roman episcopate of Pius (ca. 140-55).[79] Debates about the *Shepherd* had their high point in the second century, a time contemporary with Bishop Pius I of Rome, a period still within living memory of the author.[80] The heretical groups mentioned at the end belong to the second century. Also, if the fragment is late, it is harder to explain the omission of so many of the catholic letters, with only Jude and two letters of John included. Moreover, while sometimes called a "canon," the "fragment" in fact is different from canon lists of the fourth and fifth centuries. It more reasonably resembles a preface or introduction to a New Testament collection and gives the status quo on debates about the reception of several writings by Christ-believing groups. Metzger said that the tone of the fragment is more like an explanation than an act of legislation about the limits of a catalog of books.[81]

Other Christian authors just after Irenaeus appear to share a similar perspective in their acknowledgment of the authenticity and authority of the four Gospels. Clement of Alexandria rejects a logion from the *Gospel of the Egyptians* on the grounds that it is not found in the "four Gospels that have been handed down to us."[82] In an exposition about the rich young ruler, Clement refers to the Gospel of Mark as one among the "acknowledged Gospels."[83] Eusebius has a surviving fragment from Clement's *Hypotyposeis* where Clement receives a tradition from the "primitive elders" about the order of the Gospels: the Gospels with genealogies came first, then Mark was written in Rome, and then finally John, the spiritual Gospel.[84] Clement's view of the uniqueness and weight of the four Gospels was thought to be part of a long-standing tradition.[85]

In the first decades of the third century, Irenaeus's position becomes suddenly normative. At the dawn of the third century, Hippolytus wrote two eschatological works, a commentary on Daniel and a treatise on the Christ and the anti-Christ. Drawing a comparison between Christ and the river

---

79. The attempt of Sundberg and Hahneman to interpret "most recently, in our time" as meaning "post-apostolic time" is an epic failure: see Charles E. Hill, "The Debate over the Muratorian Fragment and the Development of the Canon," *WTJ* 57 (1995): 437-52; idem, *Who Chose the Gospels?* 97.

80. Cf. Tertullian, *On Modesty* 10.

81. Metzger, *New Testament Canon,* 200; Campenhausen, *Formation,* 244-45.

82. Clement of Alexandria, *Strom.* 3.13.93; cf. Irenaeus, *Adv. Haer.* 1.27.2; 3.1.1; 3.11.9.

83. Clement of Alexandria, *Who Is the Rich Man That Shall Be Saved?* 5.

84. Eusebius, *Hist. Eccl.* 6.14.5-7.

85. Hill, *Who Chose the Gospels?* 74.

of Eden with vivid imagery, "Christ, himself, being the river, is preached in the whole world through the fourfold Gospel."[86] Further to that, Hippolytus places the Gospels in a scriptural chain with the Law, the Prophets, and the Apostles.[87] Tertullian possessed a high esteem for the four Gospels. Sometime between 207 and 213 he wrote his lengthy *Against Marcion*, in which he defends the four Gospels over against Marcion's mutilation of Luke. He depicts the four Gospels as authoritative sources of faith.[88] In light of that, it seems hard to imagine that Irenaeus, out in lonely Lyons, could command such currency for his innovative views on a fourfold Gospel by authors spread as far as Alexandria, Antioch, Carthage, and Rome within a few decades. It is more likely that he represented what was already happening on the wider scene as the Gospels were already known and highly regarded as a collection of sacred writings for diverse Christ-believers.

There is also manuscript evidence for the widespread popularity of the four Gospels. Christians were allegedly "addicted" to the codex, and it certainly was the preferred textual medium for sacred Christian literature in the second and third centuries. Codices were the overwhelmingly preferred medium for writings that were deemed to be Scripture and later "canon." Codices were ideal for carrying a collection of Paul's letters and a collection of all four Gospels. The employment of a quasi-documentary script rather than formal book hand meant that the codices were inscribed with a view to intramural circulation.[89] All four Gospels would not fit onto a single scroll, but they could be compressed into a single codex. We have examples from the late second and early third centuries of single Gospel codices (P.[53], P.[66], P.[69], P.[70], and P.[90]), codices containing two or more Gospels (P.[75] and possibly P.[4, 64, 67]),[90] and a fourfold Gospel codex (P.[45]). Why Christians preferred the codex is a debated question. It could stem from simply enlarging notebooks

---

86. Hippolytus, *Commentary on Daniel* 1.17.

87. Hippolytus, *De Christo* 58.

88. Tertullian, *Adv. Marc.* 4.2.5.

89. Harry Gamble, "The Book Trade in the Roman Empire," in *The Early Text of the New Testament*, ed. C. E. Hill and M. J. Kruger (Oxford: Oxford University Press, 2012), 33.

90. T. C. Skeat, "The Oldest Manuscript of the Four Gospels?" *NTS* 43 (1997): 1-34 (cf. Stanton, *Jesus and Gospel*, 74), believed that P.[4] (Luke) and P.[64, 67] (Matthew) come from the same codex, but the claim is contested by Peter Head, "Is P.[4], P.[64] and P.[67] the Oldest Manuscript of the Four Gospels? A Response to T. C. Skeat," *NTS* 51 (2005): 450-57; idem, "Graham Stanton and the Four-Gospel Codex," in *Jesus, Matthew's Gospel and Early Christianity*, ed. R. Burridge, D. Gurtner, and J. Willitts (LNTS 435; London: Clark, 2011), 93-101; Scott D. Charlesworth, "T. C. Skeat, P.[64] + [67] and P.[4], and the Problem of Fibre Orientation in Codicological Reconstruction," *NTS* 53 (2007): 582-604.

containing Jesus' words into a codex, a desire to distinguish their literature from Jewish and pagan documents, perhaps cost since codices may have been 25% cheaper than scrolls, convenience of consultation and transportation, to provide a physical format to enhance the authority and prestige of the fourfold Gospels, or perhaps in imitation of a Pauline letter collection.[91]

In contrast, a fairly even split of texts and fragments of "other" Gospels are found in scrolls rather than codices, and these scrolls look as if they were designed primarily for private reading.[92] Many obviously circulated widely among like-minded readers, but they lack the telltale signs of "catholicity" associated with codices used for documents regarded as Scripture, namely, standardized codices and standardized *nomina sacra,* indicators of consensus and collaboration among Christian groups.[93] The fact that most of these non-canonical fragments are found not in codices but on scrolls would indicate that the copyists and/or users for whom copies were prepared did not regard them as possessing scriptural status.[94]

Further to that, it is surely interesting that many church fathers did not know about several of these so-called Gospels. Whereas Bart Ehrman thinks that the *Gospel of Peter* was just as popular as the Gospel of Mark, Bishop Serapion of Antioch had never heard of the *Gospel of Peter* before the church at Rhossus brought it to his attention. However, we can assume that Serapion knew all four canonical Gospels because his predecessor Theophilus compiled a Gospel harmony.[95] While Irenaeus had his own collection of "other" Gospels, including the Valentinian *Gospel of Truth* and the Sethian *Gospel of Judas,*[96] these are never once mentioned by either Clement of Alexandria or Origen, the two authors who cite "other" Jesus books more liberally, nor

91. Cf. Hurtado, *Early Christian Artifacts,* 61-83; David C. Parker, *An Introduction to the New Testament Manuscripts and Their Texts* (Cambridge: Cambridge University Press, 2008), 13-20; Bokedal, *The Scriptures and the Lord,* 128-56.

92. Unknown fragment: P. Eg. 2 (codex); P. Oxy 5072 (codex); *Gospel of Thomas:* P. Oxy 1 (codex), P. Oxy 655 (unused roll); P. Oxy 654 (opisthograph [re-used roll]); *Gospel of Mary:* P. Ryl. 463 (codex); P. Oxy 3525 (roll); *Gospel of Peter* (?): P. Oxy 4009 (codex); P. Oxy 2949 (roll); Fayyum Gospel (roll). Hill, *Who Chose the Gospels?* 28-32, also points out that the codices for *Gospel of Peter* (?) and *Gospel of Mary* were miniature size and not suited for public reading.

93. Scott Charlesworth, "'Catholicity' in Early Gospel Manuscripts," in *The Early Text of the New Testament,* ed. Hill and Kruger, 37-48.

94. Hurtado, *Early Christian Artifacts,* 56-58; Hill, *Who Chose the Gospels?* 26-28.

95. Bart Ehrman, *Lost Christianities: The Battle for Scripture and the Faiths We Never Knew* (Oxford: Oxford University Press, 2003), 22.

96. Irenaeus, *Adv. Haer.* 1.31.2, featuring *Gospel of Judas* (1.3.1); writings of the Caprocratians (*Adv. Haer.* 1.25.4-5); *Apocryphon of John* (1.29.1); and *Gospel of Truth* (3.11.9).

are they known to the catalogs of Eusebius and the Gelasian decree. Consequently we must wonder precisely how widely many of these "other" Gospels circulated beyond their point of origin.

Next we strike on the real reason why the four Gospels collection came together. For a start, the four Gospels were the earliest ones written, and they had a big head start on other Jesus books.[97] The "Holy Internet" of the early Christian movement was composed of a myriad of churches who were in close and constant contact with each other. Paul Trebilco has argued that the first Christians understood themselves as both a global phenomenon and a localized phenomenon.[98] On the international side, Christian literature displays an acute awareness by Christians of being part of a worldwide movement (e.g., Rom 1:8; Col 1:5-6; 1 Pet 5:9; Heb 13:24; *1 Clem.* 1.1; *Mart. Pol.* 8.1) and a sense of possessing a common bond with other Christian communities (e.g., 1 Cor 1:2; 1 Thess 2:14; 1 Pet 5:9; Rev. 2:1–3:22). They shared writings as directed or as collected (1 Thess 5:27; Col 4:16; *Mart. Pol.* 21.1; Polycarp, *Phil.* 13.2; Eusebius, *Hist. Eccl.* 4.23.11; Jerome, *De vir.* 17). It follows that the formation of the fourfold Gospel collection was not due to a top-down episcopal imposition, but emerged out of the networking of literature among proto-orthodox believers in the late first and early second centuries.

From the very genesis of the Gospels, they seem to have been widely circulated and well read. The author and benefactors of the Gospel of Mark passed the document on to other Christian groups, who themselves took inspiration from Mark to write their own Gospels, and their Gospels in turn circulated in similar fashion. Sometime after that, two or more of the Gospels were collected together, leading eventually to a fourfold collection. That collection itself became a portable Jesus library, holding great utility and attraction for proto-orthodox churches. The broad and brisk dissemination of the four Gospels presumes a lively interest in texts among Christian communities combined with an efficient means for their reproduction and distribution.[99] As such, Bovon is entirely correct that "The four Gospels were assembled because the groups who respected individual texts were in contact and accepted the validity of other communities' texts."[100] The single greatest factor for the development of the fourfold Gospel collection was not Marcion's single Gospel canon but an international network of churches

97. Cf., e.g., Hahneman, *Muratorian Fragment,* 94.

98. Paul Trebilco, "'Global' and 'Local' in the New Testament and in Earliest Christianity," Inaugural Professorial Lecture, September 21, 2006, University of Otago, New Zealand.

99. Gamble, "Book Trade in the Roman Empire," 34.

100. Bovon, *New Testament and Christian Apocrypha,* 320.

with a varied yet common theological ethos, who traveled widely, shared and copied each other's works, and placed them in a literary medium specifically designed for widespread usage.

As to exactly when some bright spark decided to put the four Gospels into a single collection, presumably a codex, we cannot be certain. We are left estimating at what date. Stanton is among those who cautiously intimate that it must have happened by 150, by the time of Justin.[101] Slightly earlier is E. J. Goodspeed's suggestion: by ca. 115-25.[102] Even earlier is Theo Heckel, who finds evidence from the final redaction of John and from Papias for a date between 110 and 140.[103] Together, Papias, the editors of John 21, the author of the longer ending of Mark, and the author of the *Epistula Apostolorum*, all indicate familiarity with and fusion of the four as sacred texts, and that would push us toward the date that Heckel suggested.

Some will respond that we cannot speak of a fourfold Gospel "canon" in the second century. The point is valid, but requires some explanation. By the end of the second century, there is no universally held concept of a closed canon, a definitive and final catalog of religious books to which none can be added. A closed canon emerged gradually in the fourth century. However, the architecture for the canon, specifically, a fourfold Gospel canon, is clearly in place by the mid-second century. The four Gospels were certainly functioning as Scripture for many and were the only Gospels that realistically stood a chance to be canonized later on account of their widespread usage and their esteem among both proto-orthodox and heterodox churches in the east and the west. What is clear is that there is a developing consensus from the early second century and onward that these four Gospels are the definitive apostolic accounts of Jesus' life, passion, and resurrection. The second century, then, was very much the womb for canonical development, and what was decided by the councils about the canon in the fourth century was a natural outcome from what was said about Christian literature in the

101. Stanton, *Jesus and Gospel*, 63-91.

102. E. J. Goodspeed, *The Formation of the New Testament* (Chicago: University of Chicago Press, 1937), 37-38.

103. Heckel, *Vom Evangelium des Markus zum Viergestaltigen Evangelium*, 353: "The starting point is the presumed effective-history of the Fourfold Gospel collection. The time span in which the collection originated with a formal title can be narrowed between the years AD 110-140" (Ausgangspunkt der Wirkungsgeschichte ist die vermutete Entstehungszeit der Vierevangeliensammlung. Die Zeitspanne, in der die Sammlung entstanden sein dürfe, konnte zunächst mit den Überschriften auf die Jahre zwischen 110 und 140 n.Chr. eingegrenzt werden).

second century. Stanton goes so far as to say that "By the end of the [second] century the early church seemed to be within a whisker of accepting a 'canon' of four written gospels, no more, no less."[104] To be more precise, the second century shows a three-stage process of the four Gospels acting as Scripture (i.e., sacred texts for Christ-believing groups), then operating as an "open canon" (i.e., part of a list of authorized books, albeit still open to adaptation and use alongside other Jesus literature), and then moving on the trajectory toward a "closed canon" (i.e., an authoritative collection of sacred books).[105] The second century gives us not a formal canon, but rather a canonical trajectory.

Others will suggest that even talk of a proto-canon in the second century is illegitimate because many authors of this period cite Jesus traditions and Jesus books other than the four Gospels — a statement that can be affirmed as long as it is qualified. A principled preference for the four Gospels did not require relegating all other Jesus literature to the dustbin. Justin, Irenaeus, Clement of Alexandria, and Origen are prime proof of the fact, overwhelmingly using the four Gospels but citing other traditions in some instances. The reason is that, if anything in the first two centuries was canonical, it was not a particular set of texts, but the words of Jesus and the apostolic testimony to Jesus.[106] What the proto-orthodox claimed was that the words of Jesus and the apostolic testimony to Jesus were faithfully deposited (though not exclusively found) in the four Gospels. Thus, the willingness to use "other" Jesus literature is no substantive argument against the existence of a widespread and widely regarded fourfold Gospel collection.[107]

In this context, Irenaeus's arguments for the authority of the fourfold Gospel rehearse what was either the pragmatic reality or the theological status quo for many churches. His remarks about the importance of the fourfold Gospel are not an innovation but an explanation for what was oth-

---

104. Stanton, *Jesus and Gospel*, 92.

105. On these three phases of canonization, see Allert, *High View of Scripture*, 50-51.

106. My experience has been that many divinity students find it shocking that some ancient authors felt free to "tinker" with the texts by welding them into a harmony (like Justin or Tatian), adding endings (Mark 16:9-20 and perhaps John 21), interpolating apocryphal stories (John 7:53–8:11), deliberately changing the text to be more orthodox (Matt 24:36), making a loose citation of Gospel texts, and unashamedly using agrapha, sayings not found in our "canonical" Gospels. However, we must remember that the first several generations of Christians, while they recognized the Old Testament and several Christian writings as sacred and even authoritative, also recognized that authentic accounts of what Jesus said and did could be found elsewhere as well.

107. Contra *inter alia* Hahneman, *Muratorian Fragment*, 94, 100.

erwise widely held.[108] It was his principle of exclusivity — no more and no less than these four — which was arguably the *novum* about the parameters of Christian literature, and even that may not have been entirely unique to him, for it seems to have caught on with great ease in some quarters.

II. The Foundation and Function
for the Fourfold Gospel Collection

Irenaeus's justification for there being no more and no less than four Gospels, by attributing a special quality to "four-ness," based on his allegorical interpretation of Ezekiel and Revelation, does not sound like a very compelling reason to have four Gospels. Burridge even calls Irenaeus's argument a "convoluted" attempt to justify four Gospels.[109] Yet Irenaeus appears odd only because his argument is not rationalistic but aesthetic. He perceives a fittingness and proportion to four with respect to how redemptive realities express themselves in the world.[110] Campenhausen says Irenaeus here is "so bizarre to our way of thinking, [but] is entirely in keeping with the theological taste of his age and environment."[111] It was an argument that captured the imaginations of others, including Augustine, who wrote that there are four Gospels "for the simple reason that there are four divisions of that world through the universal length of which they, by their number as by a mystical sign, indicated the advancing extension of the Church of Christ."[112]

Irenaeus's aesthetic argument is really the precipice to his mountain of other arguments for the integrity of the apostolic gospel over against competing varieties. He draws attention to the circumstances in which each of the four Gospels was written, with special attention paid to their apostolic connections.[113] On top of that, the four Gospels have a certain consistency and coherence with the Law and Prophets, they accord with received tradition, and they therefore constitute the only "true and reliable" testimonies to Jesus.[114] More precisely,

---

108. Stanton, *Jesus and Gospel*, 322.

109. Richard A. Burridge, *Four Gospels, One Jesus? A Symbolic Reading* (2nd ed.; Grand Rapids: Eerdmans, 2005), 166.

110. Eric Osborne, *Irenaeus of Lyons* (Cambridge: Cambridge University Press, 2001), 175-78.

111. Campenhausen, *Formation*, 199.

112. Augustine, *Harmony of the Gospels* 1.2.3.

113. Irenaeus, *Adv. Haer.* 3.1.1.

114. Irenaeus, *Adv. Haer.* 3.1.2; 3.11.9.

the gospel of the Gospels is christologically rooted: it is given by Christ. The bishop wrote, "For the Lord of all gave to his apostles the power of the Gospel through whom also we have known the truth, that is, the doctrine of the Son of God."[115] Elsewhere he says that "[I]t is clear that the Word . . . gave us the Gospel in four forms but united with one Spirit."[116] Though the Gospels are rooted in a chain of apostolic tradition, they are in reality authorized by Christ, and their plurality is checked by the bond of the Spirit. In addition, Irenaeus often introduces each Gospel as "one according to X" rather than "Gospel according to X" as found in later textual witnesses.[117] The difference is subtle but significant, implying as it does that there is one Gospel according to various authors.[118] In view of that, the gospel of the Lord is manifested in the "Gospel of the Apostles," the fourfold testimony of the apostolic tradition, given by Christ and held together by the Spirit, and this gospel comprises the "pillar and ground" of the faith of the churches, narrating as it does, "that there is one God, Creator of heaven and earth, announced by the law and the prophets; and one Christ, the Son of God."[119]

Subsequent to Irenaeus, many other authors recognized that within the fourfold Gospel is embedded this one gospel about Jesus Christ. The first appearance of titles in the Gospels, in P.[66] and P.[75], attest "Gospel *according to* X," meaning the *one* Gospel *according to* Luke or John.[120] Augustine in his commentary on John refers in passing to "the four Gospels, or better in the four books of the one Gospel."[121] Origen proffered the thought that "Now the Gospels are four. These four are, as it were, the elements of the faith of the Church, out of which elements the whole world which is reconciled to God in Christ is put together."[122] And further that "Since [Jesus] is the one of whom all the evangelists write, so the Gospel, although written . . . by four is one."[123] In the minds of those like Irenaeus and Augustine, the foundation for the four-in-one Gospel is that the Gospels together provide a coherent and complementary account of the gospel of Jesus Christ, a multifaceted

---

115. Irenaeus, *Adv. Haer.* 3. *Praef.*

116. Irenaeus, *Adv. Haer.* 3.11.8.

117. Cf. Irenaeus, *Adv. Haer.* 3.1.1; 3.11.8.

118. Annette Yoshiko Reed, "ΕΥΑΓΓΕΛΙΟΝ: Orality, Textuality, and the Christian Truth in Irenaeus' *Adversus Haereses*," *VC* 56 (2002): 20 n. 33.

119. Irenaeus, *Adv. Haer.* 3.1.1-2; 3.11.8.

120. Cf. Hengel, *Fourfold Gospel and the One Gospel*, 59.

121. Augustine, *Commentary on John* 36.1.

122. Origen, *Commentary on John* 1.6.

123. Origen, *Commentary on John* 5.4.

message to be sure, which was received from Christ and transmitted through the Apostles to the churches. Four Gospels, through their unity-in-diversity, make up what an anonymous anti-Montanist writer called "the gospel of the new covenant" (τῆς τοῦ εὐαγγελίου καινῆς διαθήκης).[124]

The four Gospels exhibit a plurality and unity that both encourages and restricts christological reflection. As a plurality, they demonstrate that no single Gospel, no one narration, and no solo story possesses a monopoly on describing who Jesus is. It takes the richness and diversity of four different accounts to come close to penetrating into the mystery of the man and his mission. In fact, the plurality of the Gospels stimulates us to write, preach, teach, paint, and sing about Jesus in ways that are far from monolithic but celebrate the diverse ways that Jesus Christ quickens our hearts, fills us with joy, drives us to Godward devotion, and inspires us to love others. At the same time, as a unity the four Gospels are in a sense constricting, setting the boundaries as they do for all christological discourse. They mark out the theological zone in which our discussion and devotion to Christ takes place. This proves that certain images of Jesus are out of bounds. The purely human Jesus, or the phantasm Jesus, or the Jesus as an angel view, or the neo-liberal California Jesus, or the ultra-conservative anti–big government Jesus, or the Nazi Aryan Jesus, or the armed communist liberator Jesus — all these are moving beyond the playing field. Such images do not reflect Jesus as he was, Jesus as he is known to his followers, or Jesus as he will be at the end of the ages. On plurality and unity, Richard Burridge puts it well: "By opting for *four* pictures, rather than one, in the Christian tradition, the early Fathers provided a spur to the production of new images of this person in every generation. By selecting *only* four, they mapped out the ball park where those who wish to remain in the tradition must play."[125]

There are good reasons also for putting the Gospels at the gateway of the New Testament canon. At the head of the New Testament, writes Eusebius, are "the holy τετρακτύν of the Gospels."[126] The adverb τετράκις means "four times"[127] and the noun is often translated as the holy "tetrad" or "quaternion" of the Gospels, though I much prefer the translation "quartet" for the theological resonance with which the Evangelists play together. Metaphorically speaking, placed where they are, the Gospels are an opening

---

124. Eusebius, *Hist. Eccl.* 5.16.3; cf. Irenaeus, *Adv. Haer.* 3.11.8 and the "four-formed Gospel" (τετράμορπηον τὸ εὐαγγέλιον).

125. Burridge, *Four Gospels, One Jesus?* 179 (italics original).

126. Eusebius, *Hist. Eccl.* 3.25.1.

127. LSJ, 802.

musical movement to introduce the New Testament canon. With artistic wonder, they combine motifs and melodies from the Old Testament score and then burst forth with a glorious new sound of gospel music played in their holy quartet. The Gospels provide the main theme music (much like how the famous James Bond tune operates in Bond movies) for the rest of the New Testament.

The position of the Gospels as the gateway into the New Testament provides a strong impetus to make sure that Christian faith is shaped around Jesus and around his teaching, his death, and his resurrection. The Gospels are preliminary because they are the primal sources of faith for followers of Jesus. Tertullian put it quaintly: "Of the apostles, therefore, John and Matthew first instill faith into us; whilst of apostolic men, Luke and Mark renew it afterwards."[128] In more recent times, Meredith Kline has proposed that the fourfold Gospel operates in the New Testament in much the same way that the Pentateuch functions for the Old Testament: as a testimony to God's redemptive work, a ratification of the covenant, and the definition of the way of life for God's people.[129]

The most earnest reflection on the place and function of the four Gospels in the biblical canon comes from Origen in his John commentary. The Gospels come first because "the Gospel is the first-fruits of all the Scriptures," and it is thus to the Gospels that one devotes the first-fruits of one's efforts.[130] Origen anticipates an objection, namely, how can the Gospels be the first-fruits of Scripture when they canonically precede Acts and the epistles? To which he responds that what the Apostles wrote in the epistles was itself "gospel," on the grounds that they "intended to strengthen belief in the mission of Jesus."[131]

There is no question that the words and deeds of Jesus continued to be rehearsed in the early church. Within the "Holy Internet" of Christian networks in the first two centuries, the teachings of Jesus went more viral than "Gangnam Style" on YouTube in our own decade. There are echoes of the Jesus tradition in Paul's letters and even in the Revelation of John. Paul even prioritizes Jesus tradition over his own apostolic instruction (1 Cor 7:10-14). The New Testament authors urge readers collectively to "fix our eyes on Jesus" (Heb 12:2). The various writings of the apostolic fathers weave together,

---

128. Tertullian, *Adv. Marc.* 4.2.2.
129. Meredith G. Kline, "The Old Testament Origins of the Gospel Genre," *WTJ* 38 (1975): 1-27.
130. Origen, *Commentary on John* 1.4.
131. Origen, *Commentary on John* 1.5.

almost unconsciously, the various sayings of Jesus into their exhortation and treat them with preeminence. The Gospels exerted a mammoth influence on the liturgy and worship of the primitive churches and continued to be a primary source of inspiration for faith under adversity. The great North Africa theologian Augustine (354-430) wrote in the opening of his *Harmony of the Gospels,* "In the entire number of those divine records which are contained in the sacred writings, the gospel deservedly stands pre-eminent. For what the law and the prophets previously announced as destined to come to pass, is exhibited in the gospel in its realization and fulfillment."[132] For Augustine, the preeminence of the Gospels rests on their fulfillment of Old Testament prophecies and in their deposit of apostolic preaching. An ancient Syriac document, allegedly recounting the instruction of the Apostles, enjoins: "The apostles further appointed: At the conclusion of all the Scriptures let the Gospels be read, as being the seal of all the Scriptures and let the people listen to it standing upon their feet: because it is the Gospel of the redemption of all men."[133] The author of this work considered the Gospels as the "seal" or final capstone in the building of Scripture and thus worthy of special honor. As long as Christianity cherishes its memory of Jesus Christ and deliberately stands under his dominical authority, then the Gospels will possess a canonical and theological priority as first among equals. The Gospels, as the ushers who lead us to Jesus, should rightly be considered the canon within the canon because Jesus himself is the epicenter of Christian faith.[134]

Young and ambitious theologians, especially those concerned with relating the text to the missional situation of the church in the twenty-first century, would be wise to keep exploration and exegesis of the fourfold Gospel uppermost in their studies. While no one would ever want to surrender diachronic study of the Gospels (i.e., examining them in terms of their own historical, social, theological, and narrative textures and their impact), this can be complemented with synchronic study (i.e., reading the four together as Scripture for the church). Such a dual focus, the diachronic and synchronic, can be undertaken jointly in order to appreciate and appropriate the tetrevangelium as a meaningful document for modern readers with all types of questions.[135] It is time to get past the seductive historicism which

---

132. Augustine, *Harmony of the Gospels* 1.1.1.

133. *Teaching of the Apostles* 9.

134. After writing this paragraph I read Pennington, *Reading the Gospels Wisely,* 229-58, which argues a similar point.

135. For an introduction to the Gospels in this vein, see Edward Adams, *Parallel Lives of*

says that only an individual text and the historical realities connected to it have any abiding significance for the present. Or else, we must avoid the haughty approach that one must dissolve the canonical form and instead engender an endless proliferation of images of Jesus with no commitment to any prior theological dogma, all in order to escape the authority of the episcopally-driven Gospel-shaped faith of the ancient church and its contemporary manifestations.[136]

III. Conclusion

The adoption of the four Gospels by the proto-orthodox church is a remarkable feat of Christian history. At the dawn of the second century, the Jesus tradition had crystallized into what are now the canonical Gospels, yet oral tradition and secondary orality remained quite alive, "other" Gospels were being composed, soon after Gospel harmonies began to be written, and there were obviously other options on the table besides the adoption of a fourfold Gospel collection.

As many Christians evaluated the literary options before them, gradually it seems, the four Gospels came to be held with special regard and a particular authority. The reasons are complex but can be summarized, appropriately, with a fourfold answer: (1) The four Gospels constituted the writings thought to most reflect the preaching, practice, and piety of the majority of churches. (2) These were the writings that were shared and copied the most frequently around various Christian networks. (3) The four Gospels were those thought to have connections to the apostolic generation, either to the Apostles themselves (Matthew and John) or to apostolic associates (Luke and Mark). And (4) various "other" writings, though in some cases thought to be useful, proffered a portrait of Jesus that was not as appealing to the masses as the four Gospels since it did not accord with the faith inherited from an earlier generation.

Irenaeus's argument for the reliability of the four Gospels was not innovative or unprecedented. The bishop of Lyons was simply tapping into the vein of the proto-orthodox church when he set forth a theological justification for the apostolic gospel in its four witnesses. In doing so he defended

---

Jesus: A Guide to the Four Gospels (Louisville: Westminster John Knox, 2011), and Pennington, *Reading the Gospels Wisely.*

136. On similar concerns to those raised here, see Watson, "Fourfold Gospel," 50.

the theological and literary status quo against perceived deviants, who were promoting a different type of Jesus literature for a different type of Christ-belief. What may have been innovative, however, even if it met with approval in the minds of others, was Irenaeus's claim to exclusivity — no more and no less than four — and his allegorical rationale for the special quality of the quaternion of Gospels.

In the tradition of Irenaeus and Origen, I would be prepared to argue that it makes much sense to place the fourfold Gospel at the head of the canon. To begin with, the Gospels provide a transition point between the old economy of the Law and the new economy of the Messiah. In addition, the four Gospels, by virtue of their placement in the new covenant collection, ensure that readers of this book will be immersed in an evangelical ethos and ingrained with a christocentric focus. In other words, they are a fourfold rehearsal of the fact that the Bible is about the gospel of the Lord. According to the Gospels, Christianity is not a system of neo-platonic philosophy lodged inside a Jewish casing, not German existentialism waiting to be set free from its religious mythology, not a conservative or liberal political program looking for legitimation in religious tracts. Rather, the Gospels show that Christianity is about following Jesus the Christ. Finally, the Gospels are reminders that the words and deeds of Jesus must be uppermost in the minds, hearts, prayers, thoughts, and devotion of the church. The Gospels urge that those who bear Christ's name must be willing to believe in him and follow him, through Galilee and Judea, through Gethsemane and Golgotha, through to the empty tomb and one day into the kingdom of heaven.

Excursus
The Text of the Gospels in the Second Century

There is a regrettable paucity of extant texts from the second century with no complete copy of any one of the Gospels.[137] The available texts from this period consist entirely of a handful of incomplete papyri leaves. In addition, the precise number

137. Strongly recommended as an introduction to the New Testament Gospels in the second century are Larry W. Hurtado, "The New Testament in the Second Century: Text, Collections and Canon," in *Transmission and Reception: New Testament Text-Critical and Exegetical Studies,* ed. D. C. Parker and J. W. Childers (Piscataway: Gorgias, 2006), 3-27; Scott D. Charlesworth, "The Gospel Manuscript Tradition," in *The Content and Setting of the Gospel Tradition,* ed. M. Harding and A. Nobbs (Grand Rapids: Eerdmans, 2010), 28-59; Stanley E. Porter, "Textual Criticism and Oldest Gospel Manuscripts," in *Encyclopedia of the Historical Jesus,* ed. C. A. Evans (New York: Routledge, 2008), 640-44.

of manuscripts thought to derive from the second century is contested by textual critics.[138] Generally, however, the following are regarded as originating in the second century or early third century.

Possible Second-Century Papyri and Their Approximate Dates[139]

	Contents	Jaroš	Nestle-Aland	Orsini-Clarysse
P.[4]	Luke	ca. 150	200-299	175-200
P.[5]	John	150-200	200-299	200-300
P.[52]	John	80-125	100-125	125-175
P.[64] + [67]	Matthew	75-100	200-225	175-200
P.[66]	John	100	200-225	200-250
P.[75]	Luke, John	150-200	200-225	200-250
P.[77]	Matthew	100-150	100-299	250-300
P.[90]	John	100-150	100-199	150-200
P.[103]	Matthew	100-150	100-299	200-300
P.[104]	Matthew	75-125	100-199	100-200
P.[108]	John	ca. 200	200-299	200-300
P.[109]	John	ca. 150	200-299	200-300

Given that the second century was an important century for the textual transmission of Christian writings, a key matter for discussion has been the stability of the texts of the Gospels during this time period. Not only is there a distance between an *autograph* (i.e., the original document) and a scholarly *Ausgangstext* (i.e., the earliest form of the text recoverable by critical reconstruction), but the old papyri are separated from textual archetypes by nearly a century. We know from the apostolic fathers and patristic citations that Gospel citations could at times be made very freely without concern for verbatim replication of a text, and such lack of precision could have

138. Hill, *Who Chose the Gospels?* 249-50, has a larger table conveniently listing which papyri various textual critics ascribe to the second and third centuries. How Koester, *From Jesus to Gospel*, 39, maintains that "there is no second-century manuscript evidence" remains baffling to me.

139. Based on Karl Jaroš et al., eds., *Das Neue Testament nach den älten griechischen Handschriften. Die handschriftliche griechiche Überlieferung des Neuen Testaments vor Codex Sinaiticus und Codex Vaticanus* (Mainz: Rutzen, 2006); Kurt Aland, *Kurzgefasste Liste der griechischen Handschriften des neuen Testaments* (Berlin, 1994), available with updates at http://www.uni-muenster.de/INTF/continuation-manuscripts.hml; Pasquale Orsini and Willy Clarysse, "Early New Testament Manuscripts and Their Dates: A Critique of Theological Palaeography," *ETL* 88 (2012): 469-72.

passed into copying of the Gospels. There are also clear and often massive textual variations in other Jesus books like the *Protoevangelium of James* and the *Infancy Gospel of Thomas* in both wording and content, and this provides analogies for the way in which the canonical Gospels might have been initially transmitted.[140] The first generations of Christian copyists were probably not professional scribes, and few if any early manuscripts were produced under the close scrutiny of a Christian *scriptorium*. A survey of the critical apparatus of NA28 provides scores of instances where second-century papyri attest readings that are improvements, clarifications, or even well-intended fixes to Gospel texts. Our earliest complete codex of the four Gospels and Acts, P.[45], is characterized by Barbara Aland as a "free" manuscript: "Superfluous elements and repetitious words are dropped, parallels are restored, conjunctions are inserted and intended meanings are clarified."[141]

Even pagan critics of Christianity like Celsus could point to endemic variations in the texts of the Gospels as evidence for the incorrigible incoherence of Christian accounts of Jesus. According to Origen, Celsus argued "that certain of the Christian believers, like persons who in a fit of drunkenness lay violent hands upon themselves, have corrupted the Gospel from its original integrity, to a threefold, and fourfold, and many-fold degree, and have remodelled it, so that they might be able to answer objections."[142] In other words, Celsus alleged that Christians tinkered with their own texts to try and wiggle out of the many problems that the texts raised.

In light of evidence such as this, many have maintained that the texts of the Gospels in the second century were largely in flux and susceptible to wide-scale alteration. Koester professes that all the evidence "points to the fact that the text of the Synoptic Gospels was very unstable during the first and second centuries."[143]

---

140. Cf. François Bovon, *Studies in Early Christianity* (Grand Rapids: Baker, 2005), 209-25; Christopher M. Tuckett, "Forty Other Gospels," in *The Written Gospel*, ed. Bockmuehl and Hagner, 239 n. 4.

141. Barbara Aland, "The Significance of the Chester Beatty Papyri in Early Church History," in *The Earliest Gospels: The Origin and Transmission of the Earliest Christian Gospels. The Contribution of the Chester Beatty Gospel Codex P45*, ed. C. Horton (JSNTSup 258; London: Clark, 2004), 113.

142. Origen, *Contra Celsum* 2.27. In the same passage, Origen answers Celsus's objection: "Now I know of no others who have altered the Gospel, save the followers of Marcion, and those of Valentinus, and, I think, also those of Lucian. But such an allegation is no charge against the Christian system, but against those who dared so to trifle with the Gospels. And as it is no ground of accusation against philosophy, that there exist Sophists, or Epicureans, or Peripatetics, or any others, whoever they may be, who hold false opinions; so neither is it against genuine Christianity that there are some who corrupt the Gospel histories, and who introduce heresies opposed to the meaning of the doctrine of Jesus."

143. Koester, *From Jesus to Gospel*, 52, though in another work (*Ancient Christian Gospels*, 318) Koester is somewhat less skeptical, at least of Matthew, stating that "it still seems to

Biblical scholar-celebrity Bart Ehrman concluded that "proto-orthodox scribes of the second and third centuries occasionally modified their texts of Scripture in order to make them coincide more closely with the christological views embraced by the party that would seal its victory at Nicea and Chalcedon."[144] Even Martin Hengel, an erudite yet relatively conservative historian, noted that during the second century "Gospel texts were still to some degree 'fluid.' They could be changed — perhaps influenced by a 'richer' parallel tradition — as is evident from the numerous harmonizing supplements and also from isolated additions of an interpretative and supplementary kind."[145]

However, the textual tradition of the Gospels in the second century was not as chaotic as some imagine. Against Koester, apart from his eccentric denial of the existence of second-century papyri except for P.[52], he commits a category fallacy by thinking that written texts were fluid to the same degree that oral tradition could be fluid. We do better to distinguish the relatively free style of quotations used in patristic citations, influenced by oral tradition, secondary orality, Gospel harmonies, or catechetical praxis, and the transmission of the text itself in the specific context of early Christian book culture.[146] We must also remember that genre often determined the precision in patristic citations. The church fathers could cite biblical texts rather freely in their polemical treatises or sermons, but normally followed the texts very closely in their biblical commentaries.[147]

While Ehrman's basic thesis is correct — changes were introduced into the textual tradition by proto-orthodox scribes often motivated by christological concerns — the vast majority of changes seem accidental or geared toward harmonization. We do well to remember that varying scribal tendencies were operative in this period ranging from the closely controlled to more careless copying practices. While formal Christian *scriptoria* were unlikely to have operated in the early or mid-second century, the widespread adoption of the *nomina sacra* and the common use of the codex for sacred texts does indicate an emerging scribal culture in Christianity conducive

---

be the most plausible assumption that the manuscript tradition of Matthew's Gospel has preserved its text more or less in its oldest form. To be sure, there are variations in the manuscript transmission. But unlike the Gospels of John and Mark, there are no indications, internal or external, that an originally Hebrew or Greek text of the Gospel of Matthew underwent substantial alteration before the emergence of the archetype(s) of the text upon which the extant manuscript tradition depends."

144. Bart D. Ehrman, *The Orthodox Corruption of Scripture: The Effect of Early Christological Controversies on the Text of the New Testament* (Oxford: Oxford University Press, 1993), 275.

145. Hengel, *Four Gospels and the One Gospel of Jesus Christ*, 26.

146. Hengel, *Four Gospels and the One Gospel of Jesus Christ*, 28.

147. Gordon D. Fee, "The Text of John in *The Jerusalem Bible*: A Critique of the Use of Patristic Citations in New Testament Textual Criticism," in *Studies in the Theory and Method of New Testament Textual Criticism*, ed. I. A. Sparks (Grand Rapids: Eerdmans, 1993), 335-43.

to and conscious of accurate transmission of its revered texts. To take Ehrman to task more broadly, a juxtaposition of his scholarly and popular works suggests that they are mostly incommensurable. It is impossible to maintain simultaneously a New Testament text that was uncontrollably unstable *and yet* controllably changed to conform to proto-orthodox christology.

Importantly, the emergence of new papyri freshly published from the Oxyrhynchus collection in recent decades is revising older views about the alleged volatility of the second-century Gospel texts.[148] Kurt and Barbara Aland have categorized the early manuscripts according to the categories of "Strict," "at least Normal," "Normal," "Free," and "like D," indicating varying degrees of conformity to a hypothetical exemplar. The significance of their taxonomy is where the majority of second-century witnesses seem to fit. Those listed in the table above are classified by the Alands thus:

Second-Century Gospel Papyri according to the Alands' Categorization[149]

Strict	At Least Normal	Normal	Free	Like D
$P.^{64}$ + ^{67}, $P.^{75}$, $P.^{77}$, $P.^{103}$, $P.^{104}$, $P.^{108}$, $P.^{109}$	none	$P.^4$, $P.^5$, $P.^{52}$, $P.^{90}$	$P.^{66}$	none

It is staggering that eleven out of twelve witnesses of possible second-century mss. are categorized as either "strict" or "normal" and that the only "free" text is $P.^{66}$.[150] Even if we omitted $P.^5$, $P.^{103}$, $P.^{108}$, and $P.^{109}$ from the cohort of second-century texts, we would still have an overwhelming majority of second-century texts that were copied in a studious manner. On the whole it looks as if we encounter micro-level variations within a broader aegis of macro-level stability.[151] Moreover, $P.^{75}$ has a close affinity with the majuscule B (Codex Vaticanus). This does not prove that an Alexandrian text-type, which B is considered to be, existed as a deliberate recension in the second century (such family "types" seem to have properly emerged only after the fourth century), but it does demonstrate that good mss. were accepted and copied in later centuries. In the case of $P.^{75}$ and B, we have evidence of a reliable

---

148. Cf. discussion in Peter M. Head, "Some Recently Published NT Papyri from Oxyrynchus: An Overview and Preliminary Assessment," *TynBul* 51 (2000): 1-16.

149. Cited from Charles E. Hill and Michael J. Kruger, "Introduction," in *The Early Text of the New Testament*, ed. Hill and Kruger, 11.

150. Importantly, a "free text" does not mean a corrupted or inaccurate text but a reliable copy that was subjected to a polished editorial process.

151. Michael W. Holmes, "From 'Original Text' to 'Initial Text': The Traditional Goal of New Testament Textual Criticism in Contemporary Discussion," in *The Text of the New Testament in Contemporary Research: Essays on the Status Quaestiones*, ed. B. D. Ehrman and M. W. Holmes (2nd ed.; Leiden: Brill, 2012), 671-75.

textual phenomenon that was clearly anterior to them and may reach back into the later part of the first century.[152] Given that most textual variations are thought to have been introduced in the second century, the consistency and coherence of the second-century witnesses builds confidence that no wide-scale alteration took place, that in fact a stable text that was carefully transmitted for the most part seems to have been normative. In light of this, Scott Charlesworth rightly concludes:

> In the absence of conclusive proof it is methodologically unsound to assume that the first 150 years of textual transmission were characterized by heightened fluidity. Scribes made changes, but the early gospel text was transmitted accurately *en bloc*. "Normal" and "strict" approaches to copying gainsay the contention that the high fluidity of early gospel MSS renders impossible the recovery of the "original" text. Instead, the earliest attainable gospel text should generally be very close to the autograph or "original" text as it existed at the end of the composition process and the beginning of the transmission process.[153]

152. Gordon D. Fee, "P.[75], P.[66], and Origen: The Myth of Early Textual Recension in Alexandria," in *Studies in the Theory and Method of New Testament Textual Criticism,* ed. Sparks, 272.

153. Charlesworth, "Gospel Manuscript Tradition," 58.

Bibliography

Abbott, E. A. *The Corrections of Mark Adopted by Matthew and Luke*. London: Black, 1901.

Abel, Ernst L. "The Psychology of Memory and Rumor Transmission and Their Bearing on Theories of Oral Transmission in Early Christianity." *JR* 51 (1971): 270-81.

Abramowski, Luise. "The 'Memoirs of the Apostles' in Justin." In *The Gospel and the Gospels*. Edited by P. Stuhlmacher. Grand Rapids: Eerdmans, 1990, 323-35.

Achtemeier, Paul J. "*Omne Verbum Sonat:* The New Testament and the Oral Environment of Later Western Antiquity." *JBL* 109 (1990): 3-27.

Adamczewski, Bartosz. *Q or Not Q? The So-Called Triple, Double, and Single Traditions in the Synoptic Gospels*. Frankfurt am Main: Peter Lang, 2010.

Adams, Edward. *Parallel Lives of Jesus: A Guide to the Four Gospels*. Louisville: Westminster John Knox, 2011.

Aland, Barbara. "The Significance of the Chester Beatty Papyri in Early Church History." In *The Earliest Gospels: The Origin and Transmission of the Earliest Christian Gospels. The Contribution of the Chester Beatty Gospel Codex P45*. Edited by C. Horton. JSNTSup 258; London: Clark, 2004, 108-21.

Aland, Kurt. *Synopsis of the Four Gospels: Greek-English Edition of the Synopsis Quattuor Evangeliorum*. 12th ed.; Stuttgart: German Bible Society, 2001.

Albl, Martin C. *And Scripture Cannot Be Broken: The Form and Function of the Early Christian Testimonia Collections*. Leiden: Brill, 1999.

Alexander, Loveday. "Luke's Preface in the Context of Greek Preface-Writing." *NovT* 28 (1986): 48-74.

———. *The Preface to Luke's Gospel*. SNTSMS 78; Cambridge: Cambridge University Press, 1993.

———. "Ancient Book Production and the Circulation of the Gospels." In *The Gospels for All Christians: Rethinking the Gospel Audiences*. Edited by R. Bauckham. Grand Rapids: Eerdmans, 1998, 71-111.

———. "What Is a Gospel?" In *The Cambridge Companion to the Gospels*. Edited by S. C. Barton. Cambridge: Cambridge University Press, 2006, 13-33.

Alexander, Philip S. "Rabbinic Biography and the Biography of Jesus: A Survey of the

Evidence." In *Synoptic Studies*. Edited by C. M. Tuckett. JSNTSup 7; Sheffield: JSOT, 1984, 19-50.

———. "Orality in Pharisaic-Rabbinic Judaism at the Turn of the Eras." In *Jesus and the Oral Gospel Tradition*. Edited by Henry Wansbrough. JSNTSup 64; Sheffield: Sheffield Academic, 1990, 159-84.

Allert, Craig D. *A High View of Scripture: The Authority of the Bible and the Formation of the New Testament Canon*. Grand Rapids: Baker, 2007.

Allison, Dale C. "The Pauline Epistles and the Synoptic Gospels: The Pattern of the Parallels." *NTS* 28 (1982): 1-32.

———. *The Jesus Tradition in Q*. Harrisburg: Trinity, 1997.

———. *Jesus of Nazareth: Millenarian Prophet*. Minneapolis: Fortress, 1998.

———. "The Historians' Jesus and the Church." In *Seeking the Identity of Jesus: A Pilgrimage*. Edited by Beverly R. Gaventa and Richard B. Hays. Grand Rapids: Eerdmans, 2008, 79-95.

———. *Constructing Jesus: Memory, Imagination, and History*. Grand Rapids: Baker, 2011.

Andersen, Øivind. "Oral Tradition." In *Jesus and the Oral Gospel Tradition*. Edited by Henry Wansbrough. JSNTSup 64; Sheffield: Sheffield Academic, 1991, 17-58.

Anderson, Paul N. *The Christology of the Fourth Gospel: Its Unity and Disunity in Light of John 6*. Valley Forge: Trinity, 2006.

———. *The Fourth Gospel and the Quest for Jesus: Modern Foundations Reconsidered*. London: Clark, 2006.

Aune, David E. "The Problem of the Genre of the Gospels: A Critique of C. H. Talbert's *What Is a Gospel?*" In *Gospel Perspectives 2: Studies of History and Tradition in the Four Gospels*. Edited by R. T. France and D. Wenham. Sheffield: Sheffield Academic, 1981, 9-60.

———. *Prophecy in Early Christianity and the Ancient Mediterranean World*. Grand Rapids: Eerdmans, 1983.

———. "The Gospels as Hellenistic Biography." *Mosaic* 20 (1987): 1-10.

———. *The New Testament in Its Literary Environment*. Philadelphia: Westminster, 1987.

———. "Greco-Roman Biography." In *Greco-Roman Literature and the New Testament*. Atlanta: Scholars, 1988, 107-26.

———. "Prolegomena to the Study of Oral Tradition in the Hellenistic World." In *Jesus and the Oral Gospel Tradition*. Edited by Henry Wansbrough. JSNTSup 64; Sheffield: Sheffield Academic, 1991, 59-106.

———. "Luke 1:1-4: Historical or Scientific *Prooimion?*" In *Paul, Luke and the Greco-Roman World: Essays in Honour of Alexander J. M. Wedderburn*. Edited by A. Christophersen, C. Claussen, J. Frey, and B. Longenecker. JSNTSup 217; Sheffield: Sheffield Academic, 2002, 138-48.

———. "Gospels, Literary Genre of." In *The Westminster Dictionary of New Testament and Early Christian Literature and Rhetoric*. Louisville: Westminster John Knox, 2003, 204-6.

———. "Jesus Tradition and the Pauline Letters." In *Jesus in Memory: Traditions in Oral and Scribal Perspectives*. Edited by W. H. Kelber and S. Byrkog. Waco: Baylor University Press, 2009, 63-86.

———. "The Meaning of Εὐαγγέλιον in the *Inscriptiones* of the Canonical Gospels." In *Jesus, Gospel Traditions and Paul in the Context of Jewish and Greco-Roman Antiquity: Collected Essays II.* WUNT 303; Tübingen: Mohr, 2013, 2-24.

Bagnall, Roger. *Early Christian Books in Egypt.* Princeton: Princeton University Press, 2009.

Bailey, Kenneth E. "Informal Controlled Oral Tradition and the Synoptic Gospels." *Themelios* 20 (1995): 4-11.

———. "Middle Eastern Oral Tradition and the Synoptic Gospels." *ExpT* 106 (1995): 363-67.

Baird, William. *The History of New Testament Research.* 3 vols.; Minneapolis: Fortress, 1992-2013.

Barnett, Paul W. *Jesus and the Logic of History.* NSBT 3; Leicester: Apollos, 1997.

———. *Jesus and the Rise of Early Christianity: A History of New Testament Times.* Downers Grove: InterVarsity, 1999.

———. *Finding the Historical Christ.* Grand Rapids: Eerdmans, 2009.

Barrett, C. K. *Jesus and the Gospel Tradition.* London: SPCK, 1967.

———. "John and the Synoptics." *ExpT* 85 (1974): 228-33.

———. *The Gospel According to St. John: An Introduction with Commentary and Notes on the Greek Text.* 2nd ed.; London: SPCK, 1978.

———. "The First New Testament?" *NovT* 38 (1996): 94-104.

Barton, John. *Holy Writings, Sacred Scripture: The Canon in Early Christianity.* Louisville: Westminster John Knox, 1997.

———. "Marcion Revisited." In *The Canon Debate.* Edited by L. M. McDonald and J. A. Sanders. Peabody: Hendrickson, 2002, 341-54.

Barton, Stephen C., Loren T. Stuckenbruck, and Benjamin G. Wold, eds. *Memory in the Bible and Antiquity: The Fifth Durham-Tübingen Research Symposium.* WUNT 212; Tübingen: Mohr, 2007.

Batovici, Dan. "The Second-Century Reception of John: A Survey of Methodologies." *CBR* 10 (2012): 396-409.

Batten, Alicia J. *What Are They Saying About the Letter of James?* New York: Paulist, 2009.

Bauckham, Richard. "For Whom Were the Gospels Written?" In *The Gospels for All Christians.* Edited by R. Bauckham. Grand Rapids: Eerdmans, 1998, 9-48.

———. "John for Readers of Mark." In *The Gospels for All Christians.* Edited by R. Bauckham. Grand Rapids: Eerdmans, 1998, 147-71.

———. *James: Wisdom of James, Disciple of Jesus the Sage.* NTR; London: Routledge, 1999.

———. "The Eyewitnesses and the Gospel Tradition." *JSHJ* 1 (2003): 28-60.

———. *Jesus and the Eyewitnesses.* Grand Rapids: Eerdmans, 2006.

———. "Historiographical Characteristics of the Gospel of John." *NTS* 53 (2007): 17-36.

Baum, Armin. "Ein aramäischer Urmatthäus im kleinasiatischen Gottesdienst. Das Papiaszeugnis zur Entstehung des Matthäusevangelims." *ZNW* 92 (2001): 257-72.

———. *Der mündliche Faktor und seine Bedeutung für die synoptische Frage. Analogien aus der Antiken Literatur, der Experiemtnalpsychologie, der Oral Poetry-Forschung und dem rabbinischen Traditionswesen.* TANZ 49; Tübingen: Francke, 2008.

———. "Matthew's Sources — Written or Oral? A Rabbinic Analogy and Empirical

Insights." In *Built upon the Rock: Studies in the Gospel of Matthew.* Edited by J. Nolland and D. Gurtner. Grand Rapids: Eerdmans, 2008, 1-23.

―――. "The Original Epilogue (John 20:30-31), the Secondary Appendix (21:1-23), and the Editorial Epilogues (21:24-25) of John's Gospel." In *Earliest Christian History.* Edited by M. F. Bird and J. Maston. WUNT 2.320; Tübingen: Mohr, 2012, 227-70.

Beasley-Murray, George R. *John.* WBC; Dallas: Word, 1987.

Becker, Jürgen. *Jesus of Nazareth.* Translated by James E. Crouch. New York: De Gruyter, 1998.

Bellinzoni, Arthur J. *The Sayings of Jesus in the Writings of Justin Martyr.* Leiden: Brill, 1967.

―――, ed. *The Two-Source Hypothesis: A Critical Appraisal.* Macon: Mercer University Press, 1985.

Berger, Klaus. "Hellenistische Gattung im NT." *ANRW* 2.25.2 (1984): 1031-1432.

Bilezikian, Gilbert. *The Liberated Gospel: A Comparison of the Gospel of Mark and Greek Tragedy.* Grand Rapids: Baker, 1977.

Bingham, Dwight J. *Irenaeus' Use of Matthew's Gospel in Adversus Haereses.* Leuven: Peeters, 2010.

Bird, Michael F. "Should Evangelicals Participate in the 'Third Quest for the Historical Jesus'?" *Themelios* 29.2 (2004): 4-14.

―――. "Bauckham's *The Gospels for All Christians* Revisited." *EJTh* 15 (2006): 5-13.

―――. *Jesus and the Origins of the Gentile Mission.* LNTS 311; London: Clark, 2006, 83-93.

―――. "The Marcan Community, Myth or Maze?" *JTS* 57 (2006): 474-86.

―――. "Who Comes from the East and the West? The Historical Jesus and Matt 8.11-12/ Luke 13.28-29." *NTS* 52 (2006): 441-57.

―――. *A Bird's-Eye View of Paul: The Man, His Mission, and His Message.* Nottingham: InterVarsity, 2008.

―――. "Passion Predictions." In *Encyclopedia of the Historical Jesus.* Edited by C. A. Evans. New York: Routledge, 2008, 442-46.

―――. "Textual Criticism and the Historical Jesus." *JSHJ* 6 (2008): 133-56.

―――. *Are You the One Who Is to Come? The Historical Jesus and the Messianic Question.* Grand Rapids: Baker, 2009.

―――. *Colossians and Philemon.* NCCS; Eugene: Cascade, 2009.

―――. "Sectarian Gospels for Sectarian Christians? The Non-Canonical Gospels and Bauckham's *The Gospels for All Christians.*" In *The Audience of the Gospels: Further Conversation about the Origin and Function of the Gospels in Early Christianity.* Edited by Edward W. Klink. LNTS 353; London: Clark, 2010, 27-48.

―――. "Synoptics and John." In *Dictionary of Jesus and the Gospels.* Edited by J. B. Green, N. Perrin, and J. K. Brown. 2nd ed.; Downers Grove: InterVarsity, 2013, 920-24.

Bird, Michael F., and James Crossley. *How Did Christianity Begin? A Believer and Non-Believer Examine the Evidence.* London: SPCK, 2008.

Black, Matthew. *An Aramaic Approach to the Gospels and Acts.* 3rd ed.; Oxford: Clarendon, 1967.

Blackburn, Barry. *Theios Anēr and the Markan Miracle Traditions: A Critique of the Theios*

Anēr Concept as an Interpretive Background of the Miracle Traditions Used by Mark. WUNT 2.40; Tübingen: Mohr, 1991.

Blank, Reiner. *Analyse und Kritik der formgeschichtlichen Arbeiten von Martin Dibelius und Rudolf Bultmann*. Basel: Reinhardt, 1981.

Blomberg, Craig L. *Jesus and the Gospels: An Introduction and Survey*. Leicester, England: Apollos, 1997.

————. *The Historical Reliability of John's Gospel*. Downers Grove: InterVarsity, 2002.

————. *Making Sense of the New Testament: Three Crucial Questions*. Grand Rapids: Baker, 2004.

————. *The Historical Reliability of the Gospels*. 2nd ed.; Downers Grove: InterVarsity, 2007.

————. "The Gospels for Specific Communities *and* All Christians." In *The Audience of the Gospels: The Origin and Function of the Gospels in Early Christianity*. Edited by E. W. Klink. LNTS 353; London: Clark 2010, 111-33.

Bock, Darrell L. *Studying the Historical Jesus: A Guide to Sources and Methods*. Grand Rapids: Baker, 2003, 163-79.

————. *The Missing Gospels: Unearthing the Truth behind Alternative Christianities*. Nashville: Nelson, 2006.

Bockmuehl, Markus. *Seeing the Word: Refocusing New Testament Study*. STI; Grand Rapids: Baker, 2006.

————. "Whose Memory? Whose Orality? A Conversation with James D. G. Dunn on Jesus and the Gospels." In *Memories of Jesus: A Critical Appraisal of James D. G. Dunn's* Jesus Remembered. Edited by R. B. Stewart and Gary R. Habermas. Nashville: Broadman & Holman, 2010, 31-44.

Boismard, M.-É. "The Two-Source Theory at an Impasse." *NTS* 26 (1979): 1-17.

Boismard, M.-É., and P. Benoit. *Synopses des quatre Évangiles en Français avec parrallèles des apocrypes et des pères*. Paris: Cerf, 1972.

Boismard, M.-É., and A. Lamouille, with G. Rochais. *L'Évangile Jean. Commentaire*. Paris: Cerf, 1977.

Bokedal, Tomas. *The Scriptures and the Lord: Formation and Significance of the Christian Biblical Canon*. Lund: Lund University Press, 2005.

Bonz, Marianne Palmer. *The Past as Legacy: Luke-Acts and Ancient Epic*. Minneapolis: Fortress, 2000.

Boring, M. Eugene. "Mark 1:1-15 and the Beginning of the Gospels." *Semeia* 52 (1990): 43-82.

————. *The Continuing Voice of Jesus: Christian Prophecy and the Gospel Tradition*. Louisville: Westminster John Knox, 1991.

————. *Mark*. NTL; Louisville: Westminster John Knox, 2006.

————. "The 'Minor Agreements' and Their Bearing on the Synoptic Problem." In *New Studies in the Synoptic Problem: Oxford Conference, 2008*. Edited by P. Foster, A. Gregory, J. S. Kloppenborg, and J. Verheyden. BETL 239; FS C. Tuckett; Leuven: Peeters, 2011, 227-51.

Bornkamm, Günther. *Jesus of Nazareth*. Translated by Irene McLuskey, Fraser McLuskey, and James M. Robinson. London: Hodder & Stoughton, 1973.

Bibliography

Botha, Pieter J. J. "Mark's Story as Oral Traditional Literature: Rethinking the Transmission of Some Traditions about Jesus." *HTS* 47 (1991): 304-31.

———. "New Testament Texts in the Context of Reading Practices of the Roman Period: The Role of Memory and Performance." *Scriptura* 90 (2005): 621-40.

Bovon, François. *Luke 1: A Commentary on the Gospel of Luke 1:1–9:50.* Translated by Christine M. Thomas. Minneapolis: Augsburg, 2002.

———. *Studies in Early Christianity.* Grand Rapids: Baker, 2005.

———. *New Testament and Christian Apocrypha.* Edited by G. E. Snyder. Grand Rapids: Baker, 2009.

Bowman, J. W. "The Term *Gospel* and Its Cognates in the Palestinian Syriac." In *New Testament Essays.* Edited by A. J. B. Higgins. FS T. W. Manson; Manchester: Manchester University Press, 1959, 54-57.

———. *The Gospel of Mark: The New Christian Jewish Passover Haggadah.* Leiden: Brill, 1965.

Brannan, Rick, ed. *Greek Apocryphal Gospels, Fragments, and Agrapha: Introductions and Translations.* Bellingham: Logos Bible Software, 2013.

———, ed. *Greek Apocryphal Gospels, Fragments, and Agrapha: Texts and Transcriptions.* Bellingham: Logos Bible Software, 2013.

Brodie, Thomas L. *The Quest for the Origin of John's Gospel: A Source-Oriented Approach.* Oxford: Oxford University Press, 1993.

Brooks, Stephenson H. *Matthew's Special Community: The Evidence of His Special Sayings Material.* JSNTSup 16; Sheffield: JSOT, 1987.

Brown, Charles Thomas. *The Gospel and Ignatius of Antioch.* SBL 12; New York: Lang, 2000.

Brown, Raymond E. *The Gospel According to John.* AB; 2 vols.; New York: Doubleday, 1966.

———. *Introduction to the New Testament.* ABRL; New York: Doubleday, 1997.

———. *An Introduction to the Gospel of John.* Edited by F. J. Moloney. ABRL; New York: Doubleday, 2003.

Bruce, F. F. "Some Notes on the Fourth Evangelist." *EQ* 16 (1944): 101-9.

———. "When Is a Gospel Not a Gospel?" *BJRL* 45 (1963): 319-39.

———. "Paul and the Historical Jesus." *BJRL* 56 (1974): 317-35.

———. *Paul: Apostle of the Heart Set Free.* Grand Rapids: Eerdmans, 1980.

———. *The Epistles to the Colossians, to Philemon, and to the Ephesians.* NICNT; Grand Rapids: Eerdmans, 1984.

Brueggemann, Walter. *First and Second Samuel.* Int; Louisville: John Knox, 1990.

Bryan, Christopher. *A Preface to Mark: Notes on the Gospel in Its Literary and Cultural Setting.* Oxford: Oxford University Press, 1993.

Bryan, Steven M. *Jesus and Israel's Traditions of Judgement and Restoration.* SNTSMS 117; Cambridge: Cambridge University Press, 2002.

Bultmann, Rudolf. *History of the Synoptic Tradition.* Translated by J. Marsh. 2nd ed.; New York: Harper & Row, 1963 (1921).

———. *Jesus and the Word.* Translated by Louise Pettibone Smith. London: Ivor Nicholson & Watson, 1935.

————. "The Study of the Synoptic Gospels." In *Form Criticism: A New Method of New Testament Research*. Edited by F. C. Grant. New York: Harper, 1962, 7-75.

————. "The Significance of the Historical Jesus for the Theology of Paul." In *Faith and Understanding*. London: SCM, 1969, 220-46.

————. *The Gospel of John: A Commentary*. Translated by G. R. Beasley-Murray, R. W. N. Hoare, and J. K. Riches. Philadelphia: Westminster, 1971.

Burge, Gary M. *Interpreting the Gospel of John*. Grand Rapids: Baker, 1992.

Burkett, Delbert. *Rethinking the Gospel Sources: From Proto-Mark to Mark*. London: Clark, 2004.

Burney, C. F. *The Poetry of Our Lord: An Examination of the Formal Elements of Hebrew Poetry in the Discourses of Jesus Christ*. Oxford: Clarendon, 1925.

Burridge, Richard A. "Gospel." In *A Dictionary of Biblical Interpretation*. Edited by R. Coggins and J. L. Houlden. London: SCM, 1990, 266-68.

————. "About People, by People, for People: Gospel Genre and Audiences." In *The Gospels for All Christians: Rethinking the Gospel Audiences*. Edited by R. Bauckham. Grand Rapids: Eerdmans, 1998, 113-45.

————. *What Are the Gospels? A Comparison with Graeco-Biography*. 2nd ed.; Grand Rapids: Eerdmans, 2004.

————. *Four Gospels, One Jesus? A Symbolic Reading*. 2nd ed.; Grand Rapids: Eerdmans, 2005.

————. *Imitating Jesus: An Inclusive Approach to New Testament Ethics*. Grand Rapids: Eerdmans, 2007.

Butler, B. C. *The Originality of St. Matthew*. Cambridge: Cambridge University Press, 1951.

Byrksog, Samuel. *Jesus the Only Teacher: Didactic Authority and Transmission in Ancient Israel, Ancient Judaism and the Matthean Community*. CBNTS 24; Stockholm: Almquist & Wiksell, 1994.

————. *Story as History — History as Story: The Gospel Tradition in the Context of Ancient Oral History*. WUNT 123; Tübingen: Mohr, 2000.

————. "A New Perspective on the Jesus Tradition: Reflections on James Dunn's *Jesus Remembered*." *JSNT* 26 (2004): 459-71.

————. "A Century with the *Sitz im Leben*: From Form-Critical Setting to Gospel Community and Beyond." *ZNW* 98 (2007): 1-27.

————. "The Eyewitnesses as Interpreters of the Past: Reflections on Richard Bauckham's *Jesus and the Eyewitnesses*." *JSHJ* 6 (2008): 157-68.

————. "A New Perspective on the Jesus Tradition: Reflections on James D. G. Dunn's *Jesus Remembered*." In *Memories of Jesus: A Critical Appraisal of James D. G. Dunn's Jesus Remembered*. Edited by R. B. Stewart and Gary R. Habermas. Nashville: Broadman & Holman, 2010, 59-78.

Campenhausen, Hans von. *The Formation of the Christian Bible*. Translated by J. A. Baker. Philadelphia: Fortress, 1972.

Capes, David G. "*Imitatio Christi* and the Gospel Genre." *BBR* 13 (2003): 1-19.

Carrington, Philip. *The Primitive Christian Calendar: A Study in the Making of the Marcan Gospel*. Cambridge: Cambridge University Press, 1952.

Carson, D. A. "Current Source Criticism of the Fourth Gospel." *JBL* 97 (1978): 411-29.

Bibliography

Carter, Warren. *John: Storyteller, Interpreter, Evangelist.* Peabody: Hendrickson, 2006.

Casey, Maurice. *Aramaic Sources of Mark's Gospel.* SNTSMS 102; Cambridge: Cambridge University Press, 1998.

———. "An Aramaic Approach to the Synoptic Gospels." *ExpT* 110 (1999): 275-78.

———. *Jesus of Nazareth.* London: Clark, 2010.

Catchpole, David. *Studies in Q.* Edinburgh: Clark, 1992.

———. "On Proving Too Much: Critical Hesitations about Richard Bauckham's *Jesus and the Eyewitnesses.*" *JSHJ* 6 (2008): 169-81.

Charlesworth, James H. "Tatian's Dependence upon Apocryphal Traditions." *HeyJ* 15 (1974): 5-17.

———. *Jesus within Judaism: New Light from Exciting Archaeological Discoveries.* London: SPCK, 1989.

Charlesworth, Scott D. "T. C. Skeat, P.⁶⁴ + ⁶⁷ and P.⁴, and the Problem of Fibre Orientation in Codicological Reconstruction." *NTS* 53 (2007): 582-604.

———. "The Gospel Manuscript Tradition." In *The Content and Setting of the Gospel Tradition.* Edited by M. Harding and A. Nobbs. Grand Rapids: Eerdmans, 2010, 28-59.

———. "'Catholicity' in Early Gospel Manuscripts." In *The Early Text of the New Testament.* Edited by C. E. Hill and M. J. Kruger. Oxford: Oxford University Press, 2012, 37-48.

Chilton, Bruce D. "An Evangelical and Critical Approach to the Sayings of Jesus." *Themelios* 3 (1978): 78-85.

———. *Profiles of a Rabbi.* Atlanta: Scholars, 1989.

———. *Pure Kingdom: Jesus' Vision of God.* Grand Rapids: Eerdmans, 1996.

———. *Rabbi Jesus.* New York: Doubleday, 2000.

Collins, Adela Yarbro. *The Beginning of the Gospel: Probings of Mark in Context.* Minneapolis: Fortress, 1992.

———. *Mark.* Hermeneia; Minneapolis: Fortress, 2007.

Colwell, Ernest C. *John Defends the Gospel.* Chicago: Willet, Clark, 1936.

Cook, John G. *The Structure and Persuasive Power of Mark: A Linguistic Approach.* Atlanta: Scholars, 1995.

Crook, Zeba Antonin. "The Synoptic Parables of the Mustard Seed and the Leaven: A Test-Case for the Two-Document, Two-Gospel, and Farrer-Goulder Hypotheses." *JSNT* 78 (2000): 23-48.

Crossan, John Dominic. *The Historical Jesus: The Life of a Mediterranean Jewish Peasant.* San Francisco: HarperCollins, 1991.

———. "Itinerants and Householders in the Earliest Jesus Movement." In *Whose Historical Jesus?* Edited by William E. Arnal and Michel Desjardins. SCJ 7; Waterloo: Wilfrid Laurier University Press, 1997, 7-24.

———. *The Birth of Christianity: Discovering What Happened in the Years Immediately after the Execution of Jesus.* San Francisco: HarperCollins, 1998.

Dahl, Nils A. *Jesus in the Memory of the Early Church.* Minneapolis: Augsburg, 1976.

———. *Jesus the Christ: The Historical Origins of Christological Doctrine.* Minneapolis: Fortress, 1991.

Davids, Peter H. "The Gospels and the Jewish Tradition: Twenty Years After Gerhardsson." In *Gospel Perspectives 1: Studies of History and Tradition in the Four Gospels.* Edited by R. T. France and David Wenham. Sheffield: JSOT, 1983, 75-99.

———. "James and Jesus." In *The Jesus Tradition outside the Gospels.* Edited by David Wenham. Sheffield: JSOT, 1985, 63-84.

Davies, W. D. "Reflections on a Scandinavian Approach to the 'Gospel Tradition.'" In *Neotestamentica et patristica. Eine Freundesgabe, Herrn Professor Dr. Oscar Cullmann zu seinem 60. Geburtstag uberreicht.* NovTSup 6; Leiden: Brill, 1962, 14-34.

———. *The Setting of the Sermon on the Mount.* Cambridge: Cambridge University Press, 1964.

Denaux, Adelbert, ed. *John and the Synoptics.* BETL 101; Leuven: Leuven University Press, 1992.

Dewey, Joanna. "Mark as Aural Narrative: Structures and Clues to Understanding." *STR* 36 (1992): 45-56.

———. "Mark — A Really Good Oral Story: Is That Why the Gospel of Mark Survived?" *JBL* 123 (2004): 495-507.

Dibelius, Martin. *From Tradition to Gospel.* Translated by Bertram Lee Woolf. Cambridge: Clarke, 1971 (1919).

———. *Die Formgeschichte des Evangelium.* Berlin: Evangelische, 1969.

———. *James: A Commentary on the Epistle of James.* Translated by M. A. Williams. Hermeneia: Philadelphia: Fortress, 1976.

Dickson, John. "Gospel as News: εὐαγγελ- from Aristophanes to the Apostle Paul." *NTS* 51 (2005): 212-30.

Diehl, Judith A. "What Is a 'Gospel'? Recent Studies in Gospel Genre." *CBR* 20 (2010): 1-26.

Dodd, C. H. *The Apostolic Preaching and Its Developments.* London: Hodder & Stoughton, 1936.

———. *Historical Tradition in the Fourth Gospel.* Cambridge: Cambridge University Press, 1963.

———. *The Founder of Christianity.* New York: Macmillan, 1970.

Downing, F. Gerald. "Contemporary Analogies to the Gospels and Acts: 'Genres' or 'Motifs'?" In *Synoptic Studies.* Edited by C. M. Tuckett. JSNTSup 7; Sheffield: JSOT, 1984, 51-64.

Draper, Jonathan. "The Jesus Tradition in the Didache." In *Gospel Perspectives 5: The Jesus Tradition outside the Gospels.* Edited by David Wenham. Sheffield: JSOT, 1985, 269-87.

———. "The Jesus Tradition in the Didache." In *The Didache in Modern Research.* Edited by Jonathan A. Draper. Leiden: Brill, 1996, 72-91.

Dulling, Dennis C. "Social Memory and Biblical Studies: Theory, Method, and Application." *BTB* 26 (2006): 2-3.

Dungan, David. "Mark — The Abridgement of Matthew and Luke." In *Jesus and Man's Hope.* Pittsburgh: Pittsburgh Theological Seminary, 1970, 51-97.

———. "Theory of Synopsis Construction." *Bib* 61 (1980): 305-29.

———. "Synopses of the Future." *Bib* 66 (1985): 457-92.

————. "Synopses of the Future." In *The Interrelations of the Gospels.* Edited by D. L. Dungan. BETL 95; Leuven: Leuven University Press, 1990, 317-47.

————. "Let John Be John: A Gospel of Its Time." In *The Gospel and the Gospels.* Edited by P. Stuhlmacher. Grand Rapids: Eerdmans, 1991, 293-322.

————. *The History of the Synoptic Problem: The Canon, the Text, the Composition, and the Interpretation of the Gospels.* New York: Doubleday, 1999.

Dungan, David L., Allan J. McNicol, and David B. Peabody, eds. *Beyond the Q Impasse: Luke's Use of Matthew.* Valley Forge: Trinity, 1996.

Dunn, James D. G. "Prophetic 'I'-Sayings and the Jesus Tradition: The Importance of Testing Prophetic Utterances within Early Christianity." *NTS* 24 (1977-78): 175-98.

————. *The Living Word.* Philadelphia: Fortress, 1987.

————. "Let John Be John: A Gospel for Its Time." In *The Gospel and the Gospels.* Edited by P. Stuhlmacher. Grand Rapids: Eerdmans, 1991.

————. "Jesus Tradition in Paul." In *Studying the Historical Jesus: Evaluations of the State of Current Research.* Edited by Bruce Chilton and Craig A. Evans. NTTS 19; Leiden: Brill, 1994, 155-78.

————. *The Epistles to the Colossians and to Philemon.* NIGTC; Grand Rapids: Eerdmans, 1996.

————. *The Theology of Paul the Apostle.* Grand Rapids: Eerdmans, 1998.

————. "Can the Third Quest Hope to Succeed?" In *Authenticating the Activities of Jesus.* Edited by Bruce Chilton and Craig A. Evans. NTTS 28; Leiden: Brill, 1999, 31-48.

————. "Jesus in Oral Memory: The Initial Stages of the Jesus Tradition." In *Jesus: A Colloquium in the Holy Land.* Edited by D. Donnelly. London: Continuum, 2001, 81-145.

————. "Altering the Default Setting: Re-Envisaging the Early Transmission of the Jesus Tradition." *NTS* 49 (2003): 139-75.

————. *The Epistle to the Galatians.* BNTC; London: Black, 2003.

————. *Jesus Remembered.* CITM 1; Grand Rapids: Eerdmans, 2003.

————. "On History, Memory, and Eyewitnesses: In Response to Bengst Holmberg and Samuel Byrskog." *JSNT* 26 (2004): 473-87.

————. *A New Perspective on Jesus: What the Quests for the Historical Jesus Missed.* Grand Rapids: Baker, 2005.

————. "Kenneth Bailey's Theory of Oral Tradition: Critiquing Theodore Weeden's Critique." *JSHJ* 7 (2009): 44-62.

————. *Jesus, Paul, and the Gospels.* Grand Rapids: Eerdmans, 2011.

————. "Remembering Jesus: How the Quest of the Historical Jesus Lost Its Way." In *Handbook for the Study of the Historical Jesus.* Edited by T. Holmén and S. E. Porter. 4 vols.; Leiden: Brill, 2011, 1:183-205.

————. "The Gospel and the Gospels." *EQ* 85 (2013): 291-308.

du Toit, David S. "Redefining Jesus: Current Trends in Jesus Research." In *Jesus, Mark and Q: The Teaching of Jesus and Its Earliest Records.* Edited by M. Labahn and A. Schmidt. JSNTSup 214; Sheffield: Sheffield Academic, 2001, 82-124.

Dvorak, James D. "The Relationship between John and the Synoptic Gospels." *JETS* 41 (1998): 201-13.

Easton, B. S. *The Gospel before the Gospels*. London: Allen & Unwin, 1928.

Eddy, Paul R., and Gregory A. Boyd. *The Jesus Legend: A Case for the Historical Reliability of the Synoptic Jesus Tradition*. Grand Rapids: Baker, 2007.

Edwards, James R. "The Gospel of the Ebionites and the Gospel of Luke." *NTS* 48 (2002): 568-86.

———. *The Hebrew Gospel and the Development of the Synoptic Tradition*. Grand Rapids: Eerdmans, 2009.

Edwards, M. J., and Simon Swain, eds. *Portraits: Biographical Representation in Greek and Latin Literature of the Roman Empire*. Oxford: Clarendon, 1997.

Ehrman, Bart. *The Orthodox Corruption of Scripture: The Effect of Early Christological Controversies on the Text of the New Testament*. Oxford: Oxford University Press, 1993.

———. *Lost Christianities: The Battle for the Scripture and the Faiths We Never Knew*. Oxford: Oxford University Press, 2003.

———. *Jesus, Interrupted: Revealing the Hidden Contradictions in the Bible (and Why We Don't Know About Them)*. New York: HarperOne, 2009.

Ehrman, Bart, and Ziatko Pleše. *The Apocryphal Gospels: Texts and Translations*. Oxford: Oxford University Press, 2011.

Eitzen, Kim Haines. *Guardians of Letters: Literacy, Power, and the Transmitters of Early Christian Literature*. Oxford: Oxford University Press, 2000.

Elliott, J. K. "The Relevance of Textual Criticism to the Synoptic Problem." In *The Interrelations of the Gospels*. Edited by D. L. Dungan. BETL 95; Leuven: Leuven University Press, 1990, 348-59.

———. "Which Is the Best Synopsis?" *ExpT* 102 (1991): 200-204.

———. "Printed Editions of Greek Synopses and Their Influence on the Synoptic Problem." In *The Four Gospels 1992*. Edited by F. Van Segbroeck, C. M. Tuckett, G. Van Belle, and J. Verheyden. BETL 100; FS F. Neirynck; Leuven: Leuven University Press, 1992, 337-57.

———. *The Apocryphal New Testament*. Oxford: Clarendon, 1993.

Ellis, E. Earle. *The Gospel of Luke*. NCB; London: Nelson, 1966.

———. "Traditions in 1 Corinthians." *NTS* 32 (1986): 481-502.

———. "Gospel Criticism: A Perspective on the State of the Art." In *The Gospel and the Gospels*. Edited by P. Stuhlmacher. Grand Rapids: Eerdmans, 1991, 26-52.

———. "The Synoptic Gospels and History." In *Authenticating the Activities of Jesus*. Edited by Bruce D. Chilton and Craig A. Evans. NTTS 28; Leiden: Brill, 1999, 49-57.

———. *The Making of the New Testament Documents*. Leiden: Brill, 2002.

Ennulat, Andreas. *Die "Minor Agreements" Untersuchungen zu einer offenen Frage des synoptischens Problems*. WUNT 2.62; Tübingen: Mohr, 1994.

Evans, Craig A. *Jesus and His Contemporaries: Comparative Studies*. Leiden: Brill, 1995.

———. "The Passion of Jesus: History Remembered or Prophecy Historicized?" *BBR* 6 (1996): 159-65.

———. "Mark's Incipit and the Priene Calendar: From Jewish Gospel to Greco-Roman Gospel." *JGRChJ* 1 (2000): 67-81.

———. "Life of Jesus." In *Handbook to Exegesis of the New Testament*. Edited by Stanley E. Porter. Leiden: Brill, 2002, 427-76 .

Bibliography

————. "Sorting Out the Synoptic Problem: Why an Old Approach Is Still Best." In *Reading the Gospels Today.* Edited by S. E. Porter. Grand Rapids: Eerdmans, 2004, 1-26.

Farmer, William. *The Synoptic Problem: A Critical Analysis.* New York: Macmillan, 1964.

————. "The Lachmann Fallacy." *NTS* 14 (1968): 441-43.

————. *Jesus and the Gospel: Tradition, Scripture, and Canon.* Philadelphia: Fortress, 1982.

————. "The Minor Agreements of Matthew and Luke against Mark and the Two Gospel Hypothesis." In *Minor Agreements: Symposium Göttingen, 1991.* Edited by G. Strecker. Göttingen: Vandenhoeck & Ruprecht, 1993, 163-208.

————. *The Gospel of Jesus: The Pastoral Relevance of the Synoptic Problem.* Louisville: Westminster John Knox, 1994.

————. "The Case for the Two-Gospel Hypothesis." In *Rethinking the Synoptic Problem.* Edited by D. A. Black and D. R. Beck. Grand Rapids: Baker, 2001, 97-135.

Farrer, Austin M. "On Dispensing with Q." In *The Two-Source Hypothesis: A Critical Appraisal.* Edited by A. J. Bellizoni. Macon: Mercer University Press, 1985, 321-56.

Fee, Gordon D. "A Text-Critical Look at the Synoptic Problem." *NovT* 22 (1980): 12-28.

————. "P.75, P.66, and Origen: The Myth of Early Textual Recension in Alexandria." In *Studies in the Theory and Method of New Testament Textual Criticism.* Edited by I. A. Sparks. Grand Rapids: Eerdmans, 1993, 247-73.

————. "The Text of John in *The Jerusalem Bible:* A Critique of the Use of Patristic Citations in New Testament Textual Criticism." In *Studies in the Theory and Method of New Testament Textual Criticism.* Edited by I. A. Sparks. Grand Rapids: Eerdmans, 1993, 335-43.

Ferreira, Johan. "The Non-Canonical Gospels." In *The Content and Setting of the Gospel Tradition.* Edited by M. Harding and A. Nobbs. Grand Rapids: Eerdmans, 2010, 209-30.

Fitzmyer, Joseph A. "The Priority of Mark and the 'Q' Source in Luke." In *Jesus and Man's Hope.* Edited by D. G. Buttrick. Pittsburgh: Pittsburgh Theological Seminary, 1970, 1:131-70.

————. *A Wandering Aramean: Collected Essays.* Missoula: Scholars, 1979.

————. *The Gospel According to Luke.* 2 vols.; AB; Garden City: Doubleday, 1981.

————. "Luke's Use of Q." In *The Two-Source Hypothesis: A Critical Appraisal.* Edited by A. J. Bellinzoni. Mercer: Mercer University Press, 1985, 245-57.

Fledderman, Harry T. *Mark and Q: A Study of the Overlap Texts.* BETL 122; Leuven: Leuven University Press, 1995.

Flusser, David, and Huub van de Sandt. *The Didache: Its Jewish Sources and Its Place in Early Judaism and Christianity.* Minneapolis: Fortress, 2002.

Fortna, Robert. *The Fourth Gospel and Its Predecessor: From Narrative Source to Present Gospel.* Philadelphia: Fortress, 1988.

Foster, Paul. "Is It Possible to Dispense with Q?" *NovT* 45 (2003): 313-37.

————. "Are There Any Early Fragments of the So-Called *Gospel of Peter?*" *NTS* 52 (2005): 1-28.

————. "The Epistles of Ignatius of Antioch and the Writings That Later Formed the New Testament." In *The Reception of the New Testament in the Apostolic Fathers.* Edited by A. Gregory and C. Tuckett. Oxford: Oxford University Press, 2005, 159-86.

Foster, Paul, Andrew Gregory, John Kloppenborg, and Jozef Verheyden, eds. *New Studies in the Synoptic Problem: Oxford Conference, April 2008*. BETL 239; FS Christopher Tuckett; Leuven: Peeters, 2011.

Fredriksen, Paula. *Jesus of Nazareth, King of the Jews*. New York: Vintage, 1999.

Frenschkowski, Marco. "Marcion in arabischen Quellen." In *Marcion und seine kirchengeschichtliche Wirkung*. Edited by G. May and K. Greschat. Berlin: de Gruyter, 2002, 39-63.

Frey, Jörg. "Das Vierte Evangelium auf dem Hintergrund der älteren Evangelientradition. Zum Problem Johannes und die Synoptiker." In *Johannesevangelium, Mitte oder Rand des Kanons? Neue Standortbestimmungen*. Edited by T. Söding. Freiburg im Bresgau: Herder, 2003, 60-118.

Freyne, Seán. *Galilee, Jesus and the Gospels: Literary Approaches and Historical Investigations*. Philadelphia: Fortress, 1988.

—————. *Jesus, A Jewish Galilean: A New Reading of the Jesus-Story*. London: Continuum, 2005.

Fuchs, Albert. *Sprachliche Untersuchungen zu Matthäus und Lukas. Ein Beitrag zur Quellenkritik*. Analecta Biblica 49; Rome: Biblical Institute Press, 1971.

—————. *Spuren von Deuteromarkus*. 5 vols.; SNTU 5; Münster: Lit, 2004-7.

Funk, Robert W. *Honest to Jesus: Jesus for a New Millennium*. San Francisco: HarperCollins, 1996.

—————. *The Acts of Jesus: The Search for the Authentic Deeds of Jesus*. San Francisco: HarperCollins, 1998.

Funk, Robert W., and Roy W. Hoover, *The Five Gospels: The Search for the Authentic Words of Jesus*. San Francisco: HarperCollins, 1993.

Furnish, Victor Paul. *II Corinthians*. AB; New York: Doubleday, 1984.

Gamble, Harry. *Books and Readers in the Early Church: A History of Early Christian Texts*. New Haven: Yale University Press, 1995.

—————. "The Book Trade in the Roman Empire." In *The Early Text of the New Testament*. Edited by C. E. Hill and M. J. Kruger. Oxford: Oxford University Press, 2012, 23-36.

Gardner-Smith, P. *Saint John and the Synoptic Gospels*. Cambridge: Cambridge University Press, 1938.

Gathercole, Simon. "The Gospel of Paul and the Kingdom of God." In *God's Power to Save*. Edited by C. Green. Nottingham: InterVarsity, 2006, 138-54.

—————. *The Gospel of Judas*. Oxford: Oxford University Press, 2007.

—————. *The Composition of the Gospel of Thomas: Original Language and Influences*. SNTSMS 151; Cambridge: Cambridge University Press, 2012.

—————. "The Titles of the Gospels in the Earliest New Testament Manuscripts." *ZNW* 104 (2013): 33-76.

Gaventa, Beverly R., and Richard B. Hays. "Seeking the Identity of Jesus." In *Seeking the Identity of Jesus: A Pilgrimage*. Edited by Beverly R. Gaventa and Richard B. Hays. Grand Rapids: Eerdmans, 2008, 1-24.

Georgi, Dieter. *The Opponents of Paul in Second Corinthians: A Study of Religious Propaganda in Late Antiquity*. Philadelphia: Fortress, 1986.

Gerhardsson, Birger. *The Origin of the Gospel Traditions*. Philadelphia: Fortress, 1979.

————. *The Gospel Tradition.* Lund: Gleerup, 1986.

————. "The Gospel Tradition." In *The Interrelations of the Gospels.* Edited by David Dungan. Leuven: Leuven University Press, 1990, 497-545.

————. "The Path of the Gospel Tradition." In *The Gospel and the Gospels.* Edited by Peter Stuhlmacher. Grand Rapids: Eerdmans, 1991, 75-96.

————. *Memory and Manuscript: Oral Tradition and Written Transmission in Rabbinic Judaism and Early Christianity.* 2nd ed.; Grand Rapids: Eerdmans, 1998.

————. *The Reliability of the Gospel Tradition.* Peabody: Hendrickson, 2001.

————. "The Secret of the Transmission of the Unwritten Jesus Tradition." *NTS* 51 (2005): 1-18.

Gerlach, Karl. *The Antenicene Pascha: A Rhetorical History.* Leuven: Peeters, 1998.

Gero, Stephen. "Apocryphal Gospels: A Survey of Textual History and Literary Problems." *ANRW* 2.25.5 (1988): 3969-96.

Glover, R. "The *Didache's* Quotations and the Synoptic Gospels." *NTS* (1958): 12-29.

Gnilka, Joachim. *Das Matthäusevangelium II.* HTK; Freiberg: Herder, 1988.

Goodacre, Mark S. *Goulder on the Gospels: An Examination of a New Paradigm.* JSNTSup 133; Sheffield: Sheffield Academic, 1996.

————. "Fatigue in the Synoptics." *NTS* 44 (1998): 45-58.

————. *The Synoptic Problem: A Way through the Maze.* London: Sheffield Academic, 2001.

————. *The Case Against Q.* Harrisburg: Trinity, 2002.

————. "Scripturalization in Mark's Crucifixion Narrative." In *The Trial and Death of Jesus: Essays on the Passion Narrative in Mark.* Edited by G. van Oyen and T. Shepherd. Leuven: Peeters, 2006, 33-47.

————. *Thomas and the Gospels: The Making of an Apocryphal Text.* Grand Rapids: Eerdmans, 2012.

Goodacre, Mark, and Nicholas Perrin, eds. *Questioning Q: A Multi-Dimensional Critique.* Downers Grove: InterVarsity, 2004.

Goodspeed, E. J. *The Formation of the New Testament.* Chicago: University of Chicago Press, 1937.

Goodwin, C. "How Did John Treat His Sources?" *JBL* 73 (1954): 61-75.

Goulder, Michael. *Midrash and Lexicon, the Evangelist's Calendar: A Lectionary Explanation of the Development of Scripture.* London: SPCK, 1978.

————. "The Order of a Crank." In *Synoptic Studies: The Ampleworth Conferences of 1982 and 1983.* Edited by C. M. Tuckett. JSNTSup 7; Sheffield: JSOT, 1984, 111-30.

————. *Luke: A New Paradigm.* 2 vols.; JSNTSup 20; Sheffield: JSOT, 1989.

————. "Luke's Compositional Options." *NTS* 39 (1993): 150-52.

————. "Luke's Knowledge of Matthew." In *Minor Agreements: Symposium Göttingen, 1991.* Edited by G. Strecker. Göttingen: Vandenhoeck & Ruprecht, 1993, 142-62.

————. "Is Q a Juggernaut?" *JBL* 115 (1996): 667-91.

————. "Ignatius' 'Docetists.'" *VC* 53 (1999): 16-30.

————. "Self-Contradiction in the IQP?" *JBL* 118 (1999): 506-17.

Grant, Robert M. "The Fourth Gospel and the Church." *HTR* 35 (1942): 95-116.

Green, Joel B. "Passion Narrative." In *DJG*. Edited by Joel B. Green, Scot McKnight, and I. Howard Marshall. Downers Grove: InterVarsity, 1992, 602-4.

—. "The Gospel According to Mark." In *The Cambridge Companion to the Gospels*. Edited by Stephen C. Barton. Cambridge: Cambridge University Press, 2007, 139-47.

Gregory, Andrew. "Prior or Posterior? The *Gospel of the Ebionites* and the Gospel of Luke." *NTS* 51 (2005): 344-60.

—. "The Non-Canonical Gospels and the Historical Jesus — Some Reflections on Issues and Methods." *EQ* 81 (2009): 3-22.

Gregory, Andrew F., and Christopher M. Tuckett. "2 *Clement* and the Writings That Later Formed the New Testament." In *The Reception of the New Testament in the Apostolic Fathers*. Edited by A. Gregory and C. Tuckett. Oxford: Oxford University Press, 2005, 252-92.

Guelich, Robert. "The Gospel Genre." In *The Gospel and the Gospels*. Edited by P. Stuhlmacher. Grand Rapids: Eerdmans, 1991, 172-208.

Gundry, Robert H. "Matthean Foreign Bodies in Agreements of Luke with Matthew against Mark: Evidence That Luke Used Matthew." In *The Four Gospels 1992*. Edited by F. van Segbroeck et al. BETL 100; FS F. Neirynck; Leuven: Leuven University Press, 1992, 2:1466-95.

—. *Mark: A Commentary on His Apology for the Cross*. Grand Rapids: Eerdmans, 1993.

—. *Matthew: A Commentary on His Handbook for a Mixed Church under Persecution*. 2nd ed.; Grand Rapids: Eerdmans, 1994.

—. "A Rejoinder on Matthean Foreign Bodies in Luke 10,25-28." *ETL* 71 (1995): 139-50.

—. "ΕΥΑΓΓΕΛΙΟΝ: How Soon a Book?" *JBL* 115 (1996): 321-25.

—. "The Refusal of Matthean Foreign Bodies to Be Excised from Luke 9,22; 10,25-28." *ETL* 75 (1999): 104-22.

—. "The Symbiosis of Theology and Genre Criticism of the Canonical Gospels." In *The Old Is Better: New Testament Essays in Support of Tradition Interpretations*. WUNT 178; Tübingen: Mohr, 2005, 18-48.

Guthrie, Donald. *New Testament Introduction*. 4th ed.; Leicester: Apollos, 1990.

Hadad, Moses, and Morton Smith. *Heroes and Gods: Spiritual Biographies in Antiquity*. New York: Harper & Row, 1965.

Hahneman, Geoffrey M. *The Muratorian Fragment and the Development of the Canon*. Oxford: Clarendon, 1992.

Halverson, John. "Oral and Written Gospel: A Critique of Werner Kelber." *NTS* 40 (1994): 180-95.

Hannah, Darrell D. "The Four-Gospel 'Canon' in the *Epistula Apostolorum*." *JTS* 58 (2007): 598-633.

Harnack, Adolf von. "Gospel: History of the Conception in the Earliest Church." In *The Constitution and Law of the Church in the First Two Centuries*. London: Williams & Norgate, 1910, 275-331.

Hartin, Patrick. *James and the "Q" Sayings of Jesus*. JSNTSup 47; Sheffield: JSOT, 1991.

———. "James and the Jesus Tradition: Some Theological Reflections and Implications." In *Catholic Epistles and Apostolic Tradition*. Edited by Karl-Wilhelm Niebuhr and Robert W. Wall. Waco: Baylor University Press, 2009, 55-70.

Harvey, A. E. *Jesus and the Constraints of History*. London: Duckworth, 1982.

Häusser, Detlef. *Christusbekenntnis und Jesusüberlieferung bei Paulus*. WUNT 2.210; Tübingen: Mohr, 2006.

Hawkins, J. C. *Horae Synopticae*. Oxford: Clarendon, 1909.

Hawthorne, G. F. "Christian Prophets and the Sayings of Jesus: Evidence of and Criteria for." *SBL Seminar Papers 8*. Missoula: Scholars, 1975, 105-29.

Head, Peter M. *Christology and the Synoptic Problem: An Argument for Markan Priority*. SNTSMS 94; Cambridge: Cambridge University Press, 1997.

———. "Some Recently Published NT Papyri from Oxyrynchus: An Overview and Preliminary Assessment." *TynBul* 51 (2000): 1-16.

———. "The Role of Eyewitnesses in the Formation of the Gospel Tradition: A Review Article of Samuel Byrskog, *Story as History — History as Story*." *TynBul* 52 (2001): 275-94.

———. "Is P.[4], P.[64] and P.[67] the Oldest Manuscript of the Four Gospels? A Response to T. C. Skeat." *NTS* 51 (2005): 450-57.

———. "Graham Stanton and the Four-Gospel Codex." In *Jesus, Matthew's Gospel and Early Christianity*. Edited by R. Burridge, D. Gurtner, and J. Willitts. LNTS 435; FS Graham Stanton; London: Clark, 2011, 93-101.

———. "Textual Criticism and the Synoptic Problem." In *New Studies in the Synoptic Problem: Oxford Conference, 2008*. Edited by P. Foster, A. Gregory, J. S. Kloppenborg, and J. Verheyden. BETL 239; FS C. Tuckett; Leuven: Peeters, 2011, 115-56.

Heckel, Theo K. *Vom Evangelium des Markus zum Viergestaltigen Evangelium*. WUNT 120; Tübingen: Mohr, 1999.

Henaut, Barry W. *Oral Tradition and the Gospels: The Problem of Mark 4*. JSNTSup 82; Sheffield: Sheffield Academic, 1993.

Hengel, Martin. *Judaism and Hellenism: Studies in Their Encounter in Palestine during the Early Hellenistic Period*. 2 vols.; Philadelphia: Fortress, 1974.

———. *The Son of God: The Origin of Christology and the History of Jewish-Hellenistic Religion*. Translated by J. Bowden. Philadelphia: Fortress, 1976.

———. *Acts and the History of Earliest Christianity*. Philadelphia: Fortress, 1980.

———. *The Charismatic Leader and His Followers*. Translated by James C. G. Greig. Edinburgh: Clark, 1981.

———. *The Johannine Question*. London: SCM, 1989.

———. *The Pre-Christian Paul*. Translated by John Bowden. Philadelphia: Fortress, 1991.

———. *The Four Gospels and the One Gospel of Jesus Christ*. Translated by J. Bowden. Harrisburg: Trinity, 2000.

———. "Eye-Witness Memory and the Writing of the Gospels." In *The Written Gospel*. Edited by M. A. Bockmuehl and D. A. Hagner. Cambridge: Cambridge University Press, 2005, 70-96.

Hengel, Martin, and Roland Deines. "E. P. Sander's 'Common Judaism', Jesus, and the Pharisees." *JTS* 46 (1995): 1-70.

Hezser, Catherine. *Jewish Literacy in Roman Palestine*. TSAJ 81; Tübingen: Mohr, 2001.

Hill, Charles E. "The Debate over the Muratorian Fragment and the Development of the Canon." *WTJ* 57 (1995): 437-52.

————. "Justin and the New Testament Writings." In *Studia Patristica* 30. Edited by D. A. Livingstone. Leuven: Peeters, 1997, 42-48.

————. "What Papias Said About John (and Luke)." *JTS* 49 (1998): 582-629.

————. "The *Epistula Apostolorum*: An Asian Tract from the Time of Polycarp." *JECS* 7 (1999): 1-53.

————. *The Johannine Corpus in the Early Church*. Oxford: Oxford University Press, 2004.

————. "Ignatius, 'the Gospel,' and the Gospels." In *Trajectories through the New Testament and the Apostolic Fathers*. Edited by A. Gregory and C. Tuckett. Oxford: Oxford University Press, 2005, 267-85.

————. "The Fourth Gospel in the Second Century: The Myth of Orthodox Johannophobia." In *Challenging Perspectives on the Gospel of John*. Edited by J. Lierman. WUNT 2.219; Tübingen: Mohr, 2006, 135-69.

————. "Papias of Hierapolis." *ExpT* 117 (2006): 309-15.

————. *Who Chose the Gospels? Probing the Great Gospel Conspiracy*. Oxford: Oxford University Press, 2010.

Hill, Charles E., and Michael J. Kruger. "Introduction." In *The Early Text of the New Testament*. Edited by C. E. Hill and M. J. Kruger. Oxford: Oxford University Press, 2012, 1-19.

Hincks, Edward Y. "The Probable Use of the First Gospel by Luke." *JBL* 10 (1891): 92-106.

Hirsch, E. *Frühgeschichte des Evangeliums*. Tübingen: Mohr, 1941.

Hobbs, Edward C. "A Quarter-Century without 'Q.'" *Perkins School of Theology Journal* 33 (1980): 10-19.

Holladay, Carl R. *Theios Anēr in Hellenistic Judaism: A Critique of the Use of This Category in New Testament Christology*. Missoula: Scholars, 1977.

Hollander, Harm W. "The Words of Jesus: From Oral Traditions to Written Record in Paul and Q." *NovT* 42 (2000): 340-57.

Holmes, Michael W. "From 'Original Text' to 'Initial Text': The Traditional Goal of New Testament Textual Criticism in Contemporary Discussion." In *The Text of the New Testament in Contemporary Research: Essays on the Status Quaestionis*. Edited by B. D. Ehrman and M. W. Holmes. 2nd ed.; Leiden: Brill, 2012, 637-88.

Holtzmann, H. J. *Die synoptischen Evangelien. Ihr Ursprung und geschichtlicher Charakter*. Leipzig: Engelmann, 1863.

————. "Zur synoptischen Frage." *Jahrbücher für protestantische Theologie* 4 (1878): 145-88, 328-82, 533-68.

————. *Lehrbuch der historisch-kritischen Einleitung in das Neue Testament*. Leipzig, 1885.

Honey, T. E. Floyd. "Did Mark Use Q?" *JBL* 62 (1943): 319-31.

Hood, Jason B. *Imitating God in Christ: Recapturing a Biblical Pattern*. Downers Grove: InterVarsity, 2013.

Hooker, Morna D. "Beginnings and Endings." In *The Written Gospel*. Edited by Markus

Bibliography

Bockmuehl and D. A. Hagner. FS Graham Stanton; Cambridge: Cambridge University Press, 2005, 184-202.

Horbury, William. "'Gospel' in Herodian Judean." In *The Written Gospel*. Edited by M. Bockmuehl and D. A. Hagner. Cambridge: Cambridge University Press, 2005, 7-30.

Horsley, Richard A. *Galilee: History, Politics, People*. Valley Forge: Trinity, 1995.

———. *Hearing the Whole Story: The Politics of Plot in Mark's Gospel*. Louisville: Westminster John Knox, 2001.

———. "Oral Tradition in New Testament Studies." *Oral Tradition* 18 (2003): 34-36.

Horsley, Richard A., Jonathan A. Draper, and John Miles Foley, eds. *Performing the Gospel: Orality, Memory, and Mark: Essays Dedicated to Werner Kelber*. Minneapolis: Fortress, 2006.

Huck, A., and H. Greeven, eds. *Synopse der drei ersten Evangelien mit Beigabe der johanneischen Parallelstellen*. Tübingen: Mohr, 1981.

Huggins, Ronald V. "Matthean Posteriority: A Preliminary Proposal." *NovT* 34 (1992): 1-22.

Hughes, Graham. *Hebrews and Hermeneutics: The Epistle to the Hebrews as a New Testament Example of Biblical Interpretation*. SNTSMS 36; Cambridge: Cambridge University Press, 1979.

Hultgren, Arland J. *The Rise of Normative Christianity*. Eugene: Wipf & Stock, 1994.

Hultgren, Stephen. *Narrative Elements in the Double Tradition: A Study of Their Place within the Framework of the Gospel Narrative*. BZNW 113; Berlin: de Gruyter, 2002.

Hurtado, Larry. "Gospel (Genre)." In *DJG*. Edited by J. B. Green, S. McKnight, and I. H. Marshall. Downers Grove: InterVarsity, 1992, 276-82.

———. "Greco-Roman Textuality and the Gospel of Mark: A Critical Assessment of Werner Kelber's *The Oral and the Written Gospel*." *BBR* 7 (1997): 91-106.

———. *Lord Jesus Christ: Devotion to Jesus in Earliest Christianity*. Grand Rapids: Eerdmans, 2003.

———. *The Earliest Christian Artifacts: Manuscripts and Christian Origins*. Grand Rapids: Eerdmans, 2006.

———. "The New Testament in the Second Century: Text, Collections and Canon." In *Transmission and Reception: New Testament Text-Critical and Exegetical Studies*. Edited by D. C. Parker and J. W. Childers. Piscataway: Gorgias, 2006, 3-27.

———. "Manuscripts and the Sociology of Early Christian Reading." In *The Early Text of the New Testament*. Edited by C. E. Hill and M. J. Kruger. Oxford: Oxford University Press, 2012, 49-62.

Ingolfsland, Dennis. "Kloppenborg's Stratification of Q and Its Significance for Historical Jesus Studies." *JETS* 46 (2003): 217-32.

Iverson, Kelly R. "Orality and the Gospels: A Survey of Research." *CBR* 8 (2009): 71-106.

Jaffee, M. S. *Torah in the Mouth: Writing and Oral Tradition in Palestinian Judaism 200 BCE–400 CE*. Oxford: Oxford University Press, 2001.

Jaroš, Karl, et al., eds. *Das Neue Testament nach den älten griechischen Handschriften. Die handschriftliche griechiche Überlieferung des Neuen Testaments vor Codex Sinaiticus und Codex Vaticanus*. Mainz: Rutzen, 2006.

Jeremias, Joachim. *New Testament Theology*. Translated by John Bowden. London: SCM, 1971.

Jervell, Jacob. "The Future of the Past: Luke's Vision of Salvation History and Its Bearing on His Writing of History." In *History, Literature, and Society in the Book of Acts*. Edited by Ben Witherington. Cambridge: Cambridge University Press, 1996, 104-26.

Johnson, Luke Timothy. *The Writings of the New Testament: An Interpretation*. Rev. ed.; London: SCM, 1999.

Johnson, Luke Timothy, and Wesley H. Wachob. "The Sayings of Jesus in the Letter of James." In *Authenticating the Words of Jesus*. Edited by B. D. Chilton and C. A. Evans. NTTS 28.1; Leiden: Brill, 1999, 431-50.

Johnson, William A. "Towards a Sociology of Reading in Classical Antiquity." *AJP* 121 (2000): 593-627.

―――. *Readers and Reading Culture in the High Roman Empire: A Study of Elite Communities*. Oxford: Oxford University Press, 2010.

Jones, Brice C. *Matthean and Lukan Special Material: A Brief Introduction with Texts in Greek and English*. Eugene: Wipf & Stock, 2011.

Kähler, Martin. *The So-Called Historical Jesus and the Historic Biblical Christ*. Translated and edited by Carl E. Braaten. Philadelphia: Fortress, 1988 (1896).

Käsemann, Ernst. "The Problem of the Historical Jesus." In *Essays on New Testament Themes*. Translated by W. J. Montague. London: SCM, 1964, 17-47.

Kee, Howard Clark. "Aretalogy and Gospel." *JBL* 92 (1973): 402-22.

―――. *The Beginnings of Christianity: An Introduction to the New Testament*. London: Clark, 2005.

Keeder, Kylu. *The Branches of the Gospel of John: The Reception of the Fourth Gospel in the Early Church*. LNTS 332; London: Clark, 2006.

Keener, Craig. *A Commentary on the Gospel of Matthew*. Grand Rapids: Eerdmans, 1999.

―――. *The Gospel of John: A Commentary*. 2 vols.; Peabody: Hendrickson, 2004.

―――. *The Historical Jesus of the Gospels*. Grand Rapids: Eerdmans, 2009.

Keightley, G. M. "The Church's Memory of Jesus: A Social Science Analysis of 1 Thessalonians." *BTB* 17 (1987): 149-56.

Keith, Chris. *Jesus' Literacy: Scribal Culture and the Teacher from Galilee*. LNTS 413; London: Clark, 2011.

―――. "Memory and Authenticity: Jesus Tradition and What Really Happened." *ZNW* 102 (2011): 155-77.

―――. "The Indebtedness of the Criteria Approach to Form Criticism and Recent Attempts to Rehabilitate the Search for an Authentic Jesus." In *Jesus, Criteria, and the Demise of Authenticity*. Edited by C. Keith and A. Le Donne. London: Clark, 2012, 25-48.

Kelber, Werner. *The Oral and the Written Gospel*. Philadelphia: Fortress, 1983.

―――. "The Case of the Gospels: Memory's Desire and the Limitations of Historical Criticism." *Oral Tradition* 17 (2002): 55-86.

―――. "The Generative Force of Memory: Early Christian Traditions as Processes of Remembering." *BTB* 36 (2006): 15-22.

————. "The Work of Birger Gerhardsson in Perspective." In *Jesus in Memory: Traditions in Oral and Scribal Perspective.* Edited by W. Kelber and S. Byrskog. Waco: Baylor University Press, 2009, 173-206.

Kelber, Werner, and Samuel Byrskog, eds. *Jesus in Memory: Traditions in Oral and Scribal Perspectives.* Waco: Baylor University Press, 2009.

Kelhoffer, James A. *Miracle and Mission.* WUNT 2.112; Tübingen: Mohr, 2000.

————. "'How Soon a Book' Revisited: ΕΥΑΓΓΕΛΙΟΝ as a Reference to 'Gospel' Material in the First Half of the Second Century." *ZNW* 95 (2004): 1-34.

Kennedy, George A. "Classical and Christian Source Criticism." In *The Relationship among the Gospels: An Interdisciplinary Dialogue.* Edited by W. O. Walker. San Antonio: Trinity University Press, 1978, 125-55.

Kim, Seyoon. "Jesus, Sayings of." In *DPL.* Edited by Gerald F. Hawthorne, Ralph P. Martin, and Daniel G. Reid. Downers Grove: InterVarsity, 1993, 474-92.

Kirk, Alan, and Tom Thatcher. "Jesus Tradition as Social Memory." In *Memory, Tradition, and Text: Uses of the Past in Early Christianity.* Edited by Alan Kirk and Tom Thatcher. Semeia 52; Leiden: Brill, 2005, 25-42.

Klein, Hans. *Bewährung im Glauben. Studien zum Sondergut des Evangelisten Matthäus.* Neukirchen-Vluyn: Neukirchener, 1996.

Kline, Meredith G. "The Old Testament Origins of the Gospel Genre." *WTJ* 38 (1975): 1-27.

Klink, Edward W., ed. *The Audience of the Gospels: The Origin and Function of the Gospels in Early Christianity.* LNTS 353; London: Clark, 2010.

Kloppenborg, John S. "*Didache* 16:6-8 and Special Matthean Tradition." *ZNW* 70 (1979): 54-67.

————. *Formation of Q: Trajectories in Ancient Wisdom Collections.* Philadelphia: Fortress, 1987.

————. *Q Parallels: Synopsis, Critical Notes and Concordance.* Sonoma: Polebridge, 1988.

————. *Excavating Q: The History and Setting of the Sayings Gospel.* Minneapolis: Fortress, 2000.

————. "Is There a New Paradigm?" In *Christology, Controversy, and Community: New Testament Essays in Honour of David Catchpole.* Edited by D. Horrell and C. M. Tuckett. NovTSup 99; Leiden: Brill, 2000, 23-47.

————. "The Reception of the Jesus Tradition in James." In *The Catholic Epistles and the Tradition.* Edited by Jacques Schlosser. BETL 176; Leuven: Peeters, 2004, 91-139.

————. "The Emulation of the Jesus Tradition in the Letter of James." In *Reading James with New Eyes: Methodological Reassessments of the Letter of James.* Edited by Robert L. Webb and John S. Kloppenborg. LNTS 342; London: Clark, 2007, 121-50.

————. "The Reception of the Jesus Tradition in James." In *Catholic Epistles and Apostolic Tradition.* Edited by Karl-Wilhelm Niebuhr and Robert W. Wall. Waco: Baylor University Press, 2009, 71-100.

————. "Synopses and the Synoptic Problem." In *New Studies in the Synoptic Problem: Oxford Conference, 2008.* Edited by P. Foster, A. Gregory, J. S. Kloppenborg, and J. Verheyden. BETL 239; FS C. Tuckett; Leuven: Peeters, 2011, 51-86.

Knox, John. *Jesus: Lord and Christ.* New York: Harper, 1958.

Koester, Helmut. *Synoptische Überlieferung bei den apostolischen Vätern.* Berlin: Akademie, 1957.

―――. "One Jesus and Four Primitive Gospels." In *Trajectories through Early Christianity.* Eugene: Wipf & Stock, 2011 (1971), 187-93.

―――. "The Structure and Criteria of Early Christian Beliefs." In *Trajectories through Early Christianity.* Eugene: Wipf & Stock, 2011 (1971), 211-29.

―――. *Ancient Christian Gospels: Their History and Development.* London: SCM, 1990.

―――. "Epilogue: Current Issues in New Testament Scholarship." In *The Future of Early Christianity: Essays in Honor of Helmut Koester.* Edited by Birger A. Pearson. Minneapolis: Fortress, 1991, 467-96.

―――. "History and Development of Mark's Gospel (From Mark to Secret Mark and 'Canonical' Mark)." In *Colloquy on New Testament Studies: A Time for Reappraisal and Fresh Approaches.* Edited by B. Corley. Macon: Mercer University Press, 1991, 35-57.

―――. "Written Gospels or Oral Tradition?" *HTR* 113 (1994): 293-97.

―――. "Gospels and Gospel Traditions in the Second Century." In *Trajectories through the New Testament and the Apostolic Fathers.* Edited by A. Gregory and C. Tuckett. Oxford: Oxford University Press, 2005, 27-44.

Köstenberger, Andreas. "John's Transposition Theology: Retelling the Story of Jesus in a Different Key." In *Earliest Christian History.* Edited by M. F. Bird and J. Maston. WUNT 2.320; Tübingen: Mohr, 2012, 191-226.

Kuhn, H. W. *Ältere Sammlungen im Markusevangelium.* Göttingen: Vandenhoeck & Ruprecht, 1971.

Kümmel, W. G. *Introduction to the New Testament.* Nashville: Abingdon, 1966.

―――. *The Theology of the New Testament.* Translated by John E. Steely. London: SCM, 1976.

Kürzinger, Josef. *Papias von Hierapolis und die Evangelien des Neuen Testament.* Regensberg: Pustet, 1983.

LaBahn, Michael. *Jesus als Lebensspender. Untersuchungen zu einer Geschichte der johanneischen Tradition anhand ihrer Wundergeschichten.* BZNW 98; New York: de Gruyter, 1999.

LaGrand, James. *The Earliest Christian Mission to "All Nations" in the Light of Matthew's Gospel.* Grand Rapids: Eerdmans, 1999.

Lambrecht, Jan. "Q Influence on Mark 8,34–9,1." In *Logia: Les paroles de Jésus — The Sayings of Jesus.* Edited by J. Delobel. BETL 59; Leuven: University of Leuven, 1982, 277-304.

Lane, William L. *The Gospel of Mark.* NICNT; Grand Rapids: Eerdmans, 1974.

Lang, Manfred. *Johannes und die Synoptiker. Eine redaktiongeschichtliche Analyse von Johannes 18-20 vor dem markanischen und lukanischen Hintergrund.* FRLANT 192; Göttingen: Vandenhoeck & Ruprecht, 1999.

Laufen, Rudolf. *Die Doppelüberlieferungen der Logienquelle und des Markusevangeliums.* BB 54; Bonn: Hanstein, 1980.

Layton, Bentley. *The Gnostic Scriptures: A New Translation with Annotations and Introductions.* London: SCM, 1987.

Bibliography

Le Donne, Anthony. *The Historiographical Jesus: Memory, Typology, and the Son of David.* Waco: Baylor University Press, 2009.

———. *Historical Jesus: What Can We Know and How Can We Know It?* Grand Rapids: Eerdmans, 2011.

Lee, Sang-Il. *Jesus and Gospel Traditions in Bilingual Context: A Study in the Interdirectionality of Language.* Berlin: de Gruyter, 2012.

Lemcio, Eugene E. *The Past of Jesus in the Gospels.* SNTSMS 68; Cambridge: Cambridge University Press, 1991.

Leo, Friedrich. *Die Griechisch-römische Biographie nach ihrer literischen Form.* Leipzig: Teubner, 1901.

Lightfoot, R. H. *History and Interpretation in the Gospels.* London: Hodder & Stoughton, 1935.

———. *St. John's Gospel: A Commentary.* Edited by C. F. Evans. Oxford: Clarendon, 1956.

Lincoln, Andrew T. *The Gospel According to Saint John.* BNTC; Peabody: Hendrickson, 2005.

Lincoln, Bruce. "Thomas-Gospel and Thomas-Community: A New Approach to a Familiar Text." *NovT* 19 (1977): 65-76.

Lindars, Barnabas. "The Language in Which Jesus Taught." *Theology* 86 (1983): 363-65.

Lindsey, Robert L. "A Modified Two-Document Theory of the Synoptic Dependence and Interdependence." *NovT* 6 (1963): 239-63.

Linnemann, Eta. *Is There A Synoptic Problem? Rethinking Literary Dependence of the First Three Gospels.* Translated by R. Yarbrough. Grand Rapids: Baker, 1992.

Longstaff, Thomas R. W., and Page A. Thomas, eds. *The Synoptic Problem: A Bibliography, 1716-1968.* Macon: Mercer University Press, 1988.

Lowe, Malcolm. "The Demise of Arguments from Order for Marcan Priority." *NovT* 24 (1982): 27-36.

Lührmann, Dieter. "Jesus: History and Remembrance." In *Jesus Christ and Human Freedom.* Edited by E. Schillebeeckx and B. van Iersel. New York: Herder & Herder, 1974, 42-55.

Lummins, E. W. *How Luke Was Written: Considerations Affecting the Two-Document Theory with Special Reference to the Phenomena of Order in the Non-Markan Matter Common to Luke.* Cambridge: Cambridge University Press, 1915.

Luz, Ulrich. "Korreferat zu W. R. Farmer, The Minor Agreements of Matthew and Luke against Mark and the Two-Gospel Hypothesis." In *Minor Agreements: Symposium Göttingen, 1991.* Edited by G. Strecker. Göttingen: Vandenhoeck & Ruprecht, 1993, 209-20.

MacDonald, Dennis R. *The Homeric Epics and the Gospel of Mark.* New Haven: Yale University Press, 2000.

Mackay, Ian D. *John's Relationship with Mark.* WUNT 2.182; Tübingen: Mohr, 2004.

Mallen, Peter. *The Reading and Transformation of Isaiah in Luke-Acts.* LNTS 367; London: Clark, 2008.

Manson, T. W. *The Sayings of Jesus.* Oxford: Oxford University Press, 1937.

———. "The Quest of the Historical Jesus — Continued." In *Studies in the Gospels and Epistles.* Manchester: Manchester University Press, 1962, 3-12.

————. *The Teaching of Jesus: Studies in its Form and Content.* Cambridge: Cambridge University Press, 1963.

Marcus, Joel. *Mark 1–8.* AB; New York: Doubleday, 2000.

Marshall, I. Howard. *The Gospel of Luke.* NIGTC; Grand Rapids: Eerdmans, 1978.

Martin, Ralph P. *New Testament Foundations.* 2 vols.; Grand Rapids: Eerdmans, 1975-78.

————. *James.* WBC; Waco: Word, 1988.

Martyn, J. L. *History and Theology in the Fourth Gospel.* Rev. ed.; Nashville: Abingdon, 1979.

Marxsen, Willi. *Mark the Evangelist: Studies on Redaction History of the Gospel.* Nashville: Abingdon, 1969.

Mason, Steve. *Josephus, Judea, and Christian Origins: Methods and Categories.* Peabody: Hendrickson, 2009.

Massoux, Edouard. *The Influence of the Gospel of Saint Matthew on Christian Literature before Saint Irenaeus.* 2 vols. Translated by A. J. Bellinzoni and N. J. Belval. Macon: Mercer University Press, 1990.

McDonald, Lee Martin. *The Formation of the Christian Biblical Canon.* Peabody: Hendrickson, 1995.

————. "The Gospels in Early Christianity: Their Origin, Use, and Authority." In *Reading the Gospels Today.* Edited by S. E. Porter. Grand Rapids: Eerdmans, 2004, 150-78.

McIver, Robert K. *Memory, Jesus, and the Synoptic Gospels.* Atlanta: Society of Biblical Literature, 2011.

McIver, Robert, and Mark Carroll. "Experiments to Determine Distinguishing Characteristics of Orally Transmitted Material When Compared to Material Transmitted by Literary Means, and Their Potential Implications for the Synoptic Problem." *JBL* 121 (2002): 667-87.

McKnight, Scot. *Interpreting the Synoptic Gospels.* Grand Rapids: Baker, 1993.

————. *A New Vision for Israel.* Grand Rapids: Eerdmans, 1999.

————. "A Generation Who Knew Not Streeter: The Case for Markan Priority." In *Rethinking the Synoptic Problem.* Edited by D. A. Black and D. R. Beck. Grand Rapids: Baker, 2001, 65-95.

————. "The Jesus We'll Never Know." *Christianity Today* 54.4 (2010): 22.

————. *The Letter of James.* NICNT; Grand Rapids: Eerdmans, 2011.

————. "Matthew as 'Gospel.'" In *Jesus, Matthew's Gospel and Early Christianity.* Edited by D. M. Gurtner, R. Burridge, and J. Willitts. LNTS 435; FS Graham Stanton; London: Clark, 2011, 59-75.

McKnight, Scot, and Terence C. Mournet, eds. *Jesus in Early Christian Memory.* LNTS 359; London: Clark, 2007.

McNicol, Allan James. "The Composition of the Synoptic Eschatological Discourse." In *The Interrelations of the Gospels: A Symposium.* Edited by D. Dungan. BETL 95; Leuven: Leuven University Press, 1990, 157-200.

Meier, John P. *A Marginal Jew.* ABRL; 4 vols.; New York/New Haven: Doubleday/Yale University Press, 1991-2009.

————. "The Present State of the 'Third Quest' for the Historical Jesus: Loss and Gain." *Bib* 80 (1999): 459-87.

―――. "The Parable of the Wicked Tenants in the Vineyard: Is the Gospel of Thomas Independent of the Synoptics?" In *Unity and Diversity in the Gospels and Paul.* Edited by C. W. Skinner and K. R. Iverson. FS Frank Matera; Atlanta: Society of Biblical Literature, 2012, 129-45.

Meijboom, Hajo Uden. *A History and Critique of the Origin of the Marcan Hypothesis, 1835-1866.* Translated by J. J. Kiwiet. Macon: Mercer University Press, 1993.

Metzger, Bruce M. *The Canon of the New Testament: Its Origin, Development, and Significance.* Oxford: Clarendon, 1987.

Meyer, Ben F. *The Aims of Jesus.* London: SCM, 1979.

―――. "Some Consequences of Birger Gerhardsson's Account of the Origins of the Gospel Tradition." In *Jesus and the Oral Gospel Tradition.* Edited by Henry Wansbrough. JSNTSup 64; Sheffield: Sheffield Academic, 1991, 424-40.

Millard, Alan. *Reading and Writing at the Time of Jesus.* New York: New York University Press, 2000.

Moll, Sebastian. *The Arch-Heretic Marcion.* WUNT 250; Tübingen: Mohr, 2010.

Moloney, Francis J. "Recent Johannine Studies. Part Two: Monographs." *ExpT* 123 (2012): 417-28.

Momigliano, Arnaldo. *The Development of Greek Biography.* Cambridge: Harvard University Press, 1993.

Morgenthaler, Robert. *Statistische Synopse.* Zurich: Gottelf, 1971.

Morris, Leon. *Studies in the Fourth Gospel.* Grand Rapids: Eerdmans, 1969.

Moule, C. F. D. *The Phenomenon of the New Testament.* London: SCM, 1967.

―――. *The Birth of the New Testament.* London: Black, 1981.

Mournet, Terence C. *Oral Tradition and Literary Dependency: Variability in the Synoptic Tradition and Q.* WUNT 2.195; Tübingen: Mohr, 2005.

Mussie, G. "Greek in Palestine and the Diaspora." In *The Jewish People in the First Century.* Edited by S. Safrai and M. Stern. 2 vols.; Amsterdam: Van Gorcum, 1974-76, 2:1040-64.

Neirynck, Frans. *The Minor Agreements of Matthew and Luke against Mark.* Leuven: Leuven University Press, 1974.

―――. "John and the Synoptics: The Empty Tomb Stories." *NTS* 30 (1984): 161-87.

―――. *The Minor Agreements in a Horizontal-Line Synopsis.* SNTA 15; Leuven: Leuven University Press, 1991.

―――. "Recent Developments in the Study of Q." In *Evangelica II: 1982-1991.* Edited by F. van Segbroeck. BETL 99; Leuven: Leuven University Press, 1991, 409-64.

―――. "The Minor Agreements and the Two Source Theory." In *Minor Agreements: Symposium Göttingen, 1991.* Edited by G. Strecker. Göttingen: Vandenhoeck & Ruprecht, 1993, 25-64.

―――. "The Reconstruction of Q and IQP and CritEd Parallels." In *The Sayings Source Q and the Historical Jesus.* Edited by Andreas Lindemann. Leuven: Leuven University Press, 2001, 55-93.

Neusner, Jacob. *Method and Meaning in Ancient Judaism.* Missoula: Scholars, 1979.

―――. *The Origins of Judaism, Volume II: The Pharisees and Other Sects.* New York: Garland, 1990.

Neville, David J. *Arguments for Order in Synoptic Source Criticism.* Macon: Mercer University Press, 1993.

―――. *Mark's Gospel — Prior or Posterior? A Reappraisal of the Phenomenon of Order.* JSNTSup 222; London: Sheffield Academic, 2002.

New, David S. *Old Testament Quotations in the Synoptic Gospels and the Two-Document Hypothesis.* SBLSCS 37; Atlanta: Scholars, 1993.

Nineham, D. E. "Eye-Witness Testimony and the Gospel Tradition." *JTS* 9 (1958): 13-25, 243-52.

Noll, Mark. *Between Faith and Criticism: Evangelicals, Scholarship, and the Bible in America.* Vancouver: Regent College, 1988.

Orchard, Bernard. "Are All Gospel Synopses Biased?" *TZ* 34 (1978): 157-61.

―――. *A Synopsis of the Four Gospels in Greek: Arranged According to the Two-Gospel Hypothesis.* Macon: Mercer University Press, 1983.

―――. "The 'Neutrality' of Vertical-Column Synopses." *ETL* 62 (1986): 155-56.

Orsini, Pasquale, and Willy Clarysse. "Early New Testament Manuscripts and Their Dates: A Critique of Theological Palaeography." *ETL* 88 (2012): 443-74.

Osborne, Eric. *Justin Martyr.* Tübingen: Mohr, 1973.

―――. *Irenaeus of Lyons.* Cambridge: Cambridge University Press, 2001.

Osborne, Grant R. "History and Theology in the Synoptic Gospels." *TrinJ* 24 (2003): 5-22.

Paffenroth, Kim. *The Story of Jesus According to L.* JSNTSup 147; Sheffield: Sheffield Academic, 1997.

Pagels, Elaine H. *The Johannine Gospel in Gnostic Exegesis: Heracleon's Commentary on John.* Nashville: Abingdon, 1973.

―――. *The Gnostic Gospels.* New York: Random House, 1979.

―――. *Beyond Belief: The Secret Gospel of Thomas.* New York: Random House, 2003.

Pahl, Michael W. *Discerning the "Word of the Lord": The "Word of the Lord" in 1 Thessalonians 4:15.* LNTS 389; London: Clark, 2009.

Painter, John. *Mark's Gospel: Worlds in Conflict.* NTR; London: Routledge, 1997.

Pairman, John. "Mark as Witness to an Edited Form of Q." *JBL* 80 (1961): 29-44.

Park, Yoon-Man. *Mark's Memory Resources and the Controversy Stories (Mark 2:1-3:6): An Application of the Frame Theory of Cognitive Science to the Markan Oral-Aural Narrative.* Leiden: Brill, 2009.

Parker, David C. *The Living Text of the Gospels.* Cambridge: Cambridge University Press, 1997.

―――. *An Introduction to the New Testament Manuscripts and Their Texts.* Cambridge: Cambridge University Press, 2008.

Patterson, Stephen J. "Can You Trust a Gospel? A Review of Richard Bauckham's *Jesus and the Eyewitnesses.*" *JSHJ* 6 (2008): 194-210.

Peabody, David B. *One Gospel from Two: Mark's Use of Matthew and Luke: A Demonstration by the Research Team of the International Institute for Renewal of Gospel Studies.* Harrisburg: Trinity, 2002.

Penner, Todd C. "The Epistle of James in Current Research." *CRBS* 7 (1999): 257-308.

Pennington, Jonathan T. *Reading the Gospels Wisely: A Narrative and Theological Introduction.* Grand Rapids: Baker, 2012.

Bibliography

Perkins, Pheme. *Introduction to the Synoptic Gospels.* Grand Rapids: Eerdmans, 2007.

Perrin, Nicholas. *Thomas and Tatian: The Relationship between the Gospel of Thomas and the Diatessaron.* Atlanta: Society of Biblical Literature, 2002.

———. *Thomas: The Other Gospel.* Louisville: Westminster John Knox, 2007.

Perrin, Norman. *What Is Redaction Criticism?* London: SPCK, 1970.

Pervo, Richard I., and Mikael C. Parsons. *Rethinking the Unity of Luke and Acts.* Minneapolis: Fortress, 2007.

Pesch, Rudolf. *Das Markusevangelium 1,1–8,26.* HTK; Freiburg: Herder, 1976.

Petersen, William L. *Tatian's Diatessaron: Its Creation, Dissemination, Significance, and History in Scholarship.* Leiden: Brill, 1994.

———. "From Justin to Pepys: The History of the Harmonized Gospel Tradition." *Studia Patristica* 30 (1997): 71-96.

———. "The Genesis of the Gospels." In *New Testament Textual Criticism and Exegesis.* Edited by A. Denaux. FS J. Delobel; Leuven: Peeters, 2002, 33-65.

———. "The Diatessaron and the Fourfold Gospel." In *The Earliest Gospels: The Origins and Transmission of the Earliest Christian Gospels.* Edited by C. Horton. London: Clark, 2004, 50-68.

Peterson, Jeffery. "Order in the Double Tradition and the Existence of Q." In *Questioning Q: A Multi-Dimensional Critique.* Edited by M. Goodacre and N. Perrin. Downers Grove: InterVarsity, 2004, 28-42.

Petzke, Gerd. *Das Sondergut des Evangeliums nach Lukas.* ZWB; Zurich: Theologischer, 1990.

Piper, Ronald A. "The One, the Four, and the Many." In *The Written Gospel.* Edited by M. Bockmuehl and D. A. Hagner. Cambridge: Cambridge University Press, 2005, 254-73.

Pitre, Brant. *Jesus, the Tribulation, and the End of the Exile: Restoration Eschatology and the Origin of the Atonement.* Grand Rapids: Baker, 2005.

Pittner, Bertram. *Studien zum lukanischen Sondergut.* ETS 18; Leipzig: Benno, 1991.

Poirier, John C. "The Q Hypothesis and the Role of Pre-Synoptic Sources in Nineteenth-Century Scholarship." In *Questioning Q: A Multi-Dimensional Critique.* Edited by M. Goodacre and N. Perrin. Downers Grove: InterVarsity, 2004, 13-27.

———. "The Synoptic Problem and the Field of New Testament Introduction." *JSNT* 32 (2009): 179-90.

———. "The Composition of Luke in Source-Critical Perspective." In *New Studies in the Synoptic Problem: Oxford Conference, 2008.* Edited by P. Foster, A. Gregory, J. S. Kloppenborg, and J. Verheyden. BETL 239; FS C. Tuckett; Leuven: Peeters, 2011, 209-26.

Pokorný, Petr. *From the Gospel to the Gospels: History, Theology and Impact of the Biblical Term "Euangelion."* BZNW 195; Berlin: de Gruyter, 2013.

Porter, Stanley E. *The Criteria for Authenticity in Historical-Jesus Research: Previous Discussion and New Proposal.* JSNTSup 191; Sheffield: Sheffield Academic, 2000.

———. "Luke 17.11-19 and the Criteria For Authenticity Revisited." *JSHJ* 1 (2003): 201-24.

———. "Textual Criticism and Oldest Gospel Manuscripts." In *Encyclopedia of the Historical Jesus.* Edited by C. A. Evans. New York: Routledge, 2008, 640-44.

Pryor, John. "Justin Martyr and the Fourth Gospel." *The Second Century* 9 (1992): 153-69.

Rasimus, Tuomas, ed. *The Legacy of John: Second-Century Reception of the Fourth Gospel.* NovTSup 132; Leiden: Brill, 2010.

Redman, Judith C. S. "How Accurate Are Eyewitnesses? Bauckham and the Eyewitnesses in Light of Psychological Research." *JBL* 129 (2010): 177-97.

Reed, Annette Yoshiko. "ΕΥΑΓΓΕΛΙΟΝ: Orality, Textuality, and the Christian Truth in Ireaneus' *Adversus Haereses.*" *VC* 56 (2002): 11-46.

Reed, Jonathan L. *Archaeology and the Galilean Jesus.* Harrisburg: Trinity, 2000.

Reicke, Bo. *The Roots of the Synoptic Problem.* Philadelphia: Fortress, 1986.

Richardson, Peter, and P. Gooch, "Logia of Jesus in 1 Corinthians." In *Gospel Perspectives 5: The Jesus Tradition outside the Gospels.* Edited by David Wenham. Sheffield: JSOT, 1985, 39-62.

Riesenfeld, Harald. *The Gospel Tradition.* Oxford: Blackwell, 1970.

Riesner, Rainer. *Jesus als Lehrer. Eine Untersuchung zum Ursprung der Evangelien-Überlieferung.* WUNT 2.7; Tübingen: Mohr, 1988.

———. "Jesus as Preacher and Teacher." In *Jesus and the Oral Gospel Tradition.* Edited by Henry Wansbrough. JSNTSup 64; Sheffield: JSOT, 1991.

———. "Luke's Special Tradition and the Question of a Hebrew Gospel Source." *Mishkan* 20 (1994): 44-52.

———. "Paulus and die Jesus-Überlieferung." In *Evangelium — Schriftauslegung — Kirche.* Edited by Jostein Ådna, Scot Hafemann, and Otfried Hofius. FS P. Stuhlmacher; Göttingen: Vandenhoeck & Ruprecht, 1997, 346-65.

———. "From Messianic Teacher to the Gospels of Jesus Christ." In *HSHJ.* Edited by Tom Holmén and Stanley E. Porter. 4 vols.; Leiden: Brill, 2011, 1:405-46.

Riley, Gregory J. "Words and Deeds: Jesus as Teacher, Jesus as Pattern of Life." *HTR* 90 (1997): 427-36.

Rist, John M. *On the Independence of Matthew and Mark.* SNTSMS 32; Cambridge: Cambridge University Press, 1978.

Robbins, Vernon K. *Jesus the Teacher: A Socio-Rhetorical Interpretation of Mark.* Philadelphia: Fortress, 1984.

Roberts, C. H. "Books in the Graeco-Roman World and the New Testament." In *The Cambridge History of the Bible I: From the Beginnings to Jerome.* Edited by Peter R. Ackroyd and Craig F. Evans. Cambridge: Cambridge University Press, 1970, 48-66.

———. *Manuscript, Society and Belief in Early Christian Egypt.* London: Oxford University Press, 1979.

Roberts, C. H., and T. C. Skeat. *The Birth of the Codex.* London: Oxford University Press, 1987.

Robinson, James M., Paul Hoffman, and John S. Kloppenborg, eds. *The Critical Edition of Q.* Minneapolis: Fortress, 2000.

Rodriguez, Rafael. "Reading and Hearing in Ancient Contexts." *JSNT* 32 (2010): 151-78.

———. *Structuring Early Christian Memory: Jesus in Tradition, Performance, and Text.* LNTS 407; London: Clark, 2010.

Rolland, Philippe. "Les prédécesseurs de Marc. Les sources présynoptiques de Mc, II, 18-22 et parallèles." *RB* 89 (1982): 370-405.

————. "Marc, première harmonie évangélique?" *RB* 90 (1983): 23-79.

————. "A New Look at the Synoptic Question." *EJTh* 8 (1999): 133-44.

Rordorf, W. "Does the Didache Contain Jesus Tradition Independently of the Synoptic Gospels?" In *Jesus and the Oral Gospel Tradition*. Edited by Henry Wansbrough. JSNTSup 64; Sheffield: Sheffield Academic, 1990, 394-423.

Rowland, Christopher. *Christian Origins*. London: SPCK, 1985.

Sabbe, M. "The Johannine Account of the Death of Jesus and Its Synoptic Parallels (Jn 19,16b-42)." *ETL* 70 (1994): 34-64.

Sanday, William. "The Conditions under Which the Gospels Were Written, in Their Bearing upon Some Difficulties of the Synoptic Problem." In *Oxford Studies in the Synoptic Problem*. Edited by W. Sanday. Oxford: Clarendon, 1911, 3-26.

Sanders, E. P. *The Tendencies of the Synoptic Tradition*. SNTS 9; Cambridge: Cambridge University Press, 1969.

————. "The Overlaps of Q and Mark and the Synoptic Problem." *NTS* 19 (1973): 453-65.

————. *Jesus and Judaism*. London: SCM, 1985.

————. *Judaism: Practice and Belief, 63 BCE–66 CE*. London: SCM, 1992.

————. *The Historical Figure of Jesus*. London: Penguin, 1993.

Sanders, E. P., and Margaret Davies. *Studying the Synoptic Gospels*. London: SCM, 1989.

Sanders, James A. "The Ethic of Election in Luke's Great Banquet Parable." In *Essays in Old Testament Ethics*. Edited by James L. Crenshaw and John T. Willis. New York: Ktav, 1974, 246-71.

Sandmel, Samuel. "Parallelomania." *JBL* 81 (1962): 1-13.

Sandnes, Karl Olav. "*Imitatio Homeri?* An Appraisal of Dennis R. MacDonald's 'Mimesis Criticism.'" *JBL* 124 (2005): 715-32.

Sawyer, John F. A. *The Fifth Gospel: Isaiah in the History of Christianity*. Cambridge: Cambridge University Press, 1996.

Schadewaldt, Wolfgang. "Die Zuverlässigkeit der synoptischen Tradition." *Theologische Beiträge* 13 (1982): 198-223.

Schenk, Wolfgang. "Der Einfluß der Logienquelle auf das Markusevangelium." *ZNW* 70 (1979): 141-65.

Schillebeeckx, Edward. *Jesus: An Experiment in Christology*. Translated by Hubert Hoskins. London: Collins, 1979.

Schmid, Josef. *Mathäus und Lukas. Eine Untersuchung des Verhältnisses ihr Evangelien*. Freiburg: Herder, 1930.

Schmidt, Karl L. *Der Rahmen der Geschichte Jesu. Literarkritische untersuchungen zur Altesten Jesuberlieferung*. Berlin: Trowitzsch, 1919.

————. "Die Stellung der Evangelien in der allegemeinen Literaturgeschichte." In *EUCHARISTERION*. Edited by H. Schmidt. 2 vols.; FRLANT 19; FS H. Gunkel; Göttingen: Vandenhoeck & Ruprecht, 1923, 2:50-134.

Schniewind, Julius. *Euangelion. Ursprung und erste Gestalt des Begriffs Evangelium, Untersuchung*. Gütersloh: Bertelsmann, 1927.

Schoedel, W. R. *Polycarp, Martyrdom of Polycarp, Fragments of Papias*. Camden: Nelson, 1967.

Schoeps, H. J. *Paul: The Theology of the Apostle in the Light of Jewish Religious History.* London: Lutterworth, 1961.

Schreiner, Thomas R. *Paul: Apostle of God's Glory in Christ.* Downers Grove: InterVarsity, 2001.

Schröter, Jens. "The Historical Jesus and the Sayings Tradition: Comments on Current Research." *NeoT* 30 (1996): 151-68.

————. *Erinnerung an Jesu Worte. Studien zur Rezeption der Logienüberlieferung in Markus, Q und Thomas.* WMANT 76; Neukirchen-Vluyn: Neukirchener, 1997.

————. "Von der Historizität der Evangelien. Ein Beitrag zur gegenwärtigen Diskussion um den historischen Jesus." In *Der historische Jesus. Tendezen und Perspektiven der gegenwärtigen Forschung.* Edited by J. Schröter and R. Brucher. BZNW 114; Berlin: de Gruyter, 2002, 163-212.

————. "The Gospels as Eyewitness Testimony? A Critical Examination of Richard Bauckham's *Jesus and the Eyewitnesses.*" *JSNT* 31 (2008): 195-209.

————. "Remarks on James D. G. Dunn's Approach to Jesus Research." In *Memories of Jesus: A Critical Appraisal of James D. G. Dunn's Jesus Remembered.* Edited by R. B. Stewart and Gary R. Habermas. Nashville: Broadman & Holman, 2010, 129-43.

Schüling, Joachim. *Studien zum Verhältnis von Logienquelle und Markusevangelium.* FB 65; Würzburg: Echter, 1991.

Schulz, Siegfried. *Die Stunde der Botschaft.* Hamburg: Furche, 1967.

Schürmann, Heinz. "Die vorösterlichen Anfänge der Logientradition. Versuch eines formgeschichtlichen Zugangs zum Leben Jesu." In *Der historische Jesus und der kerygmatische Christus.* Edited by H. Ristow and K. Matthiae. Berlin: Evangelische, 1962, 342-70.

Schweitzer, Albert. *The Quest of the Historical Jesus.* Translated by W. Montgomery. London: Black, 1945.

Scott, James M. *Luke's Preface and the Synoptic Problem.* Unpublished dissertation, University of Aberdeen, 1985.

Shellard, Barbara. *New Light on Luke: Its Purposes, Sources, and Literary Context.* London: Clark, 2004.

Shepherd, Massey H. "The Epistle of James and the Gospel of Matthew." *JBL* 75 (1956), 40-51.

Shiell, William D. *Delivering from Memory: The Effect of Performance on the Early Christian Audience.* Eugene: Pickwick, 2011.

Shiner, Whitney. *Proclaiming the Gospel: First-Century Performance of Mark.* Harrisburg: Trinity, 2003.

Shuler, Philip L. *A Genre for the Gospels: The Biographical Character of Matthew.* Philadelphia: Fortress, 1982.

Simons, Eduard. *Hat der dritte Evangelist den kanonischen Matthäus benutzt?* Bonn: Georgi, 1880.

Skarsaune, Oskar. "Justin and His Bible." In *Justin Martyr and His Worlds.* Edited by S. Parvis and P. Foster. Minneapolis: Fortress, 2007, 53-76.

Skeat, T. C. "The Oldest Manuscript of the Four Gospels?" *NTS* 43 (1997): 1-34.

Smith, Dwight Moody. "When Did the Gospels Become Scripture?" *JBL* 119 (2000): 3-20.

————. *John among the Gospels.* 2nd ed.; Columbia: University of South Carolina Press, 2001.

Smith, Justin Marc. "About Friends, by Friends, for Others: Author-Subject Relationships in Contemporary Greco-Roman Biographies." In *The Audience of the Gospels: The Origin and Function of the Gospels in Early Christianity.* Edited by E. W. Klink. LNTS 353; London: Clark 2010, 49-67.

Smith, Morton. "A Comparison of Early Christian and Early Rabbinic Tradition." *JBL* 82 (1963): 169-76.

————. "Prolegomena to a Discussion of Aretalogies, Divine Men, and the Gospels and Jesus." *JBL* 90 (1971): 74-99.

————. *Jesus the Magician.* New York: Harper & Row, 1978.

Smith, Murray J. "The Gospels in Early Christian Literature." In *The Content and Setting of the Gospel Tradition.* Edited by Mark Harding and Alanna Nobbs. Grand Rapids: Eerdmans, 2010, 181-208.

Snodgrass, Klyne. "The Gospel of Jesus." In *The Written Gospel.* Edited by M. Bockmuehl and D. A. Hagner. Cambridge: Cambridge University Press, 2005, 31-45.

Soards, Marion L. "The Question of a PreMarkan Passion Narrative." *Bible Bhashyam* 11 (1985): 144-69.

————. *The Passion According to Luke: The Special Material of Luke 22.* JSNTSup 14; Sheffield: JSOT, 1987.

————. "Oral Tradition before, in, and Outside of the Canonical Passion Narratives." In *Jesus and the Oral Gospel Tradition.* Edited by H. Wansbrough. Sheffield: JSOT, 1991, 334-50.

Sparks, H. F. D. "St. John's Knowledge of Matthew: The Evidence of John 13:16 and 15:20." *JTS* 3 (1952): 58-61.

————. *A Synopsis of the Gospels, Part 2: The Gospel According to St. John with the Synoptic Parallels.* London: Black, 1974.

Spencer, F. Scott. *What Did Jesus Do? Gospel Profiles of Jesus' Personal Conduct.* Harrisburg: Trinity, 2003.

Stanley, David. "Imitation in Paul's Letters: Its Significance for His Relationship to Jesus and to His Own Christian Foundations." In *From Jesus to Paul: Studies in Honor of F. W. Beare.* Edited by Peter Richardson and J. C. Hurd. Waterloo: Wilfred Laurier University Press, 1984, 127-41.

Stanton, Graham. *Jesus of Nazareth in New Testament Preaching.* SNTSMS 27; Cambridge: Cambridge University Press, 1974.

————. "Form Criticism Revisited." In *What about the New Testament?* Edited by Morna Hooker and Colin Hickling. London: SCM, 1975, 13-27.

————. *Jesus and Gospel.* Cambridge: Cambridge University Press, 2004.

Stein, Robert H. "The Matthew-Luke Agreements against Mark: Insight from John." *CBQ* 54 (1992): 482-502.

————. *Studying the Synoptic Gospels: Origin and Interpretation.* 2nd ed.; Grand Rapids: Baker, 2001.

Stewart, Robert, and Gary R. Habermas, eds. *Memories of Jesus: A Critical Appraisal of James D. G. Dunn's Jesus Remembered.* Nashville: Broadman and Holman, 2010.

Still, Todd D., ed. *Jesus and Paul Reconnected: Fresh Pathways into an Old Debate*. Grand Rapids: Eerdmans, 2007.

Stoldt, Hans-Herbert. *History and Criticism of the Marcan Hypothesis*. Translated by D. Niewyk. Macon: Mercer University Press, 1980.

Strange, J. F. "Galilee." In *DNTB*. Edited by Craig A. Evans and Stanley E. Porter. Downers Grove: InterVarsity, 2000, 391-98.

Strange, W. A. "The Jesus-Tradition in Acts." *NTS* 46 (2000): 59-74.

Strauss, Mark L. *Four Portraits, One Jesus: An Introduction to Jesus and the Gospels*. Grand Rapids: Zondervan, 2007.

Streeter, B. H. *The Four Gospels: A Study of Origins*. London: Macmillan, 1930.

Stroker, W. D. *Extracanonical Sayings of Jesus*. Atlanta: Scholars, 1989.

Stuckenbruck, Loren T. " 'Semitic Influence on Greek': An Authenticating Criterion in Jesus Research?" In *Jesus, Criteria, and the Demise of Authenticity*. Edited by C. Keith and A. Le Donne. London: Clark, 2012, 73-94.

Stuhlmacher, Peter. "Jesustradition im Römerbrief." *Theologische Beiträge* 14 (1983): 240-50.

―――. "The Pauline Gospel." In *The Gospel and the Gospels*. Edited by P. Stuhlmacher. Grand Rapids: Eerdmans, 1991, 149-72.

Sullivan, Clayton. *Rethinking Realized Eschatology*. Macon: Mercer University Press, 1988.

Talbert, Charles H. *What Is a Gospel? The Genre of the Canonical Gospels*. Philadelphia: Fortress, 1977.

―――. "Once Again: Gospel Genre." In *Genre, Narrativity and Theology*. Edited by M. Gerhart and J. G. Williams. Semeia 43; Atlanta: Scholars, 1988, 53-73.

―――. *Reading Acts: A Literary and Theological Commentary on the Acts of the Apostles*. New York: Crossroad, 1997.

Talmon, Shemaryahu. "Oral Tradition and Written Transmission, or the Heard and the Seen Word in Judaism of the Second Temple Period." In *Jesus and the Oral Gospel Tradition*. Edited by Henry Wansbrough. JSNTSup 64; Sheffield: Sheffield Academic, 1991, 121-58.

Tasker, R. V. G. *John: An Introduction and Commentary*. TNTC; London: Tyndale, 1960.

Taylor, Nicholas. *Paul, Antioch and Jerusalem*. JSNTSup 66; Sheffield: Sheffield Academic, 1992.

―――. "Palestinian Christianity and the Caligula Crisis, Part II: The Markan Eschatological Discourse." *JSNT* 62 (1996): 13-41.

Taylor, Vincent. *Behind the Third Gospel: A Study of the Proto-Luke Hypothesis*. Oxford: Oxford University Press, 1926.

―――. *The Formation of the Gospel Tradition*. London: Macmillan, 1949.

Taylor, W. S. "Memory and the Gospel Tradition." *TT* 14 (1959): 470-79.

Thatcher, Tom. "The Gospel Genre: What Are We After?" *ResQ* 36 (1994): 129-38.

―――. "The New Current through John: The Old 'New Look' at the New Critical Orthodoxy." In *New Currents through John: A Global Perspective*. Edited by T. Thatcher and F. Lozada. Atlanta: Society of Biblical Literature, 2006, 1-26.

―――. *Why John Wrote a Gospel: Jesus — Memory — History*. Louisville: Westminster John Knox, 2006.

————, ed. *Jesus, the Voice, and the Text: Beyond the Oral and Written Gospel.* Waco: Baylor University Press, 2008.

Thatcher, Tom, and Anthony Le Donne, eds. *The Fourth Gospel in First-Century Media Culture.* LNTS 426; London: Clark, 2011.

Theissen, Gerd. *Sociology of Early Palestinian Christianity.* Translated by J. Bowden. Philadelphia: Fortress, 1978.

————. *The Shadow of the Galilean.* Translated by J. Bowden. Philadelphia: Fortress, 1987.

————. *The Gospels in Context: Social and Political History in the Synoptic Tradition.* Translated by Linda M. Maloney. Minneapolis: Fortress, 1991.

————. *The New Testament: A Literary History.* Translated by Linda M. Maloney. Minneapolis: Fortress, 2012.

Theissen, Gerd, and Annette Merz. *The Historical Jesus: A Comprehensive Guide.* Translated by J. Bowden. Minneapolis: Fortress, 1998.

Thomas Robert L., ed. *Three Views on the Origins of the Synoptic Gospels.* Grand Rapids: Kregel, 2002.

Thomas Robert L., and F. David Farnell, eds. *The Jesus Crisis: The Inroads of Historical Criticism into Evangelical Scholarship.* Grand Rapids: Kregel, 1998.

Thompson, M. M. "The Historical Jesus and the Johannine Christ." In *Exploring the Gospel of John.* Edited by R. Alan Culpepper and C. Clifton Black. Louisville: Westminster John Knox, 1996, 21-42.

Thompson, Michael. *Clothed with Christ: The Example and Teaching of Jesus in Romans 12.1–15.13.* JSNTSup 59; Sheffield: JSOT, 1991.

————. "The Holy Internet: Communication between Churches in the First Christian Generation." In *The Gospels for All Christians: Rethinking the Gospel Audiences.* Edited by Richard Bauckham. Grand Rapids: Eerdmans, 1998, 49-70.

Tiede, David. *Charismatic Figure as Miracle Worker.* Missoula: Scholars, 1972.

Tolbert, Mary Ann. *Sowing the Gospel: Mark's World in Literary-History Perspective.* Philadelphia: Fortress, 1996.

Travis, S. H. "Form Criticism." In *New Testament Interpretation: Essays on Principles and Methods.* Edited by I. Howard Marshall. Grand Rapids: Eerdmans, 1977, 153-64.

Trobisch, David. *The First Edition of the New Testament.* Oxford: Oxford University Press, 2000.

Tuckett, Christopher M. *The Revival of the Griesbach Hypothesis: An Analysis and Appraisal.* SNTSMS 44; Cambridge: Cambridge University Press, 1983.

————. "On the Relationship between Matthew and Luke." *NTS* 30 (1984): 130-42.

————. "Synoptic Problem." In *ABD,* 4:268.

————. "Synoptic Tradition in the Didache." In *The New Testament in Early Christianity.* Edited by J.-M. Sevrin. Leuven: Peeters, 1989, 173-230.

————. "The Minor Agreements and Textual Criticism." In *Minor Agreements: Symposium Göttingen, 1991.* Edited by G. Strecker. Göttingen: Vandenhoeck & Ruprecht, 1993, 135-41.

————. "The Existence of Q." In *The Gospel Behind the Gospels: Current Studies on Q.* Edited by R. A. Piper. Leiden: Brill, 1995, 19-47.

————. *Q and the History of Early Christianity: Studies on Q.* Edinburgh: Clark, 1996.

————. "Q and the Historical Jesus." In *Der historische Jesus. Tendenzen und Perspektiven der gegenwärtigen Forschung*. Edited by J. Schröter and R. Brucker. BZNW 114; Berlin: de Gruyter, 2002, 213-41.

————. "The *Didache* and the Writings That Later Formed the New Testament." In *The Reception of the New Testament in the Apostolic Fathers*. Edited by C. Tuckett and A. Gregory. Oxford: Oxford University Press, 2005, 83-127.

————. "Forty Other Gospels." In *The Written Gospel*. Edited by M. Bockmuehl and D. A. Hagner. Cambridge: Cambridge University Press, 2005, 238-53.

van De Sandt, Huub. "Matthew and the *Didache*." In *Matthew and His Christian Contemporaries*. Edited by D. C. Sim and B. Repschinski. LNTS 333; London: Clark, 2008, 123-38.

Vansina, Jan. *Oral Tradition as History*. Madison: University of Wisconsin Press, 1985.

Verheyden, Joseph. "Justin's Text of the Gospels: Another Look at the Citations in *1 Apol.* 15.1-8." In *The Early Text of the New Testament*. Edited by C. E. Hill and M. J. Kruger. Oxford: Oxford University Press, 2012, 313-35.

Vickers, Brian. "The Kingdom of God in Paul's Gospel." *SBJT* 12 (2008): 52-67.

Vielhauer, Philipp. *Geschichte der urchristlichen Literatur. Einleitung in das Neue Testament, die Apokryphen und die Apostolischen Väter*. Berlin: de Gruyter, 1975.

Vines, Michael E. *The Problem of Markan Genre: The Gospel of Mark and the Jewish Novel*. Leiden: Brill, 2002.

von Wahlde, Urban C. *The Gospel and Letters of John*. ECC; 3 vols.; Grand Rapids: Eerdmans, 2010.

Votaw, Clyde H. *The Gospels and Contemporary Biographies in the Greco-Roman World*. Philadelphia: Fortress, 1970.

Wachob, Wesley H. *The Voice of Jesus in the Social Rhetoric of James*. Cambridge: Cambridge University Press, 2000.

Wagner, J. Ross. *Heralds of the Good News: Isaiah and Paul in Concert in the Letter to the Romans*. Leiden: Brill, 2003.

Wansbrough, Henry. "Introduction." In *Jesus and the Oral Gospel Tradition*. Edited by Henry Wansbrough. JSNTSup 64; Sheffield: Sheffield Academic, 1991, 9-15.

Watson, Francis. "The Fourfold Gospel." In *The Cambridge Companion to the Gospels*. Edited by S. C. Barton. Cambridge: Cambridge University Press, 2000, 34-52.

————. "Veritas Christi: How to Get from the Jesus of History to the Christ of Faith without Losing One's Way." In *Seeking the Identity of Jesus: A Pilgrimage*. Edited by Richard B. Hays and Beverly R. Gaventa. Grand Rapids: Eerdmans, 2008, 96-114.

Watts, Rikki E. *Isaiah's New Exodus in Mark*. BSL; Grand Rapids: Baker, 1997.

Weeden, Theodore J. *Mark — Traditions in Conflict*. Philadelphia: Fortress, 1971.

————. "Kenneth Bailey's Theory of Oral Tradition: A Theory Contested by Its Evidence." *JSHJ* 7 (2009): 3-43.

Weiss, Johannes. *Das älteste Evangelium. Ein Beitrag zum Verständnis des Markus-Evangeliums und der ältesten evangelischen Überlieferung*. Göttingen: Vandenhoeck & Ruprecht, 1903.

Weissenrieder, Annette, and Robert B. Coote, eds. *The Interface of Orality and Writing*. WUNT 1.260; Tübingen: Mohr, 2010.

Wenham, David. "Source Criticism." In *New Testament Interpretation*. Edited by I. Howard Marshall. Grand Rapids: Eerdmans, 1977, 139-52.

———. "Paul's Use of the Jesus Tradition: Three Samples." In *Gospel Perspectives 5: The Jesus Tradition outside the Gospels*. Edited by David Wenham. Sheffield: JSOT, 1985, 7-37.

———. *Paul: Follower of Jesus or Founder of Christianity?* Grand Rapids: Eerdmans, 1995.

Wenham, John. *Redating Matthew, Mark, and Luke: A Fresh Assault on the Synoptic Problem*. Downers Grove: InterVarsity, 1992.

Westcott, B. F. *Introduction to the Study of the Gospels*. 8th ed.; London: Macmillan, 1895.

Wiles, Maurice. *The Spiritual Gospel: The Interpretation of the Fourth Gospel in the Early Church*. Cambridge: Cambridge University Press, 1960.

Wills, Lawrence. *The Quest of the Historical Gospel*. London: Routledge, 1997.

Windisch, Hans. *Johannes und die Synoptiker. Sollte der vierte Evangelist die älteren Evangelien ergänzen oder ersetzen?* Leipzig: Hinrich, 1926.

Wise, M. O. "Languages of Palestine." In *DJG*. Edited by Joel B. Green, Scot McKnight, and I. Howard Marshall. Downers Grove: InterVarsity, 1992, 443-44.

Witherington, Ben. *The Christology of Jesus*. Minneapolis: Fortress, 1990.

———. *Paul's Narrative Thought World: The Tapestry of Tragedy and Triumph*. Louisville: Westminster John Knox, 1994.

———. *Jesus the Seer: The Progress of Prophecy*. Peabody: Hendrickson, 1999.

———. *The New Testament Story*. Grand Rapids: Eerdmans, 2004.

Wrege, Hans-Theo. *Das Sondergut des Matthäus-Evangeliums*. ZWB; Zurich: Theologischer, 1991.

Wright, N. T. "The Paul of History and the Apostle of Faith." *TynBul* 29 (1978): 61-88.

———. *The New Testament and the People of God*. COQG 1; London: SPCK, 1992.

———. *Who Was Jesus?* London: SPCK, 1993.

———. *Jesus and the Victory of God*. COQG 2; London: SPCK, 1996.

———. *The Challenge of Jesus*. London: SPCK, 2000.

———. *Judas and the Gospel of Jesus: Have We Missed the Truth about Christianity?* Grand Rapids: Baker, 2006.

———. *How God Became King: Getting to the Heart of the Gospels*. London: SPCK, 2011.

———. *Simply Jesus: A New Vision of Who He Was, What He Did, and Why He Matters*. New York: HarperOne, 2011.

Yarbrough, Robert W. "The Date of Papias: Reassessment." *JETS* 26 (1983): 181-91.

Young, Stephen E. *Jesus Tradition in the Apostolic Fathers: Their Explicit Appeals to the Words of Jesus in Light of Orality Studies*. WUNT 2.311; Tübingen: Mohr, 2011.

Zimmermann, Ruben. "Memory and Form Criticism: The Typicality of Memory as a Bridge between Orality and Literality in the Early Christian Remembering Process." In *The Interface of Orality and Writing*. Edited by A. Weissenrieder and R. B. Coote. WUNT 1.260; Tübingen: Mohr, 2010, 130-43.

Index of Names and Subjects

192-94; and literary relationship with John, 194-211; similar Old Testament citations in, 137-38; similar outline of, 132-34, 161; similar parenthetical and redactional material in, 134-36; similar wording in, 128-32

Talbert, Charles, 237, 242-43
Talmon, Shemaryahu, 86n50, 92n82
Tasker, R. V. G., 196n187
Tatian, 194, 302n10, 305-7, 316, 323n106
Taylor, Nicholas H., 50n95, 125n1
Taylor, Vincent, 23nn6-7, 49, 113-14, 118, 126n3
Taylor, W. S., 98n96
Teacher of Righteousness, 63; as authoritative teacher, 26; conflict stories of, 32; as "movement founder," 35-36
teachers, and the Jesus tradition, 63-64
"telephone game," 4
testimonia, 46-47
textual criticism, and Gospel titles, 188, 254-55, 257, 268-69, 325
Thatcher, Tom, 5n11, 79n12, 98n96, 99, 117n153, 194n182, 202n204, 243n85
Theissen, Gerd, 21n2, 31n31, 34, 38n47, 60n132, 82n26, 89n62, 90, 110, 121n169, 122n174, 125n1
theography, in Gospels, 229
theology, and history, 37, 48, 69-73, 76, 80, 105, 117, 121, 123
Theophilus (compiler of harmony), 304, 306, 316, 320
Thomas, Page A., 127n5
Thomas, Robert L., 148nn40-41
Thompson, M. M., 55n114
Thompson, Michael B., 27n15, 116n149, 186n163, 280
three-source theory. *See* Holtzmann-Gundry hypothesis
Tiede, David, 233
titles, of Gospels, 2, 188, 240, 254-69, 288-89, 325
Tolbert, Mary Ann, 234
tradents: and form criticism, 117-18; imprint of, 69, 77; as remembering

Jesus, 103-4; role of, 51, 57, 60-62, 94, 113, 251n124
tradition: use of παραδίδωμι, 51-52, 88, 245, 251n124; transmission of, 51-52
Travis, S. H., 115n146
Trebilco, Paul, 321
triple tradition, 127-28, 144, 153, 159-60, 168; and the Mark-Q overlaps, 142, 182, 184; minor agreements in, 175-80
Trobisch, David, 256n143, 257n149, 258n150
Tuckett, Christopher M., 28n18, 141n15, 142nn16-17, 143n22, 165n95, 169, 177, 182-85, 261nn161-62, 265n187, 287n257, 332n140
two- (four-)source theory, 149-51, 156, 173; and the Mark-Q overlaps, 180-84, 186; and the triple tradition, 175-80
Tyndale, William, 1

Ur-Gospel, theory of, 143-47
Ur-Mark, 126, 150; and the Lachmann fallacy, 161n86; problems with, 145, 155, 157-58, 178, 180

Valentinians, 190n173, 247, 289; and εὐαγγέλιον, 267-68; and fourfold Gospel, 314-15; and John, 294n283, 302
Valentinus, 266-68, 314-15, 332n142
van de Sandt, Huub, 64n148, 261n161
Vansina, Jan, 62n139, 63n145, 90
Vaticanus (B), Codex, 188, 255, 257, 334
Verheyden, Joseph/Jozef, 127n5, 250n117
Vespasian, 7
Vickers, Brian, 16n46
victory, as good news, 6-20
Vielhauer, Philipp, 287n257
Vines, Michael E., 229-30
vita. See biography
Votaw, Clyde, 236, 276n234

Wachob, Wesley H., 29n25
Wagner, J. Ross, 13n36
Wahlde, Urban C., 201
Wansbrough, Henry, 39n49, 105n116

Index of Scripture and Other Ancient Texts